CW01270769

The Diaries of John Gregory Bourke
Volume 3

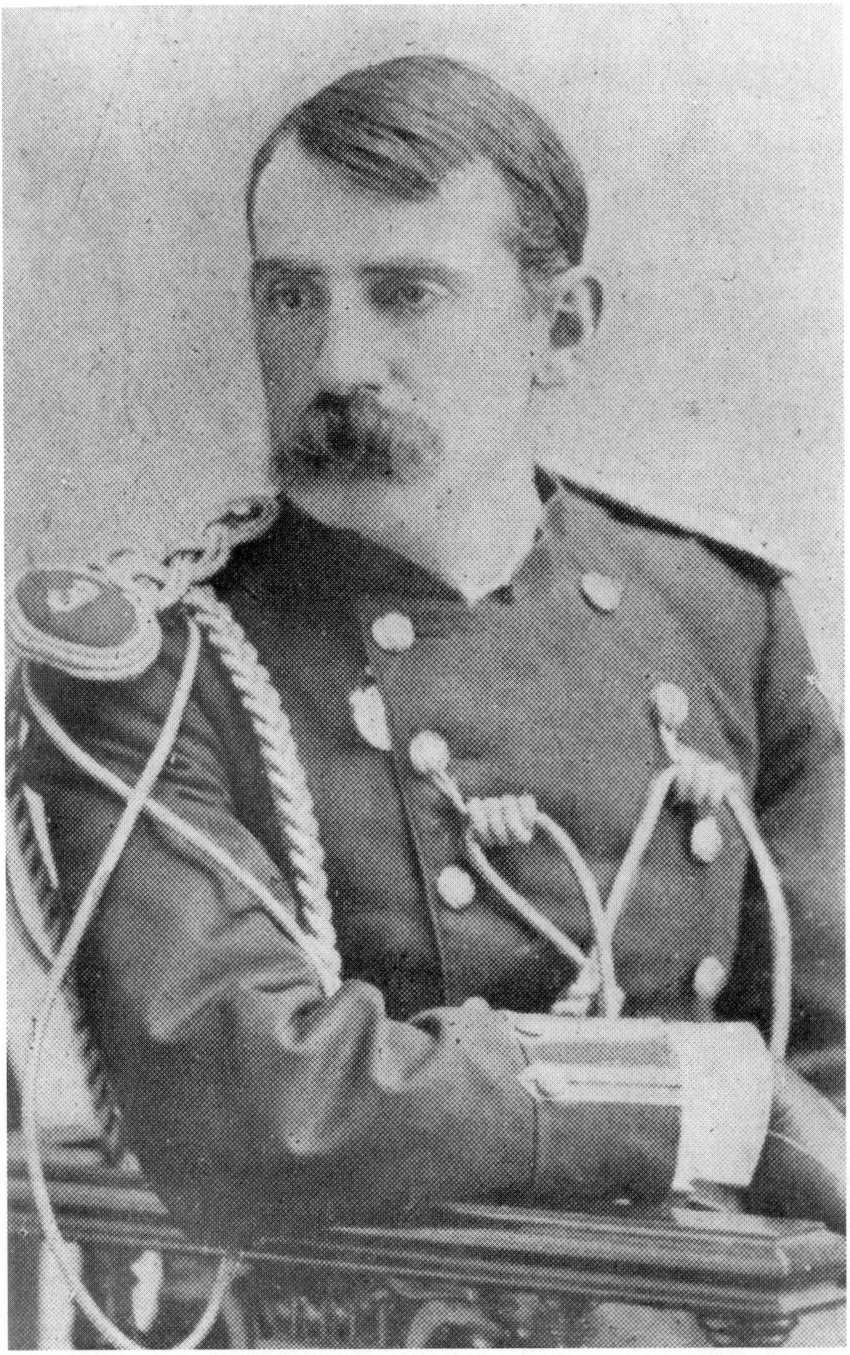

The Diaries of John Gregory Bourke

VOLUME 3
June 1, 1878–June 22, 1880

Edited and Annotated by
Charles M. Robinson III

University of North Texas Press
Denton, Texas

©2007 Charles M. Robinson III

All rights reserved.
Printed in the United States of America.

10 9 8 7 6 5 4 3 2 1

Permissions:
University of North Texas Press
P.O. Box 311336
Denton, TX 76203-1336

The paper used in this book meets the minimum requirements of the American National Standard for Permanence of Paper for Printed Library Materials, z39.48.1984. Binding materials have been chosen for durability.

Library of Congress Cataloging-in-Publication Data
Bourke, John Gregory, 1846–1896.
　　The diaries of John Gregory Bourke / edited and annotated by Charles M. Robinson III.
　　　p. cm.
Includes bibliographical references and index.
　　　ISBN-10 1-57441-196-9 (cloth : alk. paper)
　　　ISBN-13 978-1-57441-196-6 (cloth : alk. paper)
　1. Bourke, John Gregory, 1846–1896—Diaries. 2. Soldiers—West (U.S.)—Diaries. 3. Indians of North America—Wars—1866–1895—Personal Narratives. I. Robinson, Charles M., 1949– II. Title.

E83.866 .B75 2003
978'.02'092—dc21
2002152293

All illustrations are held by the United States Military Academy Library, West Point, NY. Cover and frontispiece photo of John Gregory Bourke is courtesy of the National Park Service, Little Bighorn Battlefield National Monument.

To Paul L. Hedren

[I]t matters not whether the grievances of our Indians be true or false, exaggerated or under-estimated, the fact that the word of our Government is mistrusted by every tribe on the continent cannot be denied and is a black blot upon our national escutcheon.
—John Gregory Bourke, Diary, 26:19

It seems to me to be an odd feature of our judicial system that the only people in this country who have no rights under the law are the original owners of the soil: an Irishman, German, Chinaman, Turk or Tartar will be protected in life and property, but the Indian commands respect for his rights only so long as he inspires terror for his rifle.
—Brigadier General George Crook,
Letter copied in Bourke, Diary, 29:34–35

Contents

Acknowledgments ix
Introduction to Volume 3 1

Part 1. The Life of a General's Aide
Background 15
1. Nostalgia, a Society Wedding,
   a Day at the Races, and a Parting 19
2. The Bannock Uprising 35
3. Retrospective on the Sioux War and Crazy Horse 53
4. The Death of Crazy Horse 65
5. The Developing Frontier 79
6. Sojourn in the Mountains and a Visit to Denver 97

Part 2. The Cheyennes and the Poncas
Background 113
7. Cheyenne Life 117
8. Hunting the Refugees 144
9. Misery on the Trail 160
10. The Ponca Affair 177

Part 3. Americanizing the Frontier
Background 205
11. Of Irish Lords and Irish Soldiers 208
12. "It Is of Such Stuff that Good Commonwealths Are Made" 225
13. Fort Craig to Camp Grant 249
14. Back to the Present 276

Part 4. The White River Ute Uprising
Background 291
15. Merritt's Ride 294
16. Camp Under Fire 317
17. From Field to Staff 338

Part 5. Staff Duties and Nostalgia
Background 364
18. Procuring Mules and Mounts 366
19. Phil Reade and Old Jerry 388
20. More Horses, More Nostalgia, and Miscellaneous Rambling 400

Appendix 1: Persons Mentioned in the Diary............................ 420
Appendix 2: Authorities. Personal notes of the Campaigns
    Conducted by Brig. General George Crook.................... 503

Bibliography 518

Index 529

Acknowledgments

A large group of people have made this series possible, particularly Ron Chrisman, director, and Karen DeVinney, managing editor, University of North Texas Press, for whom this is an on-going, and sometimes seemingly endless project.

Special thanks go to Robert Wooster for his review and valuable comments on each volume, and to Sherry Smith for her equally valuable suggestions for this volume. Friends who have followed this project and encouraged it from its inception include Lt. Col. Thomas T. Smith, U.S.A., Frances Vick, retired director of the University of North Texas Press, Jerome A. Greene, Robert Utley, and Patricia Stallard.

Thanks also to the Rev. Michael Coleman, archivist, Diocese of Kansas City, for background on the history of the Roman Catholic Church in Kansas City.

The United States Military Academy, West Point, New York, provided copies of photographs pasted in Bourke's manuscripts.

The administration of South Texas College, McAllen, Texas, Dr. Shirley A. Reed, president; Juan Mejía, vice president for instruction; Shirley Ingram, director of Human Resources; Dr. Magaretha Bischoff, dean, Liberal Arts and Social Sciences; and Dr. Christopher Nelson, chairman, Department of History and Philosophy, have provided both latitude and encouragement for this project.

Finally, almost from the beginning of my writing career some twenty years ago, Paul L. Hedren has provided criticism where it was due, praise where it was due, and in all cases, friendship and encouragement. For that reason, this volume is gratefully dedicated to him.

Military Division of the Missouri

— overland routes

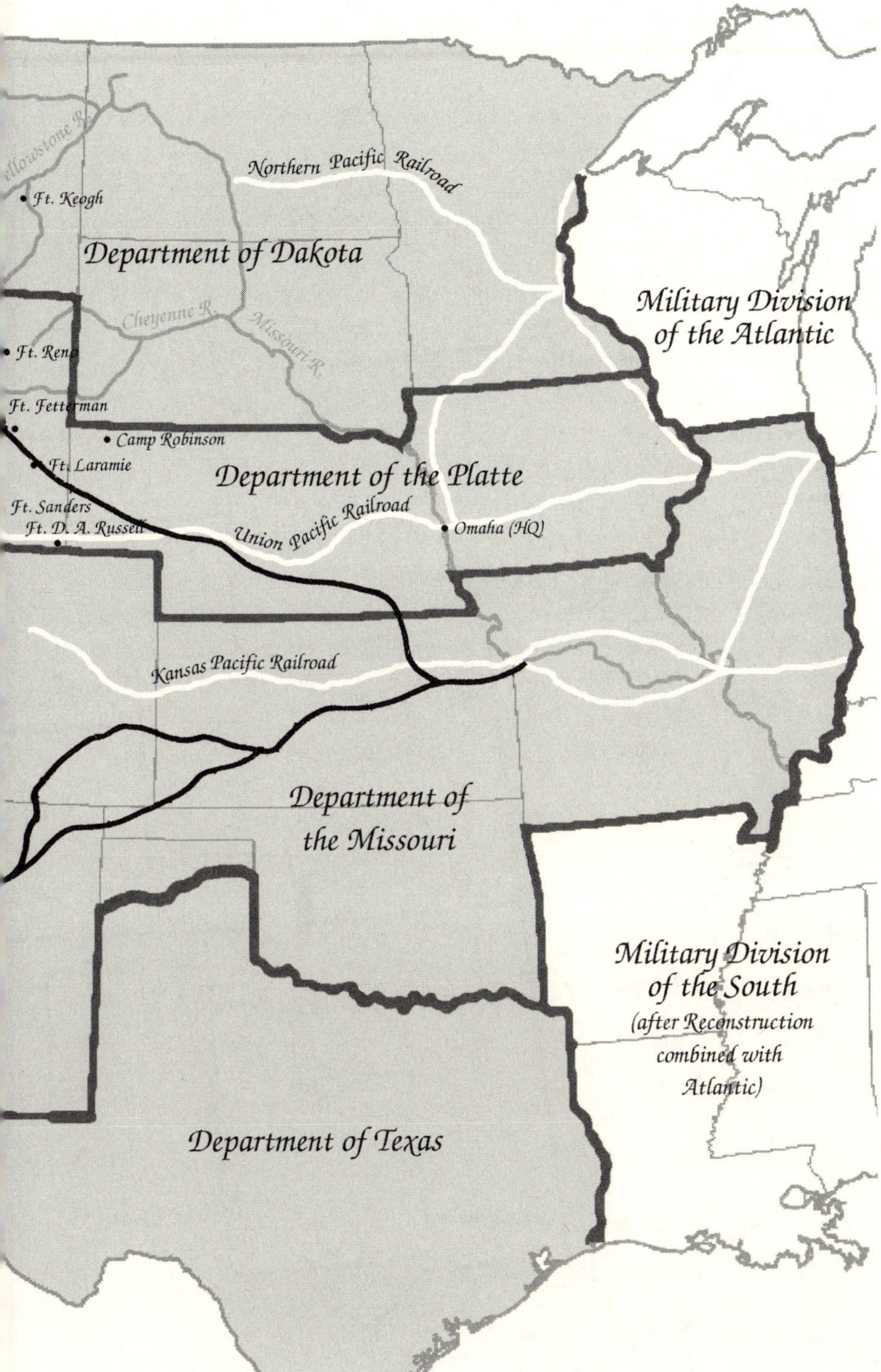
Yellowstone R.
Ft. Keogh
Northern Pacific Railroad
Department of Dakota
Military Division
of the Atlantic
Cheyenne R.
Missouri R.
Ft. Reno
Ft. Fetterman
Camp Robinson
Ft. Laramie
Department of the Platte
Ft. Sanders
Ft. D. A. Russell
Union Pacific Railroad
Omaha (HQ)
Kansas Pacific Railroad
Department of
the Missouri
Military Division
of the South
(after Reconstruction
combined with
Atlantic)
Department of Texas

Map

Montana
- Ft. Keogh
- Ft. Custer

Idaho
- Ft. Boise
- Ft. Hall

Wyoming
- Ft. Fetterman
- Ft. Laramie
- Rawlins
- Ft. Fred Steel
- Laramie
- Ft. Sanders
- Cheyenne
- Ft. D.A. Russell
- X Milk Creek Fight

Dakota Territory
- Ft. Robinson
- Ft. Niobrara
- Sidney Barracks

Utah
- Salt Lake City
- Ft. Douglas

Kansas
- Ft. McPherson

- Denver

- Ft. Mojave
- Camp Hualpai
- Prescott
- Ft. Whipple
- Camp Verde
- Ft. McDowell
- Tucson
- Ft. Lowell
- Ft. Bowie

- Santa Fe
- Ft. Craig
- Ft. Cummings

Rio Grande

Texas

Introduction to Volume 3

Volume 3 of this series covers John Gregory Bourke's diaries from June 1, 1878, through June 22, 1880, and manuscript volume 23 to half-way through volume 34. During this period, the notebooks progressively deviate from the standard daily journal to a "stream-of-consciousness." Increasingly, Bourke is aware that he is writing for posterity. He shifts from the word "journal," referring more to his "note-books" and "scrapbooks." This, in part, reflects more time on his hands. For almost the first time in the ten years since he graduated from West Point, Bourke was neither in the field nor preparing for a new field expedition. He could look back on events so far, which gives several interesting retrospectives on his early days in Arizona. He also was able to enjoy the amenities of the East and the urban Midwest, and when he did accompany General Crook, it was in the capacity of administrative inspection, as in the Bannock uprising and site selection for what became Fort Niobrara, Nebraska.[1] In fact, Crook rarely appears in this volume; more often, Bourke is on his own.

---

1. Fort Niobrara was established in 1880 on the Niobrara River, to protect cattlemen and settlers from whatever roaming bands of Indians might remain, and as an additional control over the Indians at the Spotted Tail Agency. It was abandoned in 1906 and is now a national wildlife refuge. Frazer, *Forts of the West*, 89.

He found time to dedicate all of manuscript volume 24 to a retrospective on the Sioux War, which includes a long dissertation on Crazy Horse, whose death he called "an event of such importance, and with its attendant circumstances pregnant with so much of good or evil for the settlement between the Union Pacific Rail Road and the Yellowstone River that I do not feel that it would be proper for me to pass it over with the condensed account given in my notes of July and August last year [1877]."[2]

Throughout the narrative, Bourke refers to various letters and telegrams which he included at the end of this volume under the heading:

Authorities.
Personal notes of the Campaigns conducted by Brig. General George Crook, U.S. Army, against the Sioux Indians in Nebraska, Wyoming, Montana, Dakota—1876–1877.

This includes correspondence surrounding the surrender and death of Crazy Horse as well as an account provided by Billy Hunter, one of the mixed-blood interpreters, of the chief's death. Because of the continuing interest, as well as the controversy, surrounding Crazy Horse, I have deviated from my usual practice of deleting all but the most relevant correspondence, and have included Bourke's "Authorities" as Appendix 2.[3]

Bourke betrays a grudging admiration for Crazy Horse, calling him a "truly great man,"[4] and in his summation, he unintentionally contributes to the modern Crazy Horse mystique.

> A dead lion is of no account in the regard of those who lately were wont to trouble at his faintest roar; thus, Crazy Horse being dead, an exaggerated importance has attached to the war with the Nez-Percés, but how much more costly in blood, treasure, time and material would have been that war had

---

2. Bourke, Diary, 24:1; Bourke's account of these months is published in Robinson, *Diaries*, Vol. 1, Chapters 18–19, and Vol. 2, Chapters 1–4. Crazy Horse had become a sort of symbolic "boogey man," whose actions—real and imagined—during the Great Sioux War had unnerved both Crook and his counterpart in the Department of Dakota, Brig. Gen. Alfred H. Terry. The surrender of Crazy Horse's band, in May 1877, was considered to be more or less the end of significant Lakota resistance. See Robinson, *General Crook*.

3. Bourke, Diary, 24:1; Bourke's account of Crazy Horse's surrender is in Robinson, *Diaries*, Vol. 2, Chapter 14.

4. Bourke, Diary, 24:49.

Crazy Horse broken away and rallied around him the disaffected elements of the Dakotas and obliged us to fight 3000 or 4.000 skilled warriors instead of 3 or 400.[5]

The comment is absurd. There is no real evidence that Crazy Horse planned to go to war, and it is doubtful that he could have, even if he had wanted. Only a few pages earlier, Bourke had noted that the Northern Plains tribes were thoroughly beaten and divided into too many quarreling factions to offer any further resistance, as Crazy Horse himself was aware.[6] Meanwhile, the flight of the Nez Percés under Joseph garnered national attention—and sympathy—and Joseph himself emerged as a heroic figure.[7]

Three other key events during this period were the Cheyenne Outbreak of 1878–79, the Ponca Affair, and the White River Ute Uprising, both in 1879. The Cheyennes and Poncas will be discussed in the introduction to Part 2 of this volume, and the Utes in the introduction to Part 4.

The Cheyenne and Ute crises contain the most action in this volume. For those accustomed to the nearly continuous scouting expeditions and Indian fights of Volumes 1 and 2 of this series, at least half of Volume 3 will appear almost mundane. Bourke spends a great deal of time in Omaha, Kansas City, and St. Louis. He visits factories and foundries. He is a member of a remount board that buys horses in Kentucky for the cavalry. And he takes advantage of every opportunity to enjoy local society.

Bourke visiting factories and horse farms does not correspond to the image of Bourke the soldier and the ethnologist. For that reason, readers might wonder why I bothered to include these sections; indeed, I initially considered omitting them. Bourke, however, realized—and commented—that he was witnessing a transformation. The United States now fronted two oceans. The North-South sectional conflicts that for so long had hindered national development were resolved. There was a feeling of unbridled optimism as the

---

5. Ibid., 24:39.
6. Ibid., 24:34–36.
7. The Nez Percé War began in the spring of 1877 when a band of young warriors, resentful of relocation to a reservation, attacked and killed several white settlers. Fearing retaliation, Joseph, Looking Glass, and several other chiefs led their bands in a trek of a thousand miles across Idaho and Montana, seeking refuge in Canada. Pursued by troops, Joseph finally surrendered on October 5, 1877, less than a hundred miles from the border. See Beal, *"I Will Fight No More Forever,"* and Greene, *Nez Perce Summer, 1877.*

nation rapidly grew into a major industrial and economic power. Noting the shipment of California wine to Germany, he writes, "This new and important demand will stimulate our wine-growers to new energy and beyond question American wine will within the next twenty years assume a high place in the list of our staple resources." He even went so far as to predict that the American West would be ideal for ratite culture.[8] In the case of wine, his foresight was correct, the disaster of Prohibition notwithstanding. As for ostriches and emus, the attempt made almost a century after Bourke's death never lived up to expectations.

The horse-buying visits give a better view of Bourke's racial attitudes. Until this point, most of his references to blacks have involved soldiers, and he has been favorably impressed. Here, however, he ventures to parts of the country where there are large numbers of black civilians, and his impressions are less positive. In Kentucky, he writes:

> The blacks flock to the towns like Lexington whose streets they *throng*, either as downright idlers or pursuing such apologies for labor as polishing boots, waiting on hotel tables or running errands. It disgusted me greatly to be accosted half a dozen times to the block with the question, "shine yer butes, Boss?"[9]

He has made many previous references to restaurants, and no doubt his orderly regularly polished his boots. But as he has never referred to these as "apologies for labor," he seems to feel that there is something particularly menial about it if blacks do it. That, together with appellations like "niggers" and "darkies," shed light on his views, which were in line with most whites of his era, regardless of his Union Army service.

Likewise, he is completely unsympathetic over the problems of Johnson Whittaker, who became West Point's only black cadet following the graduation of Henry Flipper in 1878. Whittaker contended that he had received a threatening note, and, on the night of April 5–6, 1880, he was bound, beaten, and slashed. A hastily

---

8. Bourke, Diary, 33:529–30.
9. Ibid., 33:499.

convened board of inquiry determined Whittaker had written the note and inflicted the injuries on himself as a means of avoiding the examinations. Following the story, Bourke commented, "[A]s the injuries of which he made so much ado are now found to have been too trivial for mention, the burden of proof in the whole business is thrown upon Whittaker & such sympathizers as may still adhere to him."[10] Whittaker, however, demanded a court-martial to clear his name. He was found guilty, but in 1882, President Chester A. Arthur threw out the verdict on the grounds that a court-martial was not legally applicable to the case. By then, however, Whittaker had been dismissed from the academy for failing his examinations.[11]

Bourke's view of the Whittaker Affair no doubt is based in part on his racial attitudes, and also because he was what might be called "all West Point." References to the academy and to classmates abound in the narrative. In fact, on April 25, 1880, he was offered an appointment as assistant professor of Spanish at West Point. Although he initially accepted, eventually he opted to remain with Crook.[12]

This volume not only covers the Plains and Midwest, but also digresses to Bourke's time as a young junior officer, fresh out of West Point, and experiencing his first introduction to the Southwest. Recalling a march from his first post, Fort Craig, New Mexico, to Camp Grant,[13] Arizona, he writes:

> I wish I could remember as vividly and in proper sequence the general features of the topography of the line of march. My memory is constituted in such a way that I retain for a

---

10. Ibid., 34:572.
11. The Whittaker Affair is described in John F. Marszalek, *Court-Martial: A Black Man in America*.
12. Once before, in 1872, Bourke had been called to West Point, as an instructor in French and Spanish. Crook, however, had blocked it, saying his services were needed in Arizona. In this instance, Bourke noted in his entry for July 26, 1880, that he asked the War Department to revoke the appointment to the academy, although he did not give a reason. Porter, *Paper Medicine Man*, 20–21; Bourke, Diary, 34:639.
13. Fort Craig was established on the Rio Grande, to provide protection against Apaches and guard the road along the Rio Grande in New Mexico. It was abandoned and transferred to the Interior Department in 1885. Camp Grant was established in 1865 on the San Pedro River near its confluence with Aravaipa Creek. Located on the site of the abandoned post of Fort Breckenridge, it guarded the road between Tucson and Sacaton. An Indian reservation was established briefly at Grant in 1872, but after the Indians were reconcentrated at San Carlos later that year, the post no longer was necessary. It was abandoned in 1873, a new Camp Grant having been established at the head of Sulphur Springs Valley. Frazer, *Forts of the West*, 4–6, 8, 98; Altshuler, *Starting With Defiance*, 28–30.

long time the impressions made upon me by individuals, but in a sense of locality I am lacking in details but always capable of describing the character of a district with an approach to correctness; even if my account of the lesser meanderings of roads and streams be somewhat at fault.[14]

Yet this period of Bourke's life gets only three paragraphs in *On the Border With Crook*,[15] and without the lengthy diary entries of New Mexico and Arizona, we would know little about this early part of his career.

Here, and elsewhere throughout the diaries, Bourke pokes fun at the quirks and foibles of the Irish soldiers who made up such a large part of the frontier army. Both his parents were from Ireland, but they were well-to-do, and not refugees from famine or clearances that so often made up the Irish immigrant class. He expresses sympathy with the Irish country people caught up in the famine of the late 1870s, and resents the apparent indifference of the British government to their suffering.[16] Nevertheless, he was thoroughly Americanized, apparently devoid of any romantic fantasies of an ancient, heroic Ireland that so often permeate Irish-American mythology; he seems to view immigrant and home-country Irish as a species that was interesting, and perhaps a little odd. His parodies come to full fruition as he recollects an encounter between Sir Rose Price, an Irish baronet, and two Irish officers in the U.S. Army, Col. John Joseph Coppinger, and "Old Jemmie" Henton, blistering (in his own humorous way) their accents, vanities, and mannerisms.

Yet there was no malice in his accounts. Lengthy descriptions of Capt. Gerald Russell, 3rd Cavalry, whom he first met as a new lieutenant fresh from the academy, show a young officer's admiration for a crusty, vain, but extremely competent old soldier who ruled his troops with just the right balance of terror and paternal affection. A shrewd Irish peasant who, in his own view, has done well in his adopted country, Russell boasts of his background to emphasize his achievements. In the "Jerry Russellisms," the Western movie fan

---

14. Bourke, Diary, 30:189.
15. Bourke, *On the Border*, 3.
16. This famine was in no way as severe as the one of the 1840s, but served to point up the abuses in Irish land law that kept the country people impoverished and on the verge of starvation. No British government seemed capable of arriving at a solution. Churchill, *Great Democracies*, 343.

can easily hear Victor McLaglen. Bourke describes a drinking bout the night before a scouting expedition against Apaches, in which Russell and other senior captains had to be carried to their cots by the junior officers. It is a humorous scene that portrays these battle-hardened veterans as human beings, capable of kindness and sentimentality.

The second half of this volume contains frequent references to General U.S. Grant, who seemed to be a major news topic as the 1880 election approached. After completing his second term in March 1877, Grant and his wife, Julia, departed for Great Britain to visit their daughter, Nellie, who had married into the English gentry. The vacation turned into a two-and-a-half-year, round-the-world tour, with the Grants feted from London to Tokyo. There being no constitutional prohibition on a third term at the time, Grant was considered a contender in 1880, and his biographer, William S. McFeely, calls the trip "a campaign tour unlike that of any previous candidate for the presidency." The world tour was followed by a tour throughout the United States, along with Cuba and Mexico. Through 1879 and the first half of 1880, Bourke has little doubt that Grant would make a political comeback and become the nation's first three-term president. Indeed, when the Republicans held their convention, he was the strongest candidate, but failed to get a clear majority. The convention delegates deadlocked, and the compromise ticket of James A. Garfield and Chester A. Arthur was chosen, one that Bourke calls "essentially weak." The Democrats nominated Maj. Gen. Winfield S. Hancock, another Civil War hero, for president and William Hayden English for vice president. "This ticket," Bourke writes, "will be a formidable one and, beyond reasonable doubt, will carry success."[17] He was mistaken. Garfield won the election, although with a fractional margin. Taking office in 1881, he was assassinated a few months into his administration, and Arthur assumed the presidency.

Throughout the diaries, Bourke inadvertently dispels the image of the frontier army as being somewhere in what the British might call "the back of beyond." Certainly this was the case in the antebellum army, entering the Great Plains and Southwestern deserts for the first time. By the time Bourke went West, however,

---

17. Bourke, Diary, 34:583–84. Grant's tour and third term ambitions are discussed in McFeely, *Grant: A Biography*, Chapters 26 and 27. The quote is from page 478.

the situation was rapidly changing. Although reading material was limited, and army officers as a general rule were not well informed, neither did they live in a vacuum. The post libraries of frontier forts might not have had a wide variety of books, but newspapers and magazines, while slightly dated, were available. Opportunities for self-improvement did exist if the officers and soldiers chose to utilize them.[18] Arizona was in the midst of development, and was adjacent to already-cosmopolitan California. The completion of the transcontinental railroad in 1869 began to open the most remote regions of the frontier. Even at Fort Laramie, Wyoming, which in 1876 neared the furthest extension of what Easterners might term "civilization," the officers and ladies performed theatricals that Bourke called "capitally interpreted."[19]

Field service was more isolated, but even then, railroad, telegraph, and regular courier service kept the soldiers informed. In camp at Goose Creek, Wyoming, following the near disastrous Rosebud Fight of June 17, 1876, the mail brought regular contact with the outside world. "Our newspaper files were very complete," Bourke noted, "representing prominent New York, Philadelphia, San Francisco, Washington, Chicago, Omaha and Cheyenne publications." Besides American political news (1876 was an election year), there even was the report of a palace revolt in Constantinople, half-way around the world.[20] In various places in this volume, Bourke comments about the Zulu wars in South Africa, including the British disaster at Isandhlwana on January 22, 1879, and the death of Prince Louis Napoleon, who was killed in action while serving in the British Army in the Natal.

Format of the Edited Diaries

Editing a work like the Bourke diaries is not necessarily confined to transcription, but also to rendering the text into a readable form while preserving the author's original flavor and intent. Purists, such as Wayne R. Kime, who achieved the monumental task of preparing the Richard Irving Dodge journals for publication, adhere strictly to the original text, including cross-outs and insertions. On the opposite side of the coin, Lt. Col. Thomas T. Smith, former assistant

18. Knight, *Life and Manners*, 57, 83.
19. Robinson, *Diaries*, 1:208.
20. Ibid., 344.

professor of military history at West Point, took Cpl. Emil Bode's German syntax, fractured spelling, and erratic punctuation and rendered them more easily understood by the casual reader.[21]

With Bourke's diaries, I have chosen the middle ground between these two positions, and have undertaken a basic format to preserve as much as possible the flavor of the manuscript, while making it intelligible to the reader and without being cumbersome.

Beyond the exceptions listed in the introduction, I have followed the format of the first two volumes of this series, which is to say:

<u>Orders and Clippings</u>. By and large, clippings are simply correspondents' versions of events that Bourke himself recounted in detail. Because of the enormity of this material, and its availability elsewhere, it has been deleted in favor of Bourke's own manuscript text. In some instances, this includes entire volumes that are nothing more than collections of clippings and copies of orders.

<u>Abbreviations, Spelling, and Grammar</u>. Bourke used many abbreviations. The @ symbol often appears as a substitute for the word "or." While I have tried to remain as faithful as possible to the original text, for the sake of clarity I have spelled out the more common abbreviations, such as cardinal directions, "left," "right," "miles," and "road," as well as those he used frequently, such as "good grass and water," and "creek." For those that are less common or obvious, I have inserted the missing letters in [brackets], except when the abbreviations are scattered, requiring several sets of brackets within one word; in such cases, I have spelled out the word in brackets. When a word is illegible, but the meaning can be inferred, I have placed the probable word with a question mark in [brackets?]. If the meaning cannot be inferred, I have written it as [*illegible*]. Otherwise, I have transcribed the text as is, with all its inconsistencies, such as "tipi," "teepee," and sometimes even "tépi," all of which he used to designate the conical Indian lodge. Names of individuals suffered in the same fashion. All such instances have been noted in the biographical sketches in Appendix 1.

Interestingly enough, as the years progressed, Bourke tended to pay more attention to spelling out words, as well as to punctuation and capitalization. Consequently these become less of an issue in this volume than in Volumes 1 and 2. Nevertheless,

---

21. See Smith, *A Dose of Frontier Soldiering*.

differences exist, and words that Bourke commonly misspelled, or were spelled differently in the nineteenth century, such as "accomodation" and "Mississipi" have been copied without any particular notation.

Punctuation and Capitalization. Bourke tended to use periods and commas *outside* quotation marks rather than within. I lean toward leaving Bourke's punctuation intact except for cases where it renders the text absolutely confusing. Capitalization was erratic. For example, in giving times of day, he might use a.m./p.m., A.M./P.M., or am./pm. I have preserved his capitalization as much as possible. Paragraphing was also erratic, with new paragraphs sometimes indented, but often flush with the left margin.

Emphasis. Bourke emphasized words by underlining them. Most of the time (but not always), he underlined names of people and places, dates, and geographical features of interest. Yet some of his emphasis seems little more than whimsy and, more than a century later, appears to have had no practical reason. In an effort to make it more readable, I have deleted the emphasis except where it enhances the impression he was trying to convey. Bourke occasionally annotated the entries after the fact, as new information came to hand. His notes are indicated by an asterisk (*) while mine are numbered. I have replaced Bourke's brackets with parentheses, to avoid confusing his texts with mine.

Personalities, etc. Often individuals are named with no explanation as to who they were. Bourke was, after all, writing for his own future reference and knew the people in question. I have attempted, in Appendix 1, to identify as many as possible, and in the case of army officers, have been relatively successful. After more than a century, however, it has not always been possible to identify Indians, enlisted soldiers, or civilians.

The basic intent of the biographical sketches essentially is to explain who these people were, and why they went west. The criteria for the extent of the sketches are based on three factors: their importance in history, their importance to the narrative, and the availability of material on them. In many cases Bourke might make only a passing reference, such as, "I encountered Lieut. X," this being the only reference to Lieutenant X in the entire narrative. Because of that, and because many such officers did not attain historical prominence, the sketch is minimal. Others, mentioned frequently, and/or historically important in their own right, receive more detailed treatment.

Where Bourke uses the local name for plants, or names that might not be widely known, I have attempted to identify them and put the botanical name in the notes; I did not do so for commonly known plants. Bourke's designations of the territories have been preserved, and when they do not reflect the modern name of the state, I have inserted the state in [brackets]. In my own commentaries, I have used the modern state names.

<u>Military Ranks</u>. Bourke tended to use brevet ranks for officers who had attained them in the Union Army. Thus we see a reference to "General John H. King, Col. 9th Infantry," the former being his brevet rank and the latter being his active rank at the time of writing. The biographical sketches of officers in Appendix 1 include both active and brevet ranks.

Part 1
The Life of a General's Aide

Background

This section covers a period of relative peace on the frontier. Concerned mainly with office work, and inspection and procurement assignments, Bourke offers more detail on daily life in the Midwest and along the frontier. Little, if any, of this material appears in *On the Border With Crook*, or in his other writings, so this is a fresh view of his activities, attitudes, and opinions.

Among other things, he attended the wedding of Lucy McFarland, a second cousin of First Lady Lucy Hayes,[1] to his old classmate, Eric Bergland. This event, which occurred in June 1878, appears to have been written in retrospect, although not necessarily by any great length of time. The prenuptials were written after the fact, because, in discussing a courtesy call to her home, he commented, "Miss Lucy McFarland, at the time of this writing Mrs. E. Bergland, pleased me very much as a talented, refined and good-hearted lady of great personal attractions."[2] Yet it was close enough to the event to paste in a newspaper clipping describing the wedding.

---

1. The term "first lady," which has no legal or constitutional standing, was used for the first time with Lucy Hayes, the first presidential wife with a college education, which she used to promote social causes. See Appendix 1.
2. Bourke, Diary, 23:12.

Bourke, still a bachelor at the time, appreciated the young women at the celebration: "During all my travels and experience, I have never seen so many beautiful young women together as there were at this wedding. Nothing but my diffidence prevented my falling in love with some one of them: to being able to tune my nerves up to making a particular choice, I fell in love with them all."[3]

Bourke recorded a frontier in transition. He attended cultural events in theaters filled with gun-toting rowdies. He listened to a post commander's plans for lining his fort's parade ground with shade trees and building an artificial lake. He described a modern mill where heavy machinery extracted silver from ore. He also came to know cattlemen in the rapidly developing Territory of Wyoming, observing that only three years earlier, hostile Indians traversed the region at will. Now, however, one saw "thousands and thousands of fine fat cattle peaceably grazing and increasing in value to the undisguised satisfaction of their owners."[4]

This development did not always extend to the military. On a visit to Rock Island Arsenal, he marveled at officers quarters, and thought how much better frontier officers might live "if only the tenth part of the moneys wasted on these palatial structures had been properly applied to the legitimate purpose of maintaining an Army."[5] Like many people, then and now, he blamed the army's problems—and by extension those of the nation—on self-interested "professional politicians . . . the grandest lot of 'dead beats', thieves and scoundrels outside of jail."[6]

Many of the people mentioned in this volume were companions from expeditions during the Great Sioux War. One person, however, is noticeably missing from the bulk of this, and subsequent volumes: Azor Nickerson, Crook's senior aide-de-camp, with whom Bourke had worked closely since 1872. At Crook's behest, Nickerson was promoted to major and assistant adjutant general on June 16, 1878, which led to his assignment in Washington and separation from Crook's staff. During their last meeting, in Wyoming in late July, Bourke wrote, "We could only stammer out the stereotyped phrases of kindly feeling, but knew that no empty conventional expressions

---

3. Ibid., 23:17.
4. Ibid., 25:3–4.
5. Ibid., 23:31.
6. Ibid., 23:15.

BACKGROUND 17

could adequately convey the regard and esteem in which we mutually held each other."[7]

Bourke also followed Col. Ranald Mackenzie's incursions into Mexico. Previously, in 1873, Mackenzie had led a substantial raid some sixty miles into the Mexican interior, smashing Kickapoo and Lipan camps at Remolino, in order to stop their depredations in Texas. The attack, unauthorized but tacitly encouraged by General Sheridan, created a furor but had the desired effect. After serving with Crook in the Department of the Platte during the Great Sioux War, Mackenzie had been transferred back to Texas, where Indians and bandits again were raiding back and forth across the border with relative impunity. As commander of the Subdistrict of the Nueces, at Fort Clark, Texas, he sent or led several expeditions into Mexico. By now, however, Mexico was capable of military retaliation, and for awhile it appeared the two countries might go to war. Like many Americans of his era, Mackenzie believed that Mexico would be better off if completely absorbed into the United States, and so did Bourke.[8] Commenting on Mackenzie's exploits on the Mexican border, he noted:

> With (3) or four strong columns of invasion, aggregating a greater of a million of men, we could within two years be able to plant *strong colonies*, at eligible points, connected together and with our Rio Grande and Rio Gila systems by Rail Road and telegraphs and with these fortified colonies as foci we could easily establish such relations of commerce and manufactures with the Mexicans as would make our possession of their Territory not alone tolerant but agreeable. Intercourse with these colonies would make the Mexicans see the necessity of having their children taught our language and with a knowledge of our language would naturally come to desire to learn more of our customs. By strictly respecting the religious convictions of the people, by encouraging marriages between *American* men and *Mexican* women and above all by establishing a secure and remunerative market for all Mexican supplies, we could it seems to me,

---

7. Ibid., 23:67.
8. Mackenzie's activities are covered in Robinson, *Bad Hand*, Chapter 16, and Pierce, *Most Promising Young Officer*, 196–201.

soon reduce and pacify and even do much to *Americanize* our *Spanish-Indian* neighbors.[9]

Typically, he expressed the viewpoint that American men would marry Mexican women, and not the reverse.

9. Bourke, Diary, 25:19–20.

Chapter 1

Nostalgia, a Society Wedding, a Day at the Races, and a Parting

[June 1, 1878]

The present year, 1878, has been rendered illustrious in its century, by the discoveries of the celebrated scientific electrician, Mr. [Thomas] Edison: in other note-books, allusion occurs to the telephone, one of the emanations of his inventive genius.[1] This one must chronicle the "phonograph", or sound-writer, which has for its singular office the preservation and reproduction of all sounds, confided to its cylinder.[2] What with our improvements in machinery, rail-roading, hotel-keeping, telegraphy, printing and photography, it would seem as if but little more was needed to make good man's boast that he is the lord of creation.

June 1st. Left Omaha, and Council Bluffs, by the Kansas City, St. Joe and Council Bluffs R.R. for St. Louis, where a quick connection

---

1. Bourke is mistaken. The telephone was invented by Alexander Graham Bell in 1876.
2. Edison patented the phonograph in 1878, by embossing the groove on tinfoil. Although it did reproduce sound, it was not commercially viable, and Edison did little work on it for another ten years, until Alexander Graham Bell, his cousin Chidchester Bell, and Charles Sumner Tainter patented the Grammophone, which used an engraved wax cylinder. Faced with the competition, Edison improved his invention, and introduced the "Perfected" phonograph to market. Reiss, *Compleat Talking Machine*, 154–56.

was made in the Grand Union dépôt with the Ohio and Mississippi R.R. for Cincinnati. On the latter train was pained to find my old friend, Lieut. E. L. Keyes, 5th Cavy., and mother, travelling from Texas to Washington. Keyes, a bright intellect ruined by addiction to liquor, promised at one time to be an ornament to the service, but dissipation brought about his dismissal and, to my unfeigned regret, I saw that he was still a victim to his degrading passion and steadily running down hill.

In 1872, Keyes and myself, formed part of the detachment, which, under command of Col. Coppinger, 23d Inft., sailed from San Francisco, in the good steamer, "Newbern", to the mouth of the Colorado river, in the Gulf of California. The voyage of some 2.000 miles occupied 13 days, a period long enough to enable us to become pretty thoroughly acquainted with each other, outside of the pleasant comradeship of the occasion, not much can be said of the journey. The arid cliffs of Baja California, Sinaloa, and Sonora,[3] gave us a very unfavorable idea of Mexico; a school of dolphins, glistening in the sun, a long shark, or, semi-periodically, a whale, or what we land-lubbers thought must be whales or sea-serpents, helped to kill time pretty well; then at meridian, we used to "haul the log" or "take the sun" with Captain McDonough, an odd genius, (since drowned at sea.) The astronomical part of business didn't interest us very much; strictly speaking, I never thought that our worthy skipper knew how to handle a sextant; he preferred running his ship along the coast, of which every promontory and indentation was perfectly well-known to him; but, if he couldn't manage a sextant, he could make a very acceptable toddy, and every day, just as soon as the log had been read and the bearing determined, proofs of his skill in his favorite line were in eager demand by a throng of thirsty young officers. As McDonough was a perfect skinflint about his whiskey, strategy had to be brought into play whenever we felt like having more than one round of the enticing beverage; there was only one vulnerable point in the skipper's character; it was his Achilles' heel, but we found it out almost intuitively and assailed him there every time with success. He was very fond of telling us about his "viges";

---

3. States in northwestern Mexico. Baja California (now partitioned into two states—North and South) is the peninsula on the west shore of the Gulf of California, while Sonora and Sinaloa are on the east shore. Sonora borders Arizona, and Sinaloa is immediately to the south of Sonora.

his "vige" to Callao,[4] his "first vige" out from Liverpool, his "second vige" to Puget Sound, and so on.

To these we listed with intense gravity and interest, more or less simulated. Our patience never went without its reward. The Captain's throat was certain to become parched and we shared in the toddy, brewed for its refreshment.

Peace be to his Ashes. Softly let the waves of the Gulf of Cortez sing his requiem. He was the biggest liar I ever met, and some of his stories of adventure were masterpieces of mendacity.

Colonel Coppinger, our worthy commander, was one of the neatest men in his dress I ever knew: the one apprehension that clouded upon his mind was that one large batch of recruits would not keep themselves clean. To insure absolute cleanliness among them became almost a mania with him: every fine morning, he would have large squads stand out on the forecastle [of the ship], while water was thrown over them from the force pumps.

This seemed to tickle the soldiers amazingly: the voyage was made very pleasantly, only one man lost and he drowned through his own cursèd carelessness and disobedience of orders, while we were steaming into the mouth of the muddy Colorado.

Then as we got upon the river steamboat, "Cocopah", Jack Mellon, Master,[5] and steamed up the channel to Ehrenburg, (400) and odd miles, it seemed as if our troubles had, only commenced.[6] We couldn't make more than (60) miles a day against the swift current, and, while the sun lasted, groaned on account of the heat and at night suffered a little from the mosquitoes, but not much, for it was then in the month of November (1872).

When we could come to a "wood-landing",[7] everybody rushed ashore. Our "roustabouts" were Cocopah Indians and Mexicans,

---

4. In Peru.

5. Mellon was a renowned Colorado River pilot who, in 1874, was master of the steamer *Gila*, carrying Lt. John W. Summerhayes and his wife, Martha, to Fort Mojave. Martha Summerhayes remembered Mellon as "then the most famous pilot on the Colorado, and he was very skilful [sic] in steering clear of the sand-bars, skimming over them, or working his boat off, when once fast upon them." Bourke mentions the *Gila* in the next paragraph. Summerhayes, *Vanished Arizona*, 36ff.

6. The first attempt at steam navigation on the lower Colorado appears to have been in 1852, when the steamer *Uncle Sam*, delivered in pieces by schooner, and assembled at the mouth of the river, reached Fort Yuma in December of that year. She ran aground and sank after a year or two of service. After another false start, in 1854, steam service finally began on a regular basis in the fall of 1855, and continued throughout most of the remainder of the century. Bancroft, *Arizona and New Mexico*, 490.

7. A depot where the steamer would put into shore to take on more wood for fuel.

who worked to my unpracticed eye very faithfully: this wasn't the first mate's opinion and the way that man poured out profanity and tobacco juice from his mouth was a caution. The "roustabouts" never seemed to mind him in the least, and probably fancied he was praising their good looks whenever he "damned their eyes". About half way up from Point Isabel, (the miserable collection of hovels at the mouth of the river,)[8] to Fort Yuma, Cal.,[9] (the first point inside of the American lines,) we met the steamboat "Gila", commanded by Captain Mellon's friend and comrade of years, Captain Steve Thorn.

The meeting was very funny: the two men were of the same general type—red-faced, broad-shouldered, warty-knuckled, deep-chested, profane, good-hearted, honest old fresh water mariners, who could out-drink, out-smoke, out-chew, or out-swear any two men in Arizona—and that's saying a good deal. Each was very proud of his boat, and as this periodical meeting was always looked forward to with fond anticipation—the respective commanders were arrayed sumptuously in their "nobbiest" apparel. Each wore black doe-skin pantaloons, and a white linen shirt which would have been very presentable, if it had not been disfigured with so much jewelry. Neither wore a collar, but Mellon's garment was buttoned at the neck, while Thorn's lay open carelessly, exposing a red-flannel undershirt beneath. In the matter of jewelry, Thorn completely eclipsed our more unpretentious commander, but either could have equipped a Jew pedlar with the amount carried on his person. Thorn had, besides the usual studs, and cuff-buttons, not far from half a dozen breast-pins, all of them bounteous in material and one or two of good workmanship. He had a good-sized gold anchor, held by a small cable to a gold cross, and, if I remember correctly, he also wore a gold anvil, almost big enough for the uses of a blacksmith. But, he didn't have any hat, at least not at that moment, while Captain Mellon,

---

8. Not to be confused with Point Isabel, Texas, near the mouth of the Rio Grande, which gave access by steamer to Fort Brown and Fort Ringgold.

9. Fort Yuma was established as Camp Independence in 1850 on the Colorado River about half a mile below the mouth of the Gila. A few months later, in March 1851, it was relocated to a low hill on the west bank of the Colorado, opposite the present city of Yuma, Arizona. The post subsequently was abandoned, but reoccupied and renamed Fort Yuma in 1852. Initially established to protect the emigrant routes and control local Indians, it later became a supply depot for military posts in Arizona. It was abandoned in 1883, when the railroads rendered it redundant, and was transferred to the Interior Department the following year. An Indian school and mission now occupy the site. Frazer, *Forts of the West*, 34–35; Altshuler, *Starting With Defiance*, 67–72.

in a brand new, black silk "plug", presented by admiring friends in San Francisco, fairly obscured the glories of Solomon.

As the steamboats, bumped their prows together and the gang of "roustabouts" were, under the jealous supervision of two screaming and swearing first mates, actively fastening cables and running gangway planks between them, two streams of simultaneous objurgation burst from the lips of our rival skippers.

"Easy thar with your blank, blank, blank, old canal-boat, you horny-handed, land-lubber".

"Avast you bilious-eyed, blabbering mouthed mud-turtle—don't talk to your boss, your master, you dash, dash, dash, dash, son of a sea-cook". I didn't hear all the conversation; about the time, I descended to the lower deck, the air was blue and hot and sulphureous [sic] with profanity, but our gallant Captain was already silencing his less accomplished adversary. At Fort Yuma, our party broke up; myself, under orders to rejoin General Crook, at Prescott and the others, under Colonel Coppinger, to proceed, by easy marches, to their proper stations.

Fort Yuma fully merited all the bad reputation given it in the camp-talk of the Army, as the hottest and most dreary post in our country. During the time of our stay, there wasn't much to be seen, except now and then a squad of Cocopah, Yuma or Mojave, Indians lazily floating in the water which appeared to all intents and purposes to be their native element:

Give one of those Indians enough blue mud with which to plaster his hair as a shield against the sun and a cottonwood log to support him partially in the water, and he will be happy as any king and float on the turbid bosom of the Colorado, until he meets an upcoming steamer, whereon he knows he is always welcome to ride back to his little patch of squashes and melons, with which he will surfeit himself until the humor take him for another float in the river, or until some other Indian challenge him to a game of cards—the ruling passion of all these tribes. I am wandering away from my text—seemingly, but not in reality, as Keyes* has been in my mind all this time. He was a most jovial companion, one fitted for better things than the life of a drunkard.

*[Bourke's footnote] Lt. Keyes, 5th Cavalry, dismissed for drunkenness, April 1877.

These reminiscences, awakened by meeting with him, are inserted because I fear that the note-books of that date, 1872, have been mislaid, destroyed or stolen.[10]

[Bourke returns to the present, which is to say, June 1, 1878]

At Cincinnati, I rested for a day at the Grand Hotel, a hostelry very inferior to the hotels of Chicago or San Francisco, but to be noted as one of the first to employ the telephone, which was there used to connect the Office with the Stable, six blocks distant. Here I had the great pleasure of meeting my old class-mate, Saml. Tillman, as well as [James Alfred] Dennison (of 68)[11] who has since resigned and is now enjoying himself as a gentleman of leisure, in Baltimore. They informed me of the death of Major and Bv't. Brig. Genl. L. H. Pelouze, of the Adjutant General's Corps.

June 4th. We three took the Kentucky Central R.R. to Lexington, and from the slowness of our ride had ample opportunity for an inspection of the beauties of the famed Blue Grass Region, and of Paris, Cynthiana and other little towns. At Lexington, in the Phoenix Hotel a quaint, old-fashioned rookery, very clean, with good table and good beds, but with an air of "going to seed" about it that I cannot describe, we found good accomodation [sic] and a number of old friends, viz. Price, P. M., Rockwell, C. H., and Bergland of our class ('69), [Rezin G.] Howell (of '64), [William C.] McFarland of '72, and [George Brinton] Walker, of '72. We had a great deal to talk about and our tongues rattled so that strangers might have thought our room was a girls' boarding school, but all things have an end, as well as a conversation. Our ablutions were soon completed, but we were not allowed time to change our clothing, as Mr. Henry Clay, (grandson and namesake of the distinguished senator,) was waiting to take us out for a drive. We got into two carriages and trotted along the streets of the town, which can boast a number of fine residences, some few good stores and a general air of thrift and wholesomeness, but withal offers many an odd surprise in the juxtaposition of dingy negro [sic] cottages, squalid blacksmith shops, or livery stables and elegant residences, the abodes of the cultivated, rich and influential people of the city.

---

10. Bourke probably is correct. The earliest extant volume in the West Point collection commences on November 20, 1872.

11. Heitman states Dennison entered West Point in 1866, and was commissioned in 1870, indicating he graduated that year, rather than 1868. Heitman, *Historical Register*, 1:367.

After sun-down, we called en masse at the residence of Mr. McFarland, to pay our respects to the bride elect, his daughter, and her bridesmaids. The young ladies were very bright and entertaining and the hours flew by until nearly midnight; when we took our departure. Miss Lucy McFarland, at the time of this writing Mrs. E. Bergland, pleased me very much as a talented, refined and good-hearted lady of great personal attractions. At midnight, Bergland entertained us all at supper, his "last shriek for freedom". Our party broke up about (2) in the morning, but as there was a liberal supply of 26 year old Kentucky whiskey in our rooms upstairs, our adjournment from the supper table did not signify that we were going to bed. We saw the sun rise before any such idea was thought of.

June 5th. Mr. Clay again escorted us to the points of interest within and about Lexington: we visited the training grounds and stables of Mr. [H. P.] McGrath, Col. Withers and Mr. Treacy, whose horses are highly considered in this region.

The red stallion, Cassius M. Clay, now over 26 years old, was a finely preserved specimen of equine power and grace. Almost, a noble animal, whose descendants are making a fine record as family carriage horses of speed, power, beauty, and above all extreme gentleness—and many other notabilities of the turf, whose names unfortunately, I cannot remember.

By all the gentlemen mentioned above we were treated most courteously; I may as well here mention also Mr. Buford and Mr. Morton, and also Mr. Preston, son of General Preston, our former minister to Spain, who called upon us in his father's name, very soon after our arrival. Our next visit was to the cemetery, which is at once the sacred field and the public park of the town.

It is maintained in a style worthy of all praise and is, beyond question, the most beautiful abode of the dead I ever saw.

Each plot of ground is kept trimmed and sodded, ornamented with choice flowers; and very generally, a pretty iron railing encloses a monument of granite or polished marble upon which may be read the names of the best families of Kentucky.

In one corner, cluster the graves of the Union dead, each mound marked by a pretty little head and foot-piece of white marble. Similarly, in another corner, are to [be] found the burial-places of the gallant, even if misguided men, who perished in support of the "Lost Cause".

There is a monument to the Union heroes, and also a beautiful shaft to the memory of the Confederates. One cannot help feeling proud of those rebels; they displayed in the highest degree the virtues of valor, fortitude and devotion to their principles. Slavery extirpated and the bad blood, engendered by long years of bitter political discussion, let out by the sharp edge of the sword, there is some reason to hope that our people may become united and homogenous,—a result which can never be *fully* accomplished until some method shall have been devised for exterminating the "professional politicians" who infest our land,—they are the grandest lot of "dead beats", thieves and scoundrels outside of jails.

The cenotaph to Henry Clay is a fine piece of masonry, polished Aberdeen granite, I think, (80) or (90) feet high.

The residence of Henry Clay, Ashland, some 3 miles outside of Lexington, is preserved by the State of Kentucky in the same condition as that in which it was left at the time of her great son's death. There the visitor may see the Library, bed-room, dining-room, the cozy little nook in which he did so much of his studying and the picturesque walks along which he so often sauntered.

Our last visit of the day was to the house of Colonel Preston, a long, one-story building pleasantly arranged in grounds, of nearly a square in extent, plentifully studded with outrageous [?] oak-trees. This mansion was as tastefully arranged on the inside as we had been led to suppose it might be from its exterior appearance. It was a source of regret to Tillman and myself, (we went in company) that none of the family could be seen; the young ladies, who were out driving, are reputed to be among the loveliest in their State.

At (7) in the evening, we assembled at the mansion of Mr. McFarland, which I should say was one of the most elegant in Lexington, and there found a large concourse of invited guests, nearly all of whom were relatives of the family. Of the ladies present, it must be stated in simple justice that they sustained the reputation of the Blue Grass Region for having as beautiful, finely-formed, graceful and animated young ladies as there are in the world.

During all my travels and experience, I have never seen so many beautiful young women together as there were at this wedding. Nothing but my diffidence prevented my falling in love with some one of them: to being able to tune my nerves up to making a particular choice, I fell in love with them all. The officiating clergyman, Mr.

Christy, of the Presbyterian church, delivered a brief, but very sensible and affecting address. The bride looked sweet and lovely in a dress of white silk or satin, trimmed with lace or illusion of some kind. She was a very sweet girl. The young lady, whom I had the honor of escorting, Miss McPheeters of Saint Louis, Mo., was dressed in white silk and illusion also, if I remember aright, and presented an appearance at once stately and charming. The wedding supper was a summary of all that money could purchase in the fine markets of Cincinnati, O[hi]o. or Louisville, Ky., aided by the fullest exertion of the powers of local cooks and confectioners. Fruits, of every description and of the finest quality, creams, ices, bonbons, wine—everything to tempt the palate, made a glittering and costly array. With feasting and dancing, the wedding reception was kept up in full vigor until 3 in the morning, at which hour, the brides-maids were placed in carriages and under the escort of the groom's men taken to their homes.

Bidding them good night and good bye, we returned to our Hotel, but remained up all night, talking over old times at the Point and the varied scenes in which we had been thrown since last we had met.

June 6th, We left Lexington, viâ the Cincinnati and Southern Rail Way. With us we had the pleasure of having Lt. and Mrs. Bergland, on their bridal tour, and Miss Scott, of Cincinnati, one of the brides-maids. The others drove down to the R.R. dépôt to say farewell. . . .

By the Cincinnati Southern, passengers are taken into Cincinnati, across the fine new iron bridge spanning the Ohio river at this point. This structure stands high in the list of those which would be called "first class" in all parts of the world, and is one of which the "Queen City" may well be proud.

When we reached the terminus, our pleasant party scattered in every direction. I was sorry not to have time to make a more extended inspection of the exceptionally fine markets through which I strolled on my last visit, or to attend an evening concert at some one of the numerous beer gardens on the hills overlooking the city, where the performances are said to be of a high order of merit.

As I entered the sleeping car, Lieut. R. P. Brown, 4th Infantry, accosted me, and in his company, I made the journey to Saint Louis. Early the next morning, we were at the Illinois side of the immense iron bridge, arching over the "Father of Waters."[12] By this connection, Saint Louis, in the matter of R.R. facilities, almost equals Chicago. As soon as the train touched the Missouri side, it entered a deep, dark tunnel, running entirely under the city and emerging only in the suburbs, where we found ourselves in the large edifice known as the Grand Union Dépôt, where all tracks converge and every accomodation needed by the traveller is at hand.

The Lindell Hotel, Saint Louis, is an extremely large building, well-constructed and arranged, but devoid of many of the modern conveniences. My room was 163,—on the best floor or as good a floor as any in the house,—but it was a narrow, low-ceiled den, with one petty window, and without even a stationary wash-stand.

The clerk said he could do no better, on account of the great throng drawn to S Louis to witness the races. The fine rotunda of the Lindell was one surging mass of people, strangers "doing" the races and an outside swarm of people come to the metropolis to prey on those less cunning than themselves. In the Hotel, I met Genl. [Daniel] McClure, of the Pay[master's] Dep't. and Col.[William H.?] Johnson of the Same Corps: the latter had served in Oregon with General Crook and made many inquiries about him. With Col. Johnson, was Mr. Halliday, his gentlemanly clerk, who offered his services to show me the city. I cannot say that I am particularly impressed with this place. My opinion of it remains pretty much as it was in 1869, the last time I was there.

It certainly had great capabilities for the future, and must erelong take its stand as one of the busiest cities in the world. Blocks of elegant private residences attest the wealth and refined taste of its citizens, while its numerous R.R.'s may be cited in evidence of their being alive to their own interests: Chicago, to me, is far ahead in enterprise and is also better placed, St. Louis is hot and insalubrious.

Mr. Halliday escorted me to the Race Grounds, pointing out on the way Forest Park and such public and private edifices as were most worthy of notice. The race-track was as fine a piece of ground for the purpose as I ever saw. Neither dusty nor heavy for the horses, and so laid out that from the Grand Stand every step taken

---

12. I.e. the Mississippi River. The Mississippi sometimes is mistakenly referred to as "Big Muddy," but that, in fact, is the Missouri River. The distinction was well-known in the nineteenth century.

by each horse was distinctly visible to every one of the thousands of spectators.

I tried to estimate the numbers in the audience, but couldn't satisfactorily do so. There was any number from 9.000 to 11.000 present. Major [Edward B.] Grimes, A.Q.M., and Captain Luke O'Reilly, 19th Infantry, were on the grounds: I had a few words of conversation with each of them.

The horses assembled were beautiful creatures. Miss Malloy, Hardy, D'Artingan [sic] and five or six others were perfect in form and action. It is impossible for me, much as I love fine animals, to take much interest in the turf, on account of the number of villains and rascals who seem to have control of all racing matters in our country. Better take a seat and look at what is going on, without venturing to wager money on a race when the chances are so great that it is already "sold out".

The second day previous to my visit, the fine horse McWhirter, running on this course, had broken both his legs and had to be shot to put him out of his misery.

In the... races, Hark-Away, Miss Malloy and Hardy were the winners.

Of the whole return trip from S'Louis to Omaha, about 500 miles, (Omaha is about 925 or 950 miles from Lexington, Ky.) Not much remains to be stated. Ass't Surgeon Springer was in the same car with me—he on his way to Arizona. At Hamburgh, Iowa, a washout, occasioned by an overflow of the Missouri river, detained us nine hours. When I arose from sleep, I found my friends Lt. E. Pratt, 23d Infantry, and wife, were on the car, having joined us during the night at Fort Leavenworth, Kansas.[13]

We made the best of our forlorn situation, which we knew couldn't last very long. By (2) in the afternoon, the break was repaired and before sun-set; we were in Omaha.

June 18th 1878. Started for Chicago in company of Genl. Crook. We took the Chicago and N-Western line, which has lately com-

---

13. Fort Leavenworth was established in 1827, and is the oldest United States active military post west of the Mississippi. During the last half of the nineteenth century, it was headquarters for the Department of the Missouri, a subdivision of the vast Military Division of the Missouri which comprised much of the central two-thirds of the United States. During the 1850s and '60s, it was the depot for supplies for all military posts of the Rocky Mountain region, and remained a primary frontier defense unit throughout most of the Indian Wars. Frazer, *Forts of the West*, 56.

menced to run "Hotel" cars of a pattern not to be credited until seen. These cars cost $30.000 each and contain every improvement the experience of the past quarter of a century in Rail-Road management has been able to suggest. The wheels are of papier maché, made under hydraulic pressure, and bound with steel rims: these cause the cars to move very smoothly over the fine steel rails and good, firm road-bed of this company, which has now become known as one of the best-constructed in the world.

The interiors of these cars are embellished with ornate and costly inlaid work, executed in Europe by skilful [sic] artists. The finishing is in Hungarian maple, a curiously grained wood, firm, hard and receiving an attractive polish. The restaurant was very well supplied, but the prices charged we found to be very dear. While in Chicago, stopped, as usual at Grand Pacific Hotel.

Coming back from Chicago, by the Rock Island line, I visited the Rock Island Arsenal, partly to see the arsenal itself and partly to call upon my class-mate, D. M. Taylor, who was then stationed there. By himself and wife, I was received very warmly and courteously entertained during my stay. Col. Flagler, the Commandant, Lt. James Rockwell, (1868.) and Captain Martin, were also extremely cordial and made me feel that I was among old friends.

Col. Flagler took me around the buildings and about the grounds—the former amount in value to something over $5.000.000 and are as Colossal in size as they are grand in design and commodious in arrangement. The material used is the Joliet (Ills.) Stone, of a light cream color which contrasts prettily with the deep green of the foliage embossing the Arsenal and Warerooms. Altogether, there are a dozen buildings, each not less than 300 feet by (60) to (100) feet wide. The Island belongs entirely to the General Gov't. and has been laid out in pleasant drives and delightful little parks, where the Qrs. of the officers cluster very prettily. These Qrs. are extravagant in plan and appearance: at least such was the idea which struck me when I saw one and thought how much comfort might have been brought to the poor devils of officers on the frontier, if only the tenth part of the moneys *wasted* on these palatial structures had been properly applied to the legitimate purpose of maintaining an Army. It is my belief that if the Ordnance Corps had a few more such men as Colonel Flagler, it would stand higher in military estimation than it now does. The general verdict of the

Army is that the Ordnance Corps just now is rather a thin outfit.[14] On My way back from Rock Island to Omaha, our car was robbed by sneak thieves, who had taken berths at one of the way stations; by this I lost ($40.)

In speaking of Chicago, I should make mention of how favorably its big hotels, the Palmer and the Grand Pacific (where we staid) impressed me, who so lately had been in the caravansaries of St. Louis and Cincinnati. The two hotels spoken of are equal to any in this country, which means that they are superior to almost any in the world.

In Omaha, the main topic of conversation was the Army Bill, passed by Congress in the last throes of adjournment. It may be à propos to say that the Congress just in session has been thus far a severe test of the potency of that Article of War which forbids any disrespectful comments being made against the National Legislature and there have not been wanting evil-minded men who have boldly asserted that it has been composed of as big a lot of fools, dead-beats and bummers as ever disgraced our history. There have been few, if any, thieves in the present Congress; parties are so evenly divided now that there is no certainty of concealment for any great length of time of any villainy that may be attempted: our "statesmen", God forgive me for using such a word in speaking of dumb, driven cattle, are content with playing the baboon and do not aspire to the nobler intellectual flights of thievery which distinguished the Republican Majority immediately after the War.

The immediate effect upon ourselves was the removal of Hd.Qrs. to Omaha Barracks,[15] (4½) miles from the city. This gave a great deal of trouble to officers having families and was a bad move so far as the transaction of Government business was concerned, but the Barracks is a beautiful post, one of much attractiveness and which can be made, at slight expense, still more charming.

14. This period saw what author Douglas C. McChristian has called "a long struggle between the Ordnance Department and the common soldier." There was an immense supply of surplus equipment from the Civil War that remained on hand for more than a decade after the war ended. While it often was of poor quality, and totally unsuited for the frontier, a parsimonious Congress was unwilling to appropriate adequate funds for new equipment. Consequently, the Ordnance Department took what was on hand, altering and modifying it, without actually improving it. See McChristian, *U.S. Army in the West* (quote from page 34).

15. Omaha Barracks was established in 1868 on the right bank of the Missouri River within the present city limits of Omaha, Nebraska. It was designated Fort Omaha in 1878. The post was replaced by Fort Crook in 1895, but has been reactivated several times, and the government has retained the military reservation. Frazer, *Forts of the West*, 89.

Captain A. H. Nickerson, who for so long a time, had been my friend and associate upon the staff, received the appointment of Major and Ass't. Adjt. General, vice Pelouze, deceased. For the vacancy there was a great struggle, over seventy candidates presenting themselves, all backed more or less powerfully and many of them men of great powers, enlarged experience and fine records. Neither in fitness nor in experience was there one to compare with Nickerson, who had filled with such especial acceptance the onerous and delicate position of Chief of Staff for General Crook; during the war of the Rebellion, desperate wounds sealed his devotion and courage, while since the War, instead of hunting a soft place, as so many of our officers do, he accompanied General Crook to the field upon all his arduous campaigns against the hostile Indians and made his presence felt at all times and in all places.

Nickerson's claims were supported by the Governors of every state and Territory in which he had served in Indian campaigns, viz: Arizona, Nevada, Washington T[erritor]y., Oregon, Utah, Wyoming and Nebraska; by Senators [William B.] Allison of Iowa, [Algernon S.] Paddock and [Alvin] Saunders of Neb., [John B.] Gordon of Georgia, and [Daniel W.] Voorhees of Indiana.
Gordon, then a General in the Confederate Army, was wounded in front of and at same time with Nickerson, at Antietam.

General Crook sent the following telegram to President Hayes.

Omaha, Neb., June 16th, 1878

President Hayes,
  Washington, D.C.
    I urgently solicit Captain Nickerson's appointment as a favor to myself and assured that he is the best selection that can be made. His record during and since the War, his severe wounds, cultivated mind and high tone of character as known to me for more than twelve years, are the qualifications upon which I base my recommendation.

      (Signed) George Crook

And again after the appointment had been made and confirmed.

Omaha, June 16th 1878

President Hayes
  Washington, D.C.
    Permit me to thank you most sincerely for the appointment

of Nickerson.

It was a deserved recognition of a soldier, who, not content to rest upon the laurels gained during the War, has each year acquired fresh distinction in arduous and perilous service on the Border.

(Signed.) George Crook,
Brigadier General.

The following orders, which it will appear were not issued until after Nickerson had received his commission and been relieved from duty at General Crook's Hd.Qrs., are inserted at this point to maintain unbroken the chain of reference to a gallant comrade and sincere friend, whose equal we shall not soon have with us again.

HEADQUARTERS DEPARTMENT OF THE PLATTE,
Omaha Barracks, Nebraska, July 17, 1878.
GENERAL ORDERS,
No. 8.

In obedience to Paragraph 2, Special Orders No. 148, current series, Adjutant General's Office, Major *A.H. Nickerson*, Assistant Adjutant General, is relieved from duty at these Headquarters.

The Brigadier-General Commanding, cannot let pass this occasion for making known his deep sense of obligation for the valuable and distinguished services rendered him by Major *Nickerson*, during the twelve years that that officer has been a member of his military family, and for congratulation upon a promotion so richly deserved, which will assuredly secure a general recognition for the high qualities of mind and character which have won the warm regard and esteem of those from whom he is now to be separated.

BY COMMAND OF BRIGADIER GENERAL CROOK:
ROBERT WILLIAMS,
Assistant Adjutant General.

OFFICIAL:
[*Signed*] John G. Bourke,

Aide-de-Camp.

I might fill several pages with the extracts from the Omaha newspapers, showing the esteem and regard in which Captain (or Major) Nickerson was held by his neighbors, civil, as well as military and also of the regret manifested at the separation from our little circle of this bright and genial member, with his fine wife and sweet little daughter, but such clippings are more appropriately used in my Scrap Book than in this Journal which records my personal experiences and expresses my personal views.[16]

16. This is an interesting comment, considering how often Bourke used the journals as a reflection of his experiences and views, as well as a scrap book.

Chapter 2

♦
♦
♦
♦
♦

The Bannock Uprising

Compared to the other outbreaks of the 1870s, the Bannock Uprising was a small affair, caused by the usual problems of expanding white settlement and the government's inability to adequately plan and implement an Indian policy. Although the Bannocks were friendly, and some of their warriors had scouted for Crook in 1876, grievances had been building for several years. The Bannocks and Shoshones shared a reservation in Idaho, centered around agencies at Fort Hall[1] and Ross Fork. Here they continued to hunt, as well as harvest the quamash camas (camassia quamash), a bulb that was a staple of their diet. Encroaching white settlement, however, depleted the game, and settlers' hogs began eating the camas bulbs. As was so often the case, government rations were inadequate and poorly distributed. Facing famine, the Bannocks grew restless, and the army put them under surveillance. Random violence broke out in the summer of 1877.[2]

---

1. This refers to the second Idaho post designated Fort Hall. The first Fort Hall was established in 1849 and abandoned less than a year later because of a shortage of forage. The second Fort Hall was established in 1870 between the Snake and Portneuf Rivers, near a Hudson's Bay post of the same name. Fort Hall was abandoned in 1883 because of heavy development in the area, and advances in transportation that allowed rapid deployment of troops into southern Idaho from Fort Douglas, Utah. Frazer, *Forts of the West*, 44–45.

2. The Bannock outbreak is discussed in Brimlow, *The Bannock Indian War of 1878*. The history of the tribe is covered in Madsen, *The Bannock of Idaho*.

The trouble centered around Fort Hall, in southern Idaho, which was in the Department of the Platte, prompting Crook and Bourke to visit, so the general could personally assess the situation. In a bristling letter to divisional headquarters, he wrote:

> [W]e have promised faithfully to feed and clothe them and teach them to earn their own living, and they insist upon our living up to our contract, or they will, if driven to the war-path, wreak vengeance upon the unprotected ranchmen and miners near them.
>
> Then, too, they are dissatisfied because while they, who have been for years our steadfast friends and allies, are nearly starving, the Sioux—so lately our bitter enemies—have twice the amount of supplies provided them.[3]

Ultimately, most of the Bannocks remained calm, in part because of Crook's influence over the chiefs. About 150 hostile warriors crossed into Oregon, where they fell under Brig. Gen. O. O. Howard's jurisdiction. Chased back into Idaho, they were rounded up and distributed among various military posts to give them a chance to calm down before being returned home.[4]

En route to Fort Hall and the meeting with the Bannock leaders, Crook and Bourke passed through Utah. Here Bourke demonstrated an attitude toward Mormonism which, while certainly less vitriolic than his earlier writings,[5] nevertheless was condescending:

> Passengers on train to-day are of the same general type of poor, ignorant and squalid European peasantry who have come here to find homes, which are certainly better than those they have left over the water. Mormonism can't degrade such people and if it make them honest, industrious and laborious, even if they remain ignorant and benighted, a great good will have been accomplished.[6]

---

3. Crook to AG, MilDivMo, April 3, 1878, 1:413, George Crook Letter Books. The Plains Indians commonly complained that if they maintained the peace, the government treated them with indifference and neglect, but if they started trouble, the government would try to buy peace with better rations and annuities.
4. Robinson, *General Crook*, 220.
5. See Robinson, *Diaries*, Vol. 1, Chapter 7.
6. Bourke, Diary, 23:47.

July 15th, 1878. General Crook, Lt. [Walter S.] Schuyler, A.D.C., and self left Omaha for the Shoshonee and Bannock at Fort Hall, Idaho. Weather was fearfully hot. Mr. R.E. Strahorn and wife were on train with us, on their way to the "parks" and springs of Colorado. The *Chicago Times* received to-day, contained a telegram, announcing resignation of Captain Alex. Moore, 3d Cavalry. Moore was tried by General Court Martial, at Cheyenne, in January 1877, for cowardice in presence of enemy, in attack upon the village of the Indian chief, Crazy Horse, on Powder River, Montana, March 17th, 1876.[7]

Enough was proved to bring in a sentence of suspension from rank, pay and command for (6) months. With this cloud upon his reputation, Capt. Moore felt it [to] be incumbent upon him to resign from the service.

Dashing along the plains of Nebraska, covered with a rapidly ripening harvest of golden grain, we could see the developing power of this great West which, under our own eyes, during the past three years, has been growing like a young giant. Omaha is reaching out in every direction, new houses springing up, new enterprises inaugurated and a general air of prosperity evident. Stock Yards have been established: a lead works for the manufacture of white paint from the raw material obtained from the smelting works, a nail factory to utilize the old iron from the R.Rs. converging at Omaha, a starch factory to work up the grain yield of the state,* an Opera House (also only in contemplation,) and a great number of subsidiary enterprises too numerous to mention. The Union Pacific and B. and M.[8] R.Rs., the great highways traversing the state, are planning new feeders to tap every section of this great Trans-Missouri Country.[9]

Above this Bourke inserted: (contemplated)

7. The attack, frequently discussed in Volume 1 of this series, actually was against a band of Cheyennes who were bound for Fort Laramie in compliance with a government mandate, a fact which Bourke and Crook both later discovered, but never admitted. Crazy Horse's Oglalas were some fifty miles away at the time of the fight. See also Robinson, *General Crook*, 169–71.

8. Burlington & Missouri River.

9. Omaha was occupied as early as 1820, when the army established Fort Atkinson immediately to the north. The city itself can be traced to the establishment of the Council Bluffs and Nebraska Ferry by Iowa promoters in 1853. The following year, when the Omaha Indians ceded their land to the federal government, and Nebraska Territory was created, the Iowa group platted a town across from Council Bluffs, which they named for the Indians. Acting Governor Thomas B. Cushing chose Omaha as the capital of the new territory, which it remained until 1867, when Lincoln was specifically established as the seat of government. From its earliest years, however, Omaha was an important transportation center, first for wagon roads, and later for railroads. The settlement of the Nebraska back country further boosted the city's importance. Lamar, *New Encyclopedia*, 821–23.

In viewing the evidence of our nation's solidarity, we forgot the paucity of intellect in the National Councils and the petty policy which curtailed our incomes.

We chatted about the Peace Congress in Paris, where Beaconsfield[10] attained such distinction, and by the terms of which Great Britain acquired possession of the Island of Cyprus and paramount control in Mesopotamia. If nothing occur to change this appointment Great Britain will within ten years dwarf the other Powers by her swollen proportions. Gibraltar, Cyprus and Malta give her the ownership of the Mediterranean, this, with Mesopotamia, more than counterbalances Russia's future acquisition of Constantinople. England's victory is the victory of money over impecuniosity: if Russia were not bankrupt, the war would go on until Cossack troopers watered their steeds by the Dardanelles and to my mind, it seems that a resumption of hostilities is merely a question of the pecuniary strength and not one of will or inclination.[11]

July 16th, Read with pain and astonishment, the telegrams giving a brief account of the death by drowning of my old friends, Lieuts. [John Anthony] Rucker and [Austin] Henley, 6th Cavalry.[12] At the time of the fatal accident, these young officers were stationed at Camp Supply, Arizona,[13] in charge of Apache Indian scouts. A cloud-burst, caused a stream of water to pour down along an arroyo, running through camp, and imperilled the safety of men and government property. Lieut. Henley dashed into this torrent, hoping to swim it and reach his men on the other side. His horse became

---

10. Benjamin Disraeli, Earl of Beaconsfield, British prime minister, and a key architect of the British Empire.

11. Bourke refers to the Fourth Russo-Turkish War of 1877–78, which secured independence for Romania, Serbia, and Montenegro, and autonomy for Bulgaria, and Bosnia-Herzegovina. Suspicious of a growing Russian hegemony, Disraeli dispatched units of the British Mediterranean Fleet to take up station in the Dardanelles and protect the Ottoman capital of Constantinople. In return for guaranteeing protection against the Russians, Britain received the right to occupy Cyprus as a base, although technically it remained Ottoman territory. This war inspired Tchaikovsky's "Marche Slave." The outbreak is mentioned in Bourke's diary entry for April 23, 1877. See Robinson, *Diaries*, 2:277; Palmer, *The Decline and Fall of the Ottoman Empire*, Chapter 10.

12. July 11, 1878.

13. Bourke refers to the second post known as Camp Supply (the first being a temporary encampment for the California Volunteers in 1863). Camp Supply was established in April 1878 in White River Canyon, forty-two miles south of Fort Bowie. In October of that year, it was renamed Camp Rucker, in honor of Lt. John A. Rucker, who drowned in the rescue attempt mentioned by Bourke, and who, coincidentally, was the brother-in-law of Lt. Gen. Philip H. Sheridan. In 1880, it was designated as a picket station, and later downgraded to a heliograph station. Altshuler, *Starting With Defiance*, 51, 54.

frightened and was swept off his feet by the foaming waters. Rucker, without a thought of self, plunged in to rescue his friend and former class-mate. But he too fell a victim to the remorseless fury of the waves and was swept out of sight before his panic-stricken men could throw him a rope. The Indian and white soldiers made a prolonged search for the bodies which were not found for some hours: resuscitation was impossible and the Army had to mourn the loss of two exceedingly bright and promising officers. Both Rucker and Henley belonged to the Academy during the term of my Cadetship. Rucker, a finely formed, reckless, dashing, good-natured young fellow had too much of the devil in him to avoid demerits, which cut short his career, altho' he had brain enough if he would only apply himself. He was a fine rider, an expert athlete and man of great muscular development.

Henley had been a private soldier in the Regular Army during the latter days of the War: his soldierly bearing, intelligence, vivacity, studiousness, and courage, won the regard of his Regimental officers who united in a petition to the President for the appointment of Henley as a Cadet. This was done and the wisdom of the choice was manifest. Henley did extremely well in studies and was graduated in 1872, and appointed to the 6th Cavalry, to which Regiment, Rucker had by this time also been assigned upon the application of his father, General Rucker of the Q.M. Dep't., and perhaps also through other influence, as his sister a charming young lady, about that time married Lieut-General P. H. Sheridan.[14]

Henley's parents, he often told me, were very poor: they lived in the vicinity of Easton, Penna, and made their living from a small farm and vegetable garden. For both these boys I had formed a high opinion and deep regard, which was not at all diminished when I heard of the gallant manner in which they had distinguished themselves in Kansas and in Arizona, while in action with hostile Indians.

At Cheyenne, parted with our friends the Strahorns. On the dépôt platform, met Lts. [William Bayard] Weir, [George Oscar] Eaton, [Alpheus Henry] Bowman, Robinson,[15] [Jacob A.] Augur, and Messers Wilson and Woodworth, with Mrs. and Miss Cham-

---

14. Irene Rucker, who married Lt. Gen. Philip H. Sheridan. Lieutenant William H. Brown committed suicide in 1875, supposedly distraught because of the marriage. See Volume 1, page 394, in this series.

15. Bourke knew several lieutenants named Robinson. Given time and place, this probably was William Wallace Robinson Jr., 7th Cavalry.

bers, Mrs. Rodgers, Mrs. Merritt, Mrs. Hart, Mrs. Montgomery, Mrs. Hamilton, Mrs. and Miss Nash. Mrs. Merritt and Mrs. Hart were en route to Fort McKinney[16] to join their husbands: most of the others came with them as far as the E. Bound train, on which we saw Lt. [George] Palmer, 9th Infantry.

Lt. Augur was a class-mate of mine and with Mrs. Merritt and Mrs. Hart we were already quite well acquainted. We passed a very pleasant afternoon in their society and were very sorry when the end of their journey arrived.

At Laramie City and Fort Sanders,[17] saw Mr. Zano [?] and Lt. [Horace] Neide. At Laramie City received a dispatch from Nickerson, urging the General's return to Omaha to meet the Secretary of War, who was expected there the next day: but this, General Crook was, unable to do.

At Rock Creek, the Government was building a new warehouse for the storage of freight, for Fort Fetterman[18] and Fort McKinney, which reaches these posts by an excellent new road, which leaves the R.R. at this point. This road had just been completed by a detachment of soldiers under command of Lt. [Joseph] Keefe, 4th Infantry. A military bridge has also been built over the Rock creek.

At St. Mary's, Major [Thomas Tipton] Thornburgh and Capt. [William Henry] Bisbee, were waiting for us and rode in our car to Fort Steele.[19] Across the North Platte river, at this point there is a Howe truss bridge of considerable length crossed by the Rail Road which almost immediately after cuts across the [military] Reservation.

16. Fort McKinney was established on October 12, 1876, as the new Cantonment Reno to supply Crook's Powder River Expedition. In 1877, it was designated Fort McKinney, in honor of Lt. John A. McKinney, 4th Cavalry, who was killed in the Dull Knife Fight of November 25, 1876 (see Volume 2 of this series). In 1878, the fort was relocated to the confluence of Clear Creek and the Powder River, just west of the present city of Buffalo, Wyoming, and the original site was redesignated McKinney Depot. The post was abandoned in 1894, and the following year the buildings were given to the state, which used it as the State Soldiers's and Sailors' Home. Frazer, *Forts of the West*, 182–83.

17. Fort Sanders was established three miles from Laramie in 1866, to protect emigrant routes, the Denver-Salt Lake stage route, and Union Pacific construction crews. It was abandoned and transferred to the Interior Department in 1882. Not to be confused with Fort Laramie, which is in extreme east-central Wyoming near the Nebraska line. Frazer, *Forts of the West*, 185.

18. Fort Fetterman was established in 1867. It was abandoned in 1882, and turned over to the Interior Department two years later. The post buildings became a tough cow town that served as a model for the town of Drybone in Owen Wister's *The Virginian*. It is now a Wyoming state historic site. Frazer, *Forts of the West*, 180–81.

19. Fort Fred Steele was established in 1868 at the crossing of the Union Pacific Railroad over the North Platte River, to protect the railroad and the Overland Trail. The post was abandoned in 1886 and transferred to the Interior Department. Frazer, *Forts of the West*, 186.

Inside the post we had the pleasure of meeting Mrs. Thornburgh and Mrs. Chase, Surgeon [Calvin] De Witt and Lieut. Geo. N. Chase, 4th Infantry.

Since entering the mountains, the weather had been very cool and exhilarating.

Shortly after passing Evanston, Wyo., encountered a flight of grasshoppers, and as we entered the Cañons of the Wahsatch, temperature became very warm, but not very oppressive.

At Ogden, Colonel [Charles Warren] Foster, A.Q.M., and Mr. Kreuger were awaiting us: also met Lt. Ludlow and Lt. Loring of the Wheeler Survey[20] and Mr. Barkalow, of Omaha.

Colonel Foster and Judge Highbee took us for a drive about Ogden and give [sic] us an insight into the growth and beauty of the town: it is truly very well placed for drainage and comfort and nesting at the foot of the towering Wahsatch commands a picturesque view of the mountain and Valley and Lake scenery combined. Every house is embowered in groves of fruit trees, all the streets are finely shaded and there are also reservations of public squares to afford a maximum of breathing space. There are very few costly buildings, but many cosy cottages, showing a high average of comfort among the inhabitants. The new Court-House is a presentable building of brick and stone. From its cupola is obtained a grand view of the country, hundreds of miles in extent.

The Catholic Church is building a fine stone schoolhouse:—altogether, the town looks thrifty and progressive. Our sleep this night was most refreshing: cool breezes, reduced the temperature to a point at which covering was not regarded as torture.

July 18th. Was surprised and delighted to be accosted by my old class-mate, Shirley, of Mississipi, [sic] who was with me at the Point for two years: since leaving the Academy, he has engaged in cotton planting on the Yazoo (River), but was now on his way to Logan, Utah, for the restoration of his health, and travelled with us to that point. With him was a very bright young lady, Miss Park and her grand-mother, an old lady 86 yrs. of age. It was surprising to see

---

20. This survey was conducted throughout the 1870s by George Montague Wheeler of the Topographical Engineers. Initially begun as a survey of eastern Nevada and Arizona, it eventually expanded to include much of the territory west of the 100th Meridian that had not been surveyed up to that point. Ultimately the plan was to map about 1.5 million square miles, but rival civilian surveys lobbied Congress to terminate the project two years before its completion. Thrapp, *Encyclopedia*, 3:1544–45.

how bravely the old lady bore the fatigue of the long journey out from Washington. Took dinner at Logan, in a newly-opened building: appearances rather slipshod, but food tolerably well-cooked and in variety. Fresh raspberries and currants of excellent flavor:—everything raised in the immediate vicinity.

The lumber used at Logan is white and red pine from the peaks of the Wahsatch. This is cut early in Spring, while snow is still hard and allowed to run down the steep mountainsides: it rushes down with such velocity that if one of the logs deviate from the marked path and strike rock, the log will generally split from end to end.

Passengers on train to-day are of the same general type of poor, ignorant and squalid European peasantry who have come here to find homes, which are certainly better than those they have left over the water. Mormonism can't degrade such people and if it make them honest, industrious and laborious, even if they remain ignorant and benighted, a great good will have been accomplished.

With us was Mr. [Philatus] Norris, the Superintendent of the Yellowstone Park: a gentleman of great intelligence and extended travel in our Western Country.

Reached Oneida, the present terminus of the R.R. at 8.30 P.M: this is a mushroom village of canvass and balloon framed shanties with no signs of permanency. Saw here Major [Montgomery] Bryant, 14th Infantry. Travelled in four-horse ambulance to Ross' Fork Agency: on leaving Oneida, ran into a chuck-hole. General Crook was severely cut in the scalp by being bumped against [wagon cover] bows. Night at first cool and agreeable but towards morning so chilly that my teeth rattled. At and beyond Pocatello, where we changed teams, the dust became so thick that we were nearly stifled; once or twice came near upsetting in the dark. Reached Schilling's Ranch (Ross Fork,) at 3.45 A.M: here we found Colonel [Thaddeus H.] Stanton, Mr. Chase, his clerk, and Lt. [Richard Thompson] Yeatman who kindly turned out of their beds to let us have a nap. Awakened at 7 A.M. for breakfast, which we ate with but little appetite. Captains [Augustus Hudson] Bainbridge, and [John Morrison] Hamilton, Lt. [Robert] London and Major Danielson [sic], (the Indian Agent,)[21] came over to see us.

21. William H. Danilson.

The Bannock Uprising

Major Danielson drove us to look at the Indian farms: they have (350) A[cre]s (300) A[cres] sown broadcast in Wheat, and (50) A. in potatoes and garden truck, such as peas, tomatoes, beans and beets of which the Indians are becoming very fond.
At the Agency, there are only (200) A., the rest being in nooks and valleys adjacent. The wheat certainly looked fine. From the wheatfields, drove to the Agency for a conference with the leading men of the Shoshonees and Bannocks. There met Genl. Kimball and his son, Lt. Kimball, 14th Inft.: the other white men were General Crook and his Aides de Camp, Lieuts Schuyler, and Bourke, Captains Bainbridge and Hamilton and Major Danielson, the Agent. The speakers for the Indians were Captain Jim and Major George.
General Crook. Jim[,] how long since you came from Boisé?
Jim. I don't know. The Major knows.
Major Danielson. Jim came to the Agency about a month ago: about the time of the outbreak.
General Crook. How many people stay over at Boisé?
Jim. I don't know. I have never counted them. Probably (20) or (25.)
General Crook. How do they live over there?
Jim. Some men over there give them flour and a little to eat and they hunt a little.
General Crook. How many Bannocks went on war path?
Jim. I don't know: Major (Danielson) may know.
General Crook. How many Shoshonees?
Jim. Eight lodges that I know of; that's all I could see together.
General Crook. Are they in the Steen's Peak Country where Jim and I campaigned some years ago?
Jim. Yes. Some of the same Indians you were fighting then are there now. I don't know what has become of their brains. They promised you they'd go to farming. I don't know why they have broken the peace after shaking your hand. I have kept your hand and have not thrown it away. Here is an old letter I want you to see. (Showing the one given him years ago by General Crook when in Oregon.) I want you to give me another one like this: this is getting old.
(New letter given him, as requested.)
General Crook. You know the way of Indians pretty well. What do you think these Pa'-Utes and Bannocks mean?
Jim. I don't know what they do want to go to war for. I don't know their minds or their hearts or what they are going to do.

General Crook. Are they coming back by Stein's [sic] Mtn?
Jim. I don't know anything about where they are or where they are going, only what I hear from the papers; I can form no idea: There is no danger of their coming in here by ones and twos, or of people going out from here to them. They would be too much afraid of the white men.
General Crook. What has caused them to go on the war-path?
Jim. An Indian, by the name of Issie-po-po-nan-die, came to the Agency this spring and told us that all of Wash-akie's Indians and all of the Utes and other Indians were going to War. Buffalo Horn told the same thing.
General Crook. Did they have any intention of going to war when I was here last Spring?
Jim. Yes. When you were here, they were just lying to you.
General Crook. How do you like farming?
Jim. We like it: we all want to farm. You can see our wheat-fields. I was farming on Indian creek when the troubles began. Then I ran away and came here. One of my friends, Charlie Curtis, a white man, has charge of my farm. I had water-melons, wheat, potatoes, onions, apples and peaches. I like apples. I planted them: a white man gave me the seed and told me that in ten years the trees could grow and I should have plenty of them.
General Crook. You ought to farm on the Reservation, then the white man couldn't take your farm away from you.
Jim. I want to go to Washington when the war is all over. After the war is over, I want to go back to see how my apple trees are getting along.
General Crook. See your agent about that.
Jim. I don't want to do wrong. I have shaken the white man's hand and I will hold on to it. Whatever you tell me, I will obey, and tell the other Indians to do the same.
General Crook. When the troops push the Bannocks where will they go?
Jim. I don't know; they can't come in here. There are too many white men here & won't let them come in.
General Crook. Have they their families with them?
Jim. Yes, Sir.
General Crook. Are any families here of those who are out fighting?
Jim. None.

General Crook. Have those on the war-path plenty of arms and ammunition?

Jim. Some are armed and have plenty of ammunition. Some have good arms, but not all.

General Crook. Do you hear frequently from Washakie?

Jim. An Indian came here a little while ago and told me Washakie said all his Indians were going to stay there (at Camp Brown.)[22] Tin-doy's band say the same thing. Tin-Doy's people are Shoshonees principally with a few Bannocks.

General Crook. Why did those eight lodges of Shoshonees go out?

Jim. Because they listened to Buffalo Horn when he was lying to them: they couldn't see or hear and hadn't any brains. There are a lot of Indians just the same way. If you speak, they can't hear, and if you tell them anything that is good, they won't listen to you. The Indians that are there, their hearts are all good. When they look at their farms and see their wheat and potatoes, it makes them feel good. It makes my heart glad and feel good to see you and talk to you. When I was young, I used to fight, but I am getting old now and don't want to fight. When the Indians hear that you have been looking at what they have done, it will make them feel good.

General Crook. I understand that Egan (a chief.) was killed in a fight lately.

Jim. When I heard of the fighting, I am not going there. I am not going around with my eyes shut: the first thing I'd know, I'd know nothing. I want to get sick and die and not die any other way.[23] A long time ago, when the first letter[24] came here from Washington, I said "Yes" to it and I don't want to talk two days.

General Crook. You see the whites are coming in all around you and you had better keep the peace with them.

Jim. I know that. The land I farm, I know it belongs to me and no one can take it away.

General Crook. Better plant your apple trees on the Reservation, so that no white man can take them away.

---

22. Camp Brown was established in 1871 on the Wind River in west central Wyoming, to protect the Shoshones. In 1878, it was renamed Fort Washakie, in honor of the paramount Shoshone chief. It was permanently abandoned in 1909, and turned over to the Interior Department to use as headquarters for the Shoshone Agency. Frazer, *Forts of the West*, 186–87.

23. I.e., he wanted to die of natural causes, and not in battle.

24. Treaty.

Jim. I know that. The Indians love this place because they know that when they plant wheat here the white men can't take it away: there is no salmon here, no camas.** There are choke-cherries and service-berries up in the mountains, but no yamp [sic], no camas and no salmon.

General Crook. Better become like white men. They don't have everything they want. They must plant what they want. The white men are putting hogs on the camas grounds and they'll soon eat it all up. Better plant what you want:—apple-trees, camas and wheat and when you die, your children will have something.

Jim. I know you are telling me the truth.

General Crook. You have plenty of land here now: better get some of it for yourself and go to farming.

Jim. If I was farming, I wouldn't do like some white men; if *their* horses reached over and got a mouthful of wheat, *I'd* not get mad.

General Crook. All men are not alike.

Jim. That's so: some *Indians* have very little hearts.

General Crook. And white men too: you have to get spy-glasses to see their hearts.

Jim. Yes. Indians and white men are very much alike.

General Crook. Camas is good, but meat is good too. You must get cows to eat up the grass and give you plenty of meat.

Jim. When you were here before there were no farms, there were no farms like we have now; when you come again, maybe we'll all have farms.

General Crook. That's right; the world wasn't made in a day. You must commence with small things.

Jim. The Indians who want to learn farming must take two years to learn.

General Crook. Each family ought to get at least one cow and raise calves; but, even if the Agent have [sic] no beef, they mustn't kill their cows; they must kill jack-rabbits and eat them in preference.

***Bourke's note:* The "camas" or "cammas" is an [esculent?] in high repute among the Bannocks & other tribes. The plant grows in damp, meadow land, is about (2) to (3) feet, purplish-green stem, often bi-furcated and topped by a blue or white flour [sic]. The bulb is the part used: being very starchy, when baked in hot coals, it has a very pleasant, sweetish taste, not unlike baked apples or pears. Pigs are very fond of it and root it out of the ground in great quantity, to the annoyance of the Indians, who relish this food so highly. This bringing of hogs in upon the Camas grounds, I am inclined to suspect has had not a little to do with engendering the bad feeling of which the present hostilities have been the culmination.

Jim. I have five head now.
General Crook. I am glad to hear it.
Jim. That's the way I got a start: six years ago, I got a calf from a big herd going through here: now I have lots of calves. I found another calf the other day. The herds going through often leave calves that cannot travel and I look out for them. I am afraid to go over to the Post any more. A soldier got on my back and told me to go home and go quick. When the Captain, (Bainbridge.) comes here, we don't tell *him* to go home. I don't think *he* told the soldiers to say that.
Captain Bainbridge. The Indians are always welcome to come over to the Post.
Jim. I believe that. You always treat us right and are glad to see us and shake us by the hand.
Captain Bainbridge here explained to General Crook that, last winter, while the ponies which had been taken from the Indians, were at his post, he gave orders to the sentinels to allow no Indians to go near the herd, for fear they might try to stampede it.
Jim. We want permission to go over to the Post when we please. We don't carry arms with us.
General Crook. You must ask your agent.
Jim. I am going to listen to what you have to tell me, and I am going to do it. I don't want my young men to listen to anything wrong. Major Danielson knows how my breath is. I don't lie to him. Whenever I want anything, I come to him. I don't think Captain Bainbridge can say I lied to *him*. I've always told him a straight story. Some of our young men lie when they talk; some *Indians* lie plenty; some white men do the same. They told me that when I'd commence farming, they'd build me a house. I want a house so I can live like a white man. They have told me that for (4) or (5) years. Every year they are going to build me a house, but they don't do it.
Agent Danielson. I have the saw mill ready now and will build him a small house this Fall.
General Crook (to Jim.) That winter when we campaigned together, we didn't have even a tent.
Jim. I was told the Great Father said if we would come on the Reservation, he would build us all houses.
General Crook. Well, that's your own fault: you haven't all come in. When you were at the other Agency, houses were built for you, but you used to burn them up for fuel. Now that you mean business, we

can build houses for you right away.

Jim. Are there those who've been farming, all to get houses this Fall?

Agent Danielson. The Great Father told me to build a school-house with the first lumber saved. I am going to build Major George a house, because I promised him, but I'll ask the Great Father and, if he will allow it, I'll build them all houses after the school-house is finished.

Major George. Are the cars (i.e. Rail Road.) to come along here?

General Crook. Yes.

Major George. Well when they come through our Reservation, won't we be entitled to ride on them? I want a pass to go on the cars to Salt Lake, to buy goods, and trade.

General Crook. Major Danielson has written to Washington about it.

Jim. I want you to write the Great Father and tell them how well we are doing with our farms. When the answer comes back from the Great Father, I want to see it. I want to know if the Great Father talks good and if he is going to give us wagons and other things.

General Crook. Major Danielson has sent a letter about that to Washington.

Jim. I want to know if I am made the leading man here, after a while, if I ain't going to get pay like Wash-akie?

(Mem[orandum]. Wash-akie, principal man of the Camp Brown (Wyo.) Shoshonees, gets by treaty $(500) per annum.)

General Crook. Wash-akie don't get any pay after this year, unless there should become [a] new understanding at Washington.

Jim. I think I ought to get paid; I think we all ought to get paid.

General Crook. I think that that was part of the treaty. Wash-askie was to get so much for five years and this is the last year.

Jim here remarked that when the R.R. reached their Reservation, (the Utah and Northern R.R.) He wanted to ride on the cars all the time. He didn't want to ride like the Pi-Utes, who had to go on the freight cars, but he wanted a ticket like a white man and a car all to himself, with plenty of cushions on it, so he could sleep all night. (i.e. a Pullman Car.) He wanted General Crook to write about this to the Great Father and to put his hand down strong on the paper, so his words would "go straight['] and to use black ink, that the letters might not rub out &c.

The conference here ended in a grand hand-shaking and how! how!ing, after which we were very glad to get back to Mr. Schilling's and partake, of a palatable lunch.

Left Ross Fork, a few minutes after mid-day and drove leisurely to Oneida, (42½ miles.[)] The clouds of dust in the road reminded me,—and in no feeble way either, of similar journeys in the valleys of the Gila and Salt Rivers, in Arizona. At Oneida, Colonel Stanton and Mr. Chase were awaiting us; also Major Bryant and his bride.

The hotel was composed of a number of tents, two being used for sleeping apartments one for the bar-room and another for refectory. We tasted the liquors at the bar and found the lemonade genuine, but the "French Brandy" I very strongly suspect, was spurious.

We soon turned into bed, sleeping (3) or four men in a "room", to call by that name the divisions in the tent made by suspending cotton strips across from wall to wall and to the height of five or six feet from the floor. We had the advantage of hearing all the snoring of our neighbors;—there was no extra charge for this.

Major Bryant was especially active during the night; but Colonel Stanton was not much behind in his music. Among the passengers on the R.R. train with us was Miss Harvey, of Helena, Montana, who was travelling to Brooklyn, there to join relatives for a tour through Europe. She was very bright, genial and entertaining—a pleasant travelling companion on this dreariest of Rail Roads.

She told me a very funny anecdote of a young Presbyterian divine, who, from frequently visiting at her home, had become acquainted, after a fashion, with the Chinaman employed as cook by her mother. The clergyman was anxious to convert the Mongolian and the latter felt grateful for the many little attentions shown him by the theologian. Being discharged for some fault, "John", went to the parson and told him he had determined to set up in business for himself, a business that would pay "big money",—so big indeed that if the preacher would accomodate [sic] him with a loan of money to make a start, he would engage to pay him one half his gains as interest. The young divine, anxious to gain influence with the people of the Celestial Kingdom and win this representative over to Christianity, consented without critically examining the project, to advance the money; but, to his horror and dismay, found, before it was too late, that his pig-tailed friend was going to open what he styled "a gam-min

Hell".[25] The Chinaman retired in high dudgeon at what, I suppose, he considered the "Melican Man's too muchee dam fool pigeon".

At Logan, we had a good homelike meal of raspberries, in plenty, and rich, thick cream as the chief item.

Plodded slowly along behind the Iron horse on the R.R. with its steep grades, abrupt curves, and innumerable deviations from a right line: it was built originally for local traffic only, so it winds around from town to town, wasting many valuable hours by so doing.

Minden is the name of the place where we met the "up-train", loaded with a contingent of newly-converted Scandinavians—Mormons just from Denmark. Our train brought down a car-full of their friends, who greeted the new-comers with warm shakes of the hand and with some good singing.

Weather has been quite warm on this trip, but not debilitating. When we read the telegrams, telling of the heat-wave, creeping down on the Missouri Valley and on the Eastern States, which in Saint Louis alone in one day, prostrated one hundred and fifty persons, nearly fifty of whom died,—of poor men and women dying in their bed, we felt that we ought to bear without complaint the slight increment of solar fervor to which we were exposed during the day, particularly, while we had such tonic breezes at night.

Our bed last night was a shabby enough affair, covered with one dirty blanket and one dirty sheet, but Schuyler and I cuddled up in it and slept like cherubs.

Nearing Ogden, in the Bear River and Salt Lake valleys, the ground partitioned off into large fields of wheat and corn, or planted in fruit trees bending under the weight of ripening clusters gave a most pleasing impression of the value of the land and the industry of its owners.

At Ogden, met besides the officers seen on our out-come, Lt. [Stephen John] Mulhall, 14th Infantry, and Bvt. Col. J.B. Campbell, 4th Artillery. Called at Colonel Foster's residence this evening and remained with him and Miss Foster until about nine P.M., when we returned to our Hotel. Retired at 11 P.M. and enjoyed a refreshing nap.

July 21st. Left Ogden and the Salt Lake Valley, with its ripening peaches, apricots, plums, and apples, and its ripe raspberries and started back for Omaha.

In Weber Cañon, our train ran over and killed a horse belonging to a party of emigrants, camped alongside the track.

25. I.e. Gambling hell.

Near Evanston, passed a Westward Bound train, having on it Lieut. [Benjamin Harrison] Randolph 3d Artillery, Qr. Master of the Wheeler Expedition, an old West-Point friend whom I had not seen for years.
Weather very pleasant. Sky Cloudy.
At Green River, Wyo., were joined by Col. R. D. Clark [sic], Paymaster and Mr. [Cuthbert] Mills.
At Rock Creek, saw Lt. Keefe, whose company had just gone into camp at that place after finishing [the] new road between [Union] Pacific R.R., and Fort Fetterman.
At Laramie City, Major Nickerson came on our train, and rode with us to Hazard.
Day very cloudy and cool.
When the time came to say Good Bye to Nickerson we all felt how strong are the links of sympathy and good feeling which unite soldiers who have served together as long as we had.
We could only stammer out the stereotyped phrases of kindly feeling, but knew that no empty conventional expressions could adequately convey the regard and esteem in which we mutually held each other.

At Cheyenne and Sidney met a number of friends, nearly the same as mentioned in outgoing trip. Mr. Hooker of the C.R-I and P. R.R.[26] rode on the train with us as far as Sidney.
At Grande Island, Neb., Col. [Gilbert Saltonstall] Carpenter, 14th Infy. came aboard and travelled to Omaha.
July 23d. A Cool morning with pleasant breeze brought us back to Omaha, where we soon experienced anew the tortures of Tartarean Heat and sultriness. . . .

Hd.Qrs. Dep't. of the Platte,
Commanding General's Office,
Omaha Barracks, Neb.,
July 27th, 1878.

Assist.' Adjt. General,
    Military Division of the Missouri,
        Chicago, Illinois.
Sir,
    I have the honor to report that, during my recent visit to the Shoshonee and Bannock Agency, at Ross' Fork, Idaho, I had sat-

---

26. Chicago, Rock Island and Pacific.

isfactory interviews with the principal men in the presence of Mr. Danielson, the Agent.

The Indians seemed well disposed and anxious to keep the peace; many of those now there are becoming interested in farming and have sown this Spring some (300) A. in wheat, and about (5) Acres in Potatoes and Garden truck. Those fields which I inspected with Agent Danielson certainly looked fine and promised an encouraging yield.

From my conversation with the chiefs, many of whom I have known for years, I am satisfied that not more than one hundred and fifty fighting men are absent from the Agency, presumably with the hostiles, and of this number many are but indifferently armed.

I would respectfully invite attention to the importance of changing the post of Fort Hall, just as soon as the completion of the Utah and Northern Rail Road, now approaching the Snake river fork of the Columbia, shall enable the Division Commander to determine the proper position of the site.

The terminus of this Road is now at Oneida, Idaho, one hundred and Twenty seven miles South of Ross' Fork Agency and I understand it is the intention to push the Road to the latter point or even to Snake River before snow falls.

              Very Respectfully,
                Your Obedt. Servant,
                  (Signed.) George Crook,
                    Brigadier General.

Chapter 3

Retrospective on the Sioux War and Crazy Horse

[August 1, 1878][1]

The death of the renowned chief Crazy Horse was an event of such importance, and with its attendant circumstances pregnant with so much of good or evil for the settlement between the Union Pacific Rail Road and the Yellowstone River that I do not feel that it would be proper for me to pass it over with the condensed account given in my notes of July and August last year.

At that time, altho' I appreciated fully the future value of an exact and truthful narration of this event and accordingly kept an eye upon all notes, memoranda, telegrams and reports, official or semi-official, bearing upon the state of affairs at Red Cloud and Spotted Tail Agencies (Nebraska,) prior to and terminating in the death of this truly great warrior and statesman, the back-bone of Dakota hostility to the white man and the white man's government yet I was so pressed for leisure,—being obliged to travel with General Crook to Camp Brown, Wyoming, and other places, on account of the Nez Percé war which was then at its height, that I was obliged to postpone to some more eligible occasion the completion of a task which should have been performed during our stay at Red Cloud Agency.

1. Date inserted in manuscript diary at West Point.

Yet, as I have a vivid recollection of all that which took place under my own observation, as my memory is likewise fortified by copious notes and as I have in my possession all the documents bearing upon the case, I am content to let this journal pass as a true and *almost* impartial account of Crazy Horse's death.

I say *almost* impartial, because no white man can write impartially the history of our Indian conflicts; it is against human nature to write with mathematical even mindedness of wars and contests in which one'sself [sic] or one's own people has taken a part, however insignificant.

Therefore, all that I can promise is that I will guard carefully against any bias or prejudice and that I will fortify each statement by a reference, when practicable, to the authority for making the same.

To understand the topography of the region comprehended in 1876–7–8, under the title of the military departments of Dakota and of the Platte, commanded at the time mentioned by Generals Terry and Crook respectively and forming the most important position of the Military Division of the Missouri then under Lieutenant-General P. H. Sheridan, it would be well to carefully consult the map prefaced to this little volume, for which I am indebted to the courtesy of Captain [William S.] Stanton, Corps of Engineers, Chief Engineer of the Department of the Platte.[2]

Of all the chieftains of the widely scattered nation of American savages known as the Sioux[*] or Dacotah or Lacotah,[**] there was not one who in 1874 and 5 was the cause of more solicitude to the United States government than the subject of this sketch. Ta-Shunca-uites or the Crazy Horse was known to the American settlers and officers upon the North-Western border as the leader of a band of his people who had become the terror and the scourge of the feeble villages in Montana and Wyoming.

To all overtures made him by the Great Father he had turned a deaf ear: no reservation had ever seen him or any of his band and his persistent hostility, & brilliant success in eluding the troops sent in pursuit of him had gained him so great an influence with the young men of his own nation that the reservations along the Missouri and

[*]*Bourke's note*: A French Canadian contraction from Chippeway *Na-wah-don-ni-Sioux*=enemies.

[**]*Bourke's note*: Da-cotah or La-cotah in the language of the Sioux is generally supposed to have some affinity with the word Cotah or Codah–friend.

2. The map was not included in the extant volume. See map on page ix.

in Northern Nebraska had become so many depôts of supplies where recruits and material in any amount would be furnished him at a moment's notice.

How long such an inflamed and threatening state of affairs would have been borne is hard to say: probably the venturesome ranchmen, miners and freighters of Montana would be in just as much peril to-day if it were not that the discovery of gold in the Black Hills on the reservation set aside for the Sioux precipitated the bloody and costly war of which the death of Crazy Horse was one of the closing episodes.[3]

The different bands and divisions of the Great Sioux nation have been given in a preceding note-book;[4] I am consequently spared the trouble of any reference to them at this time, or of giving an epitome of the causes leading to the war of 1876–77, which in truth had been coming on so surely for so many years that it would be very difficult to specify when the conduct of the Indians first became avowedly hostile and when it ceased to be friendly.

The discovery of gold in the Black Hills may be regarded as the point from which the preponderance of bad feeling is to be dated. The principal chiefs from that time, seeing that their Reservations were to be invaded by gold-seekers, began to yield to the clamors of their young men and call for pecuniary indemnity or else covertly encourage war.

In September 1875, the Commission, of which Senator Allison of Iowa was chairman, met at Red Cloud Agency, Nebraska, and laid before the Indians, (who had assembled to the estimated number of 25.000,) the terms of the General Government.[5] The savages became highly enraged that for a while it looked as if the lives of

---

3. Army losses from February 1876 through December 1877 were 283 killed and 125 wounded, the majority of which were from the Little Bighorn on June 25, 1876. The number of civilians, Indian auxiliaries, private citizens, or hostile Indians is not known. The monetary cost of the war was placed at $2,312,531.44, a phenomenal amount for an Indian campaign, and one incurred in the midst of a major economic depression. Robinson, *Good Year to Die*, 336.

4. Robinson, *Diaries*, 2:155–56, 202–3.

5. This commission was an effort to purchase the Black Hills and the "unceded Indian lands" of Montana and Wyoming, both of which had been guaranteed to the Indians in the Fort Laramie Treaty of 1868. The subsequent discovery of gold in the Black Hills had led to such a large influx of miners that the government was unable to evict them according to the terms of the treaty. The non-treaty bands boycotted the council, and the reservation bands that did attend felt they already had made enough concessions. The government's offer of $6 million for outright purchase was rejected, as was an offer to lease mining rights to the region. Ultimately, the Indians fell to quarreling among themselves, and the negotiations collapsed. Robinson, *Good Year to Die*, 37–40; DeLand, *Sioux Wars*, 15:272–75; Department of Interior, *Report of the Commissioner of Indian Affairs*, 1:33–34.

the Commissioners were not worth an hour's purchase and so far as any understanding was arrived at, the Commission might just as well never have left Washington.

Little Big Man, Crazy Horse's right hand man and who had come down from Powder River to represent his superior on this occasion, was especially noticeable for his violence.

To the coolness and intrepidity of Captain [James] Eagan [sic], 2nd Cavalry, the salvation of the who[le] Commission and the white spectators was generally attributed. I was not present during the last days of this Commission, as the whole business seemed so farcical that Captain Nickerson and I left Red Cloud Agency shortly after the commission had assembled and returned to Omaha, satisfied that there was nothing to be learned by remaining.

The Commission having separated without accomplishing anything, the Indians became more and more bold each day: the Secretary of the Interior (Zach Chandler,) determined to strike a crushing blow against Crazy Horse's band, then supposed to be in camp on Powder River. A summons was first sent to this chieftain to come in to the Agency at once and remain there, or failing in that, to take the consequences.

A full account of the winter campaign which resulted upon his refusal and of the whole Sioux war is to be found in my journals, from Feby. 17, 1876 to May 10 1877.[6] From these journals it will be gathered that General Crook's pet scheme of enlisting auxiliaries from among the Sioux themselves to aid in the reduction of the persistently hostile of their tribe, was frustrated by the antagonism of [William] Vandeveer [sic],[7] the Inspector and [James S.] Hastings, the Indian Agent at Red Cloud Agency: the summer campaign was consequently arduous, unduly protracted and void of result.

Had General Crook taken with him in June, one hundred Sioux scouts, it is my opinion that Custer and his brave comrades would yet have been alive.[8]

    6. See Robinson, *Diaries*, Volumes 1 and 2.
    7. Bourke despised Vandever, whom he considered to be a pawn of the Indian Ring, a group of Eastern contractors who enriched themselves at the expense of the Indians, and which he believed was responsible for much of the trouble. See entry under Appendix 1.
    8. Bourke may be been sincere in his belief. Nevertheless, this passage attempts to absolve Crook of any blame for the disaster at the Little Bighorn, which many modern historians believe he must share. Crook failed to immediately notify General Terry that he had been turned back at the Rosebud, leaving Terry and Custer to believe that he was en route to meet them. In fact, he was hunting and fishing at his base camp at Goose Creek, Wyoming. Robinson, *General Crook*, 179; Carroll, *Court Martial of Frederick W. Benteen*, i–ii.

The disasters of that terrible summer (1876) opened the eyes of our imbecile government. The clamors of the people could no longer go unheeded and the administration of the Indian agencies (of the Sioux nation,) was immediately turned over to the care of the war [sic] Department.

General Crook's first action was to depose Red Cloud and Red Leaf, who had behaved in a manner that augured badly for the solidity of their good feelings towards the whites and next he organized his winter expedition which accomplished such wonderful results. This was composed of ten companies of Cavalry (6 of the 4th 2 of the 3d and 2 of the 5th,) under General R. S. Mackenzie and fifteen cos. of Infantry and Artillery (four of the 4th Art. 6 of the 9th Infantry and the others of the 4th and 14th Infantry,) under Lt. Col. R. I. Dodge, 23d Infantry. The most peculiar feature of this command has now to be noted; our contingent of Indian scouts was composed of one hundred Pawnees from the Indian Territory, one hundred Shoshonees and Bannocks from the Wind River and Snake River regions in Wyoming and Idaho, one hundred Arapahoes from Red Cloud Agency and one hundred Sioux and Cheyennes from same place.

I am gliding rapidly down the current of these important events for the simple reason that in my other note-books they have been exhaustively treated: I shall not allude further to this campaign, except to say that on the 25th of November, 1876, our Cavalry forces, under General Mackenzie, were led by our Indian allies to the village of Dull Knife, the Cheyenne chief, on the banks of a little fork of Powder River, debouching from a steep and dark cañon in the Big Horn Mountains. This village of nearly *200* lodges was totally destroyed, and the vast herd of 2000 ponies captured (750) killed, wounded or stampeded in great numbers over the country. The Cheyennes lost all their worldly effects and indeed escaped with nothing but the arms in their hands and a few cartridges, not to mention the great loss of life and the numbers of wounded and frozen in the cold weather which set in at this time.

Over seven hundred ponies were captured and brought away and of those which did not fall into our hands, great numbers were badly wounded and others afterwards killed for food or died from overwork and exposure.

Many of the enemy's dead fell into our hands, and great pools of blood upon the trail of the retreating hostiles showed us they were carrying away many wounded.

Among our own loss[es] we had to mourn the gallant John A. McKinney 1 Lieut. 4th Cavalry (for full particulars of that fight, see my note-book of proper date.)[9]

The bitter coldness of the weather, (the mercury nearly congealed in the bulb.) Assured us that the Cheyennes must be suffering terribly, destitute as we knew them to be of clothing, blankets, furs and provisions; but we never learned until after their surrender at Red Cloud Agency how truly effective the blow had been.

The Cheyennes, under Dull Knife and Standing Elk, made their way along the base of the Big Horn Mountains, and by following the thread of the Powder and Tongue river, within 15 or 20 miles of the Yellowstone, where they expected to find help and sympathy.

But for some reason, Crazy Horse received them with very slight manifestations of pity and made them feel that their presence in his camp was only tolerated and not desired.

The Cheyennes, after remaining a few days with Crazy Horse, determined to leave him, and surrender at Red Cloud Agency, provided they should be assured of kindly treatment.

The first detachment (of 385.) under Little Wolf reached Camp Robinson,[10] (Red Cloud Agency.) Neb., in January–February, 1877, and, after being dismounted and disarmed, was allowed to send back some of its people to hurry up the remainder of the tribe.

Few persons, excepting General Crook, attached much importance to Little Wolf's assertion that the Cheyennes had become hostile to the Sioux and wished to help us against them, in retaliation for Crazy Horse's bad treatment, but the truth came out when one thousand more surrendered at Red Cloud Agency early in April.

The destitution of these people was extreme; their clothes were in tatters; for lodges they had branches of trees or half-burned tépi poles, covered with pieces of skin, horse-hides, half-scorched buffalo-robes, and even gunny-bags, picked up from the deserted camp of our command on the Belle Fourche, in December and January.

9. Robinson, *Diaries*, Vol. 2, Chapter 9.
10. Camp Robinson was established in 1874 to control the Indians of the Red Cloud and Pine Ridge Agencies. It was redesignated Fort Robinson in January 1878. During the Second World War, it was used as a dog training center for the K-9 Corps. It was abandoned in 1948, and is now a Nebraska state park. Buecker, *Fort Robinson and the American West*; Schubert, *Outpost of the Sioux Wars*.

They said that after the engagement of Nov. 25th, the weather became so cold in the mountains that many of their wounded died and in one night fourteen little children froze to death in their mothers' arms. They would have surrendered to us at once, but were afraid, on account of our Indian allies. One night they sent spies into our camp to learn what Indians we had with us; but when these had crept slowly along through the brush and approaching one of our camp-fires, heard their *own* language spoken, they skulked back in precipitation to their own people and counselled them to go to Crazy Horse.

The chilling reception accorded them in his camp embittered them as already stated and they made up their minds that, if General Crook would accept them as auxiliaries, to enlist as soldiers under him and go out to fight Crazy Horse and the Northern Indians.

To explain away any seeming delay in the execution of this plan, I will say that the engagement took place Nov. 25th 1876, that the Cheyennes did not all reach Crazy Horse's village until 15 or 20 days after, that they remained with him until January 1877, when the first detachment of the Cheyennes left him and moved to Camp Robinson, Neb., which post it reached early in February. From Camp Robinson back to Tongue River is nearly (300) miles as the crow flies; to traverse this distance in mid-winter where snow covers the grass and the hillsides are slippery with ice is a toilsome undertaking even for *Indian* runners and when the worst season of the year for its journey. So it came along slowly but surely, through mud and slush and snow as fast as broken down men and women could urge broken down ponies to drag it.

Their best ponies had fallen into our hands during the MacKenzie fight, hundreds of others had been injured by our bullets or by running against rocks and trees during the stampede, had been eaten for food or broken down by extra work and insufficient forage while exposed to the bitter cold of winter.

The great number of widows and orphans and people with frozen limbs and half-closed wounds was a melancholy souvenir of the Mackenzie fight. Such of the wounded as yet needed medical help were promptly attended to by the surgeon at the post. One strapping big fellow was in miserable plight; he had been shot squarely through the hips and the right leg was so bent back that the sole of the foot rested against the flank; the knee-joint had ancylosed and to add to his sufferings the right heel and toes were frozen off. I must here take occasion to praise the stoical fortitude of these Indians, many of whom were wounded in what I should call a horrible manner, but they didn't seem to mind it much and went to the post surgeon more, as it were, out of compliment to him than regard for their own safety.

In conversation with them, they would from time to time astonish us by showing a freshly healed scar which they had received on the hill back of their village that cold November day which the Cheyennes are never to forget.

Such wounds would keep an *American* soldier in bed for months; the free life, pure air and simple food of these people must have much to do with the rapidity of their convalescence.

In my note-books, written upon the spot, I gave such complete details of the surrender of these Cheyennes that I may well spare myself any further reference to them, but I can, without stringing out this account too much state the fact that one of the half starved Cheyennes ate himself into a surfeit and died soon after reaching Camp Robinson.[11]

Of the Cheyennes who came in in February, Little Wolf, one of their head chiefs in the fight with Mackenzie, was enlisted as a soldier to go out after the hostile bands, and, April 11th, old Turkey Legs and other chiefs of the Cheyennes came to see General Crook; they said they wanted to go out and fight the Northern Indians, (Crazy Horse's band.) and spoke of the ungenerous treatment they had received from them when in trouble.

Turkey legs who was paralyzed and unable to do much physical labor, was evidently a man of acute mental powers and a good talker. He said he claimed for his people that "They were the best fighters on the plains" and, turning to Generals Crook and Mackenzie, "you who have fought us know what we are".

The spirit of these first comers was reflected by the later arrivals: indeed the change in the attitude of the Cheyennes was truly wonderful. One year previous, they had been the boldest warriors and most intractable Indians at this Agency; now, they appeared as docile and subdued as if they had never been on the war-path.

These Indians dread nothing so much as an encounter with our Indian allies; white troops they despise.

11. Robinson, *Diaries*, Vol. 2, Chapter 13.

High Bear, a surrendered Sans Arcs, told Major [George Morton] Randall, at Spotted Tail Agency, Neb., in April (1877.)
"I want to be a soldier now and work for the Great Father". ["]When you had white soldiers, I wasn't afraid because I don't care anything for them. I used to sleep well when you had white soldiers, but now you have my own people fighting against me, I don't know what to do. My squaws are too frightened to sleep at night and the children can't go to sleep.

["]We don't know when your Indian scouts may lead you into one of our villages to destroy it just as the Cheyennes had their village taken this winter. We feel so suspicious now that when a strange *Sioux* comes into our village we think he is one of your soldiers and set young men to watch him and follow him back.

["]I can't fight you in this way and I want to make peace and stay at peace."

While these things were occurring at Camp Robinson, events of almost equal importance were transpiring at Camp Sheridan,[12] 45 miles distant.

At that point, Touch the Clouds, with his own band of Minneconjous and the band of Sans Arcs under Roman Nose, (whose village had been destroyed by General Crook's troops at Slim Buttes, Dakota, Sept. 9th 1876.) surrendered early in April:—a few days earlier in fact than the Cheyennes did at Camp Robinson, but I have with propriety given prominence to the Cheyenne surrender, it having been prior both in time and consequence and the greater celerity with which the Sans Arcs and Minneconjous traveled was due entirely to the superiority of their animals and equipment while the Cheyennes as already stated, were burdened with many sick and wounded and had lost everything in their fight with Mackenzie, in November.

Charging Bear, one of Roman Nose's band of Sans Arcs, captured by us at Slim Buttes and who owed his life to Gen'l. Crook, was now a soldier, ranking as Corporal in the Company of Indian scouts. His influence with his surrendered relatives was very strong and gratitude impelled him to act as recruiting agent for General Crook.

12. Camp Sheridan was near the Spotted Tail Agency, on the west fork of Beaver Creek, twelve miles above its confluence with the Niobrara River. It was one of two posts established in 1874 to control the Lakotas and protect the agencies, the other being Camp Robinson at Red Cloud. It was replaced by Fort Niobrara in 1880. Frazer, *Forts of the West*, 89–90; Heitman, *Historical Register*, 2:544.

It was hard to say whether Cheyennes or Minneconjous were more desirous of furnishing soldiers, but the Cheyennes [capped the chinaso?] by telling General Crook he could have every man of their tribe if he wanted to go fight Crazy Horse.

We have digressed from the main line of this story very much, but not more than has been necessary to give a complete bird's eye view of the situation.

We now return to Crazy Horse who by this time had moved into the North West corner of the Black Hills and formed his village on the Belle Fourche of the Cheyenne river, where he watched the progress of events, keeping himself in constant communication with his people at Red Cloud and Spotted Tail Agencies.

He saw now that the game was up: he had either to surrender within six weeks or prepare himself to be hunted to death by the vindictive Cheyennes, just as soon as the troops got ready to resume the campaign.

The great secret of General Crook's success in Indian warfare, is based upon three facts. Firstly, while he is not the only American general who has employed Indians to fight Indians, he is the first to initiate and successfully rival Julius Caesar's famous plans of making the shattered fragment of conquered tribes furnish, as an earnest [demonstration] of their peaceful intentions, a contingent of auxiliaries to assist in the reduction of their persistently hostile relatives. While other commanders have employed Crows, Rees and Gros Ventres to fight Sioux and Cheyennes, they have never dared to enlist any large bodies of the two last tribes to fight their own people.

General Crook, on the contrary, has fought and whipped Pi-utes with Pi-Utes, Snakes with Snakes, Apaches with Apaches, Cheyennes with Cheyennes and Sioux with Sioux.

Nor has he discarded the services of other tribes, but the large employment of *subdued* hostiles to fight unsubdued hostiles is the key-note of his strategy; is what has made him by placing the jealousy of tribe against tribe, complete master of the situation, independent of the whin[in]g caprices and superstitions to which other commanders much defer, and given him as thorough a knowledge of the enemy's position and plans as if he were sitting in their Council Lodge.

The transportation of troops has all his life been a favorite study with him: in campaign he strips officers and soldiers down to the clothing on their backs and does this by that most widely obeyed of all General Orders—Example.—

No one can truthfully say that in any campaign, General Crook took with him for his own comfort more than he allowed the humblest soldier, and for this reason, his columns have always been noted for the velocity and for keeping so close to the heels of the Indian scouts that scarcely have the latter detected the presence of a hostile village before the Cavalry and Infantry Battalions have pushed forward, surrounded and stormed it.[13] *Lastly*, his reticence: General Crook will never tell what he is going to do, will never speak of what he had done. His soldiers, consequently, when they start on a campaign, are always prepared to encounter the worst privations and hardships and to take things just as they come.[14]

To preserve the chain of narration, I will mention that early in January [1877], an embassy sent by the Red Cloud Indians to find the Northern bands and induce them to come into the Reservation was obliged to visit General [Nelson A.] Miles' post at the mouth of Tongue River[15] While approaching that post, they were murdered in cold blood by some of the Crow Indians allowed to loaf about the Garrison.

One of these friendly Sioux Indians was Sitting Bull of the South,[16] a man of great prominence among his people, a firm friend of the whites and a strong supporter of General Crook in his efforts to manage the Indians.

In May, 1876, he had entered heartily into General Crook's scheme for the enlistment of a body of Indian scouts, which was frustrated at the time by the opposition of Indian Inspector Vandeveer and Indian Agent Hastings.

13. Bourke completely ignored—as he generally did—the situation at the Rosebud, which Capt. Anson Mills, Third Cavalry, accurately summed up with the observation, "I did not think that General Crook knew where [the hostile Indians] were, and I did not think our friendly Indians knew where they were, and no one conceived we would find them in the great force we did." The closest Bourke ever came to admitting Crook narrowly averted disaster was in *On the Border With Crook* (311) where he said the Rosebud "was a trap." Mills, *My Story*, 398.

14. This characteristic, which Bourke apparently considered admirable, was cordially resented by many of the officers, who often came away from officers' calls with no idea of what Crook expected of them. They also attributed the "worst privations and hardships" more to poor planning and organization than to any virtues on Crook's part. Bourke, *On the Border*, 109; Robinson, *A Good Year to Die*, 57; and *General Crook*, 194–95.

15. Later permanently established as Fort Keogh, Montana.

16. An Oglala chief, designated "of the South," to distinguish him from the great Hunkpapa chief who was a key leader of the hostiles. See biographic sketch in Appendix 1.

The death of this chieftain, Sitting Bull of the South, was a heavy blow to our national credit with the plains Indians: it shook their faith in our professions of good will and satisfied them that we were not to be trusted and that the Indians who, bearing white flags, entered our forts and Reservations should like the victims descending into Hell, "leave all Hope behind."[17]

17. Quote from Dante, *Divine Comedy*, Canto III.

Chapter 4

♦
♦
♦
♦

The Death of Crazy Horse

Bourke's retrospective continues.

When, finally, after many days of waiting, it was announced at Red Cloud Agency that Ta-Sunca-Uit-Co, Crazy Horse was on his way in to surrender it was understood at once that our campaigning days in the Department of the Platte were over and that the Sioux problem, as a problem, was solved. No further resistance was to be expected from a coalition of the bands of this great nation; the leader, who could organize such a coalition and hold its elements together by the force of his intellect and will, was about to bury the hatchet.

Sitting Bull,[1] who has gained such a reputation from the jottings of journalists, has not and never has had the influence possessed by Crazy Horse.

He is without power among the Southern Dakotas whose reservations have always been magazines of men and material for Crazy Horse.

Any trouble which Sitting Bull may make will be that which any other ill-disposed Indian demagogue may make; trouble demanding prompt and energetic measures for its suppression, but not taxing

---

1. In this case, Bourke means the hostile Hunkpapa chief.

to the utmost the resources of our military Establishment.

I venture to say that had not General Crook been in command of the Dep't. of the Platte and the measures of Crazy Horse been frustrated by the far-reaching calculations of our Commander, the regular army would have been increased to 50.000 men and its annual cost to $40.000.000 before this insurrection, (for such it was worthy to be called.) could have been suppressed.

The entry of Crazy Horse's band into Red Cloud Agency was one of the most impressive spectacles I ever witnessed. In the bright, exhilarating sunlight of a May morning, (May 6th, 1877.), the long column of swarthy warriors descended the grass-covered hills overlooking the Agency and debouched upon the plain about a mile from the Government buildings.

First came Lieut. [William Philo] Clark, with 1st Sergeant Red Cloud and the company of friendly Sioux soldiers, then Crazy Horse, with Little Hawk, Little Big Man, He Dog and Big Road—his head men. Then the warriors of the tribe in solid rank, showing fine discipline; lastly the women and children, with the camp equipage and pack animals. There was not the usual number of dogs, many probably had been devoured as food. The entire column was not much under two miles in length. As the Indians approached the Agency, the warriors broke out into a low chant, which gradually swelled into a loud song of gladness—the Hymn of Peace, as our Indians said. As the procession filed out to the place chosen for its encampment, its animation and bustle were very marked, but there was none of the charging at full speed on horse-back and firing of guns and pistols which Indians are always so fond [of] when first coming to a new village of their people.

The erection of the lodges at once commenced and, in less than half an hour, they were all in position to the number of One Hundred and Forty Six, but as most of the lodges contained two families each, the aggregate strength of the band was found to be nearly Eleven hundred.

The day previous to the entry into the Agency, Lt. Clark had gone out to meet Crazy Horse and had shaken hands with him and smoked the pipe of peace. It was remarked that Crazy Horse did this while sitting on the ground and that he extended his Left hand, saying that it was the "heart-hand"[2] and he wanted this peace to be forever.

2. I.e., the hand closest to his heart.

The Death of Crazy Horse 67

He Dog bestowed upon Lieut. Clark a war-bonnet, war-shirt, and a fine buffalo robe, in token of good-will: Crazy Horse gave all his war-equipment to Red Cloud, his near relation.

The herds of ponies and horses brought in by this band were simply immense: experts estimated the number of animals at from (2200) to (2500.) My own opinion was (2200) or (2300.)

As soon as the lodges were erected, the surrendered Indians were called upon to give up their arms: Crazy Horse first laid down on the ground seventy-six, but Lieut. Clark at once told him that that was too thin—everything must be given up, and that he would now search the lodges.

In this work, he was assisted by the guides and interpreters, Frank Gruard and Billy Hunter,* and a detachment of Indian and white soldiers. Only One hundred and seventeen guns could be found, but these were taken away without any evidence of acrimony or ill-feeling.

But what struck me as a fact of great significance was the presence of our Cheyenne scouts, armed to the teeth and concealed behind one of the knolls commanding Crazy Horse's Camp and not over 100 yards away. I accidently rode in among them while taking a short cut back to my quarters. Standing Elk and Little Wolf smiled rather grimly and looked as if they would like some excuse for pitching into the tribe they hated so bitterly.

Our friends, the Arapahoes, to the number of 150, were assembled at Camp Robinson, under Sharp Nose and White Horse, apprehending some treachery on the part of Crazy Horse. All the Agency Indians seemed to distrust Crazy Horse personally very much, but to have great confidence in the friendly feelings of the Indians with him.

Some of our Indians said in my presence that Crazy Horse didn't at all like the idea of coming in but that his head men were satisfied with the inutility of further resistance.

That evening, I visited the village and had an opportunity of seeing Crazy Horse and his associates.

Crazy Horse's face was of a quiet and melancholy cast, dogged, tenacious and resolute. He was very taciturn and reserved, speaking to no one, Indian or white.[3] At the time of my coming to his lodge, a

---

*Bourke's note: See Hunter's account, at end. *[Appendix 2]*

3. In *On the Border With Crook* (414–15), Bourke elaborated, saying:
   I saw before me a man who looked quite young, not over thirty years old, five feet eight inches high, lithe and sinewy, with a scar on the face. The expression

squaw was making coffee and another one making arrangements for the evening meal. Crazy Horse was seated upon the ground, when Sorrel Horse, the Indian who accompanied me, moved forward and told Crazy Horse that I was one of Three Stars (General Crook's) Officers.[4] [(]Crazy Horse had never yet seen General Crook, who had been called away to Chicago a few days previously to consult General Sheridan.) but he had heard about him long ago and learned of him from the other Indians. He leaned forward, grasped my hand very warmly and grunted "how!" This was the extent of our conversation and as Frank Gruard was waiting to take Crazy Horse down to supper at his home, I sauntered about the village, scrutinizing the faces of the other chiefs and seeing what was to be seen. (My note book of the proper date has a very full description of this village)[5]

Frank Gruard had for five years been Crazy Horse's prisoner and was well thought of by that chieftain. We all believed that if anybody could make Crazy Horse unbosom himself, Frank was the man. But no such result was obtained. Crazy Horse remained during the whole of his life the same strange combination of genius, moroseness, generous love for his own people and hatred of the white man.

Little Hawk, the second in command, was about the same size as Crazy Horse, 5' 8", and like him lithe and wiry. His countenance was more kindly his speech more fluent. On his breast appeared the silver medal received by his father from President Monroe, in 1817.

Little Big man, the chief who did so much to break up the Red Cloud Commission, in 1875, had the look of a shrewd politician and, altho' his face did not strike me as a good one, I remember it impressed me as an able one.[6]

Day by day, as he remained at Red Cloud, Crazy Horse became more and more melancholy and sullen, withdrawing into himself as he felt his power waning away.

---

      of his countenance was one of quiet dignity, but morose, dogged, tenacious, and melancholy. He behaved with stolidity, like a man who realized he had to give in to Fate but would do so as sullenly as possible.

    4. "Three Stars" refers to the individual stars of a brigadier general, one on each shoulder strap, and a third possibly sewn or pinned to his hat. It would not have referred to three stars in a line on his shoulder strap, the designation of a lieutenant general, and a rank that Crook never achieved.

    5. Robinson, *Diaries*, 2:297–99.

    6. Again, in *On the Border With Crook* (415), Bourke wrote of Little Big Man, "He and I became better friends afterwards, and exchanged presents."

As he well knew, the total number of Indians surrendering at Red Cloud and Spotted Tail Agencies was very great. (Note. It was a little over [4400]. J.G.B.) Few, if any, of these Indians would ever take to the war-path again, because dissensions had been introduced among them with so much skill that the weakness of factions had been made to replace the solidity of harmony.

Crazy Horse took in the situation without delay: he saw that General Crook had arrayed Spotted Tail against Red Cloud and had, besides, alienated completely the former good feeling of the Cheyennes and Arapahoes.

Were Crazy Horse to take to the field again, he would have to fight his way out from the heavily-garrisoned Agency, would be instantly pursued by every man the Cheyennes and Arapahoes could raise and even if aided by Red Cloud would be opposed by Spotted Tail, or if encouraged by the latter, bitterly antagonized by the former.

After his enlistment as a soldier, which enlistment was made at his own request, Crazy Horse had his eyes still more completely opened to the power General Crook had gained over the Indians at the Agency. Of all three tribes there assembled, numbering all told not quite (15.000) souls, (1200) were Arapahoes, (1400) to (1500) Cheyennes and the remainder Dakotas. Of these last Crazy Horse's own band numbered 1100 and the Minneconjous and Sans Arcs who had formerly associated almost exclusively with his people (1000) more.

The Indian soldiers were equally apportioned among the various tribes; they acted as a police force, and exercised a system of espionage which made conspiracy impossible. Then too, as time flew by, Crazy Horse found that his own people were tampered with by their fellow-soldiers and began to give evidence of a strong leaning to the white man's administration.

Little Big Man was one of the first to weaken, but the others fell into line so rapidly that Crazy Horse soon found himself without any support whatever.

This was in the summer of 1877. General Crook had promised the Indians that if all came in and no hostiles remained on this (South) side of the Yellowstone, he would not object to their having an escort of a Battalion of Cavalry, while they engaged in a Buffalo hunt in the Big Horn Mtns. to the West of Fort McKinney; but from this promise he afterwards withdrew upon the recommendation of some of the Indian chiefs, who suspected and indeed detected a growing disposition on the part of Crazy Horse to make trouble and, if possible, to incite the Sioux to recommence War.[7]

About the 1st of June, the Cheyenne Indians asked to be sent to the Indian Territory to join those of their people already there: this request was granted and the band started down across country under charge of Lieut. [Henry Ware] Lawton, 4th Cavalry, a fine soldier, and a small detachment from that Regiment.[8]

After the departure of those warriors, Crazy Horse daily grew more insolent and intractable thinking that perhaps he could manage matters better to suit himself.

The Sioux chiefs, one by one, gave up the desire for a buffalo hunt, until at last Crazy Horse was the only one of prominence who adhered to it, but with such persistence that no one doubted it was to serve only as a pretext for getting away from the Agency never to return.

Early in August, Crazy Horse was invited by General Crook to become one of the delegation of (30) Indians whom Commissioner [Ezra] Hayt had asked to have sent on to Washington to consult with the Great Father on the question of removing the Agencies to the Missouri River. At first Crazy Horse assented, but solely upon condition that no Indians should go but those whom he selected and that all should be from his band.[9]

Lieut. Clark told him in as kind a way as possible that his band was only a small part of the total at the Agency and that Red Cloud, Spotted Tail and Sharp Nose were also big chiefs and should be consulted by the President relative to the welfare of their people.

Crazy Horse then sullenly answered he wouldn't go.

From that time, affairs daily grew more serious and only wanted an excuse for being brought to a head. This excuse was soon found in the Nez Percé war then waging.

Joseph and his band, pressed by General [Oliver O.] Howard, had retreated from the basin of the Columbia river, across the Rocky

---

7. There is a strong possibility that other chiefs, fearing Crazy Horse's influence and the possibility of more trouble, spread rumors to undermine his position with the whites. See Clark, *Killing of Chief Crazy Horse*, 28.

8. There is no indication the Cheyennes actually requested transportation to the Territory, but rather resigned themselves to a decision of the government. Monnett, *Tell Them We Are Going Home*, 5.

9. The various correspondence concerning Crazy Horse is found in Appendix 2.

Mountains, and taken refuge in the Yellowstone Park with the evident intention of working their way farther East. General Crook was ordered to organize an expedition to head off the Nez Percés, who were supposed to have the intention of coming into the Bannock and Shoshonee country: as guides for this column, he enlisted a band from these two tribes and also called upon the Sioux for a quota of one hundred men.

That number was at once made up of their best young men and an additional one hundred presented themselves to serve without pay. Crazy Horse now said that he would move out slowly towards the north with his whole village and when our column overtook him, he would join it and go fight the Nez Percés: but this manoeuvre was entirely too transparent and he was told he must remain where he was. He hereupon grew very sulky and said he would not allow any of his young men to go upon the proposed expedition. Our Indian spies said that Crazy Horse had lately been in correspondence with the Indians who had escaped into British America[10] and that he had determined to leave the Reservation and join them.

This information was not credited at first, but each day it was repeated and finally it was learned that in a council with his own band, Crazy Horse had proposed breaking away from the Agency even if he had to go alone.

On the 31st of August, he told Lieut. Clark in council that he didn't intend to stay any more and would leave at once. General Bradley, then in command of Camp Robinson and Lt. Clark, who had charge of the Indian soldiers, kept General Crook fully posted on every turn of affairs and it was at last decided by General Sheridan and General Crook that Crazy Horse should be made a prisoner, his band disintegrated and scattered among the other bands and himself sent to some place East.

General Crook started on his way to Camp Brown, Wyo., there to assume, if necessary, the command of the expedition to head off the Nez-Percés: on his way, he telegraphed to General Bradley to "round up" Crazy Horse at once not thinking it worthwhile to go in person to the scene, as Crazy Horse's power had been so thoroughly undermined and the Nez-Percé problem was then apparently more deserving of attention.

10. I.e. Sitting Bull and the remnants of his band.

But General Sheridan did not share in this feeling; in his opinion, any disturbance that Crazy Horse might raise was far more to be dreaded than the whole power of an insignificant band like the Nez-Percés.

A dead lion is of no account in the regard of those who lately were wont to trouble at his faintest roar; thus, Crazy Horse being dead, an exaggerated importance has attached to the war with the Nez-Percés, but how much more costly in blood, treasure, time and material would have been that war had Crazy Horse broken away and rallied around him the disaffected elements of the Dakotas and obliged us to fight 3000 or 4.000 skilled warriors instead of 3 or 400. Joseph was a brave and dextrous chieftain, but not more brave, not more dextrous than Crazy Horse and not to be mentioned on the same page where resources were to be counted.

General Crook and self arrived at Red Cloud Agency, Neb., Sept 2d [1877], with the intention of superintending the "round up", which was to have occurred at once, had not unexpected events caused its postponement.

Colonel [Julius Wilmot] Mason, with three companies of the 3d Cavalry, had just reinforced the garrison from Fort Laramie:[11] Red Cloud, Spotted Tail, Sharp Nose and the other head men had been sounded and answered that they considered the safety of all demanded the deposition of Crazy Horse and the dismemberment of his band. But that very day, news came that the small party of Lame Deer, recently broken up by General [Nelson] Miles, was making its way in to Red Cloud Agency to surrender and might be there in a very few hours: that morning seventy three men, women and children surrendered at the Agency.

There was much reason to fear that if Crazy Horse's village should not be completely surrounded and his warriors not all captured, those that escaped might get mixed up among those of Lame Deer's band and some of the latter might be killed or wounded.

Such a misfortune was especially to be averted at this moment, since the advance members of the Lame Deer village asserted that General Miles had dealt treacherously with them and after persuad-

---

11. Fort Laramie was established as an American Fur Company trading post in 1834. In 1849, it was purchased by the federal government and garrisoned as a miitary post until 1890, when it was abandoned. Much of the post has been preserved or restored, and it is now a national historic site. Frazer, *Forts of the West*, 181–82.

ing them to surrender had murdered Lame Deer and his two companions who had gone down to Miles' camp to make terms.

I may as well here give the whole story as these Indians told it. They said that General Miles had attacked their village at day-break, had set fire to their tépis, (between 50 and 60 in number.) and routed themselves to the hills; that they lost a good many of their ponies, but from the hill-sides kept up a galling fire on the troops, of whom they killed six, while their own loss thus far had only been three, slightly wounded. They also claimed to have sent a party in upon Miles' rear, who killed the detachment guarding his ammunition train and ran off three mules loaded with six boxes of cartridges, (i.e. *6000* metallic cartridges.) General Miles called upon the Indians to give up and Lame Deer with two companions[12] concluded to go down and arrange stipulations, thinking there was no use in remaining out in the mountains during the winter, without lodges.[13]

When Lame Deer and the two other Indians laid down their guns, General Miles ordered an officer to pick them up; remembering the cold-blooded murder of Sitting Bull of the South, at Miles' post on Tongue river, a few weeks before,[14] these Indians at once apprehended duplicity of some sort and seized their guns to fight for their lives; in the mêlée, they were all killed, which being perceived by their comrades who were watching affairs from the neighboring hill-tops, they took to the brakes and scattered in all directions, satisfied that the white men were all murderers. A repetition of such a criminal piece of carelessness would have jeopardized General Crook's plans and impaired his influence; hence his anxiety in a military point of view, to avoid it; aside from any abhorrence he might feel for the needless shedding of blood.

To give Crazy Horse one last chance for self-vindication, General Crook sent him word that he wanted to hold a council with him that day (Sept. 3d) and hear what he had to say for himself. As the General started for the Council Building, one of our friendly Indians a soldier, named Woman's Dress, came up alongside the ambulance and said there must be no Council held, that he was down with Crazy Horse's people the preceding night and heard that chieftain

---

12. Greene, citing Miles, mentions only two Indians, Lame Deer and Iron Star. Greene, *Yellowstone Command*, 208–10.
13. The Lame Deer Fight actually occurred on May 7, 1877, one day after Crazy Horse surrendered at the agency.
14. Actually four months.

tell his band he was going to leave the Reservation at once, but that, before leaving, he was going to the Council and would then and there stab General Crook, believing he was the one soldier the Dakotas had to be afraid of. He stated that during the interview, he would address some angry words to General Crook, which were to be the signals for his followers to get ready and when General Crook replied, Crazy Horse was to stab him with a knife which he was to keep concealed under his blanket and then the other Indians were to rush on, kill Lieut. Clark and any other officers and white men who might be present and in the confusion break away from the Reservation. The Indian was so earnest in his statement and had proved himself so perfectly trustworthy that General Crook gave full credit to his story and instructed General Bradley to make the "round up" already ordered without waiting for any Council.[15]

September 4 [1877], General Crook and self left Camp Robinson for Fort Laramie and Cheyenne, Wyo., going through to Fort Laramie by daylight and then catching the Black Hills Stage for Cheyenne 93 miles farther, which place we reached next day @ 1.30 P.M., in time for the Western Express, (U.P.R.R.)[16] For Green River, Wyo., 330 miles by rail.

We reached Green River at 8 in the morning, took breakfast, climbed aboard the stage, a most miserable "dug-out", plodded along up Green River valley and all along its tributaries, the Big Sandy, Little Sandy, and Dry Sandy, past "Starvation ranch", which a rude inscription, scrawled on the door, informed us was "one mile from water, six miles from wood and two inches from Hell".—on through South Pass, & Atlantic City to Camp Stambaugh[17] in the Rocky Mountains, some 9000 feet above the sea. Here we were very courteously received by Capt. Bisbee, who had just taken station at the post, and invited to breakfast.—a very excellent one it was too—by

15. Crook easily would have believed this. On September 8, 1872, he had survived a remarkably similar assassination attempt during a council with Yavapais at Camp Date Creek, Arizona. The Indian scout who reported the supposed Crazy Horse conspiracy was Woman's Dress, who was jealous of the chief's prestige. Baptiste "Big Bat" Pourier vouched for it to Crook and Clark. The rumor appears to have been encouraged by Frank Grouard who, despite his outward cordiality, apparently nursed old hatreds from his period of Oglala captivity, and who may or may not have heard about the earlier incident at Date Creek. See Robinson, *General Crook*, 125–26; and *Good Year to Die*, 338; De Barthe, *Frank Grouard*, 337–39; William Garnett in Clark, *Killing of Chief Crazy Horse*, 77–78.

16. Union Pacific Rail Road.

17. Camp Stambaugh was established in 1870 between Atlantic City, Wyoming, and the Oregon Trail, eight miles north of the Sweetwater River to protect miners adjacent to the Shoshone Reservation. The post was abandoned in 1878. Frazer, *Forts of the West*, 185.

Mr. Baldwin, the post trader, whose charming wife and daughter, did their best to make our stay pleasant.

From Stambaugh to Camp Brown, a distance of (45) miles, we were driven by one of the General's former scouts, Texas Bob [Eckles], on a wild, harum-scarum specimen of the frontiersman; our horses were Texas mustangs, unbroken and wild as could be. They ran away with us at one time, but our driver was an expert; our ambulance strong and the roads the mountains, fortunately not rocky. Still it was by a stroke of good luck that we came out with-out a scratch and reached Brown about dark (Sept. 7th).

General Crook busied himself with the preparations for the expedition to head off Joseph and the Nez-Percés, but as telegrams informed him that the Nez-Percés instead of coming South to the Shoshonee country had turned North East and started to effect a combination with the River Crows, he saw it was no use to wait at Brown, so leaving Genl. [Wesley] Merritt, 5th Cavy., in command of the corps of observation, he started back, Sept. 9th for Omaha. (1000 miles distant.)

At Camp Robinson, in the meanwhile, all had been excitement. The troops moved out from their camps early in the morning of the 4th of Sept., the Cavalry under Col. Mason, the Indian soldiers under Lieut. Clark; General Bradley superintending the whole movement. Crazy Horse's village was six miles from the Post. When the troops came in sight of the spot where the village had been they found it deserted and knew that the enemy had left during the night or early in the morning. Upon the skirts of some of the hills near by, a few of the lodges yet lingered, not being able to move fast enough to escape the observation of our keen-eyed scouts. Our column pushed forward, pressing the runaways so closely that out of the Seventy Three lodges which had remained faithful to the fortunes of Crazy Horse, over fifty were captured before noon and our scouts closely pressed the remainder, now making for the Spotted Tail Agency, (45 miles East of Red Cloud.) Lieut. Clark stimulated the exertions of his scouts as much as possible, even offering Mini-Wa-nichi (No Water,) the head man, a reward of ($200.) if he would catch Crazy Horse.

Couriers were sent in hot haste to Camp Sheridan, the military station at the Spotted Tail Agency, and everybody there, red and white, was put on the qui vive[18] for the whole party of fugitives.

18. Taken from the French. In this particular instance, it means, "on the lookout."

Before noon, every lodge had been picked up except Crazy Horse's, but shortly after sun-set he was apprehended by our Indian soldiers and delivered to Major [Daniel Webster] Burke, the Post commander.

The Indians seemed to comprehend the necessity of surrendering him to the Military authorities, feeling assured that if he once got away from the agency, he would in less than no time stir up anew the embers of war which they had begun to perceive it was to their own interest to extinguish.

Crazy Horse was taken in an ambulance the next day, to Camp Robinson, under charge of Major Burke, Touch the Clouds, Swift Bear and High Bear.

By some mistaken courtesy, his stiletto and revolvers had not been taken from him. At the door of the Camp Robinson guard-house, he made a sudden attempt to escape, striking out with great force, to hew "a way for himself["] with his knife. Little Big Man jumped upon his back, throwing his arms over Crazy Horse's arms, but not succeeding in this soon enough to escape a fierce thrust in the wrist, which, luckily for him did not make a bad wound. In the excitement and confusion occasioned, Crazy Horse was stabbed in the abdomen. By whom I cannot say, nor do I think that this is a point which can with satisfaction be determined. There are two conflicting accounts, each sustained by a number of adherents. One is that the sentinel on post No 1, in front of the Guard House, inflicted the fatal thrust;[19] the other, is that Little Big Man, enraged at the wound given him by Crazy Horse, wrenched his stiletto from him and stabbed him. Either story is plausible enough: in either way, the wound could have been made. As the stiletto Crazy Horse had would make a wound like that which caused the death of this truly great man, it was not easy to come to any conclusion from the medical examination to which, of course, the patient was at once subjected. Permission was granted to Crazy Horse's father, to Touch the Clouds, and to other friends of the dying man, to remain by his bedside and to ease his last moments by such friendly offices as he might desire. Crazy Horse spoke but little; he knew that the hand

---

19. In one of his last articles, the late John Carroll wrote that when the commotion began, the guard, Pvt. William Gentles, instinctively raised his rifle. As that moment, Little Big Man grabbed Crazy Horse, who lost his balance and fell against Gentles' bayonet which pierced him through both kidneys. Carroll, "Man Who Killed Crazy Horse," 41.

of death was upon him and with a calmness and fortitude worthy of all praise awaited the approach of the dread messenger.

To such tender inquiries as were addressed to him from time to time, he returned brief answers, but his conversation was laconic as had ever been usual with him.

He said he blamed no one for his death; he had tried to leave the Reservation and escape to the north, and failed. He had intended to kill all he could before leaving; he had tried to kill Little Big man and the soldiers standing near him. He didn't have any ill-will towards them for what they had done.

At midnight, the soul of the Great Implacable took its flight and the last Great Organizer of the North American savages had entered the happy hunting grounds of his people.[20]

I confess that in reading the telegrams conveying the news of his death,[21] I felt, combined with the contentment of knowing that our borders ever for the future to be free from any *extended* war, a sentiment of regret for the gallant savage who had so skilfully [sic] combined against our people all the bands of his widely-scattered nation and resisted with so much science and daring the forces sent against him.

Crazy Horse was greater than Tecumseh; he united in himself all the qualities of a great ruler:—generous to a fault, skilfull, cool in battle, ever in advance of his warriors, his recklessness in the moment of conflict commanded the respect which his shrewdness and sagacity in the council chamber retained. Modesty and reticence were marked features of his character; he was the only perfectly modest Indian Chief I ever saw.

Cocheis, the famous leader of the Arizona Apaches, was a much handsomer man and perhaps equally able as a statesman, but he never attained the eminence of Crazy Horse who swayed the tribes from the Saskatchewan to the North Platte.

In coming years, the encroachments of settlers upon the hunting ranges of the red men will provoke other wars in which many valuable lives will be lost and many millions expended, but the United States will never again be forced to cope with an aborigine who is a

---

20. Bourke's account in *On the Border With Crook* (421–23) does not vary greatly from that given here. Likewise, the eyewitness accounts in Clark, *Killing of Chief Crazy Horse*, may differ in detail, but follow essentially the same scenario. Most agree, however, that Crazy Horse died of a bayonet wound.

21. See Appendix 2.

match in the field for the whole miserable skeleton called its army and in the Council for the shrewdest men Civilization could pit against him.

Much notoriety has been given Sitting Bull: the slender claim of that chieftain to a place in the same rank with Crazy Horse may be shown by the fact that since Crazy Horse's death, his influence has shrunk to a shadow:—all that he had formerly came from Crazy Horse who let the boastful Sitting Bull arrogate to himself a reputation to which he was not entitled.

When Crazy Horse had ceased to breathe, Touch the Clouds laid his hands upon his dead comrade's breast and said, "it is well, he has looked for death and it has come."

The common sense of the Indians at the agencies enabled them to see that Crazy Horse's death was the result of his own folly, and the leading chiefs exerted themselves to allay the excitement among their bands.

The Indians said that Crazy Horse had always told them a bullet couldn't kill him and they looked upon the manner of his taking off as supporting in a great measure the pretensions he had always made as a prophet and great medicine man.

His remains were taken to Spotted Tail Agency for burial: a photograph of the rude grave in which this renowned chieftain now reposes is given on this page.

Crazy Horse's Grave at Camp Sheridan, Neb.

Chapter 5

♦
♦
♦
♦
♦

The Developing Frontier[1]

With no military campaigns, Bourke's routine duties took him not only through the Department of the Platte, but elsewhere in the West as well. He writes virtually nothing of this in On the Border With Crook, or his other published works, yet his observations published here and in Chapter 6 allow us to see how rapidly the West was developing even as mop-up operations continued against various Indian bands.

In Chapter 6, he is impressed with the rapid growth of Denver, at this time less than two decades old, but already a large, cosmopolitan city, whose markets, he notes, "are equalled by but few places in the world. . . . I should say it was far ahead of Omaha in all that concerns a city's comfort & welfare."[2]

---

1. Manuscript volume 25 begins at this point. Although it is listed at West Point as running from August 19 to September 9, 1878, it actually includes material on the Ponca Indians and their legal case against the federal government, in the spring of 1879. The record of Crook's conference with the Ponca leaders appears to have been written at the time, and supplemented later by newspaper clippings, one notation being made as late as December 5, 1880. These are placed in their chronological sequence.
2. Bourke, Diary, 25:63. Denver was created on April 6, 1860, with the merger of the competing villages of Denver and Auraria, both of which had been established about eighteen months earlier. Although the first ten years were sluggish, Denver began to boom in 1870, as a smelting center and railroad hub. In 1880, it had a population of 35,629. See Lamar, *New Encyclopedia*, 296–99.

79

Taking a ride on one of Colorado's famous narrow-gauge mountain railroads, he passed Idaho Springs, "a summer resort, rapidly acquiring prominence on account of its valuable mineral springs, hot and cold," arriving in the mining community of Georgetown. "There were numbers of tourists in Georgetown, ready to go to the Colorado Parks, which are most accessible from this point," he wrote, but added, "reports of a threatened Indian outbreak among the Utes deterred them."[3]

August 19th 1878. General Sherman who had been in Omaha since the preceding day, left for New Mexico. General Crook started same afternoon for the East.

August 20th. Lieut. Schuyler and self took the U.P. train for Salt Lake, under orders to proceed to Camp Douglass.[4] The first day's journey was so similar in its general features to the others already described, that there is no use in doing more than refer to it. It will live long in our memories as one of the most oppressive and sultry of days. The first part of the night was extremely dusty and quite too warm to allow us to sleep with comfort.

August 21st. Had the pleasure of seeing Lieut. [Hayden] Delaney, who had entered train during night at North Platte. The flues in our engine boiler burnt out, causing us a disagreeable detention of several hours. In the seat next to mine in the Pullman car was a very bright and interesting boy not over ten years old, who devoted himself to the care of his almost blind father. He read to him from the guide books and kept on explaining in his childlike, but very quaint way, the various localities of interest and beauty as we passed along.

The boy told me it was their first trip West of the Mississippi and that they were coming on account of his father's health: I was invited to make an examination of his journal which I did to my great pleasure and amusement, astonished occasionally by the boy's shrewdness and perceptiveness.

At Cheyenne, we met Captain and Mrs [Calbraith Perry] Rodgers,[5] Mrs Chambers and her daughter, Major and Mrs. [James?] Gilliss, Lieut. Eaton and Lt. & Mrs. [John Haskell] King. Also met Mr and

    3. Ibid., 25:66.
    4. Camp Douglas (which Bourke often spelled with a double "s") was established in 1862 east of Salt Lake City, to protect the Overland Mail and telegraph, control the Indians of the region, and watch over the Mormons, whose loyalty was suspect. It was upgraded to a fort in 1878. Frazer, *Forts of the West*, 166.
    5. Rodgers was killed by lightning three days later. See p. 84.

Mrs Strahorn, Mr Slack and Dr Corey. Lieut Delaney left us at Cheyenne.

A gentle rain began to fall at Cheyenne and continue throughout the day.

The scenery from Dale creek bridge never looked more charming; the purling brook, one hundred feet beneath us, flowed gently over its rocky beds between banks of fresh verdure and large blocks of granite. This week, an affluent of the South Platte river offers fair sport to the fisherman seeking trout. I think I have elsewhere noted the strange peculiarity that all the waters of the South Platte are trout-bearing, while not one of those flowing from the North Platte contain any, altho' the sources of these respective tributaries are often not more than ten or twenty feet apart.

At Rock creek, Mr [Francis] Wolcott, who had been with us from Cheyenne, left to go to his stock-ranch on Deer Creek, near Fort Fetterman. The increasing importance of the cattle-interests of Wyoming, Montana and Colorado can only be fully appreciated by men like myself who, by travelling constantly in this country keep themselves posted in everything relating to its development. Where only three years ago the hostile Sioux and Cheyenne roamed at will, there are now to be seen thousands and thousands of fine fat cattle peaceably grazing and increasing in value to the undisguised satisfaction of their owners.

The cattle-men of Wyoming rank among her most intelligent and enterprising citizens: not rarely, we meet with men of the stamp of Mr Wolcott, who has been highly educated, has seen much of the world and manifests refined taste and mental cultivation. At his ranch, he has a fine Library, which is used constantly by its owner and his friends.

Finished this afternoon the last volume of Miss [Louisa May] Alcott's *Little Women*, a sweet, natural little story which has given me an exalted opinion, of its author's powers.

Also advanced in the *Annals of a Fortress*, by Viollet Le Duc,[6] the French Engineer. This sketch gives a more comprehensive, bird's-eye view of the successive stages of improvement in the art

---

6. Eugène Emmanuel Viollet-le-Duc (1814–79) was a French architect, whose restorations included the cathedral of Notre Dame in Paris, and the walled city of Carcassonne. *Annals of a Fortress: Twenty-two Centuries of Siege Warfare* has been reprinted many times, into the current century. http://en.wikipedia.org/wiki/Eug%C3%A8ne_Emmanuel_Viollet-le-Duc

of defending and attacking camps and cities than the whole course of Engineering at West Point.

In the Sleeper next to us was a party of Spanish Americans, returning from the Paris Exposition to their homes in Guatemala. I had a little conversation with them and found them bright and entertaining. They gave a very good acc't. of their own country, its resources and commerce; spoke of the rapidly increasing coffee trade with San Francisco and the wish their countrymen had that more Americans might come with their energy, pluck and capital to develop Guatemala.

One of these Spaniards was a Doctor—a very old man—whose services were demanded about dusk by a young lady, (in one of the Pullman cars,) who had made herself sick by an over-indulgence in pea-nuts. It fell upon my lot to act as interpreter while the Doctor prescribed; the young lady was too squeamish to have the Doctor go into her car to see her—an over-delicacy which offended the old gentleman, who thereupon declined giving any advice beyond that of refraining from eating or drinking anything until morning, saying that he couldn't tell what was the matter with the patient until he had seen her—a remark so axiomatic that the gentleman who came to interview the Doctor admitted at once the correctness of the position he had assumed. The young lady recovered during the night much to my relief as I was decidedly perplexed and embarrassed. My Spanish is good enough for any ordinary conversation or to procure for myself anything I desire, but I was afraid that some word or phrase might go wrong while making an interpretation for others, especially in such a critical case as sickness.

Near Evanston passed [R. Lyman] Potter, the "wheel barrow fiend", pushing his barrow towards the Setting Sun, to gain the wager of $1000 that he would walk from ocean to ocean, wheeling a barrow, within 150 days.[7] At Weber, the Mormon girls sold our passengers delicious peaches at exorbitant prices.

7. Bourke's information was not entirely accurate. R. Lyman Potter and L. P. Federmeyer raced by foot from San Francisco to New York, each pushing a loaded wheelbarrow. The combined weight of wheelbarrow and contents could never be less than one hundred pounds. The race was contrived as a publicity stunt by newspaper magnate George Hearst, father of William Randolph Hearst, who offered a $2,000 prize to the winner. A referee was sent ahead to check the weight as each man arrived in town, and validate it with the local postmark. Federmayer won the race, leaving San Francisco on December 8, 1878, and arriving in New York on July 23, 1879, a walk of 4,500 miles in 227 days. http://americahurrah.com/SanFrancisco/Federmeyer.htm

Rained in heavy showers all the afternoon.

Were received at the dépôt in Salt Lake by General [John E.] Smith and Col. Stanton, and by them driven to Camp Douglass. We whiled away a couple of hours in pleasant conversation with the ladies of Colonel Stanton's household and in rummaging among the many fine books in his Library, which certainly excels in numbers as well as in literary and pecuniary value that of any gentleman in this part of the country. A refreshing repose crowned the end of the day and of our journey.

Saturday,[8] August 23. Finished the last few pages of Le Duc's treatise on Fortification.

Colonel Stanton directed my attention to a book lying on the table—*Absaraka, the Land of Massacre*, by Colonel [Henry B.] Carrington of the Army. The book is not badly written, but full of errors calculated to deceive the ignorant and unwary.

Nothing but the insufferable conceit of the author could have suggested the publication of this work. Too much of a coward to see service either during the war or since, he is one of those who trusted to political influence for his appointment and to a restless pen to achieve a reputation.

Officers who served under Colonel Carrington at old Fort Kearney,[9] in 1866, tell me he was known there as a most contemptible coward.[10]

---

8. This is an error. August 23, 1878, was a Friday.

9. Fort Phil Kearny (which Bourke almost inviarably spelled "Kearney") was established in 1866, about fifteen miles north of present city of Buffalo, Wyoming. Together with Forts Reno and C. F. Smith, it was intended to protect the Bozeman Trail. The post was abandoned in 1868, under the terms of the Fort Laramie Treaty, and the Indians then burned the buildings. It is now a Wyoming State Park. Not to be confused with Fort Kearny, Nebraska, which was named in honor of Stephen Watts Kearny. Frazer, *Forts of the West*, 183.

10. *Absaraka, the Land of Massacre* was an attempt by Carrington, who commanded both the post of Fort Phil Kearny and the district, to justify his inaction during the massacre of Capt. William Judd Fetterman and eighty men near the fort on December 21, 1866. Earlier, on December 6, Carrington himself had led a squad of men into essentially the same trap, and had barely escaped. This made a profound impression on him, and he later claimed he verbally ordered Fetterman to stay within range of support, although no one else heard the order. Carrington was roundly criticized for failing to relieve Fetterman, even though those in the fort could hear the distant gunfire. In fact, Fetterman's departure with eighty men had so reduced the garrison as to render it vulnerable. It should be remembered that in 1866, Congress was in the midst of massive post-Civil War reductions in the army, and the garrison strength of Phil Kearny suffered accordingly. Carrington's requests for additional support were received with indifference by his superior, Bvt. Maj. Gen. Philip St. George Cooke, who nevertheless pressured him for an offensive operation against the Indians. Besides allegations of cowardice stemming from the massacre itself, virtually all the officers of the garrison formed an anti-Carrington faction; most had distinguished themselves as combat soldiers during the Civil War, while Carrington spent the war behind a desk. Additionally, many officers of the Regular Army never really understood Indian fighting, and Fetterman's total contempt for Plains Indian military strength and tactics was another key factor in his destruction.

Drove to Salt Lake City and visited the Museum. This is a repository of relics, illustrative of Utah's history and progress. Much trash has been accumulated, but the careful student can find several hours' work in examining the specimens of the stone age, pottery, fossils and Indian trinkets: of the last named, the collection, although small was quite good. I noticed some fine baskets from Arizona; these are woven so tight that they will hold water: pottery from New Mexico, Arizona, Colorado and Utah, the older specimens showing a great advance over the newer, which in some cases it could be seen had been made over baskets as moulds, while the former had evidently been manufactured on a wheel: stone implements, such as "metates" for grinding corn and crushing seeds;[11] pestles, hammers and axes, garments of various kinds, (made of skin,) I found bones of "mammoth" and buffalo. The great numbers of fossil bones of the buffalo found within the limits of Utah, shows that the "habitat" of this animal once extended far to the West of the Rocky Mountains.

The curator of the museum told me the Indians had a tradition that once upon a time a great many seasons ago, there came a very heavy and long-continued cold spell which caused all the buffalo to die.

From the museum went to some of the stores, with which Salt Lake is so abundantly supplied. Having already described several of these in my notes of last year, I shall merely say that the business of the present season appeared to be decidedly brisk, altho storekeepers generally complained of dull times.[12]

August 24th. We were horrified to read in the dispatches in the *Salt Lake Tribune* an account of the death by a stroke of lightning, of Captain Rodgers, 5th Cavalry, an old and esteemed friend. The dread calamity occurred while in his tent on the road between Rock Creek and Fort Fetterman. He had taken refuge in his tent to escape a fearful rain-storm; with him were to Indian (Arapahoe,) scouts, one on each side. The bolt struck Rodgers at the base of the skull

---

Whether Carrington did order Fetterman to stay within range of support is academic. There was enough blame to go around, although Carrington was the convenient scapegoat. See Dee Brown, *The Fetterman Massacre*, and Utley, *Frontier Regulars*, Chapter 7.

11. The *metate* is a flat slab of stone, about twelve inches long, the top surface of which has been smoothed, used as a bed for grinding corn. The grinding stone, or *mano* (literally: "hand") is shaped like a rolling pin and used in generally the same manner. *Metates* and *manos* still are used in Mexico and the American Southwest.

12. There are substantial gaps in Bourke's diaries for 1877–78, and he may be referring to observations in the lost volumes. He does, however, describe Salt Lake City at length in 1875. This may be found in Robinson, *Diaries*, Vol. 1, Chapter 7.

and ran down his back and legs, burning his body in a curious way, as if he had been sitting upon a hot gridiron. Poor Rodgers was one of the most popular young Captains in the Army, had seen much [that was] valuable, acquired a distinguished reputation and was held in high esteem by superiors, associates and inferiors.

At breakfast, the one topic of conversation was the sad fate of our friend:—indeed, we made very little breakfast at all, scarcely tasting the fine melons, plums, peaches and grapes Mrs. Stanton had prepared for us. In my opinion, the Salt Lake Valley will before long become a formidable competitor of California in the fruit market.

Surgeon [Bennett A.] Clements invited me to visit his Hospital. It is a large structure of red sandstone with fine, broad porticoes and spacious surroundings. The ventilation is perfect and accomodations excellent. The number of patients is always small, owing to the salubrity of the climate. From the second story, the view obtained of Salt Lake and the city is very attractive. It is the intention to surround the Hospital next year with a row of shade trees and to sow the sertilage [sic] in grass seeds, which improvements will add not a little to the charms of the place.

Doctor Clements and I had a long talk about our previous experience together in the campaign of 1876,[13] and of his first entry into the valley of the Salt Lake, 20 yrs. ago, when he marched with General Albert Sidney Johnston's Command through the Timponague Cañon which the Doctor pronounced one of the finest genic scenery in the world.[14] As this is a place I hope to be able to visit soon I hope to supplement with [the] Doctor's very interesting description with my own notes.

As a pleasant means of passing our day, drove to town and then to the Warm Springs for a bath; these Springs contain Carbonate of Lime, Chlorine and Hydrochloric Acid, Sulphur, Carbonic and Sulphuric Acids, and other chemicals, and remain at a uniform temperature of 120°F. They bear in many points a decided resemblance to the Warm Springs near Camp Brown, Wyo and like them give to the bather a sensation of coolness, freshness, and cleanliness, but not altogether free from languor.

13. See Clements' report in Robinson, *Diaries*, Volume 2, Appendix 2.
14. This refers to Johnston's expedition to Utah in 1858–60, which resulted in the replacement of Brigham Young as governor with Alfred Cumming. Utley, *Encylcopedia of the American West*, 302; Thrapp, *Encyclopedia of Frontier Biography*, 2:735.

At the Townsend House, called upon Mr. Hart of Chicago, a friend of my friend, Col. Farrar, and a gentleman whom I had the pleasure of meeting at the Chicago Club, this Spring.

Sunday, August 25th Breakfast over, we gathered on the porch to listen to the music of the band at Inspection and Guard Mounting, and to look upon the picturesque valley spreading out for miles beneath us.

Lieut. Schuyler started on a bear hunt, intending to travel about twenty miles up the Cañon and to remain out all night.

Colonel Stanton and I not having lost any bears and being somewhat blasé on the subject anyhow, thought a day's quiet would be good enough for the likes of us, especially since we had both been bone tired and had never gotten entirely rested. The chances of seeing and shooting a bear were so slim and the attractions of the Library so great that the latter prevailed. I finished the perusal of Sir Thomas More's *Utopia*, a book to be read more on account of its great author than for any especial artistic merit in its construction; so far as the latter is to be regarded De Foe's *Robinson Crusoe*, Rev. Hale's "Man Without a Country," and some of Jules Verne's works display much more realistic power than can be discerned in the *Utopia*, and had they been written in the credulous age in which the *Utopia* appeared,—I mean to use the term credulous only so far as it implies a willingness to swallow every wonderful story travellers might choose to tell of the newly explored regions of American & Africa,—they would have been accepted as true by the greater part of Europe.

By one thing in the *Utopia*, I was greatly surprised and pleased—the fluidity of style, the easy-rolling sentences, perfectly comprehensible by the humblest reader of our vain day. The praise for such a work must indeed be great, since the fashion of that Age was to write all learned treatises in Latin, and Roger Ascham, Queen Elizabeth's instructor, a contemporary with or perhaps subsequent to Sir Thomas More, devoted his abilities, in a work called the *Schoolmaster*, to demonstrate the propriety and wisdom of writing for the English people in the English Language![15] The *Utopia* was dedicated to

---

15. Roger Ascham (1515–68), sometimes called the most likeable of the early humanists, served as tutor to Queen Elizabeth I, and upon her accession became her secretary. *The Schoolmaster* (the Elizabethan title is *The Scholemaster*) was a treatise on education begun in 1563, and published posthumously in 1570. Sir Thomas More's work introduced the word "Utopia" as an earthly paradise. It describes a fictional voyage by a Portuguese navigator to

Erasmus of Rotterdam, the great Reformer, who held it and its great author in paramount esteem. Yet here were Stanton and myself, two pygmies, dissecting and criticizing the thoughts, and ideas of two men whose shoes we would not be worthy to latch; probably on the same principle that a musquito [sic] thinks he is entitled to bite an elephant, if he wants to.

Utah's mining resources are rapidly developing and drawing in among the Mormons, who confine themselves exclusively to agriculture and manufactures, a new class of people,—miners, speculators and frontiersmen, who make and lose money with a rapidity that is something astonishing. The "Antonio" mine near here has just paid its 32nd dividend within 19 mos., each dividend being 50 c[ents]. A share and the number of shares being, I think, 100.000.

Other leads promise yields fully as large altho' not yet developed to so great an extent. This morning, I heard a story, of a Mr. Keyser, a successful miner in Brigham Cañon who has just been married. He has more money than education and is, if the truth must be told, somewhat behind in his knowledge of etiquette. Having made up his mind to take up his cross, he naturally consulted a friend whom he asked to "help him out." "Certainly, old man, what can I do for you?". Well, said Keyser, whose notions of the necessary ceremonies were somewhat confused, "*I want you to give me away*". The friend, like the good fellow he was, promised to do all that was required, and nobly fulfilled his word. The bride, of course, looked charming and the groom, poor wretch, was declared by the old women to be the very image of happiness. The friend stood by his side "to give him away", and when the Judge had pronounced the formula which sealed away his bachelor happiness, the newly-made husband rushed to the door and shouted down the narrow lane of grog-shops, dead-falls and gambling hells which formed the town—"turn 'em loose, set 'em up for the boys", whereupon the expectant bartenders began to dispense over their counters to the eager throng of thirsty customers all the forms of Hell-Fire whiskey, French Brandy, (from Oshkosh,) and Port Wine, (from Milwaukee,) and other deadly

---

the mythical island of Utopia, where a communal people governed themselves in peace and harmony. It has certain parallels to the late Medieval *Amadis de Gallia* and James Hilton's later *Lost Horizon*. More, who was executed on a matter of religious principle during the reign of King Henry VIII, had not yet been canonized by the Roman Catholic Church, or doubtless Bourke would have referred to him as "St. Thomas More." http://www.luminarium.org/renlit/aschbio.htm

beverages, which from not immediately killing the inhabitants of these mountains have caused the climate to be regarded as one of the salubrious wonders of the world. If the firing of revolvers, yells of drunken men, howling of dogs and music! of such instruments as were available would serve as a criterion, the wedding might be pronounced a grand success; not so "toney" as if held in a 5th Avenue Mansion, but much more hearty and enthusiastic.

While mentioning mining resources, I should say that the Sulphur deposits of Southern Utah will soon be made available. There is much talk even now of establishing a manufactory of Sulphuric Acid in Salt Lake. Sulphuric acid is used to a great extent in manufactures, principally in the preparation of Carbonate of Soda, but Sulphur itself is needed for making matches, for bleaching and dying establishments and commands at all times a very remunerative price.

Dined to-dy with Lt. and Mrs. [William W. Mc]Cammon, who had as their other guests Captain Alfred Smith, 8th Infantry, and his sister, Mrs. Bascom, (son and daughter of General John E. Smith, post commandant.) And Miss Lindsay of Salt Lake.

Went to divine service in the evening and listened to a very good sermon from Chaplain [Thomas B.] Van Horn, one of the worthy and earnest men of his grade in the Army.

The public journals are discussing affairs on the Rio Grande and General Mackenzie's raids into Mexico—are regarded generally as the prelude to more serious complications. A war with Mexico is almost inevitable.

We have one of three courses to pursue: we must crush Mexico completely, a system of action repugnant to the dictates of humanity: we must render it tributary, which would be antagonistic to republican government, or we must occupy it and absorb its population. This last plan is the only one by which we can hope to succeed and yet it is the one most difficult of prosecution. With (3) or four strong columns of invasion, aggregating a greater of a million of men, we could within two years be able to plant *strong colonies*, at eligible points, connected together and with our Rio Grande and Rio Gila systems by Rail Road and telegraphs and with these fortified colonies as foci we could easily establish such relations of commerce and manufactures with the Mexicans as would make our possession of their Territory not alone tolerant but agreeable. Intercourse with these colonies would make the Mexicans see the necessity of having their children taught our language and with a knowledge of our language would naturally come to desire to learn more of our customs. By strictly respecting the religious convictions of the people, by encouraging marriages between *American* men and *Mexican* women and above all by establishing a secure and remunerative market for all Mexican supplies, we could it seems to me, soon reduce and pacify and even do much to *Americanize* our *Spanish-Indian* neighbors.

The student will see that some of my ideas have been borrowed from Machiavelli, whose *Prince* I have just perused with much pleasure and profit.

I give as my opinion that Machiavelli is one of the best abused and least understood authors that have [*sic*] ever written. His treatise upon Government, (*the Prince*) is a very exact description of the method employed by sovereigns in the administration of their Kingdoms; and where censure has most been levelled against Machiavelli has been just where he least deserved it, unless he be deemed a fit subject for reprehension on the same principle that a skillful painter should be criticized for depicting the blemishes in the countenances of his sitters.

In one chapter, however, Machiavelli avows that princes are not bound to fulfil their promises:—it was the acceptance of this idea which cost Charles 1st his head.[16]

Monday, Aug.[26] To my great relief, Schuyler returned from his bear hunt: knowing the ferocious character of these monsters of the mountains, we had not been without forebodings during the whole time of our comrade's absence and seeing him return to us safe and sound, we plied him with questions which for some moments, such was his modesty in speaking of his own prowess he was disinclined to answer. Importunity finally overcame reluctance and obtained the following outline of a most thrilling and blood-curdling adventure. Schuyler, with the soldier who was to act as his guide, had proceeded up the cañon not more than five miles when they came to the lodges of some wood-choppers and charcoal burners who confirmed the

---

16. *The Prince* is a dissertation on government by the Florentine civil servant Niccolô di Bernardo dei Machiavelli (1469–1527), consisting of political theory and advice based on his study of public policy throughout history. Machiavelli's basic thesis is that a ruler should govern according to realistic needs and conditions rather than altruism, and avoid radical changes that might unsettle the citizenry. Bourke's reference to King Charles I is a poor example, because Charles I attempted to impose absolute rule as a matter of royal prerogative, whereas Machiavelli cautioned that absolutism is valid only if it serves a practical purpose.

story that bears had lately been seen in their vicinity. With renewed precautions our young hero and his companion, pushed along up the difficult path to the summit of the range where all traces of a bye-way disappeared and further progress was only possible by breaking through a matted jungle of stunted undergrowth. While doing this a crackling of branches was heard and, horror of horrors! two ferocious, blood-seeking monsters were dashing towards them and not two hundred yards away.

The soldier started to run, seeing that by remaining they would be at a disadvantage, but Schuyler stood to his post, resolved to die bravely sooner than flee.

His face blanched and drops of cold perspiration stood upon his brow: he thought of his home, so far away, and the sweetheart who would wildly howl to the mail-carrier for a letter from her darling who had been lunched upon by a bear in the Wahsatch and consequently wasn't very likely to continue the correspondence. It is a terrible thing to be torn to pieces and devoured by a wild animal—and Schuyler felt that nothing but a miracle could save him from such a fate, but *the miracle occurred*. The bears turned out to be two nanny-goats which had escaped from a herd in the Valley, and run wild in the mountains. Schuyler bore with philosophic resignation all our banking upon the subject and said he would willingly trust to Time, which he knew one day would give him the laugh upon us.

After breakfast, General Smith took me about the post, to the Company Quarters, to the warehouse of the Q.M. Dep't., (where we saw a large pile of corn which had spoiled from having heated, because bought when too new,) then to the Guard-House and finally to the Ordnance Magazine. This last is of stone, with wooden pent roof and remarkably dry; no chloride of Calcium or other chemical has to be used to keep away dampness. We put on India-rubber shoes before entering, and then proceeded to examine the ammunition: there is a large quantity of this, as well as guns & equipments belonging to the Territory of Utah stored here for protection. The field guns, carriages and limbers belonging to the post are of antiquated patterns, worn out and worthless except to ornament the parade-ground and perhaps for moral effect. The vents of the guns are extremely large. Much obsolete ammunition and other Ordnance stores have accumulated here since the establishment of the post by General [Patrick] Connor, in 1862.

General Smith wants to put a fence around the [military] Reservation, to prevent petty depredations now so frequent; to plant a row of trees about the parade and to fill in with water and make a lake out of some ugly ravines which now disfigure the post. These improvements will greatly enhance the beauty of the reservation. With $15.000 and the labor obtainable from a garrison of six cos. which he considers to be the about the normal strength of the post, he feels confident of being able to complete it in all its details and make Camp Douglass, a credit to the service.

He expressed himself much in favor of the idea that Regimental Commanders should be ordered twice each year to inspect the Companies of their respective Regiments with a view of learning of their discipline and tone.

In the evening, Colonel Stanton, Lieut Schuyler and I took a little walk going out as far as the pretty cemetery of the post, where rest the remains of many brave soldiers, a great percentage were killed or died of wounds received in actions with the hostile Utes and Shoshonees who infested this region during our civil war.

A monolith of sandstone commemorates the services of the California and Nevada Volunteers who did such hard work here under General Connor.[17] The roll of dead was quite large as was also that inscribed under the carved heading—"Killed while on vidette duty".

A neat sandstone wall had been built across the enclosure, but this is at present much disfigured because some of the people living close to the post have been in the habit of sneaking up, during dark nights and carrying away the capping stone which they use for building material.

At night, we went to a largely advertised ["]Spiritualistic Manifestation". The crowd was great and the collection of money quite large. As far as the performance itself, too much cannot be given to the managers, for the dexterity with which bells were rung, tambourines played, guitars twanged &c. &c. &c., by a lady sitting with hands bound inside a cabinet, closed by a curtain.

17. This refers to troops under Col. Patrick E. Connor, Third California Infantry, commander of the District of Utah and Nevada. Connor established Camp Douglas in 1862, to put down Indian raids, and also to oversee the Mormons whose loyalty was suspect. Connor's troops defeated the Bannocks and Shoshones in Idaho in January 1863, effectively ending the Indian disturbances and opening the region to settlement. He also suppressed the Utes and Gosiutes, who he suspected were being encouraged to raid by the Mormons. For this he was promoted to brigadier general of Volunteers. Thrapp, *Encyclopedia of Frontier Biography*, 1:308–9; Utley, *Frontiersmen in Blue*, 222–26.

There was no "materialization", and if there had been, as our party was armed with glass-pipes and plenty of putty, we confidently relied upon our ability to rout the spirits without much trouble. The audience was unusually turbulent and demonstrative: cat-calls, whistling, yells and cries of all kinds filled the air, but finally impatience gave way to hilarity and it looked as if each spectator was doing his best to make the exhibition ridiculous. There was a committee appointed from the audience of four persons who did their full duty in inspecting the cabinet, tying knots and such work, but nothing would satisfy the jolly concourse of hoodlums in the galleries. Each time that Mr. Bishop, the manager would announce that a trick had been concluded and that the Committee reported they found the knots still tied, he would add in his blandest tone: "Ladies and Gentlemen! Can I do anything more for you?" Then fierce would come the howls from scores of throats:—"shoot the committee"! which would set everyone to laughing so heartily that nothing could be seen or done for the next five minutes. An old man, very wise in his own conceit, but very officious and stupid in the view of the audience, made himself a nuisance by pushing forward with the Committee to examine, and by standing in the way and obstructing business. Some one in the audience roared out, "won't somebody please kill that old man?", which exasperated him so much that he drew out a card and called to the audience that there was his name as well as his address for anybody who would like to try the job. As might be understood, this increased the din and uproar to a frightful extent: cries of "oh! shoot that old man! Shoot his spectacles!" and others of like ridiculous import, rent the air: the boys in the gallery squealed, kicked, screamed and howled.—and in the midst of the turmoil, we retired almost sick with laughing.

Tuesday. Colonel Stanton, Lieut [Charles Henry] Warrens, Lt. Schuyler and myself started in ambulance about 9 a.m., moved rapidly up Valley of Salt Lake, which appeared to good advantage with its multitude of thrifty farms; about six miles from post turned in to Parley Park Cañon, which has pretty scenery, but nothing to compare with that which we saw in American Fork Cañon last year. The road up this cañon is very narrow; much difficulty is experienced in passing wagons. Met a number of wagons, loaded with coal from Coalville, near the head of Weber creek which rises near Parley Park. The seam from which the coal is taken is almost eight feet wide and yields an inexhaustible supply of good, hard, merchantable fuel to the people of Salt Lake. The cost of transporting it in wagons down from the Mtns. raises its value very much before reaching its market, where it commands eight dollars per ton. The construction of a narrow gauge tramway, either for steam or horse power, to this coal ledge would reduce the price in Salt Lake at least one half and be a good, paying investment for the capitalist who might engage in it. At 11 o'clock, halted to give our animals, rest, water and a nibble of grass. Passed up the cañon to the "divide", where we entered Parley's Park, a mountain meadow, about 2 miles in Diameter, producing a good grass, but not suited for fruits, vegetables or the cereals, (being too cold.)

Did not see any great quantity of timber: a few pine, balsam firs and red pine on the crests of the ridges and some quaking asp[en] in Parley Park.

Descended into the valley of Ontario Creek by a gentle grade and after a ride of 30 miles drove up in front of the McHenry House, [at] Ontario Gulch, or Park city, as it is commonly called. This "city" is a straggling line of frame shanties on either side of a narrow ravine; some of the houses are neat but generally rough and unfinished looking. (The water from the gulch flows to a branch of Weber creek.)

A stroll of half a mile brought us to the Ontario Mill where we hunted up the Superintendent to whom I presented our letter of introduction from Mr. Chambers, one of the principal owners.

Our letter secured us a very cordial reception and we at once began the tour of the immense building, the asst. superintendent explaining as he went along, the uses and purposes of the machinery, the value of each particular grade of ore and the method of its reduction. The "Oneida" ledge is 3000 ft. long, between one and two feet wide, and has been developed to a depth of 500 feet: the ore runs from $100 to $200 to the ton, and enough ore is "in sight" to keep the mill going for two years. Forty stamps are at work, run by a (250) horse power Engine, [(]made in San Francisco,) with a sixteen foot Driving Wheel and a 5 ft. by 20 in. cylinder.

The entire cost of mill was $250.000.[18]

This company employs (165) men, but gives indirectly occupation to about 300.

18. The dollar of that era was roughly $12–13 in modern currency.

The monthly expenses are $30.000; the monthly gross yield $125.000 to $145.000, leaving for a net yield to be distributed in dividends $95.000 to $115.000 monthly. Shares are now worth about $50 each. The stamps are old-fashioned and crush only about 50 Tons per diem, which is only half of what can be accomplished by the new model.

The ore is a friable and decomposed quartz, very easily milled. Ten tons of coal, (worth $8.50 per ton,) are consumed each day and the same number of cords of wood. The mill runs Sunday and Monday, as to stop it would cost the company not less than $3.000.
The whole theory of reduction may be simply stated in a few words; the ore must be crushed to a fine powder and incorporated with quicksilver which takes up the precious metals, from which it is afterwards separated by sublimation.

The ore is first put through the "rock-crusher", a proceeding which seemed to me to be unnecessary, such was the soft, clayey condition of the material: afterwards, it is run under the stamps which grind it speedily to such a fineness that it will sift through wire-screens, with meshes 2500 to the inch; it is then looked upon as fit for the "amalgam pans" and is so hot that it will almost burn the fingers.
The "amalgam pans" are large, cylindrical vats, each of which is charged with (3000) pounds of the levigated ore and 300 pounds of Quicksilver. By the revolution of flat, circular iron plates about vertical axes, (the pans being filled up with water,) the mixture is agitated and the mercury speedily combines with the precious metals.

The whole contents of the "pans" are now run off into another and lower set, called the "condensers", in which, by the principle of decantation the earthy matters are separated from the "amalgam", the former running off with the water from the top and the latter running out at the bottom into tubs with canvass bottoms which allow the uncombined mercury to run into receptacles provided for it, while the amalgam is kept until it *hardens*, (which is a sign that it has gathered up all the silver it is able to hold.) And there is carried to the "retorts", which sublime the mercury and leave the silver to be run into coarse blocks. (The mercury is afterwards condensed and saved for future use.)

This is an outline of the process employed, without dwelling upon the various appliances for measuring "charges" of mercury &c.

When the ore contains much "base metal", it must first be roasted: this is a very curious operation, the finely pulverized rock being thrown down *through* a sort of reverberatory furnace, where fierce flames seize upon it and burn out every trace of sulphuret. The value of the silver lost by this mill is something to wonder; nearly half in fact, so that ores which "assay" $200 to the Ton, don't "work" over $100. An immense pile of "tailings", said to be worth $100.000 to $150.000 has been collected below the mill and here an industrious Swede works, by permission of the Company to which he pays ($10) per diem for the concession. It is said he makes $75 daily, by using a kind of "concentrator", which saves much of the silver.

    Returning to the McHenry House, we were surprised to find an excellent bill of fare, comprising various kinds of fresh fruit, 3 or 4 styles of meat and as many of vegetables, well cooked and served and all for the reasonable price of 50 c[ents].
After dark, we drove to Kimballs' Ranch, down the Parley Park cañon, some six miles. Here we were presented to a party of young Mormon ladies, among them Miss Jennings whom I met in Salt Lake last year.
They did their best to make the evening pass agreeably, entertaining us with a number of sweet and tender ballads, sung with good expression, and with conversation which showed them to be well-educated, intelligent and observing. I could not help feeling sorry to think that the future of these bright, pure-minded girls would very probably be ruined by a polygamous union, without happiness or even worldly advantage.
Mr. Kimball, the father, came to this valley in 1848 and got his first start in the world by hauling freight for General Johnston's column in 1857.
Wednesday. August 28th. Perhaps, I ought to give here a glowing account of our fishing excursion and go into ecstasies over the clear stream, with the schools of finny beauties, delightful weather and all that sort of thing; but I cannot. In plain prose, we got up long before sun-rise, worked our way up the creek through wet grass which soaked our feet, and ankles, failed to get a single bite before the rays of the sun had struck the water and then caught only such wee little bits of things that Schuyler threw one or two of his back into the water. I didn't take any rod with me: a fortunate circumstance, as there was not fish enough to go around. What little I know

of the habits of trout will keep me from ever going after them before daylight. They are the most curious of fish in some respects that I have ever seen: no one rule will do on two separate occasions. The fisherman has to study the inhabitants of each pond or creek and learn their ways before he can hope for much success.

The stream itself is a beautiful one: no trees to bother you, no bushes to catch the line and water so clear that everything can be seen in it as if a mirror.

Passed one fine spring on our way home and stopped for lunch at another which poured out a larger stream of pure icy-cold water across the road.

A fine view was presented by the sun's setting behind the Oquirrh Mtns. The clouds lazily floating in the Western horizon gleamed like burnished gold & the contrast of purple peaks and gloomy, cavernous valleys was very effective.

Made our farewell calls on the ladies of the garrison. Passed the evening at the Quarters of Colonel [Frank Eugene] Trotter, with all the officers of the Post:—an enjoyable Bachelors' party.

Chapter 6

Sojourn in the Mountains and a Visit to Denver

Thursday, August 29th. Bade farewell to our good friends, the Stantons and started at 6 in the morning for Salt Lake, to take the train for the East. On the cars, fell into conversation with a gentleman from Arizona; his description of the overt progress made in that Territory amazed me greatly. He showed me a mining map [marking] the locations of the various ledges, mills &c. in what are known as the "Globe", ["]Mineral" and "Pinal" districts.
I scouted all over that region in 1870-1-2-3, when it was the chosen haunt of the Apaches, who defied every effort of our Government to subdue them until General Crook was sent to take the field against them. How well his work was done, it is not necessary here to say, but for his important services, Crook was made Brigadier General in response to the demands of the whole Pacific Coast. It was with great interest that I listened to the account of the progress of a Territory which in my day was such a wild and hostile region.

The Yellow Fever, the papers still tell us, is making deadly advances in Louisiana, Mississipi [sic], and Tennessee. All communication, except telegraphic, with the infected cities is cut off: we read of whole towns depopulated, abandoned by their terror-stricken inhabitants; of families dying without medical attendance, of dead bodies lying unburied and of all the other horrible accompaniments of the Plague.

On the train received a telegram from Major Thornburgh, asking me to go with him as far East as Hazard, Wyo., and there meet the train, upon which would be his brother, (Congressman Thornburgh.) Postmaster-General Key and others.

When the trains met, we entered the special car in which we found the Postmaster General and family, Mr. and Mrs. Thornburgh, Mr. Harrison and the rest. None of the party, except Mr. Thornburgh impressed me as being of much depth. The Postmaster-General looked like a plain, bluff farmer, of no great intellectual powers. It has been my misfortune, perhaps that none of the public men whom I have met of late years, have been of a high mental average; some few, like General Grant, for instance, as powerful-minded, honest of purpose, and endowed with good, common sense.

Returned to Fort Steele, with the Postmaster General's party. Mr. Herbert Thayer and I occupied same seat and as old friends passed the hours in pleasant talk until we reached his home at Rock Creek station.

At Fort Sanders, the 2nd [?] Infantry Band played a complimentary march and the officers and ladies of the Garrison came to the train to pay their respects to the Postmaster General and the ladies with him.

Sunday, Sept. 1st. Major Thornburgh, Lieut. [James Herbert] Spencer and Lieut. Bourke, with a small party of soldiers, left Fort Steele for a visit to the "pinery", 50 m. off in the mountains. We journeyed due South keeping in the valley of the North Platte which we crossed, about a mile South of the post and then took across the bluffs, leaving the river between 1½ and 2 miles to the Right (West.) Seven miles out, came to Stockwell's Ranch, where we had to cross Pass creek, a bright little tongue of water joining North Platte. At this ranch there is also a very fine spring. At Bennett's (or Forney's) ranch 22 miles from Fort Steele, halted to change teams and to take lunch. The scenery thus far had been tame; the Mtns. to the east of us, i.e. the range comprising Elk, Sheep and Sheridan (or Agassiz.) Mtns. looked in grander proportions than when gazed at from the Rail Road, but did not appear very attractive from the absence of timber. In the valley of the North Platte, which we had once more entered[,] a straggling fringe of cottonwood lined the banks, but no other trees were to be discerned. Our line of direction had been nearly South all day. Lunch was soon ready and our little party had appetite enough to enjoy it. We were all dirty and uncouth in appearance and probably as much on that account as any other felt a mutual "trampy", brotherly regard. With feet cocked on table, hats on head, faces sun-burned and hands crusted with dust, we, that is today the gentlemen, "Tom", the settler, and the young boy who cooked (!) for the march, enjoyed the tempting lunch of cold beef sandwiches, apples and whiskey toddy produced from our huge baskets; there was enough for ourselves and the drivers of our conveyances. We didn't take long to finish our meal and without great delay were again whirling along the road behind a fresh team.

Immediately after leaving Bennett's we forded the North Platte once again, and kept up its valley, close to the stream, not more than 2 miles at farthest from it until we came to Jack creek, like all the other tributaries, of good size and sweet, cold water. After crossing Jack creek, our course made a greater angle with that of the river. A few miles farther on, we crossed both forks of Hot Spring creek then Cow creek and finally Calf creek, wh[ich]. joins it. There were one or two springs of considerable volume of cold, clear water, and there is said to be a fine Hot Spring, a short distance off the road, at the head of the creek of the same name.

Major Thornburgh did some fine Shooting at long range, but altho' we could see he hit an antelope, (at 350-400 yards.) the animal got away. A Hawk on the wing was not so fortunate; as he was sailing over our heads, a bullet from the major's rifle pierced him through the body and felled him to the ground. Excepting this shooting our itinerary of this day would have been void of incident, had not Lt. Spencer's wagon run into a chuck-hole and sent him flying into the air: I was afraid he was going to be seriously hurt, but Spencer was quick as a cat and landed on his feet with the skill of an acrobat.

Crossing Calf creek, we saw that we had entered the timber line: our path became steeper, road rougher and pine trees began to cluster thickly about us. Before half an hour had elapsed, we reached the camp made by our advance party and dismounted from our wagons. This camp was happily located on a shelving bench, giving fine drainage, alongside of a sparkling little brook (joining Calf creek.) and at the feet of noble, shady firs and pines, through whose topmost branches the wild winds of the mountains sang paîans of never-ending gladness. A stroll around our bivouac led me to see some pretty good grass close by for our horses, and to examine the icy, crystalline waters of the little streamlet which was to be our water-supply for drinking and our mirror for the toilet. This last idea is strictly poetical; the water was too cold and we too indifferent to make much of a toilet. Our men had killed a couple of antelope and a hare before we arrived and thus secured an abundance of good meat. While we were enjoying the fine view spread below us in the valley almost to Ft. Steele, the cooks were busy in preparing supper to which we were quickly called. Fried antelope, fried potatoes, bread, butter and coffee, all washed down with a fine julep Maj. Thornburgh concocted from the wild mint growing along the banks of the creek, made, with our appetites and good humor, a finer supper than Delmonico ever spread before a guest.

After supper, Major Thornburgh, one of the finest rifle shots in *America*, hit with a rifle, 5 times in succession, a condensed milk can which Lt. Spencer threw up in the air for him to shoot at, and also knocked into kingdom come a five cent nickel, under same circumstances. This was about as good marksmanship as I had ever seen. Thornburgh was born in the mountains of E. Tennessee where, as he told me, he used to take part in the shooting matches, which had for the centre of the bull's eye a silver dime. The best shots would hit this (3) times out of 5, at one hundred yards and that too with a rifle so rudely made that the marks of the village blacksmith's hammer were yet discernible in the barrel.

Our tent was pitched under the spreading pines whose resinous odors are to match the sweetest perfume, but, altho' we were greatly refreshed by the cool air of the night, none of our party could get to sleep until nearly daylight, the coffee being so strong that it kept us from closing our eyes. Towards morning, the air became so chilly that the shelter of *four* blankets was most acceptable and we gladly hugged the buffalo robes that made our coverlets.

Monday. Sept. 2nd. At a very early hour, before sunrise, Major Thornburgh awakened the camp. The air was very crisp, and a heavy frost whitened the grass. We had had a "running" guard of one sentinel all night to look after stock and guard against fire. The active cooks soon had breakfast hissing on the fire and said we should have just about time enough to wash our hands before finding our meal ready. So to the brook we went with rather gruesome countenances, the water being cold as ice and our fingers and cheeks tingling with fire after our rough ablutions had been finished.

Breakfast over,—and it was a palatable meal eaten with hunger and good-humor as our only sauce—the work of the day was laid out in felling a straight and shapely pine, whose future destiny was to grace the parade-ground of Fort Steele, as a flag-staff.

Muscular arms and horny hands were already swinging the sounding axe: a few moments hard work and the lofty trunk began to tremble; the cutters redoubled their blows; a crash is heard, the tree bends gracefully a few inches, stops for one instant, bends still more, pauses again for perhaps a second and then with a loud groan falls prostrate to the ground.

Its beautiful branches, like the tresses of a lovely woman, form its chief beauty; but the remorseless axe has already stripped them from the parent trunk, which in a very business-like way, has been measured and found to run a little over (110) feet in length and four in circumference at the butt.

While the axemen were stripping off the bark and rough-hewing the mainmast, the rest of our camp had an exciting hunt after a bad-tempered rattlesnake which had made a spring for one of our men near the brook.

We pursued him with axes, branches of trees & shot-guns, but he eluded our efforts and took refuge in the impenetrable jungle in the darker recesses of the Forest.

A march of ten miles, over the mountains in a Southerly direction, climbing nearly all the way over steep mountains covered thickly with burnt and fallen timber, brought us to a beautiful lake, whose waters find their way through Battle creek and Green River to the Colorado of the West. On this march, we passed several important tributaries of the North Platte, the principal one being Cow creek, upon a streamlet joining which I think I have already noted our camp was situate[d]. Close by the bank of this lake, there is a little log shanty, erected by mining prospectors who, no doubt were induced to explore these mountains by the great quantities of "float" quartz visible on our trail yesterday and to-day.

In this cabin, pasted or tacked to the walls, are a series of cards, recording the names of the few hardy adventurers who have penetrated to this asylum either for pleasure or profit.

The lakelet is a gem in its way; the very difficulty of access to it

I think adds not a little to its beauty when you finally clamber to its rocky shore and look across the lengthening expanse of water. The hills closing in about it are covered with pine timber, most of it burned or blown down in the great conflagerations which swept these mountains, 5, maybe 10 years ago, destroying hundreds and thousands of acres of excellent fuel, within sight of the ranches along the U.P.R.R., to whose inhabitants it would have proved of such great value.

It was nearly sunset when we got to the lakelet, but before supper our party of five, (i.e. Major Thornburgh, Lt. Spencer, Privates Rodman and Tupan and myself.) had caught enough trout for supper that night and breakfast the next morning. My catch was the smallest of all—only twelve—as I broke my line and a fish ran away with my hook—but the others caught all the way from 35–50 each.

For the night, we made down our bedding under a clump of pine trees, close to a bubbling spring and convenient to good pasturage for our animals. Major Thornburgh made all hands a cheering toddy and then we lay down to a rest, but not immediately to sleep. The bright stars twinkling in the sky were so bright and lovely, no one thought of sleeping and there we lay for several hours chatting about any subject that presented itself and each declaring that the ceiling of our sleeping apartment was ornamented more grandly than any we had ever seen.

Tuesday. Sept. 3rd. Another heavy frost this morning. Major Thornburgh proposed that he and Lt. Spencer should start out along the trail and hunt for elk, black-tailed deer or bear, and await upon the summit of the "divide" for the two soldiers and myself who were to go back to the Lake which we expected to reach about (7½ o'clock), fish for trout until 10 and then rejoin our comrades with the spoils.

This programme was carried out in all its essential features: Rodman, Tupan and I forced our way through fallen [timber] to the far end of the lake whereupon a spot which should have filled Izaak Walton's wildest dreams of applicability and appropriateness, I took my stand armed with Major Thornburgh's splendid rod and tackle. There was nothing wanted excepting a good fisherman at the end of the pole, and I felt that General Crook or some other enthusiastic sportsman should have had my place. It was a boulder of granite rising about 10 or 12 feet above the surface of the water, and presenting an area on top of perhaps 12 feet square. Beneath it the dark, green unrippled water looked like a mirror of purest glass. It would be hard to say how much depth there was near me; but it must have been considerable. At first, I thought ten feet, then twenty and finally (30) @ forty. Thornburgh afterwards told me that near the banks, it measured forty feet and a ranchman who had been there said his party made a raft of pine logs, floated it to the center and paid out one hundred & fifty feet of line without touching bottom. However, there I was upon this boulder, overhanging the crystal waters in which, disporting themselves in its depths, darting and flitting from point to point, could be seen the red-streaked and black-speckled beauties I hoped so soon to entice to my hook.

Baiting with a fine fat grasshopper, I let my line down until the hook floated upon the surface, where I suffered it to play idly for a moment and in a freak of mischief, drew it away from the first trout or two which approached it. This game exasperated them so much that it occurred to me they must in some manner of summoned others of their tribe from the watery depths; because dozens of them in another moment were darting about just under the surface and even leaping into the air to seize the enticing bait. The sun's rays had kissed the water and at [the] same instant a fine, fat young trout made a spring for the grass-hopper, caught the hook in his jaws and started away with it, intending, I suppose, to run over to the other side of the Lake; his plans were never realized. In a second, he was dangling in the air, in one more he was squirming and twisting in my hand and in a third he lay gasping and flapping on the rock, a willow withe thrust through his gills. Oh! it was grand sport to look over and see dozens of the bright little creatures swimming about, to throw the line, watch them seize the bait and draw them out in triumph from the limpid element. Eight separate times, I caught and landed two fish, one on each hook: but through my own carelessness, four of them were allowed to squirm off from the rock. Within two and a half hours that I kept my post, I must have lifted nearly two hundred fine trout out of the water, but I succeeded in bringing only one hundred and three back to Fort Steele, losing about as many as I caught, because I didn't know very well how to secure them.

During the same time, Private Rodman, whose pole was a cottonwood sapling caught one hundred and Forty Five and Private Tupan, similarly equipped, took in One hundred and twenty Two. They used the same bait as I, grasshoppers until the trout became

excited and would bite anything and then trout-eyes which do pretty well, altho' not half so good as grass-hoppers.
After we had picked up our things and shouldered our rifles, it was no joke to work our way back to the place of our last night's bivouac. Luckily, the fish were all "pan-fish", but even small as they were, their weight oppressed us grievously, before we got them back to our campfire. There in the clear little spring brook, we had to set to work and clean them:—a task which took us not less than three or four hours.
We then laid them in layers on beds of freshly moistened sedgegrass, with which and gunny-sacks, we wrapped them up securely for transportation on the back of our sturdy pack-mule. "Muley" was something of a philosopher—a cynic—and it wasn't Fancy altogether that led me to believe the curl of his under-lip was expressive of contempt for my ignorance of packing; but at last the load was made up, put on the poor beast's back, tied after a fashion, and with a sublime dependence on Good Luck, we made ready to commence the ascent of the mountains.
It was getting well along in the afternoon; swollen-bellied clouds, black as ink, glowered at us from the neighboring pinnacles; the vivid flash of lightning and the deep-voiced thunder warned us that a mountain tempest would soon be upon us. In the distance, a couple of rifle-shots fired one in quick succession of the other were recognized as a signal from our comrades and answered with four whose echos reverberating across the rocks were immediately heard by Thornburgh, who, with Spencer, rejoined us as soon as they could descend the declivity. Trusting to Thornburgh's unerring skill as a woodsman, we set out upon the trail, creeping slowly up the mountain side, with cold rain drops, beating against our heads, soaking through our clothes, or dripping down into our boots. But we didn't mind it much; our catch of fish had been wonderful and a little rain would help to clean us.—
From the top of the ridge back to our "flag-pole" camp was mostly downgrade and we had the beaten path of yesterday to follow. We pushed along energetically, our noble old mule hanging to our heels. How it happened that he didn't throw his load more than once, I can't tell; but such is the fact and we felt jubilant over it, too. The drenching rain, shrouding in mist the nearest mountain tops and almost hiding the path along which we marched, did not, as we at

first feared it might; prevent our reaching camp that night. Thanks to Thornburgh's great skill as a woodsman, we made our way without much difficulty and with considerable rapidity to the bivouac of our flag-pole party, where a cup of hot coffee and good warm bedding awaited us. Almost at once after supper, we jumped under cover, and made up our minds to go to sleep as soon as we could; but a pitiless, pattering rain beat against the canvass all night and kept us awake until it was almost morning.

Wednesday, Sept. 4th. Our flag-pole was very neatly rough-hewed and trimmed and altho' quite short, (only 60 feet.) on account of the tornadoes of wind which occur at Fort Steele during the autumn and winter, was pronounced a beauty by all of our party. It was loaded upon two sets of wheels and brought down from the mountains under the personal supervision of Maj. Thornburgh who as soon as it was on the road in the level plain, gave his horses the rein and drove rapidly back to Ft. Steele.

The following table of distances taken from the odometer may be considered almost exact.

From Flag Pole Camp to Fort Steele

	Miles
Flag-Pole Camp to Jones' Ranch	5.11
" " " " Wagner's "	. 1
Spring C[ree]k. came from [where] Grassy Bottom commenced [Flag-Pole Camp to] Bangs' [Ranch]	14.1
Had Spring Ck. on Left to Bang's where we crossed it: end of Grassy Bottom.	
[Flag-Pole Camp to] North br[anch]. Hot Spring Creek	16.14
N. Platte river on our Right, and converging toward our line.	
[Flag-Pole Camp to] Jack creek	21.58
[Flag-Pole Camp to] 1st crossing, N. Platte River.	24.44.
[Flag-Pole Camp to] Bennett's (Forney's.) Ranch	24.94.
High Grassy Plateau, between these two Ranches.	
[Flag-Pole Camp to] Stockwell's Ranch	34.40
Fine Spring at this Ranch: also crossing of Pass creek.	
[Flag-Pole Camp to] 2nd crossing. N. Platte River	39.58
[Flag-Pole Camp to] Fort Fred. Steele	40.95

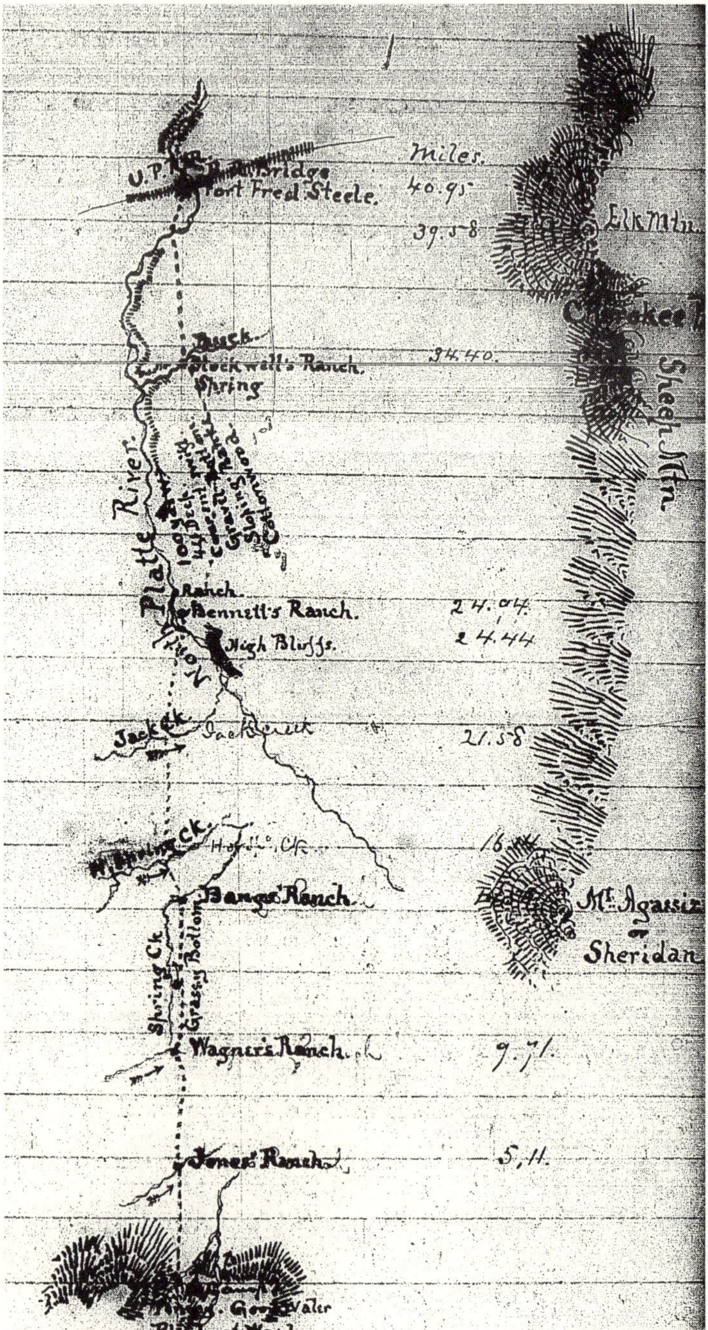

U.P.R.R. Bridge
Fort Fred Steele.
Miles.
40.95
39.58
Elk Mtn.
Buck
Stockwell's Ranch.
Spring
34.40.
Sheep Mtn.
Platte River.
Ranch.
Bennett's Ranch.
24.04.
High Bluffs.
24.44
North
Jack Ck.
21.58
16
Bangs' Ranch.
Mt. Agassiz or Sheridan
Spring Ck.
Grassy Bottom
Wagner's Ranch.
9.71.
Jones' Ranch.
5.11.
Plenty of Wood.
Grass Fair.

Thursday, Sept. 5th, 1878. Remained all day at Fort Steele.
Friday, Sept. 6th. Left Fort Steele at 5 o'clock in the morning. Was pained to hear of the total destruction by fire of the Grand Central Hotel of Omaha and the great damage to the office of the *Omaha Herald*. The Grand Central cost $300.000, was one of the most imposing hotel-buildings in the West and its loss at this time will be very severely felt.

After reaching Hazard, changed to cars of the Colorado Central Rail Road and traversed the fertile plains of the Centennial State to Denver. Put up at Chaupiot's Hotel which I was told was the best in that part of the country. The cooking was admirable, attendance all that could be desired and the rooms clean, large and handsomely furnished.

Denver impressed me as one of the most go-ahead cities I had ever seen. Its people are enterprising and ambitious, its situation for trade, travel or health cannot be surpassed and within the next century, or sooner if we have a foreign war, it may be the capital of the United States.

That evening I dropped in at a performance by Callender's "Georgia Minstrels", and was much amused. The audience was very large—fully as large as the hall would admit and many people had to stand. There is not burnt cork about these minstrels; they are all genuine darkies and their performances are not so much imitations as reminiscences of plantation life.

One of them, in the course of some burlesque song imitated hens, cocks and little chickens with such fidelity to nature that it was hard to believe there was not a lot of barn-yard fowls concealed behind the scenes.

Saturday, Sept. 7th. In the morning, took a little stroll along 14th Street, the finest in Denver. There are a great many fine residences, all of them with grassy lawns and fountains in front, trailing vines growing about the porticoes and every sign of comfort and refinement. Denver is abundantly supplied with excellent water from the South Platte river; has good gas, and a finely organized fire Dept. At present time, the R.Rs. are the Denver and Rio Grande with a mileage of 250 m., the Denver Pacific, 125, the Kansas Pacific 450 m., and the Colorado Central 131.—all these having branches and feeders. Then the Atchison, Topeka & Santa Fé and the Burlington & Missouri River R.R.'s are contemplating the construction of branch lines into Denver. The markets of this little city are equalled by but few places in the world; all varieties of game & domestic meat, fruits, vegetables and cereals, besides imported liquors and fine groceries of all descriptions can be obtained at fair prices in the large and well-conducted establishments for which Denver is noted. I should say it was far ahead of Omaha in all that concerns a city's comfort & welfare.

Like Omaha, none of the streets are paved, but Denver has the advantage of being built upon a soil of gravel, which is as good as could supply: the scenery to the West of Denver is very exhilarating; Pike's and Long's Peaks are in full view, snow-crested and majestic, the cañons and streams at their base being accessible without trouble by the various Rail Roads.

Took the afternoon train on the Colorado Central for Golden, where we changed to the "narrow gauge" and began the ascent of the cañon of Clear Creek.

The curves are so sudden that the train takes every point of the compass and scarcely ever can the occupants of the rear car see the Locomotive. The engineering skill displayed in the construction of this little road is of the very highest order.

Grand as the scenery of the Clear Creek Cañon must be conceded to be, it cannot be compared to that of the American Fork Cañon, in Utah, but there is a remarkably beautiful body of water in Clear Creek, which extorts the admiration of every beholder. Leaping over great blocks of granite or dashing angrily and vainly against the rocky walls which confine its channel, the current goes roaring down toward the Platte, now white with foam, now turbid with the sediment of the gold miner's sluices. Tunnels, shafts, prospect-holes and even finely-proportioned mills of brick are to be seen every few yards; the amount of the precious metal taken from this creek in the past has been very great and is still paying handsome returns to all those intelligently engaged in it.

On way up, passed the Idaho Springs, a summer resort, rapidly acquiring prominence on account of its valuable mineral springs, hot and cold.

About dark, reached Georgetown, a bustling mining town, claiming to have 5.000 inhabitants. This little town is prettily situated in a narrow gorge, with streets so steep that the houses at one end of a block are perched in the air high above those at the other end. There were numbers of tourists in Georgetown, ready to go to the Colorado Parks, which are most accessible from this point, but reports of a threatened Indian outbreak among the Utes deterred them. The weather during the day of my stay was extremely disagreeable, cold and damp, with occasional drops of rain and flakes of snow. The Barton House is a fair enough hostelry, without attractions enough of itself to keep me in Georgetown on a rainy day. I had contemplated going up to the summit of the Argeuta Pass and perhaps into the Middle Park, but everything considered[,] it appeared to me that I had better defer a tour through these mountains until an earlier date next year.

Sunday, Sep't. 8th 1878. Left Georgetown on an "excursion" train: passengers nearly all Dutch and Irish on their way to a "Turner" picnic in Denver. At Idaho Springs, met Mrs. Dodge, wife of my friend, Lieut Fredk. Dodge, 23rd Infantry. We had a long conversation about mutual friends and in this manner passed the 5, or nearly five, long weary hours it [took] us to make (from 7 to 11.45 A.M.) the 36 miles between Georgetown and Golden. At Golden, which in ordinary weather would be considered a bright little village of say 1000 @ 1500 inhabitants, I had to make out as best I could for the remainder of that dreary, drizzling, rainy day, without books, without newpapers later than a week old and without companions. The cold rain and snow kept everyone indoors, where the mental capacity of the individuals in the "gents" sitting room was something painful to encounter. As I didn't take part in the conversation, my ears were at full liberty to take in everything that was said: one fellow wanted to burn every ship, another damned and God-damned the banks; one [illegible] looking youth, smoking a cigar that didn't seem to be doing him any good, thought it was the damn-n-n preachers that were ruining the country, for upon one point they were all agreed and that was that the whole country was going to the demnition [sic] bow-wows.

Good God! I thought and these are the intelligent(!) thinking voters upon whose suffrages the destinies of a great nation depend! I was bilious, I suppose, or dyspeptic; anyway I was cross and looked at things mundane through cerulean spectacles; a glass of whiskey warmed me up and made me feel better-humored, but not enough to enjoy the society of my enforced companions.

The young clerk admitted that Golden was rather dull that day, but said he, ["]if you will only wait over for a week, we can show you something next *Sunday* when we are to have a picnic here with two military bands." I reluctantly tore myself away from such promised attractions and next morning,

Monday, Sept. 9th, 1878, was at the dépôt waiting for the train for Cheyenne. That was an hour late: going up the heavy grade and curve just north of Golden lost us another hour, as the rails were so wet and slippery, it was all we could do to move with engines in front and rear. But at last we reached the Union Pacific R.R., at Hazard, where the train going West passed us, having on board General John C. Fremont, who has been appointed Governor of Arizona Territory. Schuyler joined me at Cheyenne, where on the platform were Lieut. Weir, and other friends.

Next day, we reached Omaha in safety, no accident having happened to our train, altho' attacks from organized bands of train-robbers are now to be looked for at any time. The authorities of the Union Pacific R.R. are apprehensive of some dire calamity such as the train being run off the track and sacked by desperate plunderers and have appealed to General Crook for guard to be detailed with each passenger train. This request has been granted, but the number available for each train is so small that a few determined robbers could clean them out without much trouble.

Part 2
The Cheyennes and the Poncas

Background

The Cheyenne Outbreak and the Ponca Affair involved northern tribes that had been transported to the Indian Territory. The Northern Cheyennes who surrendered to Crook as the Great Sioux War drew to a close, were relocated to congregate them with their Southern Cheyenne cousins, who already were established in the Territory. The Poncas were victims of a bureaucratic error in the Fort Laramie Treaty of 1868, in which their lands on the Missouri River were ceded to the Lakotas as part of the Great Sioux Reservation. At the close of the Great Sioux War, the government decided to concentrate the Lakotas on those lands for ease of management. The Poncas, who never in history had opposed the government, then were removed to the Territory. In the cases of both the Cheyennes and the Poncas, the trauma of the move, the sudden change in climate, and the neglect of the government all contributed to suffering and death.[1]

1. The records of the Cheyenne Outbreak are found in RG 393. Special File. Military Division of the Missouri, Little Wolf's Cheyennes, March–June 1879, and the George Crook Letterbooks. An excellent recent account is Monnett, *Tell Them We Are Going Home*. The Ponca Affair has been the subject of extensive writing over the years, including Howard, *The Ponca Tribe*; Tibbles, *Buckskin and Blanket Days* and *Standing Bear and the Ponca Chiefs*; Jackson, *Century of Dishonor*; and, most recently, Mathes and Lowitt, *The Standing Bear Controversy*. The material in this introduction is drawn from this sources.

The Cheyenne Outbreak began on September 9, 1878, when a band under Dull Knife and Little Wolf bolted the reservation and started north. Initially, they held their own, driving off a detachment of soldiers, and attracting a certain amount of public sympathy. In Kansas, however, some warriors began a rampage of murder, rape, and plunder. The main band, however, continued on, and, after crossing the North Platte River in Nebraska, split into two groups. Little Wolf took his people to the Tongue River country of Montana, where Nelson Miles, who never had favored relocation, allowed them to settle. Dull Knife's band, however, surrendered near Fort Robinson, where they were interned pending transportation back to the Territory. Equally determined not to go, they barricaded themselves into a barracks.

To force them into submission, the post commander, Capt. Henry Wessells, withheld food and water. Although he since has been vilified, in the subsequent investigation he pointed out this action was done with the tacit consent of both Crook and Sheridan, and his correspondence bears him out. Unbeknownst to the soldiers, the Cheyennes had disassembled their weapons, concealing the pieces in their clothing. On January 9, 1879, they reassembled them, and that night, attacked the guards and escaped. Most were recaptured over the ensuing weeks. Some were returned to the Territory, while others, including Dull Knife, were allowed to settle with the Oglalas at Pine Ridge, in what is now South Dakota.

Bourke's attention naturally was drawn toward the Cheyennes by the outbreak, and in his diary, he allows himself time to reflect on the humanity of these people against whom he sometimes has been called upon to fight. "They are formidable competitors in the field as well as most astute in council," he notes. "From my acquaintance with them at Red Cloud Agency in 1877, and my service against them, I formed a very high opinion of their general character and always found them truthful and to be relied upon."[2]

In discussing childbirth, he blasts the notion that Indian women are somehow more resilient, and their husbands more stoic or indifferent than their white counterparts.

> Many Cheyenne women are attacked with puerperal fever and not infrequently deaths occur in labor. All the stupid

2. Bourke, Diary, 26:26.

nonsense we read about the lack of peril, the immunity of *Indian* women while passing through the ordeal of the curse primeval, is silly bosh. Upon marches, and especially when pressed by an enemy or compelled by hunger to move a village from one situation to another, Cheyenne women have brought forth their children unaided and even when exposed to cold and fatigue, but the rule is as I give it above—that both they and their husbands and friends appreciate the gravity of their condition and make every effort to diminish its pains and perils.[3]

Farther on, he adds, "The cardinal virtues among the Cheyenne are Valor, Generosity, Prudence and Tenderness for family."[4]

Bourke used the opportunity to make substantial notes on Cheyenne life and culture, including child rearing, education of warriors and women, marriage, dress, and other aspects. That which he did not gather from first-hand observation he learned from Ben Clark, a scout who had lived many years among them and had married into them.

He also had some observations on Interior Secretary Carl Schurz, whom he, and many others, considered responsible for the sufferings of the Indians, particularly after the Ponca Affair attracted national publicity. In Bourke's view, Schurz was

> keen, subtle and mendacious in character, quick to perceive the weak points of an adversary's arguments, and perfectly brazen in the suggestion of plausible explanations to cover the shortcomings of his Department, he has, without being personally dishonest, done more to protect and strengthen the thieves of the Indian Ring than any champion who has ever assumed that task.[5]

Like the Cheyennes, the Poncas found the Territory unendurable. When the son of Chief Standing Bear died, early in 1879, the chief was determined to bury the boy in their old homeland. He and a band of followers transported the body back to the Missouri River

3. Ibid., 26:28–29.
4. Ibid., 26:36.
5. Ibid., 32:438.

country, molesting no one, and attracting a substantial amount of support among citizens of the area through which they passed. Upon arrival, they were interned at Omaha Barracks pending a forced return to the Territory. Standing Bear (probably encouraged by General Crook), sought an injunction against the federal government to prevent the move. The landmark case was tried in Omaha before U.S. District Judge Elmer Dundy, with Crook as one of the witnesses. The question came down to whether American Indians had legal standing in court and could, in fact, bring suit. Judge Dundy ruled in the affirmative. Just as Indians were required to obey the laws of the United States, he said, so were they entitled to the protection of those laws.

The treatment of the Poncas infuriated Bourke. Recording the initial meeting between Crook and the Poncas, he wrote, "This conference is inserted verbatim merely to show the cruel and senseless way in which [the] Government of the United States deals with the Indian tribes who confide in its justice or trust themselves to its mercy."[6]

Bourke also included two clippings of Thomas Henry Tibbles' coverage of the Ponca Affair in the *Omaha Herald* because, he said, they "will be found both interesting, and accurate, and much more elaborate than mine."[7] I have omitted the clipping concerning the conference with Crook because much of it is the same as Bourke's own account, with additional background detail available in any of several works listed in the bibliography. I did, however, include the *Omaha Herald* account of the subsequent suit to recover their reservation, which Bourke used in lieu of recording it himself.

In the West Point arrangement of the diaries, the volume concerning the Ponca Affair is placed ahead of the volumes dealing with the Cheyennes. I have reversed the order to maintain Bourke's chronology.

6. Ibid., 25:71.
7. Ibid., 25:88.

Chapter 7

Cheyenne Life

This chapter almost could have been called "The General and the President's Son," because Webb C. Hayes, son of President Rutherford B. Hayes, accompanied Crook and Bourke on an expedition to the West. At Sidney Barracks, Nebraska,[1] however, Crook conferred with a group of Cheyennes about the Outbreak from the Indian Territory, and Cheyennes then became the focal point of Bourke's writing. The Indians were particularly pleased that Webb attended the meeting, because, as the son of the Great Father, he could give President Hayes a first-hand account of their grievances. He very likely did, because the president was genuinely concerned about Indian welfare, and was more prone than his immediate predecessors to standing up against special interest groups that so often harmed the Indians.[2]

It is obvious that Bourke knew less of Crook's personal life than he might have believed. The general tended to keep his private relations separate from his official ones, and the Hayes family was

---

1. Sidney Barracks (which Bourke sometimes spelled as "Sydney") at the present town of Sidney, Nebraska, was established in 1867 as an outpost of Fort Sedgwick, Colorado. It became a separate post in 1879, and was redesignated Fort Sidney. It was abandoned and transferred to the Interior Department in 1894. Frazer, *Forts of the West*, 90.

2. Bourke, Diary, 26:11.

a case in point. Bourke wrote off Webb's presence with the comment that he was along because Crook was "the old friend of his father" dating back to the Civil War, and that of Crook's "skill as a hunter no doubt his father had sometimes spoken."[3] In fact, the relationship was much stronger than the usual wartime comraderie; they were like a second family. Not only did Rutherford Hayes frequently exchange letters with Crook, but so did the children. When his military duties allowed, Crook and his wife, Mary, often visited Spiegel Grove, the Hayes mansion in Fremont, Ohio, and Webb Hayes became a surrogate son to the childless couple. The general followed his education and career, and Webb stood by Mary at Crook's funeral.[4]

[September 26, 1878] The journey from Omaha to Sidney, Neb., has been alluded to and described so often in my note-books, that in this I feel excused from saying anything more than I made it; Sept. 21st and Sept. 22nd, 1878, in company with General Crook, Lieut Schuyler, A.D.C., Mr. John Collins of Omaha and Mr. Webb Hayes, son of his Excellency, the President.

Mr. Hayes came on a visit to General Crook the old friend of his father, who during the war had commanded a Brigade and a Division in the Corps led by Genl. Crook. The intimacy and good feeling engendered during perilous service, had continued into the poping times of Peace and extended to a younger generation. Mr. Webb Hayes was anxious to see something of Far Western life in company with General Crook of whose skill as a hunter no doubt his father had sometimes spoken.

Contrary to my expectation, I found Mr. Hayes a very pleasant, companionable sort of a young man—not at all spoiled by the elevation of his father and the amount of flattery Washington parasites must lavish upon him. He presents much the appearance of the picture of his mother—medium size, dark hair and eyes, dark complexion, mouth large, teeth good, expression gentle and frank. In age he might be (24) or (25), though from his beardless face, he might pass for at least three years younger. Pretty soon we got talking unreservedly together and became acquainted with

3. Ibid., 26:1.
4. The Crook-Hayes connection is discussed in detail in Robinson, *General Crook*, and Hoogenboom, *Rutherford B. Hayes*. The George Crook Collection at the Rutherford B. Hayes Presidential Center in Fremont, Ohio, preserves extensive correspondence, not only between Crook and President Hayes, but also between Crook and Webb Hayes.

the rapidity so peculiar to railroad and steam boat travelling. Mr. Hayes had but lately been graduated from Cornell University (Ithaca, N.Y.), and Schuyler being a native of that town many persons there were of whom they could talk as common acquaintance. He told us a very amusing story of the artfulness with which a young Sophomore at Cornell obtained a copy of the questions to be asked his class at the approaching Examination. The rule of the university is that each professor prepare his own questions, then have them put in press and after correcting the proof, see that the type is distributed in the case. All efforts, of the pupils of the particular class of which I speak, to obtain copies of the Examination papers had resulted in mortifying failure; but the genius of one indomitable young scape-grace rose superior to adversity. Dressing himself in a very natty walking suit, he wended his way carelessly down towards the Printing Office at the door of which he saw Professor ____ busy in the preparation of his manuscript. The Professor didn't see anything harmful in the mere presence of the young man, especially since he looked upon himself as being too smart for any dodges the student might attempt to play upon him. But in this estimate of relative capacity he found himself sadly mistaken. The young man sauntered carelessly around the printing office, apparently lost in wonder and admiration of the Art preservative, until he saw the old Professor adjust his spectacles and prepare to read the final proof.

Then and not till then did this innocent young man feel tired: there were several chairs in the room, but he preferred sitting down upon the form which held the type of the list of questions to be propounded on the morrow, and as it so happened that he was wearing a pair of white pantaloons, a very fine impression was immediately taken. Before the old Professor got through with the revision of his proof, that noble young man was thoroughly rested and on his way to his rooms where a detachment of breathless class-mates was awaiting his arrival. The examination of that class next day was justly regarded as one of the most brilliant ever held in Cornell.

In the car next to ours, was Senator [John J.] Patterson, of South Carolina, Chairman of the Committee on Territories and a party travelling to the Pacific Coast. Among these was a Captain Garrick Mallery, of the Army, who is at present on detached service under the Secretary of the Interior, preparing articles on

American Ethnography.[5]

Approaching Columbus, Neb., the fine appearance of the crops and the fatness of the cattle extorted general admiration and praise. This little town is building up with great rapidity; within the last few months the Roman Catholics have commenced and almost completed a large monastery for Franciscan monks, and as an educational establishment.

Fifty miles East of Grand Island, the eccentric of our locomotive broke:[6] this detained us so long that we did not get in to Grand Island until midnight. Consequently, we had no supper and many of the passengers grumbled not a little. We were worse off, I thought, at North Platte, next morning where a perfectly vile breakfast was served up at an exorbitant price. This fleecing of passengers by conscienceless eating house sharks is the greatest blot upon American railroading: along the Union Pacific line, there are some very well served tables, but just as many where the Bill of Fare is an offense against decency and the price extorted an act of highway robbery.

Met Mr. Leech [sic], a young man, who has distinguished himself lately by his pursuit and capture of the highwaymen who last summer, stopped the express train at Big Springs, Neb., and made away with $60.000 *in gold*. Mr. Leech, at time of robbery, was a clerk in a store at Ogallalla: the day after the depredation, two men, strangers, came to the store and bought a pair of boots. From their conversation he gathered that they were getting ready for a long journey.

Trifling as was this incident, it served him as a clue to follow their trail a long distance to their camp, where he saw them and their confederates sitting around the fire counting out their money and

---

5. Garrick Mallery (d. 1895) was a captain of the First Infantry, who first entered the army as a captain of Volunteers during the Civil War. He finished the war with brevets to colonel of Volunteers and lieutenant colonel of the Regular Army. Like Bourke, Mallery became interested in American Indian culture during service in the West. He pioneered research into Indian winter counts with *The Dakota and Corbusier Winter Counts*. He was placed on detached duty to work on the monumental *Handbook of American Indians North of Mexico*, but soon abandoned it for his own field work in American Indian pictography and sign language; the *Handbook* was completed by Frederick F. Hodge. Mallery's two-volume *Picture Writing of the American Indians*, published in the Tenth Annual Report of the American Bureau of Ethnology in 1893, remains in print, as does his *Sign Language Among North American Indians*. Mallery was one of the founders of the American Anthropological Society, and served as its president for several years. Heitman, *Historical Register*, 1:686; Fletcher, "Colonel Garrick Mallery," 79–80; http://www.accessgenealogy.com/native/tribes/preface.htm

6. The eccentric is a sort of auxiliary crank that causes the valves to open and close in the steam chest of the locomotive. This, in turn, forces the pistons in and out causing the drive wheels to turn. http://www.railway-technical.com/st-glos.html#E

tying it up in the legs of old pantaloons, to be slung over the backs of horses. Leech made his way back undiscovered, got to the Rail Road, telegraphed to the Union Pacific authorities what he had seen, followed the thieves to Texas and succeeded in killing or capturing the last one of the gang and in recovering the major portion of the money.[7]

We also fell into conversation with a Mr. Fulton, a young Englishman of intelligence and education, who gave us a good idea of the interest felt by his young countrymen in the sheep and cattle interests of Colorado. Great numbers of them are already in business in that state and many more, with small capitals, will soon be on their way there. The whole of Middle Park, is now owned by English cattlemen, who intend fencing it in on the north and south to prevent their cattle from straying.

At Sidney, we met Ben Clark, Major Thornburgh, Captains [Thomas Bredin] Burrowes and [John D.] Devin and Lieuts. [George Breckenridge] Davis, [Albert] Austin, Palmer & [Robert Armstrong] Lovell; also Major [George Alexander] Gordon, the post commander, who took General Crook to his quarters.*

In the afternoon General Crook had a long conference with the Cheyenne Indians, in their camp one mile from town: none of these Indians were chiefs, but several of them were warriors of prominence. They belonged to the party who, after Mackenzie had destroyed their village at the head of Powder River in the Big Horn mountains, had made their way down to the mouth of Tongue river where they surrendered to Colonel Miles, the Commander of the troops in that vicinity. The rest of the Cheyennes of the north, (1200 @ 1300) in number had surrendered to Genl. Crook at Camp Robinson, Neb., in April 1877, had been removed from there to a location in the Indian Territory, with which they had become much dissatisfied and not having their grievances redressed, had determined to break away from the Reservation and force a path for themselves to their old homes, in Nebraska. They told the Agent, Mr. [John D.] Miles, that if unmolested, they would go peaceably, but if hindered, they would fight.

* *Immediately after this, Bourke inserted:* Maj. Gordon died Oct. 26th 1878.

7. This was the robbery of the Union Pacific eastbound train, on September 18, 1877, by a gang that included noted desperado Sam Bass. The storekeeper who tracked them down was M. F. Leach. The robbery and Leach's subsequent efforts are described in Miller, *Sam Bass & Gang*, beginning with Chapter 5.

While our party was assembling in front of the tent of Lieut. [H. M.] Creel, 7th Cavalry, I noticed one of the Cheyenne Indians making himself a whetstone from a piece of greenstone or hard rock of some kind, which he patiently hacked with a knife and hatchet. He worked carefully and quietly and I suppose by the time the stone would be ready for use, he would have employed not less than two days' hard and constant labor in its preparation. The white men present were General Crook, with his Aides de Camp, Lieuts. Bourke and Schuyler, Mr. Webb C. Hayes, Major Thornburgh, Lieuten' G.B. Davis, 5th Cavalry, Ben Clark as interpreter, with young Bill Roland, as assistant.*

The Indians were Little Chief, who had decorated himself by painting hands & hair a deep yellow; Ridge Bear, Red Hat, who had a very well defined moustache, White Thunder, a gray-headed, superannuated old man, and Crazy Mule.

General Crook. We stopped here to see you all again and hear what you have to say. I haven't anything particular to say, but if you have anything to say, I will be glad to hear it, but I have no intention of holding a Council. From what I have seen of the Cheyennes here and in the South, I like them very much. They are good fighters and I think would be good friends.

Little Chief. As you are here, I'll tell you we had a council with General Sheridan at Chicago; we intend to obey the counsels we have received. You can see these people how poor they are; the blankets they have received from the Government are all in rags. We understood we were going to get more to eat than we do. The sugar don't hold out, neither does the beef. We would like to get plenty of ammunition. We have heard that there is plenty of game below here,—antelope and some buffalo South of the Platte: we want pistols to run the buffalo with. We belong to the soldiers: we were told we could keep the arms and horses given us and we want to be assured of that. We like very well to be with the soldiers; we like them first rate, but we want more rations than we are getting. We are glad the great Father's son is here to hear what we have to say and tell it to his father and the other big chiefs. Tell them we don't want to do anything foolish. I am glad you have come here and given us a chance to talk with you. We all feel very much troubled at the news of those Indians going North; they are liable to get into fights

*Bourke originally included Mr. John S. Collins, of Omaha, but crossed out the name.

and some of our friends and relatives may be killed. We have given ourselves up to [the] Government and don't think the Government ought to keep anything from us. We shan't do anything on the sly. None of us are chiefs, but all are warriors of the Cheyennes. We speak alike, one for all and want you to put it down straight. We are very glad you have come and seen us just as we are; you can see we are very poor. By your coming, we may get better blankets. Those we have, you can see, are nearly worn out. We were told that that, (meaning the Indian Territory,) was a very good country but we now know differently. *This* country is the land of our fathers and we like it best—we have never owned *that* country & have heard that all the people down there die off, so we like this country best. When we find our agent down there cheats us, we want to throw him away and get a good man in his place. If he don't give us our rations, we want to get a soldier who won't cheat us. We were told in Chicago that any of those agents caught stealing our rations and annuity goods should be removed and we should have soldier chiefs in their places. We also understood that when we got there, (Indian Territory) if we couldn't get along with those fool Southern Cheyennes, we could leave them and get our own country back. These Black Hills as long ago as we can remember, belonged to us,—long before the Sioux were there;—our dead fathers are buried all over there and we hate to leave it, but because the Government wants us, we are going down South. We are not fools, we have our senses; but we are going down there because we have to. That's all I have to say.

 Ben Clark here explained that the Cheyennes receive one half pound hard tack each, (that is adult or child.) and one and a half lbs. beef *net* each and eight lbs. Sugar, & three of Beans and four of coffee to the one hundred Rations. ["]They have killed several hundred antelope since leaving the Missouri River, selling their skins and eating the meat. They expect, from what they hear, to get buffalo this side of the Republican river, forty miles South of the Platte, in the Sand Hills, of S. Nebraska. I don't think there are many buffalo there. The Utes were down there hunting a month ago I have been issuing limited quantities of cartridges, on the way down. I gave them two hundred and fifty at Camp Robinson at rate of five a week. They used them in killing antelope and brought the meat in. Little Chief and Ridge Bear haven't made any trouble on the trip. Lieut. [John Burgess] Johnson prevented me from starting (from Camp Robinson.) the day I fixed, but it was just as well I didn't meet them (the refugee Cheyennes.) on the Kansas Pacific Rail Way.["] Ben Clark also said that these Cheyennes are great meat eaters and that it was no unusual thing for a grown man to consume from ten to twelve pounds of flesh-food in one day.

General Crook. ["]I am very glad to have had this talk and to hear them talk so sensibly. When they were at Red Cloud (Agency.) they were in my country.[8] While in the Missouri and in the South, they were not.[9] Now, while they are passing through my country, I want to hear what they have to say. I take a great deal of interest in them and want to hear good of them. I can and will give them some ammunition to hunt with on their own. I don't know much about *that* country (meaning the Indian Territory.) I hunted there last winter. It looks like a good country. Bill Roland (here pointing to young Bill Roland, a half-breed Cheyenne.) wants to go down there. He likes it better than this country and I understand that those people (Cheyennes.) down there, left because you didn't come in sooner. They became impatient to see you and came as much to meet you as anything else. Last night I got a dispatch from the Commanding Officer down there, General Pope, that they were away beyond the Arkansas and the soldiers after them. If they should escape those soldiers, there are a great many other soldiers at Red Cloud just come in from the Black Hills, and if they succeed in getting through from Red Cloud, these people will be allowed to go to them.

"That is one reason why I wanted you to stay here till this matter was settled. If you had gone down and met those others, I was afraid they might have induced some of you to go away and get you into trouble. Somebody is bound to get hurt pretty soon. When this matter is settled I'll let you know: you know I always tell you the truth. If those Indians, (i.e. the refugee Cheyennes) go back, you can go on down: if those Indians are allowed to go to Red Cloud (Agency.) I'll ask to have you sent to join them.

"The Government wants to get you all together. When I was in Chicago, the other day, General Sheridan told me it was his intention to send there those now at [the] mouth of Tongue River, so as to get you all together."

---

8. I.e., the Department of the Platte.
9. The Department of the Missouri under Brig. Gen. John Pope.

The conference here terminated and the Indians left, but Little Chief came back and said, "It is getting close to winter; we want to get off as soon as we can. We want to stay two days down here (on Republican river.) and hunt buffalo."

General Crook. Just as soon as the matter is settled, you'll get a telegram.

After the conference, I had a talk with Ben Clark, whom I had the pleasure of meeting several years ago, when he was a scout for General Crook in the campaign made in the winter of 1876, in the Tongue and Powder River country. Ben's life has been a singular one; for twenty-one years, he has lived among the Cheyennes, among whom he found a wife to whom he was devotedly attached. Upon her death, five years ago,[10] he sent to Saint Louis for a marble headstone, which now stands on her grave on the Reservation near Fort Reno, Indian Territory.[11] He has lately made a trip in Government service as far as Fort Walsh, British America,[12] to induce a fragment of the Nez Percé tribe now with the bands of Sitting Bull, to leave the Sioux and rejoin their own people in the United States. Ben thinks that the buffalo are nearly extinct; he estimates that there are now only (250.000) left in the northern herd, on the Saskatchewan, and not over 25.000 in the Southern herd on the Llano Estacado in Texas.[13]

Late in the afternoon, we were called upon at the Rail Road Hotel, by the officers of Major Thornburgh's Command. It is opportune to say here that this command (organized to repel the advance of a small band of refugee Cheyennes who had stolen out from their Reservation in the Indian Territory,) was composed of the "scrap-

10. Bourke may have been referring to an early wife, or may even have been mistaken. In his entry for Ben Clark, Dan Thrapp (*Encyclopedia of Frontier Biography*, 1:274–75) mentions only one Cheyenne wife, who died on May 16, 1913, fourteen months before Clark himself. Both, however, are listed as buried in the cemetery at Fort Reno, Oklahoma.

11. Fort Reno, Oklahoma. Not to be confused with Fort Reno, Wyoming, which figured in the Great Sioux War of 1876. This post was established in 1874 on the North Canadian River, to protect the Cheyenne-Arapaho Agency at Darlington, on the opposite side. The post was abandoned in 1908, and became first, a remount depot, and then a quartermaster's depot. It is now a livestock research station. Frazer, *Forts of the West*, 123.

12. Fort Walsh, Saskatchewan, was established in 1875 by the North West Mounted Police to enforce the law and maintain peace on the Canadian frontier. In 1878, following the Great Sioux and Nez Percé Wars in the United States, it became headquarters for the NWMP to deal with Indian refugees from those wars. The post became obsolete when the Canadian tribes agreed to accept reservations, and was abandoned in 1883. In 1942, the Royal Canadian Mounted Police, successor to the NWMP, reoccupied the property and used it until 1968 as a remount ranch. Fort Walsh is now a national historic site, located near the present town of Maple Creek, Sask. www.oc.gcca/lhn-nhs/sk/walsh/indez_e.asp.

13. The Llano Estacado (Staked Plain) is the high plains area of the Texas Panhandle.

ings" of the Department of the Platte. Individually, the companies or fragments of companies were good enough but the organization presented what might be called the "incoherency" always to be detected in corps formed of various organizations suddenly jumbled together. There was one company of the 14th Infantry from Camp Douglas, near Salt Lake, one of the 9th Infy. from Omaha Barracks, one of the 9th Infy., from Cheyenne (dépôt), Wyo.,[14] one of the 4th Inf. from Fort Fred Steele, Wyo., one of the 5th Cavy. from Fort McPherson, Neb.,[15] one (a mere skeleton) of the 7th Cavalry, from Fort Abraham Lincoln, Dakota,[16] and a small detachment of the 3d Cavalry, from Camp Robinson, Neb.

And this force had been suddenly assembled to head off the flight of a band of savages who had absconded from their Reservation because they felt that our Gov't. was lying to them; it matters not whether the grievances of our Indians be true or false, exaggerated or under-estimated, the fact that the word of our Government is mistrusted by every tribe on the continent cannot be denied and is a black blot upon our national escutcheon.

At [the] same time that General Crook was thus harassed and worried about the Cheyennes, telegrams came pouring in from Idaho and Montana, appealing for aid against hostile Bannocks, who have been depredating in that section for months.

Called in the evening upon the ladies of the garrison of Sidney Barracks, meeting the families of Colonel Gordon, post commander, Col.[Thomas C.] Devin, Cap't. [Michael John] Fitzgerald, Lieut. [William Barrett] Pease, Dr. [Curtis E.] Munn, Maj. [Henry Goddard?] Thomas, and Lt. [John Arthur] Baldwin.

Also, Maj. Thornburgh, Cap't. Burrowes, Lt. Spencer, Lt. Bowman, Dr. Marston, Lt. [William Foster] Norris, Cap't. [Edward Gustave] Mathey, Lt. Creel, Lt. G.B. Davis, and Lts. Palmer & Lovell.

14. Cheyenne Depot was the official designation of a subpost of Fort D. A. Russell, at Cheyenne, Wyoming. Often referred to as "Camp Carlin" or "Russell Depot," it was discontinued in 1890. Frazer, *Forts of the West*, 184–85.

15. Fort McPherson was established in 1863 on the South Platte River, eight miles above its confluence with the North Platte. It was abandoned in 1880, and transferred to the Interior Department in 1887. The post cemetery is a national cemetery. Frazer, *Forts of the West*, 90.

16. Fort Abraham Lincoln was located at the confluence of the Heart and Missouri Rivers across from present-day Bismarck, North Dakota. It was established at Fort McKean on June 14, 1872, but on November 19 of the same year was redesignated as Fort Abraham Lincoln. The post was abandoned in 1891, and the structures were dismantled by area residents for building materials. The partially reconstructed post is now a North Dakota state park. Frazer, *Forts of the West*, 111–12.

Monday, Sep't. 23rd, General Crook, Lt. Schuyler and Mr. Webb Hayes left for Fort Steele, (Mr. Collins had kept on in his journey yesterday.)
General Crook directed me to remain with Major Thornburgh's command, do everything in my power to make it a success and to report to him everything that might occur.
Lieut. [Walter Scott] Wyatt, 9th Infantry, arrived this morning from Omaha Barracks and reported for duty with Captain Burrowe's [sic] Company
Lieut. [Thomas Sidney] McCaleb, arrived from Fort McPherson to attend a General C't. Martial, in session at Sidney Barracks.

Before noon, I visited in company with Dr. Munn, the post surgeon, the fine Hospital just completed and not yet occupied. The ventilation, by ridge windows and apertures in the flooring under the stoves, pleased me very much: altho' I was acquainted with the method theoretically, I had never seen it in actual operation before. The latrines, kitchens, ward and dining rooms were all excellently managed, the bedding of newest styles and mattresses of woven wire.
Before starting for Fort Steele, General Crook instructed Major Thornburgh to call upon telegraph operators along the line of Rail Road for any information they might receive regarding the advance of the Cheyennes: also to ask citizens living in the district through which they were likely to come to advise him without fail of everything they might discover of whereabouts of the hostiles, and for all such information a liberal recompense was promised. While the General was anxious to have everything possible done for Major Thornburgh in whom he placed great reliance, he didn't seem at all sanguine of our success: indeed it didn't require much military learning to see that the command assembled at Sidney was very poorly prepared to take the field against anything. It had no pack-mules, no guides and no scouts. With a few Indians as trailers, a great deal might be hoped for. Major Thornburgh told me that he asked Genl. Crook to let him have some Arapahoes from Camp Brown, but that the General told him the distance was too great to admit of their being brought on in time to join the Expedition. As more than half our men were dismounted, Genl. Crook directed me to telegraph the Comdg. Officer, Fort McPherson, to send to Sidney every serviceable public horse at his post; and Lt. W. B. Weir, Ordnance Officer, and

Cheyenne dépôt, Wyo., for all the Cavalry equipment needed. The great trouble in all exigencies like the present is that our little army is found unprepared—nominally 25.000 strong, it is in reality not over 22.000 @ 23.000 in the aggregate, and it has imposed upon it more work than could be done by a strength of 50.000. Each little station along the line of the Union Pacific Rail Road is now anxious to possess some of the troops congregated at Sidney; last night, Ogallalla telegraphed an urgent appeal for a company of troops, but Major Thornburgh couldn't comply, as his force was too small to admit of being scattered in fragments.

Dined to-day with Dr. Munn and family; after dinner, listened to some very agreeable music on the zither, an instrument of sweetness and power, Miss Thomas, the young daughter of the Paymaster, played upon the violin and Miss Munn upon the guitar.

Sept. 25th On the Westward-bound train this a.m. were Lt. Keefe, 4th Infantry, three young graduates of the Mily. Academy, Colonel [Horace Blois] Burnham, Judge Advocate of the Dep't. Platte, and Mr. [William H.] Lyon of the Bd. of Indian Commissioners. Horses for the command arrived from McPherson at 4 o'clock this morning; saddles arrived from Cheyenne last night. As the horses were unshod and there were no suitable nails at Sidney, I ordered Lt. Baldwin, 9th Infantry, Post-Quartermaster, to purchase in open market such quantities as he might require for shoeing the fore feet.

The weather to-day has been quite windy, but nothing like the bad storm of dust which annoyed us yesterday, making walking or riding almost an impossibility.

Seventeen families came in from the ranches on the South Platte to-day, scared by the reports of the Indian advance. Major Thornburgh and his subordinates have been continuously employed all day in distributing horses, saddles and equipments among the men of the two Infantry Companies, Bowman's of the 9th and Spencer's of the 4th, which are to be mounted.

In my conversations with Ben Clark, I have been successful in eliciting much information of considerable value upon the ethnography of the plains tribes, specially the Cheyennes, among whom, as I have mentioned already, he has lived for over 21 yrs. continuously. Clark is a man of clear intellect, expressing himself in good language, honest and truthful in his statements and accurate in his deductions. The Cheyennes call themselves *His-tàs*, a derivative probably from the verb É-histà=to wound, to slash. Now in the sign-language, as I have said in another note-book, the mark for Cheyenne is made by drawing the right forefinger across the Left wrist. This would mean either "to cut" or else "striped". Generally the first meaning has been assigned and many people call the Cheyennes the "cut-fingers,["] just as for similar reasons the Sioux have been known as the "cut-throats". But the Cheyenne say that the whites first heard of them through the Comanches who wished to describe them as the people who had arrows with "striped" features, because the Cheyenne arrows were always feathered from the wings and tails of the wild-turkey. A misinterpretation of the sign caused them to receive the name I speak of.[17]

In general character, the Cheyenne are extremely fierce, cruel, skilled in battle, unequalled in horsemanship, precise as marksmen. They are formidable competitors in the field as well as most astute in council. From my acquaintance with them at Red Cloud Agency in 1877, and my service against them, I formed a very high opinion of their general character and always found them truthful and to be relied upon. (See my note-books of 1876–1877.)[18] Bancroft, in his history of the Native Tribes of the Pacific Slope, says the Comanches and Cheyennes are unequalled as horsemen.[19] The language of the Cheyennes is mellifluous and sonorous, but from a curious manner of eliding and apocopating. They have made many of their words so hard to distinguish, that their language is scarcely more easy for an American to learn than is the Arapahoe. As among all other tribes the women have a jargon of their own, using expressions which the men do not consider sufficiently dignified for their use. I noticed one very curious fact in their language: the word for nose is Nay-é-ve, but in all compounds, they use "May-é-his"="red-nose".* General

*In the half-line below May Bourke wrote red, and below é-his, he wrote nose.

17. According to George Bird Grinnell (*Cheyenne Indians*, 1:3–4), the Cheyennes call themselves *Tsistsistas*, which translates more or less as "people." As for the sign, Grinnell said it has variously been attributed to striped feathers on arrows, as well as a practice of slashing themselves as a sacrifice.
18. This material is contained in Robinson, *Diaries*, Volume 2.
19. Bourke refers to a passage in Hubert Howe Bancroft's *Native Races* (1:517–18), which states:
> Of all North American Indians the Comanches and Cheyennes are said to be the most skillful riders, and it would be difficult to find their superiors in any part of the world. Young children, almost infants, are tied by their mothers to half-wild, bare-backed mustangs, which place thenceforth becomes their home. . . . A favorite horse is loved and cherished above all things on earth, not excepting wives and children.

Custer, whose sanguine complexion and sun-peeled nose obtained for him the appellation from the Southern Cheyennes when they first met him in his campaign of 1866–67.[20] The Northern Cheyennes always called him "Long Hair". This fact of having two words in use for common objects would be a philological indication to my mind that the Cheyennes are the result of a merging at some distant day of two distinct ethnic streams, just as in English we have the Saxon word Bull and the Norman word Beef for the same thing.

They call an elk "móe", and a horse móe-ini, this shows of course from the fact that the word for horse is a compound of the word for elk, that they knew the latter animal before they knew the former, as we might suppose to be the case. The word for "moon" is "night-sun".

The most convenient point of departure in narrating the peculiarities of the Cheyenne Indians, is, it seems to me, their birth.

During the critical period of maternity, their women are carefully attended by mid-wives, and supplied with everything in the way of good food or warm herb-teas that the limited resources of their cuisine will admit. Many Cheyenne women are attacked with puerperal fever and not infrequently deaths occur in labor. All the stupid nonsense we read about the lack of peril, the immunity of *Indian* women while passing through the ordeal of the curse primeval, is silly bosh. Upon marches, and especially when pressed by an enemy or compelled by hunger to move a village from one situation to another, Cheyenne women have brought forth their children unaided and even when exposed to cold and fatigue, but the rule is as I give it above—that both they and their husbands and friends appreciate the gravity of their condition and make every effort to diminish its pains and perils.

For months before and after delivery, husbands do not approach their wives.* The child, when born, is washed in warm water, clothed and handed to its mother. No traces of the "coewade" [?] have been observed among the Cheyennes. The birth of a boy is the occasion for much rejoicing; sometimes, feasts are spread to which all friends are invited. Children are treated with great kindness—are rarely

---

Above this, Bourke inserted: Abortion is known among them.

20. This refers to the campaigns of 1867–69, during which Custer attacked and destroyed a group of Cheyenne villages on November 27, 1868. See Hoig, *Battle of the Washita*, and Greene, *Washita*.

punished, sometimes girls may be slapped by their mothers, but boys scarcely ever are struck. For games and amusements, the boys have fishing lines and bows and arrows from the time they can first stand up. They are also placed upon horseback and taught equitation while they are only able to crawl. When a boy is five or six years old, he is able to shoot birds off from the limbs of trees.

They also have tops, rudely whittled out of hard wood, the extremities of the vertical axis often terminating in brass pins: these are "whipped" with buckskin strings.

Little girls have dolls and have imitations of "travaux",[21] with poles, baskets &c, in which they sling their dolls, frequently using a little puppy as a horse. They also make toy cradles for their dolls.

A favorite game with little girls is "foot-ball", the projectile being made of buck-skin, stuffed with buffalo hair, and balanced on foot.

As they grow older, girls from ten to fifteen years of age are very fond of "shinny",—but this is rarely, if ever, played by boys or young men. This game is exactly the same as ours with established bases, sides and rules. The forfeit is a feast to be given the victors by the vanquished. Both sexes and all ages are greatly addicted to card-gambling: they procure their cards from traders and do not make them of horse-hide as do the Apaches. One of their card games bears too close a resemblance to our "muggins" to be mistaken; in it, the unfortunate loser's face is blackened amid the jeers of the other players and the bystanders. They play casino generally and many of them are familiar with both forms of "monte".

[They] are very fond of "odd or even", played with small pebbles: they have no game of colored sticks like the Pacific Coast Indians,[22] but do possess their game with lances, arrows and hoops.

An arrow placed upright as a mark has the others thrown at it; the one nearest takes the prize. Or arrows are thrown simply for display of skill in throwing; casts of thirty to forty yards with the hand are not uncommon. A hoop is rolled along the ground and lances thrown after it; the most skilful [sic] players are those who can pass the lance through the hoop while rolling. Or, they will hold a bow ver-

21. A now-obsolete plural of "travois."
22. Among the modern plains Indians, the Comanches in the vicinity of Apache, Oklahoma, play stick games. I have seen games where a considerable amount of folding money is strewn about the pit in wagers. They often are accompanied by a respectable amount of barbecued brisket on side tables.

ticle [sic], take an arrow by the feathered end, tap it smartly against the taught [sic] string and as it rebounds from the hand, determine the value of the stroke by noting where it strikes the ground with reference to an arrow inserted in the ground as a "pointer".

The young warriors are extravagantly fond of horse-racing; their favorite racers and war ponies are well looked after. Upon them can generally be seen some painting—a mark of a human hand in yellow, black or red paint; red flannel or feathers in main [sic] and tail or even a piece of skin or horn of the antelope, in the belief that by wearing those charms the horse will become swift enough to catch the fleet venison.

The young married women have a game for indoors, at which they pass many hours of their time: it is played with brass needles, six inches long, to which are attached threads of sinew, filled with beads; at ends of threads are four large rings and four bones, (from the legs of the prairie dog,) which bones are perforated with holes. Taking the needle in her fingers, the squaw swings the rings and perforated bones in the air and essays to catch them on the needle.

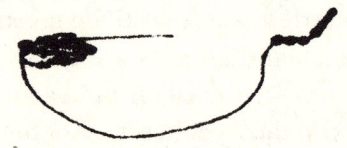

The counting is determined by the number of rings thus secured. The women have sewing "bees", with hash and gossip, just as among the whites: and when a family is about to make a new lodge all the women folks of the village are invited to take a part in the work which is really very laborious. The most experienced old woman is deputized to superintend the "cutting out", no small task when we consider that from ten to twenty buffalo cow skins are needed for each lodge and that there is just as much paring, gusseting, piercing and stretching required as in the most elaborate American dress. The sewing is done in sinew, taken from the buffalo hump.

As they grow to maturity, the young Cheyennes aspire to become great warriors; the general tenor of their education is to make them capable of enduring fatigue, undergoing privations and despising danger.

Contrary to general apprehension on the subject, the Sun Dance is not the ordeal to which all young men must submit before securing recognition as brave soldiers; while I am not ready to say that there are any warriors in this tribe who have not subjected themselves to this test, I do know from Ben Clark, Frank Gruard, old Friday of the Arapahoes, Billy Hunter, and Lieut. Clark, (2nd Cavalry,) that the Sun Dance is a propitiatory act, a vicarious sacrifice for the whole tribe, as well as a personal oblation to the Great Spirit, whose wrath, they suppose can be conciliated by self-mutilation and torture. There are many young bucks who have passed through this terrible suffering two and three, occasionally even four times.... [T]he Sun Dance must take place in the month of June as the medicine lodge in which much mummery is practised during the ceremony, has to be made of *leafy* boughs; farther to the South, the Cheyennes celebrate it sometimes as early as *April* when the foliage first appears. Having fasted from food and drink for (2) days and gone without sleep for two nights, the candidate for these honors has the clothing stripped from the upper party of his body, slits are made in the skin of his shoulders, breast and arms, through which are passed ropes of hair or buffalo hide, having attached the heads of buffalo, elk or the domestic cattle. The young man must pull and strain until he has torn loose from these impediments; sometimes, he faints away with pain. In such a case his friends may march in and stamp on him and pull and haul until they tear the ropes through the flesh and liberate the prostrate victim. . . . The cardinal virtues among the Cheyenne are Valor, Generosity, Prudence and Tenderness for family.

About this time, if he amounts to anything at all, the young man, has a voice in the public councils; here, they behave like other Indians, serious, seemingly impassive and stolid, but on all other occasions when among themselves, they are cheerful, chatty and even hilarious, and greatly given to telling stories.

The young men marry at any time from 18 to 20, generally when about 20 or 21. An Indian may have as many wives as he feels he can support, but monogamy seems to be getting more and more the rule. When in permanent camps, the Cheyennes are very neat and cleanly in dress and person: dirty and lousy habits are derided. On marches, necessarily, all this changes to a greater or less extent according to circumstances.

The devoted Cheyenne mother scours the heads of her babies and eats the objects of her search.[23] The young men and women are very

---

23. I.e., lice.

nearly all provided with fine combs. Girls are nubile at fourteen, but ordinarily marry at a later age than is the case among the Kiowas or Arapahoes. During time of menstrual purgation, women live apart in small lodges. When two or three girls in [the] same condition are in one village, they live together, for company sake. Food is brought to them and sometimes, for medical reasons perhaps this is prepared in a peculiar way. During this time, a young girl must not enter her parent's lodge or indeed any lodge, but she is at liberty to go wherever she wants out of doors.

The chastity of women is highly regarded.

In courting, the Cheyennes use rings made of Brittania [sic] metal, German silver or silver, ornamented with carvings of lizards or other animals. When a young Cheyenne warrior becomes interested in a young girl, he proceeds to her parents' lodge, near which he takes his station, while his sister or some other female relative goes inside and hands to the young maiden a ring, made as above described. If this be refused, the young man knows that his suit is rejected; but its acceptance gives him no right to her hand but simply places him on the "anxious bench", and enrolls him as one of her suitors; she may have as many of these as she pleases, three or four being not uncommon, and a ring from each worn on the fingers. The lover now has to wait until he can catch the young maiden coming out of her lodge, when he will seize her in his arms and wrap his blanket about her. This is a formal declaration of his love. Young people may be seen sitting on the ground wrapped in [the] same blanket, and when the young lady's affections are finally enlisted on the side of her lover, she allows him to kiss her, much in the good old-fashioned way to be noticed among other nations. (This sitting, wrapped up on the same blanket can also be seen among the Apaches and Navajoes of the South-West.)

Finally, when the young lady's heart has been won, the suitor must apply for her hand, not to her parents, but to her "guardian", who is most frequently an elder brother, altho' he may be some other relative. This wardship is an odd feature. The mother and father, probably exercise great influence in the matter but externally at least, the guardian has full powers: these, he may exercise arbitrarily, and in that case, the young lady to escape a marriage repugnant to her notions, often will elope with the favored lover. Taught as she is to submit to the inevitable, the young lady often accepts with good grace the hand of her guardian's—"avisin-hit" or "bosom-friend."—that is the friend who will remain by his side in battle or any other danger.

The marriage ceremony is very simple, that is if we can consider it a ceremony at all.

The groom sends to parents of [the] bride, a present, generally of horses, proportional to the importance of her family, and her own worth.

These are led over by some of the females of his family and picketed in front of the bride's parents lodge. If these be accepted any time during the day, the young man immediately has his lodge erected, in time to receive his bride, who comes to the lodge escorted by her women-friends, while she is elaborately painted and arrayed in her best attire. It is to be remarked that she wears no plumage, nor indeed are feathers ever allowed to be worn by women, as they are looked upon as the peculiar decoration of warriors only. There are no nuptial songs, and no congratulatory ceremonies. Occasionally, the bride's parents give a feast to their friends.

There is a well-defined "honey-moon" passed in travelling to other villages of the tribe; upon arriving at such villages, the bridal pair are treated with special deference and consideration. High Wolf, who has lately married Red Hat's daughter, is at this writing, (Sept. 22nd–Oct. 4th 1877.) in the camp of these Cheyennes:—he is very attentive to his bride, who seems to dote upon him. They live apart from the rest of the band and are just as "spooney" as lovers in a fashionable novel. Ben Clark assures me that there is much affection in the married life of the Cheyennes, altho' they are careful to conceal any manifestations of it from the public gaze. Polygamy being recognized, we need not be astonished when we sometimes come across 2 or three wives living in the same lodge: the rule however is to separate from the old wife before taking a new [one].

Divorces are easily obtained; the husband simply sends his wife away. While I was in Sidney, Crazy Mule took back a wife with whom he had quarrelled and from whom he had separated. He acted as if ashamed of himself, in having admitted by his last act that his first one had been an injustice.

Here Bourke inserted a picture which is now darkened beyond recognition, possibly by the glue used to affix it to the page almost 130 years ago.

The picture on this page represents a young Cheyenne courting his sweet-heart: it is one of a series from a book in my possession, painted by the Cheyennes. The book itself, they say, was taken from the body of a soldier killed in [the] Custer Massacre.

Ben Clark presented me with the book.

I have made many inquiries concerning "totems", or clan-marks; thus far with scarcely any success. Ben Clark says, so far as the Cheyennes are regarded, a Cheyenne warrior can marry any Cheyenne girl excepting his sister or first cousin. Like the Spaniards and Mexicans, they call their cousins by the endearing title of "sister". I have, however, found that all these plains tribes, the Crows, Sioux, Cheyennes and Arapahoes have certain secret-politico-military organizations throughout the tribe and charged with the defense of its interests, in peace or war.[24] Among the Cheyennes, these are known as the Bull-soldiers, Elk-soldiers, Fox-soldiers, Dog-soldiers, and Crooked Lances. The Dog-soldiers, have been of late, by far the most famous and are the best known to our people, who for a while in 1866–67 considered them almost as a separate band.

The Cheynne scarcely ever tattoo. Painting is very commonly practised. The face is painted almost any color, preferably yellow. Black and Red are most affected as "war paint". The median line of the head is for "full dress", powdered with Chinese vermillion, and the eye-lid, at the eyes, tipped with a brush holding some of [the] same pigment. Contrary to general opinion, I must say that the North American Indians are not very dark naturally; sometimes as light almost as white babies, but exposure to the sun tans them very dark. The Moqui[25] Indians who live constantly in the shelter of stone houses are to my model of thinking, fairer than the Mexicans inhabiting the country near them.

The Cheyennes manufacture no stimulants; they are passionately fond of whiskey, obtained at times from white men and Mexican half-breeds. When their nerves are depressed, they will eat the gall of the buffalo as a tonic and exhilarant.

---

24. These are the warrior societies. In battle, they function as quasi-combat units, and in camp as a sort of civil police. Among some plains tribes, these societies have been resurrected in modern times as veterans' organizations. A notable example is the Kiowa Black Leg Society. See Time-Life, *Way of the Warrior*, 120ff.

25. I.e., Hopi.

Their ordinary language is almost free from invective; in their imprecations, the name of the Great Spirit is never used. Their expressions of contempt are Mas-sìm=fool, enhé-to-vàn=silly-head, hí-â-tam=dog, níssi-keh=bitch, O-îsh-kish=pup, and rarely, when very angry, Natsi-vis=____ mouth[26] and I-ehé-his=snot nose.

The common prayer, to call it by such a name, is, among the Northern Cheyennes, at least, Nâchi-°vettàn,°° i.e. help me (Great Spirit.) Occasionally they will ascend to the tops of lofty mountains and there remain for 3 or four days, fasting and crying, calling upon the Great Spirit to help them because they are poor Indians, want more horses &c. Bear Butte, at the North East. corner of the Black Hills[27] was once a sort of a Mecca for the Cheyennes; its summit, they imagined, was the place of resort of the spirits of their dead and to go there and remain isolated from the world for a few days, until half starved was looked upon as an act of great piety.

In smoking the pipe, each Indian has his own method of handling it, waving it to the Right or Left, upwards or downwards, in a circle or straight line and of inhaling and ejecting the smoke. From all I can gather, the act of smoking, at least in council, has much "medicine" connected with it. They are superstitious to a fault in some things; as for instance, when they hear owls hooting after dark, they are certain that their dead friends are embodied in the owls and trying to communicate with those they left on earth. They have no superstitions about food, as other tribes have; but when a Cheyenne has made a vow not to partake of certain kinds of food, he will religiously observe his contract, even where the article from which he has vowed to abstain is whiskey.

Thunder they believe to be occasioned by a large and malevolent bird—Na-nó-moh=thunder, is derived from I-ná-_=to kill. Both Cheyennes and Arapahoes fire off guns to drive away thunder and lightning. In Battle the warriors sing a monotonous chant of howls and hiaya, ya, Hi–ya-ya's, and shout to the enemy "we don't want to live until our teeth are short", alluding to the fact that the teeth of their old people are often worn down to the gums from eating dried buffalo meat which the wind fills with sand.[28] They call the enemy

°Below this Bourke wrote: me.
°°And below this: help.

26. Bourke's Victorianism is showing. He almost certainly meant "shit mouth."
27. Plainly visible to the north from the Veterans' Administration center at Fort Meade, South Dakota, about five miles due east of Sturgis.
28. Meaning the buffalo meat was dried in the sun, exposing it to grit and dust.

cowards and dogs, and defy them to come close and fight. "Chivy-mumuawitz" which literally means "hurry up and strike against us". Of their method, if any, of declaring war, I have been able to obtain very meagre and incoherent accounts, and I consider that Ben Clark's statement is a well-founded one. He says that they have made no new wars since he came among them and that all their feuds and enmities are hereditary. They admit that the Pawnees and Shoshonees are brave, but say that the Utes are braver than either. The Crows are daring horse-thieves, but don't fight well. As for the Sioux, they gained this country by sheer force of numbers and not by any especial bravery.

At this point it is appropriate to remark that for some cause, probably the incoming of the Sioux, the tribes of the plains have within the past century been much disintegrated; bands of the same nation, speaking the same language, are to be found at opposite poles, so to speak; thus, the Arickarees and Pawnees speak the same language; the upper Gros-Ventres and the Crows are the same and the lower Gros Ventres [sic] are identical with the Arapahoes. The Asiniboines and Dacotahs are of same stock; the Kiowas are closely related to the Crows and the Shoshonees to the Comanches. The Blackfeet, altho' using a different idiom, are of the same derivation as the Arapahoes.

(Upon this subject, remarks were made in my note-books of Novr-Decr 1876 and April 1877.)[29] The Northern Arapahoes call themselves Nan-na-é, but are styled by the Southern Arapahoes—Nah-thé-n_.

Of their tribal government, I couldn't obtain much more knowledge than already possessed; in one word, we may say the administration of affairs is in the hands of a senate of old men, and distinguished warriors, in which every man of the tribe, who has distinguished himself in battle, has a voice. (See preceding note books.)[30]

Old people are kindly treated, but when hard pressed by an enemy, the Cheyennes have been known to abandon them.

Their commerce with other tribes is at present reduced to a nullity; all trading is done with the whites whose stocks are greater and prices lower than could be obtained in a trade carried on by barter with their neighbors. As our money circulates freely, they have no

---

29. This material is contained in Robinson, *Diaries*, Volume 2.
30. Ibid.

wampum or shell currency. They buy with great eagerness the "hair pipe", sold by the traders; of this they make fanciful breast-plates and sometimes earrings. I don't know what this hair-pipe is made of; it is made by a man in New Jersey, who thus far has kept the secret of its manufacture to himself. It looks like porcelain or fine glass tubing, but many people think that it is made from sea-shells. The Indians value it highly and will pay almost any price for it.[31]

They take scalps in war, simply as a proof that an enemy has been slain. In holding relations of a pacific nature with other tribes, it is their custom to send a herald, armed with a pipe. Before proceeding on his mission, this envoy will fast for several days, to insure success. Dramatic societies have only lately been introduced among the Cheyennes; these are evidently organized in imitation of those among the Sioux of which a full account can be found in my notebooks of April and May 1877.[32]

They take great pleasure in the dance and will organize parties for that purpose upon the slightest pretext. In one of these, the participants take their places in couples; while dancing, the young buck will sing to the girl who happens to be his partner—"I am looking for a nice girl to live with me and be my wife and stay with me wherever I go; I think I see the girl I am looking for". The young lady answers in the same strain and then they join hands and dance together down the line. (Of the Buffalo dance a description will be given farther on.) Their literature, whether as tradition or graphic delineation amounts to nothing: they do not show much proficiency as picture-writers and are unable or unwilling to give an account of their lineage or the locality from which their progenitors migrated. My experience has been that an Indian will frame for the occasion just such a tradition as he thinks will suit the fancy or prejudice of his inquisitors.

Their lodges, formerly made of elk or buffalo cow skins, are now framed of canvass, wrapped around poles, (18 @ 24 in number.) of a length all the way up to 24 feet. These are made from the heart of pine, fir, (among Northn. Cheyennes) or cedar trees, (among Southern Cheyennes.

The saplings are selected for their straightness and flexibility and

---

31. Generally considered porcelain.
32. The material for April 1877 is found in Robinson, *Diaries*, Volume 2, Chapter 13. The notebooks for May are missing.

are trimmed down to the proper diameter, four inches. Around the inner side of [the] lodge are strewn couches made of furs spread over willow branches, with head and foot-boards of twigs, covered in like manner; pillows of buffalo hair. A fire is made in [the] center of floor, the smoke escaping through [an] orifice left in the apex of the cone.

Outside of each lodge may be seen the owner's shield and sometimes his lance, bow and war-bonnet.—also a scaffold upon which meat is "jerked". (Consult note-books of 1876–1877, for fuller description.)[33] Their villages are always arranged in [the] form of [a] circle; the space enclosed is used for dances, councils, &c.

Before starting on a buffalo hunt in the Fall of the year, they hold their "buffalo dance". In centre of camp, they erect a big lodge of boughs, covered with skins, &c., much after the manner of a "medicine" lodge. In this all the mummery of the festival is carried on. The master of ceremonies is a very important personage and orders things much to his own fancy. A grand Mardi Gras procession dances through the village, the characters represented being those of wild animals; lions, wild-cats, panthers, buffalo, elk, deer, mountain sheep, bears and wolves are cleverly imitated, the actors decked out with the heads and skins of the proper animals whose actions they assume with great cleverness.

Besides these actors proper, there are a lot of clowns, who are entirely naked, except a breech-clout; there seems to be no recognized color to be followed, each one being left to the dictates of his own fancy. The procession moves along, as I have said, much in the style of a carnival;—the ludicrous, burlesque, obscene and serious blended.

The clowns indulge in vulgar jokes to excite the laughter of the spectators. The actors meantime are faithfully carrying out their respective parts; the buffalo bulls lower their heads and rush at each other in deadly combat; the vanquished bull runs away, and the conqueror suddenly darts into the crowd, seizes some young girl and carries her off. This is the signal for great merriment. The maiden is derisively called the buffalo cow and must remain with her captor until the farce is over. While the dance is going on, all the sick and infirm are brought to the front of their lodges; the masqueraders make a grand circuit of the village and upon coming

---

33. Robinson, *Diaries*, Volume 2.

to one of the sick people march around him three times in single file—this, they think, will alleviate his sufferings. The clowns keep dancing about among the villagers and frequently try to shoot with blunt arrows, some of the young girls and if they succeed, she must follow the clown all day.

This is all there is of the dance in public, but afterwards there is a meeting in the big lodge, at which appear two young girls, eight to ten years old, naked and painted to represent buffalo calves. While in public view, these girls were kept covered with buffalo calf heads and skins; but among the Arapahoes, this part of the ceremony is carried on with less regard to decency. *They* have one full grown woman and two young girls, perfectly naked and their chief of ceremonies is not a man but a naked woman who takes the part of a white buffalo cow. This dance is considered sure "medicine" for bringing the hunters plenty of buffalo.

They are superstitious about the albino or white buffalo to this extent that when one is killed, the woman who is to tan the hide must first have a lot of mummery and incantation performed over her by the "medicine" men.

Their burial ceremonies may be delineated in a few words.[34] "Formerly they buried their dead on scaffolds, erected on poles, 6 ft. above the ground (feet of corpse to the East.); they also placed their dead on trees where there was plenty of them. When a warrior died, they painted him, put on all his finest clothes, ornaments &c. and rolled him and his implements of war, shield, war bonnet, in his finest blankets, and robes, and with them fineries contributed by friends and relations. All these were tied up on a large robe. The body then [was] placed on a travaux [*sic*], or 'Um-sto-ase', as these Cheyennes call it and taken by the relations and friends to the place of burial: a favorite horse (sometimes two or more;) led to the grave and shot. The relatives then cut their hair, which is worn full length by both men and women when not in mourning. The women gash their legs from the ankle to the knee, sometimes, a mother will cut her finger off at first joint. Their hair is left to hang loose during the period of mourning which is arbitrary in its duration. When not in mourning, men and women have their hair done up. The women

---

34. Here begins an account of Cheyenne burial customs, and their connections with Arapahos written by Ben Clark.

wear it in two neat braids; the men twist theirs up in strips of blue or red cloth or otter skin.

["]At time of burial, relations remain crying near grave until the fall of night when they return to the village, and then cry at intervals during night loud enough to be heard all over the Camp. (At foot of grave or scaffold—for I must here interpolate the remark that they now bury nearly as often in the ground as upon scaffolds—articles of food and drink are placed.) They sometimes visit a grave after several months, place articles of food and drink in kettles and leave them there. This habit is not so generally observed now as it once was; in the last year or two, they have begun to bury in ground for better security, there having been several bodies stolen from scaffolds and trees.

["]The name Cheyenne, as they are known by the whites, was given them by the French at an early day & is derived from the French for dog=chien.[35] The Cheyennes were then, and are yet, great dog-eaters, and their first French visitors were feasted so often on dog that they called them the "dog-eaters"; some of the oldest men of the tribe, yet living, say the above version is true. Their Indian name *His-tah*, means the 'Wounders'; it is abbreviated from the word, 'A-his-tah'=to wound. How they came to get that name they say they can't tell; they only know that their fathers before them called themselves 'His-tah'.

["]The range of the Arapahoe Indians, as regards their ancient and present locality, are exactly the same as the Cheyennes, they having always been a neighboring and friendly tribe and much intermarriage. They roamed the same range before and their Agency and Reservation are now together. *Their* Indian name is 'Non-nôh-a'=Tit-suckers or Sage men. *They* [are] always buried in the ground feet to the East and their other ceremonies are same as (those of) the Cheyennes.

["]Yours Respectfully,
(Sig.) Ben Clark."

The above was sent me by Ben Clark, from the Cheyenne Agency, Fort Reno, Indian Territory, Oct 2d, 1877, and was by me sent to

---

35. Grinnell (*Cheyenne Indians*, 1:2–3) acknowledges this was thought to be the case for many years, but adds it is now known that the word "Cheyenne" is a contraction of the Sioux words *Sh_ h_' y_ na*, or *Sha h_' _ la*. This literally translates as "red talkers," which means people whose language cannot be understood. Cheyenne is an Algonquian language, while the Siouan languages and dialects are in a group of their own.

Dr. H. C. Yarrow, who was compiling a work for the Dep't. of the Interior on the mortuary services of our native tribes.[36]

John G. Bourke
Aide de Camp

In our conversations at Sidney, Ben supplemented the above by saying that as a sign of mourning, Cheyennes will crop the manes and tails of their ponies: widows, mothers and sisters slash arms and legs with knives. Whenever, they pass by the graves of any of their kindred, they will halt for a time and wail.

---

36. Yarrow's book, *A Further Contribution to the Study of the Mortuary Customs of the North American Indians*, was published by the Smithsonian Institution Bureau of Ethnology in 1880. Like Bourke, Yarrow was a soldier, in this case, a surgeon in the Regular Army, although Heitman does not list him. In researching the book, Yarrow sent a questionnaire to every Indian agent, as well as agency physicians, and to army officers serving at frontier posts. The volume was one of a series of books on North American ethnology prepared under direction of Maj. John Wesley Powell, director of the Bureau of Ethnology, under whom Bourke later also would work.

Chapter 8

Hunting the Refugees

Sept. 26. Thus far no news of any kind concerning the Cheyenne refugees: Major Thornburgh has had scouts sent out along the South Platte river, to the South and East of Sidney, to watch for the first intimations of their presence. Day before yesterday, Dr. Munn told me a story he had heard from one of the cattle men employed on the ranch of the Bosler Bros. This was to the effect that on the night of the 21st, or 22d instant, a dark, but starlit night, two men of that ranch who were out hunting for stray cattle, came suddenly upon seven figures, closely wrapped, mounted on Indian ponies and moving in single file at a rapid gait, (jog-trot.) towards the North. The cattle men at first halloed at them, but the only effect produced was to make the Indians, if such they were, go faster. The cattle men then becoming alarmed, hid themselves in the hills until dawn when they took up the trail of the mysterious travellers and followed it until they came to where a beef had been slaughtered, in the way peculiar to Indians.[1] At first I was not inclined to put much credence in the story, and besides was afraid that anything

---

1. These probably were Cheyenne foragers, trying to round up livestock to feed the refugees. Because farmers and stockmen were putting up fights, the foragers tended to work by stealth, avoiding confrontation whenever possible. Monnett, *Tell Them We Are Going Home*, 74.

I might say would be repeated and great alarm and anxiety occasioned; but as the same story came to me afterwards of the same mysterious seven night-wanderers, mounted on ponies, journeying northward, I concluded and still believe that they were an advance party pushed out by the Cheyennes to scan the country or perhaps to open up communication with the Sioux at Red Cloud and Spotted Tail Agencies. Major Thornburgh has been working hard to have the mounted Infantry learn something of drill and horsemanship. They are divided into two companies under Lieut. Bowman of the 9th and Spencer of the 4th Infantry. Each morning, they drill for two hours and each afternoon for same time. There are many laughable occurrences to note, but the general good humor of the men and patience of the officers is worthy of all praise. One man at morning drill, mounted his horse in a rather clumsy way, sticking his spurs in the animal's sides and making him trot slowly out of ranks. The recruit, of course, grabbed hold of the mane and the horse feeling the spurs pressed against his flanks, started at a good round "lope" for the stable. Headed off by the members of the stable police, he started back towards the platoon, his pace accelerated at every stride and the poor devil on his back holding on like grim Death with both arms about his neck. The sarcastic yells and suggestions from his comrades didn't sooth his mortification very much and added greatly to his perplexity. "Arrah! thin, take your sphurs orf!" Och! Murther! luk at the Curcus roider! and others of the like import. The steed had by this time come to the conclusion that he had had enough of such a rider and very dexterously chucked him over his head, into a sand-bank, as he raised himself and scraped the sand from his eyes, nose and mouth, the unfortunate victim cried out reproachfully to his tormenters, "Och! thin, boi Jaysus, it's moighty aisy to say, take yur sphurs orf, but how the Hill can oi?" Taking this fellow as a fair average and he wasn't very far below it, I couldn't help thinking that our Expedition wasn't likely to accomplish anything very brilliant in the shape of a Cavalry charge.

Friday, September 27th. Colonel [William B.] Royall Insp. Genl. of the Department of the Platte, passed West on his way to Fort McKinney. A party of our scouts returned from the South Platte, reporting no signs of Indians. They say that buffaloes in considerable numbers are coming north and are now near the Head-waters of the Republican river, not more than fifty miles South of the South

Platte. The newspapers to-day contained telegraphic accounts of a fight between the Cheyennes and the troops sent to intercept them, in a cañon near Sand Creek, on the Kansas and Colorado line. In the fight, the Cheyennes retreated up the cañon to a point where they had excavated rifle-pits, hoping to induce the troops to follow. The latter camped in front of the enemy all night, intending to commence an assault at early dawn; but during the night, the Indians, not wishing to risk an engagement, decamped and pushed out to the North-West. The account was so meagre we couldn't rely much upon it.[2] Saturday, Sept. 2d. Dr. Munn drove me around the town of Sidney, growing to a place of importance; the Black Hills' traffic; and the shipment of supplies to the Sioux Indians at the Agencies to the North are the sources of considerable business.

The residence of Mr. Van Tassel, a wealthy stock raiser, is very neat in appearance and shows the good taste of the owner. The only new building of any size was a Roman Catholic church, the only church I believe in town.

Sunday. Sept. 20th. A very disagreeable storm of wind and dust arose in the afternoon and reached to greatest height about sun-down: the velocity of the blast could not have been less than (50) @ (60) miles an hour, before which the supple cottonwood trees fringing the barracks' parade bent like blades of grass. Mr. James Chambers invited Major Thornburgh and myself to dine with a small number of friends; we enjoyed the little affair greatly and as is wont to be the case at all military parties, we talked a great deal about our old friends and indulged in reminiscences of days passed away. Thanks to Dr. Munn, the post Surgeon I have been furnished with a pleasant room in the new Hospital, as yet unoccupied by patients. Here, I have a good bed, warm fire, as well as desk and stationery, with which to keep my journal.

Major Thornburg [sic] and the officers belonging to his command are in camp, with their companies, the Cheyennes, who are to go South under Ben Clark, being alongside of them.

The post of Sidney Barracks, built to be occupied by three companies of Cavalry, has at present only one, Fitzgerald's, of the 9TH

---

2. This refers to a fight on Sand (or Big Sandy) Creek, in Kansas, on September 21–22, 1878, when Dull Knife and Little Wolf dug in on high ground overlooking troops and cattlemen volunteers. Fearing the whites might be reinforced, the Cheyennes slipped away during the night of September 22, crossing the Arkansas River the following day. Monnett, *Tell Them We Are Going Home*, 63–66.

Infantry, altho' Cap't. and Bv't. Lt. Col. Devin of the same Regt. is in command. Col. G.A. Gordon, 5th Cavalry, in command at the time of our arrival, has since gone on sick leave, his health being very much in danger and life threatened.* The parade ground is a charming sward of green grass, surrounded by a row of thriving cottonwood trees; the quarters are prettily built, in the cottage style and are in very good condition. Ditches filled with water from the Lodge Pole creek, supply moisture to the roots of the cottonwoods, and serve also to lay the dust of the roads. The society at the post is very pleasant and agreeable, much of it old friends of mine; being kept very busy with my note-books, and official duties, I have very little time for making social visits, but those which I have made have been very enjoyable indeed. There has been very little, if any, time for reading, but such as has been available has been employed in re-perusing some of the chapters in *Green's Short History of the English People*—a very carefully digested book, written in a spirit of fairness and impartiality.³

Monday, Sep't. 3d. Telegram received from Colonel Williams, Assistant Adjutant General, Hd.Qrs. Dep't. of the Platte, giving intimation to Colonel [sic] Thornburgh that the Cheyennes had broken through the line of the Kansas Pacific Rail Road and that he (Thornburgh.) might be required to act.

Lieut. Davis, 5th Cavalry, with his company, "L", was at once ordered out to patrol the line of the South Platte, to cross that river and push out in direction of the Republican, and upon the first approach of the enemy, to avoid an engagement, but to watch them closely, and at the same time send couriers to Colonel Thornburgh, who would keep the main body of his troops well in hand at Sidney.

The Union Pacific R.R. was to have a train ready for us to move the command at the shortest notice possible: the work of drilling our mounted Infantry was redoubled and we now began to have some hope of getting them into shape before they could be called upon to confront an enemy.

Above this, Bourke wrote: (Since died, Oct. 27th 1878.)

3. John Richard Green (1837–83) was an English clergymen who held parishes in London as well as serving as librarian of Lambeth Palace. He was considered one of the leading amateur historians of his day. The *Short History of the English People*, to which Bourke referred, was published in 1874, and was a smooth, colorful narrative that made it the second best-selling English history book of the nineteenth century, Macaulay's *History of England* being the first. Green later expanded the project into the four-volume *History of the English People*, which was completed by his wife after his death. http://www.litencyc.com/php/speople.php?rec=true&UID=1858

Lieut. Spencer has been especially zealous and hard-working with his company.

Heard from the papers to-day of the fight of the 27th inst. in which Lieut-Col. [William H.] Lewis, of the 19th Infantry, was killed, also that the Cheyennes had certainly crossed the Kansas Pacific Rail Way on the 29th at 9 in the morning, near Carlyle Station.[4]

Major Thornburgh's Command is composed as follows:

Co. "D" 14th Infantry, Lts. Austin & Lovell	38 men.
"H" 4th Infantry, Lieut. Spencer & [Silas A.] Wolf	38
"G" 9th Infantry, Capt. Burrowes & Lt. Wyatt.	40
"A" 7th Cavy., Cap't. Mathey & Lt. Creel.	21
"L" 5th Cavy., Lts. Davis & Merrill	52
"K" 9th Infy. Lieut. Bowman & Palmer	32.

Lieuts. Merrill and Wolf, are young graduates of this year's Class at the Mily. Academy, who are on their way to join station; they volunteered to accompany the Expedition & have been assigned to duty as above stated.

In addition to the above, were Lieut Bourke, Lieut. Norris, A. A. Surgeon Marston and Lieut [Robert H.] Young. The three Lieutenants named were volunteers. Lt. Young did not arrive until later, but I put his name in at this point to keep the organization complete by itself.

Nearly all the officers of Thornburgh's command messed at the Rail Road Hotel, in Sidney, about half a mile from camp; they had a separate table and received kind attention.

Tuesday, Oc't. 1st. Nothing to-day to record.

Wednesday, Oct. 2d. [I] feel pleased to think that I have been so careful in collecting materials for this note book: the little Cheyenne war-cloud, erewhile [sic] no bigger than a man's hand is each day gathering to itself huger proportions.

To-morrow or next day, we expect to encounter the enemy in their effort to cross the Union Pacific Rail Road and while we may not perhaps be successful in foiling them, we shall certainly not be found lacking in duty.

---

4. This fight occurred on September 27, on Punished Woman's Fork, where the Cheyennes decide to make a stand against Lewis, who was trying to intercept them before they could cross the Smoky Hill River. The Indians were dug in among the bluffs of a canyon, but an impatient warrior fired too soon, warning troops of the trap. Although the Cheyennes withdrew after dark, they had lost more than sixty ponies loaded with provisions. Monnett, *Tell Them We Are Going Home*, 67ff.

Extracts from the various newspapers bearing on this subject are here inserted.

General W. T. Sherman, with Colonel A. McD. McCook, his Aide de Camp, passed through Sidney, going East this evening: they had been on a tour of inspection through New Mexico and Arizona, returning by way of San Francisco: the general made me sit down with him at table and asked me many questions concerning the situation; I then went for Major Thornburgh who came in and had a long talk with the General until the train started.

A dispatch came this evening from Colonel Williams, Assistant Adjutant General of the Dep't. to the effect that the Cheyennes when last heard from, were on Beaver creek, (which is on the South boundary of the State of Nebraska,) while Major [Clarence] Mauck, 4th Cavalry, commanding forces in pursuit, was close behind. In the opinion of Colonel Williams, the Cheyennes might be expected to cross the Union Pacific R.R., in from (24) @ 36 hours.

But at almost same time, the operator at Ogallalla transmitted to Major Thornburgh, a copy of a dispatch from Major Mauck stating that in his opinion and in that of the cattle men with him the Indians would cross the Union Pacific Rail Road on the *night of the 5th*. Messages also came from several of the stations along the Union Pacific Rail Road [(]Big Springs, Julesburgh, Ogallalla &c.) asking that troops be sent at once to relieve them from any danger of attack. Major Thornburgh has done and is doing all that mortal man can be expected to do, in preventing the Indians from doing any great damage and if possible to intercept and defeat them. While he, as well as all of officers with him, is much perplexed by the conflicting information sent him, he has made up his mind not to be thrown off his guard by sensational reports; incited by panic, but to do all in his power to secure accurate information. This is not going to be an easy task, with so many little stations, scared out of their wits and magnifying every stump into a hostile Indian and every two or three Cheyenne skirmishers into a war party.

Our wagons and ambulance have been loaded on the train* and from present indications we shall sometime to-morrow be on our way to Ogallalla, or Julesburgh, unless the Cheyennes, as they are likely to do, turn in this direction and cross to the *West* of Sidney. We cannot understand matters very well; early this morning, Lt. Davis

---

*With rations for ten days and half-forage for same time.

reported that his advance had discovered a party of twenty of the Cheyennes, coming slowly up Frenchman's creek, in a direction which would cause them to cross the Union Pacific Rail Road near Sidney. Evidently, these Indians are throwing out skirmishers in every direction to bewilder our people as to their real intentions and the real point at which they will attempt the crossing of the South Platte river and the Rail Road. Word has been sent to the people of Ogallalla, Julesburgh and Big Springs to send out scouts and make careful examination of Cheyenne movements.

On train this morning, as I omitted to mention in proper place, were Lieut. Robert H. Young, 4th Infantry, a volunteer for this Expedn. Altho' broken down in health, Young is an excellent soldier—one with a fine Indian record. He was with us on the campaign of 1876 and did good work. His services will no doubt prove of value to Maj. Thornburgh. We are not properly provided with transportation; wagons are of no account in hunting Indians; nor have we any good guides—none at all in fact. I have been deputed to select such as would apply, but haven't as yet found a single one who knew the least thing about the country between the U.P.R.R., and Camp Sheridan. The Cheyennes in leaving their agency asserted that they were going to try and force their way through to the Red Cloud Agency where they had formerly (1877.) been located, and which Agency is now somewhere near the Camp indicated. Mr. Evans, an old hunter, a man of honesty and intelligence, tells me that the country I speak of is a terrible region of sand and without wood or water: no person to his knowledge, was at all acquainted with it.

A number of brazen-faced impostors had presented themselves for employment, but a few moments' examination always discovered their fraudulent pretensions.

October 4th Fearing to leave behind him an armed and mounted band of ill-disposed, perhaps secretly hostile savages, Maj. Thornburgh determined to take away from the Cheyennes in camp near Sidney, all the horses and arms in their possession. As they numbered 45 men, besides women and children to a total of one hundred & eighty, they might, if they took a notion, be able during our absence to break away from Sidney, raid the whole of the adjacent country and make off to the north before troops could be summoned for their repression: every consideration of prudence & policy demanded such action. So at a very early hour in the morning, our mounted troops commenced drilling; their evolutions were so arranged that one company took up position on each side of the Cheyenne camp, while a small detachment moved out towards where the Cheyenne herd was grazing and got between it and their lodges.

The Infantry also were assembled under arms and in close proximity to the Cheyenne camp which was thus completely in our power. The employment of such an overwhelming force had a good effect; they made no attempt at resistance when Lt. Creel was sent among them with a small squad of men to receive their arms, but Little Chief came out to see Major Thornburgh and assure him that this band of Cheyennes intended to remain friendly and take no part with the refugees from the Territory.

About 9.40 or 10 in the morning a telegram came from Ogallalla that Indians could be seen through a telescope in the bluffs, lining the South Platte to the South of that station. The observer, I think, was a Mr. Farrow. At 11 o'clock, word was flashed over the wire that the Cheyennes had succeeded in crossing the South Platte and also the Union Pacific Rail Road at Alkali, a station five minues to the East of Ogalalla. Our command was working hard to get everything on the cars; altho' a train had been kept in readiness on a side track, it was discovered at the last moment that the engine intended for it was a "passenger", not suited for "freight" as it would not couple to the box-cars we had to use. This compelled Major Thornburgh to have his cars run along by hand, whenever he wanted to move them from place to place on the switches.[5] When our horses were run into the box cars, holes had to be cut for ventilation; the section-hands had to run after axes. The greater number of our men were recruits unused to such business; everything seemed to conspire against us. But at last, at 12:25 P.M., we were off.* The train-dispatcher promised to get us a clear track and to send us at 30 miles an hour to Ogallalla seventy-four miles: no doubt, he did his best, but there was a number of cattle-trains on the track ahead of us; at Julesburgh the main

---

*Co. "G", 9th Inf. Cap't. Burrowes & Lt. Wyatt, left [at Sidney] in charge of the Cheyenne prisoners, with Ben Clark.

5. By 1878, the modern Janney automatic, or "knuckle" coupler gradually was replacing the old link-and-pin, but was not required until 1893, when federal law finally mandated both the automatic coupler and the air brake. A locomotive equipped with one coupling system could push cars with the other system, but could not couple and pull them. Consequently, when shunting the cars to and from sidings, a gang of soldiers had to line up the length of the car on both sides, and push them. On the main line, the locomotive would have pushed the cars ahead of it. See Wheeler, *The Railroaders*, 176.

track was clogged, we were switched off on a side track and there alone lost half an hour's time. At Julesburgh, we found Lt. Davis and his company had arrived in obedience to instructions sent by Major Thornburgh; we did not wait for them, as a special train had been ordered down for their use and was already in place. We arrived at Ogallalla, precisely at 4 o'clock in the afternoon: at the station was an excited crowd of men, most cattle-herders, each of whom had his own version of everything about the Cheyennes. Thornburgh with great common sense, insisted upon seeing men who had seen the enemy and with these only would he talk. One of these stated in my hearing that the band he had seen did not number over one hundred and Fifty; this would seem to show that the Cheyennes had crossed the river in several detachments, because we know from official reports that the number escaping from the Reservation was Three hundred and Sixty.

One party of cattle-men had exchanged shots with the rear-guard of the Indians and showed us some felt hats they had found on their trail. Acting under the Major's direction, I made every effort to obtain guides—not one single man could be found who knew the country north of the North Platte. Neither could any of them be persuaded to go as volunteers. I must make two exceptions; one a Mr. [William D.] Street, a cattle man, who had been with Mauck's column and brought in the dispatches mentioned on page 68.[6] and another, Mr. [name left blank]. Both these were good, reliable persons. Mr. Street had forty-six horses stolen by the Cheyennes and was anxious to recover them, if possible. He told me that nobody in Ogallalla would let him have a fresh mount, altho' there were hundreds of horses collected at that point, run in from the vicinity for safety against the hostiles. [(] Take it for all in all, the people of Ogallalla didn't make a very favorable impression upon me.) This is the first opportunity I have had for writing that just previous to our departure from Sidney, telegrams were sent to Genl. Crook, at Ft. Steele, the A.A.G.,[7] at Omaha, to Col. [Caleb Henry] Carlton, in command of 3d Cavalry, near Camp Robinson, Neb, and to Cap't. Mauck, 4th Cavalry, in command of the troops in pursuit of the Cheyennes. All these were of the same purport and explained the position of the officers.

6. See page 149.
7. Assistant Adjutant General, i.e., Col. Williams.

The Cheyenne (Wyoming) papers received last night had a report that in an engagement on the 2d, Lt. [Patrick Thomas] Brodrick, 23d Infy. was wounded and six men killed, this mornings papers say nothing of the matter, so the whole story has a fishy flavor.[8]

At 4.25 P.M., our mounted men moved out at a fast gait, (trot and lope.) from Ogallalla, going towards the North Platte river. The day has been dark and lowery and altho' we made the ten miles in excellent time, it was just dark before the head of our column struck the river. Lt. Norris, Lt. Wolf and myself, with two orderlies had taken what we thought would prove to be a short cut to the ford, but we found out the truth of the old saw that "the longest way around is the shortest way home". A brisk gallop along the riverside brought us to the point where the Indians had crossed; their trail was broad, well-defined and seemingly not over two or three hours old. The night was getting very dark: through a thick, cold mist rising from the surface of the broad, cheerless river, we could only indistinctly see the stars. No traces [sic] of our command was to be found; trails there were in plenty, the whole valley was filled with them, both of ponies and cattle—but nothing that would help us out of our difficulty. We once more carefully examined the trail at the river-bank—there was not reason to doubt that; pony tracks and horse-tracks, but no signs of lodge poles. It has been made by not less than (150) @ 200 animals, and led straight across the river. Suddenly, on the farther bank, we saw a flash of light! It blazed up with distinctness for a few moments, died out and re-appeared, this time followed by a half a dozen smaller slights undulating in an uncertain way in the air. They could be nothing else than signals and to us, standing as we were right on the Indian trail, it occurred that they must be for the purpose of warning some stray band of Cheyennes where to cross. We had heard from Major Thornburgh,—a few moments before leaving him that he had been overtaken by a courier from Ogallalla, bringing information that another band of Cheyennes, said to be one hundred strong, was crossing the South Platte, at Dexter, a small place, to the East and South of Ogallalla. Major Mauck's command was also reported at same time as being on the South Platte. Taking this information in connection with the

---

8. In this instance, Bourke appears to have been correct. The last fight between soldiers and Cheyennes in this stage of the Outbreak appears to have been at Punished Woman's Fork on September 27.

signals, we became greatly alarmed and thought that we were in great danger of capture. We lost no time in pushing back at a fast lope, for at least three miles when, in crossing a small knoll, we saw in front and to the right of our course, on our side of the river, another fire. This made us stop to consider: we determined to reconnoitre carefully and pushed up in line until within (500) yards of the fire, when we heard voices shouting; reassured, we advanced closer, and soon heard the cracking of whips and the braying of mules. It was the rear end of our wagon train and the fires had been made on both sides of the river, to mark the ford. We got over our fright at once and plunged into the cold current; the water rose above the girths, but the ford was not bad for horsemen, and the only damage done us was a very cold wetting of our feet and ankles. The Infantry and wagons had a worse experience. Two or three of the wagons broke their tongues in the middle of the stream and had to be hauled to the opposite bank by hand, a difficult job, in so wide a river, with current so swift and cold. The poor Infantry men, who were in the wagons, had to get out and wade across on foot; one of them stripped off all his clothes and carried them over dry on top of his head. We found Major Thornburgh and the other officers, clustered around miserable little piles of burning cow-manure, trying to be as philosophical as possible. When they had by careful cross-questioning extorted the story of our scare, they bantered us without mercy.

Lt. Davis and his company got across about 9. P.M. They had been detained at Julesburgh by the great number of stock trains obstructing the track near that place. The Infantry and all the wagons did not make the passage until nearly midnight. Our Bivouac was a cheerless one; there was not a stick of timber to be found on the river bank, and the mist became so dense, cold and penetrating that with the few blankets we had, it was with great difficulty we managed to keep warm. Scouts were sent out to look for the Indian trail and observe all they could: they returned at 3 o'clock, on the morning of the 5th, reporting that they had pushed out for twelve miles nearly to the head of White Tail Creek, where they came upon the herd of the Indians. The mist was so dense they dared not trust themselves to too close a reconnaissance but they were sure the Indians had camped for the night at that place. Our command was at once aroused and ordered to saddle up; the obscurity was so great that the order took everyone as somewhat of a burlesque, but all recognized its necessity. It was impossible to discern a horse thirty yards away, a man, ten, or a wagon at forty. Few, of the command, officers or men, were able to get as much as a cup of coffee for breakfast, there being no wood at all and but little dry manure. My old friend, Lt. George B. Davis, 5th Cavalry, gave me a few exhilarating sips from a cup of coffee which he had boiled while I was engaged in writing a set of dispatches for Maj. Thornburgh. As it was plain to the most ignorant that we could do nothing with our heavy transportation, our wagons were ordered back from this point with the foot-troops under command of Lt. Austin, 14th Infy. Lt. Lovell, our A.A.Q.M.,[9] went back also. As we started out, (between 4.30 and 5 A.M.[)], it was as much as we could do to see the length of a horse in our front; the air was bitingly cold and raw, and our men shivered in their saddles as they rode. We were soon on the Indian trail, which being at this time, quite plain was followed easily at a gallop. Scouts were thrown out in front and on flanks; through the mist, men would loom up as big as Gog and Magog, and horses looked as bulky as young elephants almost. Before we had gone far, from last night's camp, a small party of cattle-men, under a Mr. Ware, joined us as volunteers: they didn't do much, if any, good as trailers but as their herds roamed in that part of the country, it was hoped they might act as our guides. Our gait was so rapid that no time was given for taking extended notes of the topographical features of the country; we kept along the narrow valley of White Tail creek, on its Left bank. This stream is not far from 12 @ 14 miles long, flows in a nearly due South course, is a fine body of water, pure and icy-cold, of from 20 to 30 feet in width and 2 @ 3 in depth. The crossings are pretty good, the bottom stiff clay, and occasionally rocks. The current is very rapid and a few picturesque falls and swirls can be seen as the head of the stream is approached. Here the bluffs draw closer to the water and the narrow valley constricts to a small cañon, with almost vertical walls. These, tho' not very high, were gashed and scarred with such a multiplicity of ravines and hollows that to withstand a large force with a few skilful [sic] men was a very easy matter. No one was surprised to hear from the advance guard that the Cheyennes had bivouacked here over night. We came upon the remains of seven beeves, which they had slaughtered for food and cooked over small fires of scrub pine wood gathered in the cañon.

9. Acting Assistant Quarter Master.

Farther on they had bivouacked without fires and in a ravine, with sides so steep that mounted troops could not approach it. A few abandoned ponies were wearily nibbling the grass, but no other signs of the Indians could we see. There lay the trail, however, and with redoubled energy we took it up, hoping almost against hope, that the fog might soon be dissipated and a clear sky be opened out to us. In the morning, our course was nearly north, with perhaps a slight general inclination to the Eastward, but by noon, when the sun's rays had begun to struggle through the heavy mist, it began to trend more to the West and by 2 o'clock, when the clouds had rolled up like a curtain and we could see in every direction with a distinctness, the Cheyennes evidently were so closely pressed that they must soon turn to fight; to avoid this, they doubled, twisted and scattered in every direction. At one moment, we were going due West, at another, straight to the South; while every few hundreds of yards, the trail would show fewer and fewer tracks. The Cheyennes were leaving it in small parties, partly through fear of a fight with our fresh troops and partly because they wished to draw us into the Sand Hills and there lose us. All day long, we pushed ahead at a killing place, Lt. Loring, who had command of the advance doing all that mortal man could to do expedite the pursuit and Major Thornburgh urging him every little while with the remark: "Mr. Loring can't you go just a little faster?"

At 4 or 5 o'clock, Mr. Ware and his comrades left us, advancing the plea that their horses were played out and that they didn't know the country in front of us. We were sorry to lose Mr. Ware, but the others didn't amount to much. We had soon come to at least 40 miles from the camp of last night on the South Platte, and since leaving the head of the White Tail creek, hadn't seen a drop of water, or a stick of timber; that is to say for 30 miles. Dispatches were sent back by the cattle men to be telegraphed to Genl. Crook's Hd.Qrs. from Ogallalla. The Indians had succeeded in their object and we were now completely at sea, in a desert of sand; with much good grass in places, and in others nothing but extended and depressed plains, whereon grew weeds and which had no doubt once been the beds of small lakes or ponds. We still kept up our pursuit, going as fast as we could to economize what little was left us of sun-light. Indian ponies were found more frequently; about 20 @ 25 had already been counted, while bundles, packages, clothing & provisions were found scattered with great regularity, abandoned by the Cheyennes in their flight. By night fall, our march had reached at least sixty miles and some persons thought it much greater than that. We could follow the trail no longer for the day, which was a most exasperating misfortune as our close proximity to the Cheyennes was shown by a series of small rifle-pits they had excavated for themselves in a "blow-out", on the crest of a small sand-hill. At this place, they had abandoned seven ponies, one of them with his pack still on his back. All these animals were covered with sweat, still damp and were completely ridden down. Packages of flour, sugar, meat and clothing were picked up and examined. I saw one black silk dress, of odd and antique pattern, probably stolen from some German settlers in Kansas. We had done all we could for the day; altho' the moon was very bright, there was such difficulty in making out the trail where it had scattered in the grass that the only thing remaining for us to do was to camp upon the trail until morning and then endeavor to pick it out again. We made a bivouac, in the form of a square, our animals picketed on the inside. They had all the grass they wanted, but were so tired and thirsty that most of them lay down the moment the saddle was taken off. There wasn't a drop of water to be seen, nor had any been visible since leaving the hand [sic] of White Tail creek; nor did we have any fuel of any kind. In every respect we passed an uncomfortable night; many of our men were badly chafed from hard riding, our horses were suffering from exhaustion and thirst and worst of all we felt that the enemy had not only broken on us, but had led us into a desert country, of which not one of us knew a single foot. Voices were heard in the distance calling as if in distress; Major Thornburgh felt satisfied it was a decoy and that some Cheyennes prowling about our camp were trying to get one or two of our men to leave camp, and when they had drawn them far enough away from the main body, they could fall upon them & kill them before assistance arrived. But their design was frustrated, because a strong little party was sent out under a non-commissioned officer, and proceeded back on the trail for several hundreds of yards without finding anyone and as each company was present or accounted for, we felt all the more assured that the cries had been raised by the Indians.

The night turned very cold about 12 o'clock. The ambulance with medical stores which Major Thornburgh had ordered to keep up

with us did not come into camp until midnight & then with mules so jaded and driver so wearied that no further good could be obtained from them. The light wagon which had been ordered to follow us, did not arrive at all. Late in the afternoon, Major Thornburgh had ordered a small detachment of men to wait for it and in case it should appear that it could not catch up with us, they were to take on their saddles what canned stuff they could and move on with the ambulance. Consequently, we were unexpectedly provided with a dozen cans of pork and beans, and fruit. Major Thornburgh very generously divided these around among the officers and the orderlies who had brought them. The enlisted men of the command had five days' rations each on their saddles, the officers nothing but a can of beans for nearly every one and a saddlebag full of hard tack. A courier reached camp at 3 o'clock in the morning of
October 6th, bringing dispatches from General Sheridan and General Crook. The general tenor of these was that the pursuit must be kept up to the very utmost and Mauck's command was to follow in our trail. Command marched at first dawn of day; morning chilly, sky partially covered with clouds. Street, Totten and Shorty, the cattle men, who had brought dispatches, took the lead; trail very indistinct. All tracks now leading due South. One of our men, Private Lacey of Co. "H", 4th Infantry, whose horse had played out, was left back on trail to await the arrival of Mauck's battalion. He was instructed to hide himself in the Indian rifle-pit, on account of danger from prowling Cheyennes. Pushing along as fast as possible, we discerned as soon as the day cleared the long line of bluffs which marked the course of the North Platte river: our great object was to get water. After marching ten miles, we turned suddenly to the left and halted on the banks of a very pretty little stream of cold, sweet water with half a dozen trees to supply us with fuel. Here we unsaddled and unbridled and led our horses down to water; they were wild with thirst and struggled hard to get to the water. It required the whole strength of two men to pull some of them back;—at first they were allowed to drink only a few mouthfuls and then were driven out to graze: at the end of half an hour, they were permitted to take as much as they pleased. Yet with all this precaution, one or two of them, narrowly escaped foundering. Lt. Young with the advance scoured the country in hopes of striking the Indian trail; his scouts found a Mr. Barngrover, who came to Maj. Thornburgh and said that we

were now on Ash creek, a small stream, almost due north from Big Springs, on the Union Pacific Railroad. He took dispatches across to the Rail Road, and also agreed to pilot our ambulance across the river, it being proved impossible to take any wheeled vehicle along with the Expedition. Sergeant Otis, "L", 5th Cavy., was sent back to last night's camp with instructions to Major Mauck, 4th Cavalry.

The want of a good pack-train and of good guides was so apparent to us all that no one cared to speak of the deficiency; without them, to pursue Cheyennes was a task almost hopeless, but we were hoping almost against hope that we might find their trail & head them off. After halting for two hours, we struck out North and North, North West for thirty miles, over a hilly, grassy country, to the Blue Water creek, not many miles from the head of which we made bivouac for the night. Saw a great number of cattle, all of them wild as deer. They had evidently been chased by the Indians and been badly scared. Had no wood for fires, but used such cow-manure as we could find. Killed a couple of fine, fat beeves, and warmed the steaks as best we could in the ashes. Passed through a fine grazing country all day, but no timber to be seen. The creek (Blue Water.) is 15 feet wide, 2 @ 3 feet deep, current of five to six miles, water sweet and pure. Bottom in many places marshy and fords generally poor. Bluffs from 50 to 75 feet in height and approaching quite close to water. Great numbers of ducks flying about in the air and very many springs of good water emptying into the creek.

Total march to-day nearly forty miles.

Chapter 9

Misery on the Trail

October 7th. Awakened at a very early hour: night had been very cold. Tried to make ourselves a cup of coffee or tea with a fire of cow-chips, but the attempt was not a success. Lt. Bowman and Lt. Palmer had quietly monopolized the fire which Major Thornburgh and I had made with so much difficulty and crowded us out. When I came back with my arms filled with dried cow-chips, I piled them on the fire and in so doing inadvertently filled up Bowman's cup on which he was trying to boil tea. When he came to taste the noisome mixture of tepid water, sage brush, weeds, grass, mud and cow-chips, Bowman, who is something of an epicure, expressed his opinion of the production in very decided and emphatic language. We didn't have much of a breakfast, but we did have a good laugh. Captain Mathey did not get into camp until late last night. He had moved down to the Platte and then over to the mouth of Blue Water. Before leaving the Platte, he sent a detachment of his company to look up his wagon—this was without orders from the Expedition Commander and without his knowledge,—a very unsoldierly proceeding. In coming up the Blue Water to rejoin us, his Co. had great trouble in crossing miry places; one (or two) of the horses was nearly drowned.

At starting on this march, the temperature was very low; our fingers and noses suffered greatly until the bright sun arose and made all bright and pleasant. After marching up the Blue Water for (5) or (6) miles, came to some extremely large springs; one poured out a volume of water of, certainly, not less than (2) or three Barrels a minute. A distance of eight miles brought us to the end of the stream, altho' there seemed to be to the West another fork, which came from a large blue lake which we afterwards saw half a dozen miles, perhaps to our Left. (West.) Our course was almost due north. Saw early this morning three black buffaloes, or what we were certain were buffaloes. Twelve @ thirteen miles from site of last night's bivouac, began to climb the first range of the Sand Hills. These are lofty dunes of loose sand, destitute of vegetation, excepting a thin coating of weeds and at rare times, patches of grass. Stagnant, reed-choked ponds of alkaline and brackish water added a great deal to the barren and bleak look of the country, which in some respects is like the desert immediately to the South of the Moqui villages in North East Arizona.[1] And here I may remark that the country at the head of White Tail Creek, reminded me very much of that as the Old Woman's Fork of the South Cheyenne is approached, (in Southern part of Wyoming Territory.)

During this day's travel, saw a few antelope: yesterday could see nothing in shape of game, excepting one or two prairie chickens, a cowbird[2] and, I think, a couple of meadow larks. Day became warmer and more pleasant towards noon: we watered at a small pond, (175 yds. long by 75 yards wide.) of slightly brackish water: of this, our animals drank a little, but to my taste it was too much like soap-suds to be palatable.

At 2 P.M., halted for half an hour, to let the animals rest and have a nibble of grass; the first halt for strictly such purpose, since starting on the trip. Moved on, our horses greatly refreshed, and found that we were entering a country full of small ponds of brackish water: one of these was of perfectly black water, unpleasant to sight and smell. Away off in the distance to the West saw a small bunch of wild cattle.

---

1. See Robinson, *Diaries*, Vol. 1.
2. *Molothrus ater*, a species of the *icteridae* (blackbird and oriole) family, found from southern Canada to northern Mexico. Peterson, *Field Guide*, 252.

Now that we had climbed the first spur of the Sand Hills, country assumed more the character of a sandy mesa, or table-land, and had less of the bluff and ridge in its contour. Traces of aquatic submersion are plain there are many sun-baked patches of ground, looking very much like beds of wood-ashes, which at some period, not very long ago either, were the bottoms of great pools and lakelets. The country improved in the afternoon, so far as grass was concerned, but the contour of the land remained the same wearisome succession of hills, and swales,—we made good marching, as the soil, altho' sandy, was firmer than in the early part of the day. As the sun's rays became more and more feeble, we made up our minds that we should have to bivouac for the night without water, but fortunately a party of Lt. Davis' men, sighted from the summit of a high hill, a set of three or four little lakes about 3 or 4 miles to the West of our course. The command changed direction at once, and in another hour had reached the banks of the nearest one: this was a large pool or lake of very indifferent water, and dangerous of access as its banks were of boggy mud and alkali. Numbers of our horses mired in going to or returning from water and gave the men a great deal of trouble to extricate them. The immediate vicinity of the lake, was a great bed of reeds, stunted sun-flowers, and what may have been dwarf rose-bushes or osiers, with some tulé and other coarse grasses, but it was so dark when we reached the spot that it wasn't an easy thing to distinguish what sort of vegetation we had about and around us. By moving back, 400 or 500 yards, we came to the declivity of a small hill where we found pretty fair grass, as well as a small quantity of stunted grease-wood. Bivouacking in the form of a square, as usual, we picketed our horses on the inside, and then pulled some of the grease-wood and started fires, upon which we cooked steaks. None of the officers had any coffee: I had a package of tea, given me by Dr. Marston. This we boiled as best we could with the water of the pond and had enough to give two or three sips to each of our mess. It was a bitter decoction, very beastly in every respect. Distance, over forty miles.

October 8th. Last night was very warm, much more agreeable than any since we left Ogallala. Camp aroused at 3.30 A.M. Made another cup of tea for breakfast. Have heard no praises of my skill as a cook; this may be on account of the inherent ingratitude of mankind or it may be that I don't amount to much as a cook. But the latter assumption is untenable. Moved at first streak of day. Lt. Loring has adhered faithfully to his instructions to keep a due North course; this he determines by a prismatic compass, and does not deviate from it except to avoid high hills, or, as we did last night, to reach water. Found a few stray steers, succeeded in killing one marked 卌 on off side.

four [sic] miles out, came to five ponds of alkaline water. Stopped a few moments at one to give animals what they wanted. No wood to be seen in any direction.

Day clear and rather warm; horses and men seem to be in better spirits than on the second day out (Oct. 5th.)

At 8.45, four couriers reached us, bearing dispatches from General Crook's Hd. Qrs.; from these we learned that all the Red Cloud and Spotted Tail Indians were on the war-path; also that Colonel Carlton's command, (3d Cavalry;) had moved East from Camp Robinson, along the line of lakes, South of the Niobrara river. These couriers also told us that Mauck's command had followed on our trail to Ash creek, picking up our wagon on the way, and from Ash creek had gone back to Sidney, Neb., where Dodge's and Dallas' commands were also expected. Great alarm was felt along the line of the Union Pacific Rail Road about the gravity of the Indian situation: guards were sent out with each passenger train to quiet the fears of travellers. (These guards are of no use, except for such a purpose.)

Lacey, the soldier of "H" Co. 4th Infy., left back in our camp of 5th, to notify Mauck of our whereabouts and intentions, was surrounded while in his rifle-pit, by a band of Cheyennes, who stole his horse and equipments and came near getting him; he was shot through the blouse, and the trigger of his rifle carried away, but the providential approach of Major Mauck's command saved his life.

Major Thornburgh answered the dispatches and sent two of the couriers back: command kept on due north, through the same sandy country, and in a belt of good grazing land, and coming to three good-sized lakes, of brackish water, but rather better than that of last night. Here we struck Carlton's trail, going due East and apparently one day old. Sent two couriers ahead at full gallop to overtake him. About twelve miles out from our bivouac of last night, we passed one of Carlton's abandoned wagons.

The region in which we now were, was a most beastly collection of hills and bluffs of heavy sand; marching in this wore out both horses and men, but we had a plain trail (Carlton's) to follow, one well beaten out, which made our progress much more easy. The hills because of great height, cut up in all directions by ravines, gulches and deep valleys, in which, to our continued disappointment, no water could be discovered, except at great distances apart, small pools of salty, soapy and semi-putrid rain. No trees to be seen anywhere and no vegetation save weeds and some patches of good gramma grass.

The frequency with which the "amole" or Arizona soap-weed[3] was seen, surprised me very much, but convinced me of the hopeless sterility of the soil.

Eighteen miles out from our bivouac, we came upon two soldiers of Company "C", 3d. Cavalry, who said that they were couriers sent from Camp Robinson, Neb., with dispatches for Major Carlton. The pack-mules they had with them had played out and they were making a halt to rest. We opened Carlton's dispatches, but found nothing newer than our own information. Major Thornburgh, seeing that the horses of these men were much fresher than ours, sent one of them, Johnson, an old soldier of Co. "C" 3d Cavalry, on to overtake the other Command and retained with his own column the two whom he had sent out early in the morning when we had first struck the trail and who had halted to await our arrival when they had caught up with the men of the 3d Cavalry, just spoken of.

Rested here an hour, during which time, Thornburgh, Loring, [William Foster] Norris and I, made a cup of coffee, from grains borrowed from one of the 3d Cavalry men, who had plenty of rations on their mule, and also wrote a note to go forward to Col. Carlton, telling him that our men were now out of rations, that the officers hadn't anything at all, excepting such as they could pick up from cattle killed in the Sand-Hills and asking him to please send us back something to eat and a pack-mule loaded with good water, provided he had come across such a thing by the time the messenger overtook him.

Carlton must have travelled very fast, to speak from what we could see on his trail. In several places, his wagons had been pulled by hand up steep bluffs of heavy sandy, and then let down in same way on the other side.

---

3. Also known as wavy-leaved soap plant (*chlorogalum pomeridianum*) a member of the lily family. The roasted bulbs yield a substance that was used to glue feathers to arrows. Spellenberg, *Field Guide to North American Wildflowers*, 574.

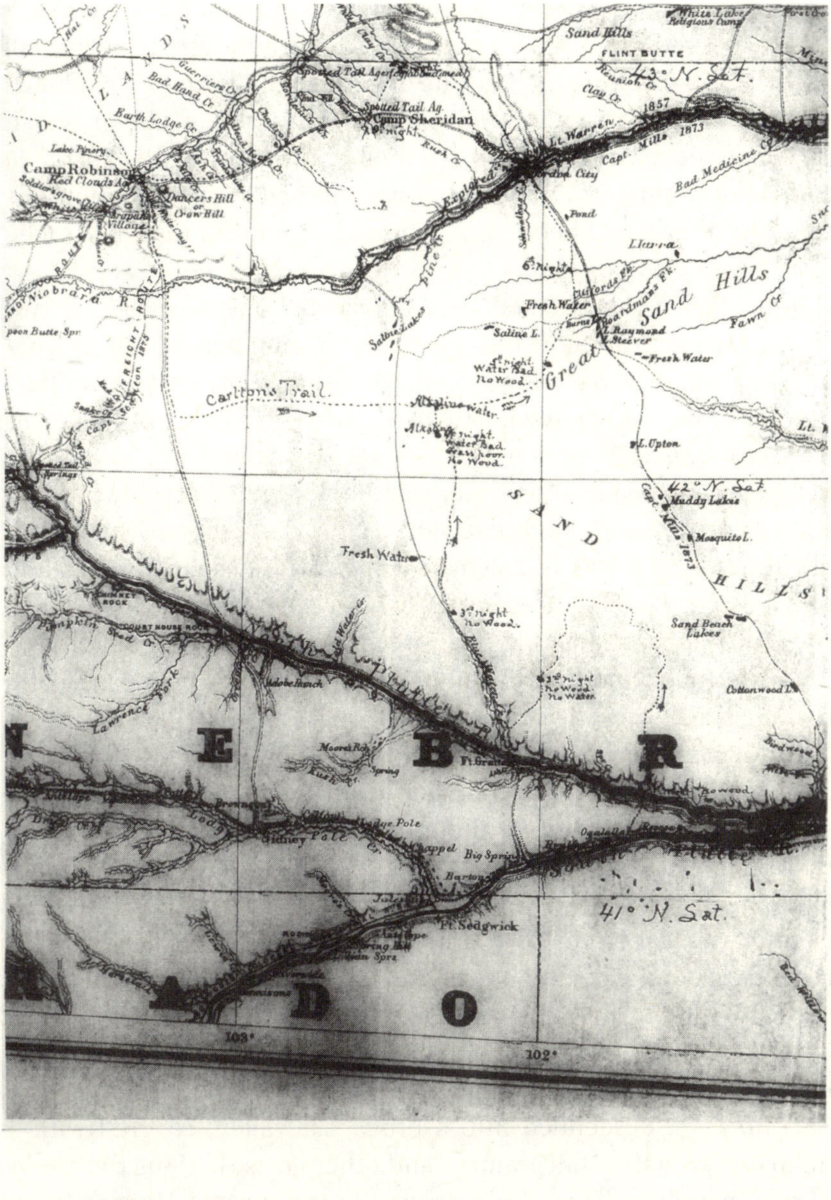
Sand Hills
FLINT BUTTE
43° N. Sat.
Reunion Cr.
Clay Cr.
Lt. Warren 1857
Capt. Mills 1873
Bad Medicine Cr.
Spotted Tail Ag.
Camp Sheridan
Bad Hand Cr.
Earth Lodge Cr.
Camp Robinson
Red Clouds Ag.
Dancers Hill or Crow Hill
Explored
Pond
6th night
Fresh Water
Saline L.
Saline Lakes
Pine Cr.
Boardman's Fk.
Sand Hills
Fawn Cr.
L. Raymond
Steever
Fresh Water
Great
Water Bad
No Wood.
Carlton's Trail
Alkaline Water
Alkaline
Water Bad
No Wood.
L. Upton
42° N. Sat.
Muddy Lakes
Mosquito L.
Capt. Mills 1873
SAND
HILLS
Fresh Water
3rd night
No Wood.
Sand Beach Lakes
Cottonwood L.
CHIMNEY ROCK
COURT HOUSE ROCK
Pumpkin Seed Cr.
Lawrence Fork
Adobe Ranch
N E B R
Moores Ro.
Spring
Ft. Grattan
Birdwood
Lodge Pole
Sidney
Chappel
Big Spring
Ogallala
Barton
41° N. Sat.
Ft. Sedgwick
A D O
103°
102°

The country along our trail continued wretched; occasionally, there were patches of grass, but the unvarying monotony of sand bluff and alkali flat was rarely thus broken and we had to plod along through weeds and forbidding vegetation which made the absence of water and foliage all the more sensible. Reached a camping place about 8 P.M., obtained water from a slightly alkaline and salty lake, a small allowance of fuel from the tail-gate of another of Carlton's abandoned wagons which we found there, and also from a pot of axle-grease in its jockey-box. The grass was fair in quality and quantity. Distance to-day, only thirty-five miles, but we had had so many detentions that our horses had been under the saddle for fourteen hours, the same as on other days.

October 9th. Awakened at 3.30 A.M. Last night was very cold; heavy frost on ground this morning—water in our canteens frozen. Started at daybreak, still on Carlton's trail, which since late yesterday afternoon has been going due north and is still so pointing. It looked as if we were never to get out of the sand-hills which still loomed up before and around us, ridge after ridge, of sandy soil, loosely covered with grass or weeds, and flat valley after flat valley of sun-dried, alkali mud. At 9.10 a.m., sighted three trees, two small pines and one a cedar, the first timber of any kind seen since we first struck the Blue Water, on the 6th. Soap-weed in great quantity on to-day's trail. A strong wind blowing all morning, directly in our faces, and making travel very disagreeable.

Tops of hills scooped out by the wind into "blow-outs". At 10 o'clock, struck an old, almost effaced wagon-trail, coming from South South East. Took this to be either that made by Captain Mills 3d Cavalry, in 1873, or one made by Col. Royal, 3d Cavalry, (then of the 5th Cavalry[)], in 1870–71.

Nothing yet heard from Col. Carlton's command. There being another fresh horse in the command, Major Thornburgh sent out the other of the two 3d Cavalrymen whom we had overtaken yesterday, with a letter to Colonel Carlton, saying that we had been entirely out of rations since yesterday and urging him to send us back some at once. At 1.30 P.M., descended into a broad flat valley, covered with a luxuriant growth of tall gramma and other grasses. Along the banks of a dry streambed, were a dozen small cottonwoods. Here we commenced to dig for water and to start fires, but the velocity of the winds was so great that we had to forego our intention.

Just then Street came back with the welcome information that he thought we had struck Clifford's fork of Snake river, and that the River itself was not more than six miles in advance & could be distinctly seen from the hill-top just in front.

We resaddled in great good humor: pressed forward and in less than five miles' journey reached Snake river, a little stream beautiful at all times, but precious in our sight at that moment. It carries a fine volume of water, clear as crystal, cold and pure as ice. It is ten ft. wide by 3 and even four in depth. Bottom firm clay, fords very good, altho' banks are somewhat steep and in places quite high. Grass-coated bluffs approach close to water's edge; these are well fringed with good timber;—cottonwood, box-elder, oak, pine, cedar, willow and ash, together with plum, cherry and gooseberry bushes—grow in this valley and upon the adjacent hills.

For first time in six days, our camp had wood, water and grass together, and all these necessaries were of excellent quality.

Here we met a detachment from Carlton's command, sent out to gather up abandoned stock. They had no reliable news other than that Carlton's camp was on the Niobrara river, at Newman's ranch, near mouth of Antelope Creek, not more than twenty miles to the north of our present position.

We first had the enjoyment of washing our faces, hands and heads in the cold, flowing stream and then we set about cooking a meal for our mess from the rations left on the pack-mules by the last of the Camp Robinson couriers. We had fried beef, tea and bread, and to wash it down, Dr. Marston surreptitiously gave me a little drink of good brandy which he had been carrying for use in case of emergency.

At 4 P.M., Mr. Gay, a guide arrived from Carlton's camp; this Gay is a squaw man, married to Spotted Tail's sister. At 4.30 P.M. Lt. Baxter, 9th Infantry, with a detachment of the 3d Cavalry, rode into camp bringing fourteen pack-mules, carrying three hundred rations and a supply of water in canteens and kegs. The water of course we didn't need any longer: the rations were immediately issued to our men, and the forage brought along for Baxter's mules & horses taken from them and divided among our animals which needed it more.

Colonel Carlton stated in his note to Major Thornburgh that he had rations enough to take both commands to Camp Sheridan for which place he thought of moving in the morning.

Distance to-day, Twenty-five miles.

October 10th Camp broke at 6 o'clock. Last night cold, morning bright and crisp. Our horses and men vigorous and in fine spirits, from a good rest and plentiful supper and breakfast. The pack-train moved along as fast as we did and appeared in good trim for active work. A very strong north wind prevailing; country became more level and better grassed as we drew near the Niobrara. A march of seventeen miles brought us to Carlton's camp at Newmann's Ranch, 40 miles East of Camp Sheridan. Colonel Carlton received us with the greatest courtesy and inquired with interest into the particulars of our experience in the Sand Hills.

With him were Captain [John Burgess] Johnson, Lieuts. [George Augustus] Drew, [Henry Rowan] Lemly, [John Charles] Thompson, [Alexander D. B.] Smead, [George Francis] Chase and [George King] Hunter and Ass't. Surgeon [Edward Buckland] Moseley,—all with the bronzed look of old campaigners, most of them having been in the field since last May.

They had no news later than our own, except that the Sioux had killed about one hundred and fifty cattle on the Niobrara, taking out the tongues, and leaving the bodies to rot.[4]

Newmann's Ranch is a log hut, of 2 or 3 rooms, one story in height, small in size and unpretentious,—small in size and unpretentious and squalid in appearance; yet its proprietor, Mr. Newmann, is one third owner of twenty two thousand head of cattle, nearly half of which range along this part of the Niobrara.

At this point, the Niobrara is twenty yards wide, three feet deep, good current, firm and hard crossing, bluffs hemming in the banks. Plenty of scrub pine & cedar available. The united command moved up Antelope Creek one & half miles for grass.

Before leaving Newmann's Ranch, its owner gave a number of us a hearty welcome to a "cow-puncher's" dinner of fried beef-steak with gravy, fresh bread, pickles, syrup and coffee. Mr. Linchard, the correspondent of the *Chicago Times*, Dr. Marston and myself ate like a trio of starved cayotes [sic].

Our camp on Antelope creek was prettily situated; the stream is

---

4. Contrary to popular belief, the American Indian was not overly sensitive to the environment. George Catlin recorded an incident in 1832, in which six hundred Sioux warriors slaughtered 1,400 buffalo, taking only the tongues, which they traded at a fur company post for whiskey. Catlin, *Letters and Notes*, 1:256.

(15) feet wide, 2 feet Deep, good current, water pure, bottom clayey and sticky, fords good but not numerous. The depth of water near a Beaver Dam below our camp was reported as not less than ten or twelve feet in depth. We found wood, water and grass in plenty. Total distance marched to-day (18½) to nineteen miles.

Paid my respects to Colonel Carlton in his tent where I found nearly all the officers of his command; everybody is pleased that the two commands have united and that we did not suffer a greater loss of men or animals during our march through the Sand Hills. Colonel Carlton sent a courier to Camp Sheridan on the 7th, but he has not since been heard of: one who left the command after he did got into Camp Sheridan all right, hence it is feared that the first one was lost.

Colonel Thornburgh also lost a courier, a man who was sent the morning of the 6th, with a written message to Captain Mathey; nothing has since been seen or known of them.* Colonel Carlton says that his guides knew nothing of the Sand Hills; one of them, Hank Clifford, after whom Clifford's fork of the Snake river was named, had been in this part of the country before, but was the first person to become confused. The Sand Hills, to quote an expression I heard employed by Mr. Linchard, the *Chicago Times*' correspondent, are a "geographical blank", known only to the Indians and not too well to them.

Major Thornburgh is confident that the Cheyennes are still in the Sand Hills; that our pursuit was so hot, they had to scatter on the 5th and that afterwards, we passed them and kept up our march at so rapid a gait that they were left far behind.

In this belief, I coincide most heartily; yet it is extremely annoying to hear from Camp Sheridan that they passed between that post and Robinson on the 6th.[5] This, if true, is a most extraordinary circumstance, and one that involves our belief that they travelled in an air line, over heavy sands, and high hills, at least one hundred and forty miles in less than two days.

Supped this evening with my old friend, Lt. [Oscar] Elting, 3rd Cavalry.

Bourke's note: Both these men have since been found.

5. This would have been Little Wolf's band, which earlier had separated from Dull Knife's. See Monnett, *Tell Them We Are Going Home*, 162.

After night-fall, Elting and I walked down to the camp of the packers, where I met Barron, Delaney and other old friends.

October 11th. Camp aroused at dawn of day. Last night clear and very cold. Water frozen in canteens. Were dilatory in moving out this morning as we did not intend making a long march and wished to let our animals have all the morning grazing they wanted. Our trail led almost due West up antelope creek [sic], along its banks we saw a thin fringe of timber, but the stream soon ran out; about 6 miles out on the Right fork of the creek, came to three willow trees and a large pool or spring of water; one and half miles farther on found water in a ravine. In the distance to our front and Right, the sky was filled with heavy columns of smoke, from fires supposed to have been ignited by the disaffected Indians of the Sioux nation. One of our stupid soldiers, a recruit, with criminal carelessness, dropped the match with which he had just lit his pipe; it fell in the thick, dry grass and in one instant, the flames were roaring and hissing all around us. Officers and men were dismounted and set to work to beat out the flames with blankets and overcoats: to unstrap these from the saddles required a little time and it was then too late to try to make headway against the conflagration. A high wind blew the flames at the rate of ten or even twenty miles straight towards Newmann's Ranch and undoubtedly wrought serious damage to the grass upon which his herds were pastured. All day long we marched through as fine a grazing country as I ever saw; altho' we intended going straight towards Camp Sheridan, which is almost due west from the mouth of Antelope Creek, we noticed that our guides, that is those with Carlton's column which was in the lead, took us well to the north and to touch the easternmost head waters of the Wounded Knee creek, thence to the head of the White Clay which we followed down for a mile before going into camp. Landscape picturesque and beautiful; as far as eye could see rounded hills appeared covered with grass and thick clumps of pine timber. Saw at foot of hills and about six miles to north of our trail, a large village of Sioux Indian lodges: in their choice of an agency, the Sioux have displayed excellent judgment and have probably the best place between the Missouri River and the Big Horn Mountains. Having marched nearly thirty miles, we went into camp, as stated, on a branch of White Clay Creek, in a beautiful situation with all the requisites of wood, water and grass in profusion. Day very warm, but a pleasant breeze blowing. The creek to-night is 12 feet wide and in Depth averages at this season not less than two feet, the bottom is clayey and in places miry; the banks are steep but not very high and are readily broken away to allow animals to get to water's edge. Water here flows with a good current, (to the north,) and is pure and sweet to the taste. Timber in plenty for fuel along banks and rich gramma grass on hill-slopes.

October 12th Last night quite cold, but somewhat warmer than its immediate predecessors. Slept soundly until 5 A.M. Colonel Carlton and the officers with him were all extremely kind and hospitable and wished us to share their blankets, tents and rations; considerations of discipline prevailed, and, let it be said to their credit not one of our officers left his command; all remained with the men, whose hardships they had more than shared, determined to finish the scout as they had commenced it.

A march of (12) to fifteen miles downgrade through a fine grazing, hilly and well watered region, brought us to Camp Sheridan, on the Beaver creek, an affluent of White Earth river. At the post we had the pleasure of meeting Cap't. [Deane] Monahan, the Commanding Officer; Lieut. Brown, 4th Infantry with a train of supplies for our command.

There was a Roman Catholic missionary, Father Brassart, who had been for five or six months among the Red Cloud Indians and was, when I met him, under orders to proceed to Fort Reno, in the Indian Territory. Mrs. Monahan prepared for us a very delicious dinner, which was very completely disposed of by our hungry officers. At 2 'o'clock, Mr. Clay Dear, Lieut. Creel, 7th Cavalry, and self, started in Mr. Dear's buggy, for Camp Robinson. On the road we met a herd of three thousand three hundred head of beef cattle—an immense column, stretching for a mile or more down the road and to a good distance on each side of it.

Reached Camp Robinson at 8 P.M., and put up at the house of Major Paddock, the post-trader. Here we met Lt. Johnson, 14th Infy., Lt. Simpson, 3d Cavalry and Lt. Goodwin, 14th Infy. To our great annoyance we learned that the stage had left an hour previous, so we had to leave over for a dreary twenty four hours: this time I improved by ascertaining the amount of stores on hand at the post, and the length of time they would last the troops expected to arrive.

Carlton and Thornburgh united had Six hundred and fifty men and at least (750) animals. Mauck, I learned, had been ordered to stay at

Sidney, but Dallas, with four or five companies of mounted Infantry was to push through the Sand Hills to Camp Sheridan. Then Maj. Tilford of the 7th Cavalry was marching towards Robinson for supplies for his command of nine companies of the 7th Cavalry, two of the 1st and two of the 11th Infy.

Camp Sheridan had not quite (8000) lbs of Bacon and 15.000 lbs. of flour, with only seven boxes of hard bread; 70.000 lbs. grain & something like (200) tons of hay: Consequently, there was nothing for Carlton and Thornburgh to do, but march down to Robinson where there were 70 Boxes of hard tack, 25.000 lbs. flour, 12.000 Bacon (and 10.000 more on way from Sidney.); 400 l[bs]. Hay and 60.000 lbs. Grain, and several large trains en route from Sidney, Neb.

It was Major Thornburgh's intention, when I parted from him, to have arranged for an interview with Red Cloud and his chiefs, and try to induce them to give up any Cheyennes who might take refuge among them and also to send out scouts from the Sioux bands to help our troops find the Cheyennes who must still be lurking in the Sand Hills. I may anticipate events and bring my narrative to a speedy close by saying that a very satisfactory interview was had, that Red Cloud furnished scouts and that Captain Johnson, 3d Cavalry, captured the first batch of the Cheyennes, 150 in number and brought them to Camp Robinson; other parties were picked up afterwards and confined at same place.[6] They gave an apparently truthful statement of having been starved on their Reservation and that they came north to get once more under General Crook, who had gained their confidence and was regarded as their best friend.

In justice to Lt. Loring, I must say that for an invalid as he was when we started, he worked like a slave; his assistance to his chief was beyond estimation and his general conduct such as to excite the admiration and emulation of every true soldier: all our officers did well[,] as well as they knew how, many of them being young and inexperienced.

October 13th, Lunched with Mr. Dear and then Creel and myself took the stage for Sidney. At every station, people had seen Indians or asserted they had which amounted to the same thing: all our passengers were in a ferment of excitement and when, shortly after midnight, our driver stopped the coach and yelled, "Here they

---

6. This was Dull Knife's band. See Monnett, *Tell Them We Are Going Home*, 112.

come! Indians!"—The effect was all that might be expected. For a few seconds, we were badly frightened, but it turned out that our fears had been raised by a drove of ponies, horses and mules, which a boy, wrapped up in a blanket à la Indienne, was driving to water from a train which had been making a forced march. Then it took nearly an hour for each one of us to swear that he hadn't been in the slightest degree alarmed so we passed the night without noticing it and at a reasonable hour in the afternoon we reached Sidney, in time for the train for Omaha. The officers of the post came down to see us, also those of Mauck's command. Mauck, Leeper, Martin, Wood &c. . . .

Oct. 15th Returned to Omaha and reported in person to General Crook.

November 1878. Almost immediately after my return from the scout made under Major Thornburgh, and after the rendition of my report . . . it became my pleasing duty to assist at the wedding of a brother officer, Lieut. James C. Ayers, of the Ordnance Corps, who had been at the Military Academy with Lieutenant Schuyler and myself and afterwards associated with us at General Crook's Hd. Quarters in Omaha, where for some months, during the summer and Fall of 1877, he performed the duties of Chief of Ordnance of the Department of the Platte.

The bride was Miss Ella Rodman, youngest daughter of the late Brigadier general T. J. Rodman of the Ordnance Corps, U.S.A., whose invention and improvements in Ordnance, as well as his work in laying out the great arsenal on Rock Island, (in the Mississipi [sic], opposite the town of Rock Island, Ills.) had given him a more than national reputation.[7] On the 28th of Oct. (1878,) Lieut. Schuyler, A.D.C., and myself left Omaha, Neb., for the scene of the ceremony (Rock Island, Ills.) Before starting for the dépôt, General Crook told me that he had received that morning a telegram from Lt. General Sheridan that Colonel Gordon, 5th Cavalry, had died on the 26th. Colonel Gordon had been on sick leave for some weeks and his

---

7. Thomas Jefferson Rodman (1815–71), commander of the Allegheny Arsenal, determined that a stronger cannon barrel could be made by cooling the casting from the inside out. The stress of the metal then worked against the stress caused by firing, creating less metal fatigue and reducing the chance of the gun exploding over extended use. This also allowed a substantially larger projectile so that Rodman guns and their successors were classified according to diameter of the bore, rather than weight of the projectile. Weaver, *Legacy in Brick and Stone*, 39–40.

death was therefore not entirely unexpected, but it was no less a sad piece of news for his friends to hear. Under General Crook, he had performed valuable and distinguished services against hostile Indians and his name occurs a number of times in my journal of the campaign against the Sioux & Cheyennes. (in 1876–1877[)][8]

While going across the fine iron bridge, over the Missouri River, Mr. P. P. Shelby, asked Lt. Schuyler and myself to look after a friend of his, a Captain Storrow, who had been, as the phrase goes, "shot to pieces" in the war of the rebellion. We did the best we could to make him comfortable on the transfer train and in taking him to the hotel car of the Chicago and North-Western train, on which he was to travel. His wounds were so severe that paralysis had attacked the lower extremities and he, who in his youth had beyond question been a splendid specimen of physical power, was now a complete wreck, merely the shell in which, bright and vigorous, his mind still dwelt. The men who risked their lives and property to make treason odious, are rapidly passing away from our midst. Scarce half a generation has grown up since the surrender of Lee at Appomatox [sic], and already the sickle of the dread Destroyer, Death, has gathered in a ghastly crop of the valorous and intellectual young men who for four long years bared their breasts to the shock of battle and, conquering, convinced a doubting world that the foundations of our Government were not built upon sand and that the waves of invasion and rebellion should beat against them in vain.

The wonderful advances in railroading in the West have already been the theme of admiration in several of the volumes of my journal: on this trip, we took our supper on the dining car of the Rock Island Road, where everything was served in a neat and attractive manner, dishes well cooked and the colored waiters attentive and pleasant-mannered.

At Rock Island, we were received by Lieut. Ayers, who drove us to the Harper House, where the best rooms of the establishment had been secured for our accomodation; a very polite invitation from the bride's mother to accept the hospitalities of her home was declined for the reason that we knew she was already entertaining a number of guests, and under the circumstances we were afraid that

---

8. See Robinson, *Diaries*, Vols. 1 and 2.

our presence might prove a source of trouble and embarrassment. We didn't see much of the Hotel, for, just as soon as we had breakfasted, bathed and made a change of garments, we were driven to the home of Mrs. Rodman; there we met the young bride, the ladies of her family and those who were to officiate at the ceremony as her maids of honor:—also her two brothers, and her brother-in-law—T. J. Butler, Esq., ex-mayor of the city, a former officer of the Ordnance Corps, and a graduate of the Military Academy where in the year 1865–1866, he commanded the Company, "C", in which I served as a "plebe." We were within a very few minutes on excellent terms with all the young ladies and remained with them until after dinner; we had then to return to our hotel to dress for the ceremony which took place at 8 o'clock. The bridal party proceeded in carriages to the new church of the Presbyterian denomination: it fell to me to have charge of Miss Black of Pittsburgh, Lieut. Schuyler, had charge of Miss McClellan of the same place, and the bride's two brothers, Messers Thomas and Burt Rodman escorted Miss Merrill and Miss Buford, respectively. The first two bridesmaids were cousins and the last two intimate friends; Miss Merrill, the daughter of Colonel Merrill, (Major of the 7th Cavalry from Fort Lincoln, Dakota,[)] and Miss Buford, a resident of Rock Island. Revd. Mr. Holcomb, an Episcopalian, performed the ceremony.

Everything connected with the affair was in elegant taste; the dresses and appearance of the young bride and her attendants, the congregation and at home, the reception, attended by the very best people of that part of the country. The presents were very elegant: one in particular struck my fancy. It was from the mechanics and artificers of the Rock Island Arsenal—a fine pair of heavy, burnished bronze andirons of the design of two corinthian [sic] surmounted by lobes, bearing in relief on the pedestal the arms of the Ordnance Corps. The reception was over by half past one in the morning of Oct. 30th. We remained in Rock Island all that day, passing our time, of course, with the bridal party until 6 in the evening when the express train bore us away to Omaha, with the most delightful recollections of the pretty and charming young ladies, of the generous hospitality shown us and with the sincerest wishes for the prosperity and happiness of the bride and groom who, at same hour, to the express train for Chicago, on their way to their new home at Fort Lincoln, Dakota.

Oct. 31st. Reach Hd. Qrs., at Omaha, Neb., and reported to General Crook.

When I returned to Hd. Qrs. Dep't. of the Platte and submitted my report of the operations of the battalion commanded by Major Thornburgh during the time I accompanied it in pursuit of the Cheyennes who had burst out from their Reservation in Indian Territory sooner than starve to death or perish from chills and fever, I little imagined that this Exodus from the land of American Pharaohs, should assume such an importance that it would one day rank with the Retreat of the Ten Thousand or put to the blush the desperation and valor of the Greeks at Thermopylae.

I feel painfully sensible of my deficiencies as an annalist, altho' I believe my theme to be worthy the pen of Xenophon or Tacitus. There is no flight of rhetoric which would not be sustained by the narrative of the achievements of this little handful of half-starved, half-frozen savages, disfigured tho' they were by the concomitants of brutal outrage upon defenseless women who fell into their hands. Had it not been for this one stain, the record of this little legion would have been grander and brighter than the stories in *Niebelungen* or *Jerusalem delivered*.

Editor's Note: The remainder of this notebook, Manuscript Volume 27 and all of Manuscript Volume 28, is taken by copies of official reports and correspondence, printed orders, and newspaper clippings concerning the outbreak. Much of the correspondence and reports can be found in Record Group 393, Special File, Military Division of the Missouri, Cheyenne Outbreak, September 1878–February 1879.

Chapter 10

The Ponca Affair

March 11th 1879. Lieutenant-General P. H. Sheridan, with Generals G. A. Forsyth, A.D.C. and Captain [James Fingal] Gregory, Engineer Officer of his Staff, and Brigadier General Crook and the writer, left Omaha, Neb., for a visit to the posts of Forts Robinson and Sheridan. The journey by rail, over the Union Pacific Rail Road, as far as Sidney, Neb., was accomplished in the usual time and without special incident. At Sidney, all the officers of the garrison had assembled to pay their respects to the Division and Department Commanders. From that point we proceeded by stage to Fort Robinson. Our vehicle was new, our horses fresh, driver experienced, careful and quick and our party very congenial and good-humored. We laid over for the night at Elliott's Ranch, and the next day reached Robinson about noon. Colonel Van Vliet, the Post Commander and his subordinates, did everything in their power to make us comfortable. Mr. Paddock, the post-trader, took charge of me, and with the assistance of his amiable wife, made my stay most agreeable.

March 14th. The forty-five mile drive between Robinson and Sheridan, was made by 2 o'clock in the afternoon, as Colonel Van Vliet had taken the precaution to send out relays half-way on the road.

At Fort Sheridan, we saw nothing beyond what has time and again been inscribed in my note-books. Captain Monahan, Lieut. [Emmett] Crawford, Doctor [William Henry] Corbusier and Lieut. [Frederick Halverson] French were very kind and attentive to all our party.

March 15th. We returned with expedition to Fort Robinson, reaching there in time for lunch and to take the stage-coach for Sidney. Captain Vroom, 3d Cavalry, and Lieut. [George Allen] Dodd, 3d Cavalry, had arrived at post and Captain Monahan and Lieut. Crawford followed closely after our party from Sheridan—These were all members of a General Court-Martial convened at Fort Robinson.

Our downward drive to the rail-road was made without trouble, altho a severe snow-storm, prevailing at the time we left the post, made us fear for the worst. We were so well wrapped up that we did not heed the cold wind or the drifting snow. At every little stream, the bodies of dead cattle, which had mired in the mud and being too weak to extricate themselves, told of the great severity of the winter just ending: other carcasses lay alongside the road, torn and mangled by wolves and cayotes. The loss to the cattle dealers of Nebraska and Wyoming has been very severe; much more so than for obvious business considerations they are willing to admit.

(During a great part of this extremely cold weather, five companies of the 5th Cavy. were out after Little Wolf's band of the Cheyennes; and at almost same time, the companies of the 3d Cavalry, from Forts Robinson and Laramie were pursuing those who had escaped from confinement at Fort Robinson. . . .

March 16th. We reached Sidney, in time for the Eastward-bound train on the U.P.R.R., and March 17th arrived in Omaha.

Editor's Note: The foregoing material is in Manuscript Volume 29. The following, concerning the Poncas, appears in Manuscript Volume 25, pages 71–88, but is inserted here to be in proper chronological order.

Conference held between
    Brigadier General George Crook,
        Commdg. Dept. Platte
        and
a small band of Indians
    of the Ponca tribe.
at Fort Omaha, Neb., March 31st 1879

The Ponca Affair

This conference is inserted verbatim merely to show the cruel and senseless way in which [the] Government of the United States deals with the Indian tribes who confide in its justice or trust themselves to its mercy.

Where the savages are numerous enough to offer armed resistance, our Government has [?] in each and every case plays [sic] the part of a craven and concedes terms beyond reason. After the savages have buried the hatchet, all subtleties of statesmanship(!) are employed to nullify the compacts so solemnly subscribed. We discover difficulties in the mode of settlement, make new definitions by which to interpret clauses in treaties which are unfavorable to ourselves or where the Indians are more thoroughly in our power, we quietly recede from our concessions or ignore every stipulation.

It was thus with the Poncas. Once they formed with their allies and blood-relatives, the Omahas—a very considerable band whose hostility was averted and alliance courted by our people. Since the completion of the Union Pacific R.R., their relative importance has diminished, settlements have surrounded their Reservation and as our Governments' good intentions are always in the inverse ration of its power, as we become stronger we become more and more indifferent to the performance of our obligations.

The Poncas had made advances in civilization; had adopted the dress of the whites; had begun to build houses and stables, to break ground, to sow crops and to collect small herd[s] of domestic animals.

Suddenly, in the spring of 1877, they were taken from their Reservation, without authority and without warning; they were dragged from their homes and taken to a point in the Indian Territory, leaving behind their ungathered crops, their farming implements, their houses and improvements. While in the Indian Territory, chills and fever broke out among them; many died (157) and the survivors, a small band, of seven lodges, determined to steal away from the Indian Territory and march across the country to their old home in the North East corner of Nebraska, (the reservation of their relatives the Omahas.)[1] Taking their families in wagons, the men marching on foot, the journey was made in two months' time.

---

1. Actually, the Ponca lands were on the Dakota side of the Missouri River, although this often was referred to as Nebraska, because the boundary was not finalized until 1874.

They had just reached the Omaha Reservation and had been warmly welcomed by their kinsmen, when the Indian Bureau called upon the military authorities to send these poor wretches back to their prison-house.

Lieut. [William Lewis] Carpenter, 9th Infantry, with four men of that Regiment, left Fort Omaha, marched to the Omaha Reservation and effected the capture of the entire band. When informed that they were to go back to the Indian Ty., the men declared that they would die just where they were and for a few moments very serious trouble was threatened: this was averted entirely by Lieut. Carpenter['s] coolness and firmness. The Indian Agent and all his employees kept away from the scene, esteeming discretion the better part of valor.

The captive Poncas wept and wailed while leaving the Omahas, whose sorrow was expressed in loud lamentation. Lt. Carpenter arrived safely at Ft. Omaha with his charge and on the 31st March, the Poncas held their interview with General Crook.

Those present were
Brigadier General George Crook,
Lieut-col. Robert Williams, Ass't. Adjt. Genl.
Lieut-col. Wm. B. Royall, Inspector General
Colonel M. I. Ludington, Chief Qr. Master,
Lieut. John G. Bourke, 3 Cavalry, A.D.C.
General John H. King, Col. 9h Infantry,
Lieut. W.L. Carpenter, 9h Infantry,
Captain A. S. Burt, 9h Infantry.
Mr. [Thomas Henry] Tibbles of the *Omaha Herald*, and
Mr. Charles Morgan, an Omaha Indian, who acted as interpreter.
Lieut. Carpenter then presented the following named Indians, who shook hands with General Crook and the other officers and then squatted in a semi-circle on the floor.
Standing Bear, Buffalo Chips, Cries for War, Yellow Horse, Long Runner, Crazy Bear, Buffalo Track, and Little Duck.
Standing Bear, the head man, was a noble looking Indian, tall and commanding in presence, dignified in manner and very elegantly dressed in the costume of his tribe. He wore a shirt made of blue flannel, having collar and cuffs of red cloth, ornamented with brass buttons: leggings of blue flannel, mocassins [sic] of deer-skin, and over his shoulders was draped a beautiful blanket, one half red, the

THE PONCA AFFAIR 181

other half blue, with the lines of suture covered by a broad band of beadwork. His hair was parted in the middle, the dividing line marked with red paint; the hair itself gathered in two tresses, one hanging over each shoulder and braided in with otter fur. The most striking feature in his attire was a necklace of claws of the grizzly bear, of which he appeared highly proud.

The other Indians were attired in the costume of the whites excepting that they wore green blankets, a la Mexicaine.*

The interpreter, Morgan, altho' a full-blooded Omaha Indian, spoke English as fluently and clearly as any American: he told me that he had served through the war as a private in the 1st Nebraska Volunteer Infantry.

General Crook. What do they want to say?

Standing Bear, (shaking hands with General Crook.)

"Brothers, I think that the Great Spirit has given me life to see all my friends here, to-day;—all that I see.

["]Brothers, You can see me, how I have been used, that I have been travelling from place to place, and that I am getting thinner each day.

["]But you can see that I am an Indian but I think I can see forward; if nothing hinders me: not only that, the Great Spirit has created us as Indians and the white people can do almost everything because they've got something to work with. But we, poor Indians can't do anything because the Almighty hasn't given a book to read but the books have been given to the white people—That's why I am weak.

["]Brothers, whenever I see any paper or any kind of a book, I always think to myself that it would be a good thing if I could read & know what was going on in the world. But, hereafter, I hope to send my children to school so they can learn like the white people. Here are my white friends. I suppose they know that we have come back from the ocean,—the great water to the East, (—The interpreter said that this referred to the ancient home of the Poncas having been along the shores of the Great Lakes—.) And that we have travelled and travelled and traveled until we have got to Dacotah Terry.[2] For a

---

Bourke's note: None of the Indians [was] painted on this occasion.

2. The apparently refers to the Ponca migration to the Missouri River, the date of which is vague. See Howard, *The Ponca Tribe,* 15ff.

good many years, I have lived there. A good many of our tribe have died there on that old Reservation.

["]The first thing we know, my Brothers, somebody came there to our Reservation, took us by the arm, made us stand up, and took us to another Reservation,—a bad place. Before I started, I wanted to have time to speak to my friends;—but they wouldn't let me.

["]We had just to leave our plows—our mill—everything that we worked with.—and start on down.

["]When I got down to Indian Territory and stayed there for a few months,—I went to see my Great Father.[3] When I went in his office, he shook hands with me—Good—We had a talk with him. I said to him—My Great Father—I have come to see you. With all my might, I hope you may do something for me as I am in an awfully bad place.

["]I told my Great Father that before I started down to Indian Territory, I had built my house with my own hand.—stables—broke land—had horses and cattle. Then somebody else came there and threw my things away.

["]My Great Father stood up and said in a few words to me: "how is this? I don't understand this. I don't know it. Who did this? I will try to find out who did this.["][4]

["]I told him:—"I am in a bad fix. I want to get out of it and go back to my old home".

["]When he said those words, I stood up again and said to him: "My Great father, I would like to ask permission to go back again to my old place where I now live and make my living. I can go home without expense [to the government]."

["]He didn't say, No or Yes but only this. "Yes, I would like you Indians to go back up there, but I think it's too late,—I think it's too far. I would like you to see if you can't find some land close by there (i.e. in Indian Ty.) and if you like it, you can take it."

["]When I got back to the Agency, I started back to look for land. I found some good looking land. I thought it might be a good place. We tried it. But something came down upon us and about one hundred

---

3. President Hayes.
4. Hayes initially had acquiesced to the removal of the Poncas upon assurances from Secretary of the Interior Carl Schurz that it was in the best interests of all concerned. Upon learning of the true situation, he regretted that decision and attempted to alleviate the problem. By then, however, the Poncas remaining in the Territory had adjusted to the new situation. Schurz never admitted he had made a mistake. Robinson, *General Crook*, Chapter 14.

The Ponca Affair

183

and fifty-seven of us died right there. A few days after that, a few Inspectors came out and visited us and asked us questions. I told one of them, I would like somebody to help me move out of that place,—that dreadful place.

["]He spoke to me this way: "my friend, I can't say anything else, but that when I get back East, I'll do all I can to get you back to your old place,—that's all, I can say,—that I will try."

["]But he didn't say that I could go back up there or that I should stay. But I was in haste to save the lives of the rest of my tribe,—I wanted them to live.

["]As I am saying, my Brothers,—I mean the soldiers and officers—I hope that all my brothers may turn in and help me to get back to the old place that I may save myself and the rest of my tribe.

["]My Brothers, It just seems this way to me; as if a big prairie-fire was coming towards me: I would take hold of my wife and baby boy and run with them to a safe place. As like if the Great River, (the Missouri.) was overflowed, I'd try to get them up on the hills, out of danger. It seems that way to me.

["]My Brothers, The Almighty has looked down upon me. He knows what I am saying. I think he has given me a reason for saying these words. I hope The Almighty may send a good spirit to my Brothers and make them think of me.

["]If any white man had land and some one would try to swindle him and he had no time to make arrangements, but was taken away to a strange place,—whenever he thought of his land, he would want to go back to see about it.

["]Oh, My Brothers and my Friends outside! I want you to look at me and take pity on me, and help me to save my women and children.

["]My Brothers and Friends—as I am saying, there is somebody clamping me down to the ground. I need help to get that man off of me, so I can stand up. I need help."

Buffalo Chips. "When the first movement was made, I didn't know anything about it. I was holding my plough-handle when they commence this movement. I had a house, built with my own hands, and a good stable,—had raised cattle and hogs and broke land so I could work it:—all that is lost by the conduct of some bad men.

["]My Brothers. Every body knows that the coldest days will freeze any man and the heat of the sun will make any man sick and kill him. There were seven lodges of us; they didn't want us to go down with the Poncas. We told the man that took us down that we were going down with our friends to see how they would like it down there. Yes. I have come up home now and my Brothers, the soldiers, have come up after me.

["]I didn't say a word; I took my brothers and just came on down. When we got up there—the Omahas gave us land. We went to work and were going to put in wheat. The first we knew some soldiers came after us and we had to drop all and come down. I look at this business this way, my Brothers. Our Government feeds me. I don't get enough but I've thought it best to till the ground and plant; that's the only way to get enough to eat. When I was in Indian Territory, it weakened me:—weakened every body; we didn't have any strength; we couldn't do anything; only let our arms drop down alongside of our bodies.["]

General Crook. When did they move down to Indian Territory?

Morgan, (the interpreter.) Sometime in May or June, 1877.

General Crook. I understand when they went down that the matter was just as they represented it; The whole matter was reported to Washington. I think myself it is a very hard case,—but it is something I haven't anything to do with. I must obey my orders from Washington, where they know all these facts and still order them down. If we intercede for them, it will do more harm than good. They can stay here a few days to feed and rest their stock and then move on down slowly, taking all their stock with them. I would telegraph on to Washington, but it would do no good.

Standing Bear. "I speak to you all. I would like today one, two or three words. I have been wandering around for the last three years, going from one place to another. I always wondered what men had done this. Yes, my Brothers, of course, I know that I cannot say No! Whatever my Brothers say to me, I am willing to do. Of course, you've got an order from the Department to send us back down to Indian Territory and, of course, we're willing to go. Of course, if I travel on down, I wish my Great Father and Brothers to let me have a little money to put in my pocket so I can spend a little once in a while on the Road. Half of my family are sick;—half are not very strong. While we travel, the sick will die and the rest of us will think we'll die before we get there.["]

General Crook. It's not our place to give them money; they must get that from Washington. We will give them plenty to eat while they are here. I know it's very hard and painful for them to go down and it's just as hard and painful for us to have to send them there.

With another general hand-shaking, the conference ended.

In talking with Morgan, I found out to my great surprise that the Poncas and Omahas who are the one people, speaking the same language and affiliating closely, are of the same ethnic stem as the Sioux, altho' Morgan strenuously disclaims any relationship. An examination of the two vocabularies would, I am sure, prove my assertion to be correct.[5]

Thus, from the little I know of Sioux, I ascertained that the following words are identical in the two dialects.

Water=Minin*ni* (Sioux) and Ni, (Ponca) Ni being an abbreviation of *mininni*, which is understood by the Poncas.

Horse=Shunca, in both languages.

Bear=Mâto, in both languages.

Salt=Minni-squia, in both languages.

The numerals are almost identical, the differences, where any exist, being one of pronunciation, merely.

Manuscript Volume 29 resumes.

From March 17th to April 14th, the following events are to be noted.

The case of the Ponca Indians.

The surrender of Little Wolf, with thirty-three lodges of Cheyennes to Lieut. W. P. Clark, 2d Cavalry, near Fort Keogh, Montana.[6] As these Indians were personally well acquainted with Lieut. Clark, and as not a shot was fired, the whole thing looks to one like an arranged surrender. . . .

The triumphant vindication of Fitz-John Porter was a source of gratification to his thousands of admirers throughout the country. His vindication was Pope's condemnation. . . .[7]

---

5. The Poncas are, in fact, a Siouan people. Howard, *The Ponca Tribe*, 4–5.

6. Fort Keogh, known in Bourke's early narratives as the Cantonment or Post on the Tongue River, was established in 1876 as a supply base for Brig. Gen. Alfred Terry's and Col. Nelson A. Miles' operations during the Great Sioux War. Construction of a permanent post began in 1877, and the following year, it was designated Fort Keogh. It remained an active post until 1900, and served as a remount depot until 1908, when it was converted into a livestock experiment station. During the First World War, it was a quartermaster's depot. It was transferred to the Interior Department in 1924. Frazer, *Forts of the West*, 82.

7. During Second Manassas, Maj. Gen. John Pope, who was unable to comprehend the situation, ordered Porter to execute an impossible maneuver. Animosity already existed between the two men, and when Porter failed, Pope brought him up on charges. Porter belonged

April 10th. Major Burt's company of the 9th Infantry suddenly ordered by special train to Hastings, Nebraska, to protect the civil authorities from the Texas cattle men, during the trial of [Isom Prentice] Olive, the man-burner. As the President declined to sustain this order, it being in contravention of the Posse-Comitatus Act,[8] the troops were ordered to return to Omaha, April 14th. The same night this decision was reversed and they were allowed to remain at Hastings for a few days, "for moral effect".[9]

The Stanley-Hazen Court-Martial convened at Governor's Island, New York Harbor, on the 7th April. This was the result of a long and bitter quarrel between the two generals named, dating back as long ago as the Battle of Shiloh, in 1862. Without knowing anything of the merits of the case, my sympathies are entirely with Stanley, who was my Commanding General at Stones River and for some months after.[10]

---

to a faction supporting Maj. Gen. George B. McClellan against Secretary of War Edwin M. Stanton, who decided to ruin him. A carefully orchestrated court-martial convicted Porter and sentenced him to dismissal. The review board mentioned by Bourke reexamined the case, exonerated him of wrong-doing, and commended him for having saved the army from complete disaster at Second Manassas. Porter eventually was reinstated. The original court-martial record is contained in *War of the Rebellion*, Series 1, Vol. 12, Part 2 Supplement. See also Warner, *Generals in Blue*, 379–80.

8. The Posse Comitatus Act was passed in 1878 in response to military involvement in Southern civil government during Reconstruction. It forbids the use of the Army for civilian law enforcement except where specifically authorized by the Constitution or by Congress. The military may lend support and technical assistance, but may not directly participate in law enforcement. The law was amended in 1956 to include the Air Force. Although it does not include the Navy and Marine Corps, the same restrictions apply by Navy Department regulation. The Coast Guard is considered a civilian law enforcement agency, and therefore is not subject to the act.

9. Isom Prentice "Print" Olive (1840–86), one of the area's leading cattlemen, was on trial for the hanging deaths of Ami Ketchum and Luther Mitchell, homesteaders with reputations as cattle thieves. Earlier they had killed Olive's brother, a deputy sheriff. After Ketchum and Mitchell were hanged, their bodies were set on fire. Whether or not Olive was responsible, he was blamed, and became known as the "man-burner." He was convicted of second degree murder and sentenced to life in prison, but after serving twenty months, he was granted a new trial and acquitted. He was gunned down in Dodge City. See Myers, "Cattleman Print Olive," 24, and Lamar, *New Encyclopedia*, 819–20.

10. As Bourke noted, the feud between William B. Hazen and David S. Stanley went back at least to Shiloh, and in the intervening time, Stanley had found numerous allies. Hazen's brusque manner, his outspoken attacks on corruption, and his opposition to the railroad corporations made him many powerful enemies. For years, General Sherman had tried to reconcile the two but neither would give. Finally, each demanded the other's court martial, and Sherman obliged by ordering them tried simultaneously. Hazen was charged with disgraceful conduct at Shiloh, false claims concerning his actions at Stone's River and Mission Ridge, and giving false testimony at former Secretary of War W. W. Belknap's impeachment. Stanley was charged with conduct unbecoming an officer and a gentleman, and conduct prejudicial to good order and discipline because of his public allegations against Hazen in newspapers. As Bourke later notes, Stanley was acquitted of conduct unbecoming an officer, but convicted of conduct prejudicial to good order, and sentenced to be admonished in general orders issued

The Ponca Affair

The arguments in the Habeas Corpus case of the Ponca Indians were heard before Judge Elmer S. Dundy, of the Supreme Court of the United States, for the District of Iowa and Nebraska, at Omaha, commencing on the 1st of May 1879.

[A. J.] Poppleton and [John L.] Webster for the Indians and U.S. Dist. Attorney [G. M.] Lambertson for the Indian Bureau. From the very first clash, it was apparent that the Government had "no case" and the decision of Judge Dundy that the Poncas should be set free occasioned much joy and no surprise.

The Indian Bureau ordered its Attorney to take an appeal.

Again the following is taken from Manuscript Volume 25:106–7 for the sake of proper chronological order.

This Ponca case was tried before his Honor, Judge Elmer C. Dundy, U.S. Dist. Court, at Omaha, Neb., May 1st 1879, and resulted in a complete victory for the Poncas.

Dec. 5th 1880. The legal points in the case were argued by Mr. Poppleton and Mr. Webster, two able lawyers of Omaha. After gaining the first victory, above referred to, suit was brought to obtain an ouster of the Sioux Indians from the Ponca Reservation. The account herein given, taken from the Omaha, Neb., Herald, of the 4th of December 1880, gives a clear exposition of the whole business.

JUSTICE AT LAST.

The Ponca Indians Recover Their Old Reservation,

Which was Wrongfully Taken from Them and Given to the Sioux.

Judge Dundy Decides the Suit in Favor of the Ill-Used Tribe.

The noted suits of the Ponca Indians to recover their reservation, which was taken from them and given to the

---

by the commanding general (i.e. Sherman). The court determined the charges against Hazen legally could not be heard because all were subject to a two-year statute of limitations that had expired in every case. Kroeker, *Great Plains Command*, 155ff.

Sioux by the treaty of 1868, and from which reservation the Poncas were removed, three or four years ago, was submitted, two or three days since, before Judge Dundy in the United States court clerk on printed arguments.

The title of the case was "Ponca tribe of Indians, plaintiff, vs. Makh-pi-sh-lu-tah, or Red Cloud, in his own behalf and in behalf of the Sioux Nation of Indians, defendant."[11]

Widespread interest has been aroused in the suit, and the story of the wrongs of the Poncas is now too familiar to require a recital anew. The cause of the Poncas has been championed from the outset by Hon. A. J. Poppleton and Hon. J. L. Webster of this city, and they have conducted the suit ably and well. Their labors have not been fruitless.

Judge Dundy rendered a decision

IN FAVOR OF THE PONCAS

in court yesterday morning, to the effect that they have a legal estate in the reservation, and are entitled to the possession thereof.

THE JUDGMENT

is substantially as follows:

This cause coming on for hearing without the intervention of a jury, and the Court being fully advised in the premises, finds that the Ponca tribe of Indians has a legal estate in the lands described in the petition, and that the Sioux nation of Indians wrongfully kept the Ponca tribe of Indians out of the possession thereof.

It is therefore adjudged by the Court that the Ponca tribe of Indians recover possession of the lands described, &c.

And thus, the heavily-used Poncas, their tribe reduced to two-thirds of its number, their houses destroyed, are at last to be permitted to return to the lands that are theirs.

"AN IMPERTINENT REPORT."

Under this caption the Boston *Advertiser*, one of the many newspapers in the east which has taken a lively inter-

---

11. This case would have been of considerably more interest to the government bureaucrats than to the Sioux. Just as the Poncas were unwillingly relocated from the Missouri River to the Indian Territory to make way for the Sioux, so the Sioux resented being relocated to the Missouri River. Already, they had come to an accord with President Hayes that allowed them to remain in their preferred haunts of Pine Ridge, Cheyenne River, and Standing Rock. Hyde, *Red Cloud's Folk*, 299ff.

est in the righting of the Poncas' wrongs, says in its issue of November 23d [1880]:

"The Indian commissioner in his annual report, given to the country yesterday, speaks of certain "meddlesome persons," who are still endeavoring to induce the Ponca Indians to defend their rights in Dakota. It would be impossible to mention here all the persons who have rendered service of this kind, to whom this creature of an hour applies the insulting epithet. But foremost among them is the judge of the United States court for Nebraska, who, in delivering the captives who came to him for justice, demonstrated this act of captivity as without defence in law, and a flagrant outrage upon human rights. Next to him should be mentioned Dr. [Robert Harper] Clarkson, the Episcopal bishop of Nebraska, who has given to a name already illustrious fresh claims to gratitude by the courage with which he has thrown the shield of his high office and good name over the cause of these outraged people, who, while differing as to the remedy, were one in denouncing the whole proceeding on the part of the United States as without justification and demanding at the hands of the government speedy and full redress. It also includes countless thousands in all parts of the land who have protested against this premeditated wrong, and who do not intend that shall be consummated as long as appeals to the honor and the conscience of the country are of any [*the rest of the clipping is missing from the diary*].

Manuscript Volume 29 resumes.
The Stanley trial developed much testimony, directly or by implication damaging to the fair fame of General Hazen.
May 9th 1879. In company with General and Mrs. Crook started for Chicago viâ the Rock-Island R.R. The wonderful improvement made in the R.R. communications of the Trans-Mississipi country during the past ten years is a matter of pride to every man whose pride can be aroused by the improvement of his country.
The three connecting lines between Omaha and Chicago, each five hundred miles long, are laid entirely with steel rails, ballasted with sand and gravel, provided with the best motive power and rolling stock and the most luxuriant and comfortable dining and sleeping

cars. Within ten years more Arizona, Idaho, Montana, Colorado, New Mexico and Oregon will be girdled with lines of rail and telegraph. In Chicago, General and Mrs. Crook became the guests of Lieut-General and Mrs. Sheridan. I took up my quarters at the Grand Pacific, one of the best kept and best appointed hotels in the world.

My first evening was taken up entirely with necessary change of clothing, supper, various purchases and a visit to the Theatre, to see *Henry VIII*. The play was sadly curtailed, not more than one Act and a portion of another being given, but the acting was very good, the interpretation of the characters of Henry, Wolsey, & Queen Catherine being decidedly impressive and faithful.

On Sunday morning, after a visit to General Sheridan's Hd.Qrs., I called upon the family of General Bradley,—then to the Chicago Club, where I lunched with my friend General Forsyth, (A.D.C. to General Sheridan) and Col. H. H. Farrar, of whom I had such pleasant impressions since our first meeting in the Big Horn Mountains in 1877. After lunch, General Forsyth very kindly drove me out along the newly-opened boulevard to the Water-works and Lincoln Park and then by way of the ever-beautiful lake side to General Sheridan's residence on Michigan Avenue. Here we dined, our party consisting of General and Mrs. Sheridan, General and Mrs. Crook, Genl. Forsyth and myself. I was delighted with Mrs. Sheridan—a beautiful and refined lady, dignified but cordial in her manners,—who made one feel on friendly terms with her at once. The dinner was a very agreeable one and it was quite late in the evening when we separated. The next morning, I had the pleasure of meeting at the Palmer House, Governor Safford and W. C. Parsons of Arizona, with whom I had a long talk about affairs in that Territory, which he pronounced to be in the most flattering condition.

Returned by that morning's train to Omaha, reaching there May 13th.

Read, while on the cars, that Indian Commissioner Hayt had been indicted by the Grand Jury of Jersey City, N.J., for falsely certifying to the financial status of a defunct savings Bank, of which he was President.

In Omaha, everything quiet, excepting that the citizens were greatly disturbed over the removal of the Q.M. Dépôt to Fort Omaha. They *now* see that the removal of the Dep't. HdQrs can have but one result—the pecuniary damage of their business. As they neglected to take proper steps in time, there is hardly any use in bolting the stable door now that the horse is stolen.

June 3d. General Crook, Lieut. Schuyler, A.D.C. and Col Ludington, Chief Quartermaster, started for Fort Hall and the Lemhi Agency, Idaho.

June 11th. I started for Kansas City, Mo., having been detailed a member of the B'd of Officers convened to inspect Cavalry horses purchased at that point.

The weather was extremely hot and sultry after recent heavy rains: it was impossible to get to sleep altho' our car was kept as cool and our bedding as light as practicable. The train stopped for some time at the inconsiderable village of Hamburgh, Iowa, interesting to me only from former associations; I was delayed there for a whole day last summer, on account of the track being overflowed by the Missouri river. I never want to see the place again if I can help it.

Saint Joseph, Mo., 125 miles South of Omaha, is a town of importance. We were awakened by the yells and cries of a crowd of rival hackmen importuning descending passengers to patronize their conveyances. We were not exactly awakened, because we hadn't as yet fallen asleep, but the doze disturbed was almost as sweet as the sleep of which it promised to be the fore-runner. After the racket and noise made at St. Joe, I lay awake, open-eyed, in a half-stupor, until I was thoroughly aroused by noticing that our train was crossing the iron bridge over the Missouri at Kansas City, when I arose and dressed hastily in time to leave the car the moment it entered the depot at 3.30 A.M. (June 12th)

The Coates House is a very fair hostelry, the best in town; cleanly kept, with rooms well-furnished and beds sweet and good. I enjoyed a nap of several hours and then plunged into a cold bath which invigorated me fully. After breakfast, I strolled about the town, which is a great R.R. center and a very bustling busy market of traffic, to all appearances. It contained many substantial brick and stone edifices, public and private, boasts of somewhere in the vicinity of 60.000 inhabitants and has an air of vigor and go-aheadativeness that augurs well for its permanence.

There is the drawback of unequal surface for building: the town is situated upon a limestone bluff, badly cut up with steep, abrupt ravines, to fill up which will cost the tax-payers thousands of dollars in time to come. There is any amount of good building material, good brick being made of clay from the front of the bluff and limestone quarried out from the same depository. The streets, altho' it was still quite early in the morning, were thronged with people, on foot, mounted or in vehicles. It was evident to me that Kansas City was doing a heavier amount of traffic than Omaha.

I likewise regretted to see that the metropolis of Western Missouri was far ahead of the chief town of Nebraska in public spirit and in desire for necessary improvement and this too in face of natural obstacles far greater than any that have yet stood in the way of Omaha's growth.

Meeting Lieut. Hall, 5th Cavalry, who was one of the members of the Board with me, I was informed that the Board had adjourned until Tuesday, June 17th. Colonel Van Vliet had gone to Fort Leavenworth, Mr. Chambers was about to start back for Omaha, and Lt. Hall was in readiness to take the morning train to his home in Saint Joseph.

This left me my own master and I was not many minutes in making up my mind to return to Omaha by the first train: the temperature was absolutely torrid and make[s] one gasp for breath. An odd feature of the street was the great number of stores, advertising lemonade for sale—and very good lemonade it was too, as we found out by testing at several places. Such a beverage is better suited to the climate of this hot valley in summer than is beer or whiskey.

The most important item of news on the lips of the frequenters of the public streets was the "Rail Road War", among the lines running from Kansas City to Saint Louis and Chicago. Tickets sold to Saint Louis for as low as $3 each and the same price was accepted for a passage to Chicago. The respective distances are 345 and 680 miles!! Such a rivalry is suicidal and antagonistic to every sound principle of commercial prosperity.

Kansas City, from a hasty inspection, I should judge to be a fine market for corn, hogs, cattle, horses &c. The stock-yards did not impress me as being especially large, but I had no really good chance to look at them and must indeed defer any attempt at describing Kansas City and its surroundings until my next visit.

Returning, I had nothing of value to note. The train was without parlor or sleeping cars, and as every seat was filled, the sky brazen, wind hot as a sirocco and charged with burning dust, comfort was not to be dreamed of. Fortunately, a dining car was attached in which for the very reasonable price of 75¢. I obtained an excellent meal of boiled mutton, with all kinds of new vegetables, strawberries &c, washed down with a glass of ice-cold beer.

There is a very good bridge across the river at Saint Joseph, making the fourth structure of the kind already in existence, viz. Omaha, Saint Joseph, Kansas City and Glasgow. One will be thrown across Bismarck, Dak., very soon, and maybe, another at Plattsmouth, Neb.

The line of this Rail Road, the Kansas City, St. Jo. and Council Bluffs, follows the valley of the Missouri, the whole way: for the part, between Kansas City and St. Joseph, I can say that these are numerous stretches of charming scenery,—heavy masses of thickly-leaved cottonwoods and elms and moss-covered bluffs which will yet pay a fine tribute of excellent building stone. Here are evidences that the Missouri occasionally forgets its usual placid dignity and swelling in angry passion sweeps over great stretches of fine country which would otherwise be made productive. Cords of drift-wood lodged against its banks gave employment to bands of fuel-gatherers. With a good system of masonry embankment, this danger will be reduced if not averted and fertile fields take the place of the broad grassy wastes lining the track for such distances.

The country is not very thickly settled and with the exception of Saint Joseph, there is no large town between Kansas City and Omaha, but there are plenty of farm-houses, well-built of brick and complete in all surroundings. Farms are generally neatly fenced in. The principal productions seem to be corn, hogs and cattle. The corn-fields all looked well.

I was so hot and so tired while jotting down the first part of these notes that I forgot to refer in fitting terms to the magnificent Union R.R. Dépôt in Kansas City; it will not merely compare favorably with the best in the country—those in Chicago, the Union in Saint Louis, that at Altoona, Pa., the N.Y. Central in N.Y., and others, but its fine system of management is worthy of imitation. Everything seems to go by clock-work.

One of the oldest inhabitants of Kansas City is Father Dunn,[12] who has been stationed here as a missionary priest of the Roman

---

12. Bourke evidently is confusing the Rev. James A. Dunn (1838–1888) with the Rev. Bernard Donnelly (1810–1880). Dunn arrived in Kansas City as pastor of St. Patrick's Parish in 1873, only five years before Bourke's visit, while Donnelly had served in the area since 1845. A native of Ireland, Donnelly was assigned as a circuit riding missionary to Independence, Missouri, and the adjacent region shortly after his ordination. After living briefly

Catholic Church for more than thirty-five years. The remarkable changes wrought during the time of his pastorate, which has seen this town grow from a little trading post doing business with the savages to be the metropolis of the South-Western country have struck the old man with a mute astonishment.

To our great relief, a refreshing thunder-storm commenced about 2 o'clock and lasted until nearly 6, making the country roads run with water. We reached Council Bluffs, Iowa, at 8 P.m., and Omaha at 9. June 12th. After a hurried supper at Wirth's restaurant, I visited the Academy of Music; where I had the pleasure of listening to that divinely-gifted songstress, Miss Annie Louise Cary and the sweet-voiced M'lle Litton, in "Mignon" and part of "Martha".

The Rough sketch . . . will give a feeble idea of the relative position of the principal towns noted on this trip. The distance from Council Bluffs to Kansas City is 196 miles: from Omaha 199½ miles.

The distances are all roughly approximated.

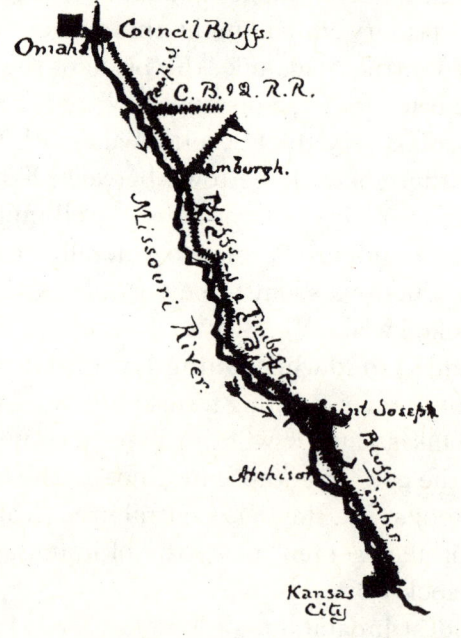

Total Distance from Omaha, Neb., to Kansas City, Missouri, 199 m.

---

in Independence, he established himself on a bluff overlooking Westport Landing, which later became Kansas City. He continued to live in Westport Landing/Kansas City until his death in 1880. Probably Bourke met both priests, and later wrote the wrong name when he recorded the visit. The Rev. Michael Coleman, archivist, Diocese of Kansas City, to Charles M. Robinson III, October 9, 2005.

June 15th General Crook, Lieut. Schuyler, A.D.C. and Colonel Ludington, Chief Quartermaster, returned from their visit of inspection to Fort Hall, Idaho and Fort Douglas, (Salt Lake,) Utah.[13]

June 19th A little boy, 12 years old, named Charley Green, came into the offices this morning to seek pecuniary assistance. He said that he had left his home in Buffalo, N.Y., sometime last month and went with a detachment of recruits for the 2d Cavalry, under Captain Whalen, to Fort Keogh, Montana Territory, (at the junction of the Tongue and Yellowstone rivers.)

From Keogh, he took the steamboat down the Yellowstone to the Missouri and down the latter stream to Bismarck, Dakota where he crossed over to Fort D. A. Lincoln.[14]

From Lincoln he started with a wagon train for the Black Hills; but becoming wearied by the slow rate of travel, he got on the stage and was carried fare to Fort Meade,[15] near Bear Butte, at the North East extremity of the Black Hills. He made no delay at that place, but rode on another stage South to Sidney, Nebraska, and from that town was given fare passage on the Union Pacific R.R. to Omaha. We helped him with small contributions, making him feel very glad; he stated that he would "this afternoon start back over the Burlington road for Chicago and from that city travel back to Buffalo".

He was a bright, talented boy, one upon whom all this travel will not be lost. I hope that the success attending his first journey may not cause him to degenerate into a worthless tramp.

The finding of the General C't. Martial which tried General D. S. Stanley for alleged defamation of General Hazen's character reached here to-day. General Stanley was sentenced to be admonished by the General of the Army in General Orders.

The impression left in the minds of unprejudiced people is that Stanley did not fully make out his case simply because under the statute of limitations much valuable testimony was excluded from the trial. Hazen is left in a worse state than he was before the case

---

13. Fort Douglas, or Douglass, was established as a camp in 1862 east of Salt Lake City, to protect the Overland Mail and telegraph, control the Indians of the region, and watch over the Mormons, whose loyalty was suspect. It was upgraded to a fort in 1878. Frazer, *Forts of the West*, 166.

14. Fort Abraham Lincoln. Bourke apparently had Fort D.A. Russell, Wyoming, on his mind.

15. Fort Meade was established in 1878, just east of the present town of Sturgis, S.D., to protect the mining district in the Black Hills. It was transferred to the Veterans Administration in 1944, and currently houses a museum and VA facilities. Frazer, *Forts of the West*, 136.

came before the public and this in spite of all the extraneous influences, political and social, brought to bear by his friends to bias public sentiment in his favor.

June 20th. News reached this country by cable that Louis Napoleon, Prince Imperial of France was killed by the Zulus near Natal, Africa, while on a reconnaisance [sic]. Since the death of his father in exile, the Prince and his mother, the Empress Eugenie, had resided in England, principally at a villa, called Chiselhurst. The education of the Prince was finished at the Military School at Woolwich, from which he graduated No 11, in a class of 45.[16]

When the news reached Great Britain that the African chief, Cetawayo [sic], king of the Zulus, had almost annihilated the English troops, under Lord Chelmsford, at Isandula [sic], the young Napoleon was the first, I think the only, young gentleman of distinction to offer his services as a volunteer.[17] He joined the English troops, in the northern part of the Cape Colony, South Africa, early in the present year, but was almost immediately prostrated by a severe attack of the malarial fever incident to the climate. As soon as he was able to go to the front, he participated with great credit to himself in a number of reconnaisances [sic], in the last of which he was ambushed by a party of Zulus who slew him with their peculiar spears, called "assagais", his body was found, stripped of its clothing and marked with seventeen wounds. His death was a glorious, but mournful termination of a career which gave every promise of becoming valuable to France and to the civilized world.

Peace to his ashes.

---

16. Louis Napoleon (1856–79), Prince Imperial of France, and only legitimate son of Napoleon III, was commissioned an officer in the British Army during his family's exile in Great Britain. His party, commanded by a Lieutenant Carey, encountered a group of Zulu warriors on June 1, 1879. Carey and the others fled, but the Prince Imperial, slowed by a defective saddle, stood his ground and was the only casualty in the party. Stacton, *The Bonapartes*, 351–52.

17. The Zulu conflict of 1879 stemmed from British efforts to federate all the white states in South Africa. Using Zulu power as a pretext for annexing the Natal, a combined British-Boer force marched into Zululand, where it was crushed at Isandhlwana on January 22, 1879, with a loss of over 1,700 men. Stung by this defeat, the British organized a massive invasion, in which Louis Napoleon was killed. Cetewayo, meanwhile, had decided on a purely defensive war that resulted in defeat for the Zulus in front of their capital at Ulundi, on July 4, 1879. Cetewayo was taken to Cape Town as a prisoner. Omer-Cooper, *Zulu Aftermath*, 47–48. In his book, *The Dust Rose Like Smoke*, James Gump draws comparisons between the British subjugation of the Zulus and the U.S. subjugation of the Western Sioux, with particular emphasis on Isandhlwana and the Little Bighorn. Similarities certainly exist, but also differences. The Sioux essentially were a tribal people with a highly individualistic warrior mentality, whereas the Zulu were an organized state, with a well-trained, highly disciplined professional army, albeit one that specialized in close combat rather than long-range firearms.

The Ponca Affair

The following letter from General Crook to Mr. Tibbles, assistant editor of the *Omaha Herald*, (the gentleman who first commenced proceedings against the Gov't. in behalf of the Poncas.) contains General Crook's views on the Indian question and for that reason is worthy of a place in this record.

> HdQrs. Dep't of the Platte,
> Commanding General's Office,
> Fort Omaha, Neb., June 19th, 1879.*

My dear Mr. Tibbles.

I have been so busy since my return to HdQrs. that I have not previously had leisure to answer your questions in reference to the management of the restive tribes, and while I believe that the views I am now about to express will cover all the salient features of the case, I am afraid there may be, in the hurry of correspondence, some omissions which, however, can be remedied whenever desired.

To begin with, my experience with the red men embraces much more than a quarter of a century, during which time I have been thrown in contact with them, both in peace and war, in all the grades of military rank from a brevet second lieutenancy to that of General Officer, and have had under my control Reservations whereon were congregated Indians in numbers ranging from several hundreds well up into the thousands. I have had, I may say, excellent opportunities for studying the character of the Indians who roam, or lately did roam, over Washington Territory, Oregon, California, Nevada, Arizona and New Mexico, Idaho, Utah, Wyoming, Nebraska, Dakota and Montana, or the tribes known at Klamaths, Pit rivers, Modocs, Apaches, Hualpais, Pimas, Caricopas, Papagoes, Yumas, Mojaves, Yavapais, Cocopahs, Moquis, Sioux, Cheyennes, Arapahoes, Pawnees, Bannocks, Shoshonees, Utes and Pi-Utes. Some of these, as the Pawnees, Papagoes and Maricopas, I have only known as friends in peace and allies in war: of the others, there have been tribes expressing friendly feelings towards our people, but sympathizing with and aiding our enemies, and others still, like the Apaches, Klamath's, Sioux, Cheyennes, Bannocks,

*Below 19th *Bourke wrote* 20th.

Shoshonees and Pi-Utes, with whom it has been my fortune, after vigorous campaigning, to have been on terms of intimacy and confidence. I have been at pains to give an outline of my experience that you may feel confident that my views and opinions are not given at hap-hazard, after brief service in this Department of military administration, but that they are the slowly-formed convictions of a deliberate judgment, based upon unusual facilities for observation; in addition to the tribes above enumerated, I have had some opportunity for studying the British management of the Indians near Puget Sound and have had under my command, Mexican Indians, representatives of the tribes known as Opata, Yaqui and Otomi.

But I will restrict my remarks to our own tribes, for obvious reasons.

Our Indians act under precisely the same impulses and are guided by identically the same trains of reasoning as would white men under like circumstances.

They are fierce, warlike and blood thirsty as long as war is the only avenue by which their young men are to gain prominence and distinction, but they are by no means slow to perceive when their best interests demand the cultivation of peaceful relations with former enemies, be they white or red. It is not to be denied that, whenever tribes, which have for generations been on the war-path, have made peace, either of their own seeking or under compulsion, some of the restless and dissatisfied spirits have resumed hostilities, dragging after them more or less of their comrades. Such a fact is to be attributed to the want of suitable employment, to the craving for eminence among their fellows, or, especially, to the general lack of tone of our system of dealing with them; yet, in face of all this, I will say, without hesitation, that our Indians have adhered more closely to the spirit of treaty stipulations than the white man or the white man's government has ever done.

The leading chiefs thoroughly understand the changed condition of affairs;—they see that they can no longer depend upon game for their support, and are anxious to obtain cattle, seeds and implements and to have their children educated.

They see the necessity of adopting the white man's way and of conforming to the established order of things. But, I am very sorry to say, they have, to a very great degree, lost confidence in our people and their promises.

Indians are very much like white men in being unable to live upon air. If you were to collate from treaties all the *promises* made to the red men and contrast them with our *performances*, you would have to admit that there was a very serious margin of compacts broken and unfulfilled upon which the Indians could ground their distrust and contempt.

We sent them too many *Commissioners*: there is no class of men for whom the Indians have less respect. Better select one tribe and stick closely to the letter and essence of the compacts we have entered into with it; such an example would not be lost upon adjacent tribes. Our method is different. Let a tribe remain at peace; we starve them. Let them go to war and spring suddenly upon our scattered settlements, we make every promise, yield every concession. Thus the Indian learns that by being "bad", he is all the more certain to be the recipient of kind treatment.

This was the very point so forcibly urged by the Bannock and Shoshonee chiefs in a talk I had with them at Fort Hall, Idaho, last summer.—"They had been our allies in the war with the Sioux and Cheyennes, but the latter who had given us so much trouble, (that is to say the Sioux), were kept well supplied whereas the tribes which had been friendly in the our of our need were exposed to starvation."

And yet thousands of our people wondered why we should have war with the Bannocks!

But, supposing that the appropriations do admit of feeding the Indians and that the Agent is a thoroughly honest and capable man;—there is now to be encountered a new and a greater danger.

The Indians have absolutely no status for claiming protection under our laws.

Let me cite the case of the Red Cloud and Spotted Tail bands of Sioux, now living on Reservations lying along the northern boundary of this Department. I am personally acquainted with the chiefs and head men of these two powerful bands which aggregate somewhere from 12.000 to 14.000 souls.

I believe that they are earnestly desirous of remaining at peace and they will remain at peace until aggressions goad them to war. You know to what an extent these two Bands have been preyed upon by organized companies of horse-thieves; during the past winter and spring alone, they have been robbed of over one thousand ponies. Their Agents, Dr. [James] Irwin and Dr. V. T. McGillicuddy, have been exceptionally zealous and capable, but they have been utterly powerless to check the evil complained of. Under the "Posse Comitatus" Act, the military arm of the Government is paralyzed. The Sioux can't understand anything about legislation in military affairs;—they don't want to understand it. All they know is that bands of white thieves boldly seize their ponies and drive them off, finding a ready sale for them among ranchmen and cattle-herders.

For all this there is no redress whatever. As I understand the law, we cannot even seize Indian property when found in the hands of well-known thieves. The Indian owner has the privilege of sueing [sic] for the recovery in the State Courts, but this would prove to be, in most cases, a very shadowy consolation.

It seems to me to be an odd feature of our judicial system that the only people in this country who have no rights under the law are the original owners of the soil: an Irishman, German, Chinaman, Turk or Tartar will be protected in life and property, but the Indian commands respect for his rights only so long as he inspires terror for his rifle.

We have conscientious, able men interested in the civilization of the aborigines, but the system, or want of system, under which they are working is a grave obstacle to success.

Between the advocates of the theory that an Indian is incapable of good and the supporters of the antipodal idea that he will never do wrong, the red man is in danger of annihilation;—of starving to death in the centre of a country which is feeding the world with its exuberant harvests, or of being killed for trying to defend rights which the Negro and Mongolian are allowed to enjoy.

The true, the only, policy to pursue with the Indian is to treat him just as we treat a white man; if he make war upon our frontier settlements, pulverize him; but after he has been reduced to submission, protect him in life and property.
Keep white thieves from plundering him, let him see that Peace means Progress; that he has a market for every pound of beef, every hide and every sack of grain, and, my word for it, he will make rapid advances.
Self-interest will impel him to imitate us, to send his children to school, to adopt our clothing, perhaps our language, and to devote his attention to raising cattle and horses, and eventually to qualify himself for citizenship.

My letter has become longer than I intended, but I wish to add another remark.

The Indian, in his nature, is in one respect, the opposite of the Chinaman. The latter is frugal even to abstemiousness and economical to the verge of perniciousness; the former will frequently, at feasts and dances, give away the bulk of his possessions to needy friends and relatives.
We must endeavour to correct this defect in the Indian character. As affairs are now managed, he has no encouragement to save. When his horses and cattle are big enough to be of service, they are driven off in herds by white renegades; when his wheat and corn and vegetables are almost ready for the market, his Reservation is changed and, sometimes, as in the case of the Poncas, he is compelled to abandon everything.

Were we to treat some of our foreign immigrants in such a manner, it would not take long to turn them into prowling vagabonds, living by robbery and assassination.

I remain, Very Truly Yours,
(Signed.) George Crook.
Brigadier General,
U.S. Army.

Part 3
Americanizing the Frontier

Background

After a retrospective on Irish officers and their often humorous quirks, Bourke spends much of this section on the rapid development of what, only a decade earlier, was raw frontier. Homesteaders were pouring into the area, willing to endure privation in order to be their own masters. Visiting one family of settlers, living in squalor in a sod hut and maintaining a subsistence farm, Bourke believed their shabbiness was more than offset by their determination to succeed. "It is of such stuff that good commonwealths are made and, no doubt, in another quarter of a century, this family will be comfortable, prosperous and well-placed," he commented.[1]

In contrast to the Eastern and Midwestern farmers, who were doing the best they could and determined to do better, Bourke was appalled by the Spartan conditions of the local cattle ranches. The cowboys seemed to be satisfied with their scant accommodations, and had no inclination to improve them, an attitude he blamed on the influence of Texas, without giving any particular reason. Even so, he developed a grudging admiration for the hard, spare life of the cowboys, their overall good nature, and their generosity. "[A]fter all," he decided, "our lives are only what we make them and . . . a

---

1. Bourke, Diary, 29:84.

cow-boy happy is better than Alexander sighing for new worlds to conquer."[2]

The ranches are part of Bourke's account of an expedition to pick a site for a new post that eventually became Fort Niobrara, Nebraska. Here we see the care and attention that went into these selections by the late 1870s. In the antebellum West, posts often were established at unsatisfactory locations because very little was known about the country. By 1879, however, there were many considerations, not the least of which were defensive, as Bourke notes: "the hills close to [one site] had such a perfect 'command' that a few Indians creeping into secluded nooks in the rocks could annoy the garrisons terribly."[3] Besides Indians, consideration was also given to availability of water, space for company quarters, support buildings, post garden, whether a parade ground would have to be graded, and various other requirements.

Yet even as the army worried about Indian snipers "annoying" soldiers in a fort, the West was industrializing, and Bourke visits Omaha's modern new factories. In the Union Pacific shops, he describes the manufacture of railroad wheels and axles from molten steel, and construction of express, mail, and paymaster cars (passenger coaches were built by Pullman in Illinois). Nail and white lead works also are on the afternoon's agenda. To those who came up after the 1950s, the innocence with which lead was treated seems almost incredible. The lead oxide produced in Omaha was used for women's face powder.[4] In fact, lead oxide-based cosmetics, as author David Stacton notes in his history of the Bonapartes, is the reason nineteenth-century society women tended to be lethargic and suffer from bad teeth. They were being poisoned.[5] As anyone who watches modern "how-to" programs on television is well aware, even lead oxide paints, which Bourke also describes, must be carefully handled for removal and disposal in many jurisdictions.

Hazards notwithstanding, progress and optimism were everywhere. Bourke's entry for August 20, 1879, is one simple sentence indicative of the times: "Telephonic communication established between Fort Omaha and Omaha."[6]

2. Ibid., 30:29
3. Ibid., 30:123.
4. Ibid., 30:223–25, 31:226–33.
5. Stacton, *The Bonapartes*, 119. Stacton was describing the effects of lead-oxide on Madame Mère, Napoleon's mother and the family matriarch.
6. Bourke, Diary, 31:233.

Bourke's duties carry him throughout the Department of the Platte, and he spends much of his time on trains. Where, only a few years before, he had to travel by horse, ambulance, or wagon, he now rides in the comfort of a Pullman. He is keenly aware of the importance of railroads in tying the country together and developing it, and watches the expansion and consolidation of railroad lines with great interest. Remembering his scouting expeditions in Arizona in 1870–72, he writes, "The giant strides making [sic] by the Atchison and Southern Pacific R.R. lines will soon bring that hitherto neglected country of Arizona into deserved prominence."[7]

The narrative is punctuated with references to railroad magnate Jay Gould, whom he calls "that wonderful genius. . . .one of the most extraordinary men the world has ever produced."[8] Gould, in fact, did rescue Union Pacific from collapse in 1874, merging it with Kansas Pacific. He continued snapping up other lines, until only he could challenge the mighty Atchison, Topeka and Santa Fe Railroad. He also controlled a substantial share of the communications industry through his acquisition of Western Union.[9] While he probably was not the ogre that the vehemently anti-Gould New York press made him out to be, Bourke's view of him, and of the industry as a whole, is overly simplistic. Bourke's background was comfortably middle-class, and his own association with railroads is that of a beneficiary. He rides on courtesy passes or at government expense, often in the company or with the blessing of high corporate officials. His views, naturally, would be their views. He ignores the other side of the coin, the sordid world of monopoly and price-gouging that was the theme of Frank Norris' railroad exposé, *The Octopus*.

7. Ibid., 32:436.
8. Ibid., 32:442.
9. Utley, *Encyclopedia of the West*, 184.

Chapter 11

Of Irish Lords and Irish Soldiers

This night, (June 20th) a Farewell Hop was given by the officers of Fort Omaha to Colonel [Edwin F.] Townsend and family. Colonel Townsend has just been promoted from the majority of the 9th to the Lieutenant-Colonelcy of the 11th Infantry, (Station, Fort Custer, Montana.)[1] The affair was a decided and pleasing success, the attendance of young people from town being quite large, notwithstanding the bad weather!

The almost continuous rains which have fallen in the Missouri Valley, during the month just ending have been of incalculable benefit to the growing crops, but have made the atmosphere so murky and damp that a great deal of sickness prevails, mostly a mild type of chills and fever.

Yet Fort Omaha never looked more beautiful. It depends upon its natural advantages alone for its attractiveness; the buildings constructed, with exceptions to be named further on, are entirely of wood, and in a condition suggesting grave apprehensions of their durability and safety. But they *look* cosy and comfortable which is

---

1. Fort Custer was established in 1877, on a bluff above the confluence of the Bighorn and Little Bighorn Rivers. Nothing now remains of the post, which was abandoned in 1898. Frazer, *Forts of the West*, 79–80.

a great advantage. The officers' cottages fronting to the East, look out over a beautiful emerald-green parade of twenty Acres, upon the broad bosom of the turbid Missouri and the bluffs on the further side.

The post, altho' built for occupancy by ten companies of Cavalry, is now garrisoned by only two of the Infantry, 9th Regiment, as well as the Hd.Qrs. and Band.

The Department Hd.Qrs. offices &c fill the Barracks on the South side. At the North East corner, or near it, is the beautiful brick building, almost finished, as the residence of General Crook. On the East side are the Engine House, from which water is forced over the grounds and to all buildings, Commissary and Q.M. warehouse (brick) nearly finished, Post Adjutant's Office, Guard House, Main Entrances and Bakery.

The new Hd. Qrs. Building, (Brick and stone,) is in process of erection, at the centre of the parade. The post is, in most respects, a delightful station and, at date of writing, has a very refined society.

The city of Omaha, four miles distance is a Rail Road center of importance and the outlet for a great amount of trade.

In some points, its citizens are deplorably wanting in public spirit. The town is to-day without paved streets, water-works, market houses, Opera House, Theatre, good Hotels, or adequate drainage. The better classes of its inhabitants are noted for their intelligence, refinement and hospitality.

The present year has thus far been characterized by a wonderful interest in mining and Railroad development in the West: hundreds of thousands and millions of dollars have been thus invested and to-day, there is no Territory, except Montana without a Rail Road. A reviving interest in the protection and development of American shipping interest, so long shamelessly neglected, is also perceptible.

June 23d. Colonel Townsend, Captain Morton, and Captain Lee, entertained the officers of the Garrison this evening with champagne &c, in celebration of their promotion: these officers and their families have played an important part in the social and military relations of the Garrison and their departure from among us, even as a consequent of well-earned promotion, is the occasion of sincere, and deep-felt regret.

June 30th. Water let in the first time from the Hale and Norcross[,] and Savage mines on the Comstock lode into the Sutro tunnel; and in eight hours had lowered the depth of the Savage mine One Hundred feet.

This Sutro tunnel is one of the greatest engineering achievements of this generation and is worthy of mention in the same breath with the Hoodae tunnel, the Suez Canal, the Menai bridge, the fine iron bridges across the Mississipi, Missouri and Ohio, and the railroads across our continent and in India.

Mr. Adolph Sutro, the originator of the idea, has most tenaciously adhered to his plans and now after years of weary, heart-breaking obstruction and repulse, sees his tunnel completed and views in the near future a vision of Golden harvests as a reward for his labors. This tunnel is over 5000 feet long and connects a point in the valley of the Carson river, Nevada, with the 2000 ft. levels of the great mines on the Comstock. These mines[,] some one hundred in number[,] have netted since 1862, about Three hundred and sixty five millions of dollars[2] to their owners and in some cases, as notably in those of the Ophir, Savage, Hale and Norcross, Gould and Curry, Sierra Nevada, Union Consolidated[,] California[,] and Consolidated Virginia, share-holders have jumped from obscurity and indigence to the affluence of Croesus or Monte Cristo.[3] Of late months, the net yield of bullion has been small, partly because the great depth now attained makes it impossible to reduce the low grade ore and partly on account of the presence of great bodies of water in the lower levels. At the depth of 2000 feet, the heat was found so great that the consumption of ice to the fabulous apportionment of 93 pounds per diem to the man was necessitated. Now this great tunnel will establish 1st a constant draught of air, inducing fair, even excellent ventilation and lower the Tophet-like temperature of the greater depths: 2nd It will cut down the enormous expenses heretofore incurred for hoisting ore which can in the future be run out on horizontal tramways and lastly, it will empty the accumulations of water which have done so much to obstruct the progress of

---

2. This is the final figure, several others having been crossed out. Bourke apparently updated this notation as time passed.

3. Croesus was king of Lydia in modern Turkey from 560 to 546 B.C. Because of rich gold deposits, he is believed to have been the wealthiest man of his age, and under his reign the Lydians were the first to mint coins for money. *The Count of Monte Cristo*, a novel by Alexandre Dumas, is about a man, falsely imprisoned, who escapes and discovers a fabulous treasure.

exploration and development. Yet more, it is suggested that as the work of excavation goes on, the water of the upper levels can be allowed to fall upon over-shot wheels working pumps which will keep the newly opened drifts and crescents as dry as powder and after having fulfilled this important duty the stream can be conducted in boxes to the mouth of the tunnel and these let into the Carson River, whose waters can be used for irrigating barren lands farther down its course.

July 2nd Received from my friend, Mr. Ben Clarke, interpreter at the Cheyenne Indian Agency, Fort Reno, Indian Territory, a book of Indian pictures made by warriors of the Cheyenne tribe. This is an important addition to my collection of such sketches and contained delineations, in a rude style, of events in the fights with Crook's troops at the Rosebud, Custer on the Little Big Horn, Mackenzie on Powder and Miles on lower Tongue river.

July 4th The anniversary of the Declaration of Independence passed quietly at Dep't. Hd. Qrs: all work, not of necessity, stopped and every office closed. Mrs. J. W. Mason, wife of Colonel Mason, 3d Cavy, an old friend of mine, was at the post, on a visit to the family of Colonel Royall, previous to starting for the West, to rejoin her husband at Fort Fetterman, Wyo.

A feeble attempt at pyrotechnical display was indulged in, most of the rockets and Catherine wheels fizzing out and the balloons burning up before they had ascended to any great height. The effect of the fire-works upon Colonel Ludington's bright dog, Don, was most dispiriting. Don had never seen such strange things before and could not be induced to go near them. The 4th being Colonel Ludington's Birth-day, we drank his health in a goblet of champagne, before going to bed.

July 5th A couple of men have been exhibiting in Omaha what they call a "headless chicken", said to have "*lived*" for nearly three months, since decapitation. I went to see the curiosity and examined it carefully. Making due allowance for any imposition that may have been practiced upon me, it struck me as a very strange affair & had all the semblance of a real decapitation. I have been informed that a chicken will exist for some days if the head be severed from the truck in such a manner as to leave a small portion of the brain at the base of the cranium attached to the neck.[4]

4. I.e., the brain stem.

Started this morning for Fort Hartsuff, Neb.,[5] in company with General Crook, Lieutenant Schuyler, A.D.C., & Captain W. S. Stanton, Engineer Corps, Engineer Officer of the Department. On the train with us, were also Captain Fred. Van Vliet, 3d Cavy., en route to his post, Fort Robinson, Mr. D. P. Foster, of New York, formerly of Arizona, and Mr. Williams and Wife of San Francisco, the later old friends of General Crook.

The weather was most propitious. The immense growing crop of the State surprised and delighted everybody as we rapidly made our way up the valley of the Platte.

Wagons, loaded with immigrants, could be seen alongside the R.R. track, at almost any moment.

At Grand Island we descended from the train to await the departure of a conveyance for Fort Hartsuff; Mr. Wiltze and his wife, the proprietors of the hotel, received us with their accustomed friendliness.

A pleasant evening stroll about Grand Isle. surprised me by the extent of the improvements and the remarkable increase of population since my last visit, which was in April, 1878, when I came out to hear Captain Nickerson's (now major and Ass't. Adjt. General.) lecture upon Gettysburgh, [sic],—a noble oration, listened to with rapt attention by a large gathering of people.

Grand Island is looking forward to another Rail Road connection, to lead from the town of Hastings, (the point of junction of the Saint Joseph and Denver [Railroad] with the B. and M.[6] in Nebraska,) up the Loup Valley to Fort Hartsuff. This will give an additional impetus to settlement, affording a market for the future productions of a vast area of arable land, yet virgin. Nebraska, Kansas, Colorado, Iowa, Minnesota and Dakota are the field of greatest activity in Rail Road construction just now, altho the great cheapness of construction and improvement in the financial outlook of the country have occasioned a general revival in the business of transportation.

No allusion to the Railroads of the Great West would be complete which did not refer to Mr. Jay Gould, the intellectual colossus who presides over the destinies of the Union Pacific and its de-

---

5. Fort Hartsuff was established in 1874 near the present town of Burwell, Nebraska, and named in memory of Maj. Gen. George Lucas Hartsuff. It was abandoned in 1881, after the establishment of Fort Niobrara rendered it redundant. The reservation was transferred to the Interior Department in 1884. See Chapters 13, 16. Frazer, *Forts of the West*, 86–87.

6. Burlington & Missouri Rail Road.

pendent lines: to him, more than to any other man that I know if, is due the development of the great business principle that long lines of Rail Road are the only ones that can be depended upon to pay well.

Aided by his subordinates, S. H. H. Clark, Superintendent of the Union Pacific, who fourteen years ago was a brakeman and has since risen by the simple force of his mental powers to his present eminence, and T. L. Kimball, a wary, shrewd manager—by the aid and upon the suggestions of such men, Gould has gradually and silently obtained control of various lines, until at this date he has an unbroken track from New York, to Ogden[,] Utah[,] and is reaching out boldly for an independent line to the Pacific; with arms stretching to the Right and Left to Montana and Arizona.

Doctor Towns, & Mr. West guided our party around town and pointed out everything calculated to interest or instruct. Mr. West is Q.M. Agent at this point and Dr. Towns was post Surgeon at Fort Hartsuff at the time of my last visit there in 1875, of which more anon.

Dr. Towns is now engaged in stock-raising on the Niobrara.

One of the first buildings in Grand Island is the new brick school-house, costing $20.000 which accomodates a daily average of 500 scholars.

This evening we had a remarkably fine sun-set. The sky would have been perfectly cloudless were it not for one large purple mass in the West which the declining sun ribbed and edged and flecked with gold.

Beneath this, floated a few slight [illegible] cloudlets of gray and gold and silver, over which the sun, like a colossal brazen ball hung immobile in the firmament, shedding rays and streaks of soft light in all directions.

July 6th Our conveyance was ready at an early hour and as soon as breakfast was over we clambered in, and saying farewell to our friends were on the road to the north. I recognized the vehicle as an old acquaintance being the same one which in 1875 had carried a party consisting of Capt. [Charles] Wheaton, Capt. Henton, Lieut. Clark, Lt. Broderick, 23d Infantry, Lt. W. P. Clark, 2d Cavalry, Sir Rose Price and myself. The officers were on duty as members of a General Court-Martial to be convened at Fort Hartsuff and Sir Rose Price, was taken along to give him a chance to see the country.[7]

Then, as now, the conveyance I rode in, was in a shaky, asthmatic condition, creaking and wheezing fearfully while going down every grade. It is the living representation of Oliver Wendell Holmes' "One Horse Shay", but may hold together for a few weeks yet.[8] Our driver, Mr. Washburne, the mayor of Grand Isle, is an old kiln-dried veteran who has rought [sic] it in every state and territory from Maine to California.

We had a very bright and cheery drive, the four horses attached to our old rattle-trap pulling it along at a respectable pace; our course being almost due North through a finely-grassed country, possessing a very good soil and settling up with remarkable rapidity.

The houses are of all materials, very many being of sod and of pisé. with a great deal of chopped hay.

Six miles from Grand Island, we crossed the Prairie Creek and eighteen miles out entered the valley of the Loup. Here we saw a brick yard, turning out a fair article of building material.

Nearby is a settlement of German Catholics, called Saint Labon, their modest little church being a prominent feature. Soon after, we crossed the Loup River on a good wooden bridge, the river being very broad[,] 200 yd.[,] shallow and full of sand-bars: and, possibly, very much swollen in spring.

The valley of the Loup is fast filling up with a very good class of people.

---

7. Sir Rose Lambart Price later wrote a book about the trip through the Western Hemisphere, entitled *The Two Americas*. In it, he expressed admiration for Americans in general, and U.S. Army officers in particular, a sentiment unusual in the British gentry of the period. Price's comments on Army officers are quoted in Robinson, *Diaries*, 2:256n10. His visit is discussed in ibid., 255–56, and 380, and later in this chapter.

8. The shay (from the French *chaise*) is a two-wheeled carriage with a single seat over the axle. The driver sits in a box above and to the rear of the passengers. Bourke is referring not to the type of vehicle in which he and his companions were riding, but to its dilapidated condition, which Holmes expressed in the poem, "The Deacon's Masterpiece; or the Wonderful 'One-Hoss Shay'."

> Have you heard of the wonderful one-horse shay,
> That was built in such a logical way
> It ran a hundred years to a day,
> And then, of a sudden, it—ah but stay. . . .
> Now in building of chaises, I tell you what,
> There is always somewhere a weakest spot,
> In hub, tire, felloe, in spring or thill,
> In screw, bolt, thoroughbrace,—lurking still,
> Find it somewhere you must and will,—
> Above or below, or within or without,—
> And that's the reason, beyond a doubt,
> That a chaise breaks down, but doesn't wear out. . . .

Saint Paul, the seat of Howard County, is a good-sized village of neat houses, planted right in the middle of a broad green prairie. Here we took dinner and a miserable meal it was; served up in a slouchy, dirty manner, with a superabundance of flies.

The vegetables were all raised in the settlement. Nebraska has for five years enjoyed immunity from the depredations of grass-hoppers which in 1874, 1875 wrought such destruction.

Four miles beyond Saint Paul, we crossed the North Fork of the Loup, ascending it for fourteen miles to the house of Wentworth, or "Buckshot", at one time a Government scout and guide of considerable reputation. On our way, we saw many broad fields of wheat, bearded out finely and most of it promising a fine yield. There was a very noticeable absence of fences, and of timber, but in many localities, groves had been planted often of fruit-bearers, but mainly of the cottonwood. Prairie-fires are guarded against in this region by fire-breaks, made by turning over the side for a width of 25 @ 30 ft: this space is often planted in corn which can be gathered before the coming of the high winds of November which spread conflagrations through the high grass.

The Loup Valley is sandy and alluvial until you reach Buckshot's, where a protrusion of sandy limestone is visible in the bluffs close at hand; this becomes pure limestone a couple of miles to the north, and at Beebe's is burnt for building purposes.

Buckshot was not at home when we alighted, but his wife took good care of us and busied herself in getting us something to eat. Their home is a neat, homelike little cottage, a pretty flower garden lying in front of leafy vines clamber[in]g on trellises against the walls: wells, spring-houses,[9] chicken-coops and other appentenances kept in a clean and sweet condition.

In the conversation maintained while waiting for dinner and from the conclusion of that meal until bed-time, Mr. Washburne gave us in a quiet, modest way, a recital of his adventures while making the overland trip to California, in 1849. The Sioux Indians were then a tribe much more numerous even than they are to-day, but inclined to friendliness and peace, but among the immigrants were many hard customers who would just as soon shoot an Indian in cold blood as eat their breakfast.

---

9. As the name indicates, a spring-house is a structure built over a spring, and used for cool storage of butter, milk, and other perishables.

About the time, Mr. Washburne made the trip, one of these desperadoes, belonging to a train moving up the Platte Valley, saw an old Sioux squaw alone and thinking it would be good fun shot her dead.

The joke was a very excellent one in its way, but not quite so happy in its general results as the perpetrator expected. A large band of Sioux happened to be in the vicinity and learning of the murder of their relative and suspecting the immigrants surrounded their camp, and demanded the surrender of the murderer. The trembling whites produced him without delay and the exasperated Indians *skinned him alive* and then burned him. From this circumstance, Raw-Hide creek, an affluent of the Elkhorn river, in Nebraska, takes its name.

On this journey across the plains, Mr. Washburne says his party encountered many Indians: 1st, a great concourse of Pawnees, number several thousands, on their way to Sarpy's store, near Omaha, to trade. 2d. an immense village of Sioux on the Platte river, 20 miles East of Fort Laramie. This village was so long that the immigrants were ten hours in passing it: the tepees were five and six deep.

On the north Platte, near the Sweetwater, they encountered a fabulously large herd of buffalo moving across their line of travel. The immigrants were so afraid that the buffaloes might charge through their camp, that they kept up their march without halting for two days and two nights, before they reached the end of the herd.

In the Big Horn country, they came across a large band of Shoshonee and Bannock Indians, with whom they found an old Frenchman deriving a good trade. Beyond the Rockies, they saw Pi-Utes and Diggers, but not in parties strong enough to be threatening.

The Loup Valley was then the hunting ground of the Pawnees and was not looked upon as habitable by white men.

A storm raging to the South of us cooled the air and enabled us to sleep soundly in spite of the devoted attentions of a host of bed-bugs.

July 7th. Awakened at 4 o'clock; air cool, balmy and invigorating. Ate heartily of a well-cooked breakfast of fried chicken, new potatoes, fresh bread and butter, coffee and milk. Moved North of the Loup, passing Beebe's, where a new house of concrete was a-building. Near this flourished a small grove of ash, elm, cottonwood and willow, while in the little ravines close by, was scrub-oak. Day cloudy, but travelling excellent.

Captain Stanton gave a most interest[in]g account of his experience at Fort Saint Philip and Fort Jackson, on the Mississipi, below New Orleans.[10] As these posts are situated on the muddy, low-lying river bottom, water can only be kept off the parade by the constant use of steam-pumps. On one occasion, the pump broke and the river water soon covered the parade with a deep, treacherous slime, in which alligators and gar-fish made themselves at home.

When the pump was again in operation, many of these animals were left high and dry by the receding water and dying, poisoned the super-heated air with the stench from their decomposing carcasses.

This effluvia and that from the stagnant pools and ditches about the fort produced aggravated forms of fever and placed all the garrison on sick-report.[11]

On to-day's march, we have seen but little timber. The Loup meandered gently down a broad valley of emerald green and were it somewhat more thickly timbered would remind one of descriptions I have read of scenery in Great Britain and Ireland. Several hundreds of Polish families and also many Bohemians have taken up land at the head of the tributaries of the Loup and are actively at work building settlements and planting crops. Two or three German families passed us this morning in carts drawn by oxen, the animals being hitched and not yoked.

10. These forts defended the main channel of the Mississippi River below New Orleans, where a force of invading ships would have to slow to round Plaquemines Bend and continue upriver. Fort St. Philip was begun by the Spaniards as Castillo San Felipe in 1793, and was remodeled and strengthened by the United States in 1812. Two years later, it withstood a British bombardment. The U.S. Army continued to maintain Fort St. Philip, and, on the opposite side of the river, began construction of a second stronghold, designated Fort Jackson, in 1824. After the outbreak of the Civil War, the two forts were taken over by the Confederates, and, in the 1862 New Orleans Campaign, fell to Union forces after a siege lasting about a week. In the 1890s, both forts were modernized with concrete emplacements for mortars and long-range coastal defense guns, and new facilities for garrison and support. They continued in service until 1922, when they were declared surplus and abandoned. Fort Jackson now is the centerpiece of a park owned and operated by Plaquemines Parish, which maintains a museum in the guardroom and magazine. Fort St. Philip is privately owned and not open to the public. See Manuel, *Coastal Castles*, 18ff.

11. Anyone familiar with Forts Jackson and St. Philip cannot avoid the suspicion that Stanton was telling a tall tale. Both forts were infamous for their flooded parade grounds, but except for rises in the river (most recently in Hurricane Katrina in 2005), the water pooled from ground seepage rather than an outside source. Additionally, they are surrounded by masonry walls, and when garrisoned and with gates and casemate shutters closed, should have been inaccessible to fish or alligators. At this time, the parade ground and galleries of Fort St. Philip are filled with silt and debris from river flooding, but that is because of abandonment and lack of maintenance.

Ord City, Loup City, (both on West side of the river.) and Scotia, are fast -growing towns. All these have newspapers. I had a chance to read several copies of the Scotia paper—the *Greeley Tribune*—and found it full of matter, original and selected. At Ord, met Lieut. Norris, 9th Infy. Approaching Fort Hartsuff, the valley of the Loup is more heavily timbered.

Fort Hartsuff is a beautiful post, altho' not located in the best available site. The Quarters for two companies, Barracks, Officers, &c are all of concrete, well-built, finely finished, with veranda and other conveniences. Water is supplied by a force-pump, operated by a windmill. The post, at time of our visit, was garrisoned by one Company ("C") [Samuel] Munson's, of the 9th Infantry. The men were at target practice, under the supervision of Cap't. Munson and Lt. [Thaddeus] Capron, who left the company and hastened over to pay their respects to Genl. Crook.

Capt. Munson took charge of Genl. Crook and Cap't. Stanton, Lt. Norris of Lt. Schuyler[,] and Lt. Capron of myself.

We were taken to visit the Company (then in tents on account of the Qrs. being cleaned.) and to the Post Garden, a finely cultivated strip of 3 Acres, yielding abundantly of Beets, Beans, Lettuce, Onions, Parsnips, Peas, Cabbage and Potatoes. We then went to the Guard-House and to the Q.M. warehouse, in which Lt. Capron was preparing a set of hanging shelves, or rather hanging boxes, to keep the company clothing and blankets from the depredations of mice. The supports were wooden slats, *covered with tin.*

The Reservoir, we were told, gave a "head" of 60 feet above the parade ground.

The changes occurring, in the country between Grande Island at Ft. Hartsuff and at Ft. Hartsuff itself since my last visit in 1875, are something wonderful and illustrated well the progressive tendency of American colonization, if such a word be the correct one to explain this connection.

Then, the town of Grand Island was a very small and comparatively insignificant affair; now its schools afford the elements of education to more than five hundred children; the settlements which in that year did not come beyond Saint Paul, only twenty-four miles this side (North) of the R.R. now reach to a point thirty miles beyond Hartsuff itself and a Rail Road extension is under way for their benefit.

Of my former trip in some particulars, I might, if so disposed, write much that is ridiculous. We had with us, as I have already remarked, a real, genuine, sure-enough, live Lord—a member of the British Aristocracy! Well, as Sir Rose Price, to all outward appearances, was a perfect gentleman, we quietly determined to treat him as such and let him feel that he was one of ourselves. Sir Rose being a sensible fellow and himself an Army officer of some considerable experience in all parts of the world, entered heartily into our companionship and we all talked, joked, told stories and tales of adventure, drank toddies, smoked or shot game all the way from Grand Island to Fort Hartsuff. This was exactly as it should be[.] Sir Rose was just as good as we were, but no better. When we reached Fort Hartsuff, then commanded by Captain and Brevet Lieutenant-Colonel John J. Coppinger, 23d Infantry, everything changed at once. Coppinger, altho' calling himself an Englishman, was really a Corkagian Mick from Ireland. He was a man of education and travel, having served in the Pope's Army, during the war with Victor Emanuel and in our own during that of the Rebellion.[12] But with all his worldly knowledge and common sense, he could not shake off the trammels of early ideas and at heart, in all cases where rank was concerned he was as thorough a snob as ever I have met. The idea that he was to have a live "Lord" under his roof was too much for him and he lost his equilibrium entirely. This conduct struck us as extremely funny, because we had extracted from Sir Rose much of his history; Sir Rose, a younger son of a younger son, had counted himself lucky in the possession of a Captaincy in the Marine Infantry, serving at Hong Kong, China, when a gouty-toed old relative "pegged out" and left him the residue of a small "estate" in Ireland,—an "estate", about as big as many a Western farmer's corn-patch, but carrying with it a Baronetcy and a small income on which Sir Rose was economically travelling around the world.[13]

To see those two confounded "tare and ages" Muldoons playing the "blarsted Hinglishmen", and talking of "Pell-Mell["], "Wotten Wo" and "Wegents Pawk"[14] would give a Government mule the blind

12. Bourke refers to the Wars of Italian Unification, in which the various Italian states, and ultimately the States of the Church, eventually were fused together in a single kingdom under Victor Emanuel II.

13. A baronetcy is one step below British peerage, which begins with baronies, but one step above a knighthood. A baronet is addressed as "Sir," as is a knight. While technically not peers, baronets have enough prestige to be listed in *Burke's Peerage* and *Debrett's Peerage, Baronetage, Knightage, and Companionage*. National Geographic, *This England*, 201.

14. Pall Mall, Rotten Row, and Regent's Park.

staggers, but the spectacle of Coppinger's obsequious deference, almost servile abjection, to the other's miserable rank was as galling as it was absurd. Now, in our party, we had old Captain "Jemmie" Henton, also an Irishman, an honest, old soldier, who had, by his own merit, won his way up from the ranks. Jemmie was not "up" in the ways of Courts or the niceties of etiquette, but had thus far succeeded in getting along admirable with the "aristocrat". But, when we reached Hartsuff, Col. Coppinger made so much of a fuss over the "Hinglishman", (from Cork,) that "Old Jimmie Henton",[15] as we called him, became bewildered. One of Coppinger's ideas was that the Americans didn't know how to address distinguished foreigners, so he instructed us that, under no circumstances, must we say "*Lord* Rose" and "*Sir* Price", but always the contrary method, i.e. "*Sir Rose*" or "*Lord Price*". We took the whole thing very quietly but it required no gigantic intellect to foretell that the demure young lieutenants meant mischief. Pretty soon, dinner was announced and in we marched, Sir Rose being very properly assigned to the seat of honor as a stranger and guest. Conversation had barely began [*sic*], in fact the ice of new acquaintance had just about cracked, when Old Jimmie Henton made a fearful break by addressing "*Lord* Rose". Coppinger looked daggers at him. Poor Jimmie's red neck and pulpy blue eyes grew redder and more pulpy, his short sandy hair stood erect and a great lump protruded from his throat. He tried to correct himself, but the more he taxed his memory for the proper title the less willing it seemed to be to respond. So he kept repeating the wrong title over and over again, his neck by this time a brilliant carmine, his eyes dodging clear out of the sockets, every individual hair on end, and cold globules of perspiration rolling down his cheeks, and the whole table, of course on the "qui vive", the Lieutenants coughing ominously and stuffing their napkins into their mouths.

Old Jimmie was in for it, surely. "*Lord* Rose, *Lord* Rose, may I help yiz to some *banes*?" Coppinger was fearfully disgusted at this ignorance of Courtly titles and could ill conceal his chagrin, but his attention was soon attracted to other quarters. The "youngsters" at the table were now "in for it" and partly to show contempt for Coppinger's snobbishness and partly through pure love of mischief began to mock in a scarcely concealed way everything that Cop-

15. Bourke varied the spelling between "Jemmie" and "Jimmie."

pinger and *Sir Wose* said to each other. We had an exceedingly lively evening, and I think that neither *Sir Wose* nor Coppinger have yet forgotten it. (Sir Rose has since written a book, descriptive of his travels, entitled the *Two Americas*.)

The Post Trader at Fort Hartsuff, formerly occupied the same position at the post of Beale's Springs, Arizona,[16] where I met him in 1871, 2, and 1873. Beale's Springs will always hold a high rank in my estimation as one of the meanest places on God's foot-stool. It was at that time garrisoned by a small company of the 12th Infantry, and under command of Captain Thomas Byrne. The Reservation and Agency of the Hualpai Indians were established at this point and troops were stationed there to protect the Agent, afford shelter to travellers and keep up a show of force. How inadequate this was may be seen from one fact. The Hualpais numbered not far from four hundred warriors, noted for their daring, celerity and physical endurance. Their country extended up to the Grand Cañon of the Colorado and included some of the lateral gashes which cut into the bosom of the earth fully as deeply as the principal chasm.

In a whole year, the entire 8th Cavalry, under an energetic and skilful [sic] commander, Maj. Wm. Redwood Price, had pursued this little band from crag to crag and cañon to cañon, the Hualpais finally consenting to Peace not because they did not have the advantage of the troops in nearly every engagement, but because they were tired of war. It is related of this campaign, that mountain howitzers were brought into service to shell the Hualpais from one of their strongholds. One shell is known to have killed two and wounded three of the enemy but in this manner. Three years after the 8th Cavalry had left Arizona, a small hunting party of young Hualpai bucks found one of these shells in the mountains. They picked it up, examined it and satisfied themselves that it must be hollow; but how to get to the inside of the iron sphere was something beyond their power. At last, the idea occurred to them that they had better *cook* it in their fire; so they thrust it in the ashes and sat around in a circle awaiting developments which soon came in the shape of a

---

16. Camp Beale's Springs was established in 1871 as a temporary camp to protect Hualpai Indians and avert conflicts between Indians and civilians. The relationship between soldiers and Indians was cordial. In 1874, however, the Indian Bureau ordered the Hualpais removed to the Colorado River Reservation, and Beale's Springs was abandoned. Altshuler, *Starting with Defiance*, 14.

tremendous explosion, knocking two of them to Kingdom Come and covering the others with ashes, sand and [beans?].

When I first went to Beale's Springs with General Crook, (in November 1871) the Hualpais were in a half-satisfied sort of a condition, ready to break out into open war upon the smallest incentive. Captain Byrne had already won their respect for his honesty, their implicit confidence in his word—but they didn't fear his power. Captain B. was determined that they should look up to him as the representative of the whole power of the Government. Calling all the chiefs and warriors to a grand council, he addressed them in words which I put down, as nearly as memory allows, as they flowed from his lips while giving his account of the affair to General Crook.

"Charlie, sez vi, (Hualpai Charley, was the principal one of the disaffected Indians.) ar yez fur pace, Charlie, sez vi, or fur war-r, Charlie, sez vi." "Oh, Cap'n, sez he to me, sez he, me dam gud Injun." ["]That's roight, Charlie, sez vi, thet's roight, becase, Charlie, sez vi, av yez is fur war-r-r, sez vi, we'll move out again yez, with moi *whole command*, sez vi, and in a month, Charlie, sez vi, there won't be a dam *Wallapoop* left aloive".

Tommy Byrne was a fine old soldier, one who loved his profession and felt a great pride in his position;—his one failing was an overindulgence in alcohol which he strictly contended he took only as "medicine", for the "*neuralgy*".

I think I can yet see the old man, narrating his interview to Genl. Crook, his face flush with excitement, making a fine contrast to his iron-gray locks and flowing, snowy beard. I have purposely rambled out of my path to jot down these reminiscences, suggested by my meeting with Mr. Moore,[17] because I have always regretted very keenly that I did not more completely keep my journals, note and scrap books during the period of my service in Arizona and New Mexico.[18] Captain Byrne played a by no means insignificant part in the task of reducing the Indians of that wild country to submission.

He had acted well during the war, was wounded and had been a prisoner in Libby,[19] for a great many months. Under his administration,

---

17. The post trader.
18. The New Mexico journals, and those from Arizona prior to November 20, 1872, are among those that are missing.
19. A notorious prisoner-of-war detention center in Richmond.

the little post at Beale's Springs was rapidly pushed to completion, if that can be styled complete which hasn't a blade of grass, a stick of timber and but a small amount of drinkable water. All day long and all the year through[,] the fierce rays of the sun beat down upon that mass of black lava, sending the thermometer away up above par and making the half-roasted garrison sigh for a flight to the timber-crest mountain range of Cubat, fifteen miles to the Eastward.

Here, old Tommy remained with his "Wallapoops", doing all that mortal could do to preserve friendly relations with them and to prevent war. Nothing gave him greater satisfaction than to see his wards advancing in the habits of civilization; the most that any of them did was to assume some teamster's cast off shirt or doff a rejected old slouch hat. Paper Collars were particularly affected by them, and the contrast between this emblem of a partial civilization and the brass ear-ring or bare legs of total savagery impressed itself upon the beholder in an instant.

The squaws of this tribe were perfectly wild for *castor oil*, smacking their lips after every dose as if they had been partaking of honey. They didn't use it for its medicinal qualities, but as a delicacy and almost drove the post surgeon wild by their importunate demands to be supplied with the drug. Tommy, in the course of time, came to be a terror to the grand army of scoundrels and dead-beats who surround an Indian Reservation, like vultures flocking to banquet upon a putrid carcass. Men caught selling whiskey to the Indians never asked him for any mercy; they knew well that they had none to receive. On one occasion, Tommy and a detachment of his men surprised an establishment all ready for business, in a secluded ravine.

The party was not exactly on the Reservation, but their intentions were obvious and as the Hualpai chiefs themselves had lodged the complaint, Captain Byrne lost no time in considering legal technicalities, but summarily seized and destroyed every particle of property and turned the rascals adrift with a total loss on their investment. In fact, the whiskey was the property of a man named Hardy, who lived on the Colorado river near Fort Mojave[20] and was a sort of a contractor, speculator, Congressional candidate, farmer

---

20. Fort Mojave was established in 1859 on the Colorado River opposite the present city of Needles, California. It was abandoned in 1890, and became an Indian school. The school was closed in 1935, and the post buildings were demolished seven years later. Frazer, *Forts of the West*, 11–12.

and anything else you please. These men were either selling the vile stuff on his account or else having purchased it from him, felt that they had a right to claim his interposition to secure "redress" from Captain Byrne.

Hardy rather prided himself upon his legal knowledge and thought he would have an interview with the military commandant and browbeat him into paying some damage to his clients. But he reckoned on false premises: old Tommy wasn't to be bull-dozed by anybody.

"But what *right* had you, Captain Byrne,["] demanded Hardy, ["]to destroy that whiskey?["]

"Roight! Roight! ez it?["], said the thoroughly exasperated Captain, ["]Captain! Damn yer sowl! Ain't oi monarch ov all I survey?" Hardy beat an inglorious retreat, but after that, always used to say that Tommy Byrne was the "damnedest [sic] fool he ever saw."

I don't wish to crowd the pages of this journal too much with anecdotes of my old friend, reserving a more complete description of him and his peculiarities until a more appropriate occasion. A goodly volume could be filled with anecdotes of himself and his Hualpai friends Charlie, Levy-Levy, Sherum, Corporal Ioz, and old head-men like Enya, cui, yu-say[21] and Ahcoo-la-wahta.

Communication with the Hualpais was ordinarily kept up through Johnny Quinn, the son of a laundress, who, not having any white play-mates, naturally took to associating with the young savages and used to run around with them, in a condition closely bordering on nudity.

It was my lot once to have to remain at Beale's Springs for four days in mid-summer. The heat was not great for that place, only 110°F, in the shade, but each lump of lava glowed with heat like the slag from an iron-furnace. We didn't have a thing to do; too hot to drill, no shade to shelter us, no mail to give us occupation. Those who played poker, did so. I got a pack of cards and wore them out playing Solitaire. This kept me from thinking of myself. Being able to play the game fairly, I succeeded with it very often, altho' I came near catching myself cheating several times.

21. Apparently a single name.

Chapter 12

"It Is of Such Stuff that Good Commonwealths Are Made"

July 8th The members of our party were up about 4 o'clock. Capt. Munson invited us all to breakfast at his house, as he was to command the escort & would have to get breakfast ready anyhow, and the other good people of the garrison would only have to arise at that unearthly hour to prepare it for our benefit.
Our preparations for the trip, thanks to Cap't. Munson's forethought and energy, were very complete: until late last night, he had been hard at work getting everything in shape and altho' our party, all told, did not number more than twenty men, it was necessary, as we were to be absent for some days in an almost unknown country, to provide for every contingency. Fuel has to be carried for the whole distance. Grain for the animals, food for officers and men, tentage, bedding, ammunition and harness. We are to have two six mule army wagons, one light spring wagon, one ambulance, and the riding animals of the escort and guides.
We have with us, Mr. Crowell, a deputy U.S. Surveyor, who has been employed in running township and section lines in this part of Nebraska for the past eight years and who understands its topography thoroughly. After the site of the new post to be constructed on the Niobrara has been determined, Mr. Crowell is to run the boundaries

of a timber reservation for Ft. Hartsuff. Our other guide is Mr. "Happy Jack" Swearingen, a happy-go-lucky sort of a fellow who has been trapping and hunting on the Loup for a long time. Jack is always out at elbows, hard up and good humored. Latterly, he has yielded to the persuasions of his well-wishers and gone to "farming"; that is to say, he had made a dug-out for himself in the side of a hill and scratched over an Acre or two of ground; he seems to have gotten the idea into his head that people are envious of his prosperity and desirous of depriving him of his possessions. Jack has kept constant watch and every time some over-curious passer-by ventures too near his cave-like habitation, he turns loose on him with his shot-gun. His friends are acquainted with this little amiable eccentricity and generally manage to give his mansion a wide berth. But barring this slight defect, Jack is said to be a good man, honest and brave, and skilled in border-life.

Our course lay North North West and North West up the North Loup, passing a number of ranches with crops of wheat, oats and barley, most of which looked well. We halted at one of these ranches, about 3 miles out, to get a few pounds of fresh butter, and six miles out stopped at another for same purpose, getting all that we needed. Made a short halt here to give our animals rest. Caught up with our heavy wagons at this point. They had left the Post some hours before we did.

Here there is a fine spring, the road making a short détour to pass around it.

Twelve miles from the Post is Pebble creek, a beautiful spring-brook of cold water, of short length and insignificant dimensions. Bottom, Pebbles and Sand. Banks, steep, clay. Approaches, verticle [sic] and twisted.

Men had to use ropes to keep the heavy wagons from overturning. The country has made an appropriation for a bridge at this place, and it will soon be completed.

Mr. Crowell tells me that there are a great number of fine springs in this vicinity and that the ravines opening into the main valley contain considerable pine & cedar timber.

The road now takes into the hills, from the top of which a very picturesque view is obtainable of the Loup Valley. If the next four years make as great a change in this valley as the past four, it will be one of the most important in the state of Nebraska. We now left the North Loup and began to ascend the Calamus, an important affluent which comes in at the junction of the two forks of the North Loup.

Some four miles up the Calamus, was a new dwelling, a rude structure of sods, with earthen floor and roof, with one door and one window and a break in the roof for the egress of smoke.
This was the "home" of a young family from Southern Illinois. Everything spoke of a bitter struggle for existence, but the woman, altho' dressed in a faded calico gown, shoeless and with unkempt hair, had a gentleness of [illegible] and courtesy of manner indicative of the refinement of true ladyhood. The father, a rough, horny-fisted fellow, made many apologies for the uncouth appearance of his home, said he had only been here a few months and had not yet raised his first crop, but hoped to have many improvements effected with time. Two lovely children, a girl and a boy, of three and two respectively, clung to their mother's skirt, their own scanty raiment rivalling hers in dirt and tatters. But, with all their discomforts and privations, this young couple looked resolute, confident in the future and happy in each other and in their children. It is of such stuff that good commonwealths are made and, no doubt, in another quarter of a century, this family will be comfortable, prosperous and well-placed.

The water from the wells in this part of Calamus Valley tastes strongly of peat, a deposit of which is struck some ten or twelve feet under the surface. Moved ten miles further to Gracie Creek, a clear, cold, swift-flowing brook, with gravel bottom. Approaches good, but grades rather steep. Scarcely any timber to be seen since striking the Calamus. Soil, near here, much thinner and apparently not so well-suited for agricultural purposes, but thickly covered with grass.
At one of the ranches near Gracie creek, we had a talk with the inmates; one, was a young widow, comely, graceful and well-formed, who said she had come out to this country with her uncle's family, bringing her year old baby. They were all from near Muscatine, Iowa, where her husband was the owner of a small farm, but last year the horses attached to the carriage he was driving ran away, killing him, breaking the vehicle to pieces and damaging themselves irretrievably. Their crop was yet in the ground and, of course, much of it was lost for want of care. Creditors grew impatient and everything had to be sold to liquidate indebtedness: but with unabated pluck, she had come to Nebraska, looking only upon the brighter aspects

of the future. A cattle ranch is nearly completed at Gracie creek. Herds of cattle were grazing nearby, but the owners were absent from home.

While lunching here, learned from Captain Munson much about the notorious Doc Middleton, chief of the gang of horse-thieves infesting the country between the Niobrara and the North Platte.

Middleton is reputed to be a man of very gentlemanly bearing, neatly dressed, the only one who in this section wears a white shirt. He is a fine horseman, an excellent shot, fearless and intrepid. By kindness to poor ranchmen and cattle-herders, he has made many friends in the country and his apprehension is almost impossible.

They tell two stories of him which speak well for the discipline maintained in his command. Once while robbing a stage-coach, one of his gang betrayed great nervousness and trembled perceptibly while holding a cocked revolver at a passenger's head. Middleton disgusted with the recruit's timidity, took the weapon away from him, slapping his face and saying, "You d–d fool, the first thing you know, you'll shoot somebody with that pistol."

At another time, he rode up to a ranch, accompanied by two of his followers, and asked the proprietor for a drink of water. While he was talking, one of his men quietly dismounted without waiting for orders. Middleton sternly asked him—"Who told you to get off that horse? Mount, at once, Sir".

Captain Munson also gave me an account of Genl. Crook's conference with O-chée-o, head chief of the Indians in Eastern Oregon and Idaho, whom Genl. Crook whipped so badly in 1867.[1]

General Crook said emphatically to this Indian that he didn't want to make peace, his business was to make war and he had all the men and materials he wanted to do it with. Before anything should be said, of Peace, O-chee-o must give up all ponies, horses and other property stolen from the whites.

["]Well,["] said Ochee-o, ["]I want to make peace, I'm tired of war and want to be your friend. I'll give back all that I've stolen, but now that we are good friends and I am giving back all that I've taken from you, don't you think that you ought to give back all that you've stolen from me?["]

General Crook couldn't see the matter in that light, but a peace

---

1. This campaign, including the fight of the caverns mentioned by Bourke a few paragraphs later, is covered in Robinson, *General Crook*, Chapter 7.

was concluded which has never been broken to this day (thirteen years.)
During that campaign a couple of miners were mysteriously murdered by Indians, but by what band could not be discovered.

The newspapers of Oregon and Northern California began a howl about the inefficiency of military management &c. The customary yarop.

The only thing known of the property in possession of the miners at the time they were murdered, was that they had a couple of yokes of oxen. General Crook found the trail of some oxen going to the village of a band of Pit River Indians and he shrewdly concluded, from the fact that these Indians did not own any cattle, that some of their young men must have been concerned in the murder and robbery. He sent Captain Munson with a small detail to their village to demand the surrender of the delinquents. The Indian agent and everybody nearby attempted to dissuade Munson from his task, but he had been ordered to perform the duty and he made the demand of the assembled chiefs. At first they evinced no willingness to do anything, but when Munson told them that if they didn't give up the murderers without delay, General Crook would move against them with all his force, they remembered the fearful pounding they had received from him in 1857, and at once produced the three young men who had perpetrated the outrage.[2] These were wrapped from head to foot in thongs of buckskin and surrendered to the soldiers, amid the wails of their female relatives.

Munson took them to the nearest settlement and turned them over to the civil authorities to await trial for murder; but that night, a mob collected, broke open the jail and took out the Indians and hanged them.

Munson also gave us a description of the "Caverns", where Genl. Crook had such a fearful time with the hostile Indians in 1867–68. Munson paid them a visit a few months after the fight and found in their gloomy vaults a number of Indian skeletons, with flesh still partially adhering to their bones. These caves were large depressions and natural tunnels in an immense lava bed, strewn with Cyclopean blocks of Basalt. A hundred men intrenched there could safely defy a thousand invaders so long as provisions held out.

2. The 1857 campaign against the Pit River Indians is discussed in Strobridge, *Regulars in the Redwoods*; Schwartz, *Rogue River Indian War*; and Robinson, *General Crook*, Chapter 2.

At one of these conferences an old duffer embraced Genl. Crook and wanted to be very friendly with him on the ground that he had "licked" him once when he was a Lieutenant, an imputation which the General indignantly denied.

Five miles after passing Gracie creek, went into camp on the Calamus, in a broad, level prairie, glittering in the reflection of the sun's rays from the thickly-growing spears of emerald green grass. Soil improving since leaving Gracie creek, and looking very well, altho' thin. It overlies a stratum of fine sand.

Calamus here forty feet Wide. two @ three feet Deep. Water clear and pure, tasting slightly of reeds. Bottom clayey and muddy, but not miry. Banks, three feet high. Approaches easily found. Banks can be broken away at any point. No timber in sight. Fuel brought along in our wagons.

Total Distance, (Odom[eter])   28 miles

The weather to-day has been charming and recalls by contrast the memory of the fearful snow-storm which visited this peaceful valley in the latter part of April 1874, when Captain [John] Mix's company of 2d Cavalry had such a narrow escape from being frozen to death. Cap't. Munson was a volunteer with Mix's Command on that trip and the account of their sufferings, as gathered from his own lips, will be found in my note-book, describing my trip to Cheyenne depôt, (Wyo.) in March '78.[3] As soon as our command reached camp this evening, teams were unhitched, horses unsaddled, all animals turned out to graze, while details of men were at once set to work erecting tents, putting up trestle-beds, with mosquito bars to keep away insects, building fires or carrying water. In another moment, our rough toilettes were completed and we were drinking a good, stiff toddy prepared under the experienced eye of Munson. Then the cook announced Dinner and each takes his camp-stool in hand and seats himself at the trestle table.

We had the appetite of wolves, ate with voracity, all the while garrulously talking.

The cook's creations received due praise. He laid before us, Ham—fresh potatoes, peas and tomatoes, good Ranch Butter, bread and something he called Pie.—all washed down with strong coffee.

---

3. There is a gap in the manuscript volumes from July 29, 1877, to March 28, 1878, so this refers to a volume that apparently has been lost.

Our repast ended, we sit in front of our tent and in the pleasant light of the declining sun look at the incoming herd of stock; the slow movement of the full-bodied mules and horses being hastened by the cracking of whips and the chirping of herders.

Those of us who feel like smoking, smoke; those who don't, don't: but all talk:—of home, of old times, of scenes in the Great War passing so fleetly from the memory of our people; of campaigns against hostile Indians, of the probabilities of a war with Mexico.[4]

Other topics are opened. We talk of mines, Rail Roads, books, the drama, music, and science;—of everything in truth and some things fairly well.

We have music too, sweet nocturnes and symphonies from sturdy-winged mosquitoes, whose bites following fast upon their songs keep our hands moving in frantic activity. Fortunately, we have bed-netting with which we hope to be able to defy the attacks we may look for in the still watches of the night.[*]

July 9th Our hopes were illusory; the mosquitoes forced their way through the meshes of the bars and play sad havoc with our feelings. Until day-break we tossed and rolled and cursed without a moment's respite from the exquisite torture. I remember having read that the Buccaneers of the Gulf of Mexico, (under Lafitte.) often punished their unhappy captives by exposing them naked to the assaults of the myriads of these little pests in the low-land of the Mississipi Delta, but I never comprehended until last night the awful character of the torture.

Early this morning, a small boy, giving his name as Abraham Lincoln Bolling, rode into camp on a sore-backed, fly-bitten horse: said he had ridden down from Long Pine creek (70 miles) yesterday; had been to Cook's (Toevar's) Ranch to get work; found the ranch in possession of three of the "pony-boys" (Middleton's men)[.] This story had been told us yesterday by two men whom we met at one of the ranches near Gracie creek.

---

[*]*Bourke's note:* Cached two sacks of grain at this point.

4. Relations between the United States and Mexico during the last half of the 1870s probably were at their lowest point since the Mexican War. Besides the cross-border raids mentioned in the introduction, problems included U.S. claims against Mexico, Mexico's dire financial situation, the country's reaction against foreign development of its resources, the initial instability of the Porfirio Díaz regime, and the U.S. refusal to recognize that regime. See Cosío Villegas, *The United States Versus Porfirio Díaz*.

We gave this bold youngster a good breakfast; he was, physically, a fine brawny sun-burned boy of (14), ragged, good-natured and independent. His shirt was hanging in shreds from his shoulders and didn't have a button upon it: the rest of his costume consisted of a pair of old Army pantaloons, rolled up about the ankles and held in place by a piece of rope girdling the waist.

His horse was really a *gray*, but so bitten by mosquitoes & green-headed flies that the oozing blood made him a *roan*.

Our course continued as it was yesterday: between North West and North North West. Country almost level: valley of Calamus here about two miles from bluff to bluff. Bluffs very low: soil sandy. No trees. Seven miles out halted to rest animals. Day cloudy and sultry. Animals suffering greatly from bites of mosquitoes. The general aspect of this country is that of a boundless, grassy plain, cut up by low sand-hills and dotted with sloughs of rain water.

Three miles farther out, crossed Bloody creek, a brook of good water, 6 feet Wide, one foot deep, slow current, bottom clayey and firm. Banks 5 @ 6 feet above surface of water. With spades and picks, a crossing was soon made for our heavy transportation. (Bloody creek is said to rise 6 miles to East of this point in a couple of fresh-water Lakes[)]. Two miles farther reached Skull creek identical in character with Bloody creek and with whose clay banks we had the same trouble excavating a road-way as with the other.

Found a few strawberries at this Brook of good color and delicious flavor, but of small size. Our guides, Crowell and Happy Jack reported having seen tracks of five Elk. Country rather poorer to-day, many weeds intermingled with the grass.

Calamus now makes a big bend to South and our course, (we had left road at Bloody Creek.) was directed so as [to] cut across.

Many springs, all of good water, pouring into the Calamus. We saw a couple of white tailed deer, and shot a sage-hen this afternoon. Camped on Calamus Creek. Plenty of good grass and water slightly reedy in taste, Fuel from Wagons.

Total Distance   25 miles.

July 10th Warned by the misfortunes of the previous night, we made every effort last night to guard against mosquitoes and succeeded fairly. A heavy storm threatened as we turned in, but nothing came of it excepting a very few drops of rain.

Camp aroused at 4 o'clock this morning and without the loss of much time, we had finished breakfast and taken up the line of march, ascending the Calamus. Mr. Crowell and Happy Jack, with two m[oun]t[e]d men pushed ahead to look up a site for to-night's camp, because we are now making our way across an unknown country, not having had any road or trail to follow since leaving Bloody Creek. For (3) or (4) miles marched nearly due West, the Niobrara here averaging not over (10) @ 20 feet in width, very sinuous, banks low and swampy and covered with a kind of sedge grass. No trees or bushes. Hills about here mantled with a yellow-ripe bunch grass. Sand-cherries very plentiful. A young mink and a sand-hill crane shot and elk-track seen.

Calamus is full of pools from seven to ten feet deep, containing fish (chub) of large size. Six miles out from last night's camp, halted and sent a party of men over to the other side of river to bring back a deer killed by Mr. Crowell. Water more than waist-deep. Grass getting richer and thicker.

The "valley", so to speak, of the Calamus continues one mile wide from bluff to bluff, the course of the stream, in places, showing patches of tulé and sedge-grasses, but there is nothing in the way of timber or foliage. The grass seems to be pretty well tenanted by prairie-chickens.

After marching seventeen miles, the command halted near the head of the Calamus, at a spring of warm, reedy-flavored water which gurgled under the shade of a clump of tulés. Captain Munson and self, with an orderly, moved ahead to see if we could discover the whereabouts of Crowell and Happy Jack who were to have met us at or near this point with information as to the location of water and grass farther on. We made a circuit of three miles without finding any trace of them. As we were jogging along, we suddenly ran right into a splendid buck, who presented a beautiful picture as he lay half-stretched on the green grass, his tawny flanks broad side to us and his wide-branching black antlers pointing to the sky.[5] He discerned us just as soon as we did him and with one convulsive jump, like as if he was shot from out of a cannon, he bounded in the air, all four legs held close up under his body, and away he went, scarcely seeming to touch the ground.

5. It being July, the black color meant the antlers were newly grown and "in velvet," i.e., covered with skin and downy hair. Later in the year, when the antlers are fully grown, the deer sheds the velvet by rubbing against trees and rocks, resulting in whitish antlers with a high polish. These are shed in spring, and the process repeats itself with new antlers.

A little beyond this point, we scared up two or three more, one of which our orderly wounded.

Captain Munson now asked me to return to Genl. Crook and say to him that he would go on a little farther to look up our guides and if he could not find them that our present position was the best one for our bivouac to-night.

Munson reached Genl. Crook almost as soon as I did, having found Happy Jack, who told him that Crowell had found two small lakes or ponds some eight miles ahead. We remained at head of Calamus to lunch, making lemonade with the sedgy water, which tasted quite good. A stiff breeze blew up and heavy clouds threatened us with a storm, but beyond the rumbling of thunder and the refreshment of the cooling breeze, nothing came of it. Started out again at 2 P.M., going about North West which has been our line almost all day. Made a total distance of 23 or 24 miles.

Bivouacked alongside of a couple of fresh-water pools, (overgrown with reeds,) supposed to find their way to the Calamus, during rainy season. Water tasted strongly of mud, grass, rushes and decomposing vegetable matter.

Dug a well four feet deep, obtaining a colder and sweeter water, but one equally turbid with that flowing under the rushes. No Wood. Grass in plenty and of good quality. General Crook saw a number of large, white swans this P.M. Mr. Crowell says that they live in these ponds all the year round and raise their young.

Sand-hill cranes, plover and prairie-chickens seen in considerable numbers to-day; also dragon-flies which are said to live upon the mosquitoes. A solitary cayote also made his appearance at a distance of three hundred yards.

July 11th We had a slight change in the weather last night, the air growing cooler and enabling us to sleep, despite the mosquitoes which swarmed in the grass under our beds making a noise like a hive of angry fees. Heavy fog this morning.

At breakfast, Mr. Crowell told us of the existence of extensive desposits of peat near the Niobrara and on State line north of mouth of Snake river. Were in the saddle before 5 o'clock. Three miles from camp passed a pond, partially covered with tule. Water good and sweet, but not very cold. Just beyond that, climbed over a range of low sand-mounds. Horses and mules nearly crazy from the bites of mosquitoes and sand-flies.

Genl. Crook, Mr. Crowell and Happy Jack kept a mile or two in advance of command, looking for game: Mr. Crowell started up two deer. Descending from the top of this low sand-ridge, saw to our Right three miles away, a pond of water, probably a mile long; and a few moments after passed alongside another, of smaller size. All morning, we travelled by pools of insignificant dimensions, under whose covering of reeds and tule water, more or less stagnant, was discernible.

We have been touching upon the East extremity of the Sand Hills of Nebraska and the soil has been cognetting between sand and clay. As much as possible, we have clung to the skirts of the sand-hills, because our wagons can advance faster than in the alluvial surroundings of the ponds and we also escape the bites of the insects which cling to the grass and tule.

At 9 o'clock, the heavy clouds of fog rolled away, leaving in full splendor the rays of the sun. Being fanned by a cooling breeze, we enjoyed this delicious Sun-bath immensely.

Genl. Crook came upon a doe and two fawns. The doe got away, but the fawns ran towards us, not being able to make out who and what we were. They were not harmed.

Twelve and [a] half miles out from last night's camp, struck one of the sources of Plum creek.

No change in character of the country. It is a well-grassed plateau, without timber, but with numerous sloughs or ponds holding rain-water. One of the soldiers captured a little fawn this morning, and it has been carried in the wagons, the soldiers hoping to tame it.

Total march to-day   22 miles.

Camped alongside of a slough, full of rain-water, supposed to be a tributary of Evergreen creek. Dug a shallow well to secure a supply of water, untainted by reeds. Grass plenty. No Wood.

Happy Jack, I learned to-day, adds a little to his yearly income, by trapping wolves for which the State pays a bounty of $2 per cap.[6] There are a few thrifty families living in the Loup Valley, who eke out their incomes by raising litters of wolf-puppies and when of mature age, killing them and claiming the usual bounty.

Heavy banks of clouds again filled the sky this evening, but no rain.

6. Meaning the bounty for a wolf scalp.

After supper, Captain Munson asked me if when I was serving in Arizona, I had ever heard the story of the *mysterious Fate of Doctor Tappan*. I had served at old Camp Grant, the military Post near which the unfortunate young man had disappeared and I listened with intense interest to Captain Munson's story, which he gave as it was current in Arizona in 1867. Tappan was medical officer for a detachment of recruits who, under a young and inexperienced officer, were marching up from Fort Yuma to join the garrison of (old) Camp Grant.

    They had reached the Cottonwood Springs within twelve miles of their destination without seeing a sign of an unfriendly Indian. A few hour's marching would end their long and weary journey. All hearts lightened at the prospect. Discipline was relaxed, no sentinels were posted, nobody dreaming of the slightest danger. Suddenly, the air is rent by the blood-curdling war-cry of the fierce Apache, and the sharp crack of rifles and the whining of arrows. The Lieutenant and several of his men were killed at first fire; Doctor Tappan and others wounded, and all demoralized. The Apaches were too busy scalping and mutilating the dead, plundering and burning the train or securing horses and mules to pay much attention to the fugitives who ran like deer in what they took to be the straightest line to the Post.

All of them reached Camp Grant except poor Tappan. A strong force was at once sent to the scene of the attack and while a part took up the trail of the savages, a strong body, accompanied by expert Mexican trailers, started for the place where Dr. Tappan was last seen by his comrades.

They had no trouble in finding it and following his tracks, strongly marked by the nails in his boot-heels. They came to a little spring or tank of water under a flat rock where Tappan had evidently knelt and drank and then written in the blood from his wound a few incoherent expressions and his full name on the smooth face of the stone. From that point, it became impossible to trail him; he had seemingly become bewildered, as his foot prints wandered round and round, crossing themselves at several points. At length, even foot-prints ceased and all that is conjectured of his last end is fearful and heart-chilling. It is believed that the wounded man was *seized and carried off* by a huge *Mountain Lion*, the tracks of a monstrous animal of this class being found running alongside of Tappan's trail, and shortly before it ended, the marks on the ground showed that the lion was bounding after Tappan at the measured rate of *Twenty Two feet to the Jump*![7]

Munson also gave an account of the wonderful escape of Wentworth,—Little Buckshot,—who was in 187–, in company with two men of Captain [James] Egan's Company of the 2d Cavalry, on a scout near the head of La Bonté creek, in Laramie Peak, Wyo. A war-party of Sioux jumped their camp at night and killed his two companions, but Wentworth himself escaped just as he sprang out of bed and ran like a frightened deer in the direction of Capt. Egan's main camp.

In doing this, he had to rush through a broad field of (nopal) cactus, and filled his feet and ankles so full of thorns that for months he was unable to leave his bed and, the inflammation became so great, the Doctors for a long time thought seriously of amputating both his feet.[8]

Mosquitoes this night make our sufferings worse than anything depicted by Milton or Dante.

July 12th Kept up a North West course, country almost the same as that already described but hills of sand occurring with more frequency. These are nearly covered with dwarf sand-cherry bushes. Six or seven miles out from camp, discerned on top of hills in our front, (dividing the waters of Evergreen from those of Schlegel Creek) the first timber on march since leaving the Loup. Camp upon a number of cattle-trails.

Genl. Crook bagged half a dozen fine fat prairie chickens. Cap't. Stanton and I each secured a young one, barely hatched. These are only half the size of a newly-hatched domestic fowl, are of a bright canary color, dotted with brown, eyes and beak, blackish-brown. One of the escort caught one almost full-grown, all of which would seem to indicate that the prairie chicken lay all through summer. We released the ungrown chicks and took care, as far as possible, not to molest hens with nests.

Locusts, in considerable numbers along trail this morning.

After marching between sixteen and seventeen miles, reached

---

7. The official record states that Assistant Surgeon Benjamin Tappan, U.S. Volunteers, was "killed 22 Mar 1866 in action with Apache Inds near Cottonwood Springs Ariz." Heitman, *Historical Register*, 1:944.

8. Bourke probably means *opuntia*, which resembles nopal. The spines of the nopal are so insignificant that they are hardly noticeable.

Creighton's Ranch, on Schlegel creek, four miles from its junction with Niobrara.

This creek is 8 @ 10 feet wide, one foot deep, water clayey in taste, valley twelve miles long, about two hundred yards from bluff to bluff, fairly grassed, timber very scarce. (Scrub Pine, cedar and oak, with a little ash.)

Creighton's Ranch is a "log and chink" structure, consisting of two large rooms, each 20' x 15' and 12' high in middle; these are separated by an open roofed space, wide enough to permit of the passage of a wagon.

One of these rooms serves as dormitory, the other as kitchen and dining room. Back of the house, is the corral, 75' square.

Ground Plan, Front View

Entering the kitchen and dining room, we took a careful survey of everything about us, the general aspect being far from inviting, altho' there was no marked want of the necessaries of life. The effect produced was that of indifference to comfort—that cursed "making things do" which blights so many frontier homes and is in such marked contrast to the "Get up and git-ativeness["] of people farther East.

Everything was rough;—we expected that, but nothing was in "ship shape". A little care would have made great changes in the appearance of this interior.

A neat-looking cook, who was evidently superior to his comrades, occupied his proper place in front of a large stove, well supplied with cooking utensils. Other pots[,] pans and kettles were hanging against the walls or arranged on the floor. Boxes, bags, sacks and cans of flour, beans, bacon and baking powder, soap, sugar, syrup, tea, coffee and fruit were piled up against the wall and in proximity to the stove. In the middle of [the] room, a rough pine table, spread with tin plates, knives and forks; in the corner, the cook's bed, of rudely hewn, cedar branches, covered with venerable army blankets and an old blue military overcoat which might have been with Washington at Valley Forge. The benches and stools, scattered about on the earthen floor were in strict keeping with the bed and table. Carbines, ammunition belts, sombreros, overalls, "chaparreros",[9] antelope horns &c hung from the logs and rafters.

The foreman, cook, and cowboys, rough, good-hearted fellows, bade us welcome in a rough, slouchy, good-natured style. The word which comes most easily to pen or tongue in describing this place, is "rough",—It is a rough life, this cow-herding and they are a rough lot of fellows who engage in it.

Wallace, the foreman, a Texan, very hospitably asked us to remain for dinner but as our own was nearly ready, we declined. The cook, while we were there, was actively prosecuting the preparations for their mid-day meal; one of the principal dishes was stewed wild-currants. The bread or biscuit was rolled with a tin fruit can.

There is not much room for the refined and aesthetic in the lives of these cattle-men; their existence is a daily struggle with sterner features which gradually banishes all that is tender and sentimental from their natures, leaving only the materialistic and practical. Of those lounging about in this room waiting the signal for dinner each was booted, pistoled, belted and spurred to the last degree. The skin of a full-grown Swan, measuring eight feet from tip to tip, lay at the door, revealling the unerring aim of somebody belonging to the ranch; and a little fawn, not more than a fortnight old[,] participated in the attention which otherwise would have been given exclusively to dogs, horses and cows. The "talk" carried on in an indolent, listless kind of way was all "cattle", seasoned with profanity. "McCann's boys hain't done no duty since the 'roundup'—They hain't by Gawd". "That bunch of cattle we seed over on Snake creek must 'a b'longed to Sharp's outfit—They must fur a fae', by Gawd."

9. Known in the West as "chaps."

["]Cooke's boys say they haint lost nary cattle at all—they h'aint, by Gawd". and so on. While they are driving and guarding thousands, millions of pounds of fresh meat each year, these cattle-herders don't get a taste of it once a week. They use a good deal of it "jerked", and surmounting every cattle-ranch may be seen a couple of tall poles, between which is stretched a hemp or raw-hide rope, sustaining large strings of beef slowly "jerking" in the sun.

Creighton's ranch employs six men. This ranch, as well as all others in this vicinity, has suffered severe losses the present spring. Out of a grand total of Twenty-Six hundred, Creighton has only been able to "round-up" thirteen hundred. Cooke's ranch has escaped with scarcely any loss worth mentioning.

The cow-boys, I should take to be skilled judges of country, good riders, careful of their cattle and fair hunters, They have a vernacular of their own, calling horses "stock" and all horned animals "cattle". A whip is a "quirt". The words "outfit" and "round-up" are most constantly on duty. The[y] use profanity with liberality and are not slow to shoot upon provocation.

We had a fine breeze this afternoon which cooled the air greatly and enticed us into making a tour of the ranch.
The general air of thriftiness referred to as noticeable in the ranch itself pervaded all its surroundings. No idea of comfort seems to have entered the heads of anybody connected with the Establishment. There are no pigs and no chickens. Milk and eggs are almost unknown quantities. No wells are dug. The water for drinking purposes being drawn from the creek in which horses, cows and dogs wallow at will.
A down East Yankee or an Ohio, Penn[sylvan]ia,or Michigan farmer going into the cattle business would speedily bring about a perfect transformation: but while Texas influences rule supreme, the slipshod, comfortless, put off-until-the-day-after-to-morrow principle will be the guide.
One quarter of a mile above Creighton's, is a fine spring, shaded by a heavy cluster of cottonwood, oak, ash and currant.
Captain Stanton finds the distance from Fort Hartsuff to Creightons's, by Odometer measurement, to be One hundred and Eleven miles, in an almost straight line.
July 13th, 1879. Had but little trouble from mosquitoes last night; the strong wind proved too much for them.

At day-break this morning, Genl. Crook formed us into two parties to examine the Niobrara valley and determine upon a suitable point for the location of a Post. The first of himself, Schuyler, Crowell and one soldier, to go down the Niobrara; the other, of Stanton, Munson, self, two soldiers, and Happy Jack, to ascend the stream at least as far as the mouth of Snake River. Our wagons to remain at Creighton's and the different parties to re-unite by sun-down.

Our party moved out about 5 o'clock, going nearly West, crossing Schlegel creek at the ranch, and then going across an elevated, level plateau, well covered with green grass, for seven miles where we got to what on some maps is called Precipice creek, on others Hell Cañon. (We followed the Gordon trail.)

This Precipice creek is nothing more than a deep and sudden gash in the bosom of the plain and were it not for the tops of the pine trees which here and there protrude slightly above the edges, its existence would not even be suspected until you stood upon the brink. It is a wild sort of a ravine; not less than two hundred and fifty feet deep and scarcely one hundred and fifty wide. The walls are a glaring white, siliceous limestone banded by several strata of good building limestone. Wherever vegetation could take a foot-hold, pine trees have sprung up, while the bottom is filled with cottonwood, scrub-oak, quaking asp[en] and other undergrowth. No water could be seen, but from indications of old camps &c., there must be some at certain seasons.

We passed around the head of this cañon, and after a brisk march of seven or eight miles more, reached Snake river, a few hundred yards above its junction with the Niobrara. The Niobrara, is a geological curiosity; it has cut a path for itself longitudinally through a ridge of limestone and may be described as flowing along a knife-edge. By examining Precipice creek and Snake river, we could see that the surface of this part of Nebraska is composed of a thin layer of rich soil, resting upon a compact bed of sand and this in its turn upon a formation of siliceous limestone.

The approach to Snake river is decidedly steep, twisted and difficult.

As a matter of necessity, it could with some little expenditure of time and labor be converted into an easy ramp, but better natural grades can no doubt be found. The cañon of Snake river is liberally supplied with pine and other timber, none of it particularly large or fine, but nearly all available for building purposes. The bottom contains a great number of grape-vines and other fruit-bearers. The river itself is sixty feet wide, 2½ feet deep, current of 3 @ 4 miles per hor., [sic] ford good with a few rock[s] in stream-bed. At the junction of the two rivers, is a large, level, flat, of not less than 600 A[cres]., which in [one] or two spots shows evidence of being subject to partial overflow. This flat bears pretty clumps of cottonwood of medium size and has a soil of mixed sand and alluvium, growing grass, sun-flowers, grape-vines, weeds, &c. and extending up the Niobrara for a considerable distance. We examined the valley of the Niobrara for a couple of miles and the cañon of the Snake for a thousand yards, finding several positions upon which posts might be planted, if compelled so to be. The objection to each of these sites was that the hills close to them had such a perfect "command" that a few Indians creeping into secluded nooks in the rocks could annoy the garrisons terribly. The expense and bother of levelling off the parades would also be considerable, but in every other respect,—supply of Wood, Water and Grass, Good soil, Building materials, Drainage, Healthfulness, Protection against Winds, non-Liability to overflow, Space for company Gardens, &c. much might be said in favor of either location. It would be essential to lay out a Reservation comprehending within its limits the junction of the two streams and running along each for a distance sufficient to keep away whiskey-venders, timber-cutters and other vermin.

Met a couple of herders, employed by D. J. McCann, who has 2500. head grazing along the stream. Moved down Niobrara three or four miles, day very warm and bright, but not enervating. This river ranges in width from 350 down to 75 feet bottom sandy, in places "quick", but generally fordable. Depth from 10 inches to three feet and half. Current 4 miles, broken frequently by sand-bars. Water soft, sweet and cool. Valley variable in breadth, but offering a number of nice spots for farming: bluffs, in some points, high and steep. Rested under the shady foliage of a grove of cottonwoods and lunched. Somehow our conversation from the death of the young Prince Imperial drifted to English History and we all thought how wonderful it would be if Fate should one day give *American* rulers to both *France* and *England*. The "legitimate" rulers of both those countries are now *American citizens*, the Bonaparte family of Baltimore and General E. O. C. Ord, U.S.A. Ord is the grandson

"It Is of Such Stuff that Good Commonwealths are Made"   243

of George IV by Mrs. Fitz-Herbert, a Roman Catholic lady of great beauty whom the licentious Prince endeavored to seduce; but his efforts resulted in such inglorious failure that to accomplish his purpose [he] married her.

The marriage, duly solemnized and witnessed, resulted in the birth of one child, (perhaps more.) the father of General Ord.

Both General Ord and Colonel Bonaparte were graduated at West Point and Commissioned in the Regular Army of the United States.[10]

Got back to Creighton's Ranch, which is not, in truth, much of an oasis, but it served well for one, when we threw ourselves from our saddles, tired and hot, from our (12) hours' ride of thirty-five miles in the blazing sun. Captain Munson immediately prepared a draught of cold lemonade for each of us; then we splashed our heads with a great plenty of water, and were ready to sit down to an appetizing dinner.

General Crook's party had reached camp a couple of hours before we did and had taken advantage of the interval to bathe in the little falls of Schlegel creek, just below the ranch. Stanton, Munson and I hoped to follow their example, but a heavy storm of wind springing up and a black pall of clouds mantling the sky, we did not judge it to be prudent to make the venture.

General Crook had made a selection of a site, which Stanton and I hope to visit to-morrow morning.

Lt. Schuyler caught two Kangaroo rats.

The storm passed away without doing any damage beyond a heavy sprinkling. We were for an hour or so very apprehensive that a steely-gray and deep brown and black cloud angrily circling over

---

10. Ord's father, James Ord, was born in London in 1786, but was never certain of his background. Officially, his parents were Ralph and Mary Ord, but General Ord's biographer, Bernarr Cresap, makes a strong case that this was a ruse to hide royal parentage, specifically the Prince of Wales (later King George IV) and Maria Fitzherbert. By "legitimate," Bourke meant that the reigning British sovereign, Queen Victoria, was not a lineal descendant of King George IV, but his niece, while Ord was his grandson. The marriage to Mrs. Fitzherbert, however, was morganatic, and was not recognized by the government. The Bonaparte mentioned is Jerome Napoleon Bonaparte (1830–93), grandson of Napoleon's youngest brother, Jerome, and his first wife, Elizabeth Patterson of Baltimore. An 1848 graduate of West Point, the grandson was posted to the Mounted Rifles (later redesignated 3rd Cavalry, Bourke's regiment). He resigned in 1854, and later entered French service as one of the many family hangers-on that surrounded Napoleon III. After the fall of the Second Empire, he returned to the United States, where he married a granddaughter of Daniel Webster. His brother, Charles Joseph Bonaparte, served as secretary of the navy and attorney general under Theodore Roosevelt. Cresap, *Appomattox Commander*, 2; Heitman, *Historical Register*, 1:229; Stacton, *The Bonapartes*, 357–60.

our heads would resolve into a cyclone and do us great harm as our camp was entirely unprotected.

The people of the Ranch shared our apprehension, and gathered in their herd of ponies, of which they had nearly forty. These are all grass-fed and consequently not able to stand a very great amount of hard work; the herder very frequently riding down two in one day.

Later in the night we had a very heavy wind and rain, lasting several hours. Wind blew strongly from South and was quite warm, but banished mosquitoes.

July 14th Sun arose like a ball of cherry and gold.

Captain Stanton, Mr. Crowell, Happy Jack, an orderly and myself, pushed out nearly due East, following down Schlegel creek, or rather parallel to it, until it bent North to join the Niobrara.

Seven miles out, reached the springs alongside of which, General Crook intends establishing the new Post. In a little ravine, three large springs of good, cold water, combine, and if properly dug out and walled, will supply enough water for all the needs of a garrison of 500 persons. The Plateau is of great size, is perfectly smooth and thickly sodded, has an excellent drainage, is surrounded for half a circle by the Niobrara which here makes a large bend and can get all the watering needed for the springs just spoken of, (which with scarcely a doubt, can send water all over the parade,) and from the half-dozen others which gush out from under the plateau in little gulches filled with oak or cottonwood. This plateau is very accessible, has all the advantages demanded and cannot be "commanded" from any of the bluffs or ridges in proximity. Close to the Niobrara is a fine grove of oak trees, many of which have lately been blown down by a cyclone. We crossed the Niobrara, at this point, one hundred and eighty feet Wide, Two and one half feet deep, Good, firm ford, Banks easy.

Went to Sharp's Ranch, at mouth of Mini-Chaduze,[11] or Rapid Creek, which is small, swift-flowing stream, well timbered with Pine, Oak, ash and Elm, but water tasting of decayed leaves. The dogs of the ranch made a great racket but the young fellow who acted as cook, soon silenced them and bade us welcome to the house. The Mini-Chaduza, he said, was 15 @ 20 feet Wide 6 inches to 2 feet Deep, Bottom, Rock, but now and then miry. Banks, steep.

11. Minnechaduze.

This cow-boy appeared very sunny in his disposition, anxious to make the best of everything. He almost insisted upon our partaking of breakfast with him, but, old campaigners as we were, the sight of his repast was enough to kill what appetite we might have had. The bread was the color of a lemon, with the amount of soda he had used, and the dish he called corn-starch was far from inviting. He seemed to be so happy and good-natured that the reflection came upon me that, after all, our lives are only what we make them and that a cow-boy happy is better than Alexander sighing for new worlds to conquer.

Having completed our examination of the country, we watered our horses, recrossed the Niobrara and pushed out directly South, climbing up a gently ascending grass-covered plateau for five miles, when we came to a low sand-ridge, plentifully studded with the "amole", or soap-weed. Thence we descended into a plain of grass, where we were beset by sand-flies.

As we were jogging along, we passed by, on our Right, a plum thicket, surrounded by tall green grass. Crowell remarked to me; "what a fine place for deer to hide in!" The words were only half out of his mouth, when up jumped two tall, finely-antlered bucks and darted over a sand-ridge before we could put our hands upon our weapons. We encountered a great number of crickets this morning. Towards noon, struck our ingoing trail and followed it to camp of July 12th, and there unbridled our horses to let them cool off and graze for a few moments.

The rain of last night had filled up the well we had dug, giving us a depth of 3½ feet of good water, which we poured on our heads, faces and arms before starting.

Another distance of eight or ten miles brought us to Genl. Crook's camp, at head of Plum creek, the points of which have already been noted.

Total Distance, (for Stanton & self)　　　　　35 miles.

Afternoon decidedly sultry.

We were pretty well tuckered out when we got to Camp, but with a generous ablution of hands, neck, chest and arms and placing wet h[an]dk[erchie]fs. upon our heads, we recovered from the effects of the heat, while for the fatigue occasioned by being (13½) hours in the saddle we had the recuperative effect of a short sigh and a toddy, which made us ready for our dinner of stewed prairie chicken and the usual accompaniments.

The mosquitoes again swarmed around us, but hadn't made much progress toward eating us up, when a fearful tempest broke out, a sonorous peal of thunder and a vivid blaze of lightning announced its arrival and for two hours or more, our little camp was the centre of a cascade of water dashing down from the sky. In the midst of it all, Captain Munson entered our tent, having been drowned out of his own bed, and took his seat on a camp stool between Schuyler and myself. He held in his hand a lighted candle which surrounded his straw-hat with a golden halo and attracted a great swarm of mosquitoes whose music, added to the other points of the picture, made Munson look like the wood-cut of a benevolent, old saint, in a cheap Roman Catholic Prayer Book.

July 15th Morning Gloomy, damp and disagreeable. Mr. Crowell, with six men, four horses and one six-mule team, [was] sent down Plum creek to run the survey for a timber Reservation for Fort Hartsuff. From the careful and detailed description given of the country passed over to this time, it will be seen that the absence of timber will be a serious drawback to its settlement by small bands of immigrants; not so, with organized colonies, backed by a little capital. For them it offers many inducements. The soil is not bad, the grass is abundant and of fine quality and timber will grow when properly protected. The greatest drawback would be from prairie fires.

Let a community of Mennonites or Trappist Monks get possession of one of these valleys and they could soon prove its value.

Fire-breaks could be ploughed out in the best positions, cattle turned out to fatten on the rich grass, the sloughs drained and the water gathered in suitable channels, houses and stables built of sod, and trees planted. Cottonwood, Willow, osier, & plum, grow naturally in this region wherever screened from wind and fire. Cherries, Raspberries, currants and strawberries, could be raised for market. Whether by individual or co-operative enterprise, I am sure that this great expanse of territory will not long remain uninhabited.

Had some trouble early this morning in crossing the bottoms, submerged by last night's rain; in the afternoon, marching [was] all [that] could be desired. Camped on the Calamus.

Distance   29 miles.

July 16th. Last night, a violent storm of rain unexpectedly burst upon us, lasting for more than an hour, when its force, in some degree abated, leaving a continuous drizzle for the rest of the time until morn[in]g. We were all glad of it, since we prefer anything to mosquitoes.

This morning, the ground is so saturated that we expect great difficulty in making head-way. Three of our mules were badly galled by their collars yesterday and for that reason we feared very little drawback, but at Bloody creek, we again struck the road and had good marching to camp, passing Skull and Bloody creek with scarcely any bother worth mentioning. At confluence of Skull and Calamus, our men caught a mess of chub. Genl. Crook shot a couple of prairie-chickens.

Our little fawn is thriving nicely and is already tame, allowing itself to be petted by everybody. A storm raging to the West of our trail; only a few drops of rain fell upon us.

Near Bloody creek, met an old man a Mr. Lewis, coming down from Cooke's Ranch. He was a grizzled old customer, and had a gnarled, knitty look which gave us confidence in his ability to complete the ride he had started to make—90 miles—from Cooke's Ranch to Fort Hartsuff, in one day. He had with him four ponies; by changing saddle from one to another, he kept them and himself fresh.

According to his report, Cooke's ranch has been exceptionally successful this winter and spring. Turning out last Fall (1340) head, they have up to date, rounded up over 1100 head with several bands in sight. They calculate now that they have escaped loss and may show a slight increase.

    Lewis had been sent out to hunt up one of their herders, a young fellow named Walker, who had wandered away from the ranch, over a week ago.

Made our camp to-night at same place as we had camped upon in coming out. Found our cached corn all right.

Distance travelled   34 miles

Jly 17th Another drenching storm last night. Sky this morning, a cold and forbidding gray, ground wet and air humid. Marched 27 miles to Fort Hartsuff, reaching there at 11 A.M.

During our absence, the wind-mill of the post had been blown down in a storm.

Loss about ($800) Estimated.

July 18th Left Fort Hartsuff in a heavy fog. Passed a sod school-house filled with happy-faced youngsters.

Stopped for the night at Buckshots. Rained during the night.
July 19th Moved to Grand Island.
Genl. Crook and Lieut. Schuyler took West train for California and Fort Steele respectively.[12]
July 20th Captain Stanton and self returned to Omaha.
Total distance travelled on trip, between 750 and 760 miles.

12. Actually, Crook was going to Fort Fred Steele, and Schuyler to California where, as the following chapter notes, he was inspecting the Murchie Mine, in which Crook and a consortium had invested.

Chapter 13

Fort Craig to Camp Grant

The newspapers contained accounts of the mortuary services of the Young Prince Imperial, at the chapel of Saint Mary, Camden Place, Chiselhurst, England, July 18th. The pallbearers were the princes of the English Royal family.

Almost on same date came the news from South Africa that Lord Chelmsford had with almost 5.000 men defeated the Zulus who had a force of 12.000. Sir Garnet Wolsely [sic] who had been sent out to relieve Chelmsford had not yet assumed command and consequently whatever credit was due for the affair belonged to Chelmsford.[1]

July 22d (?)[2] General Wm. F. Barry, (Colonel 2d Artillery,) died. About same date, a party of Government detectives had a fight with the outlaw, Middleton, on the Niobrara, in which two of the detectives and Middleton were wounded. July 31st Doc Middleton captured by a party of detectives and soldiers from Fort Hartsuff, Neb.

August 1st Lieut. W.S. Schuyler, A.D.C., returned from his trip to the Murchie Mine, Nevada County, California. This property belongs to General Crook and his friends and may be referred to more at length in these pages at a subsequent time.

---

1. This is the previously mentioned British victory at Ulundi, on July 4, 1879.
2. Bourke's question mark. Barry died July 18, 1879. Heitman, *Historical Register*, 1:195.

August 3d. The newspapers contain the notice of the death at Hudson, N.J. of general debility, on July 31st, of Major John V. DuBois (retired) late 3d U.S. Cavalry.

Major DuBois was the Commanding Officer of the first expedition with which I was concerned as a commissioned officer,—the march of a Battalion of five companies of the 3d Cavalry from the valley of the Rio Grande in New Mexico to the valley of the Gila, in Arizona. The order for the transfer of our Regiment with the 8th Cavalry came in February 1870, the rendezvous appointed for the companies being Fort Cummings,[3] and the date for the movement to commence March 1st.[4]

At that time, I was attached as 2d Lieutenant to Company "E" (Captain Alex Sutorius), our station being Fort Craig.

Fort Craig was a four company post (occupied by two cos.) surrounded by an earthen rampart with ditch and five bastions: the other company (one of the 13th Infantry, commanded by Capt. F. W. Coleman, an able and companionable gentleman,)[5] and the band and Hd.Qrs. of the 15th Infantry, occupied the adobe houses built during the war and still in fair condition.

My own Qrs. were the worst in the lot and consisted of a single room, quite large, not less than (20) feet square, with earth floor and roof, the latter caving in but still held in place by an immense cottonwood stanchion bolstering up the principal "viga" or rafter. The apartment was not palatial in any sense.

I had a small iron bedstead, a bottle-green glass mirror, a few pegs upon which to hang uniform and sabre, three pine shelves filled with books, a round pine table near which seated in one of my two chairs, I used to study by the flickering light of a brace of candles, a wash-bowl, at first of tin and later on, as I grew more opulent, of coarse stone-ware, and finally a heavy iron poker serving the double purpose of stirring up the fire, and of stirring up Espindiva,[6]

---

3. Fort Cummings was established in 1863, on the Mesilla-Tucson Road, fifty-three miles west of the Rio Grande. It guarded Cook's Springs which, together with Apache Pass, was one of the most dangerous points on the southern trail to California. Initially the post was deactivated in 1873, but was reoccupied intermittently, depending on the degree of Apache depredations until it was finally abandoned in October 1886. The reservation was transferred to the Interior Department in 1891. Frazer, *Forts of the West*, 98.

4. In *On the Border With Crook* (2–3), Bourke makes almost no mention of Forts Craig or Cummings, or the *Jornada del Muerto*, summing up all the following material in a single paragraph.

5. Heitman (1:316) lists Coleman as being in the 15th Infantry. The only Frederick William Coleman in the 13th Infantry served as a second lieutenant in 1898.

6. Bourke probably means "Espíndola."

the Mexican boy, who, in the wilder freaks of my imagination, I sometimes looked upon as a "valet".

There wasn't much to do; the post was a lonesome sort of a hole, maintained at the north end of the *Jornada del Muerto*[7] for the protection of travelers against prowling Apaches. In the morning, reveillé, then stable-call, breakfast, guard-mounting, cavalry drill, reading, lunch, reading and generally an afternoon ride of eight or ten miles, then stable call again, parade, supper and a little more reading. The whole business was novel to me and for that reason, I did not have time to get weary of it. There was considerable traveling about the country to be done, keeping me busy in moving from post to post.

The villages of Paraje, San Marcial and Contadera, none of them of any size or consequence, gave us an excuse for horse-back rides; the inhabitants were very poor and the houses, of adobe, ill-furnished, the peculiar feature being that the main room was well-supplied with settees and mattrasses [sic] upon which the men of the house could take their siesta in the afternoon, and the walls were covered with cheap looking glasses as a decoration. The men wore a costume of wide-brimmed sombrero, coarse white cotton shirt, loose pants or drawers of cotton, & moccasins in place of shoes, (altho' the latter of American manufacture were coming into general use.) The women, always were attired in loosely flowing robe of calico or gauze and instead of hats or bonnets which were unknown in that part of the Rio Grande valley, at that time, folded a black shawl or "rebosa" around the head and shoulders in such a way as to completely conceal all the face except the left eye.

In figure these were, as a rule, tall, slight, straight and graceful, the erectness of figure and graceful undulation of movement being attributed to their constant practice of carrying heavy loads of water upon the head.

In person, they were, so far as my observation extended, neat and

---

7. The *Jornada del Muerto* (literally "Journey of Death") is a ninety-mile shortcut on the old Camino Real from El Paso to Santa Fe that claimed the lives of hundreds of travelers. It runs through waterless, unforgiving country east of the Rio Grande, with the lower end at Robledo, New Mexico, and the upper, at Socorro. A testimony to its remoteness is the fact that the first atomic bomb, the Trinity test, was exploded only fifteen miles east of the *Jornada*. Bourke elaborates about the road further on. See Brodie Crouch, *Jornada del Muerto*.

clean, bathing frequently in the large "acequias" or irrigating canals which conducted the waters of the Rio Grande to the barley fields and vine-yards. Frequently, in my rides across the country, I came upon bevies of women—old matrons and pretty maidens, splashing in the limpid water, the approach of a stranger being the signal for a general scramble until they were all immersed up to their necks. They never seemed to mind it in the least and I may as well admit that I rather enjoyed these unexpected interviews.

One brief paragraph will answer for all the villages on the Rio Grande: they were built in the form of a hollow square, the interior or "plaza" being the place of rendezvous for every public purpose, markets, religious processions, camping places for travellers—everything of that kind. The houses, all of one story and flat roofed, varied in size from one room to a dozen, according to the circumstances of their owners, were built of sun-dried bricks, with roofs, made of small rafters, covered first with a layer of osier twigs over which was packed a certain depth of "gaspe" or lime cement with a mixture of gypsum. This same composition formed the flooring, except in the houses of the very poor who contented themselves with their mother-earth.

Where a family was pretentious, a carpet of rough woolen, woven in alternate black and white stripes, called "griega",[8] was spread out in the "best" rooms, but those in ordinary use went bare.

So far as food was concerned, the New Mexicans were not badly off. Chickens and sheep[,] pigs and goats were plenty and cheap, beef was not scarce, vegetables grew luxuriantly and fruit of poor quality in considerable quantity: never have I seen such large onions and beets, the former the diameter of a soup-plate and of a very mild flavor without acrid pungency. Tomatoes were good, chile excellent, great strings of it drying against the walls and upon the roofs of all the houses; potatoes scarce, but beans of the black or frijole variety, extremely cheap, and so nutritious as to equal bread in their hunger-staying qualities.

Grapes and peaches were the principal fruits and wine in some quantity was made in the valley. The wood used altogether for fuel was the mesquite, which exudes a gum equal to that from the acacia; this made so hot a fire that cotton-wood had to be added to temper its fierceness. Another curious piece of vegetation was the "amole"

8. Literally "Greek."

Fort Craig to Camp Grant

or soap-weed, whose roots gave a lather like soap and were much employed as a detergent for the scalp. The means of transportation to be found in the valley, aside from the Army wagons belonging to the various military posts, were the little "carretas',[9] drawn by one or two mules, the poor animals not much bigger than rats; prairie schooners—immense lumbering things requiring the united force of from (20) to (25) mules to pull them and their cargoes; or the old-fashioned wagon from the San Luis Valley, made in the rudest fashion, held together by raw-hide thongs, and running on wheels formed of solid sections of large pine trees.[10] Neither the wooden axle, nor the wooden wheels ever had any grease put upon them and, as may be readily imagined, the blood-chilling creaking once heard was never to be forgotten. These contrivances were at that date much used in the Northern part of New Mexico, but they once in a while made their appearance near Fort Craig and when travelling could be heard for three or four miles. The Pueblo Indians and many of the Mexicans, didn't have carts even, but hauled or packed their "plunder" from point to point on the backs of little donkeys or "burros" which I have seen carrying a load of fire-wood, eight or ten feet high.

Some of these "burros" were not very much larger than the great jack-rabbits of the country, but they were very patient and docile, flapping their enormous ears in a philosophical way, as they trudged along the sandy roads.

These preliminary pages are in no sense to be taken as a description of the valley of the Rio Grande, as I found it in 1869 and '70; a more complete account will be found elsewhere in my note-books, the remarks here made being for the purpose of introducing some slight narration of our march into Arizona of which I have nowhere preserved an itinerary.[11]

On marching down from Fort Craig, we took the right or West bank of the river, to avoid the *jornada del muerto*, ("The day's journey of the dead man".) so called because a wanderer could just about reach the end of it before dying of exhaustion and thirst. This desert

---

9. Two wheeled carts still seen (generally as yard decorations) in the Southwest. The modern version has spoked wheels and iron tires, but the classic *carreta* used solid wooden wheels.

10. Also known as Chihuahua wagons. These were giant, cargo-carrying versions of the *carreta* sometimes with two solid wheels, and sometimes with four.

11. These apparently are among the missing notebooks.

of ninety miles in length was formerly greatly dreaded there being no water upon it. Now there are two places, the "tanks" at the Aleman and Jack Martin's artesian well, so situated that marches need not be longer than 30 miles without water. At the north end of the *Jornada* is the Peak of San Cristóbal, with an upper contour rudely resembling the face of a man asleep. When we left Fort Craig, Major Coleman very politely drew up his men and band at the gate and gave us a complimentary musical salute as we defiled past them.

Before we reached Fort Cummings, we made camps at Palomitas, a little Mexican hamlet, and at Couppiugs[?], a fine source of water, both at the foot of the Eastern slope of the San Mateo Mountains.

At Cummings we met Major Dubois who assigned me to duty upon his staff as Quartermaster of the Expedition. Dubois was a short, thickset man who gave very strong evidence of having seriously impaired a mind and physique originally of respectable power. He was fond of good living and prone to over-indulgence in stimulants; of no force of character and disposed to cavil at the actions of his superiors, but kind to his subordinates. I cannot recall a single instance where he lost control of himself even for a moment or where he failed to accord to a subaltern the complete respect and courtesy as punctiliously enacted for himself. In the routine of camp and garrison life, he was well posted, but not fertile in expedients. He received me with great cordiality, explained to me my duties and the time when we were to start &c. To see that everything in the way of transportation was all right, kept me fully occupied all that day and the next: the train didn't number all told more than 31 or 32 six-mule wagons and to an experienced officer would have been a matter of but small concern: with a young officer the case assumed more importance and it really became a great strain upon my mind how to foresee all the requirements of our little battalion. There was food to be stowed away for men and officers and grain for the horses; each company loaded its own baggage so I was spared one great annoyance, but to prevent any detention from accidents to wagons or harness or mules, extra poles, jockey-sticks, hounds &c. were provided, "open links" and mule shoes packed in wagons, a few extra pieces of harness laid by, and in each jockey-box, a can of axle-grease, and other necessaries, secured. As our line of march would lie across a desert country scarcely inhabited, we supplied ourselves with a water-wagon holding several thousand gallons, and carried upon the wagons great piles of cord wood.

Everything was at last in order and the word was given to move out the next day, February 28th [1870]. That afternoon and night, I had a little leisure to become acquainted with my associates and familiarized with my surroundings. Fort Cummings was a pretty little post, garrisoned by one company of the 15th Infantry, officered by Captain Hedburg and Lieuts. [Julian R.] Fitch and [Edmund] Ryan. They treated us with the greatest cordiality and did everything possible for our comfort. The post itself was neat as a pin and pleasant enough, not too far from civilization to be dreary and possessing a pleasant climate. It was situated alongside of Cooke's Spring, and at the foot, of Cooke's Peak, a towering land-mark of great prominence in this region. The Apache had in former years been very troublesome to immigrants, but since the establishment of this garrison had made their attacks upon trains at points farther West.

A word at this point upon the organization and personnel of the Battalion; we had five Companies of the 3d Cavalry, officered as follows:

Major John V. Dubois, 3d Cavalry,   Comdr.
Ass't Surgeon [Charles] Styers. [sic]   Medl. Off.
2Lieut. John G. Bourke, (1).   A.A.Q.M.
2Lieut. W.W. Robinson (2).   Adjutant.
A. A. Surgeon Kitchen (3).   Asst. Medl. Off.
"B" 3d Cavalry   Cap't [Charles] Meinhold & Lieut [A. Sidney] Smith
"E" 3d   "   "   Alex. Sutorius.
"F" 3d   "   1st Lieut. H. B. Cushing & 2Lt. Bourke. (A.A.Q.M.)
"H" 3d   "   Capt. G. Russell & Lt. L. L. O'Connor.[12]
"L"   Cap't. Frank Stanwood & 2 Lt. W. W. Robinson (Adjutant)

Of Major Dubois, I have already spoken.

Doctor [Charles] Styers was a gentlemanly and skilful [sic] medical officer. I did not see much of him during the trip, on account of my duties. He very kindly presented me with a suit of old Spanish armor consisting of breast and back-plate, helmet and gorget, found near the Western extremity of the "Llano Estacado" or "Staked Plains". This armor was simple in style and construction and no doubt once covered the body of a Spanish or Mexican foot-soldier, who must have lost his life while on some expedition of discovery

---

12. Bourke was not consistent in spelling O'Connor's name.

or war, years and years ago.

The helmet was a plain, round casque, with hole in top from which a plume perhaps descended; this helmet was provided with a fixed visor of sheet iron and a gorget or neck-piece of hammered iron scales upon a backing of linen[.]

Back and breast-plate require no detailed description; they were merely concave plates of sheet-iron, shaped to fit the body and when in condition for service must have been held in position by buckles at the sides. The breast plate was ornamented around the edges by a line of brass buttons: I carried this old armor with me to Arizona, where the breast and back plate were stolen. The casque and gorget I afterwards gave to the wife of Judge Savage of Omaha, by whom it has been preserved with great care. The age of this armor I never could learn; it was of the style used by Infantry in the 17th and 18th century, but may have been of any period prior to our occupation of Texas and New Mexico: its preservation from rust, is attributable to the extremely dry climate of the Staked Plains where rain falls so seldom.

Lieut. W. W. Robinson, a class-mate of mine at the Milt. Academy, was, and is, a high-toned, soldierly officer, gentlemanly in all his dealings and much liked by his associates. (He has since been transferred to the 7th Cavalry.)

Doctor Kitchen remained with us for a few days, when he was relieved and returned to Santa Fé.

Captain Meinhold was an elderly man of fine physique and great personal attractiveness. (He has since died.)

Lieut. Smith, the subaltern of his company, some time after this became greatly distinguished under Lieut. Cushing, in a fight with hostile Apaches, in which forty six of the enemy were killed. (I visited the battlefield myself and saw the bodies.) In 1871, he resigned from the service.

Lieut. H. B. Cushing was a reckless man, one of the most daring and most completely regardless of consequences I have ever met. He was one of the most gallant Indian fighters in the regular army and had made the Apaches of New Mexico and the Staked Plain [sic] feel his power. Moving out from Fort Stanton[13] as a base, he had almost wiped out Cadette and Jesus La Paz on one or two oc-

---

13. Fort Stanton was established in 1855, on the Rio Bonito, to subdue the Mescalero Apaches. In 1862, federal troops evacuated and partially destroyed the post, as they retreated

casions, killing numbers of the enemy, capturing nearly all their stock, besides retaking all that they had run off from ranchmen and cattle-herders. In one of these engagements, his 2Lieut. Frank Seaton, my class-mate, was shot through the wrist and body and soon after died. As I couldn't get along with Captain Sutorius, the Regimental Commander transferred me to Cushing's company which I joined at Fort Cummings.

Cushing was of a slight figure, small, but well built, nervo-sanguine temperament, eyes, blue-gray and piercing, hair, light-brown, complexion florid. His bravery was beyond question; his judgement, as I had good reason afterwards to learn, was not always to be trusted. He would hazard everything on the turn of a card. Cushing occasionally drank rather more than was good for him, yet I cannot say that I ever saw him lose his self-control. He was a great gamester too, but with all his faults, an energetic, ambitious and daring soldier, one who never turned his back upon an enemy. (He was killed by Cocheis' band of Apache Indians near the Ojo del Oso or Bear Springs in the Mesteñes or Whetsone Mountains, South East Arizona, May 5th, 1871.)[14]

Cushing belonged to a family which had made a fine record during the Civil War. One brother, William B. was a Paymaster in the Navy; a second; "Albemarle" Cushing, won his curious agnomen in his desperate attack upon the rebel ram *Albemarle*, which he blew up with a torpedo, recklessly risking his own life in the attempt which met with a brilliant success.[15] A third brother, Alonzo, had but recently graduated from West Point, when he was assigned to the command of his Battery and took part in the momentous struggle,

---

ahead of the Confederate invasion. Confederate troops occupied Fort Stanton prior to their withdrawal, after which it was taken over by a New Mexico unit of federal troops. The post was rebuilt in 1868, and abandoned in 1896. Beginning in 1899, it was operated by the U.S. Public Health Service as a hospital for seamen with tuberculosis. Additionally, in 1941, it became the nation's first internment camp for Germans. In 1953, the State of New Mexico took over the tuberculosis sanatorium, operating it until 1966, when it became a hospital and training center for the mentally handicapped. It currently serves as a rehabilitation center. Frazer, *Forts of the West*, 103–4; http://www.fortstanton.com..

14. Bourke describes a scouting expedition with Cushing in *On the Border With Crook*, 29–33.

15. Bourke is mistaken. William Barker Cushing was the only brother who entered the Navy, and was the officer who sank the *Albemarle*. He appears to have spent his entire naval career on the line, with no indication he ever served in the Pay Department. The Cushing brothers were Milton Buckingham, Jr.; Howard Buckingham, under whom Bourke served; Walter, who died as a child; Alonzo Hersford, mortally wounded at Gettysburg; William Barker; and another brother, name unknown. See Roske and van Doren, *Lincoln's Commando*.

at Gettysburg, Pennia[.] He was shot through both hips and his men were carrying him off the field, when the gallant youngster reflecting that his Battery was holding an important place in the line and that his absence would leave it without a commissioned officer, declined to be moved and insisted upon keeping in command, sitting upon a stretcher, resting against a pile of knapsacks. He received another wound, (slight,) in one hand and before the battle ended was shot through the brain and died upon the field. His remains were afterwards interred in the Cemetery at West Point, N.Y.

When I first joined the company ("F"), it had in it[s] possession, not far from sixty to seventy Indian ponies and horses captured from the Apaches and two or three cows and one young bull, all of good mixed Durham blood which had been presented for the use of the enlisted men by the cattle-owners of New Mexico, whose herds had been recovered by this indefatigable little body of troops.

Of Captain Sutorius I can't say much: he was a negative, no-account man, a native of Switzerland, ignorant, opinionated, and considerably given to drink. Very many vacancies enlisted in the Regular Army at [the] outbreak of the Rebellion, caused by the resignation of disaffected officers who abandoned their colors to adhere to the fortunes of the seceding states. To fill these vacancies almost any old soldier was commissioned, without regard to merit, capacity or record. Sutorious was one of those thus advanced. He had been a bugler and, of his own choice, had acted as waiter for the officers mess at the post where he was stationed. He never rose with his good fortune, but remained always an ignorant, thick-headed waiter. (Dismissed [from] the service for drunkenness by sentence of General Court Martial—September, 1876.)[16]

Of a very different type, was Captain Gerald Russell; he too, was a "promotion from the ranks", only in his case, advancement was the recognition of true merit and gallant service and not the coquettish favor of blind Fortune. Russell was born somewhere in the mountains of Kerry, Ireland and had never lost the sweet, lisping brogue of his native wilds. The son of poor parents, his early advantages had been almost imperceptible and Fate apparently had destined him for the position of a cobbler in his native village. A fit of disgust, ambition or something else, induced him to immigrate to the United States where he had scarcely landed before he enlisted in the regiment of

16. See Robinson, *Diaries*, 1:382–85, 388; 2:32.

Mounted rifles, now known as the 3d Cavalry.[17] Before the war, as a non-commissioned officer, he had attracted the attention of his superiors by his great gallantry and general good qualities. Receiving promotion with almost the firing of the first gun upon [Fort] Sumpter [sic], he applied himself assiduously to his new duties and became a hard student. By one of those strange freaks of character which so frequently lead the best men astray, Russell who so humbly admitted his ignorance, was not too proud to study faithfully, but he disdained any application to the rudimentary branches of knowledge and confined himself to advanced topics in science and history.

The harvest produced was a curious and laughter-provoking jumble of philosophical and scientific theories, quaintly expressed in high-sounding phraseology, pronounced in a brogue rich as cream, and a substratum of shrewd common-sense acquired in his long military experience on the plains which contrasted oddly with an almost child-like ignorance of the ways of the world.

When I first met him, Russell was already a sufferer from hemiplangia, or paralysis of the left side, which gave to his gait and movement the funniest sort of a limp, accompanied by a simultaneous, spasmodic jerk of the left wrist and fingers. This paralysis, his friends told me, had been occasioned in the following manner: While the 3d Cavalry was at Little Rock, Ark., assembling preparatory to its march out to New Mexico, a remount of fine horses was received from Kentucky. These were soon distributed among the companies, but there remained one fine looking fiery animal which refused to acknowledge any control, men and officers alike were afraid to go near him, as fast as some bold rider jumped on his back, just so fast was there a demoralized cavalryman describing a fearfully eccentric [hurdle?] through the air.

The general verdict was against the horse; every one said what a fine creature, every one admitted it was a pity he couldn't be retained in the regiment, but at [the] same time conceded that it would be imprudent to keep such a fractious charger who might at almost any hour be the means of inflicting insuperable injury upon the trooper in charge of him.

Capt. Russell patiently and quietly listened to these remarks in

---

17. The Regiment of Mounted Rifles was designated 3rd Cavalry during a general reorganization of the U.S. Army's mounted units in 1861. See Herr and Wallace, *Story of the U.S. Cavalry*, 116.

which as a good cavalryman he felt he could not concur; to him it seemed a disgrace that a regiment of cavalry should reject a finely formed steed for no other reason than that he was a trifle too high-strung. Sooner than see him sent back to dépôt, Jerry would ride him himself, and ride him right then and there. In obedience to his instructions, the horse was blind-folded and firmly bound until Russell should be properly braced in the stirrup. This was soon done, the rider was seated like a centaur upon the horse's back, and at a given signal, the bandages covering eyes and limbs were removed and for a moment the horse stood perfectly quiet. Then he lazily turned his head and gazed in a dreamy, abstracted sort of manner at the insignificant creature who had the audacity to bestride him! Captain Russell mistook this behavior for docility and submission and pressed the horse's flanks with his limbs. Away dashed the horse, flying down the street like a winged Pegasus, Russell sticking to him as if he were glued to the saddle; for a few seconds, it was an open question which should gain the victory, man or beast; but the horse solved the problem by jumping with full force into a newly-excavated cellar where he landed himself and rider in a shockingly mangled condition. Russell was dug out with a broken leg, and broken, mashed or bruised ribs, arm and collar-bone, and placed upon a shutter to be carried off to the Hospital. Just before fainting away with the intense pain, he raised his head slightly and with a smile of triumph and defiance remarked to those about him; "vi knew dam-m well-l vi cud rride um-m!"

Captain Russell's pet grievance—the one subject upon which he was wont to expatiate upon the slightest provocation—was the decadence and degeneracy of the Regular Army. "Its moi proivate opinyun, Bor-uk, (he would say to me.) it's moi proivate opinyun, based upon exparyinze, for oive bin now nointeen yee-ers in the U-noi-tid Sta-ates Ormy, that de whole damn mil-lee-terry outfit is goin' to Hell".

His lamentations generally were pointed by a reference to the constitutional worthlessness of his 1Lieutenant—Lawrence Lu-shus O'Conner, a handsome, round voiced [sic], round-limbed "broth of a bi" from the "ould dart". Public opinion was decidedly adverse to O'Connor and credited him with being a coward; this I was never thoroughly satisfied could be the case. O'Conner was certainly worthless and being lazy and lethargic, several times failed to follow fresh Indian trails with proper energy; still, if brought face to face with an enemy, it is likely that he would have stood his ground and fought. He and his wife were great thorns in old Jerry's side. Mrs. O'C. was a bright woman, well-educated and able to write a good letter, but with a very creamy brogue. Her shrewdness and tact saved her husband from many a pit-fall, and enabled him to defy the inquisition of Courts-Martial, but we lost them both by the operations of the Benzine Board, in Dec. 1870.[18]

In October 1869, O'Connor and his better half were on their return from District Hd.Qrs. at Santa Fé where they had been in attendance on O'Connor's periodical trial for drunkenness or some offense of that kind, which came around regularly once a quarter.

Near Albuquerque they came to La Bajada ("The Descent".) a very severe grade having an overhanging vertical wall of some hundreds of feet on one side and a sheer precipice of five hundred on the other. The descent was so risky that stage-passengers always alighted and made their way down on foot, while the driver found abundant occupation in taking care of his team and slowly creeping down with a heavy brake on, wheels locked and shod and the conductor at head of the leaders. That was the only *orthodox* way of going down La Bajada in those days, but O'Connor had different ideas. He left Santa Fé close behind the conveyance which carried U.S. Marshall [sic] Pratt and his party. When Pratt reached La Bajada, of course he got out and walked down, letting his driver have as light a load as possible. He hadn't perceived O'Connor so close behind him and in fact, up to that day had never had any personal acquaintance with him. What was his astonishment to hear behind him, (when he had about reached the bottom,) a fine round Irish voice explain, "Oh! she'll git down all right, I dun' no", and to find himself, upon turning, face to face with O'Connor. "Shure! she'll git down all right, I dun' no" repeated O'Connor, and Pratt, looking up the break-neck grade, saw what had elicited this expression of confidence. O'Connor and his driver had both left their ambulance and descended on foot,

---

18. "Benzine Boards," so-called because benzine was a popular cleaning fluid of the day, was the nickname given to the retiring and reduction boards, created under the Army Appropriation Bill of 1869. The bill required drastic reductions in military personnel to conform with the post-Civil War determination to cut military expenditures. These boards determined which officers would be discharged or retained, with a board in Washington making the decision among field officers, and departmental boards selecting junior officers. O'Connor was cut by a benzine board for the Department of Arizona. Robinson, *General Crook*, 105.

while Mrs. O'C. was left to manage, as best she might, the four halfbred mules which pulled it. There was no brake, no lock, no shoe, and the mules, sawing on the feeble bits which held them, appeared ready to dash at any moment down the hill.

Pratt, in fear and disgust, cried out, "Why! My God Almighty! Man! I wouldn't drive down La Bajada *myself*!"

"No,["] replied O'Connor, ["]nur oi". However, Mrs. O'Connor got down without injury and to cement acquaintance, O'Connor presented Pratt and his party to his wife and invited them all to take a drink glibly running over the names of the most expensive wines as if they were the ordinary features of his wine-list. "Come now, gintilmin, Come now, nom-i-nate yer pi-sins—Sherry, Hock or To'-kay?"

Pratt thought he'd take a thimblefull of Sherry, another gentleman inclined to Hock, and a third concluded that To'-kay was "good enough for the likes of him".

"BUT La-rins-Lushus, Darlint!["] dextrously interposed Mrs. O'Connor, ["]don't yiz know that the Sherry, the Hock and To'-kay is all gone-intirely?" ["]But we have some rale good fishkey in the black bottle".

["]Well,["] said O'Connor, ["]damn their furrin ingray-jints any how—shure fish-key's the drink fur a gintelmin all-ways"; so the whole party "turned themselves loose" on the black bottle.

I had a very funny experience with Russell at Fort Seldon[19] [*sic*] on the Rio Grande in the fall of 1869. I had marched a detachment of recruits down the river and at Seldon had to turn over those assigned to Stanwood's and Russell's Companies.

Stanwood, who was commanding the post, directed his First Sergeant to receive the recruits and see that they had all the equipments for which he should have to receipt; but Jerry Russell didn't do business in any such style; he would receive his recruits in person. I drew them up in two ranks, upon order, called the roll and inspected, finding all right. Captain Russell, I thought, would order the detail to be marched to his Company quarters, but he first made

---

19. Fort Selden, which Bourke sometimes spelled "Seldon," was established in 1865, east of the Rio Grande about twelve miles north of Doña Ana, to protect the road along the river, and settlers in the Mesilla Valley. The post was deactivated in 1877, when the railroad replaced the wagon road, but was regarrisoned in 1882 during the Geronimo War. It was abandoned in 1889, and transferred to the Interior Department three years later. Frazer, *Forts of the West*, 102–03.

them a little speech, which I insert as nearly word for word as I can remember, altho' I have told the story so often that I am pretty confident the oration is almost exact:

"Young Min! I conghratulate yiz on bein assigned to moi thrupe, becoz previously to dis toime, I vinture to say that moi thrupe has had more villins, loyars, *teaves*, scoundhrils and I moight say, dam murdhrers dan enny udder in de Unitid States Ormy. I want yiz to pay sthrict attintion to jooty—and not become drunken vagabonds, wandhrin all over the face of Gods chreashun, spindin irvery cint av yer pay with low búm-mérs.

["]Avide all timptashuns, loikewoise all discipashuns, so that in toime yez kin become non-commissioned off-zurs; yez'll foind yer captin a very *laynent* man and very much given to laynency, fur oi niver duz toi no man up bee der tumbs unless he duz bee late for a roll-call. Sorjint dis-amiss de detachment".

Russell was at that time a bachelor and was very fond of remarking confidentially to the younger officers that he was "tinking voine-by of going back to de States and seein' wat dame Forchin'll do for me in de way of a dam noice woife."

His company never would come up to his views of discipline, "I decleer to God'lmoity! (he would say.) the base ingratoichude of dem *wearies* of moine is perficly 'stonishen! Dey hev evering dat mortil man kin want, 'cludin, food, *vew-el*, good grub, vidgitibbles and good quarthers, and here to-day they hev just smashed a ban new skilli over my nice first Sarjint's head i' all becuz dey didn't have enough toe-ma-tusses in dere God-dam supe!"

O'Connor had been sent out from Selden to follow up a fresh Indian trail which gave promise of resulting in an active skirmish. Russell had given him the picked men of the Company, mounted on the best horses and well provided in every way with rations for seventeen days. The trail led straight towards the San Agostin pass in the Organ Mountains, in which a band of Apaches had been known to lurk for some time.

O'Connor had as fine an opportunity as soul could wish for glory; but he wasn't hunting for Glory: Quietly leaving the trail he struck into the towns of Mesilla and Las Cruces, 30 miles below Fort Selden on the river, where he intended to lie "perdue" until his rations were eaten up. He ignored the fact that a new paper had recently been established in one of these towns, the *Las Cruces Borderer*, which would be glad to have him figure as an "item". In due course of time, the *Borderer* was delivered by mail at Fort Selden and the effect it produced on Cap't. Russell was very mirth-provoking. After recapitulating to me all that he had done to give "dat damn outfit O'Con-nur-r" a chance to attain distinction and dwelling bitterly upon his sneaking into "Crú-cis", Russell continued, and "din he wint to a 'Boyle at Bull's' where (quoting from the paper in his hand and hissing the words as he read) Lootinint Law-rins Loo-shis O'Con-nurr of the tur-id Cavalry appeared to the bist advantg'."

I have alluded to Russell's "scientific" acquirements; I have here interpolated an anecdote under this head, stating however that the date was long since the year of which I am now writing. It was in the last week of December, 1876. Russell and I were serving together with General Crook's Expedition against hostile Sioux and Cheyennes in Wyoming and had both started out with the cavalry column under General Mackenzie and taken part in the attack upon Dull Knife's village in the cañon of the Big Horn Mountains.[20] After completely destroying the village of (200) lodges and scattering the Cheyennes, we started back to rejoin the main command under General Crook, with whom we marched up and down the Belle Fourche, looking for other Indians.

Coming back over the Pumpkin Buttes, Christmas morning, 1876, the weather was something not soon to be forgotten; the mercury was frozen in the bulb and a howling wind froze everything solid. The leafless trees standing guard over the solidly frozen streamlets, the frozen tufts of grass and weeds, glistening under the weight of ice crystals & the forbidding, leaden sky would have been enough without the marrow chilling tempest, to remind us that winter was King in those desolate regions; but with the aid of the icy storm, our surrounding discouraged us greatly. Our eye-brows, eye-lashes, and moustaches were congealed and had it not been for the Esquimaux-like[21] clothing of fur and buck-skin which we all wore, I am certain that numbers of us would have laid down, never to rise again.

My companions were taciturn and solemn, but old Jerry Russell became rather voluble in his disquisitions upon "soy-inces". Doctor Wood broke out with the exclamation: ["]well'—of all the beastly weather that God never made!—This beats all I ever knew".

20. See Robinson, *Diaries*, Vol. 2, Chapters 9–11.
21. I.e. Eskimo-like.

"Docthur![''] interrupted old Jerry, very quietly, [''']our ansisthurs were bether prephared for sich weather than oursilves". "How was that?["] queried the young sawbones.

"Well, sor, dey hed hair ov'in haf a fut long". "Oh, I don't believe any such stuff as that, Captain,["] remonstrated the Doctor. "Oh, yiz, indade, Docthur,["] persisted Russell, ["]all histh'ry and soy-inces and thrue philosophy goes to show that our ansisthurs hed very short tails and hed hair ov'in haf a fut long; an ruder, Docthur Wood, it's moi proivit opin-yun det your grand-fodder or your great grand-fodder, enny way, must have bin in a mu-zée-um".

Wood was too nearly frozen to get angry, but he abruptly terminated his "scientific" discussion with old Russell.

I will leave Russell for the present to make some slight reference to other members of our Battalion, being able to do this as I shall have occasion further on to tell a few stories of my old friend who, albeit certain eccentricities of character, and solecisms in language, was a brave old soldier, tender-hearted as a woman, and proud of his profession.

Captain Frank Stanwood was, physically, a man far above the average: of good education and intellectual powers, he was amiable in manners and of a very witty mind and good humored disposition. His library, which he very kindly permitted me to examine on several occasions was large and well-selected, considering the embarrassments to be encountered in those days by Cavalry officers on the frontier who had the slightest taste for reading. (Stanwood was, without intending any harm, sometimes inclined to be a trifle irreverent in religious matters. I remember a visit he paid me at my quarters in Tucson, Arizona, in December, 1870, when I also had as my guest old Colonel Bobbie Pollock, Captain of the 26th Inft.[22] Bobbie, a native of the Quaker City,[23] had quitted home so young and had wandered about the world so much, (he had been in California with the first influx in 1849.) that he remembered but little of his Eastern training, excepting an hereditary prejudice against Yankees.[24]

Stanwood was a Boston boy and as such, old Bobbie had a prejudice

---

22. Heitman (1:796–97) lists Capt. Robert Pollock as serving in the 21st Infantry at the time.
23. Bourke is referring to Pollock by both his brevet (colonel) and active (captain) ranks. The Quaker City, of course, is Philadelphia.
24. By "Yankees," Bourke means true Yankees, which is to say New Englanders, rather than as a generic for Northerners.

against him, even in face of his long acquaintance with him and knowledge of his high tone of character and accomplishments.

Stanwood understood all this and loved to do everything to excite the old man's antagonism. We had all to sleep in one bed-room—the only habitable room in the house, and when it came time to go to bed, Pollock and I were talking; Stanwood interrupted by asking for silence as he was going to "say his prayers". Then clasping his hands, he devoutly and audibly thanked "God that we have been born in Boston, because Thou knowest, Oh Lord! that having been born in Boston, it is not necessary that we should be born again". Old Bobbie swallowed the whole thing as a genuine prayer, and the next morning when we were alone together commented savagely upon the ----------- conceit of "them ere ------------Boston Yankees -----------," making the air blue with profanity.)
(Stanwood died at his home in Boston, Dec. 20th 72.)

The night before we left Fort Cummings, the officers stationed there came down to our camp to pay a last visit. The officers of the Battalion were invited to meet them in Colonel Dubois' tent.

A nice little lunch was spread in an adjoining tent, to which any one could repair at pleasure. There was much pleasant converse, story telling, a little singing and a great deal of drinking. Lieut. Robinson and I being the junior "subs", and also the "staff" of the Battalion, were selected to make the toddies. Neither of us had been trained as a bartender and of course some little preliminary instruction was necessary to enable us to prepare toddies that would pass the inspection of gentlemen of such extended experience in that line as those whom we were serving. We made up in assiduity what we lacked in education; our first effort was pronounced a dead failure; our second was only a shade better. Our third extorted signs of approval. They came rather slowly or reluctantly from the lips of Captain Russell, ["]Wy dat's a moighty foine toddie; oi tink it would be a good oidee to put a little more sugar in soak".

We complied with this suggestion and kept a few lumps of sugar soaking to make fresh tumblers of toddy, as fast as those in use should be emptied. The effects manifesting themselves after a while; the party became decidedly merry. Towards midnight the visitors withdrew, with many warm shakes of the hand and cordial expressions of good will for our good fortune on the journey. Weary and sleepy, I started to seek my couch, but I found that a second

lieutenant's duty didn't cease with the departure of guests; in fact it only commenced. The plain English of the matter is that we had to act as valets for such of our elderly companions as had eaten too many ham-sandwiches, pickled oysters or articles of that kind on the bill of fare which, since the beginning of the world, have made giddy and light-headed gentlemen who have not, oh! no! by no means! been in the smallest degree affected by a dozen or more tumblers of strong punch. Stanwood had gone to bed, "straight as a string"; Dubois had crawled off, unaided, and without anything remarkable in his gait or demeanor except the persistency with which the guy-ropes of the tent wound themselves around his little, fat chubby legs. He bade us good night and blessed us all with a fervor that brought tears to our eyes and his own.
Meinhold and Russell were sad wrecks, jolly and maudlin, limp and incapable of moving hand or foot: their eyes stuck out from their heads as void of expression as grapes with the skins off. A Temperance lecturer would pronounce them both "drunk"; in the language of the frontier, "they had it up their snoots" and were rather inclined to be "high".
Not to beat about the bush too much, they were Drunk. Lawrence Lucious O'Connor was drunk too, but he didn't count, he always was drunk. We never took any notice of O'Connor except when he was sober. Cushing and Smith were able to help Robinson and myself quite a good deal; we grabbed Meinhold by the waist-band and he doubled together like a jack-knife or an old carpet-sack, but he offered no resistance as we laid him upon his bed and stripped off boots, collar and coat and covered him up with a pair of blankets.

Jerry Russell was less tractable; we found him as we got back to the tent, seated in a camp-chair, scarcely able to move a joint but trying very hard to whistle to his dog Toper. Toper, more in scorn than in anger, flapped his tail in response to these manifestations of affection, as old Jerry spoke to him:"Tó-pur, yez dam baste! yer dhrung, Tó-pur, ye'r dhrunk, Tó-pur en oi know it."
This bright little dialogue, or monologue rather because I don't remember that poor Toper spoke even so much as a bark, was varied by Russell's every now and then sinking back in his chair twiddling his thumbs and trying to sing the refrain of his favorite song—"Too-ril, loo-ril, Wan-oyed Roil-lee!" "Too-ril, loo-ril, wan-oyed Roil-l-lee".

Robinson tapped him briskly on the shoulder: "come, come,

Captain, it's time to go to bed". Russell was very obstinate: "no, no, Misther Robinson, no bid for mee dis noight". "But, Captain,["] I expostulated, ["]you must go to bed; it's long after mid-night, we are to have reveille at 5, everybody's in bed. We've just put Captain Meinhold to bed". This was a lucky remark to make; Russell and Meinhold, altho' firm friends, had between them that curious rivalry which has so often been remarked as existing between Teuton and Celt.

Russell would have staid up all night sooner than have it said that he had been driven "from the field" before Meinhold; but the yielding of his adversary, rendered him more amenable to reason. "Is dat damn outfit of Meinhold gan to bid, Bor-ruk?", he inquired.

"Why, Yes, Captain, We had to *put him to bed*. Don't you hear him snoring?"

Somebody *was* snoring and whoever it was wasn't *playing* at snoring, either, but doing his level best and getting along at a lively rate with no brake on.

I thought, under the circumstances, it would do no harm to give credit for the whole performance to poor old Meinhold, especially as the sound had such a favorable effect upon Russell.

He chuckled to himself and asked in a vague, drunken manner: "is dat damned outfit av a Meinhold gan to bid? Din oi kin *retoire* wid *hon-ur-r-r*", and as he said this, he struck his breast dramatically as if he had repeated "The old Guard dies but never surrenders". We took advantage of his mollified condition of mind and soon had the representative of old Erin's Green Isle snoring a most frantic rivalry with his comrade from the Vaterland.

My description of my comrades is accurate. Nothing has been set down in malice. To those personally unacquainted with the gentlemen of whom I have been writing, the eccentricities and oddities of character may perhaps be taken as the whole perimeter or at least the salient lines and angles; but such a judgment would be a gross injustice to them and to me: they were rather the incongruous and ridiculous element which are discernible in human nature everywhere and in no situation more so than on the remote frontier where people through a sense of isolation, seek a more intimate companionship with those who are thrown into their society and probably for the very same reason, feeling that there is no one to criticize, except close friends and intimate associates, are more careless about hiding little foibles and peculiarities from observation.

I wish I could remember as vividly and in proper sequence the general features of the topography of the line of march. My memory is constituted in such a way that I retain for a long time the impressions made upon me by individuals, but in a sense of locality I am lacking in details but always capable of describing the character of a district with an approach to correctness; even if my account of the lesser meanderings of roads and streams be somewhat at fault.

From Fort Cummings, New Mexico, to Fort Bowie, Arizona,[25] and from the latter post to Camp Grant (since abandoned) by way of Tucson, the country differs but slightly in its main features and but little more in its vegetation and animal life.

It is a vast alternation of plain and mountain, the ridges running from north to south and bearing the names of Cook's Peak, Mimbres Mountains, Steen's Peak, Chiricahua, Dragoon and Santa Catarina. None of these is much over 9500 or 10.000 feet in height, but in ruggedness they present as many obstacles to passage, except by the regular gaps, as if they were half as much higher. Pine and scrub oak, with some juniper and considerable "manzanita" grow upon the elevations or in the cañons; the plains, styled in the Spanish language "playas" or "beaches", bear a thick covering of blue and white grama grass, with the unnutritious stock grass called "sacaton", soap-weed, cactus in the varieties of ocatillo, nopal, saguaro and tuña [sic];[26] sage-brush and grease-wood, and "palo verde" as you enter Arizona.

In South West New Mexico, prairie-sage were not unusual. In Arizona, they are scarcely ever seen and only along the Eastern border. The Giant Cactus, (saguaro or pitahaya.) presents itself to view upon nearing Fort Bowie, and stands boldly against the horizon like a sentinel upon a rampart. Its usual height is not above 30 feet, but it is occasionally to be found nearer sixty.

---

25. Fort Bowie was established as a camp in 1862 in the Chiricahua Mountains to guard the eastern approaches of Apache Pass. The pass and springs located there were a key transit point for travelers and mail carriers on the road between Tucson and Mesilla, New Mexico, and a favorite ambush spot for the Indians. In 1868, it was relocated to a nearby hill overlooking the pass, and eleven years later permanently upgraded to a fort. Fort Bowie was abandoned in 1894, and now is a national historic site. Frazer, *Forts of the West*, 4; Utley, *A Clash of Cultures*.

26. The "tuna," which Bourke spells "tuña," is the fruit of the *opuntia phaeacantha* or prickly pear. Loughmiller, *Texas Wildflowers*, 33.

Giant Cactus. (Arizona.)

In no part of the United States does the Mescal or Century plant grow in the same luxuriant profusion as in Arizona. Its gorgeous velvety blossoms color the sides of the hills at all seasons and its roasted stalks and core, form the staple food of the Apache Indians. The Mescal, Saguaro, Tuña amd Mesquite are used in building.

The Mexicans tap the saguaro for its juice, which is boiled with pulverized sugar to make a palatable candy; the topmost branches bear in the month of June a fruit, in taste similar to our raspberry, greatly sought after by the wild Indians and preserved as a marmalade by the Mexicans.

The umbrella-like ribs of the decayed saguaro are spread from the rafters of houses to serve as the base of the earth or gypsum roof. Of the mescal, a highly intoxicating liquor is distilled, which has the taste and produces the effects of Scotch Whiskey; this and tiswin, a mild barley beer, flavored with cinnamon, are the staple intoxicants of Northern Mexico.

The juice of the nopal or tuña has a clarifying power, of which I have spoken at other times: the sliced leaves or "plates", immersed in muddy water will speedily cause a subsidence of any argillaceous matter held in suspension; its virtues as an anti-scorbutic have long been recognized by army officers of experience on the plains; stripped of its thorns it will sustain the lives of cattle in bad winters when hay and grass are not within reach and if the juice be mixed with sand and clay and a small addition of bullock's blood, it may be poured out in frames which hardening will make durable pavements for the interior of houses.[27]

The beans of the two varieties of mesquite[28] growing in Arizona are greatly prized by the Indians as food and are much relished by horses: the fruit of the manzanita[29] and the acorns of scrub oak, with the seeds of sun-flowers, wild gourds and various species of grass complete the diet list of vegetables in general use among the aboriginal tribes of that region.

Our line of travel lay nearly due West to Tucson, taking us through:

1st the town of Mimbres ("Osiers".) A little plaza, built of stone, on the clear mountain stream of same name which rises in the San Mateo Mountains and flows nearly due South to Laguna Guzman in the state of Chihuahua, Mexico.

2d. Hot Springs—Our battalion kept slightly to the left of these wonderful thermal springs which contain silica in solution and deposit a coating of it upon every twig or branch immersed in their waters.

3d Soldier's Farewell, the last station in New Mexico.

4th Steen's Peak. A tolerably high range with a good deal of pine towards the crest and in the ravines.

5th Fort (then Camp.) Bowie, the first point in Arizona, a military station of two Companies in the Apache pass of the Chiricahua mountains.

The Apache Indians were then making this part of America a perfect Hell upon earth. No small party could travel from station to station in South East Arizona, unless by night and with each man's hand constantly on his arms. Such settlers as braved the danger, ploughed their fields with rifles slung across their backs or strapped to the plough handle. In my journals and scrap-books of Arizona, a very complete account of this tribe and of General Crook's campaign, which resulted in their complete subjection, can be found.[30]

---

27. See Robinson, *Diaries*, 1:174.
28. *Prosopis glandulosa* (honey mesquite), and *prosopis pubscens* or (tornillo).
29. *Arctostaphylos*.
30. See Robinson, *Diaries*, Vol. 1, Chapters, 1–3.

On our march over to Bowie, Captain Russell and I became staunch friends; the old man frequently in conversation, gave me the benefit of his philosophical views, frequently calling attention to the mutual affection exhibited by his horse Charlie and mare, Katie: "I decleer to God'l'moitee, Bor-ruk, the amount of afficshun existing betwane dim two dumb animals, Chollie and Két-tee is perficly 'stonish'n". One morning, our old friend made his appearance at reveillé with his lower lip swollen out of all shape from the bite of a venomous spider or wasp.

All that we could get him to say on the subject was that "some damm-m-m baste of a *bay* stung it."

We regretfully parted with Captain Russell at Fort Bowie, of which garrison his company was ordered to form part. Captain Stanwood also separated from the Battalion at same point, en route for Camp Goodwin,[31] on the Gila river, opposite the mouth of the San Carlos.

The Post Commander of Fort Bowie was Captain Thomas Dunn, 21st Infy., a very good-hearted gentleman, but very odd in his behavior and a subject of considerable amusement to me in our after acquaintance.

From Bowie to Tucson is 110 miles, due West. Twenty eight miles out, at Dragoon Springs, we met the Battalion of the 8th Cavalry, marching over to New Mexico to take our places.

At San Pedro station on San Pedro river, 55 miles from Bowie, we saw the first Arizona station; a good enough house of adobe, with a corral of the same material. Like nearly all the stations of that day, it was kept in a most barbarous style. A story current in Arizona at that date, and popularly believed to be true, places the scene of the following experience at Duncan's (San Pedro) ranch. The stage, as the buck-board was jocularly called, deposited its load of passengers one evening for supper. One of these passengers was an Englishman, sent out from London to look into some mining property in Arizona. In dress and manner and speech, he was the typical "Bow Bells",[32] Cockney, baggy plaid trousers, clothed gaiters, short sack-coat, little

---

31. Camp Goodwin was established in 1864 as a base of operations against Apaches, and abandoned by the military in 1871. At this time, the post buildings served as a subagency for the San Carlos Reservation. The military reservation was transferred to the Department of the Interior in 1884. Altshuler, *Starting with Defiance*, 27–28; Frazer, *Forts of the West*, 8–9.

32. The true Cockney is said to be a person born within the sound of the church bells of St. Mary-le-Bone, or the "Bow Bells," London.

hat with a blue veil, umbrella and goggles,—the Henglish tourist's idea of a suitable costume for travelling in the wilds of America.

As he dismounted, he observed at the side of the main door, a small cottonwood three legged stool supporting a tin basin and a lump of rosin soap, while from a peg in the adobe wall, hung a ragged, "slazy", dirty strip of luck-a-back, facetiously intended for a towel. There was no help for it; the Englishman felt he was just a trifle dirtier than the towel;—that was the consolation. He splashed the basin full of water about his neck and head and into his ears and eyes, ridding himself of a fearful accumulation of sand and alkali dust and by closing his eyes tight, managed to get through with the towel without becoming sick.

The poor fellow thought at the time that that was the dirtiest towel he had seen; before he had been in Arizona a week, he learned to look back upon it as one of the daintiest pieces of linen that ever a lady's fair hand had embroidered.

Inside the ranch was the bare mud floor, rough counter, three pine shelves for bottles, tumblers and other paraphernalia; walls of adobe with a small looking glass and three or four advertisements of liquor firms doing business in San Francisco, and two or three stools, the companions in misfortune of the one in front of the house.

The sleepy bar-tender was in soiled shirt and with hair in ill-kept condition, because he had been too busy or sleepy for the past three months to give it any attention; but he hadn't been too busy or too sleepy to put on his six-shooters, which, like everybody else about the ranch, he wore constantly.

The supper was in strict keeping with the rest of the establishment; a bare pine table, china plates, tin cups, and knives and forks in various stages of decrepitude. There was tea, made from the native grasses of the Territory, biscuits, with an extravagant excess of soda, bacon, putrid and sour, sugar that would have delighted the soul of an entomologist, it was so full of ants and bugs & flies; stewed dried apples, each separate slice standing out sodden and distinct from its fellows, and the whole dish having a painfully strong suggestion of the Do-the-boys Hall, and as the crowning piece of the meal—sausage, in two ways—in globules and in casing. Mr. Duncan, the proprietor, had recently killed a pig, and in the exuberance of his good nature, was "going to set 'em up for the boys". The Englishman wasn't making much of a meal, to speak of; he sipped the tea mechanically and pushed the cup away from him in ill-concealed disgust; the bacon, he didn't pretend to even look at, but he thought he could find a small share of work for his teeth in trying to masticate the lumpy dried apples and soda biscuits. To do this, however, it was necessary to swallow a few flies; the first two or three made him sick. He became indignant; the meal was a transparent swindle, a glaring outrage, a trap for extorting a dollar from the unwary and unprotected. He had about made up his mind to forward an account of the affair to the British Minister at Washington, when the "garçon!" of the establishment leaned over his shoulder and hissed in his ear the question—"Gut sassige ur ball?["] The Englishman didn't like the looks of the waiter in the least; he was, as it were, the antipodes of anything to be seen in "Pell-Mell", or in any fashionable restaurant on the "Stwand".

He was hirsute, red-eyed, sun-burned, coatless and shoeless; his rolled up sleeves and revolver on hip imparted a "Dick Dead-eye"[33] tone to his make-up, which might have had a good effect on the stage, but in real life was the reverse of pleasant.

He was a prospector "down on his luck", who had taken to "slinging hash" as a temporary buttress against the assaults of famine. Once more he whispered—"Gut sassige or ball?["] The Englishman asked for an explanation of the cabalistic formula.

The reply was that "ball" sausage was plain sausage meat in globular masses, but "Gut" sausage was the same article in a bladder cuticle. The Englishman, desiring to avoid dirt as much as possible, intimated his preference for "ball": thereupon the waiter roared through the aperture in the wall between dining-room and kitchen; "ball sassige for one". The cook, an individual as hirsute, as dirty and as fully armed as the waiter, called back in an irritated tone; "---- your –soul to ----, didn't I tell you the ball's all gone", and immediately the waiter returning to the Englishman howled in his ear; "---- it the ball's all gone; take gut, you ---- take gut".

The Englishman wrote back to London that the mine he had been sent to examine was no doubt rich in ore, but that the great lack of wood and water and the great abundance of Apache Indians in Arizona were very discouraging obstacles to its development and for that reason only he felt compelled to decline the superintendency.

33. The devious villain of the Gilbert and Sullivan opera *H.M.S. Pinafore*.

Three miles, down the San Pedro, north of the station, was the hamlet of Tres Alamos, to which we had to send for barley for our command. From this station to the "Cienaga" (Swamp) is 25 miles, South of which 20 or 25 miles is the Ojo del Oso where poor Cushing afterwards (May 5th 1871.) was killed in a fight with Apaches.

To Tucson, the then capital of Arizona, is 25 miles more. I shall not make any prolonged reference to our march, the beautiful sunsets and sun-rises excelling those for which Italy is famed, the mirages, or the mournful aspect of the odd vegetation upon the mesas we covered.

I shall pay due attention to all that portion of my service in the note-books which I propose filling seriative from the great quantity of material on hand, in the form of letters sent home, rough notes, itineraries and maps made while scouting in that part of Arizona. We remained in the quaint old Mexican Presidio of Tucson for two days and then resumed our march for (old) Camp Grant, 55 miles to the north, keeping on the Western skirts of the Santa Catarina Mountains, the whole way and camping one night at the picturesque Cañada del oso.

Camp Grant, (since abandoned.) with its personnel including Col. [Isaac Rothermel] Dunkelberger, scenery, climate, fauna and flora, and topics of service there deserves and shall receive at my hands at some future date a more fitting recognition than a few brief paragraphs of notice in a journal opening under another heading.

And so ends the rough sketch of the reminiscences conjured up as I heard of poor Dubois' death; it has been commenced in haste, completed without skill, but I trust it ends appropriately by saying of my old Commander;

Peace to his Ashes.

Chapter 14

Back to the Present

General Miles, Colonel 5th Infantry, has for the past month, had a strongly equipped expedition of nearly one thousand men, all mounted, on the British Boundary north of Milk river, Montana, to drive back any hostile Sioux from Sitting Bull's Camp who might make an invasion of our territory.

Beyond attacking a small hunting party which, after a short skirmish with Miles' advance guard under Lieut. W. P. Clark, 2d Cavalry, fell back with rapidity across the line, the Expedition has been so fruitless, of results that I have made no effort to keep track of its operations. It will remain on the boundary during the remainder of the summer to patrol and observe.

August 12th [1879] Lieut. Genl. P. H. Sheridan, Brigadier General George Crook and Colonel Jeff. C. Davis, 23d Infantry, appointed a Board to meet in Chicago for the purpose of settling questions in dispute as to the positions and movements of troops at the Battle of Chickamauga, Ga., Sept. 18, 19th & 20th 1863.[1]

---

1. The Union disaster at Chickamauga, Georgia, on September 18–20, 1863, brought almost immediate recriminations, to such an extent that the Union major generals Thomas L. Crittenden, Alexander M. McCook, and James S. Negley demanded courts of inquiry. The courts, convened in Nashville in early 1864, determined that while Crittenden committed an error of judgment in withdrawing from the field, neither he nor McCook and Negley were

August 14th Lieut. Schuyler and I took a trip this morning over the Omaha and North Nebraska Rail Road to its present terminus at Tekama. We had to have a comparatively early breakfast at 7 o'clock and then drove in an ambulance to the station, a mile or more beyond Florence. Florence, an old Mormon settlement, was at one period of its existence an aspirant for commercial importance, the belief among many of the "knowing ones", in 1855–1864, being that there was the only proper point for the construction of the great bridge to span the Missouri river for the use of the transcontinental highway. Omaha carried off the prize and with the great trade brought to her doors by the Union Pacific Rail Road has waxed fat and kicked while her former rival has long since died of [inunition?]. It is hard to say when Florence died, but dead she is and dead as a door-nail. The Florence Bank, a brick building, of good size from those early days, is fast falling to pieces and the few inhabitants still remaining make such a living as they can by selling garden truck to the people of Omaha.

The Florence station is a rattle-trap shanty of cottonwood clapboards, the platform in front being too shaky and rheumatic for anybody to stand upon.

The station keeper's wife and five youngsters gazed dreamily at us as we got out of the ambulance, no doubt we were the only passengers in a month. The train was half an hour late. We made such an improvement of the interval as we could by walking about the station and conversing with the family. There was no trouble to be feared form the lateness of the train; only one runs in the day, leaving Omaha in the morning and returning in the afternoon.

In a few moments, the welcome whistle was heard; the train, mostly all baggage cars, came slowly up to the platform, stopped when we waved our hats and resumed progress as soon as we were seated. Half a dozen passengers occupied seats inside and the conductor, old Mr. Hermann,[2] not only collected fares, but acted as baggage-master, express agent, distributed mail and was also, I have been told, Treasurer of the road. This line is not quite 50 miles long, pays no dividends on its stock, but pays all expenses. An extension of 16 miles has been ordered, to commence at once.

---

censurable for their conduct during the battle. Nevertheless, the allegations and counter-allegations continued for years afterwards. *Official Records of the Union and Confederate Armies*, Series 1, Vol. 30, Part 1, 930ff.

2. Elsewhere, Bourke spells it "Harman."

I should describe the beautiful scenery, the finest in this part of the West, visible from the car-windows as we rode along, but as we had better opportunity for doing so in the afternoon, I shall not attempt it just now.

Blair, 30 miles north of Omaha, on the Missouri river, is the point of junction of the Sioux City and Pacific with the Omaha and North Nebraska. Practically, it is also the place of union with the latter road and the Chicago and Northwestern which sends many of its cars through Blair, by the ferry at this point, to Fremont, Nebraska, 25 miles West of Blair and 47 miles West of Omaha. Tekama, 40½ miles out from Omaha, is a very thinning village of 1000 pop[ulation].

Homes are as a general thing neat and cosy cottages, surrounded by groves of young trees, planted in regular rows.

Mr. Zanner, the jeweller of the town, very kindly invited Schuyler and myself to enter his store which contained a very fine stock of goods for so small a place. We became so interested in the conversation that time flew by rapidly and before we could get back to the dépôt, the train was pulling out. I ran as hard as I could for 25 or 30 yards, yelling all the while to attract the attention of our deaf old friend, Mr. Harman, whose multifarious duties, I suppose, so engrossed his care that he never thought of looking back at the dépôt. I never did know a belated passenger to overtake an outgoing train and I never knew one who wouldn't half break his neck in a frantic endeavor to do so.

We felt that we were in for it sure enough. There was no use growling. We had to make the best of a bad bargain.

The "station agent" thought we might hire a buggy, drive to the banks of the river, cross on the ferry and catch the down-going train of the Sioux City and Pacific Road which runs close to the Missouri on the other side. That hope was crushed when we learned that the ferry-boat had lately sunk.

We were now quite hungry and hunted up the best hotel in the town, the Astor house, which is the old building, erected by a detachment of regular troops a quarter of a century ago, to protect the first settlers from the Winnebago and Omaha Indians, who are now living peaceably and comfortably on their Reservations 26 miles North of Tekama.

Our dinner was such a meal as might be expected in such a place. Plenty of it, but nothing remarkable in the way of cooking.

The roast chicken and vegetables were relishable, bread fair, apple pie not bad and tea and coffee abominable.
The idea of staying all night in that place was simply awful, if there was any possible chance of escaping.
The bed-bugs, we knew from experience, would be not much smaller than good-sized lobsters and fully as voracious.

We tried the several livery stables, but none had a team for hire that would suit our purpose: but at the very last moment, a young man appeared who said he had to go down to Omaha and would take us for $5.50, if we would like to ride in an open spring wagon.

His horses were lively Colorado ponies, and as we had no baggage and the vehicle was light, there would be no trouble in rattling along the fine road between Tekama and Omaha Barracks, a trifle over 50 miles for wagons.
The driver had to wait for half an hour to do some business, water his horses and make personal preparations: we sat on the hotel porch pending his return and unconsciously listened to the conversation of our neighbors. "He sole that ar bay mar" "How much did he git fur her?["] "Hunner'n forty dollar"—and with the bay mare as a nucleus of discussion our granger friends were apparently ready for an all-night's work.

The spring wagon came up in due time and to my surprise was all that the driver had said for it. We took our seats, the lively little ponies struck out in a dashing way and Tekama was behind us.
From Tekama nearly all the distance to Fort Omaha, the scenery was most alluring; between Blair and Fort Calhoun, our eyes looked upon as romantic vistas as can be found anywhere. The sky was just hazy enough to temper the sun's heat and impart a delicious Indian-summery tone to the landscape which doubled its charms. Through breaks in dense groves of timber we caught glimpses of the broad-bosomed Missouri shining like silver, or of placid lakes and sloughs, fringed with saplings and embowered in the centre of grassy bluffs. Elms of unusual dimensions towered far above us, the boles in very many instances being as much as four or five feet in diameter and the dark, tapering branches intertwining to form vaulted arcades impenetrable to the sun.
Oak and walnut and cottonwood trees of great size formed a jungle with the matted foliage of luxuriant grape-vines and creepers. The peculiar impression left by these sombre recesses was one of agree-

able softness, not that of rugged wildness, and with our egress from each niche of foliage, the gently sloping hills of emerald looked like those which had received the careful attention of man. Near each pretty little village, and despite the features of newness or rawness here and there obtaining themselves all these villages are pretty, Herman, Blair, De Soto, Fort Calhoun,—the forest primeval was succeeded by broad acres of ripened wheat in which the brawny hands of farm laborers were gathering a grand harvest, or with still greater areas of corn which almost rivalled the trees of the forest in its height.

The farms were all fenced in; some with barbed wire, many with wooden polings, but the greater number with hedges of hawthorn and osage orange. An exhibition of taste was apparent in the plans of the buildings (many of them of brick) and in the colors with which they were painted. Barns and cribs and stacks were full and plethoric with the wealth of the fields, and the lowing herds coming in with the shades of the night, showed good breeding and good treatment.

The road was excellent. Our ponies pluckily held their own, never breaking their rapid trot except when pulled up by the driver, and before the sun had gone down behind the Western hills, we had passed the last little village, Fort Calhoun and were on the home stretch for Fort Omaha. At Blair, the driver had picked up one of his friends who wished to make a visit to the city. This passenger was rather "country-Jakey" in his looks, but talked well and had seen a good deal of the Western country.

He told us of the manner in which "lard oil" is made in Lacross[e], Wisconsin. A drove of pigs is urged down an inclined plane, bounded by a strong, high fence, inclining on each side to as to make a V-shaped enclosure. The fat porkers, pushed on by their fellows in the rear, and seeing but one way to escape, crowd into this opening, but they enter the jaws of Death. A pair of ponderous, iron cylinders revolve against each other and seize the hogs by the snout: There is scarcely a faint squeak heard before poor piggy is crushed into a shapeless plate of fat, skin, bones and bristles. From this pulp, the oil is distilled.

Close by Florence, we passed four vicious-looking tramps; dirty, ragged, vermin-eaten, sun-burned, and hairy—they passed by, going northward, or anywhere. Vice and want had made their indelible impressions upon their countenances and turned them into social outcasts, far worse than savage Indians.

We reached Fort Omaha at 8 o'clock, delighted with our day's journey and especially with the wagon-ride and narrowly escaping a wetting from the rain which began almost the moment we re-entered our quarters.

August 18th The cable dispatches announce the death, in Hampshire, England, yesterday, of Mrs. Nellie Grant Sartoris. As Miss Nellie Grant she was when I knew her slightly at West-Point, a sweet, modest little girl, not much over or under sixteen, winning friends on every side.

Her marriage to Algernon Sartoris, a booby-faced, chuckle-headed Englishman, with whom it is whispered she did not live happily, was one of those strange arrangements of chance for which there is no satisfactory explanation and upon which comment would be wasted.*[3]

August 18th Colonel C. J. Sprague, reported for duty as Chief Pay-Master, Major J. V. Furey, Dépôt Qr. Master, returned from leave of absence. Colonel Sprague and I have served together in the Departments of California and Arizona—1870, '71. '72. '73. '74. '75—and have had much to talk over in the way of old-time scenes and reminiscences. At mess lunch to-day, the conversation brought in the name of poor Brown, who at one time in Arizona occupied the position of Inspector General on General Crook's staff. (Brown was a great dandy, an incorrigible wag, a gallant soldier, and a man, in general terms of great capacity, altho' lacking in moral balance. He committed suicide in New York, in 1876 or 1877.)[4]

Upon one occasion, a party of English "luds" had come out to the plains of Nebraska to " 'unt the buffalo you know", and Brown had been requested by officers high in authority to show them every attention. Having but recently joined his company from a long leave of absence, his mess arrangements were not in a very satisfactory condition, a good cook being the chief want. Brown thought he could mend this defect by detailing some of the men from his company,

---

Across this entry, Bourke wrote in large, underscored words: This report proved to be a canard and was denied in the cable dispatches transmitted to the United States the next morning.

3. As Bourke noted, the story was unfounded. Nellie Grant Sartoris lived until 1922. He was correct, though, in stating the marriage was unhappy. McFeely, *Grant*, 402–4, 521.

4. 1875. See Appendix 1.

the occupation of each soldier prior to enlistment, being spread upon the muster-rolls. He scanned these carefully and to his great delight came upon the name of one man with the terse statement alongside of "cook". This was glorious; Brown called to his 1st Sergeant and told him to detail Barker to go with the hunting party. The Sergeant did as directed and Barker the first night out was assigned to the duties of cook. But Brown in running his eyes rapidly along the line of names had missed his direction and instead of selecting Barker, the "cook" by occupation, had picked out Barker who had been an "umbrella-maker". Barker was a stolid sort of a fellow who always obeyed orders without comment. He would just as soon cook as not and set about his task with much alacrity but with little previous knowledge.

The pièce de résistance of the dinner was a mammoth wild turkey, a bird of whose merits the Englishmen had heard much praise. This one was roasted to a healthy brown; rich gravy was trickling out from every break in the skin and a savory smell filled the tent. The carving-knife soon laid the bird open and disclosed the unpleasant fact that the gobbler had never been "drawn". There he was filled to repletion with fat green grass-hoppers! The foreigners started in dumb astonishment.

Brown was equal to the occasion. With his most seductive smile and most graceful bow he said to my-lud Arf-in-Arf—"My I help you to some of the Grass-hopper stuffing?["] The Englishmen pronounced the whole ménu a gem and Brown himself ate of the grass-hoppers until he was sick.

August 19th Lieut. M. C. Foot, Regimental Adjutant, 9th Infantry, Ass't. Surgeon R. Barnett, Lieut. Schuyler, Aide de Camp and myself carried into effect a scheme, [we] had in contemplation for some time, to examine the industries of most interest and value, in Omaha and which are of chief importance in building it up. Captain Stanton, Engineer Officer of the Department, had been included in the original member[ship], but important business intervened at the last moment and deprived us of the pleasure of his company.

We drove first in an ambulance to the Union Pacific Rail Road shops. Mr. Congdon, the Superintendent of the shops, volunteered to take us around and first conducted us to the moulding and foundry room where we examined with lively interest into all the details of making patterns and cores, ramming the sand in the moulds and reaming and shaving castings.

In this large building are prepared all the wheels, axles, pipes and castings of whatsoever sort demanded in the transaction of the business of this giant corporation. Grimy workmen, huge-muscled, dusty and moist with perspiration, moved about their work quietly and without bustle. They had a well-fed and contented look, corroborating the statement of Mr. Congdon that the Company made it a rule to pick the best men and to hold on to them after they had been selected. The main business transacted in this Department is the moulding of iron wheels and axles and other adjuncts of the running gear; three locomotives have been turned out, but the Company now finds it more profitable to buy ready made. A cast iron wheel has a life of 60.000 to 100.000 miles, or at the maximum will revolve over the line of this road, back and forth (50) times; compressed paperwheels of the new patent, with steel tires (2 inches thick.) last for at least 500.000 miles, when the tire must be replaced.

The axle is cast with a mathematical nicety of dimension; it exactly fits the wheel which is forced on under extreme pressure and becomes practically the same iron as the axle.

Mr. Congdon suggested after we had looked at the various operations of patterning and moulding, that we proceed to other departments of the works and examine them before returning to the foundry to see the running of metal and casting.

This arrangement brought us under the care of Mr. Stevens, the master car-builder, who continued the kind attentions begun by Mr. Congdon. Like him, he was an enthusiast in his work and showed the pleasure of a school boy when he observed how great was our interest in everything about us. In the car room, were new or remodeled cars for the Company Paymaster, for the U.S. Mail, for Express and for ordinary baggage purposes.

Each one, it its way, was a beauty and received warm praise. The Paymaster car was an elaborate piece of work, finely upholstered and supplied with all the modern conveniences.

The greatest care is bestowed upon the strength of all the work made in this shop; only the best of wood, iron, paint and glass can be used, economy assuring the rejection of materials in the smallest degree blemished.

The timber; oak, Georgia pine, and Michigan walnut used in these cars is extremely valuable and of itself ought to make strong frames, but there are, besides, horizontal and vertical tie-beams and braces as in the staunchest ship.

Painting cars is an operation far from being the simple one I had come to regard it: no less than eight coats are applied to each, the last one receives artistic ornamentation. The Pay-master's care bore on each side panel a vignette, representing a hand-full of "greenbacks" very cleverly done.

The Brass-foundry, electro-plating rooms and store-rooms, the last named filled from floor to ceiling with piles and bundles of all the articles needed in the multifarious transactions of a great Railroad, excited our admiration which reached its climax when we re-entered the foundry and saw the golden masses of fluid iron leap from the furnace into the kettles ready to receive it, which large cranes slowly swung around to the different moulds and almost that moment the iron took the form of an incandescent wheel.

We could fancy ourselves in company with Polyphemous & his Cyclops [sic] in the grimy recesses of Mount Etna,[5] as we stood watching the sturdy laborers working in a brilliant [comscation?] of molten slag or seized the fiery wheels and lowered them with care into the deep annealing pits along the walls.

In the lumber yard, high piles of various woods were stored, awaiting demand for use; in another yard, long rows of extra wheels and axles were arranged and in one place half a dozen examples of American ingenuity in the way of automatic couplers for freight cars, all failures. The Miller coupler buffer and platform, Mr. Stevens said, has proved a great success for passenger cars, but for freight cars there has been nothing invented that will suit, altho' nearly 2000 patents have been issued.[6] In every shady corner, were buckets of ice-water for use of the employees. Our visit was in every feature an unqualified pleasure and surprise and none of our party will be likely soon to forget it.

---

5. In *The Odyssey*, Polyphemus is a cyclops (pl. cyclopes) who imprisons Odysseus and his men in his cave, for the purpose of eating them. Using a ruse, the Achaeans manage to blind him and escape back to their ship.

6. The Miller Hook Coupler and buffer system, patented by Ezra Miller in 1866, was a precursor to the Janney knuckle system used today. It was part of a combination passenger coach platform, coupler and buffer that absorbed impact when coupling, and more evenly distributed motion. This essentially eliminated telescoping of coaches in accidents, and the uncoupling lever on the platform substantially reduced the risk of death or injury to crews when coupling and uncoupling cars. Miller's patent, which made him a fortune, was used by the major lines for passenger service until the 1880s, when it was replaced by the Janney system. http://www.midcontinent.org/collectn/woodpas/mlsw63/miller.html

From the Union Pacific shops, we drove to the Omaha Nail works. Mr. Marshall, the superintendent, escorted us through the building, explaining all features of his business as well as he could with such a rattle and clashing of heavy machinery. The material used, preferentially, is old scrap-iron, broken bolts, rusty spokes and other truck purchased from Rail Road companies. Two iron plates are taken and between them is placed a "filling" of iron scraps, much in a way to remind me of the cheap pies which sutlers used to sell to soldiers during the war. This is heated and rolled, heated and rolled, again and again, until the expert eye determines that it has the right temper and consistency, by which time it has assumed the shape of unwieldy "planks" of a bluish color, which after cooling, are cut into suitable lengths, (carrying according to the size of the nails to be made,) and thrust into the iron jaws of a nail-clipping machine which snaps at the blue plate and spits out nails like an angry bull-dog crunching a bone.

The next thing is to sort the product, to reject any unserviceable nails and pack the merchantable article in 100 pound kegs, which are immediately shipped on cars standing on a switch alongside the establishment.

The skilled labor in these works was brought from Pittsburgh; the value of the machinery and stock $5.000.

Capacity 200 kegs per diem, but an early increase [is] in contemplation.

Our afternoon ended with a trip to the White Lead works. Mr. Locke, I think it was, who chaperoned our party at this place. The contrast between this and the nail factory was very striking; there, all was grime and dust; here the neatness and cleanliness of everything had a pleasing effect with the drawback that the air was full of poison and the men employed have to keep the face covered and to drink occasionally of sulphuric acid lemonade.

All the lead needed is brought from the Omaha smelting work, the present cost being 3½ to 4¢ per lb. To be brief and to avoid technicalities, it may be said that the carbonate is obtained by subjecting a stream of the molten metal to the action of a jet of high steam; this reduces it to a state of powder which falling upon a hot iron floor and exposed to the atmosphere speedily oxidizes. This blue oxide is placed in great iron cylinders, revolving on horizontal axes and is sprinkled with water and vinegar and at same time receives the carbonic acid gas, under which treatment in a very short time it becomes the carbonate of lead, or "white lead" of commerce.

Considerable manipulation is now needed and much skill in grinding and washing. The powdered "white lead" is shipped in considerable quantities to druggists in Philadelpha, who put it in tasty little boxes and sell it as the face-powder known as "Lily-White". The last thing to be done is to grind the white lead in oil, only the cleanest and purest can be used, that from "Calcutta seed" being the whitest and best. The kegs to contain the "paint", as it may now be termed, have to be varnished inside as well as out, to preserve the white lead free from all contamination. This establishment represents a paid up and invested capital of $60.000: is working now to its fullest limit and expects to ship, the present year, 1500 Tons of Paint, at a market price, wholesale, of $150 per Ton. The product of the Omaha White Lead works is justly regarded as the whitest and purest furnished the American trade.

August 20th. Telephonic communication established between Fort Omaha and Omaha.

August 30th. General James B. Hood [sic],[7] formerly of the Confederate Army, died of yellow fever at New Orleans, La. During the war, Hood figured as one of the most gallant of the leaders opposed to the Union Armies, winning his way by desperate valor to the command of an Army. He first served under [James P.] Longstreet in the Army of Virginia and again at Chicamauga [sic], Ga., where Hood made the break through our centre which sent the grand old Army of the Cumberland reeling back in a demoralized mob to Chattanooga: in this battle, Hood lost a leg. In Sherman's movement against Atlanta, Hood did yeoman service and at last was ordered to relieve Braxton Bragg in command of the Army, just as Sherman was about to enter Atlanta.[8] Hood, with his army, escaped from our toils with some loss in men and nearly the total loss of his ammunition train which had to be blown up to prevent its falling into our hands. This train consisted of eleven locomotives and eighty-five cars laden with paper cartridges and powder in kegs. I remember well the fearful gash made in the earth's surface by this explosion which filled the ground with bullets for a distance of over a quarter of a mile. I was in Atlanta

---

7. Bourke means John B. Hood.
8. In fact, Hood relieved Joseph E. Johnston in a move that infuriated the Confederate troops. McPherson, *Battle Cry of Freedom*, 753.

almost with the first of our troops and in company with hundreds of comrades "off duty", went to visit to [sic] scene of destruction and gather pieces of broken shells, bullets &c.

After we took Atlanta, Hood waited for fresh supplies and when Sherman with 2/3 of our army commenced his march to the sea, (first blowing up Atlanta,) Hood rapidly threw himself against our rear and right, necessitating a rapid withdrawal and concentration on the part of George H. Thomas, who succeeded to the command of so much of the Army as did not accompany Sherman. Hood attacked us hotly at Spring Hill and Franklin, Tenn., but the determination and gallantry of D. S. Stanley saved us from destruction (J. M. Schofield received the credit for this, but it fairly belongs to Stanley.)

At last, Hood and Thomas, met in a fair and square fight, at the foot of Brentwood Hills, near Nashville, Tenn., Dec. 1864, and the Confederate Army was hopelessly shattered.[9]

Thomas' army pursued the fragments as far as the North East corner of the State of Mississipi, but owing to lack of supplies returned viâ the Tennessee and Cumberland rivers to Nashville, Tenn., early in 1865.

Hood was a brave and noble soldier, a pure-minded gentleman, and a shrewd and capable Division commander, but not possessed of the ability necessary to conduct the affairs of a large Army.

September 20th General Grant returned to the United States, landing at San Francisco, amid the thunder of guns, the roar of bands and the cheers of thousands of delighted citizens.

One Dennis Kearney, a blatant demagogue, who had gained some notoriety as a leader of the (so-called.) Working-men's party, threatened to have Grant burnt in effigy; this threat was the downfall of Kearney's power.

Grant's tour around the world was one grand series of ovations from the crowned heads and prominent dignitaries of all the countries

---

9. Spring Hill and Franklin were fought November 29–30, 1864, respectively, in Hood's attempt to retake Nashville. Hood's Army of Tennessee forced Union troops to withdraw from Spring Hill, but Confederate oversight left the road open so that Schofield was able to regroup at Franklin. Hood assaulted the Union line at Franklin the following afternoon, beginning an eight-hour battle which, for the Confederates, was one of the most devastating slaughters of the entire war. Once again, the Union troops were forced back, and withdrew to Nashville, but Confederate dead were almost ten times the number of Union soldiers killed, and overall casualties were twice those of the Union. Hood's failed effort to take Nashville on December 15–16 was the last major battle of the Western Theater. Foote, *Civil War*, 654ff.

he visited and was a fitting prelude to the enthusiastic reception to be accorded by the people of his own country, which I hope may find its conclusion by his inauguration as our first *Third Term President*, in 1881.

Sept. 22d. General Crook returned to Hd. Qrs. from a two months' absence in Maryland.[10]

Sept. 27th News arrived by telegraph that the important mining town of Deadwood, in the Black Hills, Dakota, was almost entirely consumed by fire last night.

Loss about $2.000.000.[11]

Sept. 28th General Crook left Omaha for Chicago, to attend the session of the Board of Officers convened to determine the positions of the troops at the battles of Stone River and Chicamauga [sic], in 1862 and 1863.

10. Crook maintained a home in Oakland, Maryland.
11. Bourke's impressions of Deadwood are recorded in Robinson, *Diaries*, 2:132ff.

Part 4
The White River Ute Uprising

Background

The White River Ute uprising had its roots in the usual well-meaning, but totally unrealistic policies of federal government. As Bourke noted, the public seemed to understand the problem. "Very generally, the Indian Bureau was blamed and not a few expressed the hope that the Indian Agent might be killed, thinking that his inefficiency or rascality had brought about the revolt," he wrote on the train from Omaha to Fort Fred Steele, Wyoming, on his way to the scene.[1]

The public assessment of the agent, Nathan C. Meeker, also was correct. Meeker was, in the words of one who knew him, "strictly honest, but utterly impractical and visionary and without any ability to manage Indians or whites."[2]

The problem was aggravated by the incursion of prospectors into the Ute country. One newspaper commented, "When the miners began filling the Middle and North Park last summer, the Ute heart suddenly became filled with badness."[3]

---

1. Bourke, Diary, 31:252–53.
2. Ibid., 31:253. The official records of the White River Ute Uprising are found in RG 393, Special File, Military Division of the Missouri, White River Utes, 1879, and Troop Movements (Ute War), October-December 1879. The Meeker massacre and subsequent events are discussed in Sprague, *Massacre: The Tragedy at White River*.
3. Undated, unattributed clipping in Bourke, Diary, 31:248.

There is little question that Meeker meant well. However, he was self-righteous, autocratic, and ignorant of the Indians under his charge. By September 1879, the situation had deteriorated to the point that he wrote the governor of Colorado asking for military protection. Although Colorado was in the Department of the Missouri, which was Brig. Gen. John Pope's jurisdiction, the nearest post was Fort Fred Steele in the Department of the Platte. Consequently, the post commander, Bourke's friend Major Thornburgh, was instructed to take a detachment to the agency, protect the personnel, enforce Meeker's regulations, and arrest the leaders of the Indian resistance pending an investigation.

As a general rule, Indian fights either were vicious, hit-and-run affairs, or outright disasters in which one side or the other was annihilated. Very rarely do we read of a detachment of soldiers, pinned down and surrounded, holding out until rescue. One instance is Maj. George Alexander (Sandy) Forsyth's stand at Beecher's Island on the Republican River in eastern Colorado in 1868. Another is the ordeal of Thornburgh's expedition after it was caught on the Milk River in western Colorado by the White River Utes.

Thornburgh, with three companies of cavalry and one of infantry, began the 175-mile trek on September 21. Five days later, he met with some of the chiefs, and reported that he did not anticipate any trouble. On September 29, however, the Utes ambushed him and his men just south of the Milk River. The command was pushed back to the river with heavy losses, including Thornburgh himself. The survivors managed to dig in, and send a courier to Fort Fred Steele for help. The Utes, meanwhile, attacked the agency, killed Meeker and nine others, and carried off the white women and children.

In response, Crook ordered Wesley Merritt, at Fort D. A. Russell, to relieve the troops pinned down on the Milk River and occupy the agency.[4] Bourke was sent to accompany him. Taking the train to Rawlins, Merritt started south, pausing only briefly to rest his troops on the Bear River, where Bourke caught up with him and was assigned to command the advance guard. He arrived on the

---

4. Fort D. A. Russell was established in 1867 to protect workers constructing the Union Pacific, and became an important supply base with a depot in Cheyenne. In 1930, the post was renamed Fort Francis E. Warren. It later was transferred to the Department of the Air Force, and now is Warren Air Force Base. Frazer, *Forts of the West*, 184–85.

Milk River October 5, having made the 170-mile march in a little less than forty-eight hours.[5]

Most of the action is covered in Chapters 15 and 16 of this section. Chapter 17, which deals with more routine matters, is included because it contains follow-up material on the Ute crisis.

5. Robinson, *General Crook*, 228–29.

Chapter 15

Merritt's Ride

September 30th Lieut. Schuyler, A.D.C., and his friend, Mr. Peyton, of New York, started on a hunt in the Rocky Mountains, north of the Union Pacific R.R. and West of Cheyenne.

My own preparations were made at same time, and orders received, to proceed to join the command of Major T. T. Thornburgh, 4th Infantry, then marching to the Agency of the White River Utes, to assist the Agent, who reported that he was in need of military force to quell the turbulent and unruly Indians on his Reservation.

October 1st. I was awakened this morning by Giney, our man, and Reynolds, the orderly, rushing in to my bed-room with the astounding information that Major Thornburgh had been killed, his command cut up and surrounded by the Utes and threatened with complete destruction. My first impulse was to treat the story as one of the canards which spring up in garrisons, no one knows from what source; but a second thought impelled me to hurry my dressing and get down to Dep't. Hd. Qrs. without delay. In its worst form, I found the first vague rumor confirmed. The first dispatches reached General Williams about 3½ o'clock in the morning. Within 20 minutes, he was dressed and at the key-board of the telegraph office in communication with post commanders ordering troops to

Rawlins with Majors Furey and Gilliss of the Q.M. Dep't.,—having supplies packed and shipped, with General Merritt, at Fort Russell who was to command the relief column, and with Generals Sheridan and Crook at Chicago. To give a more exact idea of the nature of the news recd. as well as to save myself the trouble of writing unnecessarily, I append the official telegrams as they appeared in the public journals of Oct. 1st and 2d.

ON THE WAR PATH.
MAJ. THORNBURGH KILLED.
His Command is Attacked near White
River—Heavy Loss of Soldiers,
Teamsters and Animals—Capt.
Payne Wounded.

The city of Cheyenne was thrown into a fever of excitement yesterday morning upon the receipt of the news that Maj. Thornburgh's command, which left Rawlins early last week for the White River, Colorado, agency, had found the Indians when they were not looking for them and suffered severely in killed and wounded. Nothing definite was known of the engagement of the Utes and the troops until the receipt of the following dispatches:

Omaha, Oct. 1:—At four o'clock this morning following dispatch was received here at the military headquarter by Gen. Williams, assistant adjutant general of the department of the Platte:

MILK RIVER, COL., Sept. 29, 8:30 p.m., via Rawlins. To the assistant adjutant general of the department of the Platte, Omaha Barracks, Neb.

The command, composed of three companies of cavalry, was met a mile south of Milk river by several hundred Ute Indians, who attacked and drove us to the wagon train, which had parted, with great loss. It becomes my painful duty to announce the death of Maj. Thornburgh, who fell in harness; the painful but not serious wounding of Lieut. [James V. S.] Paddock and Dr. [Robert D.] Grimes, and ten enlisted men and wagon master McKinstry, with the wounding of about twenty-five men and teamsters. I am now corralled near water, with three quarters of our animals killed, after a desperate fight since 12 o'clock m[eridian]. We hold our position at this hour. I shall strengthen it during the night and I believe that we can hold out until reinforcements reach us, if they are hurried through. Officers and men behaved with the greatest gallantry. I am also slightly wounded in two places.

    (Signed)   [John Scott] PAYNE, commanding

Other dispatches of a similar import were also received together with the following:

MILK RIVER, COL, Oct. 1, Bisbee, Ft. Steele: The existence of the command depends solely on the haste with which reinforcements are gotten here as Payne has directed me, simply to hold my camp and not advance.

    (Signed)   [Butler D.] PRICE.

Gen. Williams at once hurried into town and ordered reinforcements by telegraph, from various points in this department. The entire number of troops that can be mustered is 500, principally infantry. They will be sent forward by rail at once, and then proceed by forced marches. They will be able to reach Rawlins by to-morrow noon. They can make forty miles a day until they reach Milk river. The distance to Milk river is 200 miles from here. The point where the troops are corralled is near the reservation in Colorado. Only a few days ago dispatches were received from Maj. Thornburgh to the effect that some of the chiefs came forward and avowed a desire to hold friendly relations. The troops must have been strung along the road when they were overtaken. The country in which the fight occurred is one of the most rugged and inaccessible mountain regions on the continent. A spot difficult for military operations and splendidly adapted for Indian stratagems and ambushes. Col. Merritt, a gallant, brave and active officer, is to be put in command of the troops. A desperate fight may yet take place in order to dislodge the Indians.

    Milk River, Col., Sept. 29—Maj. Thornburgh's command was attacked in a bad cañon at noon to-day, one mile north from here on our march to the agency. The command retreated in good order to the wagon train where we are now entrenching ourselves as fast as possible.

3:30 p.m.—Maj. Thornburgh was killed instantly, during the retreat. Capt. Payne was wounded in two places slightly. Lieut. Paddock and Capt. [Edward B.] Grimes were also painfully, but not dangerously, wounded. Ten enlisted men and wagon master McKinstry were killed, and at least twenty-five men and teamsters wounded. The command is now very well sheltered, but now and then heard the guns of the new hostiles who have just arrived. Our poor mules and horses are getting it all around. The red devils fired the grass around us to burn us out.

Later. 9 p.m.—We still hold our positions, every man is busy digging trenches, and hauling out the dead animals for defense to-morrow, for we fully expect them back at daylight.

White River, Col., Sept. 29—5 p.m—Our courier, "Joe Rankin" has volunteered to carry dispatches to Rawlins.

Mr. Gordon, whose freight outfit of Indian supplies was near us when the fight commenced, has been burned by the fire, also the company wagons of Co., F., Fifth cavalry. Capt. Payne had his horse killed and Lieut. [Samuel Austin] Cherry's was also shot during the retreat. Capt. Lindwood and Lieut. Cherry are unhurt though men were killed all around them. About three-fourths of our horses and mules have been killed and should reinforcements reach us in five days we can hold out very well with our supplies and ammunition.

During the morning the following telegram was received at the office of Gov. Hoyt.

RAWLINS, WYO., Oct. 1.

To Governor J. W. Hoyt:

A special messenger from Maj. Thornburgh's command reports the major and thirteen soldiers killed and all officers wounded but one.

The citizens from the surrounding country are coming into our town for protection. I feel that our town is not safe. If we can have plenty of arms and ammunition we can and will protect ourselves.

If possible send us five hundred stand of arms on number three [train] to-day.

JAMES FRANCE.

An inspection of the armory by the person having charge of the keys of the same revealed the fact that but four guns were contained therein. There was plenty of ammunition, however, and the following telegram was sent to Mr. France.

CHEYENNE, Oct. 1.

To James France, Rawlins:

No guns in territorial armory. Have 6,000 rounds of ammunition, 45 calibre. Shall they be sent?

As no answer was received the ammunition was not sent.

Meanwhile Gen. Merritt, commandant at Fort D. A. Russell, received orders from Gen. Williams, adj. gen. department of the Platte, to send every available man at his post to the field and for himself to go and take command of the expedition. Accordingly all the available men at the Fort were at once engaged in preparing for their departure to the front. Companies D, and F, commanded by Lieut. Paddock and Capt. Payne respectively, were in the fight. There were four companies of the Fifth cavalry, and the Fourth infantry to move. There were company A, Capt. J. A. Augur; B, Capt. R. H. Montgomery; J, Capt. S. C. Kellogg; M, Capt. ____ and company I, Fourth infantry, Capt. S. P. Ferris.

After issuing orders, as stated above, Gen. Williams sent the following dispatch to Lieut. Gen. Sheridan, at Chicago:

"I have ordered Gen. Merritt with five companies from Fort D. A. Russell, two companies from Fort McPherson, all that can be spared from Fort Sanders and four companies from Fort Douglass to rendezvous at once at Rawlins. This gives 530 men; orders two companies from Fort Robinson, one from Fort Laramie and one from Fort Fetterman to march at once to the railroad to meet the emergencies. Capt. Gilliss is ordered to confer with Gen. Merritt and forward transportation. Have you any orders?

R. Williams,
A.A. Genl. Dept. of Platte

Such excellent time was managed that already that at 2 o'clock, railroad time, the train moved out, the troops cheering loudly. The train consisted of ten stock cars, one car for tents, etc., eight box cars for the men and a caboose for the officers. Two engines were attached and the train started off in good time. Rawlins was reached at a late hour last night. The expedition will start from that point this morning on forced marches of forty miles per day.

As the scene of the late fight is two hundred miles from Rawlins, reinforcements may not arrive before Monday. In the meantime the Utes will have only too much opportunity to kill off the little garrison in the cañon of death, or starve them out. However, if the red devils learn that heavy reinforcements are coming they will likely scatter off in small bands and roam over North Park, their old hunting ground. In that case they would make it a little unhealthy for the prospectors there. But they may not go over so far as the extreme eastern rim of the park.

It is the impression here that the fears of the people of Rawlins are not well grounded. The Utes are not likely to go northward, as they are civilized enough to know the advantage of keeping away from a railroad. And even if they chance to be scattered on the way to the White River, Gen. Merritt's command will drive them ahead. So Wyoming settlers are safe.

The history of the Ute troubles is brief. When the miners began filling the Middle and North Park last summer, the Ute heart suddenly became filled with badness. Colorow was especially indignant and threatened all sorts of vengeance. Winter coming on, he and his noble band of paupers feasted at the table of Father N. C. Meeker, at the White River agency. The going in of prospectors to the North Park again stirred up Colorow and he gathered some young men about him who killed what miners they could easily and warned others away. When the latter would not go, Colorow set fire to the timber with the intention of driving them out by fire and smoke.

The discontent spread to others of the White River Utes and their hearts grew worse. Meanwhile Agent Meeker had been carrying out orders of the interior department by putting up new buildings, laying in stores, and fencing in and plowing fields. This latter act was the straw that broke the camel's back. It resembled work for the Indians, so they kicked. Johnson, a sub-chief, became suddenly demonstrative two weeks ago and attacked Agent Meeker in his own house, kicking and cuffing the agent in a vigorous manner, ending by pushing him out of door. Several employes [sic] interfered and saved Mr. Meeker from further injury.

These facts were officially reported to the interior department and the case turned over to the war department. The arrest of Johnson and other refractory chiefs was ordered, hence Maj. Thornburgh started for the White River with his expedition, the fate of which is detailed above.

Thus we find an Indian war on hand at almost the beginning of winter. And with a tribe that has long been friendly with the whites and knows the power of the United States government. It is to be hoped that Ouray, the head chief of all the Utes, will exert sufficient influence to prevent the middle and southern Colorado Utes from becoming disaffected and sending reinforcements to their northern brethren.

A BRIEF SKETCH.

Maj. Thornburg, [sic] who was killed on Monday by the Utes, was a native of East Tennessee, being a brother of the Congressman J. M. Thornburg, who represented the Knoxville district in the forty-sixth congress, as a republican. The *Army Record* gives the following record of the major: "Cadet, July 1, 1863; second lieutenant Second artillery, June 17, '68; first lieutenant, April 21, 1870; major and paymaster, April 26, 1875; transferred to the Fourth infantry May 23, 1878.["] The major was transferred to the line in order to give his ambition the opportunity in the field against Indians. Last fall, it will be remembered, he commanded the expedition that followed up the renegade Cheyennes as they fled northward to the hills. He was the commandant of Fort Steele.

The forgoing gives in a nut shell the sad news as we heard it at Hd. Qrs. on the morning of Oct. 1st. The evening previous at the Autumn Exhibition, held under the auspices of Trinity Episcopal

Church, I had been conversing with Miss Clark, the sister-in-law of the unfortunate Thornburgh and had promised, when I met him, to convey many kind messages from her family. Little did the poor lady imagine what a fearful awakening her slumbers should have this morning.

For myself the news was sad and startling. Having been with Thornburgh at the Mily. Academy and afterwards served with him upon General Crook's Staff, as well as accompanying him upon his Expedition in pursuit of the Cheyennes last autumn, I had become especially well acquainted with him and in return for many favors and much hospitality extended me, bore him very warm and kindly feelings. In various note-books, I have had occasion to speak of him so much at length, that it is useless here to repeat. His skill as a rider and hunter excited my enthusiastic admiration. Physically, altho' a trifle too heavy to my eye, he was one of the best proportioned and most finely-formed men I have ever seen.

After a consultation with General Williams for the purpose of learning as nearly as possible what measures had been taken for the prosecution of the campaign, I started out on the Express train of the Union Pacific R.R., for Rawlins, Wyo., (710 miles, West of Omaha.) the point of departure of supplies intended for White River Agency. On the train with me were Colonel R. D. Clark, Paymaster, the father-in-law of poor Thornburgh, who was on his way to Fort Steele to comfort his afflicted daughter.

Another fellow-passenger was Colonel Guy V. Henry, whose soldierly impulses carried him to the front at the first intimation of hostilities. With him I conversed pleasantly, in part to revive former associations, but mainly to avoid as much as possible being thrown in contact with Col. Clarke[1] whose dejection was remarkable.

The only talk among the people on the train was about the "Thornburgh Massacre". Very generally, the Indian Bureau was blamed and not a few expressed the hope that the Indian Agent might be killed, thinking that his inefficiency or rascality had brought about the revolt.

A gentleman from Greeley, Colo.[,] remarked that he had an extended personal acquaintance with Agent Meeker and family; he regarded the Agent as strictly honest, but utterly impractical and visionary and without any ability to manage Indians or whites.

---

1. Bourke's spelling was inconsistent.

Oct. 2nd This morning, upon reaching North Platte, an extra section was added to our train, hauling the troops, horses and supplies sent out from Fort McPherson. The officers with the men were Captain P. D. Vroom and Lieut. [Allan] Jordan, 3d Cavalry, and Lieuts. [Charles Dyer] Parkhurst and [William Howard] Andrews, 5th Cavalry.

At Cheyenne, Lieut. [William Prebel] Hall, R.Q.M., 5th Cavalry, and Tom Moore, Q.M.D., came on our train to go West. The only word that can describe the excitement along our line of travel and particularly in Cheyenne, is "intense". Nothing else was talked about in any quarter.

Hearing that General Merritt's command had already left Rawlins, I telegraphed to Captain Bisbee, 4th Infantry, to hire me a buggy or some such conveyance with which to overtake it. Doctor [Bernard Gustave] Semig came aboard our train at [Fort Fred] Steele and went as far as Rawlins. Congressman Thornburgh from Tennessee, was with us from Cheyenne to Fort Steele, but I avoided a meeting for the same reasons which had governed my actions with Colonel Clarke.

Rawlins, seen in the gloom of midnight, didn't present a very favorable appearance; it would be unjust to attempt a description with the feeble opportunities I had, so I'll leave that to a later day. Colonel Gilliss, Captain Bisbee, Mr. Payton, and my old friend, Wilbur Hergus, received me very kindly.

A conveyance was in readiness, some little business such as sending telegrams and brief letters, was soon transacted and then in company with Mr. Wilbur Hergus and Lieutenant Charles Mason, 4th Infantry, our drive to overtake Merritt's Command commenced @2 a.m. Oct 3d.

No news whatever had been received from the front. Dame Rumor plied her vocation and wagged her tongue to a fearful extent. The scores of bummers and dead-beats, who in frontier villages loom into importance on occasions like this, had it all their own way and to their hearts' content prophesied all manner of disaster for Merritt. According to them, the last man of Thornburgh's command, but by that time have been killed and the Utes, only waiting to eat up Merritt, would devastate the whole country and incite the Shoshonees and Arapahoes to War.

We knew these fellows too well to put much truth in what they said, but human nature is weak and it was impossible not to be in a slight degree unnerved by these horrible stories. The night air too was unusually bleak and chilling, freezing the marrow in our bones. It blew directly from the South from the snow-laden domes of Pike's, and other peaks of the great divide.

None of us evinced a desire to talk. With a single grunt to the driver to "go ahead", each relapsed into a grim and stoical silence, scarcely broken through the night. I did not take enough notice of the country to do much in describing it. I saw that before some six or seven miles we went South West, keeping close to the Rail Road track, then we turned nearly due South, having the North star at our backs, and going up grade for a distance from Rawlins of 15 @ 20 miles. We there came upon broad stretches of sage-brush plains, hemmed in by high, almost bare mountains which, for some reason or another, brought to my mind the "paramos" on the summit of the Andes, in Ecuador, described in a volume I once read, by Hassaurek.[2]

My findings were somewhat enlivened by the information which Genl. Williams had telegraphed me that General Crook would return to Omaha to-day, and, as I apprehended, would at once leave for Rawlins. With him at the helm, I was sure that military affairs would go along smoothly.

The first white streak of dawn found us in sight of Lambert's Ranch, which had nothing specially deserving of mention about [it] except that close by the house was a small sulphur spring.

Our team was quite jaded and in anticipation of trouble with the 12 miles of heavy sand which the driver told us had to be passed just beyond this point, we were glad to listen to the ranchman's suggestion that we should take a fresh team from his stables. This was avoiding Scylla and a falling upon Charybdis.[3] The "fresh" team, as it afterwards turned out, was much worse than our own and gave us no end of trouble by balking at the foot of every hill. While the new team was feeding and receiving a sort of grooming before being

---

2. Frederick (Friedrich) Hassaurek (1832–85), native of Vienna, immigrated to the United States, settling in Cincinnati, Ohio. He served as U.S. Minister to Ecuador from 1861 to 1865. His book, *Four Years Among the Ecuadorians*, was published in 1867.
http://politicalgraveyard.com/bio/haskill-hastie.html

3. This is Bourke's second reference to these mythological beings, the first in his account of the battle of the Rosebud on June 18, 1876 (Robinson, *Diaries*, 1:329). These are two sea monsters dwelling on either side of what are presumed to be the Straits of Messina, between Italy and Sicily. Scylla had six heads with vicious teeth and would snatch sailors off their ships and devour them. Charybdis would suck the water down in a giant whirlpool. Ships trying to avoid the one invariably would fall afoul of the other.

harnessed up, we went over to the house to examine the prospects for breakfast.

Three or four rough-looking chaps were inside who told us that "the wimmin-folks hed ull skipped out fur *town*" (i.e. Rawlins.) Somebody had very evidently "skipped out". The house was in fearful disorder: clothes and provisions tumbled in confusion about on the floor. We were invited to sit down on sacks of flour and bacon, which would have been comfortable enough except that our dozing was interrupted by the cook's coming to cut meat or extract the material for making bread.

This cook didn't relish the idea of getting us breakfast. I thought then he was simply cross-grained; I am now assured that he felt diffident of his own powers. He growled out in a half apologetic tone; "Wa'all, Cap! I don't make no purtenshuns to bein' considered a dog-gone, fust-class French cook, no way". I replied in a soothing manner that if there was anything on the face of the earth I heartily despised, it was a French cook with a paper collar & his hair parted in the middle: that all French cooks ought to be at once run out of the country and that good, plain, home-like American cookery, such as I was satisfied *he* could prepare, was plenty good enough for the likes of me—with much more to the same purport.

The culinary artist was thoroughly mollified. He took equal measures of baking powder, water and flour, mixing the components into a mass which was too adhesive to be called gruel and not quite viscous enough to be regarded as dough.

This was formed into huge blocks, placed in a pan and run into the oven of the stove where a fierce fire was now roaring. In three minutes the bread was "done"; that is the cook said it was and as he was a man who had grown up with the country and weighed probably, sixty pounds more than I, it was merely courtesy on my part to accept his opinion as final.

The outside of each block was burned black as charcoal, while the interior was in a condition almost fluid.

A pot of coffee had been warmed over, and a pan of bacon, or ham, fried in thick slabs, was also in readiness.

We split the bread open, let out the raw material and scraped from the inner side of the burned crust a good percentage of the eatable food, washed it down with the coffee and tried our teeth on slices of the iron-clad ham and this done were ready for the trail again.

Merritt, the ranchman said, must be not less than 20 miles ahead, but the good bright sun was shining upon the gladdened earth, dissipating the cold mists of night and warming our benumbed limbs, so we didn't much care how many miles he was from us, we felt confident of being able to soon overtake him.

Mr. Hergus spoke to me about Agent Danforth, the predecessor of the unfortunate Meeker. Danforth was a very weak specimen himself, but his wife, a strong-minded female, managed the Agency to suit her own fancy. Her name was upon the rolls, under various disguises, drawing salary as schoolmistress, Postmaster, clerk and Doctor, to aggregate of $3200 per annum.

A few yards from Lamberts is a sulphur spring, rising from the side of a small slag mound. Two miles out, we came to a succession of springs, shaded by a thick willow copse. Up to this time, our road was quite good and no complaints could be justly made. From here on, we entered a sandy country and toilfully pushed on through dunes of impalbable [sic] fineness, covered thickly with grease-wood and sage-brush, with High mountains visible on each side.

The best of animals would have experienced trouble in making an advance across the 12 miles of this sand we had to encounter; our annoyance was augmented by the discovery that our "fresh team" was absolutely worthless, balking at the foot of every little hill and playing out before attaining the summit. We took turns in assisting the driver to beat them; our whips were soon broken, and our only hope lay in the persuasive powers of a ramrod which was well laid on at brief intervals with excellent effect.

At almost every mile, we met wagons loaded with the families and effects of refugees fleeing from danger; these all gave such alarming accounts of the condition of affairs at the front, that it was natural we should feel solicitous about overtaking Merritt without delay, and not a little alarmed by the indications of worthlessness our animals manifested.

Nearing what we thought must be the valley of Snake river, we discerned a great column of dust, undoubtedly made by the movement of Merritt[']s command. The whole country was so filled with smoke from the burning grass and timber ignited by the Indians in the mountains that we could not assure ourselves of the value of this dust-column as an indication of our proximity to the Command, until meeting a small party of settlers we learned that we were only seven miles from Snake river, which Merritt had reached shortly after noon and where he proposed remaining to rest for an hour. One of the party was obliging enough to lend me his horse and to take my place in the buggy. In less than 3/4 of an hour, the plucky little animal, I borrowed, had carried me across the sandy valley to the banks of Snake river. To my great disappointment, Merritt had already pushed ahead with his Cavalry, leaving the Infantry to follow as fast as possible in wagons. The last wagon of the Infantry command was almost ready to cross the stream, when my approach caused a delay. I found Capts. [Thomas Francis] Quinn, & [Samuel Peter] Ferris, and Lieuts. [Daniel] Robinson, [Edward Lyon] Bailey, [Carver] Howland and [Leonard Austin] Lovering, 4th Infantry, in a group about Colonel [Edwin V.] Sumner, 5th Cavy., the commanding officer of the Infantry column. The first named officers began to ply me with questions—where did *you* come from? How did *you* get here? and so on, when Sumner, with great consideration, interposed and said, "come, gentlemen, Lieut. Bourke is no doubt very hungry and we have no time to lose. Here, Bourke, pitch into this", at same time handing me a plate upon which were a couple of cold potatoes, one or two slices of bacon and some pieces of hard bread. A soldier also handed me a cup of cold coffee. My hunger was so great that I made a most satisfactory meal and was ready to continue my journey through the night. When our buggy drove up, Mr. Hergus left us, he having business to detain him on Snake river and intending to move out in the morning to overtake us.

Being very sleepy and almost exhausted, I didn't observe very clearly what sort of a country we were crossing. I remember one or two places where Merritt's wagons had to be let down ravines by hand.

The dust was fearful, ranging from 3 to six inches on a level and once stirred up by the hoofs of animals or wheels of wagons, remaining in the air for hours.

It was with much difficulty we could see the heads of the animals pulling our conveyance. The most remarkable thing to me was that not a single straggler had been left by Merritt and not more than three animals, that we could see, during the whole march down from Rawlins. We did learn at Lambert's of one soldier who came out alone to overtake his comrades, saying that he had been drinking in Rawlins and did not know when the hour of march came; he succeeded in pushing ahead and rejoining his company.

General Merritt had halted and bivouacked at Fortification creek, 90 miles South from Rawlins. I reached his Hd. Qrs. at 1.00 on the morning of the 4th and at once went to see him, but as he had fallen asleep, I contented myself with awakening Lieut. [Eben] Swift, his Adjutant and with trying to awaken Lieut. Schuyler.

I was very glad to learn that Schuyler was along, in fact I felt certain that somehow or another he would manage to be with the Expedition. I was told by Swift that Schuyler had joined them at Cheyenne, having abandoned the hunt upon which he started.

At Fortification creek, found Lieut. B. D. Price, 4th Infantry, all safe. Price had constructed a couple of very strong redoubts, connected by a trench, commanding every avenue of approach and within easy access of water.

He had with him Thornburgh's heavy wagons and his own Company, a skeleton organization of 27 men; also 7 men of the 9th Cavalry, (colored.) who reported to him that they had been sent with the wagons of Captain [Frederick Leighton] Dodge's Company and that Captain Dodge with the remainder of his men, 38 in number, hearing of the disaster which had befallen Thornburgh and the danger menacing Payne had determined to march from his camp on Bear River and try to break his way in to Payne's assistance.

This was on Oct. 1st, since which date, neither Price nor anybody else had received the slightest news from the front. Price was very glad to see me, but our conversation was extremely brief, sleep being the greatest desideratum with us all.

Captain Quinn, 4th Infantry, generously invited me to share his blankets and gave a drink of pretty good whiskey, as a "nightcap".

His tongue rattled away so much that, in spite of my drowsy protests, he broke in upon my slumbers with what he chose to call a history of his family—"They were one time, nice bi, a big family:—yes Sor, they wur Kings of R-r-rome! They used to be called the Tar-r-r-quin's, but they've dropped the tar *intirely*—some of it sticks to their Fathe yet, but they go by the name of Quinn, now. Their was a young bellow named Brutus; shure he stabbed wan of mee ansisthurs—an all for the sake of a foine ger-rul ould Tar-quinn had run off wid—shure, boi the same token we've got lots of testimony in the family to show that she gave him plenty of incourridgemint".

Hardly had I got Quinn's tongue quiet and fallen into a doze, when reveille sounded and camp was aroused to resume the march.

Fortification creek is the first water flowing into the Colorado of the West and the first one on this march containing trout.

(Snake river, 20 yds wide, 2 ft. deep, water cold, current moderately swift, ford good and of easy access.)

Oct. 4th Broke camp shortly after day-light, the men being allowed only time to prepare a cup of coffee. Moved briskly Southward, along a fair road with a few small hills, 23 @ 25 miles to Bear River. The sand and drift of yesterday, alternating with some trachytes, or what looked to me to be trachyte, on this part of march. Morning very bright and pleasant, excepting that dust was so thick that we had apprehensions of being suffocated by it. To the East, the tops and flanks of the mountains were dim with smoke. The fires, as seen late last night, were beautiful.

Bear River is about 25 miles South of Fortification Creek, has sweet, cool water, is 25 yards Wide, 2 ft deep and has a current of 4 miles an hour. Mountains on either side all day, soil very light and air heavy with dust and smoke. Hardly possible to see 20 ft. to the front.

The settlers in the Bear River valley had nearly all collected at the ranch of Mr. Ale, which, situated in the center of a broad, flat, open valley, and surrounded by good earthworks, could bid defiance to any attempt of the Utes to capture it. The ranchmen told us that hostile Indians could be seen from the bluffs, almost any moment but that no attack had yet been made, nor did they fear any. Here I made the acquaintance of Mr. Joe Rankin, the messenger who had carried the dispatch announcing Thornburgh's death and calling for help for Payne.

He rode from Milk River to Rawlins, 70 miles, in 36 hours, one of the most remarkable rides on record.

Halted at Bear River to rest animals and let the column close up. While there a party of ranchmen brought in a young boy in a wagon. The youngster had been attacked by sixteen Utes, but fortunately noticing their approach had time to jump into his wagon and pile up sacks of flour, bacon and corn as a barricade. He received one shot in the head, the bullet running around the skull, also two in the thigh.

Just after making the passage of Bear River, General Merritt called to me and asked me to take command of the Advance Guard, consisting of fourteen men, soldiers and civilians. In our front were several bad cañons, one reported to be 10 miles long, with vertical sides of considerable altitude. Advancing along this cañon, we could see that the worst reports had not exaggerated its terrors. The sides were too steep to give us any hope of promptly dislodging a determined force concealed near the summit; there were numerous lateral ravines from which our column or our pack-trains could be fired upon with perfect impunity, while close to the road we followed were clusters of large boulders and clumps of bushes to give shelter to any party, large or small, desirous of holding us in check. I had the lateral ravines examined as we approached them and until daylight entirely disappeared, kept flankers out, and a small party in advance. After dark, the arrangement was somewhat altered. Our little party was strung along in single file with intervals of 15 @ 20 yds., and communication preserved as well as could be with the head of the main column.

The civilians with me were extremely nervous and dissatisfied with the meagre force at my disposal, and finally told me it was rash and imprudent to venture farther without an increase of strength. I shared their fears and thought best to report their statements to General Merritt, who pushed Captain [Jacob Arnold] Augur to the front, with instructions to support us.

We soon reached the "divide", near which I am sure the Ute videttes were posted observing us. From a small grove of quaking asp[en], we heard a cayote howl, given in a very peculiar way, just as the Indians always signal to "fall back". We searched carefully without discovering any signs, either of animals or men except a crackling in the bushes, which might have been, and very probably was, made by an Indian creeping away. I afterwards heard that when Major [John Breckinridge] Babcock's Company approached this same spot, one of his men fell out to one side of the road to adjust his saddle; his carbine was attached to the pommel. Turning around preparatory to remounting, he was face to face with an Indian watching our forces. The latter noticing that his presence had been discovered, broke away through the bushes and escaped in the darkness.

After crossing the summit of this range, we descended through another cañon, so extraordinarily dusty that we congratulated ourselves upon being in the advance. What the officers and men moving with the main column, must have suffered, cannot be imagined.

We had the same high walls on either hand, the same facility for surprise, the same general resemblance to the topography of Arizona, which I had noticed previously on our journey.

The night became intensely cold. By bad luck, my overcoat had been left behind in the wagons and I had no means of sending for it. Schuyler came up to keep me company for which act I felt more grateful than I cared to say. Twenty one or two miles brought us to Williams' Fork, where orders overtook us to halt. Here we remained for an hour and five minutes before Augur's Company overtook us.

A kind-hearted soldier lent me an overcoat, he having two: Wrapped in this, I got over my chill and seated upon a log of wood was soon in a sweet doze. From this I was awakened by feeling something rub against my nose; it was a flask of excellent whiskey which Schuyler had brought along and to which I paid my respects without delay.

We had to cross Williams' Fork three times. In appearance and dimensions, it is very similar to Bear River, except that its valley is very narrow. Immediately, we entered another set of cañons, fully as bad as those from which we had just emerged. The gait became much more brisk from this time on, the idea being, if possible to reach the site of Thornburgh's fight before sun-rise. We had still at least 25 miles to march and Time was flying from us with eagle wings.

The first pale tinge of dawn was lighting the Eastern horizon, when we came to a little creek, by which were the ashes and iron-work of a burned wagon train and the bodies of (3) white men, one a half-brown, beardless boy, charred to a crisp, except in the face.

Here, pursuant to orders already given, we waited for General Merritt to come to the front in person. He did not delay a moment. The column closed up compactly, a few skirmishers were thrown to the front and everyone made ready for instant attack, for we were now only a very few miles from the crossing of Milk River and the Indians, if we were to have a fight at all, must soon commence and attack from the hills in our front, flank or rear.

My impression is that the Utes were not prepared for Merritt's prolonged march from Fortification Creek. Our lone halt at Bear

River must have given them the impression that we intended establishing camp there for the night. Under no other assumption, can I account for their failure to annoy us with attacks from such fine positions as we were compelled to face for forty miles. Rankin, the guide, said to General Merritt,—"It must be quite close now, General, we ought to see the fortifications from here."
"I think I see something in the haze, that looks like wagons", said one of the officers, close at hand.
We moved on a few yards farther and discerned in the gray dawn, the cluster of wagons and a low mound of earth thrown up as a trench.
"Who comes there?" rang out from a sentinel. "Friends"—Halt—Who comes there? Tell us who you are"—"General Merritt's command" and at same moment, Merritt's [sic] ordered his bugler to sound a few of the Cavalry calls; the bugler led off with "Officer's Call". All doubt as to who we were was removed from the minds of the beleaguered garrison and our approach was welcomed with tumultuous cheering, waving of hats and hands.

Officers and soldiers rushed out over the rampart and flung themselves upon Merritt and afterwards upon their rescuing comrades; their greeting was most affectionate, making it a pretty difficult matter for one to keep the tears back.

The first person with whom I shook hands was Captain [Joseph] Lawson, 3d Cavalry, who had escaped without a scratch. His horse had been killed under him, with five wounds. Next, Captain Payne, 5th Cavy. , wounded in thigh and shoulder and badly shaken up by being thrown on his head when his horse was shot down.
Then Lieut. Cherry, 5th Cavalry, who altho' one of the subalterns of the command, had shown himself inferior to nobody in the hour of peril; next Captain Dodge, 9th Cavalry, whose company of gallant colored soldiers had charged in to Payne's rescue on the morning of the 2d.
With Dodge, was my class-mate 1Lt. M. B. Hughes, whom I had not the pleasure of seeing since the day we left the Academy: Hughes was the same quiet, genial, good-natured and witty fellow he was in our Cadet days when his company was sought by every poor devil who had an attack of the "blues". Lieut. Wolf, 4th Infantry, a young officer who was out with Thornburgh, after the Cheyennes, was in the pit, unhurt. He reminded me that the morning one year

ago, (Oct. 5th, 1878.) we started out with poor Thornburgh on his memorable gallop in pursuit of Little Wolf's Band.

Doctor Grimes, the surgeon of the command had a bullet in his shoulder, but otherwise, was well and in good spirits. Lieut. Paddock, I did not at first see, but in a few moments when I had entered the intrenchment, I found the poor boy, in a sort of rat-hole, suffering from a severe flesh-wound in the hip, but preserving his spirits in a wonderful way.

One of the wounded men noticing me pass called out that he wished to speak and shake hands with me; I was surprised and pleased to find Schubert, of "E" Company, 3d Cavalry, who had been my orderly in 1869, during the time I served as subaltern in that Company. He had two severe flesh-wounds; one in the Right thigh, one in the left arm. The first question almost that he asked me was, did I remember the time we were last together in the sand-dunes near San Agostino Pass? (These are hills of comminerated selenite, which is soluble in the saliva and on this account, much wonder has been occasioned by the hills of "soluble sand". They are situated in South East New Mexico, not over 40 miles East of the site of old Fort Selden.)

To describe the appearance of Captain Payne's camp, is something far beyond my ability.

In some way or another, it recalled to my mind what I had read, during the war, of Forts "Hell" and "Damnation", in front of Petersburgh [sic], Va., where the mine explosion occurred.[4]

The wagon-train had been hastily packed, and ramparts made with sacks of flour, bacon and grain, the bodies of dead horses, feed boxes filled with clay and every other available barrier which could be utilized until the trenches were completed.

It resembled a series of coyote[5] holes, dovetailing into one another.

As a defensive point, it was utterly untenable for any length of time, being perfectly commanded by all the bluffs near by where the Utes had established pickets of sharp-shooters whose unerring

---

4. The "mine explosion" refers to the battle of the Crater, on July 30, 1864, in which several tons of gunpowder were exploded under Confederate defenses at Petersburg, blowing a massive hole and destroying a Confederate regiment and artillery battery. The Union assault force, which was supposed to take advantage of the confusion and smash through the Confederate lines, itself became confused, and was cut to pieces by the rapidly reorganized Confederates. McPherson, *Battle Cry of Freedom*, 758–60.

5. This is the first time Bourke spelled the word correctly.

rifles made it fool-hardy for any of the garrison to expose head or limbs above the trenches. Payne's Battalion had suffered a loss of 13 killed and over 40 wounded, not including in latter a considerable number of "scratches"; no one able to remain on the line troubled the Doctor for treatment, knowing that he being wounded could not do more than sufficient for the assistance of men seriously hurt. In this emergency, one of the enlisted men, Lebar, of "E" Company, 3d Cavalry, who had been a druggist in Philadelphia, rendered invaluable assistance under Dr. Grimes' supervision. [For a full list of killed and wounded see pp. 327–28.]

Every horse and mule, excepting four, had fallen a victim to the bullets of the enemy's sharpshooters; Captain Dodge's company had broken through the enemy's lines without trouble, but soon after getting into the trenches, the enemy opened upon them a severe fire, killing nearly every animal they had.

General Merritt's first care was to occupy the adjacent bluffs with strong detachments of cavalry, the posting of the pickets being entrusted to Lieut. Schuyler. Ample opportunity was given, with full sense of security for moving in and about the works and examining carefully all that was necessary to be seen or heard. The garrison was formed to have an abundance of the necessary components of the rations; an odd feature of their investment being that whenever a soldier wished a piece of bacon he would cut it out from the revetment of the rampart.

A corporal pointed out to me a man, a civilian, named Lowry, reported killed in first dispatches, who had a narrow escape from being buried alive.

The corporal said that he and two or three others had pulled Lowry out to bury him and had thrown the first earth upon him when the supposed dead man raised up and called out; "my God! What's the matter, boys!"

Whether this story be true or false, it was told me with an air of sincerity carrying great weight. Lowry when I saw him had a great deal of earth upon his face which certainly looked as if it had been thrown here, as the Corporal asserted. The wounds from which Lowry was suffering were both in head; one bullet going through from side to side between the ears and the intersection of the jaws and the other bullet remaining in brain near base. Dr. Grimes said that his death was a question of only a very short time, a very few hours.

It was gratifying to notice how cheerful the wounded men had become, and exhilaration due in some degree, I more than suspect to a stiff drink of fine whiskey which Lieut. Schuyler, playing the Good Samaritan, had administered to each one of them. There was no complaining, no grumbling; each officer and man spoke with warmth and good feeling of his comrades, living and dead, selecting no one for censure, none for special praise, unless it might be Captain Dodge and Lieut. Hughes, with their colored troops whom all lauded to the skies. Lieut. Cherry's name was likewise mentioned in a way of which he should feel proud, but in all candor it may be said that Lawson, Paddock, and the other officers were most warmly commended.

Outside of the intrenchment, 250 @ 300 carcasses of mules and horses were a ghastly and repulsive memento of the contest; the effluvia arising from them was sickening and had not Merritt arrived when he did, the putridity of decomposing flesh and entrails must have forced Payne to a desperate struggle for the possession of the heights overlooking his position, in which many more brave fellows would have been the sufferers. . . .

The ambulances and wagons, in the little fort held by Payne's troops, were pierced in scores of places by bullets and, several of them at least, so splashed with the blood of animals, which had been killed while tied to them; that they looked as if some awkward apprentice had commenced to paint them with red and had about completed a bungling job at the hour of our arrival.

The body of Major Thornburgh was brought in to the trenches very soon after our arrival; it had lain about 500 @ 600 yards outside, the locality in full view of the command, but the danger too great to justify an attempt at recovery. The poor fellow had been scalped and also cut over the forehead with a tomahawk or other sharp instrument; one bullet pierced his brain going through an eye; another also transfixing the brain, had knocked away a couple of teeth from upper jaw. A wound through the heart[,] one transversely across the body, and several others through the thighs and lower legs, made up a list of those inflicted. Under the warm rays of the sun, the skin of his face had turned completely black, that of the body and limbs remaining clear and white except that the extravasation of blood had caused great broad lines of brown to appear.

All clothing had been stolen from the corpse excepting the linen shirt, saturated with blood. The Indians knowing well who he was because they had visited his camp in friendly guise only two nights before the attack, had laid him out upon his back, one arm extended and pressed close to his side and the other, laid upon the breast, holding between finger and thumb the photograph of one of the Utes who had accepted his hospitality.
This photograph had been presented to Captain Payne who placed it in his trunk. The Utes captured one of our wagons and, ransacking the trunk in which was the photograph, found it and placed it as above described. The Indian, whose picture it was, was called Medicine Jack!

Copy, made by Eaton, of Omaha, Neb. of the original photograph.

Just outside of Payne's intrenchments were the charred remains of several wagons which had been loaded with supplies for the Ute Agency. In making their attack upon the troops, the savages had fired the grass and to save the whole command from being roasted alive, Payne had destroyed these wagons, just in time to post a zone of desolation between the enemy and his men, altho' in spite of all this, the fire kindled by the Utes made headway to our lines and ignited tarpaulins, grain sacks, bacon and saddles. In extinguishing the flames, a number of our men were badly wounded by hostile bullets.

Colonel Sumner with the Infantry Battalion and wagon-train reached camp between 8 and 9 o'clock, reported great trouble in descending the cañon between Williams' Fork and this place. Speaking for myself, I cannot claim to have seen much of the country marched over last night, as the mule I rode was so nicely gaited that I slept a great deal in the saddle. This morning, the packer to whom the mule belonged came to claim it. The man had become so exhausted by continuous marching and work that he had fallen down by the road-side completely exhausted. I gave him my seat in the wagon and used his fine mule to make yesterday's extremely long march. I was very grateful for having been permitted to use it, altho, as a matter of course, sorry to have returned it so soon.

Chapter 16

♦
♦
♦
♦

Camp Under Fire

The remains of Major Thornburgh and men [were] buried this morning, rather roughly, however, as at this time, the sharp rattle of musketry from our picket stations announced the approach of the enemy; positions were taken up without the loss of a moment, the long line of Infantry and dismounted cavalry commanding all the hills overlooking camp, producing a beautiful effect.

Being dismounted, I accompanied Col. Sumner's command, climbing up one of the steepest acclivities and posting myself with Ferris' and Quinn's men in a field of sage-brush. For a little while, the enemy was quite bold, coming up well within range and showing a disposition to make a determined fight. Fifteen of their warriors, mounted, had penetrated within less than 150 yards of where we were but as their presence was concealed by a couple of deep ravines they succeeded in escaping before we could fire a shot.

The Infantry rifles proved to be too powerful for the Utes who fell back like snow before the sun. Seeing that the game was ended I asked Colonel Sumner's permission to take a little nap under a protecting sage-bush and was speedily in the enjoyment of a delicious doze, from which I was awakened by hearing officers and men talking about a flag of truce the enemy had hoisted. There was no doubt about the matter at all: a large white flag, or signal was fluttering from the summit of a high hill to our Left, just within the extreme range of our heavy rifles.

Slowly it descended the declivity and our firing ceased until its purport could be detected. The Utes had ceased their firing, leaving little ambiguity as to the nature of the message coming to our lines. Captain [Robert Hugh] Montgomery, 5th Cavy., rode out to meet the flag-bearer, shook hands and returned with him to our lines where the stranger was presented to Colonel Compton, 5th Cavy., in command of our forces on the Left flank, who led the way to General Merritt's Hd. Qrs.

The messenger proved to be a white man, giving the name of Joseph W. Brady, of Mattoon, Illinois, and claiming to have been, for the past three months, an employee of the Uncompahgre Ute (Los Pinos) Agency. He said that he had been sent out by Ouray, head chief of the Uncompahgres, in company with ten warriors, all under Sapavanero, one of the prominent chiefs of the Los Pinos Agency; that Ouray and the Uncompahgres were anxious to keep the White River Utes from hostilities, but owing to the distance the messengers had to come across the mountains, they had not been able to avert the attack made upon Thornburgh's command, as they had only arrived in the hostile camp the night previous.

Sapavanero had sent in the flag of truce, to learn what terms would be granted to the hostiles. General Merritt replied that he would endeavor to respect the rights and property of all Indians remaining at peace, but that he had no message of any kind for those now on the war-path.

Brady spoke in such a straight-forward way that he dispelled all my prejudices and suspicions; he claimed to be an old friend of Lieut. T. E. Tine, Reg'l. Adjutant, 4th Infy.

The hostile Utes admitted having killed Agent Meeker, but made no statement in regard to the fate of the women, children and agency employees. Sapavanero told Brady that he had learned that the Indian loss in the Thornburgh fight was thirty-seven; Brady had seen no wounded among them and was the opinion that the above numbers represented their killed. The hostiles also claimed that in the war with the whites they would have (700) warriors, a claim which Brady did not credit. According to him, the White River Utes only have 250 warriors, at the most; in the attack upon

Thornburgh, they may possibly have had 300 @ 350 rifles since their complete success was so fully assured from the start that all their young boys and old men may have participated and perhaps a few of the Uintahs may have assisted.

Mr. Brady was given a cup of coffee and then departed. The Utes withdrew from our front, but left a white flag flying on the hill from which Brady had descended.

The stench from the dead bodies of horses and men was so overpowering that Genl. Merritt, to avoid sickness, moved the command back on Milk river, about a mile and a half to two miles, to a position inaccessible to any attack.

Brought with us to this camp all the wagons belonging to Payne's Command.

Our wounded bore the transfer well, with the exception of Mr. Lowry who died almost the moment he was taken out of the wagon in which he was carried.

Sky completely filled with smoke and dust. Word was sent around by Lieut. Swift, General Merritt's Adjutant, that a mail should leave camp immediately after dark: this information kept every one busy writing letters and telegrams.

To give a just idea of the excellent march made by General Merritt, I'll make a rough transcript of my own itinerary, premising that *my first* ride covers Merritt's *first two*; and that a better map will be pasted into this book further on, if one can be had.

Itinerary

Left Omaha, Neb. Oct 1st 1875 [sic],[1] 12.15 P.M.
Reached Rawlins, Wyo., 710 miles West Oct. 3d, 12.30 A.M.
Left Rawlins, Wyo., Oct 3d, 2 a.m.
Reached Lambert's Ranch 32 miles, 6.30 a.m Oct 3d.
    Breakf'd. and changed teams.
Reached Snake River, 62 miles, 6 P.M. Oct 3d
Reached Fortification Creek, 90 miles, Oct. 4, 1 A.M.
    Reported to General Merritt.
March 4th to
    Bear River, Colo., 23 miles.
    Williams Fork, Colorado, 25 miles.
    Milk River, Colorado, 22 miles.
    Reaching Milk River, Oct. 5th at 5 a.m.

1. Obviously 1879.

Rough Sketch of Merritt's March to the Relief of the Survivors of Thornburgh's Command.

Rawlins, Wyo., to Milk River, Col. 160 miles.

October 3–5, 1879.

U.P.R.R. Rawlins Sp'gs
Sp'gs
Lambert's Sulphur Sp'gs
Willows Sp'gs
Heavy Sand, 12 m.
Soldier's Well
Snake R. Perkins'
Fortification Ck. Price's Camp.
Bear R. Ale's Ranch
Cañon
Williams Fork
Cañon
Cañon Milk River

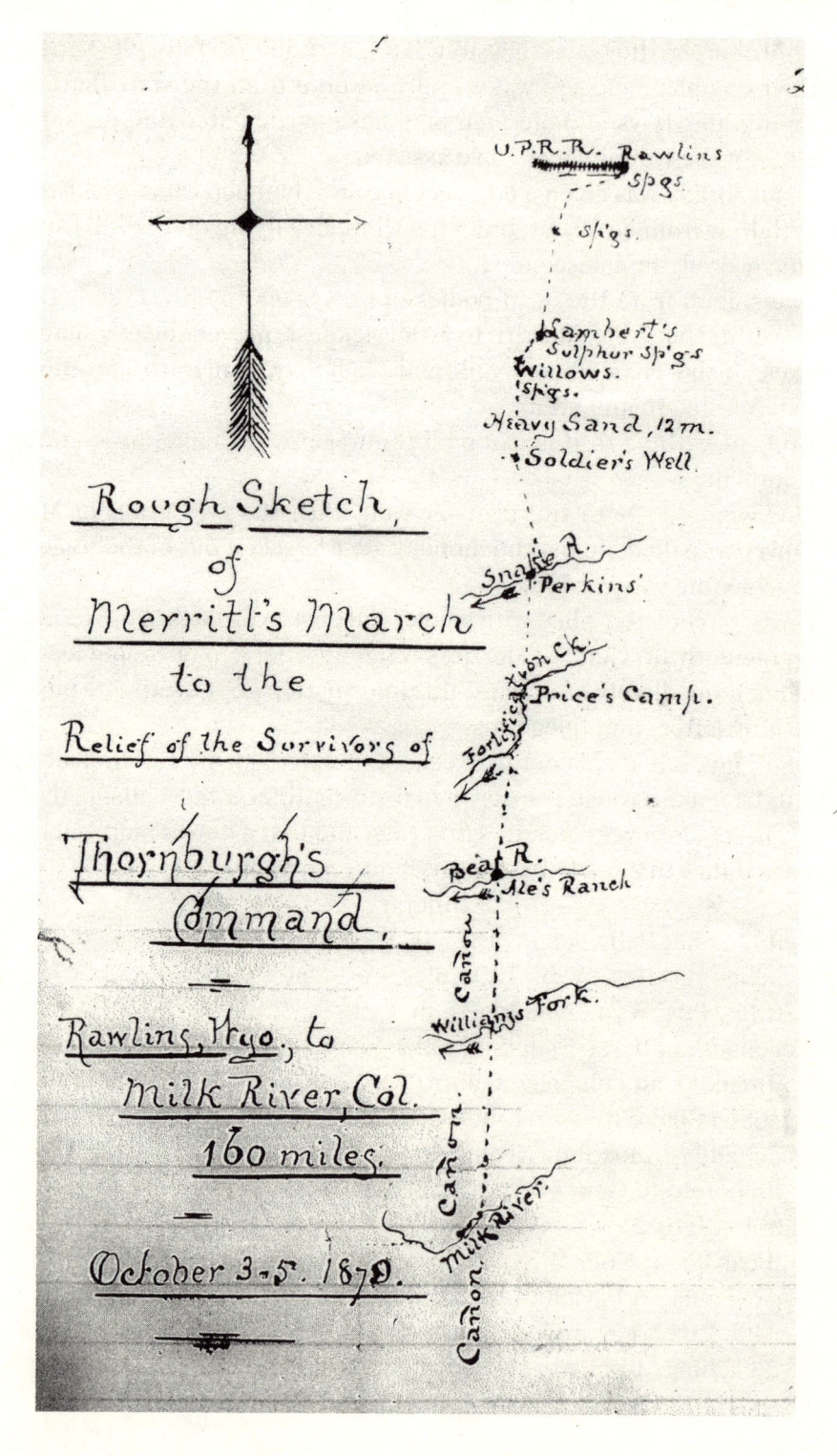

For this magnificent forced march, General Merritt and his command cannot be too highly commended. Merritt was ably assisted by his Adjutant Lieut. Swift., his Commissary and Quarter-master, Lt. [Hoel Smith] Bishop, his Ordnance Officer, Lieut. [William Bayard] Weir, and by Lieut. Schuyler who acted as his A.D.C. His battalion commanders, Compton and Sumner also should be remembered and while speaking of this wonderful forced march, it is an act of simple justice to allude to the faithfulness, intelligence and zeal of General Williams, Major Furey, Major Gilliss, Major Nash, Lt. G. B. Davis, Surgeon Summers and General Wilson, Chief Commissary, which made it possible.

Sent notes & telegraphic dispatches to General Williams, mother &c.

(Dispatch never reached General Williams was stolen from Rawlins Office.)

Captain Quinn, 4th Infantry, whose guest I am, gave an account before we fell asleep of certain experiences he had in the Army when a boy.

He was a drummer in the Florida war against Billy Bowlegs; band of Seminoles, (1855.)[2] During that year, to over-awe the surely [sic] savages, a line of block-houses had been built, but by some oversight not occupied, in the Everglades. The construction of these buildings had greatly exasperated the Indians, without leading to an open rupture. Captain [George Lucas] Hartsuff, (afterwards General Hartsuff and now dead.)[3] was sent into the Seminole country, with a petty detachment of 25 men, to examine into the condition of these block-houses; on the march, he fell in with a small band of Seminoles who surlily rejected civilities proferaed [sic] them. The block-houses were either burnt or dismantled. Disregarding these ominous indications of slumbering hostile feeling, Hartsuff continued on to the village of Billy Bowlegs where he hoped to be able to hold a conference.

Not a soul was to be seen! The fires on the hearths of the huts were smouldering to ashes and not even the bark of a dog disturbed the

---

2. This refers to the Third Seminole War, from 1855 to 1858, which was provoked by white expansion into Seminole country in southern Florida. The Seminoles, led by Billy Bowlegs, engaged in a series of hit-and-run attacks that resulted in considerable bloodshed. Bowlegs finally surrendered and agreed to accept relocation to the Indian Territory, where he died sometime in early 1864. Thrapp, *Encyclopedia of Frontier Biography*, 1:111–12.

3. Fort Hartsuff was named after General Hartsuff shortly after his death in 1874.

chilling silence. Hartsuff entered one of the largest huts, apprehensive that he might have to defend himself against attack.

This was not long delayed, from all sides, Billy Bowlegs' braves rushed to the assault, making the situation so hopeless that Hartsuff gave to his solders the command to save themselves.

Those who were still living, and able to obey the order, broke for a clump of forest close to the village. In this number was Hartsuff himself, badly wounded.

Two of the men, after long wandering through the swamps and hummocks of the everglades, found their way to a frontier post; the alarm was soon flying across the country and couriers in hot haste assembled every available detachment to march to the rescue. Quinn was with the column thus organized. The march made was extremely rapid and fatiguing but almost entirely barren of result, the Seminoles having killed, as was at first thought, the very last man of Hartsuff's command. The troops were about to relinquish the search, had made their very last march in fact, when, as tattoo was sounding, a shot broke upon the still night air, followed in a few moments by another equally distinct.

The commanding Officer of the Expedition sent out a reconnaisance at once and to the surprise and joy of everybody, Hartsuff himself was discovered nearly dead from loss of blood and exhaustion. He was on the point of giving up life in despair when the welcome sound of the bugles announced the proximity of friends and to attract attention he discharged his rifle with the result mentioned. Another episode was scarcely less thrilling. A party of young drummer boys had been formed to go outside the post to fish; Quinn had been invited to go, but having no pole or line tried to borrow one from a Corporal in the Company. The corporal in a very disobliging way refused the favor asked and, angry words following, Quinn became impudent and was hustled off to the Guard-House. The four companions who started out together *never returned*.

Next year when the Seminoles made peace, Billy Bowlegs was questioned concerning the fate of these drummer-boys; he replied that he didn't know anything of the matter personally but that some of his young warriors had told him about having captured the year before a party of four young soldiers whom they *burnt at the stake*!

Learned to-night, as we were turning in, that our losses to-day were only a couple of horses killed and one or two men wounded in Babcock's Co., and one or two men slightly wounded on our Right.

October 5th A Gentle rain fell last night, giving some hope that the terrible dust may be laid. On this march the dust has been a grievous infliction,—a perfect plague. Our clothing has been permeated by it and hands, lips, eyes, ears and noses peeled in an unsightly manner. The mules in the wagon and pack-trains have had to endure a martyrdom; many of the poor creatures have sore gums and lips from the sharp, cutting particles of sand blown in their faces.

Before I was out of bed, Hughes came to see me and have a long chat. He has been in the Rocky mountains and parts of South East Colorado, all summer in the presence of much of the noblest scenery on this continent. He told me a very funny story about our old friend and class-mate, "Deitsch" Stedman, now R.Q.M., 9th Cavalry. Stedman was on a scout with a cavalry command, under General Merritt, I believe, and had a contract surgeon for a tent-mate.

One evening, upon retiring to sleep, they placed their clothing on the ground between their beds. The camp was attacked at midnight and much confusion created. Companies sprang to their arms and fell into line, officers scurried to and fro, dressed, half-dressed and not dressed at all, bugles sounded, horses neighed and voices of men broke the stillness as they answered the roll-calls of companies. Stedman and the Doctor had been sleeping heavily and now, barely half-awake, darted out of bed and seized upon the same pair of pants. Stedman put his *right* leg into the *left* leg of the garment, the medical man thrusting his *left* leg into the *right*, and each intending to complete his toilet on the way, made a rush out of the tent to reach the line of troops. They struck against the tent-pole and for the first time the truth flashed upon them: "get out of my pants", yelled Stedman; "get out of mine", roared the Doctor and then they began pummelling each other and struggling about the tent pole. After tearing the pantaloons into shreds, they learned that the Indians had been driven back and the soldiers of the Command returned to their tents.

Captain Lawson detailed this morning in charge of a company to properly inter the dead of Major Thornburgh's Command. The bodies had been buried in the rifle pits, but were now exhumed and placed side by side in one grave.

Called upon Lieut. Paddock after breakfast and was delighted to find him bright and cheerful. He had received only one bullet in the fight, but four others had pierced his clothing.

A ranchman, from Bear River, rode into camp this morning and told Genl. Merritt that a large force of hostile Indians was on its way to attack him: every preparation was made to receive the visitors in becoming style, but they did not appear.

Devoted a couple of hours this morning to reading Longfellow's Poems, which by great good fortune, I had brought with me. The strong wind blew so much dust in my face that my literary labors were not especially agreeable, however valuable their results may prove to be in the future.

Our camp is extremely dusty; it is excellently situated for defense, every hill within rifle-shot being guarded by a strong picket, concealed behind breast-works of stone; our position is so compact that companies are huddled close upon the heels of horses and mules at the picket lines, an unpleasant feature under the most favorable circumstances, but doubly so with such quantities of dust.

We have an abundance of water from Milk River, a little grass, not much, for our horses, and enough wood, which the men returning from picket bring down on their shoulders, the march of companies bearing so many trees resemble the progress of Birnam Wood moving to Dunsinane.[4] Courier sent in to-night, with dispatches to Bear River to which point the mail is running once more.

Our pickets this evening discerned in the distance four mounted Utes moving from the direction of Bear River towards the White River Agency; doubtless, they were scouts who had been watching Bryant's and Vroom's column coming down from Rawlins to join us.

Oct. 7th. A cloudless sky and balmy temperature. Strong breeze blowing all last night filling our blankets and buffalo robes with dust. After breakfast, the Infantry battalion changed camp to a hill several hundreds of yards beyond former site, escaping much wind and consequent annoyance by do doing.

---

4. In *Macbeth*, the main character is told he "shall never vanquish'd be until great Birnam Wood to high Dunsinane Hill shall come against him." Macbeth takes refuge in the castle on Dunsinane, but Malcolm's troops cut down Birnam Wood and move forward, using the foliage to conceal their numbers and sealing Macbeth's doom.

At noon, General Merritt asked me to take a Sergeant and four mounted men and go out beyond our pickets a mile or two to examine and, if possible, determine the character of, a column of smoke or dust reported by the pickets as coming down the road. While the horses were being saddled and men putting on their arms, I accepted Major Babcock's invitation to take dinner with him. The meal was rather thin, but there was no fault to be found with the hospitality.

Lieut. Weir asked to be allowed to come along. General Merritt, greatly to my gratification, assented. Weir and I, being old friends at the Point, were good company for each other. We rode out beyond our lines and soon ran in upon a party of five men whose actions showed conclusively that they were Utes, watching the roads for hunting parties, couriers or stragglers. They retired behind a low range of hills and we took up positions in a thick chapparal on the crest of a "hog-back", overlooking a wide stretch of country. With the aid of our field-glasses, we could see that the column of dust was made by a long line of men, Indians or whites, advancing steadily but rapidly towards us. From having seen the five Indians just spoken of, I was for a while apprehensive that we were looking upon a column of Utes. This apprehension was dispelled the moment we detected the white canvas of wagon-covers descending a long hill. Then we knew it must be Vroom. The Utes meantime had quietly disappeared behind the knolls on our left, and our little party moved out to greet Vroom or whomsoever it might be.

Directly in advance of Vroom, we came upon four couriers who told us that they had been sent out from Georgetown, Col., with dispatches to Captain Dodge, 9th Cav., to take his company into the White River Agency, see what the trouble was and arrest the ill-disposed Indians.

The couriers had caught up with Vroom on Bear River, and learning from him of the condition of affairs, had wisely concluded to slacken their speed and move along with the troops as far as Milk River.

With Vroom were two companies of Cavalry; "L", (his own.) and "H", 5th. The subordinate officers were 2Lieut. Jordan, 3d Cavalry, and Lieuts. Parkhurst and Andrews, 5th Cavalry, Surgeon Calvin De Witt and eighty-six enlisted men.

Lieut. W. P. Hall, R.Q.M., 5th Cavalry, accompanied the command.

After exchanging salutations with our friends, the command resumed its march to Merritt's camp.

All day long a miserable, blustering wind has been blowing, carrying clouds of dust. Nobody is making any effort to keep clean, officers and men alike are dirty as a litter of pigs.

Another courier sent in to Bear River to-night.

Our camp-fires, placed in little gullies and ravines, fill a space of several hundreds of yards in Diameter and are the focus of attention to groups of soldiers, who, smoking their pipes, drinking coffee, or eating bacon and hard-tack, tell stories, or joke and laugh as the light of the flames or the darkness of night, alternately play over their bronzed and dusty faces.

(Mr. Wilbur Hergus, who had ridden out with me from Rawlins, but had remained at Smoke River, Perkins' Ranch, to transact business, came in with Vroom.) There was also a band of scouts, guides and trappers, none of any prominence, excepting "old Jim Baker", who has trapped and prospected in the region, between the Rio Grande and the Columbia for nearly 40 years and who was, with Kit Carson, one of Frémont's guides.

Dash, a beautiful setter dog, the property of Lieut. [Charles Adam Hoke] McCauley, 3d Cavalry, which followed Merritt's command down from Rawlins, is still in camp, almost worn out, but rapidly regaining strength under the kind care of officers and men. Dash has a hard time; the long, hurried march was enough for an ordinary canine experience, but to add to his cup of affliction, this poor animal has had his paws filled with cactus thorns and in an unfortunate interview with a porcupine his nose was filled with spines.

General Merritt sent a couple of scouts over toward the Agency to-night, with instructions to go cautiously as far as they could, examine carefully the lay of the country and the position, if any of the Indians and then return, if possible, by morning.

A wind storm howling through camp all night.

October 8th. A beautiful sky and warm breeze. Nothing needed but a heavy rain to soak the sun-dried and fire-parched earth and lay the clouds of dust and smoke filling the air.

Lieut. S. A. Cherry, Adjutant of Thornburgh's command gave me the official list of the killed and wounded which is here inserted.

Killed.

Major TT Thornburgh, 4th Infantry
1st Sergeant John Dolan, Co. "F", 5th Cavalry.
Wagoner Amos D. Miller, Co. "F", 5th "
Private John Burns,   "   "   "   "
   "   Saml. McKee,   "   "   "   "
   "   Michl. Lynch,   " "D" "   "
   "   Thos. Mooney   " "D" "   "
   "   Charles Wright   " "D" "   "
   "   Dominick Cuff   " "E" "   "
Wagon-master McKinstry.
Teamster McGuire.
Guide Lowry.

Wounded

Cap't. J. Scott Payne, 5th Cav. F[lesh]. W[ound]. Arm and side.
2Lieut. J.V.S. Paddock "   "   F.W. Thigh.
A.A. Surgeon Robt. D. Grimes, F.W. Shoulder.
Serg't. John Merrill, Co. F, 5th Cavy.
Trumpeter Fredk. Sutcliffe, "   "
   "   John McDonald, "   "
Private William Esser   "   "
   "   James T. Gibbs   "   "
   "   John Harney   "   "
Private Emil Kussman,   Co. "F" 5th Cav.
   "   Eugene Patterson   "   "   "   "
   "   Eugene Schickerdonz,   "   "   "   "
   "   Gottlieb Stieger   "   "   "   "
   "   Fredk. Bernhardt   " "D" "   "
   "   Nicholas W. Herney   " "D" "   "
   "   Thomas Lynch   "   "   "   "
   "   Ernest Muller   "   "   "   "
Serg't. Allen Lupton   " "E" 3d "
   "   James Montgomery   "   "   "   "
Corporal Charles Eichwurzel   "   "   "   "
   "   Frank Hunter   "   "   "   "
Farrier William Schubert   "   "   "   "
Private James Budka   "   "   "   "
   "   John Crowley   "   "   "   "
   "   William Clark   "   "   "   "

"	Orlando Duren	"	"	"	"
"	John Donovan	"	"	"	"
"	Thomas Ferguson	"	"	"	"
"	Marcus Hansen	"	"	"	"
"	Edwin Lavelle	"	"	"	"
"	Thomas Lewis	"	"	"	"
"	William Mitchell	Co. "E" 3d Cavalry			
"	John Mahoney	"	"	"	"
"	Thomas McNamara	"	"	"	"
"	Joseph Patterson	"	"	"	"

Teamster Nelson
    "   Cain
Train Blacksmith Rodney.
Also, a civilian freighter, name unknown.
I read a great deal of Longfellow's Poems to-day and also some little of LeSagre's *Bachiller de Salamanca* and *El Diablo Conjuelo*.[5]
Taylor, and his two companions, (the scouts whom Merritt sent out last night.) returned to-day, reporting that when near the Agency they discovered the Ute pickets and were fired upon by them.
Lieuts. Weir and Cherry, with a small party of soldiers, went out to-day to make a rough sketch of the scene of action. Lieut. Weir's work was especially good.
A strong South breeze carried to our nostrils the sickening effluvia from the carcasses of dead horses.
General Merritt, in conversation with Schuyler and myself to-day, said that while he should be glad to have us remain with the Command, he thought we could do more service to everybody by rejoining General Crook who might be in need of our assistance and to whom we could give invaluable information upon the subject of the topography of the country and the question of supplies. General Merritt concurred fully in our proposition to return to the Rail Road and rejoin Genl. Crook.

    Merritt was not sanguine of being able to do much under present circumstances; he will be hampered for supplies, and will need Indian scouts and a few pieces of artillery.

---

    5. Bourke means Alain-René Lesage, who published French editions of these works by Spanish authors. *Bachiller de Salamanca, o Aventuras de don Querubin de la Ronda* and *El Diablo Conjuelo* were Cervantes-style satires, the former by Gil Blas de Santillane, and the latter by Luis Velez de Guevara.

There are now several sutler's wagons with the command, doing a lively business and surrounded at all hours by groups of officers, soldiers and civilians.
It has at length been decided to send the body of poor Thornburgh to the Railroad, to do this a very long, deep and wide box has been made out of saddle chests, in which the remains can be buried.

A very cold wind set in towards night followed by a severe storm of rain and snow.

Oct. 9th Morning cold and gloomy. Two inches of snow on ground. Humme returned from Bear River, with mail for the Command. I was much disappointed at not receiving any letters or papers. Humme reported that he and his comrades had run in upon a party of eleven Utes, who were making coffee, some distance off the main road near Bear River. It is said that marauding bands of Utes have run off nearly all the horses from the ranches on Bear and Snake rivers. Major Bryant arrived with his command of four companies of the 14th Infantry, 165 rifles, guarding a supply train. He brought with him the following officers.

"E" Co. Capt. Trotter, 2Lt. [Frank French] Eastman.
"K" Co. "   Carpenter, 2Lt. Austin
"H" Co. "   [Samuel] McConihe, 1Lt. [Julius Edward] Quentin, 2Lt. Mulhall.
"I" Co. 1Lt. Taylor, 2Lt. Yeatman and Lieut. Leighton.

Major Bryant gave us an item of news that the major portion of the 7th Infantry from the Department of Dakota, had arrived at Rawlins and that Colonel Guy V. Henry would also have at same point a battalion of the 3d Cavalry.

Lieut. Yeatman, of Bryant's Battalion, has just been married to the sister of Lt. Mulhall. The ceremony took place immediately upon receipt of the telegram ordering the Battalion into the field and a few moments after, Yeatman bade farewell to his bride and started for Rawlins and Milk River.

Lunched with General Merritt who informed me that he intended issuing orders for the wounded to return to the Rail Road under escort of the dismounted Cavalry, Captain Dodge, 9th Cavy., in command. General Merritt, with main column would advance upon White River, but apprehended no trouble in so doing the strength of his Infantry being much too great for the Indians to make a successful resistance.

Major Thornburgh's body was exhumed and brought into camp this afternoon; also an estray pony picked up by a detachment of our packers.

Lieut. Swift gave me an exact Roster of the officers of General Merritt's column.

Oct. 10th Slept very cold last night. Captain Quinn, being on picket, had to take half the bedding, making sleep uncomfortable for each of us. Morning dawned bright and cold. Merritt promptly moved out in the direction of White River, while Dodge, (with whose command Schuyler and I were to travel,) commenced his march toward Rawlins. With our detachment were Cap't. Payne, (wounded.) Cap't. Lawson, Dr. Grimes, (wounded.) Lieut. Paddock (wounded.) Lieuts. Hughes, Cherry and Wolf. General Merritt gave Schuyler and myself horses which were too lame for further field service, but good enough for steady marching.

Mr. Wilbur Hergus equipped us with a box of canned stuff, bread, beer and other luxuries & had our baggage carried in one of his wagons, in which also he had seats reserved for our use in case of need. Bidding adieu to my kind-hearted mess-mates, Captain Quinn and Lieut. Bailey and Howland, I started out on the return march to Rawlins. Captain Dodge wishes, if possible, to get as far as Williams' Fork to-night. The distance is not great, not over 30 miles, but with wounded men there are so many delays in moving out, & so many detentions on the road and we have such a number of extra wagons (all those of Thornburgh's command.) to haul back, that we do not expect, unless we have good luck, to make camp before dark.

Seven miles out we passed the burnt wagons which had contained commissary stores for the White River Agency.

Scenery this morning, even where marred by the forest fires kindled by the savages, has been decidedly beautiful: the dawn is disappearing rapidly, except upon the highest peaks and our march has been pleasant from the absence of dust.

Ten miles out, our advance saw Indians and skirmishers were thrown out to oppose them. The supposed Indians advanced to meet us and turned out to be a detachment of soldiers and guides sent ahead from Colonel Guy V. Henry's command to inform General Merritt that Henry would camp to-night at Bear River with four companies of the 3d Cavalry and immediately behind him, Lieut.-Colonel

Camp Under Fire 331

[Charles Champion] Gilbert, 7th Infantry, with seven companies of his Regiment.

We reached Williams' Fork after sun-down and went into camp, taking every precaution against surprise, by picketing all the hills overlooking our position. Our wounded made the journey without injury. Close to this camp, alongside of road, a find coal measure crops out in the sand-stone.

Williams' Fork is a beautiful trout stream 60 ft. wide, one foot deep, flowing over pebbly bottom.

The driver of Mr. Hergus' wagon came to tell me that he would prepare supper. Our mess was composed of Lt. Schuyler, self, the driver and a wounded civilian, a nice young fellow, named Davis. The driver wasn't prepossessing in appearance. In truth, like the rest of our command he was remarkably dirty and dusty; but it was charming to see how neat and tidy he could be with favorable opportunity.

Our frying-pan was filled with water and then with a small piece of rosin soap, he began washing his dusty head and neck! Schuyler suddenly remembered a previous engagement he had with Lieut. Paddock's mess and I betook myself to Lawson's tent where I was cordially invited to take such a supper as they had there. When I returned to where the driver was, I unblushingly told him that I never ate meat for supper and wanted nothing but a cup of tea and a cracker. I tried to philosophize over the matter and think that a frying-pan was an excellent wash-basin, but I couldn't succeed in my endeavors, the mere thought of the confounded business made me suffer from nausea.

Late at night, couriers reached our camp from General Merritt who had advanced as far as the White River bottom where he camped, on account of darkness. No resistance had been made to his progress and no Indian signs had been seen, made since the snow-fall. The body of a Jew freighter Goldstein, had been found, alongside of the burnt remains of his wagon-train. In Coal Cañon, in the shaft of the mine, (worked for the Agency.) was found the body of an employee, shot through the head. Before death released him from pain, he had taken off his shirt and made a pillow of it upon which to rest his head. A Henry rifle lay by his side.

Oct. 11th Very early in the morning, our command moved out, Cap't. Dodge asked Lieut. Schuyler and self to keep with the advance-guard where we might prove of benefit in case of an attack.

The morning air was decidedly keen particularly after entering cañon. At another time, we might have paused to admire the beautiful views visible from every point: on this march, the picturesque rocks might conceal a squad of enemy's sharp-shooters, hence we were anxious to get into a country which if not so beautiful would be less dangerous for the command.

Three miles out, we overtook the two couriers who had passed through our camp with dispatches from Merritt last night. They were greatly frightened and shook their heads dubiously when questioned. Knowing that the great percentage of the so-called "guides", "scouts" and "frontiersmen" encountered out here are deplorable cowards, we didn't attach too much importance to their warning of danger. They said they had come upon a fresh pony track, made last night in the cañon and a number of older tracks farther up the road.

As our duty required, we notified Captain Dodge and then pushed on with our party to make an examination, the timid guides being very reluctant to accompany us. Sure enough, there was a fresh track and a pony track too, not three hours old. We followed it, looking carefully along the road for the others reported, without finding them. The one track seen wandered in a curious kind of a way from side to side of the road. I distrusted my abilities as a trailer, but could not help forming the conclusion that the animal whose tracks we were inspecting was an estray. My idea had scarcely been communicated to those about me, when an animal of some kind was discovered looking attentively at us from a little copse of willows a few hundred feet above us.

Our brave pair of scouts called out to be careful, we must be near an ambuscade! and darted behind a big rock. One of our party, a Colored miner from Georgetown, (by the way one of the four who had come down from Bear River with Vroom's Command and who had dispatches for Dodge to proceed to the White River Agency.) proceeded up the slope and found a poor Government pack-mule, which had strayed away from Merritt's column and had nearly scratched and torn itself to pieces in its efforts to disembarrass itself of its pack and baggage.

This occurrence raised a hearty laugh at the expense of the braggart guides, whose worthlessness and cowardice were so completely exposed.

Yet while we have to meet a multitude of pretentious scoundrels who in the moment of danger unblushingly play the craven, the exceptions are notable for modest courage and true grit. For example we have with us Gordon, known as "Black Hills" Gordon, who is as full of resolution and intrepidity as any man I have ever encountered. He brought the first dispatches out from Payne to Dodge and would have gone through to Rawlins with Rankin, had he not turned aside to ascertain the fate of his young brother who was the young boy of whose charred remains mention is made.

[on p. 310]

We hurried back word to Captain Dodge that the *Indian attack!* had been deferred and that the column might resume its march. Four miles further on, we discovered the skirmishers of Henry's advance guard and in a few moments rode up to where Henry himself was with the officers of his Battalion ("A", ["]B", ["]D" and "H", 3d Cavalry, 151 carbines.) A cordial greeting was extended us and countless questions asked. With Col. Henry we had the pleasure of meeting Mr. John F. Finerty, of the *Chicago Times*, an old campaign friend and one of the most gallant fellows on earth and the following officers, Capts. Drew, [Henry Walton] Wessells, Lts. [Francis Hunter] Hardie, Dr. [Samuel Miller] Horton, Chase, Hunter and [James Ormond] Mackey, all of 3d Cavy. Mackey is a recent graduate (1879.) but all the others have had considerable experience in Indian warfare. It is a source of pleasure to me to observe the alacrity with which the young officers, graduated this year, have hurried to the front, several of them as Volunteers. Merritt's column has six with it, and each one has done his duty well.

Colonel Henry drew up his Battalion in two lines, one on each side of road, facing inward and when the ambulance containing Thornburgh's remains moved by, gave the command "Advance Carbines", as a mark of respect to his late comrade.

Behind Colonel Henry's Battalion, we came upon General Gilbert's companies of the 7th Infantry and the officers named below: Captains [Daniel Alfred] Freeman, [Constant] Williams, [Thaddeus Sandford] Kirtland and [Walter] Clifford and Lts. [William Isaac] Reed, [Levi Frank] Burnett, [William] Quintin [sic], [Joshua West] Jacobs (R.Q.M.) Jackson (A.H.) [Charles Austin] Booth, [George Shaeffer] Young, [Lewis Douglas] Green[e], [Daniel Alfred] Frederick and [Daniel] Robinson, many of whom we had known in the Sioux campaign on the Yellowstone, in 1876.

General Gilbert asked me to issue an order in General Crook's name authorizing the transfer of a few of his weak mules with an equal number from Dodge's train, not in so bad a condition. I consented to do this as he requested, provided the comfort of the wounded should in no manner be interfered with. The application later assumed the proportions of a general exchange, taking our best mules and giving in return animals which by careless management had become almost disabled. I declined lending any countenance to such an arrangement for the reason that it was of greatest importance to have our sick and wounded taken to the R.R., than to have reinforcements reach Merritt, and moreover, a good wagon-master who looks carefully after his train is entitled to encouragement and should not, without urgent course, be deprived of good animals to cover up the derelictions of inattentive officials.

The couriers from Merritt were ordered to hurry on to Bear River. Henry, however, took their dispatches, which he forwarded by a detachment from his own Company.

Bear River was reached in good season, camp being 800 @ 1000 yds. from Ale's Ranch, the Post Office, which had been surrounded by a deep trench and was garrisoned by all the settlers, or nearly all in the valley, excepting the women and children, who had been sent to Rawlins for safety. We visited the ranch to see about mail. This was contained in a grain sack, kept in a room where lay the young man wounded so badly by the Indians [see p. 308] In another room, ten or a dozen ranchmen and herders were about to partake of the evening meal, with rough but genuine and unaffected hospitality, they insisted upon our joining them at table. The table-ware was rude and the food more substantial than delicate. Great chunks of boiled and fried beef, piles of bread, tins filled with molasses and sugar and large cups of coffee or tea standing by each plate made up the bill of fare. Every one was hungry and every one did full justice to the cook's efforts. The topic of conversation was the *immense* amount of mail coming to the ranch, for the troops.

"I swar", remarked a weather-tanned old fellow, evidently the mail carrier, ["]thar must a bin sixty poun' on the mule the last trip".
"I should say", interrupted a listener who appeared to be a critic.
"I should say, thar must a bin nigh on ter seventy". Ordinarily, the

mail matter coming down here, was not more than enough to fill a saddle-pocket, but in the present state of affairs, an extra mule was required to carry it.

The settlers assembled at Ale's had taken from a ranchman named Peak, living a couple of miles down the river, nearly (12.000) rounds of metallic cartridges which he had been openly selling to the Indians, letting them have as many as they wanted the very morning they attacked Thornburgh.

According to what Mr. McCagne and Mr. Gordon told me, this subject of selling ammunition to the Indians is a crying evil, which should be extirpated. They said that to the best of their knowledge, the Utes must have purchased in the neighborhood of a quarter of a million metallic cartridges during the present year. Comment is superfluous.

Lieut. Schuyler and I determined to leave Dodge at this point and return to Rawlins with all speed possible, to rejoin General Crook by whom we would certainly be needed. Our companions said Good Bye, we jumped into the farm-wagon Mr. Hergus had sent back, the driver gave his mule a deep cut of the lash and we were on the road. The moon was nearly dead but the bright light of the stars disclosed the trail very clearly. Fearing to meet hostile Indians at every step, we shuddered at forms which turned out to be bushes and savagely challenged horsemen who instead of replying with a rifle-shot or a sentence in Ute, talked as good English as we and halloed, "U.S. Mail", or gave their names and, advancing to our wagon, talked over the situation in the front. From Bear River to Perkins Ranch, on Snake river, is 50 miles—a distance we had to accomplish, and did accomplish, before sun-rise. Towards dawn, our weary eye-lids drooped and nothing but the danger of losing our scalps or of falling out of the wagon and getting run over, kept us from dropping into a deep slumber. On the march down, we did sleep in our saddles, but *then* we had the whole column to look after us; now it was necessary to keep awake to look after ourselves.

At Fortification creek, near Price's old Camp, we halted for half an hour to give our mules a feed. At break of day, we reached Perkins ranch, ordered a change of mules and asked for breakfast, during the preparation of which we threw ourselves on the board floor, rolled up in buffalo robes and journeyed to the land of Nod. Mrs. Perkins must be a very kind-hearted soul, because when breakfast was ready, she came to call us, but seeing how utterly worn out we were, ordered it served up to the hired men and another one to be ready for us in two hours. So, through her goodness, we enjoyed a most refreshing nap of nearly 3 hours duration, after which we ate heartily of a very good breakfast. At Perkins, we learned of a great accumulation of mail, principally newspapers, for Merritt's command; there was a barrel full of it.

October 12th Left Perkins' with the same farm-wagon, but a different team, which we had orders to exchange, if desired, upon meeting Perkins' train on the road. This we did, 8 miles out and obtained four fresh mules, putting two in harness and leading the others at tail-gate of our conveyance.

Looking back, saw a huge volume of smoke rising in our rear. A party of teamsters, whom we came upon at this moment, were very much excited by this smoke, saying that the Utes must have swept down upon Perkins' ranch and destroyed it. We convinced them of the groundlessness of their apprehensions, by saying that we thought it must be the smoke from a fire we had noticed in the timber in a little cañon a couple of miles this side of Perkins' and which fire must have been fanned by the wind into a large conflagration. (This proved to be a correct surmise.)

Fifteen miles out, passed Government train laden with forage for Merritt's troops. Twenty miles out, halted to water stock.

Our driver told me that the Navajo Indians from New Mexico travel about a great deal in the Ute country, selling their fine blankets, which could be purchased at any time at Perkins' Ranch. They ought to make good scouts if we should employ them for that purpose.

Near muddy cabin, on Left side of road, saw a large coal seam, 3 ft. Wide. The driver remarked that the whole country was full of them, the best being on Snake River, a few miles above Perkins' Ranch, where the seam averages eight feet in thickness. At Soldiers' Well, turned one team loose and hitched up the other.

Had a high wind from South all afternoon, blowing a thick dust along with us.

At Willows, rested a few moments took a cup of tea and resumed ride.

Schuyler and myself, tired out beyond description, now laid down to rest in the bottom of the wagon, the driver promising that we should lose no time in reaching Rawlins.

As we had crossed over the worst of the road, the heavy sand to the South of this point, we were greatly relieved, by the announcement that our mules were still "fresh as daisies", and if the lively clatter of hoofs was any corroboration, the driver's judgment was correct.

Fifteen miles rapid traveling brought us to a camp of soldiers by the road-side; the sentinel said it was one company, 3d Cavalry, and a train of supplies, under Colonel A. W. Evans. Everybody, but the Colonel was sound asleep, so we made no delay.

At 2.55 a.m., October 13th, we rattled up in front of the Rail Road Hotel, Rawlins, and soon were shaking hands with General [Albert Gallatin?] Brackett, Colonel Gilliss, Mr. Moore and other friends. Mr. Stilson, of the *New York Herald*, started to interview us, during which, a tramp (as I afterwards learned,) stole all my personal baggage from the platform in front of the Hotel. This loss was most serious, especially as involving the notes of our trip with General Merritt. To anticipate a little, I will say that everything was recovered, the thief being a drunken tramp who had put on my over-coat, rolled himself up in my buffalo robe and taken my hand-satchel for a pillow.

Pending this recovery, I determined to start at once for Omaha, to refit.

The train came along at five minutes of four in the morning and reached Omaha, on time, the next day, October 14th at 3.30 P.M. On the way down, I met Captain [George Mason] Downey, 21st Infantry, with whom I spoke at length of numerous old acquaintances, and Brigadier General S.V. Benét, Ordnance Corps, (Chief of Ordnance, U.S. Army), and wife, who listened with intense interest to the story of the march to relieve the survivors of the Thornburgh Expedition.

Received, while on train, telegram from General Brackett and Mr. Thomas Moore that my baggage had been recovered.

At Cheyenne, met Mrs. Merritt and Mrs. Compton, Lt. Davis, 5th Cavalry, and Captain Johnson (3d Cavy.) and [Albert Emmett] Woodson and Hamilton, 5th Cavalry. Lieut C. A. H. McCauley on the Westward bound train at Valley, Mr. Donnelly, of the *Omaha Herald* interviewed me on the train, getting information for his journal of the condition and plans of Merritt's Command. Lieut. Schuyler left our train at Cheyenne.

October 14th Arrived in Omaha and drove to Dep't. Hd. Qrs., at the Fort.

Chapter 17

♦
♦
♦
♦

From Field to Staff

In this chapter, we see the beginning of a turn in Bourke's life. Up until now, he has been very circumspect in his personal relations. If there were any women in his life, he does not mention them. The entry for New Year's Day 1880, however, states he spent the day with friends, including the Horbach family, who had a daughter, Mary, known to her friends as Mollie. Then, under February 21, he pastes a newspaper clipping that she had been involved in a carriage accident, but, while shaken, apparently was unhurt. These innocuous entries are the diary's first extant references to the woman he eventually would marry.[1]

October 17th. Ordered back to Rawlins and started on train, but at Grand Island, just as I was about turning in to bed, (our train being 3½ hours late at that point.) received a telegram from Lt. Schuyler to stop over at some point on road to meet General Crook and himself. For this reason, remained at Cheyenne (October 18th.) returning to Omaha October 19th.

The importance of the Ute war is my justification for occupying so much space in my note-books with an acc't of it, even after my personal connection had ceased.

---

1. Porter, *Paper Medicine Man*, 146.

The Interior Department sent out Genl. Charles Adams who, with the assistance of Ouray, head-chief of the Uncompahgres, penetrated to the camp of the hostiles, where he found Mrs. Meeker, Miss Meeker, and Mrs. Price and two children, whom he rescued and returned to Denver, Col.

Meantime, troops and supplies had been accumulating under Generals [John Porter] Hatch and McKenzie at Fort Garland, Col.,[2] but no forward movement allowed by their command or that of Genl. Merritt, which encamped at White River Agency, a most difficult place to supply in winter, on account of the almost absolute lack of transportation.

Young Man Afraid of his Horses, offered General Crook the assistance of one hundred Sioux warriors to act as scouts against the Utes: an offer declined because of the cessation of active movement. October 20th. Lieut. W. B. Weir, Ordnance Corps, killed by Ute Indians, while hunting. Knowing Lieut. Weir as well as I did, in former days when we were cadets together (he being one class below me.) I could in perfect justice and truth speak most eulogistically of his extreme gentleness of nature, almost feminine in its type; of his devotion to study and high order of intelligence, of the unstained purity of his heart which has preserved in all his contact with the world a modesty and rectitude rarely found among men; of the great affection entertained for him by his comrades and those under him, but feeling that a humble-jumble of a collection, such as is my note-book, is no place for panegyric, I will make no elaborate mention of my dead friend's virtues beyond what is contained in the enclosed slip, hurriedly penned for the *Omaha (Daily) Herald*, of October 24th 1879.

THE SLAIN WEIR.
Another Massacred Warrior at White River
—The Ute Ambuscade.
Personal History of the Deceased.

The information received in Omaha to the hour of going to press in regard to Lieutenant W. B. Weir's sad death at White River Agency is to the following effect: General Mer-

---

2. Fort Garland was established in 1858 near the mouth of Sangre de Cristo Pass, to replace the earlier post of Fort Massachusetts, and protect settlers in the San Luis Valley from Ute and Jicarilla Apache depredations. The post was located near a major Indian trail leading from the Rio Grande to the Arkansas River valleys. Fort Garland was abandoned in 1883, and is now a state historical monument. Frazer, *Forts of the West*, 36–37.

ritt, learning of the discovery of fresh pony tracks on the summit of the ridge, near the old White River Agency, sent a detachment of cavalry under Lieut W. P. Hall, Fifth Cavalry, to make an examination and report. With this detachment Lieutenant Weir sought and obtained permission to go as a volunteer. Hall's command was ambuscaded by the Utes and forced to fall back, having narrowly escaped destruction. Lieutenant Weir and Mr. Humme (a scout) had a few moments previous to the attack left Hall's command for the purpose of shooting some antelope, being at a short distance from the column. In doing this no one imagined any danger would be incurred, as the rosy dispatches daily given to the world from Washington have created the impression that the hostile Utes were only waiting an opportunity to surrender and be taken back to their reservation. Hall's men had heard firing in the direction of Weir's position, but supposed it was that of the hunters exclusively. When pressed by the Utes, Hall had no power to do anything but return to camp. Gen. Merritt sent out five companies of the 5th cavalry, under Col. [Charles Elmer] Compton, to make a search for Weir and bring him back dead or alive. His body was found, shot through the brain. Humme's remains were not discovered and it is probable that the Utes captured him alive. Lieut. Weirs remains will be at once sent to Rawlins for shipment to his friends.

 The reputation in the army of this young officer was most brilliant. He was regarded as one of the most promising in the ordnance corps—a fact attested by his assignment to the care of the supply depot at Cheyenne, one of the most important in the country. Not alone in intellectual powers, but in moral worth and sterling integrity, he stood preeminent. His friends will deplore in his death the loss to the service of one of the most talented and gentlemanly of all whose names have ever appeared on the official record. Lieut. Weir's parents are still living. His father, Prof. Weir, a distinguished artist, was formerly for many years in charge of the department of drawing at the Military Academy, from which position he was honorably retired on account of failing health. He is at present residing in the city of New York. Lately a sister of

Lieut. Weir, an amiable, beautiful and accomplished young lady, has been visiting him at Cheyenne Depot. To her, as to all his family and friends, the dread tiding of his premature fate will come with the crushing effect of the thunderbolt. No earthly consolation can mitigate the bitterness of this sorrow. The sympathy of friends will not be wanting, nor the solace of knowing that this noble son and brother has died on the field of duty, but these, however gratifying they may prove cannot reanimate the lifeless clay, which but little more than a week ago was the casket in which was enshrined one of the noblest and purest souls ever created.

October 22nd 1879. The remains of Major T. T. Thornburgh were consigned to the grave to-day, with appropriate military and Masonic ceremonies. A Battalion of the 9th Infantry, Colonel [William Thomas] Gentry, Commanding, acted as escort, while the Masonic body turned out in strong force. General Crook and staff and nearly all the prominent citizens of Omaha swelled the procession, the largest ever seen in Omaha. The services at the grave were too long; their prolixity, in the bitter north wind blowing all that day, robbing them of much of their impressiveness: the military participation in these was limited to the usual volley firing and dirge.
The previous night, the remains had laid in state in Masonic Hall, Omaha, which presented a beautiful and solemn sight, robed in the drapery of mourning.
Octo. 31st 1879. Major-General Joseph Hooker, U.S.A., (retired,) died at Garden City, L[ong]. I[sland]., During the late war, for a long time a salient figure in the history of our country, of late, he had fallen into obscurity.
As one of the commanders of the Army of the Potomac in its most troublous days, he will always be remembered by the veterans of the civil conflict.
November 1st. Senator Zach Chandler, found dead in his bed at Grand Pacific Hotel, Chicago. The night before, he had delivered an excellent political speech, replete with the soundest Republican doctrine. His death will prove a great loss to his party and to the country. The remains of Lieutenant Weir arrived in Omaha escorted by his brother, Charles G. Weir, Esq. of New York. (They were kept in Omaha over night under military guard.)

General U. S. Grant reached Omaha in a special train over the Union Pacific R.R.

At the dépôt, the distinguished soldier and citizen was received with the whistling of locomotives, ringing of bells, thunder of guns, and the shouts of assembled thousands. To these demonstrations of good-will, Grant modesty [sic] bowed his acknowledgments. General Crook escorted Mrs. Grant from the cars to the carriage in which Mrs. Crook awaited her, the two ladies driving to Fort Omaha, where General and Mrs. Grant were to remain over Sunday.

General Grant himself, escorted by a large procession composed of regular and militia companies, fire and benevolent associations, and industrial organizations, General Crook's staff, and everybody in this part of Nebraska who could beg, borrow or steal a horse to carry or haul him, moved through a dense throng of people to the High School, on Capitol Hill, outside of which a stand had been erected and the customary speeches of welcome and acknowledgment delivered.

Governor Albinus Nance welcomed Grant to Nebraska, Mayor Chase to Omaha; the reply Grant made was terse, pointed, sensible and good-humored.

After this succeeded the hand-shaking torture inflicted by American custom upon all great men and then a banquet at the Withnell House, covers being laid for sixty. At Fort Omaha, I had the pleasure of taking tea with Mrs. Grant, the only others present being the hostess, Mrs. Crook, her sister, Mrs. Reed and brother-in-law Mr. John Reed. I will here violate my rule not to make personal references to ladies in my note-books, by saying that Mrs. Grant, in our conversation impressed me as a very motherly, affectionate woman, devoted to her husband and children; of keen perception, tenacious purpose and unlimited ambition, but unspoiled by the world's favors. Her descriptions of the countries and people she had met were shrewd and incisive, without being scholarly or profound. It is a great pity that her education was not more thorough before commensing her round-the-world tour. I don't mean to say that she wasn't just as well fitted for profiting by her advantages as the average of our women, but her opportunities were so extraordinarily fine that had she been afforded a couple of years' leisure for reading before leaving this country, she would assuredly have returned one of the most intellectually expanded of our people.

Her sketches of her receptions in Scotland, England, France, Italy (by the Pope.) India, China, Burmah, Japan and Siam were strong and graphic without being in the least affected.

Nov. 2d. General Crook sent for me early in the morning. I arrived at his quarters while all were at breakfast, of which I was invited to partake. General Grant, contrary to the usual idea of him is full of talk at meals, very fond of badinage and poking fun in a quiet way at his wife who seems able to defend herself against all assaults. He said among other things, that he never had been a hunter and with the exception of a few ducks shot while he was on duty in Oregon, he had never been able to kill anything in his life. General Grant's countenance is wonderfully strong; his head is well shaped, pertinacity being strongly shown; his nose is the weakest feature he has, altho' of itself strong enough. His ears are the biggest I ever saw and if large ears be an indication of generous nature, as some say, he must be the most generous man in the world. After breakfast, Genl. Grant asked me to write a few telegrams for him. These were mostly replies to invitations, pouring in from all quarters, to accept the hospitalities of towns and cities on his route of travel East.

A delegation from the 1st M.E. Church called at 10 o'clock, to escort General Grant and Genl. Crook to divine service. General Crook declined the invitation as he had just received orders to start for Chicago this afternoon.

Colonel Fred. Grant and his wife, Mr. Honore, Col Sharp, Paymaster, Mr. Walker, (Secy. of the C.B. and Q.R.R.),[3] arrived in special train from Chicago.

Between 1 and 2 in the afternoon, Mrs. Grant received the children of the officers, much to the gratification of the little ones.

In the evening, Mrs. Crook held a reception in honor of General and Mrs. Grant,—a very enjoyable affair, attended by all the officers and ladies of Fort Omaha and Dept. Hd. Qrs. and a number from the town. The music furnished by the 9th Infy. band was unusually fine. (General Crook left for Chicago in the afternoon.)

Nov. 3d. Early in morning, General Grant left Fort Omaha and drove to the Withnell House in town, from which place he started for the Union Pacific R.R. dépôt, escorted by a Battalion of the 9th Infantry, Colonel Gentry commanding, a number of Army officers and citizens of prominence.

---

3. Chicago Burlington and Quincey Rail Road.

A special train of five Pullman cars was in waiting and without unnecessary delay pulled over to Council Bluffs station, Iowa. The reception there accorded was very thin in contrast with that of which Grant had been the recipient on the West bank of the [Missouri] river. Governor Gere welcomed the distinguished guest to the state of Iowa, Grant replying in a few brief, sensible words.

Mr. D. W. Hitchcock, of the C.B. and Q. R.R., one of the ablest R.R. men in the West, under whose supervision the special train had been prepared, had given his personal attention to the dining car, which was a perfect bower of rare and fragrant exotics. . . .

Here Bourke jumps from the subject of Grant back to the Merritt expedition to the Milk River.

Roster of Officers with General Merritt's Command, Oct. 8th, 1879.
‡General Wesley Merritt, Colonel 5th Cavalry,
    Commanding.
‡2Lt. Eben Swift, Regl. Adj't. 5th Cavy., Adjutant.
1Lt. W.P. Hall, R.Q.M. 5th Cavalry. joined with Vroom, Oct. 8th.
‡1Lt. H.S. Bishop, 5th Cav. Commissary
‡1Lt. W.B. Weir, Ord. Dept. Ord Officer. since killed.
‡1Lt. W.S. Schuyler 5th Cavalry and
‡1Lt. John G. Bourke, 3d Cavalry, Aides de Camp to General Crook, Volunteers.
Asst. Surgeon C. DeWitt.
    "   "   W.L. Kimball
Actg. Asst. "   Grimes.†§
‡Lt.-Col. Compton, 5th Cavalry, Comdg. Cavalry Battalion.
‡"A" 5th Cav. Capt. Augur, 1Lt. Bishop, Commissary[)] and 2Lt. [William E.]Almy.
‡"B" 5th Cav. Capt. Montgomery and 2Lieut. [Augustus Canfield] Macomb.
‡"M", 5th Cav. Captain Babcock, 2Lt. [Henry Joseph] Goldman.
‡"I"   "   "   Capt. Kellogg and 2Lt. [Luther Scott] Wellborne. [sic]
"L" 3d   "   Cap't. P.D. Vroom, 2Lt. Jordan.
"H" 5th   "   1Lt. Parkhurst and 2Lt. Andrews.
‡Major E.V. Sumner, 5th Cavalry
    Commandg. Battalion 4th Infy.
    and Dismounted Cavalry.
‡"I" 4th Infy. Captain Ferris, 2Lt. Mason, C.W.

‡"B" 4th "   "   Quinn, 1Lt. Baily, 2Lt. Howland
‡"F" 4th "   1Lt. Robinson, 2Lt. Brown
‡"E" 4th "   1Lt. B.D. Price, (2Lt. [James Alexander] Leyden.)
‡"G" 4th "   1Lt. Webster (G.O.) and 2Lt. L.A. Lovering
†"D" 9th Cavalry, Cap't. F.S. Dodge and 1Lieutenant M.B. Hughes.
†"E", 3d Cavalry, Capt. Joseph Lawson.
†"F", 5th   "   "   §J. Payne, 1Lt. Cherry.
†"D" 5th   "   §2Lt. Paddock and 2Lt. Goldman. [sic]
Battalion, 14th Infantry, Major M. Bryant, 14th Infy., Commanding. [Roster already given on p. 329]
Companies and officers present with Major Thornburgh marked thus: †
Those accompany[ing] Merritt, ‡ marked thus;
Those wounded, thus; §

Manuscript volume 32, from the bottom half of page 360 through page 421, consists of newspaper clippings and copies of official correspondence on the Ute War. Bourke's narrative resumes on November 25.

November 25th Lieut. Schuyler, A.D.C., started for California, to remain absent for several months in general charge of the Murchie mine, a valuable property, owned by Generals Crook, Sheridan, and other Army officers. Lieut. Schuyler obtained two months' leave of absence, as authority for his remaining away from Hd. Qrs.[4]
November 27th. Thanksgiving Day. A very delightful hop, attended by eighty or ninety persons, was given this evening by the officers and ladies of Fort Omaha and Dep't. Hd. Qrs., as a farewell compliment to Mrs. Royall and Miss Royall (wife and daughter of Lt-Colonel Royall 3d Cavalry, Inspector General Department of the Platte,[)] who started East next day for a prolonged visit.
November 30th General Jeff C. Davis, Colonel 23d Infantry, died at Palmer House, Chicago.
One of the bravest and most efficient and energetic officers of the late war, a leading figure in the Army of the Cumberland and the

---

4. The Murchie Mine, purchased by a consortium headed by Crook, Sheridan, Gen. Delos Sacket, and Andrew Snider, proved to be Schuyler's undoing as a member of Crook's staff. Bourke and Charles King were minor investors. Although Schuyler's initial impression of the mine was positive, it continually lost money, and proved a major embarrassment to Crook, who was the moving force behind the project. Always ready to blame someone else for any setbacks, Crook focused his wrath on Schuyler, forcing him to resign as aide-de-camp. Crook's correspondence with Schuyler throughout the project is in the Walter Scribner Schuyler Papers in the Huntington Library. See also Robinson, *General Crook*, 248ff.

last commander of the old 14th Corps. During the last years of his life, his mind had been embittered and enfeebled by disease and military disappointment, to such an extent that few of his more recent acquaintances could have recognized in him the lion-hearted soldier, who so dauntlessly faced the rebel brigades in the defeat of Chicamauga.

General Grant's triumphal tour across the continent still continues: cities vie with each other in doing him honor.

Dec 1st. Cable dispatches report grave difficulties arising in Ireland on account of high rents, short crops and atrocious misgovernment. Agrarian insurrection may be looked for at any moment, as famine is threatened especially in Connaught and other portions of the Western counties.

A consolidation effected of the Vanderbilt and Gould interests in railroads, the former disposing of his shares in Lake Shore and New York Central stock for a consideration of $25.000.000! The new combination controls a through line from Ogden, Utah to New York city, a distance of over 2500 miles.[5]

Dec. 9th Started, under orders from Genl. Crook, to Forts Douglass, Utah and Hall, Idaho. Having chronicled this same journey a number of times previously, I shall now confine my attention to such unusual features only as may present themselves.[6]

The newspapers for several weeks past have referred to the Commission appointed by President Hayes to treat with the Ute Indians for the surrender of the white prisoners held by them and also that of the Indians engaged in the massacre of Agent Meeker and employees.

The members of the Commission, consisting of General Hatch, U.S.A., Charles Adams, Esq. of Colorado, and Ouray, Chief of the Uncompahgre Utes, succeeded in effecting (as elsewhere narrated) the surrender of the white women and children of the Meeker and Price families and at this date has the promise of the delivery for

---

5. Bourke is in error. The Vanderbilt interests retained control of both the New York Central and the Lake Shore and Southern Michigan Railway. In 1914, Lake Shore merged with New York Central, which remained under the Vanderbilts until 1954. Gould blocked Cornelius Vanderbilt's attempted takeover of the Erie Railroad, but himself was ousted, after which he concentrated his interests on Union Pacific and Missouri Pacific. Some years later, however, Gould sold his American Telegraph Company to William Vanderbilt's Western Union at a substantial profit.

6. See Chapter 2 of this volume.

trial in Washington, of the young men most prominently concerned in the murder of Agent Meeker.
Whether the savages will deliver the Indians named or not is an open question, but the fact remains that no effort has been made to have justice dealt out to those who so treacherously attacked Thornburgh and his Command, while en route to support the authority of the *Interior Department* upon one of its Reservations.
Among our passengers between Omaha and Ogden was a considerable number of gentlemen interested in mining in Colorado, California, Nevada and the Black Hills of Dakota. Their outlook of the future was most rosy and their predictions full of enthusiasm. Deadwood, they said, will produce dividends for generations to come; Colorado, this year, has added $17.000.000 to the national fund of silver & gold and within 5 years will produce at the rate of *$200.000.000* per annum.
In Leadville, there are now on the dumps upwards of 50.000 Tons of ore, working over $60 to the Ton.
On the way, we encountered heavy snow and high head winds which caused us a detention of 7 *hours*. East of Ogden, passed a train containing six cars of silkworm eggs, valued at $7.500.000, going from Japan to Italy. We got to Ogden at such a late hour at night that I cheerfully accepted the invitation of my friend, Mr. France, the Pullman conductor, to remain in my bed in the car until breakfast. This courtesy saved me the trouble of arising between 2 and 3 in the morning.
December 12th Breakfast at the Beardlee House and started for Salt Lake.
Shortly after reaching the Walker House, was called upon by General Smith, commanding Fort Douglass, Lieuts. McCammon and Patterson of his Regiment and Post, and His Excellency, Governor [George W.] Emery and Terr't Marshal O'Shaughnessy, (U.S. Territorial Marshal.)

Dined with Mrs. Carpenter, (wife of Major Carpenter, 14th Inf.[)], Mrs. Patterson, wife of Lieut. Patterson, and Miss North of Salt Lake.
Mrs. Patterson, after dinner, showed me, in Miss North's apartments, some very beautiful flower painting (on silk.) executed by herself and friends.
Dec. 13th Lieut. Patterson drove me in a sleigh to the post. (Fort Douglass.) The ground was covered with snow, but the air was most

pleasant, quite warm for winter. At Fort Douglass, had a long conversation with General Smith, with whom I lunched and in whose company I called upon all the ladies of the garrison.

From what I can learn in Salt Lake, Utah is making giant strides, chiefly by the impulse given by the mining industry. The Ontario and other properties are paying enormous dividends, and the Honi silver mine of Frisco has an amount of ore "in sight" sufficient to dumbfound an Aladdin or a Monte-Cristo. Estimates run all the way from $16.000.000 to $67.000.000; the most careful one I have seen puts the figures at $27.000.000. The wealth within reach of its owners has been amply sufficient to warrant them in building an extension of the Utah Southern R.R. for 200 miles to carry their ores to market.

December 14th Received a visit from Mr. Stenhouse, Pacific coast correspondent of the *New York Herald*, who is, like myself, interested in the Murchie Mine of Nevada County, Cal.

He spoke with much confidence of the future of that mine and of many of those on the Comstock lode and in Bodie district California, all of which, or nearly all, he has visited.[7]

Paid a visit to the Hot Springs, near Salt Lake and enjoyed a refreshing bath in their waters. Started in the evening for Ogden, on my way to Fort Hall. This time the trip was made in absolute comfort. I shall never forget the first occasion of my going to Fort Hall in 1875, (when I also visited Fort Cameron, Utah)[8] and the toilsome stage journey through a horrible winter storm.

The mining development of the past two years in Montana and Idaho have spurred on the Union Pacific R.R. Co, to building the Utah and Northern Railway to the Montana boundary. The train is brand new, the most agreeable improvement being the reclining chair car, in which one can sleep almost as comfortably as in a Pullman.

December 15th. Awakened at day-break, to find myself at Ross Fork, the agency of the Shoshonees and Bannocks. (This place and these Indians have already been described at length.)[9]

---

7. When he was preparing Crook's autobiography for publication, Martin F. Schmitt discussed the Murchie Mine with Oliver Crook, the general's nephew, who said, "General Crook was an easy mark, Colonel Schuyler a would-be mining operator, and both of them, with very high salaries, died broke." Schmitt, *Major General George Crook*, 238 n14.

8. Fort Cameron was established on the Beaver River in 1872, to protect the mining district of southern Utah. Originally designated Camp Beaver, it was upgraded and renamed Fort Cameron in 1874. The post was abandoned in 1883, and the reservation transferred to the Interior Department two years later, because heavy settlement rendered it unnecessary. Frazer, *Forts of the West*, 164–65.

9. See Chapter 2 of this volume.

Telegraphed to Captain Bainbridge for an ambulance, which came at 3 P.M. and took me across Mount Putnam to Fort Hall. There was a furious North West wind blowing, which strange to say, melted the snow! I learned it was the "Chinook" wind from the Pacific ocean, and that its effects are perceptible as far as Salt Lake.

My short stay at Fort Hall was made most pleasant by Cap't. and Mrs. Bainbridge, (14th Infy.) my kind host and hostess of former years, and by Lieuts. Kimball and [Bainbridge] Reynolds & Dr. and Mrs. Boyer. I should also remember Mr. Shilling, who did all he could for me, during my detention at his home at Ross' Fork.

December 16th. Drove to Blackfoot, 8 miles, the nearest station on the Railroad.

Here a thriving town is springing up, the point of supply of Challis and Bonanza, the new mining "excitements", the absorbing topic of conversation. The "hotel", at Blackfoot is the same old dungeon in which I resided when the railroad terminus was at Franklin and Oneida. It has the same proprietor, Mr. Lewis, who has had the old rattle-trap moved up along the railroad in answer to the demands of travel. The barroom was jammed full of miners and prospectors—rough fellows in canvas, blanket or oilskin suits, but honest and good natured. The only talk was mines. "Struck it down to Challis"—"four foot ledge"—good pay-streak—["]Can't do much prospecting up ter Bur-nan-zur'n count the snow" and so forth.

But enough could be gleaned from their remarks to impress the stranger with the great value of the new District—People don't send in 60 stamp mills to this country as a joke. Such an act always means business.

One of the miners told me that the Penobscot of Montana, formerly owned by Mr. Vestal, has now 40 stamps and turns out $50.000 @ $60.000 monthly.

The "biggest" man in our party was a gambler from Challis, who had just had a fight and "gotten away" with his man. A scarcely healed scar in his neck showed where his adversary's knife had "gone for" his jugular. This man's slightest observation was listened to with the same deference as would be paid to anything coming from the lips of General Grant; to be invited to "take something" by this divinity was a honor no one, except myself, felt at liberty to decline, and to have him vouchsafe a little of his conversation to a man made the latter blush with conscious pride and embarrassment.

The gambler was really, to all appearances a warm-hearted, generous and, perhaps, brave fellow, but adulation will spoil him. By and Bye, he'll "get away" with some one else—then he'll become too "damned permiskyus", as the miners say and "something'll drap". He'll hang in his boots, if he doesn't take care.

Dec. 17th. Reached Salt Lake. Heard of Genl. Crook's narrow escape from freezing to death while out hunting on the Platte and determined to return to Omaha, where my services may now be needed.

Dec. 18th At Evanston, Wyo., received a telegram from Genl. Williams saying that the reports about General Crook were greatly exaggerated and that General Crook wished me to return to Salt Lake until further orders. On account of the Westward bound train being late, did not get in to Ogden until after midnight and consequently failed to reach Salt Lake City before the morning of Dec. 19th.

During my stay at Salt Lake, I employed my time in studying up data relating to the mining development of the whole Rocky Mountain region and the Pacific slope. For exercise, I walked each morning from the Walker House to the Hot Sulphur Springs, where I bathed and drank the waters, said by the man in charge of the establishment to be good for everything under the Sun.

A walk back through the snow, 2 miles gave me an excellent appetite for the good breakfast provided in our Hotel and a repetition of same exercise in the afternoon made me eat like a wolf at dinner.

On this journey, I have met many mining experts and people who are interested in mines. Mr. Land, of the Bodie District, Cal. has impressed me as thoroughly informed and perfectly reliable. According to him, development of the Bodie country will result as [sic] a matter of a few weeks' time.

Major D. W. Burke, 14th Infantry, called upon me: I returned the call upon himself and wife (at Continental [Hotel.]) They are interested in claims in the Frisco district, of which such fabulous stories are in circulation.

December 24th Received telegram from General Williams that General Crook wished me to return to Omaha without delay.

December 25th Xmas. Left Salt Lake city [sic] 7 A.M., the coldest morning ever recorded in that valley: -8°F. and -10°F. Between Salt Lake City and Ogden our car got on fire; flames soon extinguished.

Between Ogden and Omaha we were 5 hours behind time, most of the way. Found a number of Arizona people in car—Mr. Hinton and Mr. Armes, both owning interests in mines near Tucson. With them I was soon in active conversation and listened with open ears to their stories of the advances made by the "Tombstone" ["]Huachuca" and "Dos Cabezas" districts, over every foot of which I had scouted in 1870-1-and 1872. The giant strides making [sic] by the Atchison and Southern Pacific R.R. lines will soon bring that hitherto neglected country of Arizona into deserved prominence.

Our Xmas dinner was eaten at Evanston, Wyo., and a very creditable one it was to Kitchen Bros. the proprietors of the Hotel.

Dec. 27th Returned to Omaha, Neb.

1880

New Year's Day, 1880, passed pleasantly. Made a few calls upon lady friends in Omaha, in company with Lieuts. Fort and Miner, 9th Infantry and spent the evening at Genl. Crooks Quarters, Fort Omaha, having passed most of the day at the residence of Mr. Horbach, Omaha, with his wife & dau. & Mrs. & Miss Collins.

January 5th 1880. The newspapers of the country generally published references to the letter issued by Mrs. Meeker, alleging that she and her daughter and Mrs. Price, while captives in the hands of the White River Utes, were subjected to unmentionable outrages; that a full statement of the villainies perpetrated had been given under oath to the Ute Commission and submitted to Secretary of the Interior Schurz, but by him withheld from the knowledge of the public. The effect of this announcement will be to damage the character of Schurz, if damage be possible. An unprincipled German adventurer, unmindful of God or man, caring for nothing but self, he has, by President Haye's [sic] selection for the position he now occupies, been enabled to do a great deal toward making influence, if not respect, for himself. Keen, subtle and mendacious in character, quick to perceive the weak points of an adversary's arguments, and perfectly brazen in the suggestion of plausible explanations to cover the shortcomings of his Department, he has, without being personally dishonest, done more to protect and strengthen the thieves of the Indian Ring than any champion who has ever assumed that task.

His downfall is among the probabilities of the present winter.

Mr. T. H. Tibbles, of Omaha, who started East last spring, to collect the sum of $4.000 to defray the expenses of contesting the

eviction of the Poncas from their old Reservation on the Niobrara, Neb. (see previous notes. . . .)[10] has fully succeeded in his task.
The suit, begun at Lincoln, Neb., against the Ponca Indians, Standing Bear, et al. for remaining absent from their Reservation [in Oklahoma], was discontinued by orders from Washington.
January 17th 1880. The Edison Electric light un fait accompli. "Scientific" men, of whom our unfortunate country is full, have indulged in grave doubts as to the success of Edison's efforts in this direction. Edison has gone on experimenting and perfecting his schemes just the same as if there were no "scientific" men in existence. The value of his enterprise is established by the depreciated quotations of gas stocks and the enhancement of the shares of the company formed to introduce his new light into New York and other great cities on the Atlantic Coast. Mechanical obstacles, such as attend the manufacture of a cheap and perfect glass globe, will retard the introduction of this fine light for months, maybe a year, but its general employment in the illumination of all our cities, towns and prominent villages will mark a feature in the development of the present decade.
February 5th. Rail-road consolidation [is] the order of the day. The combination of the Union Pacific, Kansas Pacific and Denver Pacific, (with lateral branches.) under one management, marks the successful issue of plans long since matured in the keen, brilliant intellect of that wonderful genius, Jay Gould—one of the most extraordinary men the world has ever produced.
Commissioner Hayt, of the Indian Bureau, peremptorily removed for corrupt practices. In connection with Inspector Hammond, Indian Agent Hart, (San Carlos Agency, Arizona.) and others, Hayt had quietly seized upon a silver mine of immense prospective yield in Arizona. This matter getting into the public journals, an investigation was ordered.
Hayt lied like Belzebub, and Hammond swore positively that a letter which he had sent Hayt, and which somehow fell into the hands of the investigating Committee, was a forgery.
 This testimony Hammond retracted the very next morning saying he had been guilty of perjury in making it.
It required but a few moments' cross-examination to develop Hayt's

---

10. See Chapter 10 of this volume.

villainy in the particular offense specified above as well as in many others. The mine had been purchased by a Mr. Edward Knapp (Hayt.) Hayt's own son who suppressed his family name, at his father's insistence, to avert attention and paid for by a Mr. Hogencamp, of Jersey City, Hayt's own partner.

At this late date in the administration of President Hayes, it will be hard to find any gentleman to succeed Mr. Hayt and it will be impossible to find a more thorough rascal.

Mr. Barston,[11] [sic] of the Board of Indian Commissioner, a whining, psalm-singing hypocrite—discovered in illicit connection with stove contracts for the Indian Bureau.

The distress in Ireland augmenting. [Charles Stewart] Parnell, M.P., visits this country to excite American sympathy. Is received with great kindness: invited to the floor of the House of Representatives, from which he delivers a speech on the agrarian discontents of the peasantry of his country.[12]

James Gordon Bennett of the *New York Herald* made the munificent donation of $100.000 for the relief of the famine-stricken Irish. This sum is greater than the whole amount as yet subscribed by the chuckle-headed, tallow-brained, beef-legged, flat-footed English aristocracy.

February 4th The Pennsylvania Republican Convention to-day resolved to support General U.S. Grant as a candidate for President (3d Term.) The vote stood Grant 143: [James G.] Blaine 103.

Blaine and [John] Sherman (the Secretary of the Treasury,) have been for some months past busy intriguing to secure their own advancement. The former is the favorite of the petty politicians of

---

11. Bourke means O. C. Barstow, member of the Board of Indian Commissioners, who, together with A. K. Smiley, and William Stickney, formed a committee appointed by the board to investigate the Hayt affair. The Board of Indian Commissioners itself was a quasi-public entity created by Congress and consisting of nine unpaid members, who served as advisors to the president and the Secretary of the Interior. It was part of an effort to clean up corruption in the Indian Bureau and improve public perception of Indian affairs. The legislation that created the board, however, was vague about its actual legal authority and this led to jurisdictional disputes between the board and the Interior Department. Priest, *Uncle Sam's Stepchildren*, 28ff.

12. Charles Stewart Parnell, president of the Irish National Land League, and member of parliament, was the acknowledged leader of the Irish nationalist movement during this period. While visiting the United States, he and John Dillon collected over £26,000 in donations for the Irish Parliamentary Party. His career came to an end after he was named as co-respondent in a scandalous divorce case, and refused to heed his party's advice to keep a low profile. Churchill, *Great Democracies*, 345ff.; http://www.clarelibrary.ie/eolas/coclare/people/parnell.htm

the Republican party; the latter has some strength from his official patronage and hopes also to conciliate the votes of the Germans through the wire-pulling of Carl Schurz, Secy. of the Interior. He has made endeavors to gain consideration with the moneyed men of the country from the fact that resumption of the specie payments occurred during his incumbency of the chief position in the national finances. His record in this is sadly against him; as a Senator, and member of the Finance Committee, he is known to have bitterly opposed the Resumption Bill;[13] his character for personal honesty is not altogether beyond suspicion and in every essential feature he is Grant's inferior. During the hour of our country's peril in the Great Civil War, neither Sherman nor Blaine had the manliness to take up arms in its defense. Grant's services have not as yet been forgotten and may again be required to crush the treasonable designs of the Southern demagogues.

While all is going on, General Grant is quietly minding his own business, travelling in Cuba, with Lieut-General Sheridan, and the recipient of most flattering ovations from the Spaniards.

Reports have been sedulously circulated that Grant was anxious to obtain the Presidency of the contemplated Inter-Oceanic canal at Panama. Grant is too shrewd not to perceive that the commencement of such a costly enterprise is not to be thought of for the next ten years: *then* and not till then will the combined capital of England, France and Holland push it to completion to prevent the carrying trade of India, China, Japan, Australia and the Sandwich Islands[14] from passing into our hands.

While freight had to be transferred three or four times in its journey across the American continent and while high prices shut out all but the costliest goods from the advantage of quick transit, the Suez Canal absorbed the bulk of the traffic of the Eastern world. A great change is now approaching;—a change as great as that which in years gone by ruined the ports on the Mediterranean and gave wealth successively to Lisbon, Amsterdam and London. Before the end of the year 1885, we shall have not less than five through lines from Ocean to Ocean.

13. The Resumption Bill, passed in 1875, allowed the Treasury Department to acquire gold for the purpose of redeeming heavily discounted paper currency. This would have been of particular interest to the Midwest, which operated on a paper economy that often was discounted substantially below face value.
14. Hawaii.

Competition and systematic administration of these long routes will so reduce charges and express [fees] that millions of pounds of silk and tea, now forced to take an alternate route, will find their way to San Francisco and Portland, (Oregon.) and thence, by rail to New York, Boston and Baltimore. The Pacific Ocean will see noble lines of steamers ploughing its waters, and its bed will receive electric cables connecting San Francisco, with Melbourne, Honolulu, Hakodadi [Japan], Hong Kong and Shang-hai. To offset this loss of her mercantile powers, England must either declare war against us or by lending aid to the construction of a ship canal across the Isthmus of Panama give employment to her own mercantile marine.

The United States is no longer an infant, drawing nourishment from the mother countries: its development during the past three years is something beyond belief and at the same rate of increase, the next five years will make us the most powerful people on the face of the earth.

All Europe is now tributary to us for flour, corn, pork, beef, sugar, (to some extent.) cotton[,] butter, cheese, dried fruits and other production, while we are buying less and less each year in exchange and, besides, the yield of our mines will from this [time] on be doubled, trebeled and quintupled. With the annexation of the Northern States of Mexico, soon to occur, the United States will have a greater area of gold and silver bearing domain open for prospecting, developing and producing than any other nation before known in the world's history.

Feby. 5th. H. C. [sic] Boynton, a journalist of Washington filed charges against General W. T. Sherman, Commanding U.S. Army, for slander and defamation of character. General Sherman's memoirs had been severely criticized by Boynton who indicated a number of misstatements. Sherman commented upon this criticism in a manner at once acrimonious, splenetic and undignified.

For self-protection, Boynton preferred charges and instituted also a libel suit in the civil suits. For my own part, I hope Boynton may meet with success, if for no other reason than to impress upon Sherman and others in Washington that a little military or civic distinction does not empower an *American* to play the Persian satrap over his fellow-citizens.[15]

15. When Sherman's *Memoirs* originally were published in 1875, many former officers of the Army of the Cumberland felt their achievements during the Civil War had been denigrated

February 5th [sic] 1880. Adolp[h] Borie, of Philad[elphi]a, Secretary of the Navy for a time under President Grant's administration, died of general debility, aged 73.

An honest, incorruptible man, a sincere patriot and a distinguished citizen. While he made but an unimportant figure as Secretary of the Navy, he detracts nothing from the dignity of a Cabinet office and if he could have been prevailed upon to retain the position, it was the opinion of the whole country that he would have done much for the improvement of our navy.

[A]n extract form *Chicago (Ills.) Tribune* of Feby. 4th, giving a complete synopsis of the Hayt (Indian Ring) Scandal.

Chicago (Ills.) Tribune
Feby. 4th 1880
HAMMERING HAYT.
The Board of Indian Commission-
ers in New York Discuss
Hayt's Case,
And Draw-Up Their Report Sub-
stantiating Fisk's Charge
of Malfeasance.
The Mine Operations—Hammond's
Connection Therewith—A Sum-
mary of the Document.
Special Dispatch to The Chicago Tribune.

NEW YORK, Feb. 3.—The *Tribune* will tomorrow publish the following: The Board of Indian Commissioners, A.C. Brayton, Chairman, Clinton B. Fisk, William Stickney, E. M. Kingley, William H. Lyon, David H. Jerome, E.H. Tuttle,

---

to boost Sherman's own Army of the Tennessee. H. V. Boynton, a veteran of the Army of the Cumberland and now Washington correspondent of the anti-Sherman *Cincinnati Gazette*, attacked the *Memoirs*, culminating with the publication of his own volume dissecting Sherman's book and accusing him of various failures during the war. Sherman, who was convinced that his enemies in the civilian arm of the War Department were behind Boynton, contended that the latter had received a $600 government stipend and provided with clerks to copy the official records cited in the attacks. In January 1880, he told a reporter that Boynton would "slander his own mother for a thousand dollars," which prompted Boynton to threaten a libel suit. Ultimately, the matter died out, and Sherman made several quiet revisions to the 1886 edition of the *Memoirs*. Since Crook had served in the Army of the Cumberland, and there was no love lost between him and Sherman, he—and by extension Bourke—naturally would have sympathized with Boynton. See Lewis, *Sherman, Fighting Prophet*, 616–18.

and A.K. Smiley, met at the Fifth Avenue Hotel to-day. The principal business before the Board was the consideration of the report of its Investigating Committee on the charges preferred against Mr. Hayt, ex-Commissioner of Indian Affairs, in connection with the Arizona mines scandal. The Committee is composed of Commissioner O.C. Barstow, A.K. Smiley, and William Stickney. Messrs. Smiley and Stickney unite in the report. Commissioner Barstow takes exception to some of the minor points, but will, it is understood, unite with his colleagues in the main. The report is a voluminous document, and corroborates in detail the charges that have been published in the *Tribune* against Commissioner Hayt and those connected with the San Carlos Indian Agency.

IT IS SHOWN

that the proceedings which had been begun against Henry J. Hart, the Agent at the San Carlos Agency, were suddenly discontinued, and that the affidavits against Hart were never forwarded to the Department of Justice until Gen. Fisk's charges were made public. The evidence further shows that Commissioner Hayt was corresponding with Inspector Hammond, who had been sent out ostensibly to investigate the official conduct of Hayt with reference to the purchase of the silver mine, and that the Commissioner's own son, Edward Knapp Hayt, was sent to San Carlos, under the name of Edward Knapp, to make the purchase.

WHILE YOUNG HAYT

was on the way Inspector Hammond telegraphed to know who was coming out, and received a reply from Commissioner Hayt that he would know the person when he saw him.

The full text of the report will probably be made public Wednesday. Ex-Commissioner Hayt, accompanied by his counsel, Judge Bedloe, of New Jersey, was before the Board last evening. He was questioned very closely concerning his connection with the Arizona Mine and other matters at the San Carlos Agency, which have been investigated, especially the part alleged to have been taken by his son in the transactions.

HE DECLINED TO ANSWER
many of the questions, and asked the privilege of bringing witnesses to aid his side of the question. This, after discussion, was granted. Mr. Hayt's counsel made the point that his client, having been removed from his position as Indian Commissioner, the jurisdiction of the Board has ceased.

Gen. Fisk has received a letter from the Secretary of the Interior referring to the case of ex-Commissioner Hayt, of which the following is an abstract: "I find statements in the papers that I had said the matter investigated in consequence of your publications had nothing to do with the removal of Mr. Hayt. The statement is too absurd to need contradiction."

Another case before the Board was that of Maj. S. C. Bridgman, who in 1874 was appointed as Agent of the Stockbridge Indians at Green Bay, Wis. He claims that he was very badly treated by Commissioner Hayt. In order that Maj. Bridgman may have a chance to be heard, the Board of Indian Commissioners has asked Secretary Schurz to allow the case to be brought before the Commissioners.

February 5th 1880. Lieutenant C. H. Rockwell, 5th Cavalry, my class-mate was married to Miss Moulton, niece of General W. T. Sherman, at Glendale, near Cincinnati, Ohio.
Rockwell is an exceptionally fine young man, bright, brave and good looking. I hope for him and his bride the most prosperous future.
February 10th. General George Sykes, Colonel 22nd Infantry, died at Fort Brown, Texas.[16] During the war of the Rebellion, General Sykes' name occupied a position of prominence and distinction in the reports of every battle fought by the grand old Army of the Potomac.

16. Fort Brown was established in 1846, on the Rio Grande opposite the Mexican city of Matamoros, just prior to the outbreak of the Mexican War. The post was abandoned in February 1859, but reoccupied the following December, because of strife along the river. Upon the secession of Texas, federal troops evacuated the post. Confederates occupied it until 1863, when it was abandoned and burned as Union forces approached. A major reconstruction began in 1867. The post was deactivated in 1944, and in 1948 was transferred to the Brownsville Independent School District, which began a process of demolition in order to establish a college. It is now the campus of Texas Southmost College/University of Texas-Brownsville. Because of its location by Gateway International Bridge, such demolition that the school district and university did not undertake was carried on by the City of Brownsville and federal government, so that today, only a few of the old buildings remain. Robinson, *Frontier Forts of Texas*, 22–25. Heitman (1:942) lists Sykes as colonel of the 20th Infantry.

He was considered one of the coolest, most careful, but at same time one of the most gallant officers that ever wore a shoulder-strap.

Feb. 12th. The newspapers, this week, have reported, denied, and re-affirmed the princely donation by the Baroness Burdett-Coatts of the sum of £500.000 or $2.500.000 of our money to the relief of the famine-stricken peasantry of Ireland. With great prudence and circumspection she has directed that but little of this immense amount of money be distributed as alms; thinking it better to use it in providing work for the needy and deserving and in purchasing seeds, implements, clothing and medicines for the helpless.

[Queen] Victoria has given $2500, a beggarly pittance. The contributions from the United States are wonderfully large. The *New York Herald* Fund aggregates already a quarter of a million of dollars! and the additions to be expected from the collections made and making in the Catholic churches and by other channels, not to forget such contributions and ship-loads of provisions from Philadelphia, New York, Baltimore, Saint Louis and Chicago, will greatly alleviate the distress, if they do not drive it away altogether.

The English government as yet has done nothing to relieve the discontent and suffering. The suggestion has been made to commence the construction of government works such as railroads, bridges, ditches[,] macadamized ways and necessary public buildings to afford employment to numbers of the destitute.

February 21st News reached us by cable of the attempted assassination of the Czar of Russia, by the explosion of a quantity of dynamite secreted in the cellar under the guard-room of the Winter Palace. The plan of the conspirators seems to have been to explode the mine at the moment the Imperial party took their seats at the dining table. The plan was conceived with shrewdness and executed with daring; had it been successful it would have flung heavenward the mangled remains of a swarm of worthless scoundrels who have been preying like vultures upon the carcass of the country. As a measure of policy, assassination must at all times be condemned: if the attempt be unsuccessful, tyranny finds its excuse for rivetting [sic] its chains more firmly. Yet in old countries where society has crystallized into castes, where the poor are born to hopeless misery and the rich to a heritage of domination over helpless creatures whom they fail to recognize as of their own species, revolution, anarchy

even, come with what dread associations they may are preferable to a perpetuation of wrong.
The French Revolution was bad simply because it was blind and rash, not because it was unnecessary.

SERIOUS ACCIDENT
Miss Mollie Horbach Jumps from a Buggy and Fractures a Limb.

Yesterday afternoon, Miss Mollie Horbach met with quite a serious accident. She was out riding in company with Mr. Luther Drake, and when near the military bridge, a runaway team came dashing towards them, and Miss Horbach jumped out of the buggy, and thus received a fracture of one of her lower limbs near the foot. She was assisted into a home near by, where she remained until the arrival of Drs. Mercer, Coffman and McClelland, who temporarily set the limb. She was then conveyed home in an army ambulance which had been procured by Major Burke, who happened by at the time of the accident. Miss Horbach was reported quite comfortable last evening, and was receiving every possible care. Her many friends will deeply regret to learn of the accident. Mr. Drake, who did everything in his power to avert the accident, is deeply grieved that anything of that kind could have happened, especially to any one who was under his charge.
From:
The Omaha (Neb.) Republican, Feb. 24th 1880.

February 25th General Grant's progress through Cuba and Mexico has been a continuation of the ovations tendered him upon his arrival in the country last Fall. Returning to the United States, it is expected that he will journey through Texas and the Southern states where he will surely be made the recipient of unaffected hospitality and undisguised honors.

His reelection to the Presidency is to my mind, an assured fact. His principal competitors will dwindle into insignificance before the day comes for casting the suffrages of the electors.
Blaine possesses some strength, chiefly among those Republicans honestly opposed to a third term and among the chronic office-seek-

ers, disappointed during Grant's incumbency. Sherman is ruined already, exposed as a crafty, unscrupulous, cold-blooded politician: Grant is emphatically, the choice of the people and as such will, if he desire, be elected in November.

Part 5
Staff Duties and Nostalgia

Background

To the nineteenth century army, the horse was every bit as important as the tank or armored vehicle to the army of the twenty-first century. In combat, the soldier's life depended on the quality and stamina of the mount. Much of this section is taken with a remount detail to acquire new horses for the cavalry. "The business of inspecting horses for Government use is a very serious affair," Bourke writes, adding, "Not more than one horse in three has been accepted."[1] Equally important was the care the soldier himself put into an animal. Bourke recalled that Capt. Jerry Russell would not allow recruits to take horses on pass "until he was satisfied they knew how to take care of them."[2]

To purchase the horses, Bourke had been entrusted with a large amount of money, and this entailed risk. During this period, Army Regulations recognized two forms of embezzlement, viz., actual embezzlement, in which government funds were stolen, and constructive embezzlement, in which the person responsible for those funds was unable to account for them, for whatever reason.[3] Either

---

1. Bourke, Diary, 34:546–47.
2. Bourke, Diary, 33:537.
3. *Regulations of the Army of the United States*, Article 76, paragraphs 1577, 1583.

was punishable by dismissal and/or imprisonment. Bourke no doubt was aware that carelessness and inattention to government funds had been the downfall of more than one inexperienced young officer. "For my own safety," he wrote, "I shall enter in this book, as a matter of record, the numbers purchased on different dates, and of different parties, with prices paid and distances travelled."[4]

4. Bourke, Diary, 34:546.

Chapter 18

Procuring Mules and Mounts

Thursday, March 4th, 1880. Recd. the subjoined orders:[1]
   HEADQUARTERS DEPARTMENT OF THE PLATTE

   Fort Omaha, Nebraska, March, 5, 1880.
SPECIAL ORDERS,
   No. 19.
                              (Extract.)
   1. A Board of Officers to consist of Lieutenant-Colonel *William B. Royall*, 3d Cavalry, Acting Assistant Inspector General, and First Lieutenant *John G. Bourke*, 3d Cavalry, A.D.C., will convene as soon as practicable, to purchase one hundred (100) mules.
   The Board, in performance of this duty, will proceed to St. Joseph and Kansas City, Missouri, or to such other places as may be necessary. Upon completion of this duty, the officers composing the Board will return to their station at these Headquarters.
   Mr. *William Chambers*, Quartermaster's Agent, will accompany the Board to assist it in its proceedings.

   1. The discrepancy in date undoubtedly is because Bourke was given the orders before they were published as official.

BY COMMAND OF BRIGADIER-GENERAL CROOK:
ROBERT WILLIAMS,
Assistant Adjutant General.
OFFICIAL:
(Sign.) Robert Williams
Assistant Adjutant General.
Friday, March 5th. Breakfasted at 5 A.M. with Colonel Royall, and then in company with him and Mr. Chambers left Fort Omaha, at 6 o'clock to catch the early "dummy" for Council Bluffs, Iowa. There we took the local or morning train, over the Kansas City, St. Joseph and Council Bluffs R.R., for Saint Joseph, Missouri.

Reached our destination at 12:30 p.m. The only good hotel in the place, the Pacific House, was undergoing renovation from which reason we were obliged to take our quarters at the Halpin House, a wretched little rookery, of squalid surroundings.
Saint Joseph is usually a good horse and mule market, but at the time of our visit the demand for the mines of Leadville, Colorado, had completely exhausted the supply on hand, making it necessary for us to proceed to Kansas City. Saint Joseph is a fine town of some 35.000 to 40.000 inhabitants, the centre of an extended rail-road system and the seat of a thriving trade, especially in groceries.
It has of late years been overshadowed commercially by Omaha, Neb., and Kansas City, Missouri, but in the fullest sense of the term is a "strong" town. During the few hours we remained there, I saw a number of noble buildings of brick and stone, a few of architectural pretensions, blocks of comfortable dwellings, well-paved and maintained streets and other marks of vitality and public spirit. Like all the cities along the Missouri river, Saint Joseph, in the dry season, is plagued with dust. A needed attention is now paid to drainage and with a good water-system, to come with time and growing wealth, Saint Joseph will be freed from both mud and dust; a considerable amount of cutting and filling has been done in places, nothing, however, to compare in kind or quantity with that required by the configuration of the site of Kansas City.
In the afternoon [we] visited the office of the K-C., St. Jo. and C-B. R.R.,[2] where we met the Superintendent, Mr. Barnard and the General Ticket Agent, Mr. Dawes, old acquaintances. Mr. Garth, who

2. Kansas City St. Joseph & Council Bluffs Railroad, later absorbed into Chicago, Burlington & Quincy.

had been a school mate of Col. Royall's, called towards evening. His wife, a daughter of General Craig, is a sister of Lt. Louis Craig, 6th Cavalry, who was at West Point, the same time I was.

After supper, Mr. Dawes and Mr. Posgate, the Post-master of Saint Joseph, invited us to go to the Theatre, to witness the play of *Lady Challoner*, with Miss Agnes Herndon in the title rôle.

The acting, especially Miss Herndon's, was exceptionally good and the play itself well constructed. Of the Theatre much can be written in a few words: it is one of the best I have seen for a long time and may be is the very best between Saint Louis or Chicago and San Francisco. The opera-house at Salt Lake City, Utah, is the only one, I can remember, to speak of in connection with it.

Another substantial structure in Saint Joseph is the market-house, apparently well-supplied with all the necessaries and delicacies of the table.

March 6th Took the local train from Saint Joseph for Kansas City. Following our train was a "railroad bicycle", propelled by a section-master who kept up with us with apparently great ease. I conversed with him from the rear platform of the hind car and learned that it could without any trouble make twenty-five miles an hour.

Kansas City is a pushing, busy city, claiming a population of 65.000 inhabitants and having not less than 50.000. The point of departure of thirteen great Rail-roads, besides being situated on the great artery of American Commerce,—the Missouri River—it is a very hive of industry, with streets and alleys filled with a bustling crowd, resembling in a feeble manner, Broadway. It has already become the entrepôt of an immense business in corn, wheat, flour, pork and beef and is reaching out boldly for tribute from the whole Trans-Missouri Valley, from Texas north to the Union Pacific Rail Road.

At this date, Kansas City is far in the lead of Omaha, but the latter city may yet prove a formidable competitor, and no matter how affairs may turn will always be a rival worthy of respect and deserving of fear.

Kansas City required an almost fabulous amount of excavating and embanking to perfect its grades and drainage.

Much has already been done and enough to bankrupt a great community still requires attention: There are houses 100 feet above the datum line of a street in contiguity with building sites the same depth below it. Property owners claim that this peculiar configuration of the land is a blessing in disguise because during the "hard times"[3] labor was furnished the poor who now instead of being a drain upon the taxpayers for charity are a source of production and benefit to the community.

The slag taken from these hills is sold to brick-makers who make it into a beautiful and excellent article, equal to the best to be found in Philadelphia, Pennia.

The flat part of Kansas City, under the bluffs and immediately adjoining the river is reported to be the breeding place of every type of malarial disease; as the enforced abiding place of thousands of poor day-laborers, working upon the Rail-roads, it will in all probability, some coming hot summer be the seat of yellow-fever or other scourge sweeping up from the lowlands of Louisiana and Mississipi. There are two hotels—both quite good—the Coates and the Saint James. The former, at which I staid, on my former visit, is the more modern of the two houses and has every late convenience: the Saint James, however, being better situated for our purposes was chosen as our place of abode. We found it clean and comfortable and not too high in price.

Immediately after dinner, which in all this country comes between 12 o'clock and 2 P.M., the most beastly hours for the purpose that can be imagined—we set out for the horse and mule yards of Stewart and Ward, where within a few hours we inspected, accepted, branded and sent to the R.R. dépôt, thirty-four very excellent mules. The process of branding gave great amusement to a crowd of youngsters and hoodlums, who perched themselves on the fences the more conveniently to see the prancing and jumping of the animals when the hot iron touched their shoulders.

My associates, Colonel Royall and Mr. Chambers—had a knowledge of horses and mules that really astonished me, tho' I have been serving with Cavalry and pack-trains for nearly fourteen years. They seemed to know by intuition the value of each animal as brought up, and in the same time I should have devoted to the inspection of one, they could have examined and purchased a dozen.

Drove to the R.R. dépôt to look after the shipment of the mules bought this afternoon; was much disgusted to be informed that they

---

3. Probably the first years of the Panic of 1873, which had recently drawn to a close at the time of this writing.

could not leave until early Monday morning, on account of there being no train on Sunday.

Met Captain Wirt [Davis], 4th Cavalry and Lt. [Christin Cyrus] Hewitt, 19th Infantry; also Dr. Cockrill, A.A. Surgeon, U.S. Army and his brother, both sons of Senator Cockrill of Missouri[4]: Mr. Cockrill, the younger brother had been a cadet at the Milt. Academy, but failed to get through the course on account of neuralgia of the heart.

Captain Price, formerly of the rebel army, a son of the late Governor Sterling Price called to see his cousin, Colonel Royall, who presented me to him,—a genial, good-natured gentleman, of the Southern type, entirely deficient in the rock-crushing nerve-force of the money-making people of the North. I also met a Mr. Cress, (a cousin of Dr. Cockrell's, [sic]) who had been the Democratic candidate for Congress from this district in the late election; he also had been in the Rebel army, and was a very agreeable and well-informed gentleman. He questioned me closely about Arizona and expressed a determination to go there to live.

According to him, immigration in Texas was making sad encroachments upon the grazing ranges and the cattle herds were generally but surely being withdrawn more towards the North and West; this movement will restrict Kansas City's market and improve Omaha's.

Sunday, March 7th. A stupid day, passed quietly at our hotel.

Monday, March 8th. At work from early in the morning, examining mules. Accepted forty seven from Mr. H. C. Crenshaw.

March 9th. Accepted nineteen mules presented for inspection by Stewart and Ward: these made fifty three obtained from that firm and with the forty seven from H. C. Crenshaw completed our number one hundred.

Met Lt. L. E. Selree, Signal Corps, U.S. Army.

Took 10 P.M. train for Omaha, Neb., where we arrived at 7.45 a.m., Wednesday, March 10th.

Under March 10, Bourke pasted a lengthy article by Charles King about the battle of Slim Buttes in 1876. The article is essentially the same as the account King published in his book, Campaigning with Crook and Stories of Army Life *in 1890. Bourke's account of the fight appears in Volume 2, Chapter 5 of this series.*

---

4. Senator Francis Cockrell.

Procuring Mules and Mounts 371

Bourke's narrative resumes:
March 12th 1880. Count de Lesseps with Mr. Nathan Appleton and party of engineers passed through Omaha en route to San Francisco on business connected with their grand scheme of an inter-oceanic ship canal across the Isthmus of Panama. De Lesseps is the Engineer who superintended the construction of the great Suez Canal, a work for which he cannot, however, claim much on the score of originality as history shows that in very ancient times the Red Sea and Mediterranean were connected by just such a work, the lines of which are still traceable in places.
[James Buchanan] Eads, the American Engineer, who built the great bridge across the Misssissipi river at Saint Louis, opposed the plan of a canal and suggests the idea of a ship-railroad, the largest vessels to be run into immense docks or tanks of iron and timber, drawn along a number of parallel rails by 20 or 25 powerful Engines!
Sunday, March 14, 1880. Colonel Royall, Mr. Chambers and myself left Fort Omaha, Neb., at 2 P.M. for Lexington, Ky, there to buy cavalry horses, in accordance with orders received.

At Council Bluffs, Iowa, were detained three hours to await arrival of Union Pacific train which was that much behind time. Enjoyed good night's rest on the "sleeper". Reached Kansas City, Mo. at day-break and there changed to the trains of the North Missouri R.R. for Saint Louis. (The line of this road runs along the Missouri river on North side and passes through a rich farming country, but one sadly behind the 19th century in all that properly pertains to civilization.
The people at the stations and coming on the trains appeared well-fed, prosperous and good-natured, but generally illiterate and unsophisticated. The villages are harum-scarum in plan, the houses unpainted and without modern conveniences.
Good horses and mules, "likely" niggers and small boys abound at all stations, each nigger and small boy attended by a "yaller dog". The squalor and thriftlessness perceptible everywhere would be a disgrace to Tipperary. Missouri is a noble state for which kind nature has done much; ignorant, idle man—Nothing.
The number of "Jedges", "Kun-nels" and "Ma-jahs" is astonishing: empty titles always abound in the inverse ratio of a state's advancement.[)]

The Conductor and Brakeman were extremely cross; the conductor had lost a leg and, perhaps, poor man, suffered from rheumatic twinges; what was the matter with the brakeman I couldn't tell altho I was much interested in finding out, as each time he opened the door of our car to yell "Brunswick", Moberley, [Inspiration?] "Clark's Switch" &c, his tone was that of a man suffering from some grievous wrong.

The time passed drearily enough except for the "Kun-nels[,"] "Jedges" and "Ma-jahs" who cracked nuts between their jaws and talked "horse" and politics. We had just outside of Kansas City, a short but exciting race with the Express train running on the Rock-Island road—our train came out slightly ahead.

In this part of Missouri, the scenery is more than tame; it is positively distressing. Mr. Chambers staid over one train at Kansas City, and Col. Royall, at Centralia, to proceed on to Columbia, to visit his mother, now an extremely old lady.[5] It was arranged that we should all re-unite at the Planters' Hotel, Saint Louis, Mo.

As Col. Royall was leaving train, his sister, Mrs. Henderson of Saint Louis, entered. He had barely time to present me when our cars started. Thanks to this incident, the remainder of the days journey was not so stupid. Mrs. Henderson was a very handsome and bright lady, but rather spicily rebellious in political feeling.

Forty miles out from Saint Louis passed a "block-house" erected either as a defense against Indians in early days or against rebel raiders during the late war.

At Saint Charles, Mo., crossed Missouri river on a fine iron bridge going up to replace the spans which gave way under a train loaded with passengers some time since, drowning thirteen persons.

Saint Charles, 28 miles from Saint Louis, is a sleepy down of large size, once, no doubt, of considerable prominence.

Reaching Saint Louis, I went to the Planter's Hotel,—an old affair, but having excellent beds and a first-class table.

In the evening saw the *Pirates of Penzance*—Gilbert and Sullivan's new burletta,—extravagant but humorous in its outlines, with many fine scenic effects and some good music, rendered by a chorus of 50 fair voices and an orchestra of 30 pieces.[6]

5. Colonel Royall, at this time, was one month short of fifty-five, having been born on April 25, 1825. He had entered the army as a first lieutenant of Volunteers in the Mexican War, when Bourke was only a month old. Altshuler, *Cavalry Yellow and Infantry Blue*, 288–89.

6. A light opera with book by W.S. Gilbert and music by Sir Arthur Sullivan which, like so many Gilbert and Sullivan works, satirizes the British social order. The best known song from this opera is "I Am the Very Model of a Modern Major General," which pokes fun not only at the social order, but at Gilbert and Sullivan's own previous work, *H.M.S. Pinafore*.

March 16th. Saw General J. E. Simpson, of the Vandalia [Rail Road] Line, who very courteously gave to my comrades and myself the courtesies of his road to Louisville and return.

Visited the Union market, a busy place filled with all kinds of supplies for kitchen and table. Mr. Chambers, (who rejoined me at bkft.) went with me to call upon Major [William Burton] Hughes, Quartermaster, to make arrangements for the care while in transition through Saint Louis of the horses we hope to purchase in Kentucky.

Met Col. Royall in the Union dépôt, with him were Dr. Mercer and Mr. Markel of Omaha. Took Vandalia line for Louisville, (330 miles) crossing the Mississipi, on the fine Iron bridge built by Capt. Eads; the bridge proper is only 2200 feet long, but with its approaches, including a tunnel under the heart of Saint Louis, it represents a total length of over 11.000 feet or more than two miles.

March 17th Waked up at Jeffersonville, Indiana, just before we began to cross the iron bridge, spanning the Ohio river between this city and Louisville, Ky.

Put up at the Galt House, a very excellent hotel, well-built, conveniently arranged, finely furnished, and excellently supplied. It is one of the best hotels I've ever seen and that is saying a great deal in its praise. It cost $1.250.000, is well located, judiciously managed and at most reasonable charges. Louisville has improved wonderfully since my first visit in Nov. 1862, when I was an enthusiastic young soldier lad, one of hundreds and thousands of Northern boys who marched with light hearts to Southern fields to defend the nation's life and integrity. It makes me feel old sometimes when I look back even for a moment and see again those gay-hearted comrades turning their backs upon comfortable homes and loving friends only to die; oh! so many of them! on the remorseless fields of battle or in the equally pitiless prison pens of Andersonville and Macon! How many pined away in hospital, dying of slow fever or gangrened wounds—and how many others have lived these long, weary years,—objects of charity and compassion! Our camping ground in Louisville was out on the plain, as it then was, near the Louisville and Nashville R.R. Dépôt. The first night was so cold that a party of us concluded to sleep in the passenger cars in the dépôt; the kind-hearted Irishman in charge let us slip in and make ourselves comfortable beds from the cushions of the seats; the next day, with a little work, our tents were made more comfortable and much warmer. Day by day, we drilled and exercised in all kinds of evolutions, and when not engaged in military exercises, strolled in squads to view the sights of the city. Hundreds of blue coats could at any moment of a fine morning or afternoon be seen on the main street.

We remained in Louisville about one month, marching thence, through Kentucky, South to Nashville, Tenn. arriving in that city just in time to move out and take part in the memorable seven days' Battle of Stone River or Murfreesboro, (i.e. Dec. 26th 1862.–January 2d 1863.)

This day is the anniversary of our attack upon the village of the Sioux chief, Crazy Horse, on Powder river, Montana, 1876, (for a full account of which see my notebooks of that date.)[7]

Colonel Royall took me to visit the family of his friend, Mrs. Peny, in whose society and that of her charming daughters, (one of them as pretty a girl as I ever saw.) we passed a very pleasant evening. I was glad to find the young ladies were cousins of an old friend of mine at the Mily. Academy—Cadet E. F. Davis, now Lieutenant, 1st Artillery; also of Captn. E. W. Ward, retired.

General Elkins, Deputy Q.M. General called upon us at the Hotel.

March 18th Visited Kentucky National Bank to make arrangements about cashing Treasury checks. The Bank President—Murray—wished to impose an exchange of [1/3?] %=$18.50 upon whole amount, an exception to which I declined to submit as I had no authority under law to "shave" Government money. I telegraphed a statement of the situation to Col. Ludington, Chief Qr. Master and asked instructions.

Started for Lexington, Ky., by the Louisville, Cincinnati and Lexington, "Short Line", Rail Road. Country poor and thinly settled, much as in Southern Indiana. The roads leading out from Louisville are superb twin-pikes, unexcelled in the whole country.

Frankfort, the capital, as seen from the cars, is a pretty town in the banks of the Kentucky river. From Frankfort to Lexington the soil becomes much more rich and is better cultivated than it is near the Ohio river.

At Lexington, put up at Saint Nicholas Hotel, the Phoenix having burned down since my last visit. In our car, was a rude, illiterate

---

7. Described in Robinson, *Diaries*, Vol. 1, Chapter 13 of this series. In fact, it was a Cheyenne village. Crazy Horse was about fifty miles away. This was known to Bourke, but he never admitted the error despite official reports to the contrary. See ibid., 2:491–92.

negro [sic]—a man, I am certain, unable to read or write, yet gifted with marvellous [sic] powers of memory about horses. He could, without hesitation, very glibly give the pedigree, points, peculiarities and record of every horse of note on the Kentucky Turf. This exceptionally strong memory I have had occasion to observe very often among Southern darkies, brought up on stock farms or near stables.

March 19th Colonel Royall very kindly made an arrangement for me with the President and Cashier of the First National Bank of Lexington, under which I exchanged a check, of $5.000 on the Assist. Treasurer in Chicago, for its face value in cash.

Strolled about the town; streets quite muddy; found the town quite sleepy in general appearance, but with some signs of commercial awakening. Lexington has now three good [rail] roads from the Ohio river; the "Short Line" from Louisville and from Cincinnati, the Kentucky Central and the Cincinnati Southern; the latter a giant thoroughfare, 334 miles long, reaching down to Chattanooga, Tenn. The completion of this great steel rail highway has just been signalized by a banquet in Cincinnati, the largest ever known in our country. 1800 guests were invited from all parts of the South and made to partake of the hospitality of a city which had staked nearly $28.000.000 of its capital in securing connection with the Central Southern States. An immense trade is carried on in Lexington in whiskey and blooded horses. The Government tax at 9 % per gal. will this year in this state alone amount to over $10.000.000! Most of this whiskey is made by members in good standing of the Presbyterian and Campbellite[8] Churches.

Lieut. Howell, 2d Artillery, called to see me: we had been associated as groomsmen at the wedding of Miss Lucy S. McFarland, and Lieut. Bergland, Engineer Corps, U.S.A., in Lexington, Ky., June 1878. (see Note Book of that date.)[9] Lieut. Howell very courteously escorted me around Lexington, showed me the new Phoenix hotel, a fine building almost complete and took me this evening to call upon Miss Brand, one of Miss McFarland's bridesmaids, a bright vivacious, sweet young lady, whose acquaintance I most gladly renewed.

March 20th Read in the press dispatches of the suicide in San Francisco yesterday of Mrs. Belloc, wife of the Banker of that name.

---

8. Disciples of Christ.
9. Chapter 1 of this volume.

As Miss Mary Seawell, daughter of old General Seawell, of the retired list of the U.S. Army, I had the pleasure of meeting this bright, beautiful and commanding young girl at the reception tendered General Crook in San Francisco, in April, 1875, and was fortunate enough to meet her again a number of times in the same and ensuing years. Physically, she was a queenly woman, one of whose fine appearance any gentleman might be proud.

Her married life, turned out unhappily and terminated in the sad manner above stated in the cemetery where reposed the remains of her little baby.

March 20th------

The newspapers to-day contain telegrams announcing the completion of the Southern Pacific R.R. to Tucson, Arizona. No event in the history of American railroad construction illustrates more strikingly the melting away of the frost of old time apathy and ignorance which kept this grand continent in the fetters of barbarism. Tucson, founded in 1542 by the Spaniards as a mission for the Indians of Arizona has preserved in a marked degree to the present hour all the tokens of its mixed Castilian [sic] and Papago origin. Proud of its claim to being considered the oldest town within the limits of the United States, it had apparently an equal pride in being regarded as the dirtiest.[10] In all its streets and alleys, offal, dirt, straw and rubbish were allowed to lie in piles undisturbed save by the scratching of inquisitive hens or the rooting of drowsy pigs. Its swarthy caballeros proudly bestrode their half-starved "bronco" ponies hardly big enough to support the weight of the immense saddles covering them from loin to withers. In the light, fresh air of the morning, the solemn clank of the cathedral bells summoned to early mass groups of dusky maidens whose faces betrayed their Indian lineage, but in whose soft eyes lurked the witchery of Andalusia and Grenada [sic].

Jesus and José, Ramon and Miguel grew from happy, prattling babyhood to the full vigor of adolescence with scarce a care except

10. Bourke is in error, as frequently is the case when he approaches early Spanish history. The 1542 date would have been near the close of the Coronado expedition, long before any permanent European settlement in what is now the American Southwest. The earliest Spanish settlement in the Tucson area was the mission of San Xavier del Bac in 1699. A "visita" or sub-mission, San Agustín de Tuquisón, was established closer to the present site in 1757 (Bancroft's earliest date is 1763). A presidio, or garrison fort, to protect San Agustín, was founded in 1775, marking the official birth date of the city. St. Augustine, Florida, founded in 1565, is considered the oldest Spanish city in the United States. Bancroft, *Arizona and New Mexico*, 381; Frazer, *Forts of the West*, 13; http://www.tucsonaz.gov/tucson_history.html

such as must ever surround the games of early boyhood or later on attend the "mozo" who is becoming deft and skilful in use of lasso, spur and pistol. To play with marbles, tops and ball—to play all these languidly and as they were languidly laid by to take up with equal languor the cigarrito and the use of mescal—to lazily plow the fields or work in an automatic kind of a way at making adobes—these were the occupations of the male sex. Nothing was done energetically, unless we speak of riding the "bronco" ponies which was always at a furious gallop or the dancing with "dulcineas" at the frequent bailes which continued from the setting of the sun until the dawning of the same.

With the girls, the same weary lassitude marked every action, altho' the women as a class were more energetic than the men and never lacked an exquisite ease and grace of motion which would have made glad the heart of a sculptor.

Anita, Francesquita, Guadalupe and Jesusita quietly baked their tortillas; prepared the "chile con tomatos" [sic], con huevos, y "con gallina",[11] or boiled the strong coffee which was to wash down the noon-day meal and then first gracefully rolling and lighting herself a cigarrito, one would gently touch the strings of harp, or guitar and sing, in a voice not altogether unmusical, strains of love and flowers, while the others busied their hands in deft lace and needle-work or wagged their jaws in gossip about their neighbors.

Thus passed the day with these primeval people when I first knew them in 1869–70–71: nothing disturbed the monotonous routine of daily life but an occasional "carrera" (horse race.) or "pelea de gallos" (cock-fight), or perhaps Don Carlos Velasco was about to christen another olive-branch and would celebrate the event with an appropriate "spread" to which all the worthy "compadres" ["]comadres" and ["]toquilos" of the village would hasten to do full justice.

The "Americanos" (may the Devil fly away with them!) had already planted their feet in the sacred dust of Tucson and were slowly but surely drawing to their own coffers every cent in the country.

Mexican social life went on all the same, the presence of the Anglo-Saxon element making about as much difference in the life current of the place as would the casting of large stones by mischievous boys into the bed of a slow-moving brook.

11. Chile with tomato, with eggs, or with chicken.

With the coming of the iron horse all will soon be changed; the dignified, grave and courteous bearing of the Castilian will give way to the paying, obtrusive and calculating manners of the Yankee and the Jew: soon from the signs above the doors of the "tendajones"[12] will disappear the names of Velasco, Carrillo, Leon and Suastegui and flaring black and white will tell us that "Gottlieb and Co["] deal in Cheap Clothing or that G. Washington Smith has just received another invoice of "Gent's Nobby Eight Dollar Ulsters". I know it's heresy to say so, but I am just a trifle sorry to hear that Tucson is being so rapidly Americanized: I had much rather have it remain as it was, dirty, dusty, vermin-infested if you will, but for all, a link binding our breathing aggressive civilization to the years when men in their sober senses scoured this vast continent in search of fountains of youth and caskets of treasures or when benevolent, good-hearted people burned their fellow creatures at the stake for God's sake.

C. P. Huntington, President of the Chesapeake and Ohio Rail Road arrived in Lexington to arrange for the early completion of his road to this point from Norfolk, Va.: this will have an important bearing upon the future of this part of Kentucky.

Mr. Chambers ordered back, (by telegram from Genl. Williams,) to go to Kansas City, to assist Major Furey in purchasing mules for Dep't. Platte.

Paid a visit, in company with Colonel Royall, Lieut. Howell and Mr. Treacey[13] to the breeding farm of Colonel Withers, looking while there at the number of especially fine colts, brood-mares and stallions. "Almost", "Happy Medium" and other noble animals brought out for our inspection. "Almost" cost originally $15.000, but $30.000 has since reportedly been refused for him. Mr. Treacy, our gentlemanly cicerone, is the senior member of the firm of Treacy and Wilson, horse-dealers; he is a young Irishman who left his native district,—Rosecommon—25 years ago and by his fine mental endowments, keen, briar-like business aptitude and thorough integrity is winning with rapidity a competence and position of respect in this community.

Visited the rooms of the Lexington Club, an organization numbering among its members some of the best young men of the town, thanks

---

12. Small stores or stalls.
13. Bourke's spelling is not consistent. Sometimes he writes "Treacy" or "Tracy."

to Lt. Howell, they have been very attentive to Col. Royall and myself: among the frequenters of the rooms I find several gentlemen whom I had the pleasure of meeting during my former stay. One of those to whom I have been presented is Mr. James Burnam, of Richmond, Ky., who turns out to be a brother to my former classmate, A. P. Burnam, to whom I sent kind messages.

Bourke's entry for March 21 is a description of Lexington Cemetery that essentially duplicates that given in Chapter 1.

March 22d. The horse market in Lexington has proved very dull: thus far we have succeeded in obtaining only four.

In the evening, drove out with Mr. Tracy and Colonel Royall to the farm of Mr. Price McGrath.

McGrath has something of a history; a former partner of John Morrissey's, he devoted the prime of his life to gambling and horseracing, from which he derived a great fortune which in his old age he is applying to the raising of blooded stock.

Whatever his past record may be McGrath is certainly a man of great natural endowments, warm-hearted, good disposition, generous and hospitable in the extreme. His mansion is furnished in the best style and contained a half dozen paintings of merit—the subject in each case being horses.

The whiskey, for which McGrath's house is celebrated, is worthy of an emperor's table; in flavor, bouquet and strength superior to any wine I have ever drunk.

The horses on this farm, I believe have been mentioned in my notebook of June 1878,[14]—the finest of them are the thoroughbred stallions,—Aristides and Tom Bowling,—noble creatures far above the level of the brute in intelligence, docility, and courage.

The old trainer—Austin—a smart old colored man—looked after these splendid animals with more care than if they were children and kept a very sharp eye upon the little bits of negro boys, who were to take the different animals out for exercise.

March 23d. Met Colonel Tarlton, formerly a Captain in the 3d Cavalry, retired on one year's pay in Dec. 1870. Tarlton was regarded as a gallant soldier and excellent gentleman, but one who rendered himself valueless as an officer by over-indulgence in alcoholic stimulants.

14. See Chapter 1.

The horse-market in Lexington is extremely dull and has proved a bitter disappointment to us. The season no doubt has had much to do with our failure as many farmers do not care to leave the work of planting and come 20 @ 30 miles to town on the chance of selling a good horse at the exceedingly low price we are allowed to give—$115.

We have done our best to make our presence known; have had notices put in all the papers and telegrams sent as far north as Louisville and Cincinnati, but to no purpose.

Lexington has been drained of its supply for the use of Eastern and Southern markets; and altho' there must be many good Cavalry horses in the country within a radius of 50 miles, yet the reasons above given will explain our failure.

In the evening, called with Lieut. Howell upon the Misses Kirkhead, with whom we also found Miss Howard and made them a long and, to us, a delightful visit.

March 23. Reported in the newspapers this morning that Ex-President Grant, with Lieutenant-General Sheridan and party had perished at sea, in a violent gale, off Galveston, Texas. The rumor was generally discredited, still it occasioned decided uneasiness.

In the evening, Lieut. Howell took Colonel Royall and myself to call upon Miss Brand and Miss Howard; in the house of the latter, met Miss Breckenridge and several others whose names I do not remember. Kentucky ladies, as a rule, are very refined, bright and ambitious, and far superior to the men of the state who are too much addicted to gambling, horse-racing, whiskey-drinking and idleness to amount to very much.

March 24. Succeeded in buying two or three good horses at fair prices—an average of $115 each. We have some funny episodes in the dry monotony of horse buying. For instance, there is the old "nigger uncle", who wants to sell his hide-bound, wind-broken and spavined plug to "the Gubment", under the impression that Uncle Sam is buying carrion for the "Calvary". Colonel Royall is always too dignified to pay any attention to such cases so the rejection of these plugs becomes my office and I throw as much dignity into the business as possible.

Then we have the drunken young farmer who wants the Board to buy his horse, because "he knows he's a good un, bee God".

But the remorseless Board deliberately inspects that frantic steed and finds him suffering from stiff joints, curbs, splints, blindness and venerable old age and declined to buy him, notwithstanding that the drunken owner keeps up his din about the brute and "knows him to be a good hoss, bee God and out ov'n Abdallah mar[e], bee God". Then we have the drunken Irishman who is ready to "foight the mon that'll offer liss than a hundher'n twenty foive dollars for his harse"—but he is gotten rid of by reference to the immutable decree of such an intangible power as the Natl. Government which cannot be foight and which doesn't allow more than one hundred and fifteen for a horse, no matter how good.

Finally, we have the old lady who wants to sell her horse because she is now "bodin" (boarding, I suppose.) and who rapidly sketches her biography for my benefit, while we were waiting for Colonel Royall to return from dinner. She "lives six miles from town on the Harrodsburg pike, has bin a widder nigh on ter twenty four year", raised a family of children and "all ov 'em done well" her "five darters is all married and livin' comfortable,—Lizzie, Malinda, Sophonista, Susan and Bell—'ceptin' Bell whose husband was killed in the wa', he was a Cone fed rit—a very brave man,—he was killed in the wa'"—and so forth and so forth until Colonel Royall came along and most inhumanely rejected the poor old lady's horse because he wasn't big enough.

It is very tedious and unsatisfactory work so we have concluded to leave Kentucky, having purchased only thirteen horses, but all of these very fine animals.

This afternoon was given up to branding them, pulling off their hind shoes, paying all vouchers due for feed, &c. making out bills of lading for the R.R. Companies and sending necessary telegrams.

The welcome news of General Grant's safety reached us about noon. He and his party have reached Galveston, Texas, and received there the same ovations tendered in all the other cities of the Union. In Mexico, as in Cuba, every courtesy and attention has been showered upon him; he has girdled the globe with his honors and crowned with the laurels of all the nations the noble monument of his fame "against which the surge of Time shall break into spray".

Mr. Treacey drove Col. Royall and myself to see his stock-farm. He has one hundred and forty Acres of blue-grass meadow with substantial improvements. His stable sheltered forty two colts and fillyes [sic], under training. None of these was over 3 years, and the great majority under 2 years of age. While the "exercise boys" brought them out, they showed in their prancing and cavorting an appreciation of the pleasure they were exciting. Next to a beautiful woman there is no work of God's creation so well deserving of admiration as a beautiful horse. The two hours we passed here were two hours of unalloyed pleasure. Many of the animals were fabulously high in price, ranging up into the thousands, but they looked as if they were worth any money that might be asked.

Colonel Royall recd. a very kind note from Lieut. Sam Swigert, 2d Cavalry, asking us to come over to his home near Frankfort, Key., (where he is now on leave of absence.) and pay him a visit.

Colonel Royall bought of Mr. Treacey, a perfect beauty of a colt, 2 years old, deep bay with black points, gentle as a kitten but spirited as a lion.

March 25th Shipped our horses to Louisville by the L-C and L. R.R.,[15] en route to Omaha, drew my balance from bank and made ready to leave by the afternoon train.

Our eight days' stay in Lexington has been without profit to us in our official capacity, but not without benefit in other respects. We have met numbers of nice people: young ladies of beauty and refinement and young men of courteous manners and generous impulses. There are many agreeable homes, with all the surroundings that wealth and good breeding can bring. But Lexington is dying slowly of a commercial dry rot; the streets are quietly going to seed, the houses show frequent signs of decay, the young men are growing up without any future. Over a score of young gentlemen, so I was told have left Lexington and struck out for the silver mines in Leadville, Colorado, preferring to work there for their daily bread to remaining at home in idleness. In the south, all mechanical employment is relegated to the "nigger" and his compeer,—the "low white": hence, the country is overrun with wretched doctors, wretched lawyers, wretched preachers and wretched politicians—representatives of the "good families".

The blacks flock to the towns like Lexington whose streets they *throng*, either as downright idlers or pursuing such apologies for labor as polishing boots, waiting on hotel tables or running errands.

15. Louisville Cincinnati & Lexington, later incorporated into the Louisville & Nashville.

It disgusted me greatly to be accosted half a dozen times to the block with the question, "shine yer butes, Boss?"[16]
This Title, Boss, is a compromise between the word "Massa" which the negro dislikes as associated with the idea of slavery and the necessity of giving his patrons some respectful appellation to conciliate favor. "Is you all dun gwine off, 's'afternoon, shure 'nuff, Boss?" asked the waiter of me at the hotel this morning, and the same "Boss" business has followed us the whole way down from Saint Joseph, Mo., through the line of country controlled by Southern influences.
Such is the present condition of Lexington, in the near future a brighter vista is opening for this city and all the Southern country. The Cincinnati Southern and the Chesapeake and Ohio Rail Roads will bring commercial prosperity to Lexington, situated as it is in the centre of several of the richest counties of the United States.
At noon, I had the pleasure of meeting General Don Carlos Buell, who arrived in Lexington on a visit of inspection to the University. During the war of the Rebellion, General Buell for a long time commanded with distinguished ability and courage the grand old army of the Ohio, (afterwards known as the Army of the Cumberland.) He was most unjustly treated by the arbitrary, Secretary of War—[Edwin M.] Stanton—and deprived of command and position. He has always held in the hearts of the thinking soldiers who served under him a high place of honor and esteem.
In appearance, Buell is refined, scholarly, modest but dignified, gentle and winning, but bold and soldierly.
In our conversation, I told him who I was, that I was Genl. Crook's Aide de Camp, and that during the war I had served as a private soldier in the regiment raised to act as his (Buell's) body-guard.
"Then[,"] said he smiling, ["]I am especially glad to meet you, for I feel as if I had a double claim upon you.[17] I always like to meet army officers to talk over old times with them."
"If that be the case, General,["] said I, ["]you'd better let me bring up Colonel Royall who has been in the army since the Mexican

---

16. Almost immediately after Emancipation, blacks began moving from the rural areas into cities and towns. It made no difference how small the town might be, the fact that it was a town represented freedom, i.e. the ability to move about on one's own, without the constant supervision of the plantation overseer that, in their minds, was the sum total of rural life. Additionally, as more blacks moved into urban areas, they congregated into communities, giving individuals a sense of belonging. Litwack, *Been in the Storm So Long*, 310ff.

17. Possibly Buell said "double claim" because Crook also had served in the Army of the Cumberland.

war"—and suiting the action to the word, I hunted up Colonel Royall with whom General Buell was soon in a very animated conversation about old times and common friends.

Started back to Louisville; passed through Frankfort, [(]the state capitol [sic],) by day-light. The Capitol building is a very ordinary affair. The Kentucky river, at Frankfort, is crossed by a stout iron bridge. The river was well filled with rafts of valuable black walnut timber, floating down to the Railroad, to be taken to *Europe* for a market.

March 26th. Reached Saint Louis, 7.30 a.m. Breakfasted at Union Dépôt and changed cars to the train of the Missouri Pacific R.R. for Kansas city. This road runs almost parallel to the Wabash Pacific (Saint Louis, Kansas City and Northern,) upon which we had come down, so we concluded to take it back, to study a new belt of country. We were glad to have done so; the journey is made in 2½ hours less time, a great consideration to a weary traveller and the day cars are the finest I have ever seen. They are upholstered luxuriously, provided with toilette stands, towels &c., had each a colored porter to attend to passengers and all without extra charge.

This change had been brought about since the road passed into the hands of Jay Gould, the greatest Rail Road manager the world has yet seen.

The ride to-day was very pleasant. Signs of returning spring were abundant on either hand;—The hills with verdure clad, the trees new-budding in the balmy air, the purple-blossoms of the fragrant peach—The murmuring brooks—The lazy cattle and sheep peacefully grazing in the light of the sun,—made a purest picture and gave a more agreeable impression of this part of Missouri than that we had received while travelling along the other road.

At Jefferson City, the state capital, we had a glimpse of the Capitol building and of the Penitentiary where gangs of convicts were at work quarrying stone.

At Gallagher, a large batch of convicts were employed in the coal mines, under guard of armed sentinels. The refuse and screenings of this mine are so loaded with Sulphur that when the dump-piles become wet with rain, they ignite and have so remained burning in some cases for years.

The Grant "boom" for the Presidency is becoming stronger each day, while the hopes of his would-be competitors,—Blaine and Sherman—are vanishing into thin air.

The Ex-Empress Eugenie—under the incognito of the Countess de Pierrefonds—started for Zululand to visit the spot where her boy fell under the assegais of savage blacks. Raining at intervals this afternoon—a prolonged rain is needed for the area of the country we have passed over on this trip; without it crops will suffer greatly.

March 27th. Reached Fort Omaha early in the morning and found a hot breakfast waiting in the mess, having telephoned my coming from town.

A most annoying dust storm, blowing all day—one of the very worst I have ever known, Arizona and Southern California not excepted. It was impossible to see ten feet in front of one, at times.

March 30th. Had an excellent breakfast at Colonel Royall's at 4' o'clock in the morning. Met there General and Mrs. Crook, Colonel Stanton, Dr. Barnett, and Lieut. [Morris Cooper] Foote, Adjutant 9th Infantry.

Started on a special train from Omaha, at 6 a.m., for Saint Joseph, Mo., to attend a town celebration there. . . .

Our party consisted of
General and Mrs. Crook,
Mrs. [sic] French, (daughter of Chaplain French.)
Lieut. Bourke, Aide de Camp,
Cols. Royall, Ludington, Stanton & Burnham, Major Furey, Dr. Barnett, Lieuts Foote, [James] Regan and [William Edwin] Hoffman and Messers, Bennett, Chambers and Hull, the whole party under care of Mr. Barnard of the K-C., St. Jo. and C-B. R.R.

We made very good time, the first forty-two miles in exactly an hour. We had a glimpse of the great Thompson farm which last year raised 1800 Acres of corn averaging 75 Bu[shels]. to the A[cre]. Thousand of wild geese, filled the field on each side, their white plumage resembling drifts of snow.

Reached Saint Joseph, 141 miles from Omaha in four hours at the dépôt, were received by a Committee and driven in carriages to the (renovated) Pacific House and there changed our travelling clothes for full miliary uniforms to wear in the procession which was much like all other demonstrations of the kind, composed of open carriages containing distinguished guests, bands of music banding away, (2 of them belonging to the Regular Army—one to the 9th Infantry at Omaha, the other to the 19th at Fort Leavenworth.) societies in regalia—and industrial and manufacturing representations.

After the procession, we adjourned to the hotel where I had an opportunity of meeting many agreeable people. From Fort Leavenworth had come some of my classmates, Phil. Reade, and Dan Taylor—also Pope J. W. and [Ernest Howard] Ruffner of '68 and 67 respectively.—[William Jefferson] Volkmar of '68—General C.H. Smith, 19th Infantry, General [Thomas] Wilson and many others. Mr. Gale called upon me and introduced himself as the husband of Lieut Cushing's sister. Lieut. Cushing, for a long time my Commanding Officer was killed by Apache Indians in Arizona, May 5th 1871. (see my note-books passim. . . .)[18]

Was presented to Mrs. Craig, wife of my old friend, Lieut. Louis Craig, 6th Cavalry, now in Arizona. Mrs. Craig made me feel good by saying she had often heard my Arizona friends speak of me in the most complimentary terms. She afterwards presented me to many of her friends, with whom I assisted in receiving the great tragedian, [John] McCullough. We drank his health, in champagne and found him affable, unassuming and well-informed.

At 4 p.m. the invited guests to the number of 250, or thereabouts, entered the beautiful dining room of the Pacific House to partake of a banquet tendered by the Saint Joseph Board of Trade.

I will pass over the banquet—one is very much like another. I must not omit to say that we had an abundance of the best champagne to which all did full justice.

Speechmaking followed, as a matter of course, General Crook replying for the Army, and Lieut. Phil. Reade for Nebraska. Reade's remarks were very funny and kept the audience in roars of laughter. Mr. Crittenden, of the Saint Louis Chamber of Commerce, made a remarkably good address, in the course of which he told those assembled that *every ship yard* on the Ohio River, from Pittsburgh to Mound City, was now busy building barges to carry Western cereals from the Missouri and Mississipi rivers to the Ocean.

In the evening, proceeded to Tootle's Opera House to witness to McCullough's performance of *Othello*; he rendered the play with wonderful effect and received able support, especially from Iago (Mr. F. B. Waide.) and Desdemona, (Miss Forsythe, a beautiful young lady.) McCullough and Miss Forsythe were twice called before the curtain to receive the applause of the immense concourse of appreciative and intelligent spectators.

18. See pp. 256–57.

After the theatre, we were invited to a Ball, but as I was already quite worn out, I staid only long enough to meet a few nice people and pay my respects to our good-natured hosts and then to bed.

Here our party broke up; General Crook with most of the Omaha delegation returning to that point; the officers from Leavenworth, returning there, while Colonel Royall, Major Furey, Mr. Chambers and myself started,

March, 3rd, for Kansas City.

Here we put up, as usual, at the Saint James and bought

April 1st of Steward and Ward, twenty-seven and of Ivel Thomas five horses; in the inspecting, branding and shipping of which we were kept at work all day. Heavy Rain at night.

April 2d. At Pacific Hotel, St. Joseph. Rained a little in morning. Purchased a carload, seventeen horses, of E. F. Mitchell, and six of Mr. J. Couch. Shipped those purchased of Mitchell but left Couch's at his stable, at his cost of keep, to await our return from Omaha. Telegraphed to horse-dealers in Centralia and Chilocothe to gather up horses to be ready for inspection by the 10th and 12th instant. Took afternoon train for Omaha, reaching Fort Omaha by 8.30 P.M.

Had a severe but brief hail storm while en route and saw, as on down trip, immense flocks of wild white geese.

Day cloudy, cool and damp.

Chapter 19

♦
♦
♦
♦

Phil Reade and Old Jerry

April 6th 1880.

As I have spoken of my friend Lieut. Philip Reade, in my description of the banquet at Saint Joseph, I think proper to make at this point some further reference to him for the reason that he is not only one of the most original geniuses I've ever encountered, but also on acc't. of the romantic tinge given his whole life by a certain circumstance to be noted.

Reade was brought up in good circumstances—a great misfortune for him—as poverty would have stimulated his ambition and given his intellectual powers something to work for. At the Mily. Academy, he was a shrewd, bright fellow, quick as a flash to seize upon the subtle points of a mathematical demonstration, but unjust to himself in the total lack of application to study.

He had a number of escapades while there—some of them exceedingly laughable. I remember that he climbed into the recitation room of the "immortals" (in math.) of our class and during the absence of instructors and janitors set about an examination of the instructor's desk to find the list of "subjects" for the approaching "January" [examination]. Professor [Albert E.] Church[1] happened

---

1. Bourke mentions Church's death, speaking of him in high terms, in Robinson, *Diaries*, 2:384.

along at the time and took a notion to go into this very room, the door of which Phil., very fortunately had locked and, while Profr. Church was waiting for the janitor, old Luke, to come up with the key, boldly slipped down by a rope from the window and reached ground in safety. He was unsuccessful in that venture, but undismayed, for we next heard of him doing one of the boldest things ever dreamed of at West Point, that breeding-place of courage.

Reade bribed Captain Warner's negro servant and one cold morning, just after Xmas, he entered Warner's bed room at reveille dressed in the negro's coat and blacked up like a minstrel. It was so dark and Warner was so sleepy that he never suspected anything wrong, and beyond swearing at the "d–d nigger" for his clumsiness, said nothing. Reade took out Warner's boots to be blacked and returned for his clothes which he brushed with so much care that he found in the pocket of his pantaloons the memoranda of the topics each cadet in the "Immortals", (the section presided over by Warner.) would be required to discuss or demonstrate at the Examinations. Need it be said that the Academic Board was amazed at the profound knowledge displayed by the young gentlemen whose recitation marks for the preceding six months had apparently shown them to be idlers or block-heads!

Yet such was the case; the section did magnificently and for a long time, no one was the wiser; not until Phil. Reade had left the Academy did the secret leak out.

Appointed to a lieutenancy in the Regular Army, Reade drifted out to the plains of Colorado and Kansas, and there in one of the young towns, Topeka, I think, became acquainted with a lovely and talented girl whose poverty was an obstacle to her ambition to cultivate a naturally sweet and powerful voice. My friend about this period of his life had been estranged for some trivial reason from the lady he loved and in a fit of pique, compassion or romance espoused the young girl I am now writing about and immediately after the wedding ceremony sent her to Italy to receive the musical training she needed and desired. In Europe she remained for four years becoming a vocalist of artistic finish, but just as she was about to leave for America to rejoin her husband, she died.

Now comes the romantic part. Our newspapers published sensational stories alleging that Reade's wife never had died; on the contrary, she had eloped with an Italian prince with whom she was living in Switzerland,—the corpse sent to America was a body obtained from the Paris Morgue, and many other thrilling features worked in to satisfy our taste for highly-seasoned literature. I don't wish to dwell upon this theme, even supposing that any part of it were true. I shouldn't have alluded to it at all, were it not necessary for the continuity of the story. His first wife being dead, Reade unexpectedly met up with the young lady who had engaged his affections as a Cadet; in less time than it takes to mention the fact, they were married, married and now living as happy and devoted a couple as can be found anywhere.

While travelling in a Pullman car, on a Western road, Reade played an atrocious prank on a number of bald-headed old deacons who occupied adjoining berths. He waited until everybody had gotten up in the morning and then pulling on a pair of bright red striped women's stockings (which he had in his valise.) he thrust one of his legs out from the curtains enclosing his bed. The car was soon in a foment: the ladies were shocked at such brazen-faced conduct by one of their own sex, (as they supposed), while the bald-headed deacons nearly twisted their necks off in trying to get a closer look at the liberal exhibition of anatomy. Phil. waited until he was certain he must be the cynosure of all eyes and then thrusting out his bright, red head and aquiline nose applied his extended palms to the tip of the latter and gyrated his long fingers in derision at the gentlemen.

At another time, in Prescott, Arizona, he was invited by the officers of Fort Whipple[2] to attend a social hop to be given at the garrison the very evening of his arrival. He sent a very elaborate reply to the Committee, regretting his inability to attend not having any suitable clothes—his baggage had been detained—nothing could give him more pleasure than to attend as he was extremely fond of dancing, but under the circumstances &c &c &c; in brief, he wrote such a note that the Committee had nothing else to do but insist upon his coming in anything he had. Phil. made his appearance in the midst

2. Fort Whipple was established December 23, 1863, in the Chino Valley, about twenty-five miles north of Prescott, and relocated to Prescott five months later. The first telegraph linking Arizona to the outside world was established between Whipple and San Diego in 1873. In 1879, Fort Whipple was consolidated with Prescott Barracks to become Whipple Barracks. It served as departmental headquarters until 1887, when Brig. Gen. Nelson A. Miles moved headquarters to Los Angeles. Deactivated in 1922, it is now used by the Veterans Administration as a hospital. Altshuler, *Starting with Defiance*, 63–67; Frazer, *Forts of the West*, 14–15.

of the festivities, clad in a suit of pajamas; (a garment in one piece, much like a child's night-gown and used by the laboring classes in China, parts of the East Indies and Mexico.) red stockings, pointed Turkish slippers and a wig, terminating in a long Chinese queue! The ladies were terribly perplexed and offended but Reade stood his ground, insisted upon it that he had let the Committee know he had no suitable clothes, that they had urged him to come in the best he had and there he was; and there he staid, too, until the end of the Hop.

April 7th Col. Royall, Mr. Chambers and myself started for Kansas city, Mo., to continue purchase of Cavalry horses. Col. Ludington, Chief Q.M. of the Dept. turned over to me an additional $24.000 to buy two hundred more.

Read in the papers this afternoon of the shipment from San Francisco, to Germany, of One Hundred Thousand Gallons of California Wine. The vineyards of Europe have suffered so terribly from the ravages of the phylloxera[3] during the past five years that their accustomed production has been much reduced and American wine is now to be brought into use, for "filling" and "doctoring" purposes. This new and important demand will stimulate our wine-growers to new energy and beyond question American wine will within the next twenty years assume a high place in the list of our staple resources.

California and Arizona should yield immensely in wine, raisins, figs and olives, besides mescal and wild hemp for cordage, and the deserts lying along the lower Colorado and Gila could most profitably be utilized as breeding places for that valuable and easily-raised bird—the ostrich.

My old friend, Cap't. Jerry Russell, 3d Cavy., was in Omaha, all day yesterday and to-day, much to my regret, as I missed the pleasure of meeting the eccentric and good-natured old fellow. My note-books contain liberal references to old Jerry[4]. . . . but as the gallant old veteran is now progressing towards the grave,[5] I may be pardoned for again filling these pages with anecdotes which will

---

3. The grape phylloxera (*daktulosphaira vitifoliae*) is an insect that feeds on grape vine roots. Aside from primary damage caused by the insect itself, the root is susceptible to secondary infection from fungi. http://berrygrape.oregonstate.edu/fruitgrowing/grapes/phybiol.htm

4. See Chapter 13.

5. In fact, Russell outlived Bourke by almost nine years, dying on April 2, 1905. Altshuler, *Cavalry Yellow and Infantry Blue*, 291.

at least serve to recall to my own mind some very pleasant, very unusual or very trying experiences.

Jerry's life, to quote his own words, had been unusually eventful. "Fursth, a bog-throttherr, thin a cob-bler, din an im-migrant, din a 'wea-r-r-y' (i.e. his designation for a private soldier.) din a Carp-r-r-il, din a Sor-r-gint and *now* oi'm a commissioned off-sur and a Cap-tin fur loife, 's'long's oi bee-have moisilf, and a gintlemin, bee act of Con-gress, bee Jay-sus Croist".

Russell, when I first met him at his station, Fort Selden, New Mexico, a post on the Rio Grande long since abandoned, had great trouble with his 1st Lt. O'Conner, as already described. The old man received me most kindly into his "mess", which, by the way, was one of the poorest I've ever seen; a fact the good-hearted old fellow seemed to feel ashamed of as he explained apologetically that he was "now livin equinomikilly, thayin' to lay boi a little mún-ee so's to go East and see what Dame For-chin'll do--o fur me in de way of a dam-m noise woife".

He was the soul of hospitality and never, except on one occasion, failed to invite visiting officers to take "pot-luck" with him. The occasion referred to was during the time he was stationed at Fort Bowie, Arizona, a small garrison occupying the place and making it necessary to detail officers from other posts every time a General Court Martial was ordered. A party of young officers—[William L.] Sherwood, since killed in the Modoc war (in 1873),[6] [Valentine M. C.] Silva run out for cowardice in the Modoc war, in '73, Jim Riley and [John Francis] Lewis, both since resigned, and, I think Paddy Miles, all of the 21st Infantry, were ordered up from Tucson to assist in administering the decree of the blind goddess upon "pay-day drunks". Every house in the garrison was thrown open to them, excepting Russell's, but the explanation received from him was sufficiently clear and satisfactory. His cook had deserted and poor

---

6. The Modoc War originated in an 1864 treaty by which the Modocs ceded their territory on the California-Oregon boundary, and agreed to move to the Klamath Reservation in Oregon. Clashes erupted between Modocs and Klamaths, and disgusted with federal indifference, a band of Modocs led by Captain Jack returned to their own lands in 1872. When troops were sent, the Modocs fortified the lava beds south of Tule Lake, California, where less than a hundred warriors held off over a thousand regular soldiers and Indian auxiliaries. In April 1873, Brig. Gen. Edward R. S. Canby, commander of the Department of Columbia, was assassinated during a meeting with the Modocs. Eventually, they were forced to surrender, and exiled to the Indian Territory. Captain Jack and three others were hanged for Canby's murder, and two other Modocs were imprisoned at Fort Alcatraz, California. Utley, *Encyclopedia of the American West*, 295; Hoxie, *Encyclopedia of North American Indians*, 319.

Jerry having himself to "browse around" from house to house for a living, could not possibly to anything for the "in-thir-tain-mint" of the new arrivals. They begged him "not to mention it" but old Jerry refused to be comforted and took the matter greatly to heart, brooding over it more and more with the libations of the afternoon. As night wore on, the potations of most of the officers as, I'm sorry to say, was then almost the rule in Arizona and New Mexico, became deeper and more frequent and Russell's explanations of his inability to inthir-tain were growing monotonous with iteration.

About 2 in the morning, the séance broke up, the young lieutenants being stowed away in one big room, with half-a-dozen hospital cots in it. They were just tucked in nicely under the blankets and getting ready to dream of promotion, sweethearts, Indian campaigns and other subjects when they were aroused by the noise of a chair crashing upon the floor and to their horror they saw in the pale light of the morn, a figure all clad in white, holding in one outstretched hand a package of some kind and the other, uplifted, a gleaming poniard!

Their fears of assassination were promptly dispelled by old Jerry's reasoning tones. "Oi'm sor-r-ry to thrubl-ble jiz, gintil-min, but de fact is oi cud'n't slee-eep until oi'd dun somethin' fur your intirtainmint. Moi Cuke—Lloyd—diserthid las' Winsday, so oi cudn't in-tir-tain yiz at all; but av Lloyd, moi cuke hedn't diserthid, las' Winsday, oi'd a bin moity glad to intir-tain yiz all in moi 'miss'.[7]

["]But oi've brought yiz all some refrishmint which oi want to share wid yiz, an' oi'me moi'ty sorry oi can't do more fur yiz becos' moi cuke, Lloid, diserthed, las' Winsday"— As he spoke, he thrust the hunting knife, he held uplifted, into the mysterious package which discovered itself to be a can of Irish potatoes, and breaking off the cover handed to each Lieutenant in turn a mouthful upon the end of a blade.

In vain were protests and excuses: Russell would hear of no denial; he was obstinate in his resolve to do "somethin' fur dare intertain-mint", his cuke, Lloyd, had diserthid las' Win'sday and he cud ["]foind nothin' but purtaters" and in spite of all opposition, he forced his unfortunate young friends to consume the contents of the can. The next morning they were all sick:—not from the whiskey

---

7. I.e., mess.

they had drunk, of course, but from the potatoes forced down their throats at their nocturnal "int-ter-tain-mint."

While I was at his mess, he gave a lot of us his opinion of the military service in a way which was at once mirth-provoking, drunken and oracular. "It's moi proi-vit opin-yun, gintil-min, based upon ixpayroyince, becos' oi've now bin goin' an nointeen yée-urs in de U-noi-tid Steets Ormee, dat de whole Damd Milée-tery outfit's goin' to Hell".

In the management of his company, he was a stern disciplinarian, as he understood discipline—gentle to the well-behaved, but a perfect terror to the lazy and indifferent. I was talking with him one morning when a new recruit walked up to the Captain to complain that he hadn't been granted a "mounted" pass. Russell explained good-naturedly that he never gave recruits the privilege of taking a horse away from the Company picket line until he was satisfied they knew how to take care of them. Hereupon, the soldier, in a very insolent way, tore up the "application" he had written and made some impudent remark. Russell never lost his temper, but quietly called to the 1st Sergeant Cox, who was standing within hearing. "Sór-júnt Cox, I want yiz to thay'n foind a noice twenty eight poun' log fur dis young gintil-min's back; Dat'll do my man, dat'll do". (this last to the recruit.): and then turning to me he said, "Oi reckon that'll put an ind to de young gintilmin's hoi-lar-vi-tee".[8]

A great tumult sprang up one day, in his company, about meal time:—some trouble or another about the cooking, which Jerry explained to a knot of his brother-officers in the following way: "we de-kleer to God'llmoighty, gintilmin, the base ingratichood av din wea-r-r-ies ov moine's perficly 'stonishin! Oi stuff thim full ov all dat morchil man can dee-soire and yet here dey go to wor-ruk a[nd] break a bran' new skillet over moi noice fur-r-st sor-júnt's head' an' all becos' dey didn't hev enough toe-mat-tus-ses in dare God-damn-n su-u-upe". (soup.)

Marching with him from the Rio Grande to the Rio Gila (Arizona.) in 1870. I noticed his whole company or nearly the whole, marching on foot, "packing" their saddles and kits on their shoulders, while a small detachment, mounted, drove the horses along in a herd in front.

8. The soldier would either have to walk a tour, probably of several hours, carrying the log on his shoulders, or stand for several hours holding up the log on his shoulders.

Seeing my amazement, he asked me quietly—"Phat do yiz tink av dim 'wea-r-r-ees' av moin, over dare, Borruk"? Thinking to placate the old man, I answered that I thought they were a very fine lot of men and that he certainly had the very best company in the regiment. "Do yiz tink so, now, Bor-ruk?["] said he—["]well, sor-r-r, on de conthry, dare the damnedest lot ov villins, louses, búmmers, teeves an' oi moight say dam' schoundhrils'n murherers there are in dee Unoi-ted Steets Ormy".

Once in Arizona, our respective companies, Jerry's K, commanded by himself and the one I was attached to, "F", commanded by 1 Lt. H. B. Cushing, as brave a soldier as ever drew a breath, were engaged constantly in hard work with the wild Apache Indians. The traveller of to-day, who is whirled into Tucson in a sleeping car, drawn by a locomotive, will not readily believe that less than ten years ago, the Apaches made the Territory of Arizona a Hell; nor will he as he visits the wonderful mining district of Tombstone readily credit that within sight of where it now is, poor Cushing was killed by Cocheis' band and Jerry Russell time and again whipped by them.

But old Jerry's pluck was indomitable; he kept after Cocheis so long as a horse in his troop could follow the trail, or until the Apaches would scatter like crows. In the Dragoon mountains, the trail one afternoon had become very "hot", showing that our troops were gaining on the enemy. Russell halted his men long enough to let their jaded horses sip a few mouthfuls of water from the gurgling streamlet which flowed down through the cañon and engaged in conversation with Bob Whitney, his guide, as to the plan to be followed in the further pursuit when suddenly from all sides, from every pinnacle crag, bang! bang! bang! sounded the rifles of the Apaches, whose exultant war-whoop told poor Jerry only too plainly that he had been drawn into an ambuscade! He turned to speak to his guide, but at that very moment, poor Bob Whitney, reeled from his saddle, shot through the head, his brains splashed all over Jerry Russell's face! By great shrewdness, Russell managed to hold the Indians at bay until dark and then sneaked out of the cañon, (fortunately he had not ventured in very far and his halting his company to water almost at its mouth caused some of the impatient young Indians to precipitate the attack.) leaving a number of animals, but getting away with his killed and wounded.

He wrote me a long letter soon after descriptive of this fight which I remember very well contains the perfectly true but oddly expressed, idea—"Oi tell yiz wat it is, Boruk, it's dam-m-m hor-r-d wor-ruk, dis snatchin' de lor-rills from de br-r-row ov Fa-m-m-e."

The unfortunate guide, Bob Whitney, was one of the handsomest men I ever saw with a face darkened by exposure to Arizona's sun, the brick color mantling his cheeks was well set off by an abundance of fine, glossy black hair and a pair of very expressive, hazel eyes: in stature, though not much over the medium height, he was so finely proportioned that he would be considered tall. He was a good horseman and very daring scout. He showed me a number of bullet wounds received in action with Indians and, what caused me most wonder! a half-dozen long scars on his right arm, caused by arrows. Whitney was with a party of whites surprised by Indians; the fleetness of his horse saved him, but one young Indian pursued desperately determined to gain his scalp. Whitney kept his sombrero whirling in the air behind his back, warning off the arrows the Indian threw at him. As the Indian was going at full speed, he couldn't aim or pull so well as if moving more slowly, to which fact Whitney always attributed his escape, almost without a scratch, the three arrows which caught his arm ploughing up only enough of the flesh to leave deep scars.

Russell gained great popularity with the people of Southern Arizona. When the 3d Cavalry was ordered away from the Territory (in Dec. 1871.) Russell had to march his company out, by way of Tucson. While there he was the recipient of a great deal of attention, which he accepted with becoming modesty. Among other courtesies, a number of gentlemen invited him into Charlie Brown's Congress Hall Saloon, to drink to his health, in something which was labelled "Champagne".

Jerry's reply was characteristic: "moi frinds, Oi tank yiz fur yur kindness. Oi don't pur-tind to bee a foighter becos' oi've no mo-no-mée-nia for foightin' Injuns, but at same toime oi can't bear to see my frinds kilt and dare prop-per-tee goin to der-struc-shun widout doin' somethin' fur to pur-tect thim". (Loud Applause)

That night, a party of nine second lieutenants assembled in a house in Tucson, belonging to Lord & Williams, (one of the principal firms.)

The purpose of these Lieutenants in thus meeting was vague and ill-defined; it was principally to growl at the dilatoriness of promotion and in a secondary way to drink a little toddy together before parting.

Jerry Russell happened by and some one, I really can't tell who, proposed that the meeting be properly organized with Cap't. Russell as presiding officer. This motion was carried by acclamation and Jerry, with his "blushing honors thick upon him" was led to the only chair in the house, the rest of the party sitting upon the floor, à la Mexicaine, or upon the bundles of blankets in which they had slept during the preceding night.

Then it was moved and adopted that each of the party, in proper turn, should sing a suitable song, tell an original joke or story or forfeit a bottle of wine. Jerry led off in a piping treble, his cracked and husky voice rendering Moore's pretty song in a very feeling way: "Bee-lieve me av oll din indearing young-g char-rums: &c.["]⁹ This, as in duty bound, we applauded heartily.

Then Dave Lyle, (now of the Ordnance Corps but who at that time was connected with Lieut Wheeler's Survey in Arizona.) gave what he said was a Chinnook song, in the language of that tribe. It sounded like a buzz-saw.

Lieut. [William] Ross (an A.D.C. of Genl. Crook's, since resigned.) gave us very sweetly "Annie Laurie in the Trenches", by Bayard Taylor.

When it came to my turn, as I couldn't sing any more than a screech-owl, I yelled at the top of my voice a Spanish madrigal which I had often heard howled by our Mexican packers, and so it went on, each one singing as best he could, until the name of W. W. Robinson, my classmate, (now of 7th Cavy.,) was called.

Robinson, arose, said he couldn't sing a note and sooner than sing wretchedly as some of the gentlemen who had preceded him, he would gladly forfeit a bottle of wine. (Tremendous applause.) The wine was obtained without much trouble, (notwithstanding it was now past midnight,) and drunk with becoming honors. Again the roll was called by our worthy chairman, who was about this time getting to be very drunk and very dignified, and again each in turn rendered his tribute in sentimental song, until Robinson was called upon. He declined more emphatically than before—said he had never sung a word in all his life and would produce another bottle

---

9. "Believe Me, Of All These Endearing Young Charms," a staple of Irish repertory.

of wine sooner than try. Noting that Robinson was married and that wine cost $5.00 a bottle in Tucson, I expostulated with him and said "sotto voce", "Great Caesar's ghost, Rob, sing something. Anything will do on this drunken crowd"—and thus encouraged, Robinson essayed that beautiful hymn "Rock of Ages", with which he was progressing famously when Ross (W. J.) in a spirit of deviltry called the chair's attention to the fact that Robinson was trying to impose upon us with a *comic* song. "Dat's so, Mis-ther Robinson,["] said Russell, very decidedly,—["]dat's so; yiz must sing us a sintimintil song, or none at all, at all."

"Why Captain,["] replied the injured singer[, "]that's the Rock of Ages,—one of the most beautiful":—"Nivir moind, Misther Robinson[,"] replied the chair, this time with much sternness of manner—"nivir moind excusis; it may be a comic song or it may not be, but at laste the oi-jée is de-soididly objecitonable, so yiz'll pay de bottil ov woine widout furder thrubble". Which poor Robinson did with scarce-concealed disgust.

Is it necessary to interpolate the remark that shortly after this, the meeting broke up and that we carried our Chairman home to bed? I next met Jerry at Fort Laramie, Wyo., in 1875, whence we were both to start out with Col. [Richard Irving] Dodge's Expedition to explore the Black Hills;—Russell commanding his Co., and I, a member of Dodge's staff as Engineer officer.[10] Russell invited [Thomas] McMillan, (the correspondent of the *Chicago Inter-Ocean*, & a very bright, pleasant fellow.) to take dinner with him and myself. The ménu was not very deliberate; simply, vegetable soup, bread and coffee, but I'll never forget the affair so long as I live. Jerry insisted on our partaking of a couple of toddies before sitting down to table and was in decidedly high feather. He said, "Gintilmen, dis Comp'ny has a Cap'n Roussil, a Lieutinint Roussil, a sor-jint Roussil, moi cuke's name's Roussil, moi sthriker's name's Roussil[11] an' oive a devilish good lookin recruit just jined de Compn'y—his name's Roussil and oim tinkin' ov making him a Corp-r-r-il, boin-boi—Née-po-tism, Borruck, mee boi, nee-po-tism".

10. The expedition is covered in Robinson, *Diaries*, Volume 1, Chapter 9.
11. The striker was an enlisted man who moonlighted as a servant for an officer. Although the practice was outlawed in 1870, the law was observed more in the breach until specifically prohibited by Army Regulations in 1881. Even then, the position did not completely disappear. By working as a striker, an enlisted man could live in private quarters, eat better, avoid more onerous duties, and supplement his meager army pay. Knight, *Life and Manners*, 128.

Of Russell's deep studies in history and philosophy, I think, I've already spoken, but I must mention his colloquy with Captain Alfd. Taylor, of the 5th Cavalry, "since retired."
"Taylor—mee boi["]—said Russell, ["]oi'm an evo-lu-tionist—oi'm an evolutionist—To Hell wid de Pope. To Hell wid de Pope".
This was when Jerry and Alfd. Taylor were both very drunk; when sober, Jerry was a dutiful son of the Church.
After the campaign against the Sioux and Cheyennes (1876–1877.) Russell went East on a leave of absence, passing most of his time in New York City. One evening he visited the Opera House, where it happened that a great prima-donna, (who I really forget, but I think it was Nillson,) was singing her best songs. Pit, Galleries and Boxes were crowded with the wealth, beauty[,] intellect and power of the great metropolis: the blaze of light from hundreds of jets [of gas] was flashed back from crystal chandeliers and reflected again from costly jewels worn by lovely women. The scene was a grand one and to an officer fresh from the rough life of the frontier it should have been replete with interest and fascination. But poor old Jerry's heart was back with his fellow-soldiers whom he had left on the banks of the Platte. His anxious gaze wandered from tier to tier, from gallery to gallery, and, to quote his language, "in all dat vast au-jince, oi found dat oi hedn't a frind. Oi de-kleer to God'llmoighty, Bar-ruk, oi'd hev given foive dhollars for de soight av de face of wan ov des we-a-r-ries av 'K' thrupe".
Jerry at once wrote to his comrades that he was tired of life in the East and would start to rejoin, "de ridgemint boi de toime de bur-r-ds av Spring begin to pipe dare mer-r-ry lays".

So much for Jerry Russell.
We visited this afternoon one of the brick-yards of which Kansas City has twenty-five working their full capacity, and passed a profitable half hour inspecting the process of tempering the clay in the pug-mills, moulding, "edging and hacking" the bricks and burning them in the kiln.
Took lunch at Gaston's saloon, which we found crowded with business men, clerks, travellers and others. Here one gets the juiciest roast beef and the best bread in the Western country. From the quantities of malt and spirituous liquors sold here it is not difficult to believe the report that Gaston is rapidly piling up a comfortable fortune.

Chapter 20

✦

✦

✦

✦

More Horses, More Nostalgia, and Miscellaneous Rambling

April 8th 1880 and April 9th 1880. Hard at work buying horses. The dust in Kansas City, especially in and around the different horse yards is simply beyond description. There has been no rain of consequence for months, and soil is reduced to an impalpable powder which the strong shifting breezes lift in dense clouds to annoy and plague the unfortunate wretches whom business compels to remain out of doors. The business of inspecting horses for Government use is a very serious affair but with such experts as Colonel Royall and Mr. Chambers it is done through with the rapidity of clock-work. The horse is carefully examined to determine his age, condition of legs and hoofs [sic] and all joints,—his eyes are then looked into for any defects and if this preliminary inspection be passed, he is led off to one side and tied up to await the more rigid examination of trotting and running a couple of hundred yards to show his gaits and action and to bring out any obscure trouble of lungs or heart.

Not more than one horse in three has been accepted. After acceptance, each horse is branded *US* on the near[1] fore-shoulder, his description entered in the book kept for that purpose, and then

1. Left.

vouchers are made out for signature by the seller, to whom a Treasury check is at once issued and the horses, in car-load lots, driven to the R.R. dépôt for shipment.

For my own safety, I shall enter in this book, as a matter of record, the numbers purchased on different dates, and of different parties, with prices paid and distances travelled.[2]

Read in this morning's Kansas City *Herald* that a glucose factory is to be established in Kansas City: I hope soon to hear that Omaha is similarly progressive.

Glucose, or grape-sugar, is obtained from corn-starch in the following manner.

It is well known as a chemical fact that maize contains starch in the ratio of 81 p.c,[3] and that its extraction is a matter of mechanical simplicity, the ground corn being boiled with an alkaline powder, (wood ashes,) to neutralize any fermenting principle present, and then washed in cold water which carries off in suspension the amylaceous particles.

This corn-starch is stined[4] into water at a temperature of about 150°F, (tepid.) and then run into a "digester", where it is boiled for 30 minutes in dilute Sulphuric acid, (i.e. one per ct. of the sulphuric acid of commerce.) The excess of acid is precipitated by powdered lime or chalk and the glucose in solution concentrated by boiling. One Bushel of corn yields nearly four Gals. of Glucose syrup, containing less than 70 c. and selling readily @ $1.40 wholesale.

The demand must for years to come exceed the supply, as glucose is coming more and more into general use as a "table" syrup, besides being used to sweeten ale, wine, beer and whiskey, preserve canned fruits, and by confectioners and others.

Nebraska last year yielded over 82.000.000 Bs. of wheat and corn, which will always be the mainstay of her prosperity; but how much greater should her advantages be if instead of sending these products to market in the raw state, she would turn them first into whiskey, beer, high wines, glucose[,] bacon[,] beef or blooded horses!

Started by the local train, April 9th, for Saint Joseph. At the Union dépôt hotel, an exceptionally nice affair, with excellent rooms and good table, met at supper Mr. Barnard, the General manager of the

2. See pp. 410–11.
3. Parts per hundred.
4. Strained?

K-C, St. Jo. & C-B R.R. with whom I engaged in a very interesting conversation. He told me that in his travels he had been much impressed with a feature of the English railway system. The cars run into "Union" dépôts, the upper stories of which are kept in good style as hotels for the exclusive use of passengers.

Instead of getting out of a warm car into a chilling omnibus and riding all over creation to get to a hotel at midnight the weary traveller enters an "elevator", ascends one story, registers in the hotel office and is assigned a room where he sleeps undisturbed by any noise, as the floors are "deadened".

In the morning, he is awakened at the proper hour, dresses, breakfasts and is taken down to the right train with scarcely any trouble. The plan is the only correct one and should be adopted by us without any delay.[5]

April 10th. Buying horses in Saint Joseph, Mo. At night, Colonel Royall and I went to see *Conrad, the Corsair*, in Tootle's Opera House.

Before the performance commenced, I found Mr. Rice, the manager, who was, I knew the brother of my friend, Lieut. W. F. Rice, R.Q.M., 23d Infantry, and upon making Col. Royall and myself known to him, he very courteously invited us to accept a Box, an attention we gratefully declined being already provided with seats. The play was very funny and the actors well up in their parts. I laughed until my sides ached. Miss Seale and Miss Jarbeau, the two leading ladies, were extremely beautiful; the one, a blonde; the other, a brunette—both possessed of good voices, superb forms, pretty faces, piquant, graceful manners and artistic ability of a high order.

April 11th, (Sunday.) Hunted up Mr. and Mrs. Gayle, principally for the purpose of seeing the latter, the sister of the late Lieutenant Cushing, my friend and Company Commander, killed by Apache Indians, in Arizona, in 1871. Mrs. Gayle is a very handsome and refined lady, and comes of the best fighting blood in this country. One brother, "Albemarle" Cushing, blew up the rebel ram *Albemarle*—the most recklessly daring naval feat of the war of the Rebellion; another, Alonzo, was killed at Gettysburgh [sic], shortly

---

5. This still may been seen in Edinburgh, where train travelers arriving at Waverley Station may exit directly into the North British Hotel on Princes Street. In the United States, of course, the railroad hotel has been replaced by the airport hotel, and in the larger ones, trams take passengers directly from the terminal to the hotel.

after his graduation from the Mily. Academy; the third, H. B., my friend, was a most distinguished Indian fighter and lost his life in a desperate encounter with Cocheis' band of Apache Indians—and the last, has been for years, a Paymaster in the Navy, who has seen much hard service. Mrs. Gayle has the best of reasons for being proud of her four brothers.

The Court-House of Saint Joseph is the best public building in this part of the country, not counting those erected by the general government.

We arranged to take the night-train for Kansas City; this started at 12.45 a.m. Not wishing to sleep too profoundly, I dozed in one of the heavy library chairs in the Reading Room; the hotel clerk very accomodatingly placed a pillow under my head and promised to awaken me in time. My nap was rudely broken by the insolent behavior of a trio of Chicago "drummers" who had a very "good time" hallooing and coughing in my ears. Waked up;—one apologized, a second sneaked off and the third was saucy.

Licked him and took the train for Kansas City. Colonel Royall stood by me during this affray and permitted no undue interference on the part of bystanders.

All the berths taken on the "sleeper"; had to sit up until reached Kansas City, at 3.30 in the morning. Stopped at the Union Dépôt Hotel; every bed was full and we were glad to take anything in the shape of a couch we could get,—Colonel Royall sleeping on a mattress on the floor and I upon a sofa.

April 12th 1880. Buying horses all day.

Took evening train on Hannibal & St. Jo. R.R. for Liberty, Mo., 15 miles from Kansas City, Mo.

Colonel Royall wouldn't let either Mr. Chambers or myself eat any supper, because he desired us to become the guests of his old school-mate, Mr. Garth, who lived at Liberty and who had been notified by telegraph of our coming. It was our bad fortune, for one reason or another, not to reach Liberty until nearly 9 o'c. in the night, an hour much later than that at which the good people of this part of Missouri are in the habit of taking supper. Our kind hostess, Mrs. Garth, insisted on showing us to our bed-rooms at once, feeling that we might be tired and in need of rest.

For my part, I was glad enough to get promptly to bed. In our crowded car on the way up, a murderous-hearted Mick occupied the seat directly behind me and smoked a villainous pipe the fumes of which nearly killed every one near him.

However, for the sake of "devilling" Colonel Royall, I combined with Mr. Chambers in a growl about our want of food and concurred with him in the opinion that the Colonel should be fined the drinks. This punishment entailed a requisition upon the Colonel's little flask of good whiskey, which was rapidly drained before his disappointed eyes.

Had a refreshing sleep in clean, sweet beds.

April 13th. Awakened very early in the morning and ate heartily of a good, old-fashioned breakfast; everything of the best & served in home-like style. After breakfast, walked about Liberty; a small town, once of great consequence in the border trade. It has a substantial Court-House, public school and a Baptist College. Our country is cursed with one-horse sectarian "colleges" of non-instruction.

Liberty has considerable wealth; the streets are paved in places and provided with brick pavements. There are many brick and stone houses. It is the centre of a "blue-grass" region, raising herds of blooded horses and mules. Formerly, there were seventy dramshops; now, not one. Near this village were born the notorious outlaws—the James Brothers—whose depredations have caused so much terror in Western Missouri. We were told that one very snowy day, some four or five winters ago, six of their gang rode boldly into Liberty and up to the door of the principal Bank, which two of them guarded, mounted, from the outside, while the others entered presented revolvers at the heads of the Cashier and Teller, robbed the safe of $50.000 and returned. They also shot two persons—a man and a boy,—dead in cold blood—galloped slowly out of town & *escaped*!

We bought five good horses this morning of Wymore and Garth.

Had a very appetizing dinner, bade good bye to our charming hostesses, Mrs. Garth and her friend Mrs. Allen and started to return to Kansas City.

Our train was late and the station was very quiet, the only signs of life being a dozen lazy niggers loading walnut logs on platform cars on a side-track and about as many more pushing, driving and kicking a drove of squealing hogs into a stock car on the main line. By and Bye, our train hove in sight, we jumped into the Caboose, (it was a freight.) and in the course of an hour were on the bridge at Kansas City.

April 14th. Worked like beavers from early morn until 7 at night. Bought and branded 73 horses and shipped 70. Day frightfully dusty: Kansas City for sand & dust surpasses any town I ever saw. In going from Stewart & Wards Horse yards to Grant's, I was taken out of my way by a very stupid or very unprincipled car driver; on my return trip with him to the Union dépôt, to take the proper car, I was prevented from swearing by the ludicrous spectacle of a "jaw-bone controversy" between the driver and a shrill-voiced lady in intensely respectable black bombazine, who had only recently arrived from the Green Isle.

"Madam,["] said he, ["]you must put five cents in the box for your return fare".

"Foive sints is it? Indade'n'oi vil not. Phat phor shud oi pay foive sints? Didn't you teck me out av mee way, you sthupid thing? Bad lack to yiz, do yiz think oi'm made av foive sints?["] and so on, so on until the poor driver was glad enough to beat a hasty retreat.

The circus is on its way to Kansas City; the *only genuine consolidated mammoth Colossal Combination of World's Wonders, with trained elephants[,] magic mermaids, Performing Lions, Queens of the Arena, Bareback Equestrian vaulters* and all the rest of the blood-curdling announcements to fire the schoolboy heart or make the rustic swain drop his plow-handle and ride over to ask his heart's idol to take in the awe-inspiring attractions under his protecting care.

In advance of the circus was the ordinary influx of "side-shows".— the man with the "Mammoth Kansas Hog, 1512 pounds"—the slippery tongued individual with the "Magic Corn Salve,["] the modest vender of the Infallible Rheumatic Liniment, the blushing, diffident proprietor of the Peruvian Tooth-Ache Drops and Diamond Dentifrice, with the invariable dirty-fanged small-boy stepping out from amid the crowd of by-standers to have his "pie-pulverizers", cleaned and renovated; the stentorian-lunged advocate of the merits of the "Canadian Winter-green soap"—warranted to ["]make everything clean from a soiled pocket-handkerchief to a politician's conscience": the "step up and try your strength"—scales, the "Cheap Johns", starting to sell four pairs of ladies Balmoral hoses for a quarter of a dollar and ["]if that don't suit you, gentlemen, why speak out and let me know and I'll throw in another four pair and this elegant case of *ginuwine Sheffield Razors*—don't stand there, young gentlemen and tell me you can't afford to get married—while such miraculous bargains are to be had for the money["] &c. &c; and finally the "Variety Combinations" in front of which "suide" brass bands made night hideous by their assault upon big bass-drums and cymbals:—all this for the edification of a throng of country jakes, cow-boys, clod-hoppers, bog-trotters, train-men, "drummers" and cyprians patrolling the streets.

April 15th. Bought ten horses from Ivel Thomas. Took early train for Omaha. Sky cloudy. Had a slight hail storm shortly after crossing the Missouri River. Young wheat looking beautiful in broad acres of verdure; while the bluffs were purple with the buds of the wild plum or green with the fast appearing leaflets of the cottonwood, ash and elm.

The K-C, St. Jo. and C.B. R.R. is now nearly every foot "steel rail" and great gangs of laborers are hurrying on the completion of the last link; two hundred yards of rail are fastened together and laid at once. At Pacific Junction, great balls of fire were playing about the electric batteries in the Telegraph Office, an indication of a severe storm not far away.

The newspapers contain accounts of the burial alive by King Theebaw [sic] of Burmah, of seven hundred of his unfortunate subjects whose sacrifice, he hoped, would appease the Deity by whom he had been visited with the scourge of Leprosy.[6]

Cadet [Johnson] Whittaker, (colored.) of West Point Mily. Academy, found in his room bound hand and foot with a cadet belt, his head slightly bruised, nose bleeding and ear slit.

He reported having been assailed at dead of night by three disguised men, who attempted to kill or "mark him as they do hogs down South", (i.e.=["]slit his ears".) There are not wanting those who believe that Whittaker inflicted this mutilation upon himself to excite sympathy and avert the danger of being found deficient at the coming Examinations and to corroborate this belief there are, it must be admitted, many curious links of circumstantial evidence too extended for insertion in this journal, at least at this time.

6. Thibaw reigned from 1878 to 1885, from Mandalay, Britain having annexed Lower Burma (Rangoon) in 1853, after the Second Burmese War. Following the Third Burmese War in 1885, Britain took over the remainder of the country. http://www.friesian.com/perigoku.htm#konbaung

Edison, the giant of invention, has stumbled across a process; in part chemical, in part electrical, for the extraction of fine gold from the tailings of mines. There seems to be no reasonable doubt of the practical workings of his method which will add *hundreds of millions of dollars* to our national wealth.

April 16th Dined with my friends, Judge and Mrs. Savage and Mr. Will. Morris. (their son.)

In the evening, listened to the Judge's lecture before the Nebraska Historical Society, upon the "Discovery of Nebraska"—an erudite, finely worded and finely delivered discussion which alluded in terms of panegyria to the labors of the French and Spanish Catholic missionaries in early days.

According to the Judge, the Platte country was first settled by the French who under Laclede, in 1764, laid the foundation of the present city of Saint Louis; but it was "explored and described by the French and Spanish missionaries far earlier than the date just given.["]

Marquette, the gentle, noble and heroic Jesuit, the explorer and discoverer of so much of the vast region lying along the Upper Mississipi and between it and the Missouri was in this vicinity, about 1640 and made a topographical chart, (now in Montreal,) in which the position and course of the Upper Mississipi, Missouri, Illinois and Platte rivers are delineated with surprising accuracy....

After the lecture of Judge Savage, I dropped in to listen to the concluding portion of the programme of the Boston Mendellsohn [sic] Quintette Club and was delighted with the instrumental part as well as with the superb vocalization of Miss Abbie Carrington.

April 18th 1880. Sunday. The worst dusty cyclone I ever have seen; sky clouded as in midst of a thunder storm; impossible to see twenty yards in advance through the opaque masses of sand and dust which have filled the air.

April 19th Left Omaha, Neb., by the C.B. and Q.R.R., for Fairfield, Iowa, 247 miles. Reached Fairfield at 4.30 A.M. on

April 20th, Bought seventeen fine horses @ $120 each of Steward and Ward, (of Kansas City, Mo.) Branded and shipped them; took breakfast and then started on train for Saint Joseph, Mo., 244 miles.

Fairfield is a prosperous go-ahead little place of about 4000 pop. It is the point of intersection of the C.B.&Q. and the South West branch of the C, R-I and P[7] R.R.s. and the centre of considerable local traffic.

Two days before our arrival a great cyclone had swept through the down, demolishing many buildings and covering the Court-House square with sheets of tin roofing. This cyclone had crossed the country from South West Arkansas, through Missouri and part of Kansas, across Iowa and into Wisconsin, working great havoc especially in the neighborhood of Mansfield, Mo., which town it wiped out of existence, killing one hundred of its inhabitants and wounding as many more.

Reached Saint Joseph, Mo., at 8.30 P.M.

April 21st Bought twelve horses of E. F. Mitchell and four of M. J. Couch, all @ $120. Shipped them to Omaha and took afternoon train for Kansas City. Since leaving Omaha, the cars have been so crowded with passengers, the weather so unseasonably warm and the roads so dusty that travelling has been far from pleasant.

April 22d 1880 (Kansas City, Mo.) Bought thirty seven horses branded & shipped them.

The Saint James, the hotel at which we put up in Kansas City compared very poorly with the reworked Pacific House at Saint Joseph. By contrast, it appears dirty and untidy, the table poorly supplied and served and the bed rooms in very ordinary condition.

April 23d 1880. Arose at 5 in the morning and took Hannibal & Saint Joseph R.R. for Chilicothe. Sky cloudy. Day very sultry. Country passed over very picturesque in green and purple. All farm houses and residences surrounded by groves of fruit trees—apple, pear, peach, plum and cherry—loaded with their wealth of purple and snowy blossoms.

At Chilicothe, we were totally unsuccesssful in our search after horses, altho this place is considered to be a fine market in the proper season. It is situated at the intersection of the Hannibal and Wabash Railroads and will soon have a turned line built by the Burlington, to run from the Mississipi River to Kansas City. It boasts a population of 4.000, has a school-house which costs over $32.000 and is a prosperous place of trade.

There is a pretty good sized tobacco factory which we obtained permission to visit and where we were shown all the processes to

---

7. Chicago, Rock Island and Pacific.

which the leaf is subjected from the moment it is delivered at the warehouse until it emerges neatly packed in boxes, the "plug" tobacco of commerce.

Took the "down" train at 5 o'clock in the afternoon, and at Cameron, 50 miles West of Chilicothe and 45 miles East of Kansas City took supper. Cameron is at the junction of the Kansas City and Saint Joe. branches of the Hannibal road and the South West branch built by the Rock-Island to run from Fairfield, Iowa, to Kansas City.

Reached Kansas City, at 10 p.m., an hour or two before the beginning of a refreshing and long needed thunder storm. The cablegrams today inform us that [Benjamin Disraeli] Lord Beaconsfield has been forced to retire from office and that Queen Victoria has been obliged to call upon Hon. W. E. Gladstone to take the reigns of Government. Of the two men, Gladstone has always occupied the higher place in my opinion, altho' I must concede that I am not especially well acquainted with the history of either. Disraeli, is assuredly a powerful mind, but withal much of a political mountebank, the mention of whose name and career somehow suggests to me those of Carl Schurz, the spindle-shanked Mephistopheles, at present presiding over our Department of the Interior. It is only in charlatanism and demagoguery that I wish to institute a comparison, in all else, Schurz is Disraeli's inferior.[8]

April 24th. Bought twelve horses of Stewart and Ward—wore out the rest of the day as best we were able in all sorts of devices, waiting for the high train for Omaha. Walked about Kansas City, whose present wonderful growth is a source of congratulation, but at same time it is hard to see how the young city is going to maintain itself under the debt which must be incurred to properly grade, excavate and embank its streets and avenues. It is reported that Chicago parties with abundant capital, contemplate the erection of immense packing houses in Kansas city—to be the largest establishment of the kind in the world.

Sunday, April 25th 1880. Arrived back in Ft. Omaha. Genl. Crook showed me a telegram received last evening from our friend, Colonel A. H. Nickerson, Adjutant Genl'l Dept., Washington, D.C., saying

---

8. Disraeli and Gladstone both were reformers who expanded the franchise and modernized the British parliamentary system. Disraeli, however, advocated an imperial policy of British interests and responsibilities, whereas Gladstone took a moralistic stand that was a precursor to that of the United States in the post-Woodrow Wilson era. Churchill, *Great Democracies*, 298–303.

that the Secretary of War would give me the detail for the next four years of Assist. Professor of Spanish, if I would accept. Telegraphed acceptance.
Sunday May 2d 1880. General John H. King (Colonel 9th Infy.), Colonel Royall, Mr. Chambers and self left Omaha for Kansas City, Mo., where we arrived
May 2d 1880 and remained purchasing horses.
May 3d 1880. Returned to Hd. Qrs. Dept. Platte, Ft. Omaha.

Checks numbered 5000 & upward, were mine upon Ass't Treasurer, Chicago, Ill.: those running from 37000 were by Col. Ludington on same depositor.
The total amount received by me were.
Cav. & Artillery horses.   Regular Supplies.   Transportation.
[$]18000+24000=42000   500   100
Against which I drew for Regular supplies 32.25. Transpn. 18.66 and Cav. & Arty horses as above, leaving me accountable
May 5th for Reg. Supl. $467.75. Transpn $81.34. & Cav & Arty $385.

May 10th Received copy of S[pecial]. O[rders]. 99. (A.G.O.) 1880 ordering me to proceed to the Military Academy at West Point, N.Y. for duty as instructor.

May 14th 1880. Lt. W. S. Schuyler, 5th Cavy., A.D.C. to General Crook, returned to Hd. Qrs. from a long absence in California, where he has been for several months in charge of the Murchie Mine, a magnificent gold bearing property belonging to General Crook and other army officers who, unfortunately, are too poor to properly develop its riches.[9]

May 15th 1880. Transferred to Major J. V. Furey, A.Q.M., Omaha Dépôt, the balance of public money in my possession, viz: Regular Supplies $467.75. Cavy. & Arty horses $395.00. Transportation $81.34. Total $944.09.

May 15th [sic] 1880. General Crook and Lt. Schuyler, A.D.C., started for the East on business connected with the Murchie Mine.[10]

May 17th. The excitement occasioned throughout the country by the reported outrage upon the colored cadet Whittaker, at West Point, which resulted in the convention of a Court of Inquiry to examine into all the facts, culminated to-day in the establishment of Whittaker being his own assailant. One of the documents submitted by Whittaker was a note, in a disguised hand, warning him to leave the Academy, "to save trouble". This note was submitted to five experts, with 250 specimens of handwriting obtained from all the cadets, including Whittaker himself.

This examination demonstrated that Whittaker himself had written the note and as the injuries of which he made so much ado are now found to have been too trivial for mention, the burden of proof in the whole business is thrown upon Whittaker & such sympathizers as may still adhere to him.

May 22d Had the pleasure of witnessing Lawrence Barrett in Bulwer's wonderful play—*Richelieu*. It was beyond question one

---

9. By now, Schuyler had realized that, while the Murchie might pay off, it was beyond the means of the investors, and was hoping they would decide to shut down the mine. When Crook and Sheridan determined operations should continue, Schuyler lobbied for a transfer, but was bluntly told that the two generals expected him to continue. Crook even hinted that his military career might be adversely affected if he gave up at this point. Robinson, *General Crook*, 249; Crook to Schuyler, April 18, 1880, and April 28, 1880, Schuyler Papers.

10. Crook had investigated the Maynard Process for extracting gold from ore, and the samples from the Murchie Mine assayed at $30.74 a ton. Based on this, the stockholders subscribed to another assessment, but by now, were at the limit of their resources. Some already were in debt on the project. Robinson, *General Crook*, 249.

of the best pieces of acting and one of the most finely delineated characters I have seen.[11]

23d. Major A. H. Nickerson, Asst. Adjt. Genl. U.S.A., formerly A.D.C. to General Crook, arrived at Hd. Qrs. on a short visit, en route to Santa Fé, New Mexico.

May 25th. Read in the telegrams the statement of the death at Columbus, Ohio, May 24th, of my old friend, Capt. Thomas L. Brent, retired list, formerly 3d Cavy. This officer represented in his descent two of the finest families of the country,—the Lees of Virginia and the Carrolls of Carrollton, Maryland. I served with him in the 3d Cavalry, in Arizona, in 1871 and together we went through many scenes that were exciting and pleasurable and some that were hazardous. Under General Crook, in his first campaign against the hostile Apache Indians, we scouted from Tucson, Arizona, to Camp Bowie and thence north viâ the Dos Cabezas, Sierra Burrita (or Mount Graham,) and head of Aravaipa and Gabilau cañons to the Rio Gila, and still north up the Rio San Carlos and over to the Sierra Blanca at the post of Camp Apache,[12] where we replenished supplies and from Camp Apache nearly due West along the crest of the then unknown Mogollon mountains to the post of Camp Verde[13] on the stream of the same name and from there into Fort Whipple near Prescott.

The total distance marched was close to 660 miles and the time occupied—from July 11, 1871 to August 31st of the same year.[14]

---

11. *Richelieu* is a five-act play by Edward George, Earl Bulwer-Lytton (1803–73). The play was first staged to public acclaim in 1839. Although some of Bulwer's phrases, such as "the pen is mightier than the sword" (from *Richelieu*), and "pursuit of the almighty dollar" are often repeated, his heavily embellished Victorian style is dated, and, except for the historical novel, *The Last Days of Pompeii*, his work is rarely read or performed today. http://en.wikipedia.org/wiki/Edward_George_Bulwer-Lytton

12. Camp Apache was established in 1870 on the Mogollon Plateau to guard a proposed reservation in the White Mountains (later Fort Apache Reservation). Upgraded to a fort in 1879, it was pivotal during the Apache campaigns of the 1870s and 1880s. The post was abandoned and transferred to the Indian Service in 1922. Altshuler, *Starting with Defiance*, 12.

13. Camp Verde was established in 1865 on the Rio Verde to protect a nearby farming community. Initially called Camp Lincoln, it was renamed in 1868 to avoid confusion with other posts named in memory of Abraham Lincoln. With the arrival of additional troops for a permanent garrison in 1871, Camp Verde outgrew its site, and a year later was relocated to a larger area away from the river. The Rio Verde Reservation was established nearby, but was closed in 1875, when the Indians were reconcentrated at San Carlos. Verde was upgraded to fort in 1879, and abandoned in 1890. Altshuler, *Starting with Defiance*, 59–62; Frazer, *Forts of the West*, 14.

14. This expedition, which preceded the extant Bourke diaries, is discussed in *On the Border With Crook*, Chapter 8.

One day in August while the command was marching through the pine forests on the summit of the Mogollon range and along the edge of the vertical wall of basalt which faced the Tonto Basin, Brent and I were riding with General Crook, the latter slightly in our front. Suddenly, a couple of stalwart Apaches who had been lying in ambush, jumped from behind a screen of low bushes, yelled a defiant war-whoop, fired two arrows at General Crook and recklessly hurled themselves over the cliff.

Whether from the audacity of the attack, the imminent danger to which our chief was exposed, or the reckless disregard of life and limb evinced by the naked Indians as they went bounding like rubber balls from rock to rock down the almost vertical face of the precipice—or from all these causes combined, we were petrified with astonishment and didn't promptly enough obey General Crook's orders to dismount and fire upon the fleeing savages. They escaped, not however, without wounds as we could see that one of them was badly hurt in the left arm. The arrows had whistled by General Crook's head and imbedded themselves so deeply in a tall pine tree that it was impossible to extract more than half the shafts.

Shortly after this we were obliged to make a very long march, hoping to reach the Rio Verde. The country was unknown to us, our guides had never seen it before and our movements, consequently, became very uncertain. After travelling for 7 or 8 hours, the heat of the sun and the glare from the barren blocks of basalt besetting our line of march, (for we had now gotten out of the forest and were descending the open flanks, of the mountain,) became extremely annoying and the command suffered greatly from thirst. General Crook sent me with a detachment off to one flank to look for springs or creeks or water-holes. In a very few moments, I had crossed a low range of hills and found myself at the edge of a deep cañon, impossible to descend, and could see flowing at the bottom a most tantalizingly pretty streamlet; our poor mules and horses brayed and neighed piteously, but to no avail. Descent was impracticable without wings. The whole command marched alongside this aggravating little cañon for a distance, if I remember right, of fourteen miles and long after dark reached its mouth at the point where the streamlet emptied into what we took to be the Beaver creek fork of the Rio Verde. Everybody was tired out, but poor Brent so exhausted that he could only get off by falling from the saddle and immediately after was attacked with a copious haemorrhage of the lungs.

He was a genial, companionable and scholarly gentleman and a soldier whose bravery, intelligence and ambition were far in excess of his physical powers.

Bourke's narrative skips back to the present.

In company with Major Nickerson, A.A.G., Captain J. M. Lee, 9th Infantry, Mr. Jewitt, Indian trader at Spotted Tail agency, Mr. Matt. Patrick, of the Black Hills Stage line, Mr. Shelton, Cashier of the Union Pacific R.R., and Mr. L. M. Bennett, President of the Pullman Pacific Car Co., started for Cheyenne, Wyo. We had an extemely pleasant party and whiled away the hours in story and reminiscence. As a "raconteur", Capt. Lee has no superior any where. He has travelled extensively throughout our country and has held important trusts among the wild tribes of the frontier.

Possessed of keen powers of observation, a ready wit, good judgment, and a fine flow of language, he readily adapts himself to his company and rarely failed to have his audience convulsed with laughter. He told us in a ridiculously pathetic kind of style of his experience as an Indian agent in Nevada, pending the arrival of the regular appointee from whom he received a letter running something like this: "Dearly beloved friend. I start for the agency to-morrow, with my daughter, Flora, aged 21, and an 8-stop organ, one of Eestey's best. Please pave the way. Yours in Christ and Christian love" &c &c.

Nickerson gave us an intensely vivid and interesting recount of the ceremony of dedicating [sic] the Gettysburgh [sic] monument and of his participation in the fierce battle whose noble dead it commemorates.

Nickerson had been shot through the lungs in the hottest part of the battle and after lingering for weeks between life and death in a field hospital, was carried in a litter through the streets of Gettysburgh to the R.R. station, to start for his home in Ohio.[15]

The day happened to be an unusually warm one even for August and Nickerson lay panting upon his couch which the weary bearers

---

15. Describing the wound in a letter to Rutherford Hayes in 1872, Crook wrote that Nickerson's "recovery was regarded as almost a miracle. He has now a hole in his chest which you can nearly stick your fist in, and in consequence his health is delicate and at times he suffers terribly from this wound. Notwithstanding this, his ambition and zeal to do his duty has [sic] been so great, that he has been constantly on duty ever since the war." Crook to Hayes, January 4, 1872, R.B. Hayes Papers, Crook Collection.

deposited for a short moment in front of a homelike mansion of the best type. While they were resting themselves upon the steps, two ladies appeared at the lower windows of the house and inquired about the sufferer.

Upon being informed that he was a Union Officer, seriously wounded, their womanly tenderness suggested the offer of refreshments. With their own hands they prepared cool wine sherbet and also a very appetizing little lunch to both of which the wounded soldier did full justice, and with grateful voice assured them he would never forget them.

At the conclusion of the great civil war, the National Government decided upon the erection of an imposing monument to carry down to succeeding generations the memory of the gallant men who had laid down their lives upon that bloody field that our country and its institutions should not perish from the earth. When the hour came for the dedication, the little town of Gettysburgh was crammed to repletion with an immense multitude assembled from all quarters of the country. Famous generals, orators and statesmen;—men of letters, men of brains and men of money;—the President and Cabinet, the Governors of all the states represented in the battle, the Senate & House of Representatives, the Supreme Court, officers and soldiers and sailors from the Army and Navy—and last but not least, veterans who had stood shoulder to shoulder in the conflict which saw the most formidable army of the Confederacy dissolve like sand before the rush of waves.[16]

Nickerson had been appointed for the day an Aide de Camp upon the Staff of the Governor of Ohio. This position gave him ample facilities for seeing all that was worth seeing and noting all that deserved to be heard as well as serving for an excuse from all other demands upon his time. But Nickerson was determined to hunt up the ladies from whom he had received such noble courtesies: all he could remember was their name—Witheron, which, however, in a small town is a good deal—and with this as a basis, he searched for their home and was successful in finding it and making himself known to them.

His treatment was as cordial and tender as might be expected from

---

16. Bourke's time frame is off. The dedication was November 19, 1863, a little over four months after the battle.

such noble women, who had long been of the opinion that he had died of his wounds.

His description of [Edward] Everetts' classic address and of President Lincoln's soul-stirring oration was listened to with rapt attention by all our party.[17]

Again, Bourke returns to the present.
Nebraska has had scarcely any rain for the past eight months, Omaha especially being plagued with dust which sweeps along in dense columns, obstructing travel, ruining clothing & furniture and adding greatly to the tendency to indulge in profanity. To-day, black masses of rain-clouds hang down from the sky promising a copious deluge of water just in time to save the crop of cereals from total destruction.

Immigration is pouring into Nebraska, at a rate unprecedented in its history. Long lines of heavily laden wagons follow the wagon-road alongside the Union Pacific Track and population is increasing in every little town. Fremont, Columbus, Duncan, and Grand Island are now, or soon will be, points of departure for new Rail Roads, opening up new belts of country to pay tribute to the Burlington and Union Pacific Railroads.

By telegraphing ahead to my friend, Mr. Wiltze at Grand Island and Mr Rumsey, at [illegible], our party secured an excellent supper at the former place and a warm, cozy breakfast at the latter one.

May 25th After leaving Sidney, the Bluffs nearby were white with fast-falling snow. Two antelope ran out from a gulf and began a race with our locomotive, keeping up with us for more than a mile. Reached Cheyenne in another snow storm. Said Good Bye to Nickerson & Lee, and met Col. Gilliss and Col. Royall.

Mr. Bennett and I took the down train for Omaha, reaching that point on the 27th and learned to our great pleasure that a most refreshing rainstorm had blessed the parched earth during our absence.

June 1st. Genl. Crook and Lt. Schuyler returned from New York, having succeeded in making arrangements with Mr. Knapp for the introduction of the Clauser process in the mill of the Murchie Gold and Silver mining Compy.

June 3d. Lieut. Schuyler started for California.

17. Edward Everett, the foremost orator of the day, was the keynote speaker, while Lincoln was invited as an after thought. Everett, however, confessed himself to be humbled by Lincoln's words.

June 4th Major Nickerson, who had returned from Santa Fé, N.M., May 31st, started back to Washington.

June 7th. The Empress of Russia died a[t] Saint Petersburgh [sic], Russia.[18]

June 8th. The Republican Convention which had seen a stormy session in Chicago, since last Friday, adjourned after nominating a ticket composed of [James A.] Garfield of Ohio and [Chester A.] Arthur of New York. At the commencement of the session, the friends of that grand old soldier—General U.S. Grant, had strong hopes of his success as a candidate. For thirty-five ballots, the vote ran along about thus—Grant 306—Blaine 281, Sherman 91 and Washburne & Edmunds each 30, Windom 10. At the last moment the adherents of Blaine and Sherman united upon Garfield, drawing with them a sufficiency of votes from those held by Washburne, Edmunds & Windom to secure the nomination. The friends of Genl. Grant stood by him to the last. My sympathies from 1st to last have been with Genl. Grant. They are with him now!

During the progress of the balloting, a vote was given for Lieut-General Sheridan, who was called to the floor and acknowledged the compliment amid vociferous cheering.

The ticket selected is an essentially weak one and is in danger of overthrow from the Democwags.[19]

One incident of the convention was the development of the treachery of E. B. Washburne to his friend, Grant. Washburne was the recipient of 35 @ 40 votes, on each ballot and so long as the Grant, Blaine and Sherman factions were so tenacious to their leaders, he had some small hopes of being run in as a "dark horse": had he given his votes to his friend, Grant's preponderance would have been such that many adherents of the other aspirants would have given up the contest as hopeless and gone over to his side.

During the month, President Hayes retired from active service—Generals [Edward D.] Townsend and [Benjamin] Alvord,—Adjutant and Paymaster General of the Army, respectively. This action was very wise and long needed, the subjects of executive action in each case having long passed beyond their career of usefulness. The appointments to the vacancies created were [Richard Coulter] Drum—Ad-

---

18. Maria Alexandrovna, who died the previous day, was the wife of Alexander II.
19. Obviously an amalgamation of Democrat and scallawag.

jutant General and [Nathan Williams] Brown, Paymaster General, the former, a good appointment & both being made on score of seniority simply.

Cap't. [William Henry] Winters 1st Cavalry, died at his post,—Fort Lapwai, Oregon [sic],[20] June 14th. I knew Winters very well in Arizona in 1870–1, and always found him a pleasant gentleman and an exceptionally gallant soldier.

June 22d. Democratic National Convention met in Cincinnati, Ohio and after the usual preliminaries of assembling and coming to order, nominated, June 23d 1880, a ticket of Major General W. S. Hancock, of the Regular Army, and [William Hayden] English of Indiana, for Presdt. and Vice President. This ticket will be a formidable one and, beyond reasonable doubt, will carry success.

20. Bourke is mistaken about the location. Fort Lapwai is in Idaho, and was established in 1862 on the Lapwai River. It was established to keep Indians and whites separate for the protection of both, at a time when miners were crowding the boundaries of the Nez Percé reservation. The military reservation was transferred to the Interior Department in 1882, and the last troops were withdrawn two years later. Frazer, *Forts of the West*, 45.

Appendix 1

Persons Mentioned in the Diary

Due to the large number of sources for the biographical sketches in this section, footnotes or endnotes would have been impractical. Consequently, I have placed the sources in parentheses at the end of each entry. In cases where the author has only one publication in the bibliography, I have used only the author's last name. In case of multiple publications by the same author, I have placed the date of publication of the edition cited.

Military

When discussing the careers of cavalrymen, the designation of units overlapping the Civil War tends to be confusing. In mid-1861, the Regular Army had six mounted regiments, viz. First and Second Dragoons, Mounted Riflemen, and First, Second, and Third Cavalry. On August 3, 1861, Congress reorganized these regiments, designating them all "cavalry," and renumbering them as follows:

First Dragoons to First Cavalry
Second Dragoons to Second Cavalry
Mounted Riflemen to Third Cavalry
First Cavalry to Fourth Cavalry

Second Cavalry to Fifth Cavalry
Third Cavalry to Sixth Cavalry.
After the war, additional Regular Army mounted units were authorized as needed. (Herr and Wallace, 116)

ALMY, William Ellery (d. 1901) of the District of Columbia, entered West Point in 1875. Upon graduation, he was commissioned second lieutenant of the 3rd Infantry, but transferred to the 5th Cavalry in September 1879. He served in the Volunteers during the Spanish-American War, and was a major in the Puerto Rico Regiment at the time of his death. (Heitman, 1:161)

ALVORD, Benjamin (1813–84), of Vermont, was an 1833 graduate of West Point, and was posted to the 4th Infantry. He served in the Seminole and Mexican Wars, and was chief paymaster of the Department of Oregon (later Department of the Columbia) from 1854 until 1862. He spent the Civil War as a brigadier general of Volunteers in command of the District of Oregon. After the war, he served in various paymaster positions until he became paymaster general of the Army in 1872. He held that position until his retirement as brigadier general in 1880. (Warner, 4–5)

ANDREWS. Heitman does not list a second lieutenant of the 5th Cavalry by this name.

ANDREWS, William Howard (d. 1880), joined the Volunteers as a captain in 1862, and was mustered out as a brevet major. He was named first lieutenant of the 12th Infantry in 1866, and assigned to the 3rd Cavalry at Camp McDowell, Arizona, in December 1870, serving as post adjutant for the next ten months. He retired in disability as captain in 1879. (Altshuler, 1991, 10; Heitman, 1:167)

AUGUR, Jacob Arnold, entered West Point in 1865, and was appointed second lieutenant of the 5th Cavalry upon graduation. In 1871, he was promoted to first lieutenant, and in 1879, captain. After serving as major and lieutenant colonel of the 4th Cavalry, he was promoted to colonel of the 10th Cavalry in 1902. (Heitman, 1:175)

AUSTIN, Albert (d. 1886), of Connecticut, served as a noncommissioned officer in the Volunteers throughout the Civil War, promoted to first lieutenant shortly after the war's end. In 1867, he was commissioned second lieutenant of the 14th Infantry, and was promoted to first lieutenant in 1874. (Heitman, 1:175)

BABCOCK, John Breckinridge (1843–1909), a native of Louisiana nevertheless served in the Union Army during the Civil War, and was breveted to major for gallantry. In 1867, he was commissioned as second lieutenant of the 5th Cavalry, and promoted to first lieutenant the following year. He went to Arizona with the regiment in 1872. He was breveted to colonel for gallant service in action against Indians at Tonto Creek, on June 16, 1873, and at Four Peaks, Arizona, on January 16, 1874. He retired as a brigadier general in 1903. (Altshuler, 1991, 14–15; Heitman, 1:178)

BAILEY, Edward Lyon, of New Hampshire, served in the Volunteers during the Civil War, being mustered out in 1864 with the rank of colonel. He was commissioned second lieutenant in the 4th Infantry in 1867, and promoted to first lieutenant in 1876. He was a captain when he was dismissed from the service in 1893. (Heitman, 1:181)

BAINBRIDGE, Augustus Hudson of New York, entered the army in 1858 as a private in general service, but was named battalion sergeant in the 14th Infantry. He was commissioned second lieutenant in 1862, and first lieutenant in 1864. Two years later, he was promoted to captain, a rank he held for over twenty-six years, until promoted to major of the 10th Infantry. He retired as lieutenant colonel of the 4th Infantry in 1898. (Heitman, 1:182)

BALDWIN, John Arthur (d. 1903), of Iowa, was appointed second lieutenant in 1872, and later posted to the 9th Infantry in the Department of the Platte. He served in Crook's Bighorn and Yellowstone Expedition, and participated in the Battle of the Rosebud. From 1886 until 1899, he made several tours in Arizona, after which he was sent to the Philippines where he served in the Insurrection. He was promoted to lieutenant colonel of the 16th Infantry in 1902, but by now, he was in failing health. (Altshuler, 1991, 19)

BARNETT, Richards (d. 1889), of Mississippi, was appointed assistant surgeon in 1875. (Heitman, 1:192)

BARRY, William Farquhar (d. 1879), of New York, entered West Point in 1834, and upon graduation became second lieutenant of the 4th Artillery. After the outbreak of the Civil War, he was appointed brigadier general of Volunteers, and earned a brevet to major general during the Atlanta Campaign, and to brigadier general of the Regular Army for the campaign leading to the surrender of the Confederate

Army. In 1865, he was commissioned colonel of the 2nd Artillery. (Heitman, 1:195)

BENÉT, Stephen Vincent (d. 1895), grandfather of the poet of the same name, entered West Point in 1845, and upon graduation was breveted as second lieutenant of Ordnance. He remained in the Ordnance Department for the rest of his career, and in 1874, was appointed brigadier general and chief of Ordnance. He retired in 1891. (Heitman, 1:210)

BERGLAND, Eric, native of Sweden, entered the army as a second lieutenant of Volunteers in 1861. He finished the war as a first lieutenant, and entered West Point. Upon graduation, he was commissioned second lieutenant of the 5th Artillery, transferring to the Engineers in 1872. He rose through the grades, retiring as a major in 1896. (Heitman, 1:213)

BISBEE, William Henry, of Rhode Island, enlisted in the 18th Infantry in 1861, and was promoted to second lieutenant the following year. He finished the war as a first lieutenant with a brevet as captain. He was promoted to the active rank of captain in 1866, and was assigned to the 4th Infantry in 1870. He retired in 1902 as a brigadier general. (Heitman, 1:220)

BISHOP, Hoel Smith (1850–1925), graduated from West Point in 1873, and was posted to Fort Whipple as second lieutenant in the 5th Cavalry. In 1876, he participated in Crook's Big Horn and Yellowstone Expedition, and in the Bannock War in Wyoming and Idaho in 1878. He retired as colonel in 1913. (Altshuler, 1991, 35)

BOOTH, Charles Austin, of Vermont, entered West Point in 1868, and upon graduation was commissioned second lieutenant of the 7th Infantry. He was promoted to first lieutenant in 1878, and captain in 1891. As of 1903, he was major of the 17th Infantry. (Heitman, 1:231)

BOWMAN, Alpheus Henry (1842–1926) of Virginia, grew up in Pennsylvania, where he attended Pennsylvania Military Academy. In December 1861, he was appointed captain of Volunteers, and after a shaky career was mustered out as a first lieutenant. In 1866, he was commissioned second lieutenant of the 27th Infantry, and promoted to first lieutenant the following year. In 1869, he transferred to the 9th Infantry. He was promoted to captain in 1881. He served in Arizona, and in various Eastern posts, and in the Philippines. He retired in 1903 as brigadier general. (Althshuler, 1991, 38–39)

BOYER. Heitman does not list a Boyer. He may have been a contract surgeon.

BRACKETT, General. Because of the service record, Bourke probably means Albert Gallatin Brackett (d. 1896), although Heitman does not list a brevet as general. Brackett joined the army as second lieutenant of a Volunteer Infantry unit in 1847, and was mustered out the following year. In 1855, he was appointed captain of the 2nd Cavalry, renumbered 5th in 1861. He served in the Volunteers from 1861 to 1864, while retaining the active rank of major of the 1st Cavalry. He was promoted to lieutenant colonel of the 2nd Cavalry in 1868, and colonel of the 3rd Cavalry in 1879. He retired in 1891. (Heitman, 1:237)

BRADLEY, Luther Prentice (1822–1910), native of Connecticut, was appointed lieutenant colonel of a Volunteer regiment in 1861, rising to brigadier general by 1864. In 1866, he entered the Regular Army as lieutenant colonel of the 27th Infantry in 1866. He commanded Fort C.F. Smith, Montana, during the Red Cloud War. As lieutenant colonel of the 9th Infantry, he was in command of Camp Robinson, Nebraska, when Crazy Horse was killed there in 1877. Bradley was appointed colonel of the 3rd Infantry in 1879, and was commander of the Military District of New Mexico in 1881, during the Cibicue outbreak in Arizona. He took troops to reinforce Fort Apache, Arizona, and commanded a special military district created to deal with the crisis. When New Mexico was attached to the Department of Arizona during the Geronimo War, Bradley served under Crook in an effort to contain the raiding. He retired in 1886. (Thrapp, 1991, 1:157; Heitman, 1:239)

BRENT, Thomas Lee, Jr. (ca. 1846–80), entered West Point in 1861, and upon graduation was assigned to the 2nd Cavalry. In 1871, he was captain of the 3rd Cavalry in Arizona, where he served under Crook during a skirmish above the Mogollon Rim. He retired in 1876. (Thrapp, 1991, 1:165; Heitman, 1:242)

BRODRICK, Patrick Thomas (d. 1886), native of Ireland, was an 1868 graduate of West Point. He served in the 23rd Infantry under Crook in the Departments of the Columbia and Arizona. Chronically ill, he died in New York. (Altshuler, 1991, 44)

BROWN, Nathan Williams (d. 1893), of New York, entered the army as a major paymaster in 1849. He was named deputy paymaster general in 1864, and assistant paymaster in 18966. He was appointed brigadier general and paymaster general in 1880, and retired in February 1882. (Heitman, 1:253)

BROWN, Rufus Porter (d. 1892), of Ohio, entered West Point in 1862, and upon graduation was commissioned second lieutenant of the 4th Infantry. He was promoted to first lieutneant in 1876, and was a captain at the time of his death. (Heitman, 1:253)

BROWN, William Henry (1840?–75), native of Maryland, was inspector general of the Department of Arizona under Crook. He enlisted in the army in 1861, and was made second lieutenant of the 5th Cavalry later that year. He was breveted to major in 1865 for gallantry and meritorious service at Five Forks, Virginia. Crook recommended for brevets to brigadier general for service at the Battle of the Caves in 1872, and fights in the Superstition Mountains, Sierra Ancha, and Mazatzals in 1873. He committed suicide on June 4, 1875. According to Constance Wynn Altshuler, he may have been in love with Irene Rucker, who had married Lt. Gen. Philip H. Sheridan the previous day. See also NANNI-CHADDI. (Altshuler, 1991, 46; O'Neal, 57–58; Heitman, 1:254; Bourke, Diary, 2b:73)

BRYANT, Montgomery (1831–1901), native of Kansas, joined the army as second lieutenant of the 6th Infantry in 1857. He went west with the regiment in 1859, serving at Fort Mojave, Arizona, and Fort Yuma, California, until October 1861, when the 6th was transferred east. He served with distinction in the Civil War. He was promoted to major of the 14th Infantry in 1874. He retired as colonel of the 13th Infantry in 1894. (Altshuler, 1991, 47)

BUBB, John Wilson, enlisted in the 12th Infantry in 1861, and was commissioned as lieutenant five years later. In 1869, he was assigned to the 4th Infantry as first lieutenant, serving as quartermaster from 1872 to 1875. During Crook's Big Horn and Yellowstone Expedition, he was acting commissary of subsistence, and played a significant part during the campaign. (Heitman, 1:257)

BUELL, Don Carlos (1818–98), native of Ohio, entered West Point in 1837. He was assigned to the 3rd Infantry and sent to Florida where he participated in the Seminole Wars. After service in the Mexican War, he was assigned to staff duties, and was lieutenant colonel adjutant of the Department of the Pacific at the outbreak of the Civil War. He served in the Volunteers as major general, but his failure to pursue Gen. Braxton Bragg's retreat from Perryville, Kentucky, led to investigation. He was mustered out of the Volunteers in

1864, and resigned his regular commission. He settled in Kentucky where he operated an ironworks and coal mine. (Warner, 51–52)

BURKE, Daniel Webster (1841–1911), native of Connecticut, enlisted in the 2nd Infantry in 1858, serving in Minnesota, Dakota, and Nebraska. He was commissioned as a second lieutenant in 1862, serving with distinction in the Civil War. In 1876, he was captain of the 14th Infantry, serving in Crook's campaigns. He commanded Camp Sheridan, Nebraska, at the Spotted Tail Agency, when Crazy Horse surrendered, and it was at his suggestion that Crazy Horse went to Camp Robinson, where he was killed. Burke, however, had no knowledge of any plans to confine Crazy Horse at Robinson. He retired in 1899 as brigadier general. See also CLARK, Walter Philo; CRAZY HORSE. (Thrapp, 1991, 1:192–93)

BURNAM, A. P. Heitman does not list a Burnam, nor an appropriate Burnham.

BURNETT, Levi Frank, of New York, served as an enlisted Volunteer until 1864, when he was commissioned second lieutenant. He served with distinction during the Civil War, and in 1867, was commissioned second lieutenant in the 36th Infantry in 1867. He was transferred to the 7th Infantry in 1869, and promoted to first lieutenant in 1873. He was captain at the time of his retirement in 1894. (Heitman, 1:264)

BURNHAM, Horace Blois (d. 1894), served in the Volunteers during the Civil War, and finished as a brevet colonel. In 1867, he was commissioned major and judge advocate, and was promoted to lieutenant colonel judge advocate general in 1884. He retired four years later. (Heitman, 1:265)

BURROWES, Thomas Bredin (d. 1885) was appointed first lieutenant of the 18th Infantry in 1861, dismissed and reinstated. He was promoted to captain in 1864. At the time of Bourke's writing, he was captain of the 9th Infantry. He retired in 1879. (Heitman, 1:267)

BURT, Andrew Sheridan (1839–1915), native of Ohio, enlisted as a Volunteer in 1861, but almost immediately was commissioned second lieutenant of the 18th Infantry. He was promoted to the active rank of captain in 1863, and breveted to major for gallant and meritorious service during the Atlanta Campaign. After the war he was posted to Fort Bridger, Utah, and Fort C.F. Smith, Montana. With the reduction of the army he was reassigned to the 9th Infantry.

Burt participated in Crook's Big Horn and Yellowstone Expedition in 1876. He retired as brigadier general in 1902. (Altshuler, 1991, 50–51; Heitman, 1:267)

BYRNE, Thomas "Old Tommie" (c. 1827–81), native of Ireland, enlisted in the 2nd Infantry in Philadelphia in 1854. He was commissioned second lieutenant in 1862, and was breveted for gallantry at Gettysburg. He was a captain at the time of his reassignment to the 12th Infantry in 1871. He died at Fort Mojave in 1881. (Altshuler, 1991, 51–52; Heitman, 1:272).

CAMPBELL, Joseph Boyd (d. 1891), entered West Point in 1857, and upon graduation was commissioned lieutenant of the 4th Artillery. He served with distinction in the Civil War, finishing as brevet major. In 1867, he was promoted to captain of the 4th Artillery. He was a major at the time of his death. (Heitman, 1:278)

CAPRON, Thaddeus Hurlbut (d. 1890), enlisted in the Volunteers in 1861, and was commissioned first lieutenant in 1863. After the Civil War, he was commissioned second lieutenant of the 9th Infantry, and promoted to first lieutenant in 1871. He retired in 1887. Capron left a diary and series of letters on the Big Horn and Yellowstone Expedition. (Heitman, 1:281)

CARLTON, Caleb Henry (1836–1923), native of Ohio, was an 1859 graduate of West Point. He was appointed second lieutenant of the 4th Infantry, and by 1862 had risen to captain. During the Civil War he served as colonel of the Volunteers and earned two brevets. Returning to the Regular Army, he served at Forts Laramie and Fetterman from 1867 to 1869, when he was dropped under the Army Reduction Acts. A year later, he was appointed to the 10th Cavalry at Fort Sill, Indian Territory, and in 1876 was promoted to major of the 3rd Cavalry and posted to Fort D. A. Russell, Wyoming. He served in Arizona from 1882 to 1885, and later was posted to Texas. He retired as brigadier general on June 30, 1897. Bourke often spelled his name as "Carleton." (Althshuler, 1991, 58)

CARPENTER, Gilbert Saltonstall, of Ohio, entered the army as second lieutenant of Volunteers in 1861, but subsequently served in the ranks of the 18th Infantry. In 1862, he was commissioned second lieutenant, and served with distinction in the Civil War. He was promoted to captain of the 45th Infantry in 1866, and posted to the 14th Infantry three years later. He retired as a brigadier general in 1899. (Heitman, 1:284)

CARPENTER, William Lewis (1844–98), native of New York, enlisted in the 2nd Artillery in 1864. He was promoted to second lieutenant and assigned to the 9th Infantry in 1867, and promoted to first lieutenant in 1873. He served on survey and scientific expeditions, including to the Bighorn Mountains, and was elected a fellow of the American Association for the Advancement of Science. He later served in Arizona, where he was promoted to captain. (Altshuler, 1991, 58–59)

CARRINGTON, Henry Beebe (1824–1912) of Connecticut, organized several regiments of state militia in time for the outbreak of the Civil War. In May 1861, he was commissioned colonel of the 18th Infantry, and the following year was appointed brigadier general of Volunteers. Despite efforts to obtain a combat assignment, he was retained throughout the war for administrative duties. He rejoined his regiment at the end of the war, and was assigned to garrison Fort Reno, and establish the posts of Fort Phil Kearny and C. F. Smith, to protect the Bozeman Trail to the Montana gold fields. Carrington's lack of combat experience divided the officers of his headquarters, at Fort Phil Kearny, into factions, the anti-Carrington faction being headed by Capt. William J. Fetterman. The dispute culminated in the massacre of Fetterman and eighty men on December 21, 1866. The massacre effectively ended Carrington's career, and he retired in 1870. In 1889, he negotiated an agreement by which the Flathead Indians moved from their lands in the Bitterroot Valley of Montana to a reservation. See also FETTERMAN, William Judd. (Thrapp, 1991, 1:231; Brown)

CHASE, George Francis (1848–1925), 1871 graduate of West Point, was assigned to the 3rd Cavalry the following year. He participated in the Big Horn and Yellowstone Expedition, and, as first lieutenant, served in Arizona. He retired as a brigadier general in 1912. (Altshuler, 1991, 67)

CHASE, George Nathan, entered West Point in 1873, and upon graduation was posted to the 1st Infantry. A month later, he was commissioned second lieutenant of the 4th Infantry. He was first lieutenant at the time of his retirement in 1891. (Heitman, 1:297)

CHELMSFORD, Frederic Augustus Thesiger, second Baron, (1827–1905), commander of British forces in the Natal during the Zulu War. Following the disaster at Isandhlwana in 1879, Chelmsford was relieved, but before the arrival of his replacement, Sir Garnet

Wolseley, he decisively defeated the Zulus at Ulundi. This victory, bolstered by proper credit in Wolseley's dispatches, redeemed Chelmsford's reputation, and he was named Grand Companion of the Bath upon his return to Great Britain. He was a full general and Grand Companion of the Royal Victorian Order at the time of his death. (Wikipedia)

CHERRY, Samuel Austin, of Indiana, entered West Point in 1870, and upon graduation was appointed second lieutenant of the 23rd Infantry. He transferred to the 5th Cavalry on July 28, 1876. He was murdered by a soldier on May 11, 1881. (Heitman, 1:298)

CHURCH, Albert E., of Connecticut, entered West Point in 1824, and upon graduation, was commissioned second lieutenant of the 3rd Artillery. He was promoted to first lieutenant in 1836. Two years later, he was appointed professor of mathematics at West Point, a post he held until his death on March 30, 1878. Together with his immediate predecessor, Charles Davies, Church was instrumental in shaping the mathematics program at the academy. He was the author of seven textbooks. (Heitman, 1:301; http://www.dean.usma.edu/math/about/history/contrib.htm)

CLARK, William Philo (1845–84), which Bourke often spelled "Clarke," was a native of New York. He graduated from West Point in 1868, and was appointed second lieutenant, 2nd Cavalry, at Fort D. A. Russell, Wyoming. He served on General Crook's staff in 1876 and 1877, figuring prominently in the Great Sioux War, particularly with events surrounding Crazy Horse's death. Much of the acrimony between Clark and Crazy Horse that set the event into motion appears to have stemmed from Frank Grouard's mistranslation of a remark by Crazy Horse. During the Cheyenne Outbreak of 1878–79, Clark managed to round up a large band without bloodshed. His book, *Indian Sign Language*, remains definitive. He also wrote an account of Crazy Horse's death, which was edited by Robert A. Clark, and published in *The Killing of Chief Crazy Horse*, in 1976. See also BURKE, Daniel Webster; GROUARD, Frank; CRAZY HORSE. (Thrapp, 1991, 1:278; Robinson, 1995, 337–38)

CLARKE, Robert Dunlap, which Bourke spelled "Clark" (d. 1891), of Pennsylvania, joined the army as Paymaster of Volunteers in 1863. In 1867, he was appointed major paymaster of the Regular Army. He was breveted to lieutenant colonel of Volunteers for faithful and meritorious service during the Civil War. He retired in 1882. (Heitman, 1:307)

CLEMENTS, Bennett A., was assigned to departmental headquarters in Omaha. He joined the army as a first lieutenant and assistant surgeon in 1856, serving in Florida, Texas, and New Mexico. He was promoted to surgeon and major in 1863, and administered hospitals during and after the Civil War. Dr. Clements participated in General Crook's Horse Meat March, and filed a report giving the medical effects of the ordeal. He also was one of the medical officers who, in 1884, certified that Ranald Mackenzie was insane and unfit for further duty. Clements's report on the Horse Meat March is found in Greene, 1993, 97ff, and in Appendix 2 of the second volume of this series; and on Mackenzie in Robinson, 1993, 323–24. See MACKENZIE, Ranald Slidell.

CLIFFORD, Walter (d. 1883), of New York, enlisted in the 16th Infantry in 1860, and was commissioned as second lieutenant in 1863. He transferred to the 34th Infantry in 1866, and was promoted to captain a year later. In 1871, he was assigned to the 7th Infantry. (Heitman, 1:310)

COCKRILL (should be Cockrell), Heitman's does not list a surgeon under "Cockrill," "Cockrell," or "Cockerill." He is the son of Senator Francis M. Cockrell. See COCKRELL, Francis Marion.

COLEMAN, Frederick William (d. 1902), of New York, served as captain of the Volunteers from 1862 to 1864, and was commissioned in the 15th Infantry in 1866. He was promoted to captain in 1867, and resigned in 1874. (Heitman, 1:316)

COMPTON, Charles Elmer (1836–1909) of New Jersey, enlisted in the Volunteers in 1861, and was commissioned captain later that year. He was mustered out in 1866 as lieutenant colonel of the 53rd U.S. Colored Infantry, and appointed major of the 40th Infantry. In 1870, he was transferred to 6th Cavalry, serving in Texas, Kansas, and Arizona. He was transferred to the 5th Cavalry in 1879, and sent to the Department of the Platte. He retired in 1899 as colonel, and in 1904 was advanced on the retired list to brigadier general. (Atlshuler, 1991, 74–75)

CONNOR, Patrick Edward (1820–91) of Ireland, immigrated to New York with his parents in childhood. He enlisted in the army in 1839, serving in the Seminole War. Discharged, he went to Texas, where he was commissioned in the Volunteers

PERSONS MENTIONED IN THE DIARY 431

during the Mexican War. In 1861, he was in California, where he was appointed colonel of Volunteers and named commander of the District of Utah. He established Fort Douglas, and policed the roads to California. Breveted to major general, in 1865 and 1866, he led an expedition against the Lakotas and Cheyennes in the Powder River Country, where he established old Fort Reno. This expedition was deemed a failure, and damaged Connor's reputation. However, in his recent book, *Circle of Fire*, John D. McDermott makes a strong case that Connor would have succeeded, had he received adequate support from the government. He was mustered out at the end of the expedition and settled in Salt Lake City. (McDermott; Warner, 87–88)

COPPINGER, John Joseph (1834–1909), native of Ireland, was a professional soldier. He was appointed captain of the 14th Infantry in 1861, and served with distinction during the Civil War. In 1866, he was assigned to the 23rd Infantry, serving in San Francisco and Alaska before arriving in Arizona in 1872. He commanded Camp Verde until 1874 when he was reassigned to the Department of the Platte. He was breveted to colonel for service against hostile Indians. He was confirmed as brigadier general in 1896, and commanded the Department of the Platte. He retired in 1898, after being appointed major general of Volunteers. (Altshuler, 1991, 78; Heitman, 1:327)

CORBUSIER, William Henry (1844–1930), of New York, became associated with the army as a contract surgeon. In 1869, he went to Arizona where he served at various military posts, and at San Carlos Reservation. In 1876, he was appointed assistant surgeon in the army, serving in the Department of the Platte, and in Michigan, until 1884, when he returned to Arizona. In 1903, he was named chief surgeon of the Department of Mindinao in the Philippines, and the following year, chief surgeon of the Department of the Columbia. He retired as a lieutenant colonel in 1908, and in 1919, was advanced to colonel. (Altshuler, 1991, 79)

COREY. Heitman does not list a surgeon named "Cory" or "Corey." Probably a contract surgeon.

CRAIG, Louis Aleck (1851–1904), native of Missouri, was an 1874 graduate of West Point. In 1875, he joined the 6th Cavalry at Camp McDowell, and spent much of the following decade in Arizona. He became senior instructor in cavalry tactics at West Point. He retired because of ill health as major of the 15th Cavalry in 1903. (Altshuler, 1991, 83)

CRAWFORD, Emmet (1844–86), native of Pennsylvania, enlisted as a Volunteer during the Civil War and was mustered out as first lieutenant. In 1866, he was commissioned as second lieutenant in the 27th Infantry. With the consolidation of regiments, he was assigned to the 3rd Cavalry at Camp Verde in 1871, moving with the regiment to the Platte where he served in the Big Horn and Yellowstone Expedition. Crawford was promoted to captain in 1879, and in 1882 was assigned to Camp Thomas, Arizona. Upon Crook's return to Arizona, he assigned Crawford as commander of Indian Scouts and military superintendent at San Carlos. During the Geronimo Campaign, he was killed in a skirmish with Mexican militia. (Altshuler, 1991, 84–85; O'Neal, 95–96)

CREEL, Herber [sic] Mansfield, of Missouri, entered West Point in 1873, and upon graduation was posted to the 8th Cavalry. Three months later, in September 1877, he was commissioned lieutenant of the 7th Cavalry. He resigned in 1882. (Heitman, 1:338)

CUSHING, Howard Buckingham (1838–71), of Wisconsin, enlisted first in a Volunteer Artillery regiment in 1862, and the following year in the 4th Artillery. Immediately on transferring to the 4th, he was commissioned as second lieutenant. He transferred to the 3rd Cavalry in 1867, and was posted to the Southwest. He was killed in an Apache ambush in the Whetstone Mountains in 1871. (Atlshuler, 1991, 91)

CUSHING, William Barker (1842–75) known as "Albemarle" Cushing for his near-suicidal exploit that sank the Confederate ironclad ram *Albemarle*, was the brother of Howard Buckingham Cushing. William Cushing entered the U.S. Naval Academy at Annapolis, Md., in 1857, but was dismissed in his final year for reasons that have never been satisfactorily explained. With the outbreak of the Civil War, however, he was appointed acting master's mate of the Volunteer Navy. As the war progressed, Cushing gained more responsibility, and became known for planning and executing daring raids on the Confederate coast. He emerged from the war as a national hero. His last major exploit was in 1873, when, as commanding officer of the U.S.S. *Wyoming*, he managed to halt the executions of surviving passengers and crew of the American ship

Virginius, held in Cuba by Spanish authorities as blockade runners. (Roske and van Doren)

DAVIS. Artillery lieutenant. Bourke apparently means Edward Davis, who served as second lieutenant in a Volunteer unit in 1862, and was breveted for gallantry at Chickamauga. He resigned to enter West Point in 1863, and upon graduation was commissioned second lieutenant of the 3rd Artillery. He served in the artillery until 1902 when, as a major, he was assigned to the Adjutant General's Department. (Heitman, 1:357)

DAVIS, George Breckenridge (1847–1914), is best known for supervising publication of the monumental *War of the Rebellion: Official Records of the Union and Confederate Armies*. A native of Massachusetts, he entered the Volunteers as a sergeant in 1863, and was mustered out as first lieutenant. He entered West Point, and graduated in 1871, after which he was posted to Fort D.A. Russell as second lieutenant of the 5th Cavalry. He served in Arizona from 1872 to 1873, when he was assigned to the academy as assistant professor. Davis was promoted to first lieutenant in 1877, and rejoined his regiment in the Platte. In 1883, he returned to the academy as principal assistant professor of history, geography, and ethics, and assistant professor of law, and wrote *Outlines of International Law*. He was promoted to captain in 1888, and after service in the Indian Territory, was promoted to major and judge advocate. Later he served for twelve years as judge advocate general of the army. He was a major general at the time of his retirement in 1911. (Altshuler, 1991, 95)

DAVIS, Jefferson Columbus (1828–78), of Indiana, was a U.S. Army officer in the Civil War and on the frontier, with no connection to Confederate President Jefferson Davis. In fact, he was part of the Union garrison at Fort Sumter, S.C., when its bombardment began the Civil War. Davis joined the army in the Mexican War, and in 1848 was commissioned a second lieutenant in the 1st Artillery. During the Civil War he served as brigadier general of Volunteers. After the war, he was named colonel of the 23rd Infantry, and in 1867, received the transfer of Alaska from Russia to the United States. He remained in Alaska until 1869. During the Modoc uprising in California in 1873, Davis took command following the assassination of Brig. Gen. E. R. S. Canby, and successfully concluded the campaign. (Thrapp, 1991, 1:380)

DAVIS, Wirt, (1839–1914), native of Virginia, enlisted in the 1st Cavalry in 1860 and was sergeant when the regiment was renumbered as 4th Cavalry a year later. In 1863, he was commissioned as second lieutenant, and promoted to first lieutenant in 1865. He earned three brevets during the Civil War, one for action against Indians in Texas in 1872, and a fifth for the Dull Knife Fight on November 25, 1876. He served in Arizona from 1884 to 1890, and in Cuba and the Philippines. He retired as colonel of the 3rd Cavalry in 1901, and was advanced to brigadier general (retired) three years later. (Altshuler, 1991, 98–99)

DELANEY, Hayden (1845–90), native of Ohio, served as an enlisted man in the Volunteers during the Civil War. He was appointed second lieutenant of the 9th Infantry in 1867, and was breveted for service against the Paiute Indians of Oregon in 1868. He was breveted a second time for action in Col. Ranald Mackenzie's attack on the Cheyennes on November 25, 1876, during Crook's Powder River Expedition in Wyoming. He was promoted to captain in 1889, but suffered from lung hemorrhages. He died during sick leave. (Altshuler, 1991, 100; Bourke, 1980, 390–92)

DENNISON, James Alfred (d. 1900), entered the army as a private of Volunteers in 1861, finishing the Civil War with the same rank. He entered West Point in 1866, and upon graduation was commissioned second lieutenant of the 2nd Artillery. He transferred to the 8th Cavalry in 1871, and resigned the following year. (Heitman, 1:367)

DE WITT, Calvin, of Pennsylvania, served as a captain in the Volutneers from 1861 to 1863. In 1867, he was appointed assistant surgeon, and promoted to surgeon major in 1885. In 1901, he became colonel and assistant surgeon general. (Heitman, 1: 371)

DODD, George Allen (1852–1925) of Pennsylvania, was an 1876 graduate of West Point. He was posted to Wyoming as second lieutenant of the 3rd Cavalry, and served in Nebraska and Dakota. He was promoted to first lieutenant in 1880, and served in the Apache campaigns in Arizona in the 1880s. He later served in the Spanish-American War and Philippine Insurrection, and during Mexican border disturbances. He retired in 1916 as brigadier general. (Altshuler, 1991, 103–4)

DODGE, Frederick Leighton (d. 1891), native of New Hampshire, enlisted in the Volunteers in 1862, and was appointed first lieutenant in 1865. In 1867, he was named second lieutenant of the 23rd Infantry in the Department of the Columbia. He was transferred to Fort Whipple, Arizona, in 1872, and promoted to first lieutenant a year later. His regiment transferred to the Department of the Platte in 1874. In 1889, he suffered a mental breakdown, and retired two years later. A few months after his retirement, he committed suicide. (Altshuler, 1991, 105)

DODGE, Richard Irving (1827–95), 1848 graduate of West Point, was a grand-nephew of Washington Irving who shared Irving's literary bent. Like Bourke, Dodge was a prolific diarist and observer as well as a naturalist, publishing several books on western wildlife and on Indian culture. Perhaps his best known are *The Black Hills: A Minute Description of the Routes, Scenery, Soil, Climate, Timber, Gold, Geology, Zoology, etc.* (1876), and *Our Wild Indians: Thirty Three Years' Personal Experience Among the Red Men of the Great West* (1882). He spent part of the period prior to the Civil War on the Texas Frontier. Unlike many of his contemporaries, who transferred to the Volunteers to attain advancement during the war, Dodge remained in the Regular service, although he was breveted to colonel for faithful and meritorious service in the organization of the Volunteer armies. Promoted to the active rank of major in 1864, he spent much of the postwar era on the frontier. He was named lieutenant colonel of the 23rd Infantry in 1873, and promoted to colonel and aide-de-camp to General Sherman in 1882. He retired in 1891. Wayne R. Kime has edited Dodge's book, *The Plains of North America and Their Inhabitants* (1989), as well as four volumes comprising his service journals from 1875 to 1883. For all his work, it is remarkable that Dodge has received little mention in biographical encyclopedias. (Kime, 1997, 9; Heitman, 1:377)

DOWNEY, George Mason (1841–1910), was commissioned first lieutenant of the 14th Infantry in 1861, and served with distinction in the Civil War. He was promoted to captain in 1865, and was posted to Fort Whipple, Arizona, the following year. He remained in Arizona, and with the reorganization of the postwar army in 1869, he was appointed to the 21st Infantry. He spent much of the remainder of his career in the Southwest or on the West Coast, and was retired for ill health in 1888. In 1904, he was advanced to major on the retired list. (Altshuler, 1991, 108; Heitman, 1:381)

DREW, George Augustus (1832–1921), native of Michigan, was

appointed a captain of the Volunteers in 1862, and promoted to major the following year. He was breveted for distinguished service in the Shenandoah and against Richmond. He was named second lieutenant of the 10th Infantry in 1866, and promoted to first lieutenant in 1868. A year later, he was reassigned to the 3rd Cavalry. He was transferred to Camp Bowie in 1871, and to the Department of the Platte the same year. He served as acting assistant quartermaster for the Big Horn Expedition under Reynolds in 1876. He was promoted to captain in March 1879, and retired with that rank in 1896, but was advanced to major in 1904. (Heitman, 1:383; Altshuler, 1991, 108–09)

DRUM, Richard Coulter, of Pennsylvania, entered the Volunteers in December 1846, and was commissioned second lieutenant in the Regular Army two months later. He served with distinction in the Mexican War and Civil War, finishing the latter with a brevet to brigadier general for service in the Adjutant General's Department. In 1880, he was appointed brigadier general and adjutant general. He retired in 1889. (Heitman, 1:384)

DU BOIS, John Van Deusen (ca. 1833–79) of New York, graduated from West Point in 1855, and served in Texas and New Mexico as second lieutenant in the Mounted Rifles. He briefly served as colonel of a Volunteer regiment in the Civil War. He returned to his regiment, renumbered 3rd Cavalry, in 1862, having been promoted to captain, and was inspector general of the Department of the Missouri from 1864 to 1866. Promoted to major in 1869, he commanded various posts in Arizona, and later served in Nebraska and Wyoming. He retired in 1876. (Altshuler, 1991, 109)

DUNKELBERGER, Isaac Rothermel (ca. 1833–1904), of Pennsylvania, was commissioned second lieutenant of the 1st Dragoons (subsequently renumbered 1st Cavalry) in 1861. He was severely wounded at Trevilian Station, Virginia, in 1864. He finished the war as a captain, with brevets to lieutenant colonel. In 1866, he was posted to Arizona. His wound continued to trouble him, and in 1870, a board recommended disability retirement. Before action could be taken, however, he was discharged as a supernumerary, denying him retirement. In 1901, Congress rectified the matter by placing him on the retired list. (Altshuler, 1991, 114)

DUNN, Thomas Searle (ca. 1823–95) of Indiana, served in the Volunteers during the Mexican War. In 1861, he was commissioned as captain in the 12th Infantry, and served with distinction in the Civil War. In 1866, he was transferred to the 21st Infantry, and was posted to Arizona three years later. He also served in the Department of the Columbia, and commanded Fort Yuma, California. He retired as major of the 12th Infantry in 1878. (Altshuler, 1991, 114)

EASTMAN, Frank French, of Illinois, entered West Point in 1875, and upon graduation was commissioned second lieutenant of the 14th Infantry. He was promoted to first lieutenant in 1890, and captain in 1894. As of 1902, he was a major in the Subsistence Department. (Heitman, 1:394)

EATON, George Oscar (1848–1930), native of Maine, was an 1873 graduate of West Point. He joined the 5th Cavalry at Camp Verde, Arizona, and was recommended for a brevet for scouting expeditions. He may have been the model for the hero in Charles King's novel, *The Colonel's Daughter*. He served on the Big Horn and Yellowstone Expedition in 1876. Eaton resigned in 1883, and later moved to Montana, where he was a member of the State Constitutional Convention. (Altshuler, 1991, 116–17)

EGAN, James (d. 1883) called Teddy by his friends, was a native of Ireland who enlisted in the 2nd Cavalry (later renumbered 5th Cavalry) in 1856. He served with distinction in the Civil War, and was named second lieutenant of the new 2nd Cavalry in 1863. He was promoted to captain in 1868, and in 1872 was among the officers assigned to the Grand Duke Tsarevich Alexis's tour of the Plains. Egan's initiative during Reynolds's Powder River fight prevented a confused, blundering situation from becoming potentially disastrous. He retired on disability in 1879, due to wounds and injuries received in the line of duty. (Thrapp, 1991, 1:454; Heitman, 1:399)

ELKINS. Neither Heitman nor Warner lists an Elkins in the Quartermaster General's Department.

ELTING, Oscar (1831–1902) of New York, enlisted in the Volunteers in 1861. Mustered out as a corporal, he was commissioned a second lieutenant in the 3rd Cavalry in 1867, and joined the regiment in New Mexico. After serving there and in Arizona, he was detailed to recruiting duty, and rejoined his company in the Department of the Platte. Elting was promoted to captain in 1881, and the following year returned to Arizona. He also served in Texas and in Vermont prior to his retirement in 1895. (Altshuler, 1991, 121)

EVANS, Andrew Wallace (1829–1906), native of Maryland, graduated from West Point together with Crook in 1852. He served on the frontier until 1863, and was breveted for the battle of Valverde in 1862. He was named colonel of the 1st Maryland Cavalry in 1864, and was breveted for distinguished service in the Appomattox Campaign. In 1865, he was promoted to major of the 3rd Cavalry, and posted to the frontier. He went to Arizona in 1870, and served under Crook as departmental inspector general. Evans transferred to the Department of the Platte in 1876, and commanded a battalion during Crook's Big Horn and Yellowstone Expedition. He retired in 1883 as lieutenant colonel of the 7th Cavalry. (Altshuler, 1991, 123)

FARRAR, Colonel. Heitman lists several Colonel Farrars whom Bourke could have known.

FERRIS, Samuel Peter, of Connecticut, entered West Point in 1857, and upon graduation was appointed second lieutenant of the 8th Infantry. He transferred to the Volunteers and served as colonel of the 28th Connecticut Infantry. In 1866, he was promoted to captain of the 30th Infantry, Regular Army, and transferred to the 4th Infantry in 1869. He died in 1882. (Heitman, 1:417–18)

FETTERMAN, William Judd (ca. 1833–66), native of Connecticut, enlisted in the Union Army during the Civil War, and was breveted to lieutenant colonel for distinguished service. Commissioned as a captain in the 18th Infantry, he was posted to Fort Phil Kearny, Wyoming. On December 21, 1866, he led his men against a band of Indians, following a decoy party into a trap. Fetterman and his entire eighty-man command died in the fight. (O'Neal, 113–15; Brown)

FITCH, Julian R. of Ohio, served in the Volunteers during the Civil War, received brevets to first lieutenant and captain. He was commissioned second lieutenant of the 17th Infantry in 1866. He was first lieutenant at the time he was transferred to the 15th Infantry in 1869. He was cashiered together with Capt. Alfred Hedberg, 15th Infantry, in January 1873. Lieutenant Edmund T. Ryan, another officer of the 15th Infantry, mentioned by Bourke in connection with Fitch and Hedberg, was cashiered a month later. Interestingly enough, Bourke mentions these officers only in their capacity as cordial hosts to his company as it passed through Fort Cummings, New Mexico, deviating from his usual custom of noting subsequent dismissals or cashierings. See HEDBERG, Alfred; RYAN, Edmund T. (Heitman, 1:422)

FITZGERALD, Michael John, native of Ireland, served as an

enlisted man first in the Artillery then in the Ordnance from 1856 to 1861. He served as hospital steward until 1863, when he was commissioned second lieutenant of the 9th Infantry. By 1876, he was captain. He retired in 1879. (Heitman, 1:423)

FLAGLER, Daniel Webster (d. 1899), of New York, entered West Point in 1856, and upon graduation became second lieutenant of Ordnance. He served with distinction in the Civil War, earning brevets to lieutenant colonel. At the end of the war he resumed the active rank of captain, and was promoted to major in 1874, lieutenant colonel in 1881, and colonel in 1890. He was brigadier general and chief of Ordnance at the time of his death. (Heitman, 1:424)

FOOTE, Morris Cooper, native of New York, enlisted in the Volunteers in 1861, and was promoted to lieutenant the following year. In 1866, he was appointed second lieutenant of the 9th Infantry, and in 1868, to first lieutenant. He was adjutant on the Dodge-Jenney Black Hills Expedition, and later served as regimental adjutant of the 9th from 1879 to 1883. He retired as brigadier general in 1903. (Heitman, 1:427)

FORSYTH, George Alexander "Sandy" (1837–1915) is best remembered for holding out with fifty men during a six-day siege by some 750 Sioux and Cheyenne warriors at Beecher's Island, Colorado, in 1868. A native of Illinois, he enlisted in the Volunteers in 1861, and was appointed first lieutenant later that year. He served as an aide to Maj. Gen. Philip H. Sheridan, and was breveted to brigadier general. In 1866, he was appointed major of the 9th Cavalry. After serving intermittently as secretary and aide to General Sheridan between 1869 and 1881, he was promoted to lieutenant colonel of the 4th Cavalry. He served in Arizona from 1884 to 1887. A year later, he was suspended for three years on half pay for financial irregularities. He retired in 1890, and wrote two books, *The Story of the Soldier* and *Thrilling Days of Army Life*. (Altshuler, 1991, 133–34; Lamar, 381; Thrapp, 1991, 1:509–10)

FORSYTH, James William "Tony," of Ohio, entered West Point in 1851, and in 1856 was commissioned second lieutenant of the 9th Infantry. He had known Sheridan since West Point, and prior to the Civil War, they had served together in the Pacific Northwest. He served under Sheridan from 1864, distinguishing himself in the battles of Opequon, Fisher's Hill, and Middletown. He finished the Civil War as a brevet brigadier general. Forsyth served as Sheridan's aide-de-camp from 1869 to 1873, when he became the lieutenant-general's military secretary. In 1878, he was promoted to lieutenant colonel of the 1st Cavalry, and joined that regiment. In 1886, he became colonel of the 7th Cavalry, which he commanded in the slaughter at Wounded Knee in 1890. (Hutton, 153–54; Heitman, 1:430)

FOSTER, Charles Warren, enlisted in the Engineers in 1846, and served for ten years. After the outbreak of the Civil War, he became captain of the Volunteers, attaining the brevet ranks of lieutenant colonel of Volunteers, and lieutenant colonel of the Regular Army. In 1865, he was appointed captain and acting quarter master, and in 1883, major quartermaster. He retired in 1891. (Heitman, 1:431)

FREEMAN, Henry Blanchard of Ohio, served as a private in the 10th Infantry from 1855 to 1856. He reentered in the 15th Infantry in July 1861, but was promoted to second lieutenant of the 18th Infantry in October. He finished the war as a first lieutenant, with brevets to captain and, in 1894, was awarded the medal of honor for gallantry as Stone's River (Murfreesboro). In 1866, he was promoted to captain, and in 1870 was assigned to the 7th Infantry. He retired as a brigadier general in 1901. (Heitman, 1:435–36)

FREDERICK, Daniel Alfred, of Georgia, entered West Point in 1873, and was commissioned as second lieutenant in 1877. Much of his subsequent career was in the 7th Infantry, although in the Spanish-American War he was a major of Volunteers. He was promoted to major of the 21st Infantry in January 1902, and assigned to the Adjutant General's Department later that year. (Heitman, 1:435).

FREMONT, John Charles (1813–90), known as "The Pathfinder," native of Georgia, entered the army as a second lieutenant of Topographical Engineers in 1836, and assisted in Joseph Nicollet's reconnaissance of Minnesota and Dakota. In 1841, he married Jessie Benton, daughter of Sen. Thomas Hart Benton, who used his influence to boost Fremont's career. He gained fame as an explorer of the West, and an author. Although much of his writing often is credited to his wife, herself a noted author, Fremont's biographer, Ferol Egan, points out stylistic differences to show that he largely was responsible for his own work. Fremont was a key player in the seizure of California during the Mexican War. In 1856, he was presidential candidate of the newly established Republican Party. His no-compromise stand against slavery contributed to his defeat, but the campaign established the Republicans as a viable party. Bad investments reduced him to poverty, which was alleviated in part by his service as governor of Arizona Territory in 1878–83. Shortly before his death, Congress raised him to major general with appropriate retirement pay. (Egan; Thrapp, 1991, 1:519–20)

FRENCH, Lieutenant. Probably Frederick Halverson French, who was commissioned second lieutenant of the 3rd Cavalry in 1877, upon graduation from West Point, and retired as a first lieutenant in 1885. (Heitman, 1:436)

FRENCH, Chaplain. Heitman lists two chaplains named French, neither of whom are appropriate to Bourke's narrative.

FUREY, John Vincent, of New York, enlisted as a private in the Volunteers in 1861. Taking a discharge in 1862, he reentered the Volunteers two years later as quartermaster captain. He was breveted to major of the Volunteers for meritorious service in the Quarter Master Department during the Civil War. Furey was appointed captain and assistant quartermaster of the Regular Army in 1867. Although Altshuler (*Cavalry Yellow and Infantry Blue*) does not list him among the officers who served in Arizona, he was Crook's quartermaster both there and later in the Platte. He retired in 1903 as brigadier general. (Heitman, 1:441)

GENTRY, William Thomas (d. 1885) of Ohio, entered West Point in 1852, and upon graduation was breveted as second lieutenant of the 4th Infantry. He was commissioned first lieutenant of the 17th Infantry in May 1871, and in October was promoted to captain. He received brevets to major and lieutenant colonel during the Civil War. Gentry was assigned to the 19th Infantry in February 1870, and a month later promoted to major of the 9th Infantry. He was a lieutenant colonel at the time of his death. (Heitman, 1:451)

GILBERT, Charles Champion (1822–1903), of Ohio, was an 1846 graduate of West Point, and served in the 1st Infantry during the Mexican War. During the immediate antebellum period, he served in the Southwest, and also on the faculty at West Point. In 1862, he received a six-month appointment as brigadier general of Volunteers. After that he served as major of the 19th Infantry, and was promoted to lieutenant colonel of the 7th Infantry in 1868. He commanded various posts in the West. Gilbert retired as colonel of the 17th Infantry in 1886. (Warner, 173–74; Heitman, 1:455)

GILLISS. The only Gilliss listed by Heitman as quartermaster and appropriate to the era was James Gilliss of the District of Columbia. However, Gilliss was not promoted to major until 1881, and is not listed as having a brevet as major prior to that. As Bourke referred to "Majors Furey and Gilliss," most likely he simply neglected to insert "Captain" in front of Gilliss' name. Gilliss was colonel and assistant quartermaster general at the time of his death in 1898. (Heitman, 1:457)

GOLDMAN, Henry Joseph, native of Germany, entered West Point in 1873, and upon graduation was commissioned second lieutenant of the 5th Cavalry. He remained with the regiment and was captain as of 1903. (Heitman, 1:462)

GORDON, George Alexander (1833–78), native of Virginia, was an 1854 graduate of West Point. After serving in the artillery, he transferred to the 2nd Dragoons in 1855, and took part in suppressing disturbances in Kansas. He was promoted to captain in 1861, shortly before the 2nd Dragoons were renumbered as 2nd Cavalry. During the Civil War he was breveted to lieutenant colonel. In 1867, he was promoted to major of the 4th Cavalry, but was dropped during the Army Reductions. Gordon was reappointed as major of the 5th Cavalry in 1873. He served in Arizona and in the Platte, before being assigned to headquarters of the Military Division of the Missouri in Chicago. (Altshuler, 1991, 141–42)

GREENE, Lewis Douglas (which Bourke spelled "Green") of New York, entered West Point in 1874, and upon graduation was commissioned second lieutenant of the 7th Infantry. He was promoted to first lieutenant in 1888, and served as regimental quartermaster from 1889 to 1893. He retired as a captain in 1898. (Heitman, 1:475)

GREGORY, James Fingal (d. 1897), of New York, was engineer officer of General Sheridan's staff at the time of Bourke's writing. He entered West Point in 1861, and upon graduation was commissioned second lieutenant of the 5th Artillery. In 1866, he transferred to the Engineers, with promotion to first lieutenant. He became captain in 1874, and served as lieutenant colonel/aide-de-camp to Sheridan from 1881 to 1885. He held the active rank of major in the Engineers at the time of his death. (Heitman, 1::477)

GRIMES, Edward B. (d. 1883) entered the army as a captain and assistant quartermaster of Volunteers in 1862. He served with distinction in the Civil War, and was breveted to major. After the war, he was commissioned captain and assistant quartermaster of the Regular

Army. He was a major at the time of his death. (Heitman, 1:480)

GRIMES, Robert D. Heitman does not list a surgeon named Grimes. Most likely he was a contract surgeon.

HALL, William Prebel (1848–1927), native of Missouri, graduated from West Point in 1868, and joined the 19th Infantry in Arkansas. On March 31, 1869, he was dropped from the lists by army consolidations, and three months later assigned to the 5th Cavalry. After service in Kansas and Nebraska, he was assigned to Arizona, where he participated in Crook's Grand Offensive. After a year of sick leave, he returned to duty in 1875, and rejoined his regiment at Fort Dodge, Kansas. Hall was promoted to first lieutenant in 1876, and participated in the Big Horn and Yellowstone Expedition. In 1879, he and a three-man reconnoitering detail rescued an officer who was attacked by more than thirty Indians. Hall received the Medal of Honor for that action. He retired as brigadier general and adjutant general of the army in 1912. (Altshuler, 1991, 150–51)

HAMILTON, John Morrison (1839–98), native of Ontario, enlisted as a Volunteer in New York in 1861. He attained the rank of first lieutenant with a brevet to captain during the Civil War. In 1867, he was commissioned as captain of the 39th Infantry in 1867. In 1870, he was assigned to the 5th Cavalry, and was posted to Camp McDowell, Arizona, in January 1872. He was breveted to major for gallantry in action against the Tonto Apaches in the foothills of the Tortilla Mountains on January 16, 1873. After the 5th was reassigned to the Department of the Platte in 1876, he participated in Col. Ranald Mackenzie's roundup of Red Cloud's band at Chadron Creek, Nebraska, and the attack on the Cheyenne camp during Crook's Powder River Expedition. He was lieutenant colonel of the 9th Cavalry when he was killed in the Battle of San Juan Hill in Cuba in 1898. (Altshuler, 1991, 152–53; O'Neal, 130–31; Heitman, 1:493)

HANCOCK, Winfield Scott (1824–86), 1880 Democratic nominee for president, was born in Pennsylvania, and entered West Point in 1840. Upon graduation, he was posted to the Indian Territory. He served in the Mexican War, Indian campaigns, and the expedition against the Mormons in Utah. Returning east from California upon the outbreak of the Civil War, he was appointed brigadier general of Volunteers, distinguishing himself at Antietam, Fredericksburg and Chancellorsville. At Gettysburg, he received a wound that troubled him for the rest of his life. In 1866, Hancock was appointed major general in the Regular Army, commanding the Department of the Missouri. He was commander of the Military Division of the Atlantic at the time of his death. (Warner, 202–4)

HARDIE, Francis Hunter, entered West Point in 1872, and was commissioned a second lieutenant of the 3rd Cavalry in 1876. He was promoted to first lieutenant in 1881, and served as regimental quartermaster from 1884 to 1888. He was a major of the 14th Cavalry as of 1901. (Heitman, 1:499)

HARTSUFF, Albert, entered the service as assistant surgeon in 1861, and was promoted to major and surgeon in 1876. He accompanied Crook's 1876 expeditions, and assisted Dr. Clements on the Horse Meat March. He was breveted to captain and major for faithful and meritorious service during the Civil War, and to lieutenant colonel in 1866, for meritorious and distinguished service during a cholera epidemic in New Orleans. He was colonel and assistant surgeon general at the time of his retirement in 1901. (Heitman, 1:507)

HATCH, John Porter (1822–1901) of New York, was an 1845 graduate of West Point, and served in the Mounted Rifles during the Mexican War. He served throughout the West during the antebellum years, and in the Civil War was a brigadier general of Volunteers. At the close of the war his active rank was major of the 4th Cavalry. He was promoted to lieutenant colonel of the 5th Cavalry in 1873, later transferred to the 4th Cavalry, and retired at the rank of colonel of the 2nd Cavalry in 1886. (Thrapp, 1991, 2:630)

HAZEN, William Babcock (1830–87), an 1855 graduate of West Point, served with distinction against the Indians in California, Oregon, and Texas, and was seriously wounded in action with Comanches in 1859. This wound, aggravated by diabetes, ultimately caused his death almost thirty years later. He was breveted to major general for his service in the Civil War. In 1867, he was assigned to the Southern Military District in charge of the Indian tribes in Kansas and Oklahoma. As colonel of the 6th Infantry, he commanded Fort Buford, North Dakota, from 1872 to 1877. In 1880, he was promoted to brigadier general and chief of the Army Signal Corps. An outspoken critic and reformer of the army system, he made many enemies. (O'Neal, 142–44; Kroeker)

HEDBERG, Alfred (which Bourke spelled "Hedburg"), of Sweden, entered the 15th Infantry as a private in 1862, and was commissioned second lieutenant the following year. He was promoted to first lieutenant in 1864, and captain in 1865. Cashiered together with Lt. Julian R. Fitch, 15th Infantry, in 1873, he was reinstated thirteen years later by act of Congress. He was killed by Lt. James A. Maney, 15th Infantry, in 1893. Heitman offers no details, but Maney remained in the army as major of the 17th Infantry as of 1902. See FITCH, Julian R; RYAN, Edmund T. (Heitman, 1:519, 687)

HENLEY, Austin (d. 1878), a native of Ireland, entered the army as a private in the 11th Infantry in 1864. At the time he left the regiment in 1867, he was quartermaster sergeant. He entered West Point the following year, and upon graduation was commissioned second lieutenant of the 6th Cavalry. He and Lt. John Anthony Rucker were drowned in a flash flood in Arizona in 1878. During the Red River War, in 1875, a detachment under Henley virtually annihilated a band of Cheyennes at Sappa Creek, Kansas, and some historians speculate that Cheyenne atrocities committed against settlers in Kansas during the Outbreak of 1878–79 were for revenge. See also RUCKER, John Anthony. (Heitman, 1:523; Monnett, 82–83, 92–95)

HENRY, Guy Vernor (1839–99), the son of an army officer, was born at Fort Smith, Arkansas. Upon graduating from West Point in 1861, he was appointed to the 1st Artillery. He distinguished himself in the Civil War, earning brevets as colonel of the Regular Army and brigadier general of the Volunteers. He rejoined the 1st Artillery as captain, and in December 1870, transferred to the 3rd Cavalry which was posted at Camp McDowell, Arizona. In July 1871, Henry led an expedition from Camp Apache to McDowell, which established the efficiency of Indian scouts in Apache campaign. During the Battle of the Rosebud in 1876, he was severely wounded in the face, losing the sight in his left eye. He recovered and as major general of Volunteers, he commanded the Department of Puerto Rico following the Spanish-American War. He was promoted to brigadier general of Volunteers in 1898, and assumed that rank in the Regular Army following his discharge from the Volunteers in June 1899. He died four months later. (Altshuler, 1991, 164–66; O'Neal, 145–46)

HENTON, James "Old Jimmie" (1835–95). Although Bourke gives the impression that Henton was Irish, actually he was born in Liverpool. He enlisted in St. Louis in 1853, and was assigned to Benicia

Barracks, California, where he was discharged as a first sergeant in 1858. He reenlisted in 1860 in the 14th Infantry, and was promoted to second lieutenant the following year, and to first lieutenant in 1862. He was breveted to captain for gallatry at Gettysburg, and with the end of the war that became his active rank. He was transferred to the 23rd Infantry in 1866. Henton commanded Camp Date Creek from September 1872 to January 1873. He was lieutenant colonel at the time of his death. (Altshuler, 1991, 167)

HEWITT, Christian Cyrus, of West Virginia, entered West Point in 1870, and upon graduation was commissioned second lieutenant of the 19th Infantry. He remained with that regiment, retiring as major in 1901. (Heitman, 1:627)

HOFFMAN, William Edwin, entered the service as first lieutenant of Volunteers in 1862, and was promoted to captain a year later. In 1867, he was commissioned as second lieutenant of the 31st Infantry, and in 1870, was assigned to the 4th Infantry. He retired as captain in 1889. (Heitman, 1991, 1:527)

HORTON, Samuel Miller of Pennsylvania, joined the army as assistant surgeon in 1861, and in 1876 was promoted to surgeon major. He retired as a lieutenant colonel and deputy surgeon general in 1894. (Heitman, 1:543)

HOWARD, Oliver Otis (1830–1909), native of Maine, graduated from Bowdoin College and West Point, spent more than half his antebellum service at West Point. Known as "the praying general," he was a devout Congregationalist, and at one point considered resigning from the army to enter the ministry. With the outbreak of the Civil War, he resigned his commission as first lieutenant in the regular army, and became a colonel of Volunteers, and was breveted to brigadier general in September 1861. He lost his right arm in the Battle of Seven Pines. He finished the war as major general of Volunteers, and brevet major general of the Regular Army with the active rank of brigadier general. He headed the Bureau of Freedmen, Refugees, and Abandoned Lands from 1865 to 1872, after which he was a appointed special Indian commissioner. Among his accomplishments was negotiating an end to the Cochise War. He later served as commander of the Department of Columbia, where his high-handedness helped provoke the Nez Percé War. After a period as superintendent of West Point and commander of the Department of the Platte, he was promoted to major general in command of the

Military Division of the Pacific, and subsequently the Military Division of the Atlantic. He retired in 1894. He also founded Howard University, serving as its first president. See also COCHISE; JOSEPH. (Warner, 237–38; Thrapp, 1991, 2:683–84)

HOWELL, Rezin Gist (d. 1887), of Kentucky, entered West Point in 1860, and upon graduation, was commissioned second lieutenant of the 2nd Artillery. He was a captain at the time of his death.

HOWLAND, Carver, of Rhode Island, entered West Point in 1872, and was commissioned a second lieutenant of the 4th Infantry upon graduation. He was promoted to first lieutenant in 1886, and captain in 1894. He was a major at the time of his retirement in 1902. (Heitman, 1:548)

HUGHES, Martin Briggs, of Pennsylvania, entered West Point in 1865, and upon graduation was commissioned second lieutenant of the 9th Cavalry. He was promoted to first lieutenant in 1873. He subsequently was breveted to captain for gallant service against Indians in New Mexico in 1880, and in 1885, was promoted to the active rank. He was a lieutenant colonel of the 10th Cavalry as of 1901. (Heitman, 1:552)

HUGHES, William Burton (d. 1896), of Tennessee entered West Point in 1852, and after a brief brevet with the 4th Infantry, was commissioned second lieutenant of the 9th Infantry in 1856. He was promoted to first lieutenant of the 1st Infantry in 1861. In 1863, he was commissioned captain and acting quartermaster, major quartermaster in 1876, and lieutenant colonel deputy quartermaster general in 1889. He was colonel assistant quartermaster general at the time of his death. (Heitman, 1:553)

HUNTER, George King (1855–1940), native of Ohio, was an 1877 graduate of West Point. He was posted to the 3rd Cavalry in Texas in December 1877, and transferred to Wyoming the following month. Promoted to first lieutenant, he was sent to Fort Bowie, Arizona, in 1882, and participated in the Apache campaigns. He later served with distinction in the Spanish-American War and in the Philippine Insurrection. He retired in 1918 as colonel, but in 1930, was advanced on the retired list to brigadier general. (Altshuler, 1991, 173–74)

JACKSON, Allen Hyre, of New York, served in the Volunteers during the Civil War, rising to the rank of lieutenant colonel. In 1866, he was commissioned second lieutenant of the 7th Infantry, and rose to first lieutenant in 1871. He was breveted through the grades to major for service in the Civil War, and to lieutenant colonel for gallantry in the Battle of Big Hole, Montana, against the Nez Percés in 1877. He retired in 1898 as major paymaster. (Heitman, 1:566)

JACOBS, Joshua West, of Kentucky, served in the Volunteers during the Civil War, mustered out in 1865 as major. In 1866, he was commissioned second lieutenant of the 18th Infantry. By 1869, when he was transferred to the 7th Infantry, he had been promoted to first lieutenant, and served as regimental quartermaster for the next thirteen years until 1882. As of 1900, he was lieutenant colonel and departmental quartermaster general. (Heitman, 1:569)

JOHNSON, Colonel, Pay Department. The only Johnson listed by Heitman in the Pay Department is Chauncey P. E. Johnson, who served as a Volunteer in the Union Army and was mustered out in 1866. Bourke probably means William Hartshorne Johnston (d. 1896) of Ohio, who entered the army as paymaster of Volunteers in 1861, and finished the war as a brevet lieutenant colonel of both Volunteers and Regular Army. He was commissioned to the active rank of major paymaster in 1866, and retired in 1888 as lieutenant colonel deputy paymaster general. (Heitman, 1: 575, 579)

JOHNSON, John Burgess (1847–96), native of Massachusetts, was named second lieutenant of the 6th U.S. Colored Infantry in 1863. In 1870, he joined the 3rd Cavalry as first lieutenant in Arizona, remaining there until his regiment was withdrawn in 1871. He participated in Crook's expeditions of 1876. He was a captain at the time of his death. (Altshuler, 1991, 181)

JORDAN, Allan (d. 1882) of South Carolina, was an 1879 graduate of West Point. He was commissioned a second lieutenant in the 3rd Cavalry, and posted to the Department of the Platte. In 1882, his company was transferred to Arizona, where he died during a winter hunting trip, apparently of exposure. (Altshuler, 1991, 183)

KELLOGG, Sanford Cobb (1842–1904), native of New York, enlisted in that state's National Guard in 1862. He became a captain of Volunteers, serving as aid to Maj. Gen. George H. Thomas, his uncle by marriage. Commissioned as second lieutenant of the Eighteenth Infantry on February 23, 1866, and promoted to first lieutenant on May 15, he was dropped from the list by army consolidation in 1869. In 1870, he was assigned to the 5th Cavalry, and in 1871, was promoted to captain. He served as Sheridan's aide from 1871 to 1873, when he was assigned to Arizona. He accompanied his regiment to the Department of the Platte in 1875. Ten years later, he was again appointed Sheridan's aide. Kellogg was promoted to major of the 4th Cavalry in 1892, and the following year, appointed military attaché in Paris. He retired in 1898. (Altshuler, 1991, 188–89)

KEYES, Edward Livingston (1843–1917), which Bourke sometimes spelled "Keys," native of Massachusetts, joined the 5th Cavalry as a second lieutenant in 1872. During Crook's 1872–73 campaign, he was recommended twice for brevets. He later served in the Department of the Platte during the Great Sioux War. He was court-martialed and dismissed for drunkenness in 1877, studied medicine, and became a prominent surgeon. (Altshuler, 1991, 191)

KIMBALL. Although Bourke gives the assistant surgeon as "W. L. Kimball," the only surgeon named Kimball listed in Heitman for this time period is James P. Kimball, who was appointed assistant surgeon in 1867, and promoted to surgeon major in 1886. He retired on April 7, 1902, as colonel and assistant surgeon general, and died twelve days later. (Heitman, 1:598)

KING, Charles (1844–1933), soldier and author, perhaps has the record for serving over a longer period of time than any soldier in the history of the United States military. He was in virtually every conflict in which the United States was involved, from the Civil War through the First World War. A native of New York, he grew up in Wisconsin. With the outbreak of the Civil War, then sixteen, King volunteered as an orderly to his father, Brig. Gen. Rufus King. He subsequently was appointed to West Point, and upon graduation in 1866, was commissioned as second lieutenant of the 1st Artillery. Upon promotion to first lieutenant in 1870, he transferred to the 5th Cavalry. King scouted against the Apaches in Arizona, distinguishing himself in the fights at Diamond Butte and Sunset Pass. He served during the Big Horn and Yellowstone Expedition in 1876. Upon promotion to captain in 1879, he was retired on disability from an old wound received in Arizona. He then became a popular novelist and playwright, and was known as "America's Kipling" for his stores of army life. When the Spanish-American War broke out, King was appointed brigadier general of Volunteers, and commanded the District of Hawaii. He later served in the Philippines, and was adjutant general of the Wisconsin National Guard. At present, most of King's writings have been forgotten. However, his 1890 book,

Campaigning With Crook, remains a standard for the Big Horn and Yellowstone Expedition. (Altshuler, 1991, 192–93; King, 1890; Russell, *Campaigning With King*)

KING, John Haskell (d. 1888), of Michigan, was commissioned second lieutenant of the 1st Infantry in 1837. He rose through the grades until, shortly after the outbreak of the Civil War, he was promoted to major of the 15th Infantry. After service with the Volunteers as brigadier general, he was mustered out and commissioned as colonel of the 9th Infantry. He was breveted to major general both of Volunteers and of the Regular Army for gallant and meritorious service during the war. He retired in 1882. (Heitman, 1:599)

KIRTLAND, Thaddeus Sandford, of Connecticut, entered the army as a private in the 18th Infantry in October 1861, but was commissioned second lieutenant at the send of that month. In 1862, he was promoted to first lieutenant. He was promoted to captain and transferred to the 36th Infantry in 1866, and three years later transferred to the 7th Infantry. He retired as a major in 1891. (Heitman, 1:604)

KITCHEN. The only surgeon named Kitchen listed in Heitman is Samuel Kitchen, who served in the Volunteers during the Civil War, and was mustered out following the conclusion of the war. (Heitman, 1:605)

LAWSON, Joseph (ca. 1821–81), native of Ireland, joined the Volunteers as a second lieutenant in 1862. He was commissioned as second lieutenant of the 3rd Cavalry in February 1866, and promoted to first lieutenant five months later. He was posted to Camp Date Creek from 1870 to 1871, when the 3rd transferred to the Department of the Platte. He participated in the Big Horn and Yellowstone Expedition. During the Milk River fight in Colorado in 1879, command devolved on Lawson after Maj. Thomas T. Thornburgh was killed, and the senior captain, John Scott Payne, was wounded. Lawson is credited with averting a massacre. See THORNBURGH, Thomas Tipton, and PAYNE, John Scott. (Altshuler, 1991, 198)

LAWTON, Henry Ware (1843–99), native of Ohio, enlisted as a sergeant in the Volunteers in 1861, finishing the Civil War as lieutenant colonel. In 1866, he was commissioned second lieutenant of the 41st Infantry, and was promoted to first lieutenant the following year. Upon the consolidation of regiments, he was transferred to the 24th Infantry, as regimental quartermaster under Col. Ranald

Mackenzie. When Mackenzie transferred to the 4th Cavalry in 1871, Lawton went with him. As RQM, he was responsible for the logistics behind Mackenzie's many successful field expeditions against the Southern Plains Indians. Lawton was promoted to captain in 1881, and later was posted to Arizona, where he served in the Geronimo campaign. He later escorted Geronimo to Skeleton Canyon, where the chief surrendered to Brig. Gen. Nelson Miles. He subsequently was promoted to major and inspector general. During the Spanish-American War, he was appointed major general of Volunteers. He was killed in the Battle of San Mateo, during the Philippine Insurrection. Lawton, Oklahoma, site of Fort Sill, is named in his honor. See also MACKENZIE, Ranald Slidell; MILES, Nelson Appleton. (Altshuler, 1991, 198–99)

LEE, Jesse Matlock (1843–1926), native of Indiana, enlisted in the Volunteers in November 1861, and was commissioned second lieutenant eleven months later. He finished the Civil War as a captain, and was appointed an infantry officer. By the mid-1870s, he was first lieutenant of the 9th Infantry at Camps Sheridan and Robinson, Nebraska. He reported that he was in the Powder River fight in March 1876, but this was purely a cavalry action with no infantry involved. Bourke does not mention him until a visit to Camp Robinson, after the expedition ended. In 1877, Lee convinced Crazy Horse to accompany him to Camp Robinson. Upon arrival, however, Crazy Horse was placed under arrest over Lee's protests, and in the ensuing fight, the chief was mortally wounded. In 1879, Lee, now captain, was recorder for the board inquiring into the conduct of Maj. Marcus A. Reno during the battle of the Little Bighorn. He retired as a major general in 1907. (Thrapp, 1991, 2:832)

LEIGHTON. No Leighton could be found in Heitman, and the only entry under "Layton" did not fit the rank for that time.

LEMLY, Henry Rowan, of North Carolina, entered West Point in 1868, and upon graduation was appointed second lieutenant of the 2nd Cavalry. He served with Crook on the Big Horn and Yellowstone Expedition in the 3rd Cavalry, and wrote an account, "The Fight on the Rosebud," that later was included in the "Papers of the Order of the Indian Wars." He was a captain of the 7th Artillery at the time of his retirement in 1899. (Heitman, 1:627)

LEWIS, John Francis (1842–1915) of Ohio, served as a sergeant of Volunteers during the Civil War. In 1866, he was commissioned second lieutenant, and within a few months was promoted to first lieutenant. He served in Arizona from 1867 to 1871, when he was mustered out under the Army Reduction Acts. (Altshuler, 1991, 203)

LEWIS, William Henry (d. 1878) entered West Point in 1845, and upon graduation was breveted to second lieutenant of the 4th Infantry. He attained the active rank, and in 1850, transferred to the 5th Infantry. With the outbreak of the Civil War, he was promoted to captain, and in 1864, was commissioned major of the 18th Infantry. He served with the Union forces opposing the Confederate thrust into New Mexico, earning brevets to lieutenant colonel. He was appointed to active rank of lieutenant colonel of the 19th Infantry in 1873. He was mortally wounded September 27, 1878, in action against the Cheyennes on the Punished Woman's Fork, and died the following day. (Heitman, 1:631)

LEYDEN, James Alexander (d. 1897), of Tennessee, entered West Point in 1875, and upon graduation was appointed second lieutenant of the 4th Infantry. He was a captain at the time of his death. (Heitman, 1:641)

LONDON, Robert (ca. 1850–92), native of North Carolina, was assigned as a second lieutenant of the 5th Cavalry after graduating from West Point in 1873. He was posted to Camp Lowell, and later to Camp Apache, where he was recommended twice for brevets for distinguished service during scouting expeditions. He also served at San Carlos and Camp Apache. During the Great Sioux War, he participated in the Big Horn and Yellowstone Expedition. (Altshuler, 1991, 204–5)

LORING. Heitman does not list a Lieutenant Loring whose service coincides with the period mentioned by Bourke.

LOVELL, Robert Armstrong, was commissioned second lieutenant in the 14th Infantry in 1872. He was a first lieutenant at the time of his resignation in 1890. (Heitman, 1:644)

LOVERING, Leonard Austin entered West Point in 1872, and upon graduation was commissioned second lieutenant of the 4th Infantry. He rose through the grades becoming a captain in 1893. During the Philippine Insurrection, he rose to lieutenant colonel of Volunteers. In 1901, he was promoted to major of the 29th Infantry, and two years later was assigned to the Inspector General's Department. (Heitman, 1:644)

LUDINGTON, Marshall Independence, of Pennsylvania, entered

the army as captain and acting quartermaster of Volunteers in 1862, and finished the war as colonel and quartermaster. In 1867, he was appointed to the Regular rank of major quartermaster. He retired in 1903 as a major general. (Heitman, 1:646)

LYLE, David Alexander, of Ohio, entered West Point in 1865. Upon graduation, he was commissioned second lieutenant of artillery, and in 1874, promoted to first lieutenant of the Ordnance Corps. As of 1903, he was a major. (Heitman, 1:648)

McCAMMON, William Wallace (d. 1903), entered the army as a first lieutenant of Volunteers in 1861, and finished the war as a brevet major. In 1867, he was commissioned second lieutenant of the 14th Infantry, and was promoted to first lieutenant in 1873. He rose through the grades, retiring in 1902 as major of the 6th Infantry. In 1896, he was awarded the Medal of Honor for gallantry at Corinth, Miss., in 1862. (Heitman, 1:654)

McCALEB, Thomas Sidney (1853-1934), 1875 graduate of West Point, was appointed to second lieutenant of the 9th Infantry, serving in the Department of the Platte during the Great Sioux War. He later served in Arizona, the Spanish-American War, and the Philippine Insurrection, and retired as major in 1902. (Altshuler, 1991, 208)

McCAULEY, Charles Adam Hoke, entered West Point in 1866, and upon graduation was commissioned second lieutenant in the 3rd Artillery. He transferred to the 7th Cavalry in 1878, and was promoted to first lieutenant the following year. He was promoted to captain and assistant quartermaster in 1881. As of 1903, he was colonel and assistant quartermaster general. (Heitman, 1:655)

McCLURE, Daniel (d. 1900), of Indiana, entered West Point in 1845, and upon graduation was breveted second lieutenant of the Mounted Rifles. He resigned in 1850, but re-entered the service as major paymaster in 1858. He was breveted as lieutenant colonel and colonel for service in the Pay Department during the Civil War, and when the war ended was appointed colonel and assistant paymaster general. He retired in 1888. (Heitman, 1:657)

McCONIHE, Samuel (d. 1897), served with distinction in the Civil War, and was breveted through the grades to brigadier general. He was commissioned as lieutenant in the 14th Infantry in 1866, and promoted to captain in 1875. (Heitman, 1:658)

McCOOK, Alexander McDowell (1831-1903), one of fourteen members of the same family known as the "Fighting McCooks" of the Union Army, and the one who attained the highest rank. A native of Ohio, he graduated from West Point in 1852 and was assigned to the 3rd Infantry. With the outbreak of the Civil War, he transferred to Volunteers, attaining the rank of major general. At the end of the war, he assumed the active rank of captain of the 3rd Infantry, rising through the grades until his retirement as major general in 1895. Meanwhile he served on the frontier, and as aide to General Sherman, when the latter was general-in-chief of the army. There appears to have been bad blood between General Crook and McCook, but whether it was Alexander, his cousin Edward McCook, or both, cannot be determined, as Crook tended to confuse the two. This animosity dated to the Civil War, where Crook felt others received the glory while his own efforts went unappreciated. (Warner, 294–95; Robinson, 2001, 321 n43)

McFARLAND, William Campbell, entered West Point in 1868, and upon graduation was commissioned second lieutenant of the 16th Infantry. He was promoted to first lieutenant ten years later, and captain in 1892. He retired in 1899. (Heitman, 1:665)

McKINNEY, John Augustine (d. 1876), of Tennessee, entered West Point in 1867, and upon graduation was commissioned second lieutenant of the 4th Cavalry. He was killed in the Dull Knife Fight on November 25, 1876. Fort McKinney, Wyo., is named in his honor. (Heitman, 1:673)

MACKAY, James Ormond (1857–1911), which Bourke spells "Mackey," was a native of Nova Scotia and an 1879 graduate of West Point. He was assigned to the 3rd Cavalry in the Department of the Platte, and later transferred to Arizona. He was placed on medical retirement as a captain in 1900. (Altshuler, 1991, 218)

MACKENZIE, Ranald Slidell (1840–89), called "Bad Hand" or "Three Fingers" by the Indians because of an injury received to his right hand at Petersburg, was an 1862 graduate of West Point. He served with distinction in the Civil War, rising to the brevet ranks of brigadier general of the Regular Army and major general of Volunteers. In 1867, he was appointed colonel of the 41st Infantry, and in 1870, he was transferred to the 4th Cavalry. He developed the 4th into a mobile assault force, fighting the Southern Plains Indians with their own hit-and-run tactics. During the Red River War of 1874–75, he smashed a large Indian camp in Palo Duro Canyon, Texas, destroying their lodges, food stores, and pony herds, a stratagem he would repeat under Crook in Wyoming. Nevertheless, he was mentally unbalanced, which would become increasingly evident during the Great Sioux War. Promoted to brigadier general in 1882, he was institutionalized for insanity in December 1883, and invalided out of the army the following year. See MANYPENNY, George W. (Pierce, and Robinson, 1993)

MACOMB, Augustus Canfield, attended the Naval Academy from 1872 to 1876. He was commissioned second lieutenant of the 4th Infantry in 1878, and transferred to the 5th Cavalry in 1879. He was promoted to first lieutenant in 1887, and to captain ten years later. (Heitman, 1:680)

MARSTON, Doctor. Heitman does not list a surgeon named Marston.

MARTIN, Captain, at Rock Island Arsenal. This specific Martin could not be identified among the various captains named Martin in the service at the time.

MASON, Charles Winder, was commissioned as second lieutenant in the 13th Infantry in 1875, and transferred to the 4th Infantry later that year. (Heitman, 1:694)

MASON, Julius Wilmot (1835–82), native of Pennsylvania, was commissioned as second lieutenant in the 2nd Cavalry (subsequently renumbered as the 5th Cavalry), in April 1861. He earned two brevets in the Civil War, and emerged from the war with the active rank of captain. He was posted to Camp Hualpai in 1872, and was recommended for two additional brevets for the 1872–73 campaign. As commander of Camp Verde, and acting agent of the reservation, he made substantial improvements. Mason was promoted to major of the 3rd Cavalry in the Department of the Platte in July 1876, but remained with the 5th until the end of the Big Horn and Yellowstone Expedition. He joined the 3rd at Camp Robinson, Nebraska, in October 1876. He returned to Arizona in 1882, as commander of Fort Huachuca, where he died on December 19 of that year. (Altshuler, 1991, 223–24)

MATHEY, Edward Gustave, native of France, entered the army as sergeant of Volunteers in 1861. The following year, he was commissioned second lieutenant and was mustered out in 1865 as a major. In 1867, he was appointed second lieutenant of the 7th Cavalry, rising through the grades and retiring as major in 1896. (Heitman, 1:696)

MAUCK, Clarence (d. 1881), was commissioned second lieutenant of the 1st Cavalry in March 1861, and remained with the regiment at first lieutenant when it was renumbered to 4th Cavalry. He was promoted to captain in 1863, and served with distinction in the Civil War, earning brevets to captain and major. He was major of the 9th Cavalry at the time of his death. (Heitman, 1:697)

MEINHOLD, Charles (ca. 1827–77), native of Berlin, enlisted in the army 1851, possibly with previous military experience in Germany. He served in Texas and New Mexico until his discharge in 1862, after which he served as an officer of the 3rd Cavalry. During the Civil War, he distinguished himself in New Mexico, and during the Vicksburg campaign, and was promoted to captain in 1866. Sent to Arizona in 1871, he investigated the Wickenburg Stagecoach Massacre the following year, He also served in Crook's Big Horn and Yellowstone Expedition in 1876. (Altshuler, 1991, 226)

MERRITT, Wesley (1834–1910), native of New York, was an 1860 graduate of West Point. He served with distinction as a cavalry leader during the Civil War, rising to the rank of brevet major general of Volunteers. After the war, he was appointed lieutenant colonel of the 9th Cavalry, spending much of his time on the Texas frontier albeit in largely administrative functions. When Merritt's promotion to colonel of the 5th Cavalry was announced, Lt. Col. Eugene A. Carr presumed that he would continue to exercise de facto command while Merritt, like his predecessor, Col. William H. Emory, remained on detached duty. When Merritt announced his determination to assume active command, Carr (who was yet unaware of the disaster that had befallen Custer) wrote his wife, "It seems curious that the government should find it necessary to spend huge amounts of money & some blood to teach Terry, Crook, Gibbon, Merritt & others how to fight these prairie Indians when there are Custer & myself who know how to do it and are ready & willing." Upon assuming command, however, Merritt quickly made up for his lack of actual Indian fighting experience, distinguishing himself in the Great Sioux War, the Nez Percé War, and the White River Ute Uprising. During the Spanish-American War, he commanded U.S. troops in the Philippines. He retired in 1900 as a major general.(O'Neal, 166–67; Heitman, 1:706; quote from Carr to Mary Carr, July 3, 1876, Carr Papers)

MILES, Nelson Appleton (1839–1925), native of Massachusetts, was a self-made soldier, and the last general-in-chief of the United States Army before the position was abolished. A store clerk, Miles joined the Volunteers as a first lieutenant, and finished the Civil War as major general. Transferring to the Regular Army in 1866, he was appointed colonel of the 40th Infantry, and with the consolidations of regiments, was transferred to the 5th Infantry in 1869. He distinguished himself in the Red River War on the Southern Plains in 1874–75. During the Great Sioux War, he drove Sitting Bull into Canada, and defeated Crazy Horse at Wolf Mountain in January 1877. Later that year, he accepted the surrender of Chief Joseph, effectively ending the Nez Percé War. Miles hated Crook, and was openly critical of him, and Crook reciprocated in kind. Appointed brigadier general in 1880, Miles relieved Crook in Arizona in 1886. He ended the Geronimo War, although he infuriated Crook by allowing loyal government Apache scouts to be sent into exile in Florida along with the hostiles. Promoted to major general in 1890, Miles became commander of the Military Division of the Missouri upon Crook's death. In 1895, he was appointed general-in-chief, and served in the Spanish-American War. He was promoted to lieutenant general in 1900, and retired three years later. Miles was married to Mary Hoyt Sherman, niece of Sen. John Sherman and Gen. W. T. Sherman. The marriage, however, may have worked against him to some degree, in part because the Sherman brothers wanted no accusations of favoritism, and in part because General Sherman detested him. See also, JOSEPH, SITTING BULL, CRAZY HORSE. (Altshuler, 1991, 229–31; Greene, 1990; Wooster; Robinson, 2001)

MILES, "Paddy." Heitman does not list a Miles named Patrick, or by any other name appropriate to Bourke's narrative.

MIX, John, of New York, enlisted in the 2nd Dragoons in 1852, with its reorganization as the 2nd Cavalry in 1861, he was commissioned second lieutenant. He was major of the 9th Cavalry at the time of his death in 1881. (Heitman, 1:718)

MONAHAN, Deane (1836–1920), native of Ireland, enlisted in the Mounted Rifles in 1856, and appointed second lieutenant in 1862, after his regiment was redesignated the 3rd Cavalry. He was promoted to first lieutenant in 1865, and the following year assigned to Fort Union, New Mexico. In 1868, he was promoted to captain, and in 1870, participated in the Red River Expedition in Arizona.

He remained there until 1871, when his regiment was transferred to the Department of the Platte. Monahan retired in 1884, having been on sick leave for two years. (Altshuler, 1991, 234–35)

MONTGOMERY, Robert Hugh (1838–1905), native of Philadelphia, enlisted in the 2nd Cavalry (later renumbered to the 5th) in 1860, earning two brevets during the Civil War, and spending the last twenty months of the war as a prisoner. He was promoted to first lieutenant in 1865, and to captain in 1870. He was posted to Arizona in 1872, and served with distinction during the 1872–73 campaign, earning a brevet as major for gallantry at Muchos Cañones on September 25, 1872, and during a scout through the Tonto Basin in November and December 1874. During the notorious Horse Meat March of 1876, his company lost fewer horses than any other in the 5th, largely because of his attention to training. He retired as major of the 10th Cavalry in 1891. (Altshuler, 1991, 235; Heitman, 1:720)

MOORE, Alexander (1835–1910), native of Ireland, was appointed first lieutenant of Volunteers in October 1861, and was breveted to major for service during the Civil War. In 1867, he was commissioned captain of the 38th Infantry, and posted to New Mexico, where he served on scouting expeditions. In 1870, he was assigned to the 3rd Cavalry, joining it in Arizona in early 1871. Moore aroused Crook's ire in 1871, when he moved his troops openly across a plain, spoiling the chance to surprise an Apache raiding party. His failure to act decisively during the Reynolds Fight on the Powder River in March 1876, led to his court-martial and suspension. He resigned in 1879 and became a wealthy rancher. (Altshuler, 1991, 235–36; Robinson, 2001, 110)

MOSELEY, Edward Buckland, of Pennsylvania, was appointed assistant surgeon in 1874, and promoted to surgeon major in 1892. As of 1902, he was lieutenant colonel and departmental surgeon general (Heitman, 1:731)

MULHALL, Stephen John, of New York, was a private soldier from 1862 to 1876, when he was commissioned second lieutenant of the 14th Infantry. He retired as first lieutenant in 1891. (Heitman, 1:734)

MUNN, Curtis Emerson, joined the Volunteers as a hospital steward in 1861, and in 1863 was appointed assistant surgeon. He was commissioned as assistant surgeon in 1868, and served in the Crook-Reynolds Big Horn Expedition. He was a surgeon major when he retired in 1900. He died in 1902. (Altshuler, 1991, 239–40)

MUNSON, Samuel, enlisted as a sergeant in the Volunteers in 1861, but was shortly commissioned second lieutenant. Later that year he accepted a commission in the Regular Army as second lieutenant of the 9th Infantry. In 1865, he was promoted to captain. He died in 1887. (Heitman, 1:736)

NASH, William Hoit (d. 1902), of Ohio, was captain commissary of subsistence in the Volunteers during the Civil War, and in 1865 was commissioned to the same rank in the Regular Army. He received brevets to major in both the Volunteers and Regular Army for his wartime service. He was brigadier general and commissary general of subsistence at the time of his death. (Heitman, 1:741)

NICKERSON, Azor Howitt (1837–1910) served on General Crook's staff from 1866 to 1878. A native of Ohio, he joined the Union Army as a second lieutenant of Volunteers in 1861. He was breveted to major for gallantry at Antietam and Gettysburg, receiving a near-fatal chest wound in the latter battle. He entered the Regular Army in 1866. His wound left him in frail health and, although he tried to accompany Crook on his Indian campaigns, sometimes the surgeons would declare him unfit for field duty. He attempted to retire in 1882, but a scandal over a fraudulently obtained divorce from his second wife prompted the War Department to void his retirement. He resigned in 1883 to avoid court-martial. Nickerson later wrote an essay, "Major General George Crook and the Indians," which, although never published in its entirety, has become an integral part of the Crook hagiography. (Crook to Rutherford B. Hayes, January 4, 1872, R. B. Hayes Papers, Crook Collection; Heitman, 1:747–48; Altshuler, 1991, 244–45)

NORRIS, William Foster, entered West Point in 1868, and upon graduation, was commissioned second lieutenant of the 9th Infantry. He resigned as a first lieutenant in 1881. (Heitman, 1:751)

O'CONNOR, Lawrence Lucius, which Bourke often spelled "O'Conner" (d. 1874), native of Ireland, was commissioned second lieutenant of Volunteers in 1861, and was mustered out as captain in 1865. In February of the following year, he was commissioned a second lieutenant in the 3rd Cavalry, and promoted to first lieutenant in November 1866. He was discharged in 1871, as part of the overall army reduction. (Altshuler, 1991, 252)

O'REILLY, Luke, originally from Canada, entered the Volunteers as a second lieutenant in 1862, and earned a brevet as major by the end of the war. He was commissioned first lieutenant of the 39th Infantry in 1866, and was promoted to captain two years later. In 1871, he was assigned to the 19th Infantry. He was dismissed in 1879. (Heitman, 1:760)

ORD, Edward Otho Cresap (1818–83), 1839 graduate of West Point, served in the Seminole Wars in Florida, and in California during the Mexican War. He then served in the Pacific Northwest off and on until 1861, when he was appointed brigadier general of Volunteers and ordered East. When the war ended, he was in command of the Army of the James and the Department of North Carolina. Ord was appointed brigadier general of the Regular Army in 1866 and commanded the Department of the Platte until relieved by Crook. He retired as a major general in 1881, and died of yellow fever in Havana two years later. He is believed to have been the grandson of King George IV through his morganatic wife, Maria Fitzherbert. (Cresap, 2; Warner, 349–50)

PADDOCK, James V. Seaman, of Illinois, entered West Point in 1873, and upon graduation, was appointed second lieutenant of the 5th Cavalry. He was promoted to first lieutenant in 1886, and retired in 1891. (Heitman, 1:764)

PALMER, George, of Wisconsin, entered West Point in 1872, and upon graduation was commissioned second lieutenant of the 24th Infantry. Soon, however, he was transferred to the 9th Infantry, where he remained through the grades until 1902, when he was promoted to major of the 21st Infantry. (Heitman, 1:767)

PARKHURST, Charles Dyer (1849–1931), native of Massachusetts, graduated from West Point in 1872 and was posted to the 5th Cavalry at Camp Date Creek. He participated in the 1872–73 campaign, and was commended in departmental orders and recommended for a brevet. In 1875, he was transferred to Kansas, and a year later, participated in Crook's Big Horn and Yellowstone Expedition. He received a Silver Star for gallantry during the Spanish-American War. Parkhurst retired as colonel of the Coast Artillery. (Altshuler, 1991, 257–58)

PATTERSON, George Thomas Tillman (d. 1894), of Ohio, served during the Civil War as a privae of Volunteers. He entered West Point in 1868, and upon graduation was commissioned a second lieutenant of the 14th Infantry. He was captain at the time of his death. (Heitman, 1:774)

PAYNE, John Scott (1844–95), native of Virginia, was an 1866 graduate of West Point. He was assigned to the 5th Cavalry, where he was promoted to first lieutenant in 1867. After resigning, he practiced law and edited a newspaper. Payne re-entered the army as second lieutenant of the 5th Cavalry, in 1873, but by act of Congress was given the first vacancy for lieutenant in that regiment, retroactive to 1867. He served in Arizona and in the Department of the Platte, where he was promoted to captain in 1875. He served on the Big Horn and Yellowstone Expedition, and in the Wind River Expedition against the Nez Percés. In 1879, he assumed command in the Milk River fight, after Major Thomas T. Thornburgh was killed. Badly wounded in the fight, Payne was commended for gallantry. He retired in 1886. See LAWSON, Joseph, and THORNBURGH, Thomas Tipton. (Altshuler, 1991, 259)

PEASE, William Barrett, of Connecticut, enlisted in the Volunteers in 1862, and in 1863 was appointed second lieutenant of the 8th U.S. Colored Infantry. He was commissioned as first lieutenant of the 11th Infantry in 1867, and later assigned to the 9th Infantry. He retired as captain in 1887. (Heitman, 1:779)

PELOUZE, Louis Henry (d. 1878), of Pennsylvania, entered West Point in 1849, and upon graduation, was breveted as second lieutenant of the 4th Artillery. After receiving his commission, he rose through the grades, becoming captain of the 15th Infantry in 1861. He finished the Civil War as brevet brigadier general. At the time of his death, he was major and assistant adjutant general. Azor Nickerson was promoted to fill the vacancy created by his death. See also, NICKERSON, Azor Howitt. (Heitman, 1:781)

POLLOCK, Robert (d. 1901), of Pennsylvania, whom Bourke called "Old Bobbie," served in the Volunteers during the Mexican War and in the Civil War. He was mustered out in 1866 as a colonel. He was commissioned first lieutenant in the 32nd Infantry, and transferred to the 21st Infantry in 1869. He was promoted to captain in 1873, and retired ten years later. (Heitman, 1:796–97).

POPE, James Worden, entered West Point in 1864, and was commissioned second lieutenant of the 5th Infantry upon graduation. He was promoted to first lieutenant in 1879. In 1885, he became captain and acting quartermaster, rising to major quartermaster in

1891. During the Spanish-American War, he served as chief quartermaster of Volunteers. In 1902, he was commissioned lieutenant colonel deputy quartermaster general. (Heitman, 1:798)

PRATT, Edward Barton (1853–1923), native of Virginia, joined the 23rd Infantry as second lieutenant in 1872, and was posted to Arizona from 1873 until 1874, when his regiment was transferred to the Department of the Platte. He served in Crook's Powder River Expedition of 1876–77. Pratt retired as brigadier general in 1909. (Altshuler, 1991, 267)

PRICE, Butler Dalaplaine, of Pennsylvania, served in the Volunteers during the Civil War, and was commissioned second lieutenant of the 4th Infantry in 1866. He was promoted to first lieutenant in 1873. He was colonel of the 16th Infantry as of 1902. (Heitman, 1:806)

PRICE, George Frederick (1835–88), native of New York City, joined the 2nd California Cavalry as second lieutenant in 1861, and participated in several Indian campaigns over the next two years. The first reference to service in Arizona is on a reconnaissance between Salt Lake City and Fort Mojave in 1864. In 1866, he was appointed second lieutenant of the 5th Cavalry. He was posted to Camp McDowell in 1872, and soon after was promoted to captain. He was nominated for brevets twice for service in Crook's 1872–73 campaign, and was commended for moving Indians to the Rio Verde Reservation after Date Creek was closed. He also supervised construction of the military telegraph between San Diego and Tucson. Transferring to the Department of the Platte, he participated in Crook's Big Horn and Yellowstone Expedition in 1876, and was present at the Slim Buttes Fight. In 1882, he published his memoirs, *Across the Continent with the Fifth U.S. Cavalry*. (Altshuler, 1991, 268; O'Neal, 185–86; Heitman, 1:806)

PRICE, Philip M. (d. 1894) of Pennsylvania, entered West Point in 1865, and upon graduation was commissioned second lieutenant of the 2nd Artillery. He transferred to the Engineers in 1872. He was a captain at the time of his death. (Heitman, 1:806)

PRICE, William Redwood (1838–81), of Ohio, distinguished himself during the Civil War, attaining the brevet rank of brigadier general ovf Volunteers. In 1866, he was commissioned major of the 8th Cavalry, and posted to Camp Mojave, Arizona, where he commanded the District of the Upper Colorado. He was breveted to colonel for gallantry in engagements with the Hualpais in December 1868. He was sent to New Mexico, where he commanded several posts, and in 1879, was appointed lieutenant colonel of the 6th Cavalry. Sent back to Arizona, he negotiated a piece with the Chemehuevis, but by 1881, was suffering too severely from diabetes for further duty. (Altshuler, 1991, 268–69; Heitman, 1:807)

QUENTIN, Julius Edward (d. 1890), native of Germany, was captain of the Volunteers during the Civil War, and in 1866, was commissioned second lieutenant of the 45th Infantry. He was promoted to first lieutenant the following year, and was transferred to the 14th Infantry in 1869. He retired as captain in 1888. (Heitman, 1:811)

QUINTON, William, of Ireland, enlisted in the Volunteers in 1861, and was commissioned second lieutenant of the Signal Corps in 1863. In 1867, he was promoted to first lieutenant of the 33rd Infantry. He was assigned to the 7th Infantry in 1870, and stayed with the regiment until 1898, when he was promoted to major of the 14th Infantry. He retired in 1902 has a brigadier general. (Heitman, 1:811–12)

QUINN, Thomas Francis, of Ireland, served in the 2nd Artillery from 1853 to 1858, when he transferred to the 4th Infantry. In 1863, he was commissioned second lieutenant, and was promoted to first lieutenant two years later. He was breveted to captain for gallant and meritorious service during the Civil War. In 1876, he was promoted to captain, which rank he held at the time of his retirement in 1894. (Heitman, 1:811)

RANDALL, George Morton "Jake" (1841–1918), native of Ohio, was one of the most competent officers to serve under Crook in Arizona. He commanded Camp Apache from 1872 to 1874, during which it was considered the best administered post in the entire department. He also had the most outstanding scouting record of any infantry captain in Arizona. Randall was breveted to colonel of the Regular Army for gallantry at Turret Mountain and Diamond Butte in 1873, and Pinal in 1874, and for distinguished service during the Indian campaigns in Arizona. He enlisted as a private in the Volunteers in July 1861, and and commissioned as 2nd lieutenant in October. By the end of the war he had been breveted to colonel of Volunteers. He was appointed brigadier general of the Regular Army in 1901 and retired four years later. (Heitman, 1:814; Altshuler, 1991, 272–73)

RANDOLPH, Benjamin Harrison, entered West Point in 1866, and upon graduation was commissioned second lieutenant of the 3rd Artillery. He rose through the grades and was a major of the Artillery Corps as of 1903. (Heitman, 1:815)

READE, Philip, of Massachusetts, entered West Point in 1864. Upon graduation, he was commissioned second lieutenant of the 3rd Infantry, rising to captain by 1889. In the Spanish-American War, he rose to lieutenant colonel of Volunteers. As of 1903, he was lieutenant colonel of the 23rd Infantry. (Heitman, 1:819)

REED, William Isaac, of Massachusetts, served as first lieutenant in the Volunteers from 1863 to 1865, and was commissioned second lieutenant of the 5th Infantry in 1866. He was promoted to first lieutenant the same year, and assigned to the 7th Infantry in 1870. He retired as a captain in 1889. (Heitman, 1:821)

REGAN, James, of New York, entered the army as a musician of the 2nd Infantry in 1858. He served throughout the Civil War as a musician and non-commissioned officer. He was commissioned second lieutenant of the 18th Infantry in 1866, and promoted to first lieutenant the following year. As of 1903, he was lieutenant colonel of the 9th Infantry. (Heitman, 1:822)

RENO, Marcus Albert (1834–89), an 1857 graduate of West Point, was commissioned brevet lieutenant of the 1st Dragoons (later renumbered 1st Cavalry), and given the active rank the following year. He served in the Pacific Northwest prior to the Civil War, and was promoted to first lieutenant in 1861. He distinguished himself during the Civil War, earning brevet ranks of brigadier general of Volunteers, and colonel of the Regular Army. Given the active rank of captain, he served as acting assistant inspector general of the Department of the Columbia. He was promoted to major of the 7th Cavalry in 1868, and was reassigned to the Great Plains. He was posted to Fort Abraham Lincoln in 1875, and was the senior surviving officer of the regiment after the battle of the Little Bighorn. Because of the controversy surrounding the fight, he demanded a court of inquiry in 1879, which exonerated him. In 1877, he was suspended without pay for two years following court-martial for conduct unbecoming an officer and a gentleman, but was dismissed in 1880 under sentence of a second court-martial for conduct to the prejudice of good order and military discipline. Over eighty years later, he was posthumously exonerated and restored to rank, when a review board found the evidence on his conviction did not support the charges. He is buried in Custer Battlefield National Cemetery. (Thrapp, 1991, 3:1206–7)

REYNOLDS, Bainbridge (1849–1901), eldest son of Col. Joseph J. Reynolds, was born at West Point, where he graduated in 1873. He was posted to the 3rd Cavalry, was breveted for action in the Battle of the Rosebud in 1876. He served in Arizona from 1882 to 1884. He resigned in 1891 to avoid court-martial. See also REYNOLDS, Joseph Jones.(Altshuler, 1991, 277–78)

REYNOLDS, Joseph Jones (1822–99), native of Kentucky and an 1843 graduate of West Point, initially served on the Texas frontier. Resigning to enter private business in 1857, he rejoined the army at the outbreak of the Civil War. His distinguished service resulted in his being breveted to major general of Volunteers. In 1870, he was named colonel of the 3rd Cavalry and, with his brevet rank, commanded the Department of Texas. During that tenure, Col. Ranald Mackenzie hinted that Reynolds was involved in corruption with supply contracts for Fort McKavett, which Mackenzie commanded. Reynolds was transferred with his regiment to the Department of the Platte in 1872. Despite the verdict and sentence handed him by Crook's court-martial following the Powder River fight, Reynolds was allowed to retire for disability in 1877. Many historians believe that Crook should have shared a heavy amount of the blame for the fiasco. (Thrapp, 1991, 3:1210; Heitman, 1:825; Robinson, 1993, 52–53)

RICE, William Fletcher (d. 1884), native of Massachusetts, enlisted in the Volunteers in 1861, and was commissioned as second lieutenant in 1863. He was commissioned second lieutenant of the 23rd Infantry in 1866, and was first lieutenant when he arrived in Arizona in 1872. During the 1872–73 campaign he served as acting company commander, and was recommended for brevets. He commanded Indian scouts at San Carlos. In 1874, he was transferred with his regiment to the Department of the Platte. He was killed when he fell from a moving railroad train. (Altshuler, 1991, 278–79)

RILEY, James, of Maryland, entered the army as a private in the Volunteers, serving from 1861 to 1863. In 1867, he was commissioned a second lieutenant of the 37th Infantry, but was dismissed the following year. In 1869, he re-entered the army as second lieutenant of the 32nd Infantry, which was amalgamated into the

21st Infantry the same year. He served in Arizona from 1869 to 1871, when he was mustered out under the Army Reduction Acts. (Altshuler, 1991, 281)

ROBINSON, Daniel, of Ireland, served in the ranks from 1849 to 1863, when he was commissioned second lieutenant of the 7th Infantry. Dismissed in 1865, he again served in the ranks until 1866, when he was recommissioned as second lieutenant in the 7th. He was captain at the time of his retirement in 1889. (Heitman, 1:837)

ROBINSON, William Wallace, Jr. (1846–1917), native of Ohio, graduated from West Point in 1869, and was posted to the 3rd Cavalry. He served in Arizona from 1870 to 1871, when the regiment was transferred to the Department of the Platte. After so many officers of the 7th Cavalry were killed at the Little Bighorn, he was transferred to the 7th and promoted to first lieutenant. He retired as a brigadier general in 1910. (Altshuler, 1991, 285).

RODGERS, Calbraith Perry (d. 1878), of Maryland, was commissioned second lieutenant of the 5th Cavalry in 1866, and promoted to first lieutenant a year later. He became captain in 1876, and was killed by lightning in 1878. (Heitman, 1:841)

ROCKWELL, Charles Henry (1848–88), of Ohio, graduated from West Point in 1869, and was assigned to the 5th Cavalry. He served in Nebraska, Wyoming, and Arizona. In 1872, he was promoted to first lieutenant. When the 5th was transferred, he served at Fort Hays, Kansas, and Fort D. A. Russell, Wyoming. In 1880, he married General Sherman's niece, Cecilia Sherman Moulton. Rockwell was quartermaster and commander of an artillery detachment at West Point when he was promoted to captain in 1886. In 1887, he was at Camp Supply, Indian Territory, when he became ill. He took sick leave in April 1888, and died four months later. (Altshuler, 1991, 286)

ROCKWELL, James, Jr., of New York. Bourke stated that Rockwell was in the West Point Class of 1868, but Heitman (1:841) indicates he entered in 1866, and upon graduation was named second lieutenant of the 1st Cavalry in 1870. He was promoted to first lieutenant of Ordnance in 1874, and captain in 1882. During the Spanish-American War, he was lieutenant colonel and chief Ordnance officer of Volunteers. In 1900, he was promoted to major of Ordnance in the Regular Army.

ROSS, William J. (1846–1907), aide to General Crook from 1871 to 1875, was a native of Scotland who grew up in Connecticut. He enlisted in a Volunteer regiment rising to the rank of major of Volunteers during the Civil War. He was commissioned as second lieutenant of the 32nd Infantry (later amalgamated into the 21st Infantry) in 1868, and sent to Arizona a year later. On September 8, 1872, at Camp Date Creek, he saved Crook's life when he kicked a would-be assassin's rifle out of the way. When Crook was transferred to the Department of the Platte in 1875, Ross resigned and settled in Arizona. (Altshuler, 1991, 288; Robinson, 2001, 126)

ROYALL, William Bedford (1825–95), native of Virginia, was commissioned as first lieutenant of a Volunteer unit in 1846, after the outbreak of the Mexican War. After two years of service in the Southwest, including a major Indian fight in 1848, he left the Volunteers. In 1855, he was commissioned first lieutenant of the 2nd Cavalry (later renumbered 5th Cavalry). He distinguished himself during the Civil War, rising to the brevet rank of brigadier general. He served in Arizona as major of the 5th from 1872 to 1875, when the regiment was transferred out. In December 1875, he was promoted to lieutenant colonel of the 3rd Cavalry, commanding Crook's cavalry during the Big Horn and Yellowstone Expedition. He later was breveted for gallantry at the Battle of the Rosebud. In 1881, he succeeded Ranald S. Mackenzie as colonel of the 4th Cavalry. He retired in 1887. (Heitman, 1:849; Altshuler, 1991, 288–89)

RUCKER, John Anthony (d. 1878) son of Brig. Gen. Daniel Henry Rucker, and brother-in-law of Lt. Gen. Philip H. Sheridan, entered the army as a cadet in 1868, although he left West Point two years later. In 1872, he was commissioned at second lieutenant in the 6th Cavalry. He and Lt. Austin Henley, 6th Cavalry, drowned in a flash flood in Arizona in 1878. See HENLEY, Austin. (Heitman, 1:849)

RUFFNER, Ernest Howard, entered West Point in 1863, and upon graduation received dual commissions as second and first lieutenant of the Engineers. He was a lieutenant colonel of Engineers as of 1903. (Heitman, 1:850)

RUSSELL, Gerald "Old Jerry" (1832–1905), native of Ireland, enlisted in the Mounted Riflemen (later redesignated as 3rd Cavalry) in 1851. In 1862, he was promoted to second lieutenant. He distinguished himself during the Civil War, and earned a brevet. He arrived in Arizona as captain in 1870, and participated in scouting expeditions until the 3rd was transferred to the Department of the Platte. During the Powder River Expedition, he participated in Mackenzie's fight with the Cheyennes in November 1876. He served in Arizona a second time from 1882 until 1885. He retired as major in 1890, later upgraded to lieutenant colonel. See also, WHITNEY, Robert H. (Altshuler, 1991, 290–91)

RYAN, Edmund T. of New York, entered the army as an enlisted man in 1856. He was promoted to second lieutenant in the 15th Infantry. He was cashiered in February 1873, in conjunction with Capt. Alfred Hedberg, and Lt. Julian R. Fitch, also of the 15th Infantry. See HEDBERG, Alfred; FITCH, Julian R. (Heitman, 1:855)

SACKET (sometimes spelled Sackett), Delos Bennet, (1822–85), of New York, entered West Point in 1840, and upon graduation was breveted as second lieutenant of the 2nd Dragoons. He earned a brevet as first lieutenant at the battles of Palo Alto and Resaca de la Palma in May 1846, and was commissioned second lieutenant of the 1st Dragoons six weeks later. Shortly after the close of the Mexican War, in 1848, he was promoted to first lieutenant. Sacket served on the frontier, and while posted to Fort Gibson, Indian Territory, married Amanda Fields, daughter of a prominent Cherokee Indian merchant. He was major of the 1st Cavalry (later renumbered to 4th Cavalry) when the Civil War broke out. By the end of 1861, he had been promoted to colonel and inspector general. He distinguished himself during the war, earning brevets as brigadier general and major general. In 1881, he was appointed brigadier general and inspector general. In 1880, together with Crook, Bourke, Sheridan, soldier-author Charles King, and several others, Sacket formed a consortium in an ill-fated venture to develop a gold mine. When it failed, Schuyler, who was managing partner, carried the blame, and lost his position as Crook's aide-de-camp. See SCHUYLER, Walter Scribner; KING, Charles. (Heitman, 1:856; Foreman, 365; Robinson, 2001, 248–49)

SCHUYLER, Walter Scribner (1849–1932), native of New York, was an 1870 graduate of West Point. He served in Arizona from 1872 to 1875 as a second lieutenant of the 5th Cavalry, distinguishing himself in several actions during that period. After a year's leave in Europe, he joined Crook as aide-de-camp in Wyoming as a first lieutenant in 1876. He resigned as aide-de-camp and returned to his regiment the end of 1881, after a falling out with Crook over his management of a mine in which Crook had invested heavily. He was breveted several grades for gallantry in action in Arizona and Wyoming. He retired in 1913 as a brigadier general. See SACKET, Delos Bennet. (Altshuler, 1991, 294–95; Heitman, 1:867; O'Neal, 193–94; Robinson, 2001, 249–50)

SEATON, Frank. Neither Heitman nor Altshuler list a Frank Seaton, nor is it under "Seton."

SEMIG, Bernard Gustave (d. 1883), native of Hungary, served as a private in the Volunteers from 1861 to 1863, after which he became a hospital steward and medical cadet in the Regular Army. He was appointed assistant surgeon in 1874. (Heitman, 1:874)

SHERWOOD, William L. (1847–73), of New York, was appointed second lieutenant of the 21st Infantry in 1867, and posted to Arizona. He served in various posts, and in 1871, was placed in command of Camp Crittenden. In 1872, he was promoted to first lieutenant and posted to the Department of the Columbia. During the Modoc War of 1873, he was killed by Indians approaching his camp under a flag of truce. (Altshuler, 1991, 301)

SILVA, Valentine Mott Cuyler (ca. 1843–1918) of New York, enlisted in the Volunteers in 1861, and a year later, enlisted in the Regular Army as a hospital steward. After the Civil War, he was commissioned lieutenant in the 12th Infantry, and with the reorganization of the army in 1866, was transferred to the 21st Infantry. He served in Arizona from 1869 to 1872, when his company was transferred to the Department of Columbia. Promoted to captain in 1872, he resigned two years later. (Altshuler, 1991, 301–2)

SMEAD, Alexander Dallas Bache (b. 1848), of Pennsylvania, was commissioned second lieutenant of the 3rd Cavalry in 1868, and posted first to New Mexico, and then to Arizona. In July 1872, he was promoted to first lieutenant, retroactive to May of the previous year. He also served in the Department of the Platte. He resigned in 1880, and practiced law in Carlisle, Pennsylvania, but re-entered the service during the Spanish-American War as a captain of the Signal Corps. (Altshuler, 1991, 304–5)

SMITH, Alfred Theophilus, entered West Point in 1855, and upon graduation was breveted second lieutenant of the 4th Infantry. He received an active commission to the 8th Infantry in 1860, and served with distinction in the Civil War, attaining the brevet rank of lieutenant colonel. His active rank in the Regular Army at the end of the war was captain of the 8th Infantry until 1883, when he was promoted to major of the 7th Infantry. He retired in 1899 as colonel of the 13th Infantry. (Heitman, 1:893)

SMITH, A. Sidney, of Missouri, enlisted in the Volunteers in 1861, and was first lieutenant at the time of his resignation in 1864. He was commissioned second lieutenant of the 37th Infantry in 1867, and transferred to the 3rd Cavalry the following year. He was posted to New Mexico and later to Arizona, where he surprised an Apache rancheria, killing thirty Indians. He resigned in 1871. (Altshuler, 1991, 305–06)

SMITH, Charles Henry (d. 1902), of Maine, entered the army as a captain of Volunteers in 1861. He distinguished himself in the Civil War, earning brevets to major general of Volunteers and Regular Army, and in 1895 was awarded the Medal of Honor for gallantry at St. Mary's Church, thirty-one years earlier. In 1866, he was appointed colonel of the 28th Infantry, and transferred to the 19th Infantry in 1869. He retired in 1891. (Heitman, 1:895)

SMITH, John Eugene (1816–97), native of Switzerland, was brought to the United States as a child. He was secretary to Governor Richard Yates of Illinois at the outbreak of the Civil War, and became a colonel of the Volunteers. He earned brevets to major general in both Volunteers and Regular Army, and in 1866 was appointed colonel of the Infantry. He served on the frontier as commander of the 14th Infantry until his retirement in 1881. (Warner, 459)

SPENCER, James Herbert, of Massachusetts, enlisted in the Volunteers in 1861, and was promoted to first lieutenant in 1863. He was mustered out as captain. In 1866, he was commissioned first lieutenant of the 12th Infantry. In 1869, he transferred to the 4th Infantry. He retired as captain in 1885. Five years later, he was breveted for gallant service in action against Indians near Fort Fred Steele, Wyoming, in 1869. (Heitman, 1:910)

SPRAGUE, Charles Jeffries (d. 1893) of Maine, entered West Point in 1838. During the Mexican War, he was breveted to captain for gallantry at Contreras and Churubusco. He served as captain and paymaster for Volunteers from 1861 to 1867, and was breveted to lieutenant colonel, after which he was appointed to the active rank of major paymaster. He retired in 1887. (Heitman, 1:912)

STANLEY, David Sloane (1828–1902) of Ohio, was an 1852 graduate of West Point. He served on the frontier. With the outbreak of the Civil War, he turned down a Confederate commission, and accepted instead an appointment as brigadier general of Volunteers. He distinguished himself in the Mississippi and the Cumberland, finishing the war as a brevet major general of Volunteers. In 1866, he was commissioned colonel of the 22nd Infantry and returned to the frontier, leading expeditions to the Yellowstone in 1872-73. Upon Ranald Mackenzie's retirement, Stanley was appointed brigadier general and commander of the Department of Texas, a position he held until his retirement in 1892. See also MACKENZIE, Ranald Slidell. (Warner, 470-71; Thrapp, 1991, 3:1353-54)

STANTON, Thaddeus Harlan (1835-1900), native of Indiana, enlisted in the Volunteers in 1861. On October 3, 1862, he was designated paymaster, a position he held for the rest of his career. He finished the Civil War as a brevet lieutenant colonel of Volunteers. Apparently Stanton moonlighted as a correspondent for the *New York Tribune*, and in that capacity accompanied Crook and Reynolds on the Big Horn Expedition in the convenience position of chief of scouts. With no previous combat experience, he distinguished himself in the Powder River fight, and later commanded the citizens and irregulars who joined Crook on the train during the Big Horn and Yellowstone Expedition. In 1890, Stanton was breveted to lieutenant colonel of the Regular Army for the Powder River fight, and in 1895, he was appointed paymaster general of the army with the rank of brigadier general. (Thrapp, 1991, 3:1357; Heitman, 1:916)

STANTON, William Sanford, of New York, entered West Point in 1861, and upon graduation was commissioned first lieutenant of the Engineers. He was promoted to captain in 1871. (Heitman, 1:916)

STANWOOD, Frank (ca. 1842-1872), native of Maine, was commanding officer at Camp Grant at the time of the massacre of the Indians by Tucson citizens and their allies. He was on a scouting expedition with much of the garrison, however, and the fact that most of the troops were absent prompted the citizens to move against the Indians. Stanwood entered the army as a second lieutenant of the 3rd Cavalry in 1861. He finished the Civil War as a brevet lieutenant colonel, and was promoted to captain in 1866. He died of tuberculosis on December 20, 1872. Some works spell the name "Standwood," but "Stanwood" is the form on the official record, and the form used by Bourke. (Altshuler, 1991, 315; Thrapp, 1988,

85; Heitman, 1:916)

STEDMAN, Clarence Augustus "Deitsch," entered West Point in 1865, and after graduation was commissioned second lieutenant of the 9th Cavalry. Promoted to first lieutenant in 1875, he served as regimental quartermaster in 1879–80, and adjutant from 1880 to 1883. As of 1902, he was lieutenant colonel of the 4th Cavalry. (Heitman, 1:918)

STYER, Charles (d. 1896), which Bourke spelled "Styers," of Pennsylvania, served as assistant surgeon of Volunteers in 1862–63, but was dismissed. He was appointed assistant surgeon in 1867, and resigned in 1878. (Heitman, 1:935)

SUMMERS, John Edward, of Virginia, was appointed assistant surgeon in 1847, and promoted to surgeon major in 1861. He was appointed lieutenant colonel surgeon in 1880, and retired in 1886 as colonel surgeon. (Heitman, 1:936)

SUMNER, Edwin Vose, was commissioned second lieutenant of the 5th Cavalry in 1861. During the Civil War, he served in the Volunteers and was mustered out with the brevet rank of brigadier general. He remained with the 5th Cavalry, and was promoted to major in 1869. He retired in 1899 as colonel of the 7th Cavalry. (Heitman, 1:936)

SUMNER, Samuel Storrow (1842–1937), native of Pennsylvania, was commissioned second lieutenant of the 2nd Cavalry (later renumbered 5th Cavalry) in 1861. He earned several brevets during the Civil War, and emerged from the war as a captain. He was posted to Arizona from 1870 until 1876, when he joined the Big Horn and Yellowstone Expedition. He retired in 1906 as a major general. (Altshuler, 1991, 324–25)

SUTORIOUS, Alexander (ca. 1837–1905), native of Switzerland, enlisted in the Mounted Riflemen (later redesignated 3rd Cavalry) in 1854. He was commissioned second lieutenant in 1863, and was breveted for gallantry in the Civil War. He went to Arizona in 1870 as a captain, serving until 1871, when the regiment was transferred to the Department of the Platte. He was court-martialed and dismissed for drunkenness during the Big Horn and Yellowstone Expedition. (Altshuler, 1991, 325)

SWIFT, Eben, entered West Point in 1872, and upon graduation was briefly posted as second lieutenant of the 14th Infantry. He transferred to the 5th Cavalry in July 1876. He worked his way up the grades and was major of the 1st Cavalry as of 1903 (Heitman, 1:940)

SWIGERT, Samuel Miller, of Kentucky, entered West Point in 1863, and upon graduation was appointed to second lieutenant of the 2nd Cavalry. He was promoted to first lieutenant in 1869. He retired in 1903 as colonel of the 5th Cavalry. (Heitman, 1:941)

SYKES, George (d. 1880), of Maryland, entered West Point in 1838, and upon graduation, was breveted as second lieutenant of the 3rd Infantry. The following year, the rank was made active. He was promoted to first lieutenant in 1846, and captain in 1855. At the outbreak of the Civil War, he was major of the 14th Infantry. He served in the Volunteers, and was mustered out in 1866 as major general. He also held the brevet rank of major general in the Regular Army. He became colonel of the 20th Infantry in 1868. (Heitman, 1:941–42)

TARLTON, Elisha Warfield (d. 1884) of Kentucky was appointed lieutenant in the 3rd Cavalry in 1861, and captain in 1863. He was breveted to major in 1863 for gallant and meritorious service at Tuscumbia, Alabama. He was listed at a supernumerary on September 26, 1870, and honorably discharged at his own request a month later. (Heitman, 1:944–45)

TAYLOR, Alfred Bronaugh (d. 1903), native of the District of Columbia, served briefly in the Volunteers before enlisting in the 5th Cavalry in 1862. He was commissioned second lieutenant in 1863, and was breveted for service in the Appomattox Campaign. He arrived in Arizona at a captain in 1872, and was breveted for gallantry in action in the Salt River Caves fight of December 28, 1872. (Altshuler, 1991, 327; Heitman, 1:945)

TAYLOR, Daniel Morgan, of the District of Columbia, entered West Point in 1865, and upon graduation was commissioned second lieutenant of the 1st Artillery. He was promoted to first lieutenant of Ordinance in 1874, and as of 1903 was major. (Heitman, 1:946)

TAYLOR, Frank, enlisted in the army in 1860, serving until 1863. In 1867, he was commissioned second lieutenant of the 2nd Infantry, and in 1869, was assigned to the 14th Infantry. He was promoted to first lieutenant in 1876, and to captain in 1892. As of 1900, he was major of the 15th Infantry. (Heitman, 1:946)

THOMAS, Major. Probably Henry Goddard Thomas (d. 1897), joined the army as a captain of Volunteers in 1861, and earned brevets up to brigadier general of the Regular Army and major general of Volunteers in the Civil War. In 1866, he was assigned to the 20th Infantry, and promoted to major ten years later. In 1878, he transferred to the Pay Department as major and pay master. He retired in 1891. (Heitman, 1:955)

THOMPSON, John Charles (d. 1889), of Maryland, entered West Point in 1862, and upon graduation was posted as second lieutenant of the 3rd Cavalry. He was promoted to first lieutenant in 1868, and at the time of his death was a captain. (Heitman, 1:957)

THORNBURGH, Thomas Tipton (d. 1879) of Tennessee, served in a Union Volunteer regiment from Tennessee from 1862 to 1863 when he was appointed to West Point. Upon graduation, he was appointed second lieutenant of the 2nd Artillery, and promoted to first lieutenant in 1870. Three years later, he was promoted to paymaster major. In 1878, he was appointed major of the 4th Infantry. He was killed in action at Milk River, Colorado, during the White River Ute Uprising on September 29, 1879. See COLOROW; PAYNE, John Scott; LAWSON, Joseph; and THORNBURGH, Jacob N. (Heitman, 1:959)

TOWNSEND, Edward Davis (d. 1893), of Massachusetts, entered West Point in 1833, and upon graduation was commissioned second lieutenant of the 2nd Artillery. He rose through the grades, and in 1846, was breveted to captain and assistant adjutant general. He served in adjutancies for the remainder of his career, and in 1869, was appointed brigadier general and adjutant general. He retired in 1880. (Heitman, 1:967)

TOWNSEND, Edwin Franklin, entered West Point in 1850, and upon graduation was breveted second lieutenant of the 3rd Artillery. He resigned in 1856, but re-entered the army as first lieutenant of the 14th Infantry in 1861. He distinguished himself during the Civil War, and was breveted to major for gallantry at Shiloh, and to lieutenant colonel for continued and faithful service in the Ordnance Department. At the time of Bourke's writing, he was colonel of the 11th Infantry. He retired in 1895 as colonel of the 12th Infantry. (Heitman, 1:967)

TROTTER, Frederick Eugene (d. 1892) of New York, served with distinction in the Volunteers during the Civil War, and was breveted to brigadier general of Volunteers, and lieutenant colonel of the Regular Army. In 1866, he was commissioned captain of the 45th Infantry, and in 1869 was transferred to the 14th Infantry. He was major of the

24th Infantry at the time of his death. (Heitman, 1:971)

VAN HORNE (which Bourke spells "Van Horn"), Thomas Budd (d. 1895), entered the army as chaplain of Volunteers in 1862. After the war, he held post chaplaincies until his retirement in 1885. (Heitman, 1:983)

VAN VLIET, Frederick (1841-91), native of New York, was commissioned second lieutenant of the 3rd Cavalry in 1861. He earned brevets to lieutenant colonel during the Civil War, and was promoted to the active rank of captain in 1866. He served in Arizona from 1870 to 1871, when the regiment was transferred to the Department of the Platte. Van Vliet participated in the Big Horn and Yellowstone Expedition in 1876. As major of the 10th Cavalry, he served again in Arizona during the Geronimo Campaign. He died of injuries received in a wagon accident. (Altshuler, 1991, 341)

VOLKMAR, William Jefferson (1847-1901), of Pennsylvania, served in the Volunteers in 1863, before being appointed to West Point. He graduated in 1868, and was posted to the 5th Cavalry at Fort Harker, Kansas, where he distinguished himself in an engagement with the Sioux. He was promoted to first lieutenant in 1870, and two years later was sent to Arizona, where he commanded Camp Date Creek. He was detached for recruiting duty from December 1872 until 1876, when he was appointed aide to Maj. Gen. John Pope. Later he served as an aide to Lt. Gen. Philip H. Sheridan. Volkmar retired at colonel in 1900. His son, whom he named after Walter Schuyler, served as an officer of the Artillery. (Altshuler, 1991, 344-45)

VROOM, Peter Dumont (1842-1926), native of New Jersey, served as an officer of Volunteers, earning several brevets during the Civil War. In February 1866, he was commissioned second lieutenant of the 3rd Cavalry, and was promoted to first lieutenant the following July. Promoted to captain in 1876, he participated in the Big Horn and Yellowstone Expedition, distinguishing himself at the Battle of the Rosebud. He served in Arizona from 1882 to 1885, when he was appointed major/inspector general. He retired as a brigadier general in 1903. (Altshuler, 1991, 346)

WALKER, George Brinton (d. 1902), of Indiana, entered West Point in 1868, and upon graduation was commissioned second lieutenant of the 6th Infantry. He was major of the 18th Infantry at the time of his death. (Heitman, 1:995)

WARD, Edward Wilkerson (d. 1897), a native of Kentucky, was appointed first lieutenant of the Kentucky Scouts in 1861, and was mustered out of the Union Army in 1865. He was commissioned second lieutenant in the 5th Cavalry in 1869, and was posted to the Department of the Platte. He served in Arizona from 1873 to 1875, commanding Indian Scouts at Camp Apache, and serving as post commander at San Carlos. He retired as captain due to ill health in 1879. (Altshuler, 1991, 352)

WARRENS, Charles Henry (d. 1902), native of Prussia, entered the army as a first lieutenant of Volunteers in 1861, and finished the Civil War as a captain. He was commissioned second lieutenant of the 18th Infantry in 1866, and soon transferred to the 27th Infantry. He was promoted to first lieutenant the following year. He later served in the 9th and 14th Infantry Regiments. He retired as a captain in 1891. (Heitman, 1:1004)

WEBSTER, George Ogilvie (d. 1899), of Connecticut, entered West Point in 1861, and upon graduation was commissioned a second lieutenant of the 4th Infantry. He was promoted to first lieutenant in 1875. He was a major at the time of his retirement, shortly before his death. (Heitman, 1:1013)

WEIR, William Bayard (d. 1879), of New York, entered West Point in 1869, and upon graduation was commissioned second lieutenant of the 5th Artillery. In 1874, he was promoted to first lieutenant of Ordnance. He was killed during the White River Ute uprising in Colorado. (Heitman, 1:1015; Bourke, Diary, 32:348–49)

WELLBORN, Luther Scott, of Indiana, entered West Point in 1875, and was commissioned second lieutenant of the 5th Cavalry in 1879. He was a first lieutenant at the time of his retirement in 1891. (Heitman, 1:1015)

WESSELLS, Henry Walton, Jr. (1846–1929), native of New York, attended the Naval Academy for two years before enlisting in the 7th Infantry in March 1865. The following August, he received dual commissions as second and first lieutenant retroactive to July 21. He transferred to the 3rd Cavalry in 1870, joining his company in Arizona in April 1871. Eight months later, the regiment transferred to the Department of the Platte, where Wessells was promoted to captain. He commanded Fort Robinson, Nebraska, during the Cheyenne Outbreak of 1879, and was wounded in the fighting. He was retired for disability as colonel in 1901. Karl Malden's portrayal of

Wessells as an alcoholic Prussian martinet with a heavy German accent, in the 1964 film *Cheyenne Autumn* is fictitious, as is the film itself. (Altshuler, 1991, 355–56)

WHALEN, Captain. Heitman does not list a Captain Whalen.

WHEATON, Charles (1835–1913), native of Rhode Island, was commissioned as second lieutenant of Volunteers in 1861, and finished the Civil War as colonel. He was appointed captain of the 33rd Infantry in 1867, and served on Reconstruction duty before going West. He was in Arizona from 1872 to 1873, and assigned to the Department of the Platte in 1874, where he took part in Crook's Powder River Campaign. He was retired for deafness in 1889. (Altshuler, 1991, 360)

WILLIAMS, Constant, of Pennsylvania, served as an enlisted man from 1861 to 1863, when he was commissioned as second lieutenant of the 7th Infantry. He was promoted to first lieutenant the following year, and to captain in 1873. He was breveted to major for gallantry at the battle of Big Hole, Montana, in 1877, where he was wounded twice. He was colonel of the 26th Infantry as of 1901. (Heitman, 1:1039–40)

WILLIAMS, Robert (d. 1901), native of Virginia, entered West Point in 1847, and upon graduation was assigned to the 1st Dragoons (later 1st Cavalry). In 1861 he was breveted to captain and appointed assistant adjutant general, and served in the Adjutant General's Department throughout the remainder of his career. In 1865, he was breveted to brigadier general for "diligent, faithful, and meritorious service in the Adjutant General's Department during the war." He was assistant adjutant general of the Department of the Platte during Crook's administration. Williams retired in 1893 as brigadier general and adjutant general of the army. (Heitman, 1:1042)

WILSON, Thomas (d. 1901), of the District of Columbia, entered West Point in 1849, and upon graduation was breveted second lieutenant of the 6th Infantry. He was commissioned second lieutenant of the 5th Infantry in 1854. During the Civil War, he served in the Subsistence Department, attaining the brevet rank of brigadier general of Volunteers. After the war, he was captain commissary of subsistence, until his promotion to major in 1882. He was colonel assistant commissary general of subsistence at the time of his retirement in 1896. (Heitman, 1:1048)

WINTERS, William Henry (1843–80), of Ohio, enlisted in the Volunteers in April 1861, and the following August was promoted to second lieutenant. He resigned in 1862, and in 1864, enlisted in the 1st Cavalry. Winters was commissioned to second lieutenant in 1865, and a year later was sent with his company to Arizona, where he was promoted to first lieutenant, and again to captain in 1873. He served in the Apache campaigns, and the Nez Percé and Bannock Wars. (Altshuler, 1991, 375)

WOLF, Silas Augustus, of Pennsylvania, entered West Point in 1874, and upon graduation was commissioned second lieutenant of the 4th Infantry. He rose through the grades and as of 1901, was major of the 19th Infantry. (Heitman, 1:153)

WOODSON, Albert Emmett (1841–1903) native of Kentucky, went to Washington Territory in 1859. Three years later, he enlisted in the territorial volunteers, serving as a hospital steward until 1863 when he was commissioned a second lieutenant. In 1867, he was commissioned first lieutenant of the 36th Infantry in the Department of the Platte, and in 1870 was transferred to the 5th Cavalry. In Arizona, he participated in Crook's Apache campaigns, distinguishing himself in fights in the Tonto Basin. As a captain, he was on the Big Horn and Yellowstone Expedition, and in the Slim Buttes fight. He later served in the Nez Percé War and in the Philippines. Woodson retired as brigadier general in 1903. (Thrapp, 1991, 3:1593–94)

WYATT, Walter Scott, of Ohio, served in the ranks of a Volunteer artillery regiment from 1864 to 1865. He was appointed to West Point in 1867, and upon graduation was commissioned a second lieutenant of the 2nd Cavalry. He transferred to the 9th Infantry in 1872, and in 1879, was promoted to first lieutenant. He resigned in 1887. (Heitman, 1:1064)

YEATMAN, Richard Thompson, of Ohio, entered West Point in 1868, and upon graduation was commissioned second lieutenant of the 14th Infantry. He rose through the grades and as of 1900 was major of the 22nd Infantry. (Heitman, 1:1066)

YOUNG, George Shaeffer, of West Virginia, was commissioned second lieutenant of the 7th Infantry in 1875, and promoted to first lieutenant in 1882. He was a major as of 1901. (Heitman, 1:1067)

YOUNG, Robert Hunter, of Kentucky who, after distinguished service in the Volunteers during the Civil War, was commissioned second lieutenant of the 30th Infantry in 1867, and transferred to the 4th Infantry a year later. In 1890, he was breveted to first lieutenant for gallant service in action against Indians near Fort Fred Steele,

Wyoming, in 1869. He retired in 1891. (Heitman, 1:1067)

Civilians

ADAMS, Charles (ca. 1845–95), native of Pomerania originally named Karl Adam Schwanbeck, was an American soldier and diplomat. He enlisted in the Union Army shortly after arriving in the United States. After the war, he served on the frontier in the 3rd Cavalry, and in 1870, was appointed brigadier general of the Colorado militia. At the insistence of his wife, he Americanized his name to Charles Adams. In June 1872, he was appointed agent for the Utes at Los Piños, where he served for two years, becoming successful and popular, gaining Ouray's friendship and support. In the White River Uprising of 1879, he secured the release of the women and children captives, and was one of three commissioners who investigated the outbreak. In 1880, he was appointed minister to Bolivia, where he arbitrated a boundary dispute between that country and Chile. See also MEEKER, Nathan Cook; OURAY. (Johnson and Malone, 1:39)

ALLISON, William Boyd (1829–1908), senator from Iowa from 1873 until his death, was a member of the Senate Committee of Indian Affairs, among other powerful positions. A native of Ohio, he studied law, practicing in his hometown of Ashland until 1857, when he moved to Iowa. During the Civil War he served on the staff of Gov. Samuel J. Kirkwood, helping raise state regiments. During that same period, he was elected to the U.S. House of Representatives, serving until 1871. Although Allison was wealthy, he devoted his life primarily to public service, and was co-sponsor of the Bland-Allison Act that established a bimetal monetary system over the opposition of industrial and banking interests. (Wikipedia)

ARTHUR, Chester Allen (1830–86), succeeded the assassinated James A. Garfield as president of the United States in 1881. A product of the New York political machine, Arthur nevertheless was personally honest. As quartermaster general of New York in the Civil War, he had arranged the rapid and efficient deployment of over 200,000 troops at substantial savings to the federal government. Initially a believer in patronage, Arthur changed his views upon becoming president, and secured passage of the Pendleton Act that reformed the civil service, calling for competitive examinations and prohibiting dismissal for political reasons. See also GARFIELD, James Abram. (Reeves)

BAKER, James "Old Jim" (1818–98), native of Belleville, Illinois, became a trapper for the American Fur Company in 1838. Thereafter, he was a mountain man and a guide before settling in Denver in 1859. He moved to Dixon, Wyoming, in 1873. (Thrapp, 1991, 1:57)

BARRETT, Lawrence (1838–91), was one of the leading American actors of the nineteenth century. A native of Paterson, New Jersey, he began work as a call boy at the Metropolitan Theatre in Detroit at the age of fourteen, and made his first appearance as an actor within a year. He gained a reputation throughout the Midwest that allowed him to immediately secure leading roles when he moved to New York. After the Civil War, he became nationally renowned, and in 1886 began a partnership with Edwin Booth that continued until his death. See also McCULLOUGH, John. (Johnson and Malone, 1:646–48)

BELKNAP, William Worth (1829–90), native of New York, was secretary of war during the Grant Administration. Belknap was the son of Brig. Gen. William Goldsmith Belknap, who distinguished himself in the Mexican War and on the Texas frontier. He served as a volunteer during the Civil War, rising to the rank of brigadier general. He was appointed secretary of war in 1869, but in 1876, a congressional committee on War Department expenditures found evidence that he had accepted a bribe in the appointment of a post trader at Fort Sill, Oklahoma. It was generally believed in the army that the corruption was not limited to Fort Sill. He was impeached, but the Senate did not get the majority needed to convict, largely because many of the senators were satisfied with Belknap's resignation. He practiced law in Washington where he died. (Johnson and Malone, 2:147–48.)

BLAINE, James Gillespie (1830–93), was a member of the U.S. House of Representatives and Senate from Maine, speaker of the House, secretary of state during part of the Garfield/Arthur administration and under Benjamin Harrison, and Republican presidential candidate in 1884. A native of Pennsylvania, Blaine moved to Augusta, Maine, in 1854, and edited newspapers before turning to politics. He was largely responsible for the Fourteenth Amendment, but opposed military governments in the Southern states, unless there was a plan for eventual end to military rule. He is considered to have been an effective and successful secretary of state. (Wikipedia)

BORIE, Adolph Edward (1809–80) served briefly as secretary of the navy under U.S. Grant in 1869, before resigning to resume his business interests. The only significant aspect of his administration was his dislike of large numbers of warships being given Indian names, and he renamed them using terms from antiquity. After he resigned, his successor, George M. Robeson, ordered them reverted back to their original names. (Wikipedia)

CHANDLER, Zachariah (1813–79), succeeded Columbus Delano as secretary of the interior in October 1875, and held the position until the end of the Grant administration in March 1877. He reorganized the Interior Department, restoring some if its integrity with large-scale dismissals for dishonesty and incompetence. Chandler was a Republican political boss in Michigan, serving as one of that state's senators from 1857 to 1874, and again for a few months prior to his death in 1879. During the Civil War, he was a member of the Joint Committee on the Conduct of the War. See DELANO, Columbus. (Johnson and Malone, 3:618)

CLARK (or Clarke), Ben (1842–1914), frontiersman from Oklahoma. A native of St. Louis, first went west in 1855, and became post courier at Fort Bridger, Wyoming. He served in the Mormon War of 1857, a Kansas unit during the Civil War, and as scout and guide during several postwar campaigns, including Sheridan's in 1868–69, the Red River War of 1874–75, Crook's Big Horn Expedition of 1876, and the Cheyenne Outbreak of 1878. With William G. McDonald, Clark recorded the legends of the Cheyennes and Arapahoes. (Thrapp, 1991, 1:274–75)

COCKRELL, Francis Marion (1834–1915), was a former Confederate officer who later served five terms as senator from Missouri. Cockrell was elected to the Senate in 1875, and served until his retirement in 1905. During that time, he was chairman of the Claims Committee, Engrossed Bills Committee, and Appropriations Committee. Upon leaving the Senate, he was appointed to the Interstate Commerce Commission, and served until 1910, when he was appointed to a commission to fix the permanent boundary between the State of Texas and Territory of New Mexico. He was director of Ordnance for the War Department at the time of his death. (Wikipedia)

COSGROVE, Thomas, native of Texas and former Confederate cavalryman, who, together with Robert Eckles and Nelson Yarnell, lived among the Shoshones and trained their warriors in conventional cavalry tactics.

DANILSON (which Bourke spelled Danielson), William H., an army officer when appointed agent at Fort Hall in 1869, was required under the Army Appropriation Act of 1870 to chose between giving up his commission or giving up his post as agent. He chose to resign from the army and remain as agent. Danilson had entered the army as a private in the Volunteers in 1861, and by the end of the Civil War had been breveted to major. After mustering out of the Volunteers, he accepted a commission as first lieutenant of the 40th Infantry. Although the Shoshones and Bannocks at Fort Hall were prepared to give up their nomadic life and settle, Danilson was hamstrung throughout the 1870s by inadequate government appropriations. Eventually the Bannocks left in disgust, setting off a chain of events leading to the uprising of 1878. Nevertheless, Danilson managed to maintain the Indians' confidence in his own integrity. (Heitman, 1:353. See also Madsen)

DELANO, Columbus (1809–96), secretary of the interior during the Grant Administration, initially joined the administration in 1869 as commissioner of Internal Revenue. During his term, already established whiskey revenue frauds continued. The following year, he as appointed secretary of the interior, and again, a preexisting pattern of corruption in the Department of the Interior's Bureau of Indian Affairs was allowed to continue, ultimately becoming a national scandal. Under pressure from newspapers, he resigned in 1875. (Johnson and Malone, 5:217–18)

De LESSEPS, Ferdinand Marie, Vicomte (1805–94), French diplomat and construction magnate best known for building the Suez Canal. A native of Versailles, he entered diplomatic service in 1825, and spent much of his career in North Africa, where he first envisioned a canal connecting the Mediterranean with the Red Sea and Indian Ocean. After his retirement, he successfully negotiated a concession for the Suez Canal, which was constructed from 1859 to 1869. In 1882, he began construction of a projected sea-level canal across Panama which failed in part because of the engineering impracticalities, corruption, and disease. (Wikipedia)

DUNDY, Elmer Scipio (1830–96), native of Ohio, practiced law in Pennsylvania from 1853 until 1857 when he relocated to Nebraska. He was a member of the Territorial County from 1858 to 1863, and the following year was appointed U.S. Territorial Judge for Nebraska.

In 1868, he was appointed to the newly created federal court for the District of Nebraska, a post he held until his death. See also STANDING BEAR; TIBBLES, Thomas Henry. (http://www.fjc.gov/servlet/tGetInfo?jid=664)

EADS, James Buchanan (1820–87), was one of the foremost American engineers of the nineteenth century. A native of Lawrenceburg, Indiana, he became purser on a Mississippi steamer in 1838, and became aware of the economic potential of salvaging sunken boats. He patented a diving bell, and in 1842, began a successful salvage business. During the Civil War, he constructed the iron-clad gunboats that helped secure Union control of the Mississippi. In 1874, he completed what is considered his greatest achievement, the Eads Bridge across the Mississippi River at St. Louis, which many engineers considered impossible using the technology of the era. (Johnson and Malone, 5:587–89)

ECKLES, Robert (Texas Bob). See COSGROVE, Thomas.

EMERY, George W. (1830–1909), territorial governor of Utah from 1875 to 1880, was a native of Maine. After serving as a federal tax collector, he was appointed governor of Utah, where he initiated election reforms and expanded government service. Despite being a Gentile in a predominantly Mormon territory, he was a popular governor, and after his term ended, the legislature named a new county in his honor. (http://historytogo.utah.gov/people/governors/territorial/emery.html)

FINERTY, John Frederick (1846–1908), a political refugee from Ireland, became a correspondent for the *Chicago Times*, and covered more Indian war campaigns than any other professional journalist. In 1876, he covered Crook's expeditions, and his book, *War-Path and Bivouac* is one of the most complete accounts. He also covered the Ute campaign of 1879, visited Sitting Bull in exile in Canada, and covered the 1881 Apache uprising. He was a member of Congress from 1883 to 1885. (Finerty; Knight, 173–74; Lamar, 369)

GARFIELD, James Abram (1831–81), president of the United States for six months in 1881, was nominated by a coalition of Grant's enemies in the Republican Convention of 1880, mentioned by Bourke. A native of Ohio, Garfield was entirely self-made, having worked his way through Williams College, and working as a school master. In 1859, he was elected to the Ohio Senate, where he was noted for his eloquence and logic. With the outbreak of the Civil War, he was appointed lieutenant colonel of Volunteers, studied tactics, and mastered command so well that, after the Union disaster at Chickamauga that ruined Maj. Gen. William S. Rosecrans, Garfield was appointed major general. He served in both houses of Congress before his election to the presidency. He was the second president to be assassinated. See also ARTHUR, Chester Allen. (Warner, 166–67)

GORDON, John Brown (1832–1904), former Confederate general, was senator from Georgia from 1873 to 1880, when he resigned to promote the Georgia-Pacific Railroad. He later served as governor of Georgia. (Wikipedia)

GOULD, Jay (1836–92), originally named Jason, was an American railroad magnate and financier. A native of Roxbury, New York, he did odd jobs, and by the age of twenty-one had saved $5,000, which he used to obtain part interest in a tannery. Eventually he gained full control, and from there went into speculation in small railroads. In 1867, he achieved notoriety when, with two partners, he managed to wrest control of the Erie Railroad from Cornelius Vanderbilt. From that point, he began acquiring control of the major lines as they expanded across the country, as well as Western Union Telegraph. (Johnson and Malone, 7:454–55)

GROUARD, Frank (1850?–1905) claimed that he was born in the Friendly Islands, the son of an American missionary and a Polynesian noblewoman. While this is the most generally accepted version, and most probably true, his numerous detractors disputed it, some insisting that he was mulatto, and others that he was Indian-white. Grouard was a braggart, and his own accounts cannot be considered completely reliable. Despite his assertions to the contrary, he also nursed an unexplained, but deep-seated hatred for the Oglala chief Crazy Horse, possibly resulting from several years spent in Oglala captivity. The animosity ultimately became a factor in Crazy Horse's death. Despite his faults, Grouard was a great scout and an experienced frontiersman, and his services to the government were invaluable during the Great Sioux War. Bourke generally spelled the name "Gruard." See also CLARK, Walter Philo; CRAZY HORSE. (DeBarthe; Robinson, 1995)

HAYES, James Webb Cook (1856–1923), son of President Rutherford B. Hayes, and a sort of surrogate son to the childless George and Mary Crook, often accompanied Crook on hunting trips in the West, and stood with Mary at the general's funeral. Webb Hayes attended Cornell University, but left in 1875 to serve as his father's secretary when he was both governor of Ohio and president. In 1887, he and three associates founded National Carbon Company, later Union Carbide, of which he served many years as vice president. He served with distinction in the Spanish-American War, winning the Medal of Honor for valor in the Philippine Campaign. He also served in the Boxer Rebellion and the First World War. See also, HAYES, Rutherford Birchard. (Robinson, 2001; Wikipedia)

HAYES, Lucy Ware Webb (1831–89), wife of President Rutherford B. Hayes, and mother of Webb Hayes, is the first wife of a president to be referred to as "First Lady." She was considered the most popular president's wife since Dolley Madison, almost sixty years earlier, and at her death, flags throughout the nation were lowered to half-staff. Mrs. Hayes attended Ohio Wesleyan University, and as the first wife of a president to have a college degree, devoted her education and energy to social causes. She was an active abolitionist and supporter of the Temperance Movement, and during her husband's term, alcohol was not served at the White House. During the Civil War, on visits to General Hayes' headquarters, she used her free time to nurse wounded soldiers in the hospitals. (Hoogeboom; Robinson, 2001; Wikipedia)

HAYES, Rutherford Birchard (1822–1893), served under Crook as a brigadier general of Volunteers during the Civil War, and became Crook's life-long friend, supporter, and admirer, even naming one of his sons after him. Declared president after a controversial and hotly contested election, Hayes held office from 1877 to 1881. He was determined not to be distracted by campaign considerations, and therefore did not seek a second term. Consequently, in many cases the full effect of his reforms was not apparent until after he left office. Nevertheless, he was one of the more capable presidents of the last three decades of the nineteenth century. See also, HAYES, James Webb Cook. (See Robinson, 2001; Hoogenboom)

HAYT, Ezra, a New Jersey businessman with ties to the Board of Foreign Missions of the Reformed Church, was commissioner of Indian Affairs from 1877 to 1880. Hayt previously served on the Board of Indian Commissioners, and was appointed commissioner of Indian Affairs in an effort to clean up the scandal-ridden Indian service. As commissioner, he advocated several reforms, although not all were adopted by Congress. He was implicated, however, in a series of irregularities at the San Carlos, Arizona, agents and,in January 1880, Secretary of the Interior Carl Schurz replaced him. See also SCHURZ, Carl. (Prucha, 191–92)

HUNTINGTON, Collis Potter (1821–1900), railroad magnate and industrialist, was a native of Harwinton, Connecticut. He became a peddler and then a small merchant. With the discovery of gold in California, he went to Sacramento and, with Mark Hopkins, began selling supplies to miners. In 1860, Huntington, Hopkins, Charles Crocker and Leland Stanford became interested in a railroad across the Sierra Nevada to connect with a proposed transcontinental line. Their line, the Central Pacific, connected with Union Pacific in Utah in 1869. He eventually gained control of Southern Pacific and Chesapeake and Ohio Railroads, several steamship companies, and Newport News Shipbuilding and Drydock. He nephew, Henry Edwards Huntington, acquired a substantial fortune of his own, part of which went to establish the world renowned Huntington Library, Art Gallery and Botanical Gardens in San Marino, California. (Johnson and Malone, 9:408–12)

IRWIN, James, appointed agent at Red Cloud in 1877, managed to keep the various factions in line by undermining the hostiles with the agency Indians, while at the same time making it more advantageous for the erstwhile hostiles to remain quietly on the reservation. (Hyde, 300)

KEARNEY, Dennis (1847–1907), was born in Ireland and immigrated to San Francisco, where he became active in the Workingman's Party. He led protests against unemployment and taxes that he considered unjust. In 1880, Thomas Nast parodied him in a cartoon that showed a skeleton demanding "Kearneyism" which Nast defined as expropriation of other people's money and property. (http://www.spartacus.schoolnet.co.uk/USAkearney.htm)

KEY, David McKendree (1824–1900), was postmaster general under Hayes. Key served in a Confederate Volunteer regiment, finishing the war as lieutenant colonel. In 1870, he was a member of the convention that helped draft the new state constitution for Tennessee. On the death of former President and then-Senator Andrew Johnson, in 1875, Key was appointed to finish Johnson's unexpired term, but was defeated in his bid for election in 1877. He accepted Hayes's appointment as postmaster general, serving until 1880, when he resigned to accept an appointment as federal judge for the Eastern District of Tennessee. (Wikipedia)

LINCHARD, *Chicago Times* correspondent. Neither Knight nor Dary mentions a correspondent named Linchard.

McCULLOUGH, John (1832–85), American actor, who immigrated to the United States from Ireland in 1847. Living in Philadelphia, he acted in a dramatic club, and made his first professional appearance in 1857. He acted in road shows and eventually ended up in San Francisco, where he went into partnership with Lawrence Barrett at the California Theatre until 1870. In 1873, he began a series of road tours that included frequent engagements in New York, and remained a highly respected and popular actor until he collapsed on stage in Chicago in 1884. See also BARRETT, Lawrence (Johnson and Malone, 12:9–10)

McGILLYCUDDY, Valentine T. (1849–1939), contract surgeon with General Crook, and topographer for the Dodge-Jenney expedition, was a native of Michigan. He served as post surgeon at Camp Robinson, where he tended the mortally wounded Crazy Horse. He served as agent for the Oglalas from 1879 to 1886, when he was relieved in part because of disputes with Red Cloud. McGillycuddy also was first mayor of Rapid City, South Dakota, and served as president of the South Dakota School of Mines. Bourke occasionally spelled the name "MacGillicuddy." See also CRAZY HORSE. (Thrapp, 1991, 2:905; McGillycuddy)

McGRATH, H. Price. Kentucky horse breeder, whose Aristides won the first Kentucky Derby in 1875. (kentuckyderby.com)

MACMILLAN, Thomas, which Bourke spelled "McMillan," a native of Scotland, reported for the *Chicago Inter-Ocean*. Although only twenty-five years old, his poor health cut short his participation in the campaigns of the summer of 1876. Like Reuben Davenport, he had accompanied the Dodge-Jenney Expedition. Dodge described him as "very gentlemanly, hard to stuff, & with excellent good sense" who won "the liking and respect of everyone." (Knight, 171–72; Kime, 1996, 57)

MANYPENNY, George W. third commissioner of Indian Affairs for the newly formed Department of the Interior, served in tha tpost from 1853 to 1856. He spent much of his subsequent career heading Indian investigation and treaty commissions. His significance in this instance is as head of a commission formed in 1876 to force the Indians to cede the Black Hills. Manypenny's book, *Our Indian Wards* (1880) describes Indian-white relations in what is now the U.S., from the first contact in the sixteenth century up to the date of publication. He was unpopular with the military. Ranald Mackenzie, who considered his efforts to negotiate a settlement to the White River Ute crisis of 1879–80 disruptive and annoying, described Manypennny as a "chronic commissioner." See MACKENZIE, Ranald Slidell. (Prucha, 113–15, 212; Robinson, 1993, 269)

MEEKER, Nathan Cook (1817–79), Indian agent killed in the White River Ute uprising, was a native of Euclid, Ohio. An agricultural writer for the *New York Herald*, he went west in 1869, initially to study Mormon farming methods, but settled instead in Colorado, where he hoped to establish an agricultural colony at what is now Greeley. He accepted the post of White River Ute agent in 1878. Meeker's overbearing attitude and tactlessness led to his death. See also ADAMS, Charles. (Thrapp, 1991, 2:968–69)

MERIVALE, Joseph, whose name Bourke spelled "Marrivale," was a long-time resident of the Fort Laramie area, who had served the army as a guide on several occasions prior to the Dodge-Jenney Black Hills expedition of 1875. Nevertheless, during the expedition, Dodge determined that Merivale knew very little about the Black Hills, and instead used him as a courier and interpreter. (Kime, 1996, 12–13)

MIDDLETON, David Charles "Doc" (1851–1913), horse thief and outlaw, was born in Mississippi, but drifted to Nebraska by way of Texas in 1876. In 1877, he killed a soldier in Sidney, and fled to Dakota Territory, where he organized a gang of horse thieves known as the Pony Boys. A vast number of horses were stolen and traded as far away as Texas, attracting the attention of the federal government. Middleton was arrested in 1879, and imprisoned until 1883. He became a saloon operator in Nebraska and Wyoming. Despite his checkered career, he was a pleasant, outgoing person who, as Bourke noted, had more friends than enemies. (Bourke, Diary, 29:86–87; Thrapp, 1991, 2:981)

MILLS, Cuthbert, *New York Times* correspondent was one of only two persons on the Big Horn and Yellowstone Expedition whom Bourke considered to be bona fide correspondents. The other was

Barbour Lathrop of the *San Francisco Bulletin*. Knight (251) has very little information about him, not even his first name. Dary does not mention him at all.

MOORE, Thomas (1832–96) was one of the preeminent mule packers of the West and, with General Crook, streamlined the military pack transportation system to a model of efficiency. A native of St. Louis, he began his western career by traveling to California in 1850. He joined Crook as civilian chief packer in 1871, and served in virtually every major Indian campaign until 1895. He also organized transportation for hunting and camping trips by Crook and other dignitaries. His sister was Carrie Nation, temperance activist famous for smashing saloons in the Midwest. (Thrapp, 1991, 2:1011–12)

MORRISEY, John (1831–78) was born in Ireland and brought to the United States with his parents in 1833. He became a boxing champion in the 1850s, and later served as a Tammany-backed member of the New York State Assembly. In 1863, he moved to Saratoga Springs where he bought the race track. (Wikipedia)

NANCE, Albinus (1848–1911), fourth governor of Nebraska, was a native of Lafayette, Illinois. At sixteen, he enlisted in a Volunteer regiment in the Union Army, and served with distinction in the Cumberland. When the war ended he studied law, and in 1871, moved to Nebraska, where he established a practice. He entered the state legislature in 1873, and five years later became governor, serving two terms until 1883. After leaving office, he went into banking. (http://www.rootsweb.com/~neresour/OLLibrary/pbal/pages/balc0028.htm)

PADDOCK, Algernon Sidney (1830–97), senator from Nebraska, was a native of New York who moved to Omaha in 1857 and became involved in local politics. He campaigned for Abraham Lincoln in Nebraska and New York during the 1860 election, and the following year was appointed secretary for the Territory of Nebraska. He held the position until 1867, when Nebraska became a state. He served in the senate from 1875 until 1881, and again from 1887 until 1893. (Wikipedia)

PATTERSON, John James (1830–1912), was a native of Pennsylvania who served during Reconstruction as senator from South Carolina. Patterson was a Union Army veteran who moved to Columbia, South Carolina, and became involved in railroad construction. He was elected to the Senate as a Republican, and was considered by many local citizens to be a carpetbagger. He served on the Committee on Territories from 1877 to 1879. By the time his term ended in 1879, Reconstruction was over, and the Democrats had regained control of the legislature, assuring that Patterson would not be reelected. He remained in Washington until 1886, when he returned to Pennsylvania. (Wikipedia)

POURIER, Baptiste (1841–1932), called "Big Bat" to distinguish him from another scout, Baptiste "Little Bat" Garnier, was born in St. Charles, Missouri. The descendant of a long line of French fur traders and explorers, while still in his teens he accepted employment with trader John Richaud, who later became his father-in-law. Pourier became an interpreter and guide at Fort Laramie in 1869, serving in that capacity until 1880. (Gilbert)

ROWLAND, William, was a white who had married into the Cheyennes and served as interpreter at Camp Robinson. He had charge of the Cheyenne Scouts on the Powder River Expedition. Bourke spelled the name "Roland." (Grinnell, 1983, 360, 364)

SAUNDERS, Alvin (1817–99), native of Kentucky, was territorial governor of Nebraska from 1861 until statehood in 1867, and senator from 1877 until 1883. He moved to Nebraska from Iowa, were he had been involved in politics, and was one of the commissioners appointed by Congress to organize the Union Pacific Railroad. During his term in the Senate, he was chairman of the Committee on Territories. (Wikipedia)

SCHURZ, Carl (1829–1906), native of Germany, secretary of the interior under Hayes. He also was a diplomat, senator, and author, and was a power to be reckoned with in every presidential election from 1860 until 1904. Schurz had to flee Germany after the abortive revolt against the Prussian government in 1848. He arrived in the United States in 1852, and soon established himself as an orator, abolitionist, and political campaigner. He was appointed minister to Spain by Abraham Lincoln, but returned to the United States in 1862, to advocate abolition. He served in the Volunteers during the Civil War, finishing as major general. After the war, he served one term as senator from Missouri. He advocated black rights, preservation of the public domain, and reform of the spoils system. Because of the Ponca Affair, Schurz has been vilified, but his moderate approach to Indian rights was the most reasonable in view of the times. He expressed his views in an article, "Present Aspects of the Indian Problem," in the *North American Review* in 1881. Tall, spindly-legged, with a bushy beard and prominent eyes, Schurz provided ample fodder for cartoonists such as Thomas Nast, as well as for some of Bourke's more acid comments. See also, STANDING BEAR. (Warner, 426–28; Robinson, 2001, Chapter 14)

SHERMAN, John (1823–1900), younger brother of General W. T. Sherman, was senator from Ohio and cabinet minister. Sherman practiced law before entering politics. He served in the House of Representatives from 1855 to 1861, and in the Senate from 1861 to 1877, when he resigned to become secretary of the treasury under Rutherford B. Hayes. In the 1880 Republican convention, he offered himself as a compromise presidential candidate between U.S. Grant and James G. Blaine, but James A. Garfield received the nomination instead. Sherman returned to the Senate in 1881, and remained until 1897 when he resigned to become secretary of state under William McKinley He was primarily responsible for the Sherman Anti-Trust Act. (http://en.wikipedia.org/wiki/John_Sherman)

SNIDER, Nathan, former post trader at Fort Ter-waw, Calif., hunting partner of General Crook, and president of the Murchie Mine project. (Robinson, 2001, 248)

STENHOUSE, *New York Herald* Pacific Coast correspondent. Neither Knight nor Dary mentions a correspondent named Stenhouse.

STRAHORN, Robert Edmund (1852–1944), who signed his dispatches "Alter Ego," was a native of Pennsylvania. He obtained his first newspaper job when he was fourteen. In 1870, he went to Colorado, where he worked in Central City and Black Hawk before joining the Denver *Rocky Mountain News*. In addition to his regular job with the Denver paper, he also sold dispatches to the *Chicago Tribune*, *Omaha Republican*, *Cheyenne Sun*, and *New York Times*. Strahorn later settled in Spokane, Washington, and became a land developer and railroad executive, with extensive interests throughout the Pacific Northwest. (Knight, 169–71; Thrapp, 1991, 3:1376)

STREET, William D., citizen who served as a courier for Mauck's unit of the 4th Cavalry during the Cheyenne Outbreak. A native of Ohio, Street was brought to Kansas in 1861 at the age of ten. As an adult, he settled near the now-vanished town of Achilles, in northwestern Kansas, and became a leader in state affairs from that region. In 1869, he served with state troops during the mop-up of Sheridan's Indian campaign. He pioneered irrigation that helped developed agriculture in western Kansas, served as speaker of the Kansas House of Representatives, and regent of the State Agricultural College. Street also wrote two accounts of incidents in the Outbreak, "Cheyenne Indian Massacre on the Middle Fork of the Sappa," published in *Transactions of the Kansas State Historical Society*, for 1907-8, and an unpublished manuscript, "Incidents of the Dull Knife Raid, Notes of William D. Street," preserved by the Kansas State Historical Society in Topeka. (Monnett, 93; http://skyways.lib.ks.us/genweb/archives/1918ks/bios/streetwd.html)

SUTRO, Adolph Heinrich (1830-98), Prussian-born mining engineer and businessman, designed a four-mile tunnel through Mount Davidson, Nevada, to provide drainage and ventilation for the silver mines of the Comstock Lode. He completed the shaft in 1878, and sold his interest a year later for a substantial profit. He moved to San Francisco, where be became the leading landowner, serving as mayor from 1894 to 1896. (Lamar, 1087)

THORNBURGH, Jacob N. (1837-90), brother of Maj. Thomas T. Thornburgh, was a Republican member of Congress from Tennessee, from 1873 to 1879. See THORNBURGH, Thomas Tipton. (Wikipedia)

TIBBLES, Thomas Henry (1838-1928), native of Ohio, joined John Brown's Free Soilers in Kansas, and later served in various capacities on the Union side of the Civil War. When the war ended he worked for various newspapers in Omaha, and was instrumental in Standing Bear's suit to obtain legal status. When the case was resolved, he became an advocate of Indians Rights, whose writings stirred public interest. See also STANDING BEAR; DUNDY, Elmer Scipio. (Thrapp, 1991, 3:1428)

VANDEVER, William (1817-93), native of Maryland, served as United States Indian inspector under the Grant administration from 1873 until 1877, prompting Bourke (who sometimes spelled it "Vandeveer") to call him "the lying emissary of the Indian Ring." Like many of Grant's appointments, Vandever had served in the Union Army during the Civil War, and was mustered out with the brevet rank of major general. He practiced law until his appointment as Indian inspector. He had served as a congressman from Iowa from 1858 to 1871, and, after moving to California, served as a congressman from that state from 1886 to 1891. He lived in Ventura, California, at the time of his death. (Warner, 523–24)

WHITNEY, Robert H. "Bob" (1840–71), native of New York, went to Arizona where he established a reputation as a scout. He was killed by Chiricahua Apaches on October 24, 1871, when an expedition under Capt. Gerald Russell, 3rd Cavalry, was lured into an ambush in Chiricahua Pass. He was buried with honors two days later at Camp Bowie. See also RUSSELL, Gerald. (Thrapp, 1991, 3:1561)

WOLCOTT, Francis Edwin "Frank," 1840–1910, Wyoming ranch manager, first moved West in March 1870, to become receiver of the U.S. Land Office in Cheyenne. Two years later, he was appointed U.S. marshal for Wyoming Territory, but was removed in 1875, because his offensive personality cost him public support. He then became manager of the VR Ranch, owned by a Scottish consortium, near Tolland, Wyoming. Wolcott headed the faction of large ranching interests that tried to drive off the small ranchers, and was instrumental in the Johnson County War of 1892, that proved disastrous for the large interests when the small ranchers stood their ground, fought back, and invoked the law. He left Wyoming in 1894, and died in Denver. (Thrapp, 3:1587)

YARNELL, Nelson. See COSGROVE, Thomas.

Indians

AMERICAN HORSE (ca. 1840–1908), Oglala Sioux chief, sometimes confused with another Oglala chief named American Horse, who was mortally wounded at Slim Buttes in 1876. He participated in the Fetterman Massacre, but subsequently settled at the Red Cloud Agency and was not involved in the Great Sioux War. He was an associate of Red Cloud, toured with Buffalo Bill, and as a leader of the Oglalas, earned enemies by often siding with the government in controversies. He died at Pine Ridge, South Dakota. (Thrapp, 1991, 1:21–22)

BLACK COAL, Arapaho chief, who, in 1874, led his people against the government and its Shoshone allies under their powerful chief Washakie. Nevertheless, he ultimately sided with the government during the Great Sioux War. Years later, in 1891, after the Arapahoes had been placed on the Shoshone Reservation at Wind River, Black Coal challenged Washakie's authority, demanding—and receiving—equal status for the Arapahoes. See also WASHAKIE. (Hyde,

1975, 297; Hoxie, 676)

CAPTAIN JIM (Shoshone) one of the signatories of the Fort Bridger Treaty between the federal government and the Bannocks and Shoshones in 1873, and was part of a delegation that asked Idaho Gov. D. P. Thompson to represent their grievances to the government in 1876. He was also a member of the Lemhi, Shoshone, and Bannock delegation that went to Washington in 1880 to discuss white encroachment on their territory, resulting in an agreement to parcel out the lands of the Fort Hall Reservation in severalty, and sell the left-over tracts for settlement. See MAJOR GEORGE. (Madsen)

CHARGING BEAR, Oglala warrior captured at Slim Buttes, together with Big Bat Pourier negotiated the surrender of American Horse, ending the battle. He later became a corporal of Indian Scouts.

COCHISE (ca. 1824–1874) is one of the most famous American Indians, in part because of his efforts to maintain peace following the Cochise War, and in part because of Jeff Chandler's portrayal of him in motion pictures in the 1950s. The war lasted almost twelve years before Brig. Gen. Oliver O. Howard was able to negotiate a peace. At Cochise's direction, the government established a reservation centered on the Dragoon Mountains, which occupied much of the southeastern part of Arizona. It was abolished two years after his death and the Chiricahuas were concentrated at San Carlos. Cochise was the son-in-law and associate of Mangas Coloradas, who is considered perhaps the greatest of all Apache leaders. He inherited the mantle of supremacy following Mangas's death in 1863. In the nineteenth century, there was no consistent spelling of Apache names, and Bourke uses "Cochies," "Cochis," and "Cocheis," the latter of which was most common among whites. See also HOWARD, Oliver Otis. (Sweeney, 1991; Lamar, 228)

COLOROW (ca. 1810–88), Ute, apparently was a Comanche captive reared by the Utes, and who ultimately became one of their chiefs. Initially, he coexisted with the whites, but came to resent their continuing incursions. Matters came to a head after Nathan Meeker, agent of the White River Utes, deposed Colorow as chief, one of the chain of events leading to the massacre of Meeker and other agency employees in 1878. Colorow was not involved in the massacre, having led the band of warriors who ambushed Maj. Thomas T. Thornburgh at Milk River. After hostilities ended, Colorow was relocated to the Uintah Agency in Utah. Eventually, he returned to Colorado, living on the Southern Ute Reservation. He was involved in the so-called "Colorow War" of 1887, which was essentially one single skirmish in which whites and Utes shot at each other until both sides ran out of ammunition and returned home. See also MEEKER, Nathan Cook; THORNBURGH, Thomas Tipton. (Thrapp, 1991, 1:302)

CRAZY HORSE (ca. 1840–1877), Oglala war chief, drew attention not only for his mysticism and introverted personality, but also because of his red hair and pale, freckled complexion. In 1865, he was designated one of the four Oglala "shirt wearers" or leading political chiefs, but lost the position five years later following an altercation involving another man's wife. He distinguished himself in the Fetterman Massacre of 1866, and subsequently during the Great Sioux War. Arrested on September 5, 1877, he was bayoneted during a scuffle at the guardhouse at Camp Robinson, Nebraska, and died about midnight. During the latter half of the twentieth century, he became a symbol of Indian political and social resistance. See also BURKE, Daniel Webster; CLARK, Walter Philo; GROUARD, Frank; LITTLE BIG MAN; McGILLYCUDDY, Valentine T. (Hoxie, 137–39; Utley, 1997, 109–10; Nickerson, 20; DeBarthe, 117)

DULL KNIFE (c. 1810–83), was one of the four "old man" or senior chiefs of the Cheyennes. Dull Knife, the name by which he is best known, was his Lakota designation. Among his own people, he was known as Morning Star. He became known to the whites when he signed the Fort Laramie Treaty of 1868. Following the destruction of his camp by Mackenzie, on November 25, 1876, he and his band wandered until the following spring, when they surrendered. They were transported to the Indian Territory where, after two years of suffering, his band joined Little Wolf's in an outbreak. North of the Platte River, the two groups split and Dull Knife surrendered at Fort Robinson. In January 1879, Dull Knife's band staged an uprising and escape. He eventually was allowed to lived at Pine Ridge, South Dakota. See also LITTLE WOLF; MACKENZIE, Ranald Slidell; WESSELS, Henry. (Utley, 1997, 132–33)

JOSEPH (1841–1904), Nez Percé, sometimes called the Xenophon of the Indians, was leader of the Nez Percés on their monumental but futile trek toward refuge in Canada. Joseph was born Heinmot Tooyalakekt, the second son of the Nez Percé chief

Tu-ya-kas-kas and the baptized Nez Percé woman, Arenoth. When Heimnot Tooyalakekt was about two years old, his father likewise was baptized, and took the name Joseph. After the death of his father, in 1871, Heinmot Tooyalakekt, who by now also was known as Joseph, became the political chief of the Wallamotkin band of Nez Percés. In 1877, federal authorities ordered all Nez Percés on to a reservation to accommodate mining interests in their territory in eastern Oregon. This enraged some of the younger warriors, who killed several settlers. Fearing retaliation, Joseph, Looking Glass, and several other chiefs led their people on a four-month trek of over a thousand miles, across the continental divide toward Canada. Ultimately, they were forced to surrender to Col. Nelson Miles less than a hundred miles short of their goal. By now, Joseph and White Bird were the only surviving chiefs. Initially, the Nez Percés were interned at Fort Leavenworth, Kansas, and later sent to the Indian Territory, where many died of malaria. In 1879, Joseph traveled to Washington to present his case, and became a national celebrity. The result was the Nez Percés where allowed to return to the Pacific Northwest, but not to their old homeland. See also MILES, Nelson Appleton; HOWARD, Oliver Otis. (Hoxie, 309–11)

LAME DEER (d. 1877), Minneconjou chief, whose band was one of the last major holdouts in the Great Sioux War. He was killed when fighting broke out between his people and Miles's troops in his camp, on May 7, 1877. (Greene, 1991, Chapter 9)

LITTLE BIG MAN, Oglala "shirt wearer" or senior chief of Crazy Horse's band, initially was pegged—justifiably—as a trouble maker when he arrived at the Red Cloud Agency in 1872. His name had nothing to do with stature, but was to distinguish him from his father, also named Big Man. Little Big Man surrendered with Crazy Horse in 1877, pledging to General Crook that he would maintain the peace. During the scuffle in which Crazy Horse was killed at Camp Robinson, Little Big Man pinioned his arms. He always maintained the death was an accident. He settled at Pine Ridge where, in 1879, he became a policeman. See also CRAZY HORSE. (Hyde, 1975, 198, 243n 297–98)

LITTLE WOLF (c. 1820–1904), Northern Cheyenne, was chief of the Bowstring Soldier warrior society. He apparently was present during the Fetterman Massacre of 1866, and the Custer fight in 1876. It is not known, however, whether he was involved in

Mackenzie's attack on Dull Knife's Village on November 25, 1876. After the Cheyennes surrendered to Crook, he was among the group sent to the Indian Territory. In September 1878, he and Dull Knife led three hundred of their followers out of the Territory and north toward their homeland. The two bands split after crossing the North Platte River, and Little Wolf continued to Montana, while Dull Knife surrendered at Fort Robinson. Little Wolf ultimately surrendered to Miles, who enrolled him as a scout. He remained a respected figure until his death. See also DULL KNIFE; MILES, Nelson Appleton. (Thrapp, 1991, 2:862–63)

LITTLE WOUND, Oglala chief, attempted to be accommodating, but government blundering drove his band to hostility in 1865. He signed the Fort Laramie Treaty of 1868. Like Red Cloud and other chiefs, however, he understood the treaty was simply to restore peace and trade, and refused to abandon his hunting grounds to the government. Nevertheless, he settled at the Red Cloud Agency, and, together with Red Cloud, probably saved Agent J. J. Saville's life from a kangaroo court organized by Little Big Man and Pretty Bear over a dispute about rations. In 1877, he combined with Red Cloud and other Oglala leaders to support General Crook against Crazy Horse. He eventually settled at Pine Ridge. See also CRAZY HORSE, LITTLE BIG MAN, RED CLOUD. (Hyde, 1975, 155, 164, 169, 209, 297)

MAJOR GEORGE (Shoshone) was one of the chiefs who agreed in1880 to divide the Fort Hall Reservation lands in severalty. See also CAPTAIN JIM. (Madsen, 337)

NANNI-CHADDI, Apache leader whose band was annihilated by troops under Capt. William Henry Brown on December 28, 1872. A year earlier, he had met with Vincent Colyer, and promised to obey the government. The destruction of his band demonstrated that soldiers could penetrate Apache country, and locate and destroy hostile groups, no matter how well secluded or defended. See also BROWN, William Henry. (Thrapp, 1988, 127–30)

OURAY (1820–80), Ute, became chief in 1860. Over the following decade, he cultivated friendly relations with the government, and was an advisor to Christopher Carson. He made two trips to Washington, the second in 1872, when he managed to obtain some concessions from the government during the expropriation of Ute treaty lands. Unlike most Western Indian chiefs, who governed through prestige and consensus, Ouray was an autocrat who tolerated little opposition. During the uprising of 1879, he united the tribe against the White River band, forcing an end to hostilities. See also ADAMS, Charles; MEEKER, Nathan Cook. (Thrapp, 1991, 2:1094)

RED CLOUD (1822–1909), Oglala, became a powerful war chief through his own accomplishments. He appears to have taken his first scalp at sixteen, in a raid against the Pawnees. He participated in the Grattan Massacre, and was a distinguished leader against Gen. Patrick Connor's failed North Plains Expedition. During a treaty council at Fort Laramie in June 1866, Red Cloud and his followers walked out in protest of a proposal to surrender more hunting grounds to the government. This led to the Red Cloud War of 1866–68, which forced the government to abandon the Bozeman Trail and Forts Reno, Phil Kearny, and C. F. Smith. After signing the Fort Laramie Treaty of 1868, Red Cloud never again went to war, although during the Great Sioux War, his sympathies were with the hostiles. This led Crook to depose him as paramount chief of the Lakotas in favor of Spotted Tail in September 1876. Following the death of Spotted Tail in 1881, Red Cloud again emerged as paramount chief. More visionary than many of the other leaders, he saw that the survival of his people depended on adapting to government expectations. He died at Pine Ridge. See also YOUNG MAN AFRAID OF HIS HORSES; SPOTTED TAIL. Red Cloud's life is covered in Olson; Hyde, 1975; and Larson.

ROMAN NOSE, Lakota leader from the Spotted Tail Agency, was among the hostiles at Slim Buttes. After the fight, he joined Crazy Horse, but eventually, he, Touch-the-Clouds, and other chiefs broke away, surrendered, and were allowed to live at the Spotted Tail Agency. Sometime after mid-1877, however, he left and joined Sitting Bull in Canada. Not to be confused with the great Cheyenne chief Roman Nose, who was killed in a fight with Forsyth's troops at Beecher's Island, in 1868. See also TOUCH-THE-CLOUDS. (Hyde, 1974, 266 n8, 287 n3)

SHARP NOSE, Arapaho chief, led his tribe's contingent serving under General Crook in the summer and fall of 1876. Besides being a noted warrior and leader, he was praised by soldiers as one of the most outstanding guides. He was especially valuable in guiding Mackenzie's cavalry to the main Cheyenne camp on November 24–25. (Dunlay, 82)

SHUNCACA LUTU (Sorrel Horse), Brulé medicine man mentioned frequently by Bourke in 1876–77, but there is little other information about him.

SITTING BULL (1831?–90), Hunkpapa war chief and holy man, as a young man attained a superlative record as a warrior, and in 1857, was designated a war chief. His conflicts with whites appear to have begun when Montana-bound gold seekers came up the Missouri River. The government soon began building forts along the river, prompting Sitting Bull to lead his people in a five-year war. By this time, his interest had turned to spirituality, and he was known among all the Lakota tribes as a holy man. In his combined capacity of military and religious leader, he became the focal point of the Lakotas resisting the Fort Laramie Treaty of 1868, and the subsequent settlement on reservations. His warriors fought troops on a survey expedition into the Yellowstone Valley in 1872 and 1873. Rather than surrender during the Great Sioux War, he led a remnant of his people into Canada, where they remained until 1881, when he turned himself in at Fort Buford, North Dakota. He toured briefly with Buffalo Bill's Wild West Show, but spent most of his time on the Standing Rock Reservation, adopting white methods he deemed useful and rejecting those he did not. As more of the Indian lands were taken, Sitting Bull became a leader of the Ghost Dance movement at Standing Rock. He was killed on December 15, 1890, in a fight that broke out when Indian Police tried to arrest him. (Utley, 1993; Hoxie, 593–95)

SITTING BULL OF THE SOUTH (1841–76) was a name that whites gave to the Oglala leader Sitting Bull to distinguish him from the great Hunkpapa chief Sitting Bull. As a young man, Sitting Bull of the South became friends with a telegrapher, who taught him to read and write, and to use the telegraph. He was fluent in English. Following the Sand Creek Massacre in Colorado in 1864, he joined a hostile faction, and participated in several fights, including the Fetterman Massacre in Wyoming. Later he settled at the Red Cloud Agency, and accompanied two delegations to Washington. He was ambushed and killed by a group of Crows while on a truce mission to Crazy Horse. (Thrapp, 1991, 3:1315)

SPOTTED TAIL (ca. 1823–81) , was a Brulé "shirt wearer" or senior chief and war leader. Although he was involved in the Grattan Massacre of 1855, he surrendered the following month. He was detained at Fort Leavenworth, Kansas, and Fort Kearny, Nebraska, for a year, during which he learned enough about the whites to realize their numbers and technology made them an irresistible force. From that point onward, he strove to maintain peace, and obtain education for his people, while preserving their ancient culture. He did, however, lead an assault against Julesburg, Colorado, in retaliation for the Sand Creek Massacre of 1864, and government restrictions on Lakota travel along the Platte River. Soon after, he permanently ceased fighting whites, signed the Fort Laramie Treaty of 1868, and took up residence on a reservation in Nebraska. In 1876, General Crook deposed Red Cloud as head chief of the Lakotas, and designated Spotted Tail in his place. Although Spotted Tail negotiated the surrender of hostile bands, he rejected the proposition that the Lakotas be relocated to Oklahoma. In 1880, a political struggle developed among the Brulés, with opposition centering around Spotted Tail's cousin, Crow Dog. On August 5, 1881, an altercation developed between the two men, and Crow Dog shot Spotted Tail. After his death, the Brulés ceased to play a significant role in Lakota affairs. See also RED CLOUD. (Hoxie, 603–05; Hyde, 1987)

STANDING BEAR (ca. 1829–1908), Ponca, was the plaintiff in a landmark suit that gave Indians certain legal standing in court, and placed them under the protection of federal law. Following the conclusion of this case, he and his supporters were allotted land on the Niobrara River. The case had galvanized Indian rights activists, and in 1879–80, Standing Bear went on a lecture tour of the East, accompanied by Thomas H. Tibbles, and Omaha Indians Susette La Flesche (whom Tibbles later married) and Francis La Flesche. Standing Bear has received revived attention in recent years; some of the literature on the case will be found in the bibliography. See also SCHURZ, Carl; TIBBLES, Thomas Henry; DUNDY, Elmer Scipio. (Thrapp, 1991, 3:1352)

STANDING ELK, Cheyenne, led the surrender of the Cheyennes at Camp Robinson in April 1876. Most of the band had been among those devastated in Mackenzie's attack the preceding November. Having negotiated with government officials previously, he accepted the army's proposal to relocate the Cheyennes to the Indian Territory. (Grinnell, 1983, 400)

TECUMSEH (1768?–1813), Shawnee chief, native of Ohio, forced with his people into Indiana by white pressure. By the beginning of the nineteenth century, Tecumseh and his brother, the Shawnee Prophet, saw the need to unify the tribes against U.S. encroachment, and sought British assistance. With the outbreak of the War of 1812, he was appointed a brigadier general in the British Army. He led rear guard actions covering the British retreat from the Ohio Valley, although he accused them of abandoning his cause. He was killed in the Battle of the Thames in Ontario. (Thrapp, 1991, 3:1406–7)

TOUCH-THE-CLOUDS, Minneconjou, so-called because he was seven feet tall. He persuaded Crazy Horse to report to Camp Robinson for internment, leading to the scuffle that resulted in Crazy Horse's death. In mid to late 1877, he left Spotted Tail's camp to join Sitting Bull in Canada. See also ROMAN NOSE. (Hyde, 1974, 287 3n; Olson, 214)

WASHAKIE (1804?–1900), powerful and autocratic chief of the Shoshones, spent most of his life maintaining peace with the federal government. His position was reenforced in 1863, when Col. Patrick Connor defeated and subdued Shoshone dissidents who had joined Bannocks in raiding against white emigrants. In 1868, he signed the Fort Bridger Treaty establishing a Shoshone reservation in what is now western Wyoming. In the 1870s, he led his people as scouts, first against the Arapahoes, and latter as part of Crook's Big Horn and Yellowstone Expedition. He opposed some government policies, including the resettlement of Arapahoes on the Shoshone Reservation. Nevertheless, he cooperated, realizing that to oppose the government would bring disaster for his people. In 1878, at General Crook's behest, the government upgraded Camp Brown, Wyoming, on the Shoshone Reservation, renaming it Fort Washakie, in his honor. See also BLACK COAL. (Hoxie, 675–76; Robinson, 2001, 221)

WHITE THUNDER, subchief of the Brulé Orphan Band, was popular among the officers and families posted to the Spotted Tail Agency. He was among the group that escorted Crazy Horse to internment at Camp Robinson, where the latter chief was killed. (Hyde, 1974, 229, 285)

YOUNG MAN AFRAID OF HIS HORSES (ca. 1830–1900) was a hereditary Oglala chief through his father, Old Man Afraid of His Horses. He was an associate of Red Cloud, and participated in various fights along the Bozeman Trail and in the Fetterman Massacre during the Red Cloud War. He was a party to the Fort Laramie

Treaty of 1868, and thereafter worked as a sort of mediator between Indians and whites. Although he opposed the sale of Sioux lands to the government, he eventually was designated president of the Pine Ridge Indian Council. He also adamantly opposed the Ghost Dance religion. See also RED CLOUD. (Thrapp, 1991, 3:1614–15)

Appendix 2

Manuscript Volume 24, Pages 54–83

Authorities.
Personal notes of the Campaigns conducted by Brig. General George Crook, U.S. Army, against the Sioux Indians in Nebraska, Wyoming, Montana, Dakota—1876–1877.

* * *

Telegram, Washington D.C. Aug. 2d 1877, from Commissioner Hayt, asking General Crook to select a delegation of 15 or 20 Indians from Red Cloud and Spotted Tail Agencies and send them to Washington under charge of Agent Irwin, or some suitable army Officer.

* * *

Telegram. Camp Robinson, Neb., Aug. 16th 78
General Williams
I think there will be no trouble about postponing the [projected buffalo] hunt. Will try to have Crazy Horse go to Washington, but he refuses now. Can delegation be increased to 25? Would like to know soon.

(Signed) Bradley
Lt-Colonel

* * *

August 20th Lieut. Clark wrote that there would be no hunt; that there was neither restlessness nor ill-feeling among the Indians by this decision.

* * *

Telegram.   Omaha, Aug. 31st, 1877
To Genl. Crook,
Comdg Department
On West.-bound train, Fremont, Neb.
The following dispatch from Colonel Bradley just received. "Crazy Horse and Touch the Clouds tell Lieut. Clark this morning that they are going out with their bands: this means all of the hostiles of last year. Probably more troops must be brought here, if this movement is to be stopped. I think General Crook's presence might have a good effect". Please acknowledge receipt and give me your instructions.
(Sig.) R. Williams,
A.G. General.

* * *

Telegram.   Chicago, September 1st 1877.
To General Crook,
  on West-Bound train,
    Sidney, Neb.
I think your presence more necessary at Red Cloud agency than at Camp Brown and wish you to get off at Sidney and go there.
Colonel Bradley thinks Crazy Horse and others will make trouble if the Sioux scouts leave. I will ask Bradley to detain them until you reach Red Cloud. Nez-Percés on Clark's fork (note, i.e. of the Yellowstone—J.G.B.)
(sig.) P. H. Sheridan,
Lieut.-General.

* * *

Extract from telegram of September 3d, from General Sheridan to General Crook.
"I do not like the attitude of affairs at Red Cloud Agency and very much doubt the propriety of your going to Camp Brown. The surrender or capture of Joseph in that direction is but a small matter compared with what might happen to the frontier from a disturbance at Red Cloud."[1]

* * *

1. This telegram is undoubtedly in response to Crook's telegram to Bradley immediately below.

Telegram. Grand Island, Neb.,
Sept. 1st 1877.

General Bradley
    Camp Robinson, Neb.
    Your dispatch received. I cannot come to Robinson. If Spotted Tail can, with his own people and the help of the troops now at Camp Sheridan, "round up" Touch the Clouds, you have sufficient force to do the same with Crazy Horse.
If Spotted Tail has not sufficient force to do this, you might send some of your troops over to him and use those from Laramie for your command.
    The two movements should be made simultaneously, as nearly as possible. I don't think that any disturbance will be made.
If there is any danger of the Indians becoming alarmed by the arrival of troops from Laramie, you should so arrange matters that they shall arrive during the night and make the round up early the next morning.
Use the greatest precaution in this matter. It would be better not to say anything to the Indians about it until the night previous when you can consult the head chiefs and let them select their own men for the work. Delay is very dangerous in this business.
        (Signed.) George Crook,
            Brigadier General.

* * *

Telegram. Camp Robinson, Neb., Sept. 4th 1877
General Crook,
(Fort Laramie.) The Cavalry and Indians started out at 9.30 this morning, Crazy Horse's village broke up last night and when the Command got out to the ground, there were but few lodges to be seen and those making for the Bluffs; some of them came in and others were captured. We have about half the village—(40) odd lodges, and the agency Indians are after the balance and are sure to capture some of them. Crazy Horse left the village this morning with his sick squaw for Spotted Tail and we have twenty picked Indians after them who promise to bring him in. All the friendly Indians behaved extremely well, Little Big Man among them. Will telegraph you to-morrow at Cheyenne.
        (Signed.) Bradley,
            Lieut.-Colonel.

* * *

Telegram. Camp Robinson, Sep't. 4th 1877.
General Crook,
   (Fort Laramie.)

   Quite a number of lodges of crazy Horse's band left here last night: the rest commenced moving early this morning before we started.

   As soon as we got within (3) or (4) miles, they promised to give up guns and move near the Agency, but most of them scattered like a frightened covey of quail, some going to camps here and quite a number to Spotted Tail. It is impossible to tell just now how many have left. Indians here acted well and were ready and would have fought, but they wanted the Northern Indians to commence.
Crazy Horse started down the river with only his own lodge. I at once sent a party to bring him back and as soon as I learned further particulars, sent No Water with ten men to arrest him and bring him to my house. I promised No water $(200) if he accomplished his mission. I have great hopes that they will get him. Under all the circumstances, I believe it would be best to turn over the remnants of this band to the head men I spoke to you about and not try to take any ponies. We have been at work all day and can take no further action before morning. I have sent two couriers to [Agent Jesse] Lee, to keep matters quiet there and intercept any who have gone there, if possible.

   I urged the arrest of Crazy Horse strongly to Lee.
      (Signed.) Clark,
         1 Lieut. 2d Cavalry.

* * *

Telegram Camp Robinson, Neb., Sep't. 5th 1877
General Crook,
   (Cheyenne.)

   (50) lodges—73 men—have been gathered up of Crazy Horse's band and some others are being brought in. The new organization for this band will, I think, be perfected satisfactorily in a day or two. I believe not more than (20) lodges got away and went to Spotted Tail.

         (signed.) Clark
         1 Lieut. 2d Cavalry.

* * *

Telegram   Camp Robinson, Neb., Sep't. 5, 1877
Major Gilliss
    Cheyenne dépôt.
    General Crook will reach Cheyenne on Laramie stage to-day: please hand this to General Crook.
    Crazy Horse was captured last night at Spotted Tail (Agency.) Seven more lodges were brought in last night and the Indians are after the balance who went towards Spotted Tail. I think we shall get them all, Seventy Five of Lame Deer's band surrendered yesterday. They state that (500) more under Fast Bull will be in in (4) or (5) days.
            (signed.) Bradley,
                Lieutenant-Colonel.
                    * * *

Telegram.   Camp Robinson, Neb., Sep't. 5th 1877
General Crook,
    Cheyenne.
    Major Burke (Note he was the C. O. of Camp Sheridan, the Mily. post at Spotted Tail Agency.) sends word that he, with Touch the Clouds, Swift Bear, High Bear and Crazy Horse are coming in ambulance to-day. He[2] will be put in guard-house on arrival. I think he should be started for Fort Laramie to-night and kept going as far as Omaha, (2) or (3) Sioux going with him so that they can assure people on return that he has not been killed. I hope you will telegraph Genl. Bradley. Everything quiet and working first-rate.
            (signed.) Clark,
                1 Lt. 2d Cavalry
                    * * *

Telegram.   Cheyenne, Wyo., Sep't. 5th 1877
Colonel Bradley,
    Comdg. Camp Robinson.
    Accept my thanks for the successful termination of your enterprise and convey the same to Lieut. Clark and others concerned. Send Crazy Horse with a couple of his own people with him, under a strong escort, viâ Laramie to Omaha.
Make sure that he does not escape.
Keep up your efforts until you get every Indian in[,] even if you have to follow them up to Powder River.
            (sig.) George Crook,
                Brig. General.

2. Crazy Horse.

* * *

Telegram.   Cheyenne, Wyo., Sep't. 3d 1877
   Lieut. General Sheridan,
     Chicago.

Your dispatch of this day received. Crazy Horse was at the bottom of the whole trouble at both Agencies and yesterday his band was dismembered by the soldiers and our Indians, mostly by the latter. The members of his band are being distributed among the other bands. Crazy Horse is now a prisoner and I have ordered Bradley to send him down here. I wish you would send him off where he would be out of harm's way.[3] You can rest assured that everything at the Agency is perfectly quiet and will remain so. The advance of Lame Deer's party has already come in and the balance will be in in (4) or (5) days with the exception of (5) lodges that went to hunt up Sitting Bull. I have given the necessary orders about disarming them as they come in. This is the end of all trouble so far as all Sioux are concerned outside of Sitting Bull. (Here followed some remarks about the Nez-Percé Campaign.) The successful breaking up of Crazy Horse's band has removed a heavy weight off my mind and I leave here feeling perfectly easy.
                (Signed.) George Crook,
                   Brigadier General.

* * *

Telegram   Chicago, Illinois, Sep't 5th 1877.
   Captain Gillis, U.S.A.
     Cheyenne, Wyo.,

Send the following to General Crook. Your dispatch of this date received. I will send to you at Green River station, the latest news of the Nez-Percés.

I wish you to send Crazy Horse under proper guard to these Hd.Qrs.[4]
                (signed.) P. H. Sheridan,
                   Lieut.-General.

* * *

---

   3. Crook probably intended for Crazy Horse to go to Fort Marion, Florida, the usual place of exile for chiefs that the government considered incorrigible.
   4. I.e., divisional headquarters in Chicago.

Telegram.   Camp Robinson, Neb., Sep't. 5th 1877
General Crook,
Green River, Wyo.

Crazy Horse reached here at 6 o'clock: his pistol and knife had not been taken from him and in getting these, he made a break, stabbing Little Big Man in arm and trying to do other damage, but we have him all right and I think there will be no further trouble. I had selected some Indians here and cannot speak too highly of their conduct, particularly of Little Big Man. Crazy Horse's father and Touch the Clouds are now with him; the latter in the mêlée was cut in abdomen, but not seriously. The Indians I selected simply did better than I can express and deserve great credit and I hope may get it.

(Signed.) Clark,
1 Lt. 2d Cavalry.

* * *

Telegram.   Camp Robinson, Neb., Sept 5th 77.
General Crook,
   Green River, Wyo.,

In the mêlée, Crazy Horse got a prod in the abdomen, probably from a bayonet but probably [sic] from a knife when he attempted to stab Little Big Man: the latter I am trying to persuade all Indians. The Doctor reports he has no pulse in either arm and I think it will be impossible to move him to-night. His father will be allowed to move his lodge near the Guard-House and take charge of him should he be alive in the morning.

(Signed.) Clark
1 Lieut. Commanding.

* * *

Telegram.   Camp Robinson, Neb., Sep't . 5th 1877.
General Crook,
(Green River.)

If you approve, will complete arrangements for payment of scouts, discharging Crazy Horse to date August 31st, and let the chiefs who are to take charge of this band designate men to replace those whose arms have been taken away. These chiefs are doing even better than I anticipated.

(Signed.) Clark,
1 Lt. 2d Cavalry.

* * *

Telegram.　　　　　　　Camp Robinson, Neb., Sep't. 6th 1877
General George Crook,
En route to Camp Stambaugh, Wyo.

　Crazy Horse died at 11;40 P.M., last night. Some lodges have left and gone to Spotted Tail, the excitement last night being intense; but the Indians here claim that they will get them and will be responsible that none go North. Everything seems to be working well, though we have not heard from Spotted Tail. The death of this man will save trouble.

　　　　　　　　(Signed.) Clark,
　　　　　　　　1 Lt. 2d Cavalry.

* * *

　　　　　　　Hd.Qrs. District of the Black Hills,
　　　　　　　Camp Robinson, Neb., Sep't. 7 1877.

Adjutant General
　Dep't. of the Platte,
　Omaha, Neb.

　When General Crook arrived here on the 2d inst., he ordered me to surround and disarm Crazy Horse's band the next morning, but I received information on the evening of the 2d that Lame Deer's band was on the way & quite near. So General Crook directed the movement to be suspended, fearing that if the attack on Crazy Horse was made at that time, the northern Indians coming in might be alarmed and driven back.

　General Crook left here on the morning of the 4th and, under his instructions I sent out a strong force about 9 o'clock of that date to surround Crazy Horse's village about six miles below this post. The column consisted of (8) companies of the 3rd Cavalry and about (400) friendly Indians. The Indian scouts were under Lieut. Clark; the other Indians under chiefs Red Cloud, Little Wound, American Horse, Young Man-Afraid-of-his-horses, Yellow Bar, Black Coal, Big Road, Jumping Shield and Sharp Nose. The Cavalry were under command of Colonel Mason, 3d Cavalry.

　When the command reached the site of the village, they found it had broke up in the night and most of it had disappeared. A part of the lodges returned to the Agency of their own accord, and joined the friendly bands, a large number were overtaken by the friendly Indians and brought back, and a few went to the

Spotted Tail Agency. Crazy Horse escaped alone and went direct to Spotted Tail (Agency.) where he was arrested the same day by friendly Indians and was brought here under a guard of Indians on the 5th inst. My orders from General Crook were to capture this chief, confine him and send him under guard to Omaha. When he was put in the Guard-House, he suddenly drew a knife, struck at the guard and made for the door. Little Big Man, one of his own chiefs, grappled with him and was cut, in the arm by Crazy Horse during the struggle.

The two chiefs were surrounded by the Guard and about this time, Crazy Horse received a severe wound in the lower part of the abdomen, either from a knife or bayonet, the surgeons are in doubt which.[5]

He was immediately removed and place in charge of the surgeons and died about midnight. His father and Touch the Clouds, chief of the Sans Arcs, remained with him till he died, and when his breath ceased the chief laid his hand on Crazy Horse's breast and said, "It is good: he has looked for death, and it has come".

The body was delivered to his friends the morning after his death. Crazy Horse and his friends were assured that no harm was intended him and the Chiefs who were with him are satisfied that none was intended,—his death resulted from his own violence. There was a good deal of excitement among his people following his death, but it is quieting down.

The leading men of his band, Big Road, Jumping Shield and Little Big Man are satisfied that his death is the result of his own folly, and they are on friendly terms with us. Crazy Horse's band is being

---

5. One must wonder whether the surgeons were completely incompetent (unlikely), or whether they were covering for something. The Model 1873 bayonet in use at the time has a triangular blade with a maximum width of 13/16 inch at the base, and maximum depth of 13/32 inch apex to base (measurements from examples in my own collection). Although there are two varieties of the 1873 bayonet, one cold-pressed to .45 caliber from surplus earlier models, and the other specifically manufactured for the .45-caliber Springfield rifle, the specifications of the blade essentially were the same; either would have left a wound very distinguishable from the deep, flat blade of a knife. Bourke (Diaries, 24:48) tried to shrug it off by saying Crazy Horse had a "stiletto," which would have left a wound similar—but not identical—to a bayonet. A stiletto, however, is a purely fighting blade designed to stab rather than cut. As such, it was preferred in Europe and by street gangs in the Eastern cities, whereas Indians generally opted for a knife with its more utilitarian cutting edge. There is no indication Crazy Horse carried a stiletto, and they generally were not found among Plains Indians, for whom knives were tools as much as weapons. Additionally, Crazy Horse's wound punctured both kidneys which would have been consistent with the eighteen-inch blade of a bayonet.

reorganized under Big Road, a moderate, prudent man, and I think most, if not all, the band can be kept quiet.
>Very Respectfully,
>>Your obedt. Servant.,
>>>(signed.) L. P. Bradley,
>>>>Lt.-Col. 9th Infantry.

* * *

Telegram.　　　　　　　　　　Camp Robinson, Sep't. 9 1877.
Lieut. J. G. Bourke, A.D.C.
> Camp Stambaugh,
>> Courier from Spotted Tail (Agency.) with letter. No stampede of Lame Deer's party. They will all be in there in a day or two and every thing going on well. Crazy Horse's remains were taken over there for burial. The excitement caused by his death is subsiding. Indians have been making presents to his kin. Some few still making threats, but the majority consider his death a blessing to his people. Scouts in from north say all who did not come in to Camp Sheridan went north to join Sitting Bull.
>>> (signed.) Clark,
>>>> 1 Lieut. 2d Cavalry.

* * *

Telegram.　　　　　　　　Green River, Wyo., Sep't. 12th 1877.
> Lieut. Clark,
>> Camp Robinson,
>>> Have received your telegram and am glad to know that affairs are in satisfactory condition at the Agency.

Please give my thanks to Little Big Man, Touch the Clouds and others who did well.

I wish you would write me a full account of all that has taken place at Robinson since I was there, so as to reach me at Omaha.
>>>> (signed.) George Crook,
>>>>> Brigadier general

* * *

>>>>>Camp Robinson, Neb., Aug. 18th 1877.

Dear General
> I write you an outline of affairs here so that you may know that everything has been done that could possibly bring about the very desirable object of having Crazy Horse go on with the other head men.

During the summer, I feared this result and thought I had worked matters so that it would certainly be avoided. I cultivated the friendship and confidence of all the northern Indians and Crazy Horse in particular and succeeded in getting on excellent "dog-eating"[6] terms with them and him, but it is impossible to work him through reasoning or kindness. When the first telegram came, I read it in council and afterwards explained it kindly and fully to him and his head men, and afterwards to each of the latter at my house and their own lodges.

He was not pressed for a decision, hoping that the influence of his head men might be sufficient. Frank [Grouard], since his return, has also done what he could. The other Indians at the agency have no influence whatever with him. The Agent has also done his best. Yesterday your telegram came, requesting him particularly to go; it was read in *Council* at the *Agency* to all.

The agent gave him two beef cattle and I bought a lot of things of Commissary and gave them for a feast, to talk over the matter and decide.

I explained to him that in addition to the other interests involved, you wished him to come on with the others and work with you in regard to their Agency and, if possible, prevent any undesirable change. That the President wanted him to come and you were anxious to have him go; that it was important and necessary for us all to work earnestly and honestly together in this matter &c. &c. Today, he came up, said he would not go himself, but brought up the men he had selected to go; wanted Spotted Tail, Little Wound, Red Cloud and the rest thrown away and only the men he had picked out, sent on; had already said where he wanted his *Agency*, and if they wanted to know anything more, these men could tell them &c.

I kindly but firmly told him that the head men were going, and this was a matter he could only decide for himself and Band; that the men who went would not only be considered but would be the chiefs of the bands; he had been asked if he would work with the president and yourself in this matter and I wanted to know if he would do so.

He replied by stating that "he had already stated he was not going". Force is the only thing that will work out a good condition in

---

6. I.e., knew them well enough to sit together at a meal.

this man's mind; kindness he only attributes to weakness.

His head men are all right, and dead against him in this matter. Extremely reticent, very brave and generous, he has had a large reputation and influence, but his power could be easily broken at the present time,—and I believe it necessary. I am very reluctantly forced to this conclusion, because I have claimed and felt all along that any Indian could be "worked" by other means, but absolute force is the only thing for him. There is no trouble with Little Big Man, Jumping Shield and Big road, the strongest men in this band, though Iron Hawk and Little Hawk each have a good deal of influence. He Dog, also a strong man, has joined Red Cloud. I regret very much that the delegation is so small,—there should be thirty at least. The Indians are particularly anxious to have more go and I heartily wish it might be increased. The Arapahoes feel that at least Black Coal, Sharp Nose and Friday ought to go. Spotted Tail wants Joe Merivale[,] and the Indians here Hunter, and Gruard feels as though he had been e'enmost promised: this would leave but just about one man to each band.

The additional cost of transportation would not be great as a car could be chartered. The Indians would be pleased to have Dr. Irwin also go along. (I promised them I would ask for the increase.) Crazy Horse sent a delegation to Spotted Tail (Agency) secretly the other night, to try and induce the northern Indians there to come up and join him, but he got no comfort from them. I think everything will go along all right, at least until the Delegation returns, but am keeping a sharp watch, through some of the scouts I can fully trust, on both agencies, and they keep me pretty well posted.

Spotted Tail said to me a few days since, (he came up to have a talk himself.) that nothing could be done with this band until their arms and ponies were taken away and he would lie to it, but he is a Brulé.[7]

> Very Respectfully & Sincerely Yours,
> (sig.) W. P. Clark,
> 1 Lt. 2d Cavalry.

* * *

---

7. I.e., indicating there might be trouble if he attempted to disarm the Oglalas.

Camp Sheridan, Neb., Aug. 8th 1877

My dear Clark.

The Indians here are very anxious to have more go to Washington than seems to be the intention to let go. They would like that three should go from each band and I think that two at least should be allowed. Do you think that there is any prospect of having the number increased? There are five different and distinct bands here, viz; the Brulés, Loafers, Wazazies, Minneconjous and Sans Arcs. Taking two from each would make but ten from here. Please arrange to have that number go if you possibly can. They also want one interpreter. Everything remarkably quiet here.

Very truly Yours,
(sig.) Burke.

(I.E. Major D. W. Burke, the C.O. of Camp Sheridan.)

* * *

Billy Hunter's Account.

In the latter part of the summer, the Indians asked for and obtained permission to leave their Agency and go out on a buffalo hunt, and having no ammunition, an order was given allowing traders to sell to the Indians ammunition for hunting purposes. Shortly after this time, the delegation was forming to go to Washington and, in a council, it was agreed to that Crazy Horse and Little Big Man should be of the number (20:) to go.

Crazy Horse appeared to be well satisfied before and at this time. After the Indians had started on the hunt, a portion of the head men came back to prepare for the trip to Washington. Crazy Horse did not like this arrangement. He wanted to go on with the hunt and would give no definite reply as to whether or not he was willing to go to Washington.

On account of the dissatisfaction expressed by Crazy Horse, the order allowing traders to sell ammunition to Indians was revoked.

At this time, the Paymaster came up to pay off the troops, (including the Indian scouts.) And, altho' Crazy Horse was an enlisted scout, he refused to draw his pay.

Seeing that Crazy Horse was very much dissatisfied, the Commanding Officer of the Post sent for him and Little Big Man to come and talk with him. They came, and the Commanding Officer told them that the Great Father at Washington had sent word to them that he wanted them to come and see him, Little Big Man immediately gave his consent to go, but Crazy Horse would give no satisfactory reply as to what he would do.

About three days after this time, Crazy Horse came up and selected the men that he wanted to go to Washington, (selecting mostly Northern Indians) but refusing to go himself.

At about the same time, or shortly after, scouts were enlisting to join the expedition against the Nez-Percés. Crazy Horse was asked if he would go, to which he would give no reply on that day, but the next day he came up to the Post, accompanied by a large number of his young men and talked very badly. He said he would not go out with the troops, but that he would move out slowly with his entire village and when overtaken would help to fight the Nez-Percés.

This was merely an excuse which he thought would enable him to get away and go north, for at the same time he was doing all in his power to induce other Indians, (especially the enlisted scouts.) to accompany him. He did not succeed in getting away as notice was soon given that the scouts would not be required.

After this, all, except the Northern Indians, wanted to move, in one large village, to Little White Chief creek. They held councils, at same time, discussing what should be said and done by the Delegation going to Washington.

General Crook came up to Red Cloud (Agency.) about this time and was to hold a Council with the Indians; on the day appointed for the Council, General Crook, accompanied by two or three persons, started for the Indian Camp, but on the way was met by an Indian scout, Woman's Dress who informed the General that if he went into the Council he would be killed as Crazy Horse said that if the Big White Chief, (i.e. General Crook.) did not talk to suit him, he (Crazy Horse[)] would stab him.

On hearing this, the party returned to the Post.

After this, and three days before Crazy Horse was killed, General Crook sent for all of the head men to come up to the post as he wanted to talk to them. They all came except Crazy Horse.

The General then told them that they were being led astray by this chief. (Crazy Horse.) and that they must take him prisoner. The Indians proposed killing him and this proposition was agreed to by the others, but General Crook told them it must not be done as it would be murder, but insisted that he must be taken prisoner.

On the next morning after the day of the Council (i.e., Sep't. 4th,

J.G.B.) A party of Indian soldiers started for Spotted Tail (Agency.) to which place Crazy Horse had moved some time before. They arrived at Spotted Tail (Agency.) and going to Crazy Horse's lodge informed him that General Bradley had words for him from the Great Father at Washington and that he must come to (Camp.) Robinson to hear them. He came along peaceably and, accompanied by Lieut. Lee(?)* And some Indian soldiers, started in an ambulance for Camp Robinson.

They arrived at Robinson about dark,** but instead of stopping at General Bradly's [sic] Quarters, they stopped in front of the Post Guard House. Crazy Horse noticed this and remarked, after getting out of the ambulance, that "this is not General Bradley's Quarters". He was then told that he must go into the Guard-House and seeing himself surrounded by the Guard, he left the persons who were with him and ran into the Guard House alone, closely followed by Little Big Man and the Sentinel No 1, the sentinel remaining near the door-way. On entering the Guard room and seeing men in the cells, confined with chains on, he sprang back, saying "I won't go in there. It is the place where prisoners are kept". While moving back toward the door, he drew both his knifes and with one in each hand rushed towards the sentinel.

Little Big Man seeing his intention of making his escape, sprang behind him and reaching around his body, held his hands, keeping the points of his knives down. In this position, dragging Little Big Man with him, Crazy Horse came up to the sentinel, who having his bayonet "fixed", as soon as he came within reach, stabbed him. He died in a short time from the effects of this stab. The points of his own knives did not touch his body.

* * *

The above was obtained for me by my friend, Lieutenant G. A. Dodd, 3d Cavalry.

*Bourke's note: Billy Hunter is mistaken: Major Burke was the Officer who took Crazy Horse to Camp Robinson, Neb. . . . J.G.B.

**Here Bourke inserted Sept. 5th, with the footnote: Billy Hunter, like all Indians and Half-breeds, has a good memory for facts, but is not exact in dates. J.G.B.

Bibliography

Manuscript Sources

Bourke, John Gregory. Diaries. 124 vols. United States Military Academy Library, West Point, New York. Microfilm in possession of the editor.

Carr, Eugene Asa. Papers. United States Army Military History Institute, Carlisle Barracks, Pa.

Crook, George. Collection. Microfilm edition. R. B. Hayes Papers. Rutherford B. Hayes Library, Rutherford B. Hayes Presidential Center, Fremont, Ohio.

———. Letter Books. 2 vols. George Crook Collection. Microfilm edition. Rutherford B. Hayes Library, Rutherford B. Hayes Presidential Center, Fremont, Ohio.

Schuyler, Walter Scribner. Papers. Henry E. Huntington Library and Art Gallery, San Marino, Calif.

Government Documents

DeLand, Charles E. *The Sioux Wars*. Vol. 15. *South Dakota Historical Collections*. Pierre, S.D.: State Department of History, 1930.

Heitman, Francis B. *Historical Register and Dictionary of the United States Army, From Its Organization, September 29, 1789,*

to *March 2, 1903*. 2 vols. Washington: Government Printing Office, 1903.
Howard, James H. *The Ponca Tribe*. Smithsonian Institution. Bureau of American Ethnology Bulletin 195. 1965. Reprint, Lincoln: University of Nebraska Press, 1995.
United States Department of the Interior. *Report of the Commissioner of Indian Affairs to the Secretary of the Interior, 1876*. Vol 1. :Washington: Government Printing Office, 1876.
United States Department of War. Office of the Adjutant General. RG 393. Special File. Military Division of the Missouri. National Archives Microfilm Publication 1495. Washington: National Archives, n.d.
  —Roll 6. Little Wolf's Cheyennes, March–June 1879
  —Roll 7. White River Utes, 1879.
    —Troop Movements (Ute War), October–December 1879.
———. *Regulations of the Army of the United States and General Orders in Force February 17, 1881*. Washington: Government Printing Office, 1881.
———. *War of the Rebellion: Official Records of the Union and Confederate Armies*. Series 1, Vol. 12, Part 2 Supplement. Washington: Government Printing Office, 1886.
—. Series 1, Vol. 30, Part 1.Washington: Government Printing Office, 1890.

Books–Primary

Bourke, John Gregory. *On the Border With Crook*. 1891. Reprint, Alexandria, Va.: Time-Life Books, 1980.
Catlin, George. *Letters and Notes on the Manners, Customs, and Conditions of the North American Indians*. 2 vols. 1844. Reprint, New York: Dover Publications, 1973.
Clark, Robert A., ed. *The Killing of Chief Crazy Horse: Three Eyewitness Views by the Indian, Chief He Dog, the Indian-White, William Garnett, the White Doctor, Valentine McGillycuddy*. 1976. Reprint, Lincoln: University of Nebraska Press, 1988.
Mills, Anson. *My Story*. 2nd ed. Washington: Press of Byron S. Adams, 1921.
Price, Rose Lambart, Baronet. *The Two Americas; An Account*

of Sport and Travel. With Notes on Men and Manners in North and South America. Philadelphia: J. B. Lippincott & Co., 1877.

Robinson, Charles M., III, ed. *The Diaries of John Gregory Bourke.* 2 completed vols. Denton: University of North Texas Press, 2003–2005.

Schmitt, Martin F., ed. *Major General George Crook: His Autobiography.* Norman: University of Oklahoma Press, 1946. Reprint, 1986.

Smith, Thomas T, ed.. *A Dose of Frontier Soldering: The Memoirs of Corporal E. A. Bode, Frontier Regular Infantry, 1877–1882.* Lincoln: University of Nebraska Press, 1972. Reprinted 1999.

Summerhayes, Martha. *Vanished Arizona: Recollections of the Army Life of a New England Woman.* 2nd ed. 1911. Reprint, Lincoln: University of Nebraska Press, 1979.

Tibbles, Thomas Henry. *Buckskin and Blanket Days: Memoirs of a Friend of the Indians.* 1957. Reprint, Lincoln: University of Nebraska Press, 1973.

———. *Standing Bear and the Ponca Chiefs.* Originally published as *The Ponca Chiefs.* 1880. Reprint, Lincoln: University of Nebraska Press, 1995.

Books–Secondary

Altshuler, Constance Wynn. *Cavalry Yellow and Infantry Blue: Army Officers in Arizona Between 1851 and 1886.* Tucson: The Arizona Historical Society, 1991.

———. *Starting With Defiance: Nineteenth Century Arizona Military Posts.* Tucson: The Arizona Historical Society, 1983.

Bancroft, Hubert Howe. *History of Arizona and New Mexico 1530–1888.* The Works of Hubert Howe Bancroft 17. San Francisco: The History Company, 1889.

———. *The Native Races. Vol. 1. The Wild Tribes.* The Works of Hubert Howe Bancroft 1. San Francisco: A. L. Bancroft & Company, 1883.

Beal, Merrill D. *"I Will Fight No More Forever": Chief Joseph and the Nez Perce War.* Seattle: University of Washington Press, 1963.

Brimlow, George Francis. *The Bannock Indian War of 1878.*

Caldwell, Idaho: Caxton Printers, Ltd., 1938.

Brown, Dee. *The Fetterman Massacre*. Originally published as *Fort Phil Kearny: An American Saga*. 1962. Reprint, Lincoln: University of Nebraska Press, 1971.

Buecker, Thomas R. *Fort Robinson and the American West 1874–1899*. Lincoln: Nebraska State Historical Society, 1999.

Carroll, John M., ed. *The Court Martial of Frederick W. Benteen, Major, 9th Cavalry; or Did General Crook Railroad Benteen?* N.p., n.d. (Bryan, Tex.: 1981).

Churchill, Winston S. *The Great Democracies*. A History of the English-Speaking Peoples 4. New York: Dodd, Meade & Company, 1958.

Cosío Villegas, Daniel. *The United States Versus Porfirio Díaz*. Trans. by Nettie Lee Benson. Lincoln: University of Nebraska Press, 1963.

Cresap, Bernarr, *Appomattox Commander: The Story of General E.O.C. Ord*. San Diego: A.S. Barnes and Company, Inc., 1981.

Crouch, Brodie, *Jornada del Muerto: A Pageant of the Desert*. Spokane, Wash.: The Arthur H. Clark Co., 1989.

Dary, David. *Red Blood and Black Ink: Journalism in the Old West*. New York: Alfred A. Knopf, 1998.

De Barthe, Joe. *The Life and Adventures of Frank Grouard, Chief of Scouts, U.S.A.* 1894. Reprint, Alexandria, Va.: Time-Life Books, 1982.

Egan, Ferol. *Frémont: Explorer for a Restless Nation*. Reno: University of Nevada Press, 1985.

Foote, Shelby. *The Civil War, A Narrative: Red River to Appomattox*. New York: Random House, 1974.

Frazer, Robert W. *Forts of the West: Military Forts and Presidios and Posts Commonly Called Forts West of the Mississippi River to 1898*. Norman: University of Oklahoma Press, 1965. Reprinted 1972.

Gilbert, Hila, with George Harris and Bernice Pourier Harris. *"Big Bat" Pourier*. Sheridan, Wyo.: The Mills Company, 1968.

Greene, Jerome A. *Nez Perce Summer, 1877: The U.S. Army and the Nee-me-poo Crisis*. Helena: Montana Historical Society Press, 2000.

———. *Washita: The U.S. Army and the Southern Cheyennes,*

1867–1869. Norman: University of Oklahoma Press, 2004.
———. *Yellowstone Command: Colonel Nelson A. Miles and the Great Sioux War 1876–1877*. Lincoln: University of Nebraska Press, 1991.
Grinnell, George Bird. *The Cheyenne Indians*. 2 vols. 1923. Reprint, Lincoln: University of Nebraska Press, 1972.
Gump, James. *The Dust Rose Like Smoke: The Subjugation of the Zulu and the Sioux*. Lincoln: University of Nebraska Press, 1994.
Herr, John K, and Edward S. Wallace. *The Story of the U.S. Cavalry: 1775–1942*. 1953. Reprint, New York: Bonanza Books, 1984.
Hoig, Stan. *The Battle of the Washita: The Sheridan-Custer Indian Campaign of 1867–69*. Garden City: Doubleday & Company, 1976.
Hoogenboom, Ari. *Rutherford B. Hayes, Warrior and President*. Lawrence: University Press of Kansas, 1995.
Hoxie, Frederick E., ed. *Encyclopedia of North American Indians*. Boston: Houghton Mifflin Company, 1996.
Hyde, George. *Red Cloud's Folk: A History of the Oglala Sioux Indians*. Norman: University of Oklahoma Press, 1937. Reprinted 1987.
Jackson, Helen Hunt. *A Century of Dishonor: A Sketch of the United States Government's Dealings with Some of the Indian Tribes*. 1885. Reprint, Norman: University of Oklahoma Press, 1995.
Johnson, Allen, and Dumas Malone, eds. *Dictionary of American Biography*. 20 vols. New York: Charles Scribner's Sons, 1928–38.
King, Charles. *Campaigning With Crook and Stories of Army Life*. New York: Harper & Brothers, 1890.
Knight, Oliver. *Following the Indian Wars: The Story of the Newspaper Correspondents Among the Indian Campaigners*. Norman: University of Oklahoma Press, 1960. Reprinted 1993.
———. *Life and Manners in the Frontier Army*. Norman: University of Oklahoma Press, 1978. Reprinted 1993.
Kroeker, Marvin E. *Great Plains Command: William B. Hazen in the Frontier West*. Norman: University of Oklahoma Press, 1976.

Lamar, Howard R., ed. *The New Encyclopedia of the American West*. New Haven: Yale University Press, 1998.

Lewis, Lloyd. *Sherman, Fighting Prophet*. New York: Harcourt, Brace and Company, 1932.

Litwack, Leon F. *Been in the Storm So Long: The Aftermath of Slavery*. New York: Alfred A. Knopf, 1980.

Loughmiller, Campbell, and Lynn Loughmiller. *Texas Wildflowers: A Field Guide*. Austin: University of Texas Press, 1984.

McChristian, Douglas C. *The U.S. Army in the West, 1870–1880: Uniforms, Weapons, and Equipment*. Norman: University of Oklahoma Press, 1995.

McDermott, John D. *Circle of Fire: The Indian War of 1865*. Mechanicsburg, Pa.: Stackpole Books, 2003.

McFeely, William S. *Grant: A Biography*. New York: W.W. Norton & Company, 1981.

McPherson, James. *Battle Cry of Freedom: The Civil War Era*. The Oxford History of the United States 6. New York: Oxford University Press, 1988.

Madsen, Brigham D. *The Bannock of Idaho*. Caldwell, Idaho: The Caxton Printers, Ltd., 1958.

Manuel, Dale. *Coastal Castles of Louisiana and Mississippi*. Del Valle, Tex.: The author, 1999.

Marszalek, John F., Jr., *Court-Martial: A Black Man in America*. New York: Charles Scribner's Sons, 1972.

Mathes, Valerie Sherer, and Richard Lowitt. *The Standing Bear Controversy, Prelude to Indian Reform*. Urbana: University of Illinois Press, 2003.

Miller, Rick. *Sam Bass and Gang*. Austin: State House Press, 1999.

Monnett, John H. *Tell Them We Are Going Home: The Odyssey of the Northern Cheyennes*. Norman: University of Oklahoma Press, 2001.

National Geographic, Editors of. *This England*. Washington: National Geographic Society, 1966.

Norris, Frank. *The Octopus: A Story of California*. Garden City: Doubleday, Page & Company, 1901.

Omer-Cooper, J.D. *The Zulu Aftermath: A Nineteenth Century Revolution in Bantu Africa*. Evanston, Ill.: Northwestern University Press, 1969.

Palmer, Alan. *The Decline and Fall of the Ottoman Empire*. 1992. Reprint, New York: Barnes & Noble, Inc., 1994.

Pierce, Michael D. *The Most Promising Young Officer: A Life of Ranald Slidell Mackenzie*. Norman: University of Oklahoma Press, 1993.

Peterson, Roger Tory. *A Field Guide to the Birds: A Completely New Guide to All the Birds of Eastern and Central North America*. 4th ed. Boston: Houghton Mifflin Company, 1980.

Priest, Loring Benson. *Uncle Sam's Stepchildren: The Reformation of United States Indian Policy, 1865–1887*. 1942. Reprint, New York: Octagon Books, 1972.

Porter, Joseph. *Paper Medicine Man: John Gregory Bourke and His American West*. Norman: University of Oklahoma Press, 1986. Reprinted 1989.

Prucha, Francis Paul. *The Great Father: The United States Government and the American Indians*. Abridged ed., Lincoln: University of Nebraska Press, 1984.

Reeves, Thomas C. *Gentleman Boss: The Life and Times of Chester Alan Arthur*. 1975. Reprint, Newton, Conn.: American Political Biography Press, 2002.

Reiss, Eric L. *The Compleat Talking Machine*. New York: The Vestal Press, 1986.

Robinson, Charles Moore, III. *Bad Hand: A Biography of General Ranald S. Mackenzie*. Austin: State House Press, 1993.

———. *Frontier Forts of Texas*. Houston: Gulf Publishing Company, 1986.

———. *General Crook and the Western Frontier*. Norman: University of Oklahoma Press, 2001.

———. *A Good Year to Die: The Story of the Great Sioux War*. New York: Random House, 1995.

Roske, Ralph J., and Charles van Doren. *Lincoln's Commando: The Biography of Commander William B. Cushing, U.S. Navy*. 1957. Reprint, Annapolis: Naval Institute Press, 1995.

Russell, Don. *Campaigning With King: Charles King, Chronicler of the Old Army*. Edited by Paul L. Hedren. Lincoln: University of Nebraska Press, 1991.

Schwartz, E. A. *The Rogue River Indian War and Its Aftermath, 1850–1980*. Norman: University of Oklahoma Press, 1997.

Schubert, Frank N. *Outpost of the Sioux Wars: A History of Fort*

Robinson. Originally published as *Buffalo Soldiers, Braves, and the Brass: The Story of Fort Robinson, Nebraska*. 1993. Reprint, Lincoln: University of Nebraska Press, 1995.

Spellenberg, Richard. *National Audubon Society Field Guide to North American Wildflowers Western Region*. New York: Alfred A. Knopf, 1995.

Sprague, Marshall. *Massacre: The Tragedy at White River*. Boston: Little, Brown and Co., 1957.

Stacton, David. *The Bonapartes*. New York: Simon and Schuster, 1966.

Strobridge, William F. *Regulars in the Redwoods: The U.S. Army in Northern California, 1852–1861*. Spokane, Wash.: The Arthur H. Clark Company, 1994.

Sweeney, Edwin R. *Cochise, Chiricahua Apache Chief*. Norman: University of Oklahoma Press, 1991.

Thrapp, Dan L. *Encyclopedia of Frontier Biography*. 3 vols. 1988. Reprint, Lincoln: University of Nebraska Press, 1991.

Time-Life Books, Editors of. *The Way of the Warrior*. The American Indian. Alexandria, Va.: 1993.

Utley, Robert M. *A Clash of Cultures: Fort Bowie and the Chiricahua Apaches*. Washington: National Park Service, 1977.

———, ed. *Encyclopedia of the American West*. New York: Wing Books, 1997.

———. *Frontier Regulars: The United States Army and the Indian, 1866–1891*. 1973. Reprint, Lincoln: University of Nebraska Press, 1984.

———. *The Lance and the Shield: The Life and Times of Sitting Bull*. New York: Henry Holt and Company, 1993.

Warner, Ezra J. *Generals in Blue: Lives of the Union Commanders*. Baton Rouge: Louisiana State University Press, 1964.

Weaver, John R., II. *A Legacy in Brick and Stone: American Coastal Defense Forts of the Third System, 1816–1867*. McLean, Va.: Redoubt Press, 2001.

Wheeler, Keith, and the Editors of Time-Life Books. *The Railroaders*. The Old West. New York: Time-Life Books, 1973.

Articles–Primary

Schurz, Carl. "Present Aspects of the Indian Problem." *North American Review* 133, no. 296 (July 1881): 1–24.

Articles–Secondary

Carroll, John. "The Man Who Killed Crazy Horse." *Old West* 27, no. 4 (Summer 1991): 38–41.

Fletcher, Robert. "Colonel Garrick Mallery, U.S.A." *American Anthropologist* 8, no. 7 (January 1895): 79–80.

Myers, Roger. "Cattleman Print Olive Was Equally Adept as a Gunman, as More than a Few Rustlers Found out Firsthand." *Wild West*. December 2003: 22–24, 80.

Websites

http://www.accessgenealogy.com/native/tribes/preface.htm Garrick Mallery

http://americahurrah.com/SanFrancisco/Federmeyer.htm R. Lyman Potter/L.P. Federmeyer

http://berrygrape.oregonstate.edu/fruitgrowing/grapes/phybiol.htm "Phylloxera: What Is It?"

http://www.clarelibrary.ie/eolas/coclare/people/parnell.htm Charles Stewart Parnell

http://www.fjc.gov/servlet/tGetInfo?jid=664 Elmer Scipio Dundy

http://www.fortstanton.com Fort Stanton, New Mexico.

http://www.friesian.com/perigoku.htm#konbaung Kings of Burma.

http://historytogo.utah.gov/people/governors/territorial/emery.html George W. Emery

http://www.kentuckyderby.com/2004/derby_history/derby_connections/winners_at_a_glance.html Kentucky Derby

http://www.litencyc.com/php/speople.php?rec=true&UID=1858 John Richard Green

http://www.luminarium.org/renlit/aschbio.htm Roger Ascham

http://www.midcontinent.org/collectn/woodpas/mlsw63/miller.html Miller Coupler and buffer system

http://politicalgraveyard.com/bio/haskill-hastie.html Frederick Hassaurek

http://www.railway-technical.com/st-glos.html#E Steam Locomotive Glossary.

http://www.rootsweb.com/~neresour/OLLibrary/pbal/pages/balc0028.htm. Albinus Nance

http://skyways.lib.ks.us/genweb/archives/1918ks/bios/streetwd.html William D. Street.

http://www.spartacus.schoolnet.co.uk/USAkearney.htm Dennis Kearney
http://www.tucsonaz.gov/tucson_history.html City of Tucson
http://en.wikipedia.org/wiki/William_B._Allison
http://en.wikipedia.org/wiki/James_G._Blaine
http://en.wikipedia.org/wiki/Adolph_E._Borie
http://en.wikipedia.org/wiki/Edward_George_Bulwer-Lytton
http://en.wikipedia.org/wiki/Frederick_Augustus_Thesiger%2C_2nd_Baron_Chelmsford
http://en.wikipedia.org/wiki/Francis_Cockrell
http://wikipedia.org/wiki/Ferdinand_de_Lesseps
http://en.wikipedia.org/wiki/John_Brown_Gordon
http://en.wikipedia.org/wiki/Webb_Hayes
 http://en.wikipedia.org/wiki/David_M._Key
http://en.wikipedia.org/wiki/John_Morrissey
http://en.wikipedia.org/wiki/Algernon_S._Paddock
http://en.wikipedia.org/wiki/John_J._Patterson
http://en.wikipedia.org/wiki/Alvin_Saunders
http://en.wikipedia.org/wiki/John_Sherman
http://en.wikipedia.org/wiki/Eug%C3%A8ne_Emmanuel_Viollet-le-Duc

Index

A

Absaraka Indians (see Crow Indians)
Absaraka, the Land of Massacre (book), 83, 83 n9
Ascham, Roger, 86, 86 n15
Adams, Charles, 339, 346, 479
Albemarle (Confederate ironclad), 257, 257 n15
Alcott, Louisa May, 81
Alexander II (Russia), 418 n18
Allegheny Arsenal, 173 n7
Allison, William B., 32, 55, 479
Almy, William E., 344, 421
Alvord, Benjamin, 418, 421
Amadis de Gallia (book), 86–87 n15
American Horse (Oglala), 271, 493, 510
American Indians, 168 n4
Annals of a Fortress (book), 81, 81 n6

Andersonville Prison Camp, 373
Andrews, William Howard, 302, 325, 344, 421
Antietam, Battle of, 32
Apache Indians (see also under individual groups, and Indian scouts), 7, 38, 97, 251, 256–58, 271, 274–75, 395–96, 402–03
Apache Wars, 413–14
Appleton, Nathan, 371
Appomattox, 174
Arapaho Indians, 57, 67, 69, 127, 129, 134, 136–38, 142, 302
Arikara (Ree) Indians, 62, 138
Arthur, Chester A., 5, 7, 418, 479
Assiniboine Indians, 138
Atchison, Topeka & Santa Fe Railroad, 107, 207, 351

Atlanta, Battle of, 286, 287
Augur, Jacob, 39, 40, 298, 309, 344, 421
Austin, Albert, 121, 148, 155, 329, 421
Ayers, James C., 173, 174

B

Babcock, John Breckinridge, 309, 323, 325, 344, 422
Bachiller de Salamanca (book), 328, 328 n5
Bailey, Edward Lyon, 306, 330, 345, 422
Bainbridge, Augustus Hudson, 42–43, 47, 349, 422
Bainbridge, Mrs. Augustus Hudson, 348
Baker, James (Old Jim), 326, 479–80
Bancroft, Hubert Howe, 129, 129 n19
Bannock Indians (see also Bannock Uprising), 1, 35–37, 43, 45, 51, 57, 91 n17, 126, 216, 348; farming among, 44, 52
Bannock Uprising, 35–36, 35 n2, 43ff., 199
Barrett, Lawrence, 412, 480
Barnett, Richards, 282, 385, 422
Barry, William F., 249, 249 n2, 422–23
Barstow, O. C., 353, 353 n11, 357
Baxter, Lieutenant, 167–68
Beaconsfield, Benjamin Disraeli, Earl of (see Disraeli, Benjamin)
Beecher's Island Fight, 292
Belknap, William Worth, 186–87 n10, 480
Bell, Alexander Graham, 19 n1–2
Bell, Chidchester, 19 n2
Benét, Stephen Vincent, 337, 423
Benét, Mrs. Stephen Vincent, 337
Bennett, James Gordon, 353
Bennett, L.M., 415, 417
Bergland, Eric, 15, 24–25, 27, 375, 423
Bernhardt, Frederick, 327
Big Road (Oglala), 66, 510, 511, 514
Bisbee, William Henry, 40, 74, 302, 423
Bishop, Hoel Smith, 321, 344, 423
Black Coal (Arapaho), 493, 510, 514
Blackfeet Indians (non-Lakota group), 138
Black Hills, 123–24, 137, 195; gold discovered in, 55, 55 n5; commission to purchase, 55–56, 55 n5, 68; mining in, 347
Black Hills Expedition, 398
Blaine, James G., 353–54, 360, 384, 418, 480
Board of Indian Commissioners, 353, 353 n11, 356, 358
Bode, Emil, 9
Bonaparte, Charles Joseph, 243 n10

Bonaparte, Elizabeth Patterson, 243 n10
Bonaparte, Jerome, 243 n10
Bonaparte, Jerome Napoleon, 243, 243 n10
Bonaparte, Letizia (Madame Mère), 206 n5
Booth, Charles Austin, 333, 423
Borie, Adolph, 356, 480–81
Bourke, John Gregory, 8–11, 15–16, 33, 36, 38 n11, 38 n13, 43, 98, 117, 148, 179–80; and diary, 1, 34 n16, 84 n12, 121, 143, 143 n36, 255, 385, 512; on Crazy Horse, 2, 3, 37 n7, 53ff., 65–66, 67–68 n3, 72, 77; on industrialization and development, 3–4, 16, 79, 80, 206, 218, 352; racial attitudes, 4–5, 375, 382, 383; and West Point, 5, 5n12, , 410, 412; early career, 5–6, 20–21; and Irish, 6, 205, 219–21, 258–60; on politicians, 7, 26, 31; on Mexico, 17–18, 88–89, 231, 231 n4, 355; on Confederates, 25–26; on railroads and their impact, 29–30, 188–89, 192–93, 207, 212–13, 218, 277, 346, 351–52, 368, 375–76, 378, 383–84, 402, 417; on Mormonism, 36, 42, 95; on bureaucrats, 56, 56 n7; concerning George Crook, 63, 66, 117–18; on Cheyenne Indians, 114–15, 117; on Carl Schurz, 115, 351; on the Ponca Affair, 116, 179; on Webb Hayes, 118; on Indian policy, 126, 179, 291, 301; Victorianism of, 137 n26; and horse procurement, 191, 364–67, 369, 370–71, 379–82, 387, 391, 400–01, 404, 406–11; on farming and ranching, 205–06, 214–15, 227–28, 240, 280, 391, 401; on Southwestern settlements and people, 251–53, 376–78; visits Union Pacific shops and Omaha industries, 282–86; and White River Ute Uprising, 291–92, 306, 344; personal life and marriage, 338; and Murchie Mine, 345 n4, 348; on General Sherman, 355
Bowlegs, Billy (Seminole), 321, 321 n2, 322
Bowman, Alpheus Henry, 39, 126, 128, 145, 148, 160, 423
Boynton, H.V., 355, 355–56 n15
Bozeman Trail, 83 n9
Brackett, Albert Gallatin, 337, 424
Bradley, Luther Prentice, 71, 74–75, 190, 424, 503–08, 517; report on death of Crazy Horse, 510–12
Brady, Joseph W., 318, 319
Bragg, Braxton, 286
Brayton, A.C., 356
Brent, Thomas Lee, Jr., 413, 415, 424

Bridgeman, S.C., 358
Brodrick, Patrick Thomas, 153, 213, 424
Brown, Charlie, 396
Brown, Nathan Williams, 419, 424–25
Brown, Rufus Porter, 27, 171, 425
Brown, William Henry, 281, 282, 345, 425
Bryant, Montgomery, 42, 49, 324, 329, 345, 425
Bryant, Mrs. Montgomery, 49
Budka, James, 327
Buell, Don Carlos, 383, 384, 425–26
Buffalo Chips (Ponca), 180, 183,
Buffalo Horn (Shoshone), 44, 45
Buffalo Track (Ponca), 180
Bulwer-Lytton, Edward George, Earl of, 412, 413 n11
Burdett-Coatts, Baroness, 359
Bureau of Ethnology, 143 n36
Burlington & Missouri River Railroad, 37, 107
Burmese Wars, 406 n6
Burke, Daniel Webster, 76, 350, 426, 507, 515, 517 fn
Burke, Mrs. Daniel Webster, 350
Burnam, A. P., 379, 426
Burnam, James, 379
Burnett, Levi Frank, 333, 426
Burnham, Horace Blois, 128, 385, 426
Burns, John, 327
Burrowes (sometimes spelled Burroughs), Thomas Bredin, 123, 126, 127, 148, 151 fn, 426
Burt, Andrew Sheridan, 180, 186, 426–27
Butler, T. J., 175
Byrne, Thomas, 221, 222, 223, 224, 427

C

Cadette (Apache), 257
Cain (teamster), 328
Camp
    Apache, Ariz., 413, 413 n12
    Beale's Springs, Ariz., 221–24, 221 n16
    Bowie, Ariz. (see Fort Bowie)
    Brown, Wyo., 45, 45 n22, 48, 53, 71, 75, 85, 127, 504
    Carlin, Wyo. (see Cheyenne Depot, Wyo.)
    Date Creek, Ariz., 74 n15
    Douglas, Utah (see also Fort Douglas), 80, 80 n4, 83, 91, 91 n17, 126
    Goodwin, Ariz., 272, 272 n31
    Grant I, Ariz., 5, 5 n13, 236, 269, 275
    Grant II. Ariz., 5 n13
    Lincoln, Ariz., (see Verde)
    Mojave, Ariz. (see Fort Mojave)
    Rucker, Ariz. (see Camp Supply)
    Robinson, Neb. (see also

Fort Robinson), 58, 58 n10, 60–61, 67, 74–76, 124, 126, 152, 163–64, 167, 171–72, 505–10, 512, 517
Sheridan, Neb., 61, 61 n12, 75, 150, 168–72, 177–78, 512, 515
Stambaugh, Wyo., 74, 74 n17, 75, 502, 512
Supply, Ariz., 38, 38 n 13
Verde, Ariz., 413, 413 n13
Camp Apache Reservation, Ariz., 413 n13
Camp Verde Reservation, Ariz., 413 n14
Campaigning With Crook (book), 370.
Campbell, Joseph Boyd, 50, 427
Canby, Edward R. S., 392 n6
Cantonment Reno, Wyo., (see Fort McKinney)
Capron, Thaddeus Hurlbut, 218, 427
Captain Jim (Shoshone), 43ff., 494
Carlton, Caleb Henry, 152, 163–64, 166–72, 427
Carpenter, Gilbert Saltonstall, 51, 347, 427
Carpenter, Mrs. Gilbert Saltonstall, 347
Carpenter, William Lewis, 180, 329, 428
Carrington, Henry B., 83, 83–84 n9, 428
Carroll, John, 76 n19
Carson, Christopher (Kit), 326

Carey, Lieutenant (British Army), 196 n16
Cary, Annie Louise, 194
Catlin, George, 168 n4
Caverns fight, 229
Cetewayo (King of the Zulus), 196, 196 n17
Chambers, Mrs. Alexander, 39, 40, 80
Chambers, James, 146, 192
Chambers, William, 366, 367, 369, 371–73, 378, 385, 387, 391, 400, 403–04, 410
Chandler, Zachariah, 56, 341, 481
Charging Bear (Oglala), 61, 494
Charles I, 89, 89 n16
Chase, George Francis, 168, 333, 428
Chase, George Nathan, 41, 49, 428
Chelmsford, Frederic Augustus Thesiger, second Baron, 196, 249, 428–29
Cherry, Samuel Austin, 297, 311, 314, 326, 328, 330, 345, 429
Cheyenne Depot, Wyo., 126, 126 n14, 128, 230, 340, 341, 507
Cheyenne Indians (see also Cheyenne Outbreak), 3, 37 n7, 67, 69, 81, 117, 126, 144ff., 172, 174, 176, 178, 185, 199, 264, 300, 301, 311; and Dull Knife Fight, 57–59, 116, 121; break with Sioux, 59, 62; enlisted as

scouts, 59–60, 62; destitution among, 59–60, 123; wounded among, 59–60; surrender, 61, 121; transported to the Indian Territory, 70, 70 n8, 113, 121; general character, 114–15; childbirth among, 115, 130–31; confer with Crook, 121–25; name and sign for themselves, 128–29, 129 n17, 142; as horsemen, 129, 129 n19; language, 129–3; child rearing, 131, 133; recreation, 131–32; Sun Dance, 132–33; virtues, 133; courtship, marriage, and divorce, 133–36; cleanliness among, 133–34; menstrual customs, 134; warrior societies and battle, 136–39, 136 n24; use of stimulants, 136; religion and spiritualism, 137; government, 138; treatment of elderly, 138; commerce, 138–39; diplomacy 139; various cultural activities, 139; lodges, 139–40; buffalo hunting and ceremonies, 140–41; burial customs, 141–43, 141 n34; origin of name, 142, 142 n35; ledger book art, 211
Cheyenne Outbreak, 3, 113–14, 113 n1, 121, 125–28, 144ff., 144 n1, 173, 176, 178
Cheyenne River Agency, Neb., 188 n11

Chicago, Burlington & Quincey Railroad, 343–44, 407, 408, 417
Chicago Inter-Ocean (newspaper), 398
Chicago, Rock Island & Pacific Railroad, , 51, 189, 407, 409
Chicago Times (newspaper), 169, 333
Chicago Tribune (newspaper), 356, 357
Chickamauga, Battle of, 276, 276–77 n1, 286, 288, 346
Church, Albert E., 387, 388, 429
Clark, Ben, 121–25, 125 n10, 211, 481; on future of buffalo, 125; on Cheyennes, 128, 133, 135–36, 138, 141 n34, 142–43, 146, 151 fn
Clark, S. H. H., 213
Clark, William, 327
Clark, William Philo, 66–67, 70–71, 74–75, 133, 185, 213, 276, 429, 504, 506–07, 509–10, 512, 515; report on condition at agencies, 512–14
Clarke, Robert Dunlap, 51, 301–02, 429–30
Clarkson, Robert Harper, 189
Clay, Henry (Kentucky senator), 26
Clay, Henry (grandson of Kentucky senator), 24, 25
Clements, Bennett A., 85, 430
Clifford, Hank, 169
Clifford, Walter, 333, 430

INDEX 535

Cochise (Apache), 77, 257, 395, 403, 494
Cockrell, Francis, 370, 481
Cockrell, Surgeon, 370
Cocopah (Colorado River steamer), 21
Cocopah Indians, 21, 23
Collins, John, 118, 122 fn, 127
Coleman, Frederick William, 250, 254, 430
Colorado Central Railroad, 107
Colorow (Ute), 299, 4995
Comanche Indians, 129, 129 n19, 131 n22, 138
Compton, Charles Elmer, 318, 321, 340, 344, 430–31
Compton, Mrs. Charles Elmer, 337
Congdon (Union Pacific shop superintendent), 282–83
Connor, Patrick, 90–91, 91 n17, 430–31
Cooke, Philip St. George, 83 n10
Coppinger, John Joseph, 6, 20–21, 23, 219–21, 431
Corbusier, William Henry, 178, 431
Couch, M. J., 387, 408
The Count of Monte Cristo (book), 210 n3
Cox, Sergeant, 394
Craig, Louis Aleck, 368, 386, 430–31
Craig, Mrs. Louis Aleck, 386
Crater, Battle of, 312 n4
Crawford, Emmet, 178, 432
Crazy Bear (Ponca), 180
Crazy Horse (Oglala), 37, 37 n7, 54, 56, 59–60, 62, 69, 70, 70 n7, 73–75, 74 n15, 495; appraised, 2, 2 n2, 53, 65, 72, 77; death of, 53, 54, 76–78, 77 n20, 509, 510–12, 511 n5, 517; surrender of, 65–67, 73 n13; described, 67–68; undermined, 69, 70–71, 516; invited to Washington, 70, 503, 513–16; and Crook, 504–05; arrested, 506–08, 511
Crazy Horse Fight (see Powder River Fight)
Crazy Mule (Cheyenne), 122, 135
Creel, Herber Mansfield, 122, 126, 148, 151, 171, 172, 432
Creighton's Ranch, Neb., 238–41, 243–44
Crenshaw, H.C., 370
Cresap, Bernarr, 243 n10
Cries for War (Ponca), 180
Crittenden, Thomas L., 276–77 n1
Croesus, 210, 210 n3
Crook, George, 1–2, 5, 5 n12, 16–17, 23, 28–29, 32–33, 40, 40 n16, 42, 53–54, 58–62, 68–73, 68 n4, 80, 102, 110, 117, 121, 125–27, 163, 172–75, 177, 189–91, 195, 211, 218, 222, 234–35, 237, 241, 243–45, 248–49, 248 n12, 264, 276, 281, 288, 301, 334–35, 338, 341, 346, 350, 352, 367, 376, 383, 385–87, 397, 409, 413, 503; confers with Bannocks and

Shoshones, 35–37. 43ff.; on Indian Policy, 36, 36 n3, 197–201; and Indian scouts, 56, 59–60; and Little Bighorn, 56 n8; Indian fighting strategy, 62; and logistical problems, 62–63; Bourke's appraisal of, 63, 66; and the Battle of the Rosebud, 63 n13; ill-feelings toward, 63 n14; assassination attempt on, 74, 74 n15; and the Poncas, 79 n1, 116, 178; appointed brigadier general, 97; and Cheyenne Outbreak, 113–14, 117, 152, 156, 158; personal life, 117; and Bourke, 117–18; and Hayes family, 117–18, 118 n4; confers with Cheyennes, 121–22, 124–25; confers with Poncas, 178, 180ff.; in Pacific Northwest, 228–30; and Murchie Mine, 248 n12, 249, 345, 345 n4, 348 n7, 412, 412 n9–10, 417; Apache campaigns, 271, 413–14; and White River Ute Uprising, 292, 295, 302, 328; and General Grant, 342–43; and General Sherman, 355–56 n15; and Crazy Horse, 504–12, 516

Crook, Mary Dailey (wife), 118, 189, 190, 342, 343, 385

Crook, Oliver (nephew), 348 n7

Crow Indians (see also Indian scouts), 62–63, 136, 138

Crowell (government surveyor), 225–26, 232–35, 241, 244–46

Crowley, John, 327

Cuff, Dominick, 327

Cumming, Alfred, 85 n14

Curtis, Charlie, 44

Cushing, Alonzo, 257–58, 257 n15, 402

Cushing, Howard Buckingham, 255–57, 257 n15, 267, 275, 386, 395, 402–03, 432

Cushing, Milton Buckingham, 255 n13

Cushing, Thomas B., 37 n9

Cushing, Walter, 257 n15

Cushing, William Barker, 257, 257 n15, 402, 432–33

Custer, George Armstrong, 56, 56n 8, 129, 130, 130 n20, 211

D

The Dakota and Corbusier Winter Counts (book), 120 n5

Dallas, Andrew James, 163, 172

Danforth (Ute agent), 305

Danilson, William J., 42, 43, 47, 48, 52, 482

Davis (wounded civilian), 331

Davis, E. F., 374

Davis, George Breckenridge, 121–22, 126, 148–50, 152, 154–55, 162, 321, 337, 433

Davis, Jefferson C., 276, 345–46, 433

Davis, Wirt, 370, 434

INDEX 537

Dear, Clay, 171, 172
De Foe, Daniel, 86
Delaney, Hayden, 80–81, 170, 434
de Lesseps, Ferdinand, 371, 482
Dennison, James Alfred, 24, 24 n11, 434
Denver, Colo., 79, 79 n2, 107, 108
Denver Pacific Railroad, 107
Denver & Rio Grande Railroad, 107
Devin, John D., 121, 147
Devin, Thomas C., 126
De Witt, Calvin, 41, 325, 344, 434
El Diablo Conjuelo (book), 328, 328n5
Díaz, Porfirio, 6, 6n16
Digger Indians, 216
Dillon, John, 353 n12
Disraeli, Benjamin, Earl of Beaconsfield, 38, 38 n10–11, 409, 409 n8
Dodd, George Allen, 178, 434, 517
Dodge, Frederick Leighton, 109, 163, 307, 311, 313–14, 325, 329–35, 345, 434–35
Dodge, Mrs. Frederick Leighton, 109
Dodge, Richard Irving, 8, 57, 398, 435
Dolan, John, 327
Donnelly (correspondent), 337
Donnelly, Bernard, 193–94 n12
Donovan, John, 328
Downey, George Mason, 337, 435

Drake, Luther, 360
Drew, George Augustus, 168, 333, 435–36
Drum, Richard Coulter, 418–19, 436
Du Bois, John V., 250, 254–55, 267, 275, 436
Dull Knife (Cheyenne), 57–58, 264; and outbreak, 114, 146 n2, 169 n5, 172 n6, 495
Dull Knife Fight, 40 n16, 57–59, 211, 264
Dundy, Elmer, 116, 187–88, 482–83
Dunkelberger, Isaac Rothermel, 275, 436
Dunn, James A., 193, 193–94 n12
Dunn, Thomas, 272, 436–37
Duren, Orland, 328
The Dust Rose Like Smoke (book), 196 n17

E

Eads, James Buchanan, 371, 373, 483
Eastman, Frank French, 329, 437
Eaton, George Oscar, 39, 80, 437
Eckles, Robert, 75, 483
Edison, Thomas Alva, 19, 19 n2, 352, 407
Egan, James, 56, 237, 437
Eichwurzel, Charles, 327
Elizabeth I, 86, 86 n15
Elkins, General, 374
Elting, Oscar, 169–70, 437
Emancipation, 383 n16

Emery, George W., 347, 483
English, Willam Hayden, 7, 419
Erasmus of Rotterdam, 87
Erie Railroad, 346 n5
Esser, William, 327
Eugenie (Empress of the French), 196, 385
Evans, Andrew Wallace, 337, 437–38
Everett, Edward, 417, 417 n17

F

Farrar, H. H., 190
Federmeyer, L. P., 82 n7
Ferguson, Thomas, 328
Ferris, Samuel Peter, 298, 306, 317, 344, 438
Fetterman Massacre, 83 n10
Fetterman, William Judd, 83–84 n10, 438
Finerty, John Frederick, 333, 483
Fisk, Clinton B., 356–57
Fitch, Julian R., 255, 438
Fitzgerald, Michael John, 126, 146, 438–39
Fitzherbert, Maria, 243, 243 n10
Flagler, Daniel Webster, 30, 439
Flipper, Henry Ossian, 4
Foote, Morris Cooper, 282, 385
Forsyth, George Alexander, 177, 190, 292, 439
Fort
    Abraham Lincoln, N.D., 126, 126 n16, 175, 195 n15
    Alcatraz, Calif., 392 n6
    Apache, Ariz. (see Camp Apache)
    Atkinson, Neb., 37 n9,
    Bowie, Ariz., 38 n13, 269, 269 n25, 270, 272, 392, 413
    Brown, Texas, 22 n8, 358, 358 n16
    C. F. Smith, Mt., 83 n9
    Cameron, Utah, 348, 348 n8
    Clark, Texas, 17
    Craig, N.M. 5, 5 n13, 250, 250 n4, 253–54
    Crook, Neb., 31 n15
    Cummings, N.M., 250, 250 n3–4, 254–55, 257, 266, 269
    Custer, Mont., 208, 208 n1
    D. A. Russell, Wyo., 126 n14, 292, 292 n4, 295, 298
    Douglas, Utah (upgraded from Camp Douglas), 195, 195 n13, 298, 346–48
    Fetterman, Wyo., 40 n18, 51, 81, 84, 211, 298
    Fred Steele, Wyo., 40, 40 n19, 98, 100–01, 103, 105, 107, 126–27, 152, 248 n12, 291–92, 296, 300–02
    Garland, Colo., 339, 339 n2
    Grant, Ariz., (see Camp Grant II)
    Hall, Idaho, 35, 35n1, 36–37. 52, 191, 195, 346, 348–49
    Hartsuff, Neb., 212, 212 n5, 213, 218, 221, 226, 240, 246–47, 321 n3

Jackson, La., 217, 217 n10–11
Kearny, Neb., 17n1, 227n8
Keogh, Mt., 63 n15, 185, 185 n6, 195
Lapwai, Idaho, 419, 419 n20
Laramie, Wyo., 8, 37, 40 n17, 72, 72 n11, 74, 178, 216, 298, 398, 505–07
Leavenworth, Kans., 29, 29 n13, 192, 385–87
McKean, N.D. (see Fort Abraham Lincoln)
McKinney, Wyo., 40, 40 n16, 69, 145
McPherson, Neb., 126–28, 126 n16, 298, 302
Marion, Fla., 508 n3
Massachusetts, Colo., 339 n1
Meade, S.D., 137 n27, 195 n15
Mojave, Ariz., 21 n5, 223, 223 n20
Niobrara, Neb., 1, 1 n1, 61, 61 n12, 206, 212. 212n6; site selection for, 242–44
Omaha, Neb., (see Omaha Barracks)
Phil Kearny, Wyo., 83, 83 n8–9
Reno, Okla., 125, 125 n10–11, 142, 171, 211
Reno, Wyo., 83 n9, 125 n11
Ringgold, Tex., 22 n8
Robinson, Neb. (upgraded from Camp Robinson), 114, 177, 178, 212, 298
St. Philip, La., 217, 217 n10–11

Sanders, Wyo., 40, 40 no 17, 98, 298
Sedgewick, Colo., 117 n1
Selden, N.M., 262–64, 262 n29, 392
Sidney, Neb. (see Sidney Barracks)
Stanton, N.M., 256, 256–57 n13
Sumter, S.C., 259
Walsh, Saskatchewan, 125, 125 n12
Washakie, Wyo., see Camp Brown
Whipple, Ariz., 390, 390 n2, 413
Yuma, Calif., 21 n6, 22–23, 22 n9, 236
Fort, Lieutenant, 351
Fort Laramie Treaty (1868), 83 n9, 113
Fort Hall Reservation, Idaho, 35
Fort Phil Kearny Massacre (see Fetterman Massacre)
Foster, Charles Warren, 41, 50, 440
Foster, D.P., 212
Four Years Among the Ecuadorians (book), 303 n2
France, James, 298
Franklin, Battle of, 287, 287 n9
Frederick, Daniel Alfred, 333, 440
Freeman, Daniel Alfred, 333
Frémont, John Charles, 110, 326, 440–41
French, Chaplain, 385, 442

French, Frederick Halverson, 178, 441
Friday (Arapaho), 133, 514
Furey, John Vincent, 281, 295, 321, 378, 385, 387, 412, 441

G

Garfield, James A., 7, 418, 483–84
Gentles, William, 76 n19
Gentry, William Thomas, 341, 343, 431
George IV, 243, 243 n10
Geronimo War, 262 n19
Gettysburg, Battle of, 258, 415–16,
Gibbs, James T., 327
Gila (Colorado River steamer), 21 n5, 22
Gilbert, Charles Champion, 331, 333–34
Gilbert, W.S., 372, 372 n5
Gilliss, James, 80, 295, 298, 321, 337, 417, 441–42, 507–08
Gilliss, Mrs. James, 80
Gladstone, William E., 409, 409 n8
Goldman, Henry Joseph, 344–45, 442
Goldstein (freighter), 331
Gordon, "Black Hills," 297, 333, 335
Gordon, George Alexander, 121, 121 fn, 126, 147, 147 fn, 173–74, 442
Gordon, John B., 32, 484
Gosiute Indians, 91 n17

Gould, Jay, 207, 212–13, 346, 346 n5, 352, 384, 484
Grant, Fred, 343
Grant, Mrs. Fred, 343
Grant, Julia Dent, 7, 342–43; described, 342; world tour, 343
Grant, Nellie (see Sartoris, Nellie Grant)
Grant, Ulysses Simpson, 342–44, 346, 349, 356, 380; world tour, 7, 7 n17, 98, 287–88; third term prospects, 7, 7 n17, 288, 35354, 360–61, 384, 418; described, 343; Latin American tour, 360, 381
Great Sioux Reservation, 113
Great Sioux War, 2, 16–17, 54–55, 113, 125 n11, 399; losses and cost of, 55 n3
Green, Charley, 195
Green, John Richard, 147, 147 n3
Greene, Lewis Douglas, 333, 442
Gregory, James Fingal, 177, 442
Grimes, Edward B., 29, 297, 442
Grimes, Robert D., 295, 312–13, 327, 330, 344, 443
Grinnell, George Bird, 129, 129 n17, 142 n35
Gros Ventre Indians, 62, 138
Grouard, Frank, 67–68, 74 n15, 484, 513–14
Gump, James, 196 n17

H

Hale, Edward Everett, 86
Hall, William P., 192, 302, 325, 340, 344, 443
Halliday, Mr., 28
Hamilton, John Morrison, 42–43, 337, 443
Hammond (Indian inspector), 352, 356–57
Hancock, Winfield S., 7, 419, 443–44
Handbook of American Indians North of Mexico (book), 120 n5
Hannibal & St. Joseph Railroad, 403, 408–09
Hansen, Marcus, 328
Hardie, Francis Hunter, 333, 444
Harney, John, 327
Hart, Henry J., 352, 357
Hart, Mrs. Verling K, 40
Hartsuff, George Lucas, 212 n5, 321–22
Hastings, James S., 56, 63
Hassaurek, Frederick, 303, 303 n2
Hatch, John Porter, 339, 346, 444
Hayes, James Webb Cook, 117–18, 118 n4, 112, 127, 484–85; and Crook, 118; described, 118–19
Hayes, Lucy Webb, 15, 15 n1, 485
Hayes, Rutherford Birchard, 32, 117–18, 118 n4, 182 n3–4, 346, 351, 353, 415 n15, 485

Hayt, Edward Knapp, 357
Hayt, Ezra, 70, 190, 405–86, 503, investigated, 352–53, 353 n11, 356–58,
Hazen, William Babcock, 186, 186–87 n10, 189, 195–96, 444
He Dog (Oglala), 66, 67, 514
Hearst, George, 82 n7
Hearst, William Randolph, 82 n7
Hedberg (which Bourke spelled "Hedburg"), Alfred, 255, 444–45
Henley, Austin, 38–39, 445
Henry VIII, 86–87 n15
Henry, Guy Vernor, 301, 329–30, 333–34, 445
Henton, James (Old Jemmie), 6, 213, 220, 445–46
Hergus, Wilbur, 302, 305, 326, 330, 331, 335
Herndon, Agnes, 368
Herney, Nicholas W., 327
Hewitt, Christian Cyrus, 370, 446
High Bear (Sans Arc), 61, 76, 507
High Wolf (Cheyenne), 135
Hilton, James, 86–87 n15
Hodge, Frederick F., 120 n5
Hoffman, William Edwin, 385, 446
Holmes, Oliver Wendell, 214, 214 n7
Hood, John Bell, 286, 286 n7–8, 287, 287 n9
Hooker, Joseph, 341
Hopi Indians, 136, 161

Horbach family, 351
Horbach, Mary (Mollie), 338, 360
Horton, Samuel Miller, 333, 446
Howard, Oliver Otis, 36, 70, 446–47
Howell, Rezin G., 24, 375, 378–80, 447
Howland, Carver, 306, 330, 345, 447
Hoyt, J. W., 297
Hualpai Indians (see also Indian scouts), 221–23, 221 n16
Hughes, Martin Briggs, 311, 314, 323, 330, 345, 447
Hughes, William Burton, 373, 447
Humme (scout), 329, 340
Hunter, Billy, 2, 67, 133, 514; account of Crazy Horse, 515–17
Hunter, Frank, 327, 333
Hunter, George King, 168, 447
Huntington, Collis Potter, 378, 486

I

Indian scouts, 61, 69
  Apache, 62
  Bannock, 57
  Cheyenne, 58–60, 62, 67, 146
  Crow, 62
  Gros Ventre, 62
  Pawnee, 57
  Paiute, 62
  Shoshone, 57, 62

  Sioux, 62, 172, 339
Iron Hawk (Lakota), 514
Iron Shirt (Miniconjou), 73 n12
Irwin, James, 200, 486, 503, 514
Isandhlwana, Battle of (Natal), 8, 196; compared to Little Bighorn, 196 n17

J

Jackson, Allen Hyre, 333, 447–48
Jacobs, Joshua West, 333, 448
James Gang, 404
Jerome, David H., 356
Jesus la Paz (Apache), 257
Jewitt (trader at Spotted Tail), 415
Jicarilla Apache Indians, 339 n2
Johnson (Ute), 300
Johnson, John Burgess, 124, 164, 168, 172, 337, 448
Johnson, William H., 28, 448
Johnston, Albert Sidney, 85, 85 n14, 95
Johnston, Joseph E., 286 n8
Jordan, Allan, 302, 325, 344, 448
Jornada del Muerto, 251, 251 n7, 253, 254
Joseph (Nez Percé), 3, 3 n 7, 70, 72, 75, 495–96, 504
Jumping Shield, 510–11, 514

K

Kansas City, Mo., 3, 19, 191–94, 366–67, 369, 370–72,

378, 387, 400, 403, 405, 407, 408–109; as rail center, 368; industrial development in, 399, 401
Kansas City Herald (newspaper), 401
Kansas City, St. Joseph & Council Bluffs Railroad, 19, 193, 367, 385, 402, 406
Kansas Pacific Railroad, 107, 207
Kearney, Dennis, 287, 486
Kearny, Stephen Watts, 83 n9
Keefe, Joseph, 40, 51, 128
Kellogg, Sanford Cobb, 298, 344, 448–49
Kentucky Central Railroad, 24
Ketchum, Ami, 186 n8
Key, David McKendree, 98, 486–87
Keyes, Edward Livingston, 20, 23 fn, 449
Kickapoo Indians, 17
The Killing of Chief Crazy Horse (book), 77 n20
Kimball, General, 43
Kimball, Lieutenant, 43, 349
Kimball, T. L., 213
Kimball, W. L., 344, 449
Kime, Wayne R., 8
King, Charles, 345 n4, 370, 449–50
King, John Haskell, 80, 180, 410, 450
King, Mrs. John Haskell, 80
Kingley, E. M., 356
Kiowa Indians, 134, 138
Kirtland, Thaddeus Sandford, 333, 450

Kitchen, Acting Assistant Surgeon, 255–56
Knapp, Charles, 417
Kussman, Emil, 327

L

Lacey, Private, 158, 163
Laclede, Pierre, 407
Lakeshore & Southern Michigan Railroad, 346, 346 n5
Lakota (Western Sioux) Indians, 61 n12, 113
Lambertson, G.M., 187
Lame Deer (Miniconjou), 72–73, 73 n12, 496, 507–08, 510, 512
Lame Deer Fight, 72–73, 73 n13
The Last Days of Pompeii (novel), 413 n11
Lavelle, Edwin, 328
Lawson, Joseph, 311, 323, 330, 345, 450
Lawton, Henry Ware, 70, 450–51
Leach, M. F., 120–21, 121 n7
Lebar, enlisted soldier, 313
Lee, Jesse Matlock, 209, 415, 417, 451, 506, 517
Lee, Robert Edward, 174
Leighton, Lieutenant, 329
Lemhi Agency, Idaho, 191
Lemly, Henry Rowan, 168, 451
Lesage, Alain-René, 328, 328 n5
Lewis, John Francis, 392, 451–52
Lewis, Thomas, 328
Lewis, William H., 148, 148 n4, 452

Leyden, James Alexander, 345, 452
Libby Prison, 222
Linchard (correspondent), 169, 487
Lincoln, Abraham, 417, 417 n17
Lindwood, Captain, 297
Lipan Indians, 17
Little Bighorn, Battle of, 56, 136, 211; compared to Isandhlwana, 196 n17
Little Big Man (Oglala), 56, 66–67, 67 n6, 69, 76, 76 n19, 496, 505, 509, 511–12, 514–15, 517
Little Chief (Cheyenne), 122, 125, 151
Little Duck (Ponca), 180
Little Hawk (Oglala), 66, 514
Little Wolf (Cheyenne), 58, 60, 67, 496–97; and outbreak, 114, 146 n2, 169 n5, 178, 185, 312; surrenders, 185
Little Women (book), 81
London, Robert, 42, 452
Long Runner (Ponca), 180
Longstreet, James P., 286
Looking Glass (Nez Percé) 3 n7
Loring, Frederick W., 41, 156, 163–64, 172
Lost Horizon (book), 86–87 n15
Louis Napoleon (Prince Imperial of France), 8, 106, 106 n16, 242, 249
Louisville, Cincinnati & Lexington Railroad, 382

Louisville & Nashville Railroad, 373, 382 n15
Lovell, Robert Armstrong, 121, 126, 148, 155, 452
Lovering, Leonard Austin, 306, 345
Lowry (guide), 313, 327
Ludington, Marshall Independence, 180, 191, 195, 211, 385, 391, 452
Ludlow, Lietuenant, 41
Lupton, Allen, 327
Lyle, David, 397, 453
Lynch, Michael, 327
Lynch, Thomas, 327
Lyon, William H., 128, 356

M

Macbeth (play), 324 n4
McCaleb, Thomas Sidney, 127, 453
McCammon, William, 88, 347, 453
McCammon, Mrs. William, 88
McCann, D. J., 242
McCauley, Charles Adam Hoke, 326, 337, 453
McClellan, George B., 185–86 n7
McClure, Daniel, 28, 453
McConihe, Samuel, 329, 453
McCook, Alexander M., 149, 276–77 n1, 453–54
McCullough, John, 386, 487
McDonald, John, 327
McDonough (steamer captain), 20, 21
McFarland, Lucy (Mrs. Erick Bergland), 15, 25, 27, 375

INDEX 545

McFarland, William C., 24, 454
McFeely, William S., 7
McGillicuddy, Valentine T., 200, 487
McGrath, H. Price, 25, 379, 487
McGuire (teamster), 327
Mackay, James Ormond, 333, 454
McKee, Samuel, 327
Mackenzie, Ranald Slidell, 17, 57, 59–60, 88, 121, 211, 264, 339, 454–55
McKinney, John A., 40 n16, 58, 454
McKinstry (wagon master), 295, 297, 327
McLaglan, Victor, 7
MacMillan, Thomas C., 398, 487
McNamara, Thomas, 328
McPheeters, Miss, 27,
Machiavelli, Niccolô di Bernardo dei, 89, 89 n16
Macomb, Augustus Canfield, 344, 455
Macon Prison Camp, 373
Mahoney, John, 328
Major George (Shoshone), 43, 48, 497
Mallery, Garrick, 119–20, 120 n5
"The Man Without a Country" (Story), 86
Manassas, Second Battle of, 185–86 n7
Maria Alexandrovna (Empress of Russia), 418, 418 n18
Marquette, Jacques, 407

Marston, Doctor, 126, 148, 162, 167, 169, 455
Martin, Captain., 30, 173, 455
Mason, Charles Winder, 302, 344, 455
Mason, Julius Wilmot, 72, 75, 211, 455, 510
Mason, Mrs. Julius Wilmot, 211
Mathey, Edward Gustave, 126, 148, 160, 169, 455
Mauck, Clarence, 149, 152, 153, 158–59, 163, 172–73, 455–56
Mears, Frederick, 267
Medicine Jack (Ute), 315
Meeker, Nathan C., 291, 292, 299–301, 305, 318, 346–47, 488
Meeker, Mrs. Nathan C, and family, 339, 346, 352
Meinhold, Charles, 255–56, 267–68, 456
Mellon, Jack, 21–223, 21 n5
Merivale, Jospeh, 488, 514
Merrick, Mr. and Mrs., 135
Merrill, Colonel, 175
Merrill, John, 327
Merrill, Lieutenant, 148
Merritt, Wesley, 75, 456; and White River Ute Uprising, 292, 295ff., 344–45
Merritt, Mrs. Wesley, 40, 337
Mexican War, 372 n5, 383–84
Middleton, David Charles (Doc), 228, 231, 249, 488
Miles, John D., 121
Miles, Nelson Appleton, 63, 72–73, 73 n12, 121, 185 n6,

211, 276, 390 n2, 456–57; and Cheyenne Outbreak, 114
Miles, Paddy, 392, 457
Milk River Fight, 292–93, 295ff.; army casualties listed, 327–28
Miller, Amos D., 327
Mills, Anson, 166; and the Battle of the Rosebud, 63 n13
Mills, Cuthbert, 51, 488–89
Miner, Lieutenant, 351
Mini-Wa-Nichi (Lakota), 75
Miniconjou Lakota Indians, 61–62, 69
Mining, 87–88, 92–95, 97, 210, 211, 347–51, 382; impact on horse and mule market, 367
Missouri Pacific Railroad, 346 n5, 384
Mitchell, E. F., 387, 408
Mitchell, Luther, 186 n9
Mitchell, William, 328
Mix, John, 230, 457
Modoc War, 392, 392 n6
Mojave Indians, 23
Monahan, Deane, 171, 178, 457–58
Monahan, Mrs. Deane, 171
Montgomery, James 327, 344
Montgomery, Robert Hugh, 298, 318, 458
Montgomery, Mrs. Robert Hugh, 40
Mooney, Thomas, 327
Moore, Alexander, 37, 458
Moore, Thomas, 302, 337, 489
More, Thomas, Saint, 86–87 n15

Moqui Indians (see Hopi Indians)
Morgan, Charles (Omaha), 180–81, 184–85
Mormons, 50, 82, 91 n17, 95, 195 n13; Bourke's views on, 36, 42, 95
Morton, Charles, 209
Moseley, Edward Buckland, 168, 458
Mulhall, Stephen John, 50, 329, 458
Muller, Ernest, 327
Munn, Curtis Emerson, 126–28, 144, 146, 458
Munson, Samuel, 218, 225, 228–30, 234, 236–37, 241, 243, 246, 459
Murchie Mine, 248 n12, 249, 345, 345 n4, 348 n7, 412, 412 n9–10, 417

N

Nance, Albinus, 342, 489
Napoleon I, 205 n5, 243 n10
Napoleon III, 196 n16, 243 n10
Nash, William Hoyt, 321, 459
Nash, Mrs. William Hoit, 40
Native Races (book), 129 n19
Navajo Indians, 336
Neide, Horace, 40
Negley, James S., 276–77 n1
Nelson (teamster), 328
Newbern (Colorado River steamer), 20
New Orleans Campaign (Civil War), 217 n10
New York Central Railroad, 193, 346, 346 n5

INDEX

New York Herald (newspaper), 337, 348, 353, 359
Nez Percé Indians, 2–3, 70–71, 75, 125, 125 n12. 419 n20, 504, 508, 516
Nez Percé War, 3, 3 n7, 53, 70–72
Nickerson, Azor Howitt, 16–17, 51, 212, 409, 413, 415, 417–18, 459; promoted, 32–33, 40, 56; Civil War wound, 415–17, 415 n15
No Water (Lakota), 506
Norris, Frank, 207
Norris, Philatus, 42
Norris, William Foster, 126, 148, 153, 164, 218, 459
North Missouri Railroad, 371
North West Mounted Police (Canada), 125 n12

O

O'Connor, Lawrence Lucius, 255, 260–64, 267, 392, 459
O'Connor, Mrs. Lawrence Lucius, 261–62
O'Reilly, Luke, 29, 459–60
Ocheo (Paiute), 229
The Octopus (book), 207
The Odyssey (epic), 284 n5
Oglala Lakota Indians, 114
Ohio & Mississippi Railroad, 20
Ojibwa Indians, 276
Olive, Isom Prentice "Print", 186, 186 n9
Omaha, Neb., 3, 19, 29, 31, 37, 37 n9, 40, 51, 56, 75, 79, 80, 107–08, 118, 173, 175, 178, 186–87, 189–94, 206, 209, 211, 216, 248, 277–79, 291, 301–02, 337–39, 341–42, 347, 350–51, 367–68, 370–71, 382, 385, 387, 401, 406–08, 417, 507, 511–12; industries in, 282–86
Omaha Barracks, Neb., 31, 31 n15, 116, 127, 152, 178, 180, 190, 206, 208–09, 279, 280–81, 286, 295, 337, 342–43, 345, 367, 371, 385, 387, 409–10
Omaha Herald (newspaper), 116, 180, 187, 197, 337, 339
Omaha Indians, 179, 180, 184, 278
On the Border With Crook (book), 6, 17, 63 n13, 67–68 n3, 68 n6, 77 n20, 79, 250 n4
"One-Hoss Shay" (poem), 214; quoted 214 n8
Ord, Edward Otho Cresap, 242–43, 243 n10, 460
Ord, James, 243 n10
Othello (play), 386
Otis, Sergeant, 159
Ouray (Ute), 300, 318, 339, 346, 497–98

P

Paddock, Algernon S., 32, 489
Paddock, James V.S., 295, 297–98, 312, 324, 327, 330, 345, 460
Paddock, Major (post trader at Camp Robinson), 171, 177
Paiute Indians, 43, 216

Palmer, George, 40, 121, 126, 148, 160, 460
Parkhurst, Charles Dyer, 302, 325, 344, 460
Parnell, Charles Stewart, 353, 353 n12
Parsons, W.C., 190
Patrick, Matthew, 415
Patterson, Eugene, 327
Patterson, John J., 119, 347, 489–90
Patterson, Mrs. John J., 347
Patterson, Joseph, 328
Patrick (student on Black Hills Expedition), 164
Pawnee Indians, 57, 138, 216
Payne, John Scott, 295–98, 307–08, 311–18, 327, 330, 333, 345, 461
Pease, William Barrett, 126, 461
Pelouze, Louis Henry, 24, 32, 461
Petersburg, Siege of, 312, 312 n4
Picture Writing of the American Indians (book), 120 n5
Pine Ridge Agency, Neb., 188 n11
Pirates of Penzance (opera), 372 n6
Pit River Indians, 229
Pollock, Robert, 265–66, 461
Ponca Indians, 3, 79 n1, 178; transported to Indian Territory, 113, 115, 179, 180ff.; relations with government, 179; ancestral home, 179, 179 n1, 181–82, 181 n2; development, 179; confer with Crook, 178, 180ff.; origins, 185, 185 n5; legal case, 187–89, 197, 352
Pope, James Worden, 386, 461–62
Pope, John, 124, 124 n9, 185, 185–86 n7, 292
Poppleton, A.J., 187–88
Porter, FitzJohn, 185, 185–86 n7
Posse Comitatus Act, 186, 186 n8, 200
Potter, R. Lyman, 82, 82 n7
Pourier, Baptiste (Big Bat), 74 n15, 490
Powder River Expedition, 40 n16, 264
Powder River Fight, 37, 37 n7, 56, 374, 374 n7
Powell, John Wesley, 143 n36
Pratt, Edward Barton, 329, 462
Pratt, U.S. Marshal, 261–62
Preston, Colonel, 25
Preston, General, 25
Price, Butler D., 296, 307, 345, 462
Price, Philip M., 24, 462
Price, Rose Lambart, baronet, 6, 213–14, 214 n7, 219–21
Price, Sterling, 370
Price, William Redwood, 221, 462–63
The Prince (book), 89, 89 n16
Punished Woman's Fork fight, 148, 148 n4, 153 n8

Q

Quentin, Julius Edward, 329, 463

Quinton, William, 333, 463
Quinn, Thomas Francis, 306–08, 317, 321–22, 330, 345, 463

R

Randall, George Morton, 61, 463
Randolph, Benjamin Harrison, 51, 464
Rankin, Joe, 297, 308, 333
Reade, Philip, 386–91, 464
Red Cloud (Oglala), 57, 66, 67, 69, 70, 72, 172, 188, 498, 510, 513–14
Red Cloud Agency, Neb., 53, 55–58, 61 n12, 62, 65–66, 68–69, 72, 75, 114, 124, 145, 150, 163, 503–04, 516
Red Hat (Cheyenne), 122, 135
Red Leaf (Oglala), 57
Reed, John, 342
Reed, Mrs. John (Mary Crook's sister), 342
Reed, William Isaac, 333, 464
Regan, James, 385, 464
Resumption Bill, 353, 353 n13
Reynolds, Bainbridge, 349, 465
Rice, William Fletcher, 402, 465
Richelieu (play), 412, 413 n11
Ridge Bear (Cheyenne), 122–23
Riley, James 392, 465
Robinson Crusoe (book), 86
Robinson, Daniel, 306, 333, 345, 466
Robinson, William Wallace, Jr., 39, 39 n15, 255–56, 266–68, 397–98, 466
Rock Island Arsenal, Ill., 16, 30–31, 173, 175
Rockwell, Charles Henry, 24, 358, 466
Rockwell, James, 30, 466
Rodgers, Calbraith Perry, 80 n5, 84–85, 466
Rodgers, Mrs. Calbraith Perry, 40, 80
Rodman, Burt, 175
Rodman, Ella, 173
Rodman gun, 173 n7
Rodman, Private, 102–03
Rodman, Thomas, 175
Rodman, Thomas Jefferson, 173, 173 n7
Rodman, Mrs. Thomas Jefferson, 175
Rodney (blacksmith), 328
Roland, Bill (Cheyenne-white), 122–23
Roman Nose (Sans Arc), 61, 498
Roosevelt, Theodore, 243 n10
Rosebud, Battle of, 8, 56, 211
Ross, William J., 397–98, 466–67
Ross Fork Agency, Idaho, 35, 42, 49, 51–52, 348–49
Royal Canadian Mounted Police (see North West Mounted Police)
Royall, William Bedford, 145, 166, 180, 211, 345, 366–69, 371–75, 372 n5, 378–79, 380–85, 387, 391, 400, 402–04, 410, 417, 467

Royall, Mrs. William Bedford, 345
Rucker, John Anthony, 38–39, 39 n13, 467
Ruffner, Ernest Howard, 386, 467
Russell Depot, Wyo. (see Cheyenne Depot, Wyo.)
Russell, Gerald (Old Jerry), 6, 7, 255, 258–60, 262–68, 272, 364, 391–99, 467–68
Russo-Turkish Wars, 39 n11
Ryan, Edmund, 255, 468

S

St. Joseph, Mo., 191–93, 366–68, 383, 385, 401, 403, 407–08
St. Louis, Mo., 3, 19, 27–29, 50, 125, 371–72, 407
St. Louis, Kansas City & Northern Railroad, 384
Sacket, Delos, 345 n4, 468
Safford, Anson P. K., 190
San Carlos Reservation, Ariz., 357, 413 n13
Sand Creek Fight (1878), 146, 146 n2
Sans Arc Lakota Indians, 61, 69
Santillane, Gil Blas de, 328 n5
Sapavanero (Ute), 318
Sartoris, Algernon, 281
Sartoris, Nellie Grant, 7, 281, 281 n3
Saunders, Alvin, 32, 490
Savage, Judge, 256, 407
Schickerdonz, Eugene, 327
Schmitt, Martin F., 348 n7

Schofield, John M., 287
The Schoolmaster (book), 86, 86 n15
Schubert, William, 312, 327
Schurz, Carl, 182 n4, 354, 358, 490–91; Bourke's opinion of, 115, 351; contrasted to Disraeli, 409
Schuyler, Walter Scribner, 37, 43, 50, 80, 86, 89–92, 95, 110, 118, 122, 127, 173–74, 191, 195, 212, 218, 241, 243, 246, 248–49, 277–78, 282, 294, 307, 310, 313–14, 321, 330–31, 335–38, 344, 468–69; and Murchie Mine, 248 n12, 249, 345, 345 n4, 348 n7, 412, 412 n9, 417
Schwatka, Frederick, 291, 329
Seaton, Frank, 257, 469
Seawell, General, 376
Seawell, Mary, 376
Selree, L. E., 370
Semig, Bernard Gustave, 302, 469
Seminole Wars, 321, 321 n2, 322
Sharp, Colonel, 343
Sharp Nose (Arapaho), 67, 70, 72, 498, 510, 514
Shelby, P. P., 174
Sheridan, Irene Rucker, 39 n14, 190
Sheridan, Philip Henry, 17, 38 n13, 39, 39 n14, 54, 68, 71–72, 114 124, 158, 173, 177, 190, 276, 295, 298, 345, 345 n4, 380, 412 n9, 418, 504, 508

Sherman, John, 353–54, 361, 384, 418, 491
Sherman, William Tecumseh, 80, 149, 186–87 n10, 286–87, 355, 355–56 n15, 358
Sherwood, William L., 392, 469
Shiloh, Battle of, 186, 186–87 n10
Short History of the English People (book), 147, 147 n3
Shoshone Indians, 37, 43, 45, 45 n22, 57, 91 n17, 138, 199, 216, 302, 348; farming among, 44–46, 52,
Sidney Barracks, Neb., 117 n1, 121, 126–28, 135, 143–44, 146–47, 149, 152, 172, 177
Silva, Valentine M. C., 392, 469
Simpson, J. E., 373
Simpson, James Ferdinand, 171
Sign Language Among North American Indians (book), 120 n5
Sioux Indians (see also Lakota, under individual tribes, and Indian scouts), 36, 57, 65, 69, 81, 125, 125 n12, 136, 138–39, 145, 174, 188, 188 n11, 199, 200, 215–16, 237, 264, 339; and environment, 168 n4; compared to Zulus, 196 n17
Sitting Bull (Hunkpapa), 63 n15, 65–66, 65 n1, 71 n10, 125, 125 n12, 276, 499, 508, 512

Sitting Bull of the South (Oglala), 63–64, 63 n15, 73, 499
Slim Buttes, Battle of, 61, 370
Smead, Alexander D.B., 168, 469
Smiley, A. K., 353 n11, 357
Smith, A. Sidney, 255–56, 267, 470
Smith, Alfred, 88, 469–70
Smith, Charles Henry, 386, 470
Smith, John Eugene, 83, 88–90, 347–48, 470
Smith, Thomas T., 8
Snider, Nathan, 345 n4, 491
Southern Pacific Railroad, 207, 351, 376
Spencer, James Herbert, 98, 100, 102, 104, 126, 128, 145, 148, 470
Spotted Tail (Brulé), 69, 70, 72, 167, 499–500, 513–14, 517
Spotted Tail Agency, Neb., 53, 61–62, 61 n12, 69, 75, 78, 145, 163, 503, 505–07, 510, 514
Sprague, C.J., 281, 470
Spring Hill, Battle of, 287, 287 n9
Springer, Assistant Surgeon, 29
Stacton, David, 206
Standing Bear (Ponca), 115, 180, 500; legal case, 116, 352; described, 180–81; confers with Crook, 181 ff.
Standing Elk (Cheyenne), 67
Standing Rock Agency, N.D., 188

Stanley, David S., 186, 186–87 n10, 189, 195, 287, 470–71
Stanton, Edwin M., 185–86 n7, 383
Stanton, Thaddeus Harlan, 42, 49, 83, 86–87, 91–92; 97, 385, 471
Stanton, Mrs. Thaddeus H., 85
Stanton, William Sanford, 54, 212, 218, 237, 240–41, 243–45, 248, 282, 471
Stanwood, Frank, 255, 262, 265–67, 272, 471
Stedman, Clarence Augustus, 323, 472
Stenhouse (correspondent), 348, 491
Stevens (Union Pacific car builder), 283, 284
Stickney, William, 353 n11, 356, 357
Stieger, Gottleib, 327
Stilson (correspondent), 337
Stockbridge Indians, 358
Stones River (Murfreesboro), Battle of, 186, 288, 374
Storrow, Captain, 174
Strahorn, Robert Edmund, 37, 39, 81, 491
Strahorn, Mrs. Robert Edmund, 37, 39, 81
Street, William D., 152, 158, 491–92
Study of the Mortuary Customs of the North American Indians (book), 143 n36
Styer, Charles, 255, 472
Sullivan, Arthur, 372, 372 n5

Summerhayes, John Wyer, 21 n5
Summerhayes, Martha, 21 n5
Summers, John Edward, 321, 472
Sumner, Edward V., 306, 316–17, 321, 344, 472
Sutcliffe, Frederick, 327
Sutorious, Alexander, 250, 255, 257–58, 472
Sutro, Adolph, 210, 492
Sutro Tunnel, 210
Swearingen, Happy Jack, 226, 232–35, 241, 244
Swift, Eben, 307, 319, 321, 330, 344, 472
Swift Bear (Lakota), 76, 507
Swigert, Samuel Miller, 382, 473
Sykes, George, 358–59, 473

T

Tacitus, 176
Tainter, Charles Sumner, 19 n2
Tappan, Benjamin, 236–37, 237 n7
Tarlton, Elisha Warfield, 379, 473
Taylor, Alfred Bronaugh, 399, 473
Taylor, Daniel Morgan, 30, 329, 386, 473
Taylor, Nathaniel, 165
Taylor (scout), 328
Tchaikovsky, Peter Ilyich, 38 n11
Tecumseh (Shawnee), 77, 500–01

Terry, Alfred Howe, 54, 56 n8, 185 n6
Thayer, Herbert, 98
Thermopylae, 176
Thibaw (King of Burma), 406, 406 n6
Thomas, George H., 287
Thomas, Henry Goddard, 126, 473–74
Thomas, Ivel, 387, 406
Thompson, John Charles, 168, 474
Thorn, Steve, 22
Thornburgh, Thomas Tipton, 40, 98–100, 102–05, 121, 125–28, 474; and Cheyenne Outbreak, 144ff., 169, 171–75, 300–01, 311–12; and White River Ute Uprising, 292, 296, 302, 307, 318–19, 330, 337, 345, 347; death of, 294–95, 297, 300, 308, 314–15, 317, 323–24, 327, 329–30, 341
Thornburgh, Mrs. Thomas Tipton, 98, 301
Thornburgh, Jacob T., 98, 302, 492
Thrapp, Dan L., 125 n10
Tibbles, Thomas Henry, 116, 180, 197, 351–52, 492
Tilford, Major, 172
Tillman, Samuel, 24
Tin-Doy (Shoshone), 45
Tine, T. E., 318
Touch the Clouds (Miniconjou), 61, 76, 501, 504–05, 507, 509–10, 512

Townsend, Edward Davis, 418, 474
Townsend, Edwin Franklin, 208, 474
Treacy (horse dealer), 25, 378–79, 381, 382
Trotter, Frank Eugene, 96, 329, 474
Tupan, Private, 102–03
Turkey Legs (Cheyenne), 60
Tuttle, E. H., 356
The Two Americas (book), 214 n7, 221

U

Ulundi, Battle of (Natal), 196 n17, 249n1
Uncle Sam (Colorado River steamer), 21 n6
Uncompahgre Ute Agency, 318
Uncompahgre Ute Indians, 318, 339, 346
Union Pacific Railroad, 2, 40 n17, 51, 53, 74, 74 n16, 80, 102, 110, 120, 121 n7, 128, 147–51, 159, 163, 177–79, 195, 206–07, 212–13, 277, 294, 301, 342–43, 348, 352, 368, 415, 417; Omaha shops, 282, 283, 284, 285,
United States Army, 7, 8, 16; and Congress, 31; clothing, weapons and equipment, 31 n14; 90; requirements for forts, 206, 242, 244; daily routine on post, 251; reduced by Congress, 261 n18; regulations on embezzlement, 364, 365; strikers

in, 398 n11; reorganization of mounted units, 420–21; frontier expedition procedures, 173–74; public attitude toward, 196, 200–01, 278–79, 362n5; and federal Indian policy, 203, 281–82, 338; soldier's life, 236–38
Utah Northern Railroad, 48, 348
Utah Southern Railroad, 348
Ute Indians (see also White River Ute Uprising), 3, 44, 91 n17, 109, 138; incursions on land of, 291, 299, 339–40; and White River Uprising, 302, 308, 310, 312, 315–18, 324–25, 328–29, 335
Utopia (book), 86, 87, 86–87 n15

V

Vanderbilt, Cornelius, 346 n5
Vanderbilt, William, 346 n5
Vandever, William, 56, 63, 492–93
Van Horn, Thomas B., 88, 475
Van Vliet, Frederick, 177, 192, 212, 475
Verne, Jules, 86
Victor Emanuel II (Italy), 219, 219 n12
Victoria (Great Britain), 243 n10, 359, 409
Viollet-le-Duc, Eugène Emmanuel, 81–82, 81 n6
The Virginian (book), 40 n18
Volkmar, William Jefferson, 386, 475

Voorhees, Daniel W., 32
Vroom, Peter Dumont, 178, 302, 324–26, 332, 344, 475

W

Wabash Pacific Railroad, 384, 408
Waide, F. B. (actor), 386
Walker, George Brinton, 24, 475
Ward, Edward Wilkerson, 374, 475–76
Warner, Captain, 389
Warren Air Force Base, Wyo. (ex-Fort D.A. Russell), 292 n4
Warrens, Charles Henry, 92, 476
Wars of Italian Unificiation, 219 n12
Washakie (Shoshone), 44–45, 45 n22, 48, 501
Washburne, E.B., 418
Washita, Battle of, 130 n20
Webster, George Ogilvie, 345, 476
Webster, John L., 187, 188
Weir, Charles G., 341
Weir, William Bayard, 39, 110, 127, 321, 325, 328, 344, 476; killed, 339–41
Wellborn, Luther Scott, 344, 476
Wentworth, Little Buckshot, 237
Wessells, Henry Walton, Jr., 114, 333, 476–77
Whalen, Captain, 195, 477
Wheaton, Charles, 213, 477

Wheeler Expedition, 41, 41 n20, 51, 397
Wheeler, George Montague, 41 n20
White Horse (Arapaho), 67
White River Agency, 339–40
White River Ute Indians, 318–19, 351
White River Ute Uprising, 3, 291ff., 338; roster of officers, 344–45; peace commission concerning, 346–47, 351
White Thunder (Cheyenne), 122, 501
Whitney, Robert H., 395–96, 493
Whittaker, Johnson, 4, 5, 5 n11. 406, 412
Williams, Constant, 333, 477
Williams, Robert, 33, 147, 149, 152 n7, 180, 294–96, 298, 301–02, 321, 350, 367, 378, 477, 503, 504
Wilson, Thomas, 321, 386, 477
Winnebago Indians, 278
Winters, William Henry, 419, 477–78
Wister, Owen, 40 n18
Withers (horse breeder), 25, 378
Wolcott, Francis, 81, 493
Wolf, Silas A., 148, 153, 311, 330, 478
Wolseley, Garnet, 249
Woman's Dress (Lakota), 73, 74 n15, 516
Wood, Marshall William, 264, 265

Woodson, Albert Emmett, 337, 478
Wright, Charles, 327
Wyatt, Walter Scott, 127, 148, 151 fn, 478

X

Xenophon, 176

Y

Yarrow, H.C., 143, 143 n36
Yavapai Indians, 74 n15
Yeatman, Richard Thompson, 42, 329, 478
Yellow Bear (Lakota), 510
Yellow fever, 97, 98, 286, 369
Yellow Horse (Ponca), 180
Yellowstone National Park, 42, 71
Young, Brigham, 85 n14
Young, George Shaeffer, 333, 478
Young Man Afraid of His Horses (Oglala), 339, 501–02, 510
Young, Robert Hunter, 148, 150, 158, 478
Yuma Indians, 23

Z

Zulu Wars, 8, 196, 249, 385; compared to Sioux Wars, 196 n17